HIGHER EDUCATION: HANDBOOK OF THEORY AND RESEARCH

Volume I

HIGHER EDUCATION:
HANDBOOK OF THEORY AND RESEARCH

Volume I

Edited by

John C. Smart
Virginia Polytechnic Institute and State University

Published under the sponsorship of
American Educational Research Association
Division J — Postsecondary Education

AGATHON PRESS, INC.
New York

© 1985 Agathon Press, Inc.
111 Eighth Avenue
New York, NY 10011

All Rights Reserved

ISBN: 0-87586-065-6
ISSN: 0882-4126

CONTENTS

PREFACE

Contemporary research in higher education is more diverse and methodologically more advanced than ever before, and the body of literature reporting on that research is increasing at an accelerating rate. The sheer growth in size is reflected in the expanding number of journals, books, and monographs published annually with a decided focus on research topics and policy issues that are germane to higher education scholars. Growing appreciation of the complexity of topics addressed has contributed to the broader scope and increasing diversity evidenced in the literature. Methodological advances may be attributed to the continuing contributions by scholars prepared in other disciplines and to the more rigorous preparation of graduates of higher education doctoral programs.

These developments are healthy reflections of the continuing evolution of higher education from an emerging to an established academic discipline. One consequence of this normal maturation process is that the current knowledge base has become exceedingly more diverse, sophisticated, and fragmented. While such conditions may be regarded as healthy examples of the maturation process to date, so too may they be seen as inhibiting future evolution by frustrating efforts toward the development of cumulative knowledge, an essential attribute of more mature areas of scholarly inquiry.

The impetus for this *Handbook* was a belief that the further maturation of higher education as an area of scholarly inquiry is contingent upon our ability to bring order and understanding to the increasingly rich, diverse, and fragmented research findings that are presently available. The need is to pull together and synthesize our increasingly disjointed research findings in order to establish a solid foundation for future advances toward the development of cumulative knowledge.

The intent of the *Handbook* is to contribute to this long-term development by providing an annual compendium of exhaustive and integrative literature reviews on a diverse array of topics. Such volumes are common in more advanced subject matter areas and contribute to their ongoing process of evolutionary maturation. The annual volumes of this *Handbook* will seek to strike an appropriate balance between comprehensiveness and depth of coverage; the former will be apparent in the diversity of topics addressed in terms of both their subject matter and their methodological perspective, while the latter will be evident in the exhaustive treatment given each topic by contributing authors selected because of their recognized expertise in the specific specialty areas. The charge to each author is threefold: to provide an integrative review of extant research on the selected topic, to critique that research in terms of its conceptual and methodological rigor, and to set forth an agenda for future research.

The *Handbook* is organized around twelve general areas that encompass the salient dimensions of scholarly and policy inquiries in higher education. These twelve areas reflect the richness and diversity of the field in terms of subject matter interests and methodological perspectives. Associate Editors were selected to provide general leadership and direction for each area. The Associate Editors are eminent scholars in their respective areas and coordinate with me the ultimate selection of specific topics included in each volume, the choice of the contributing author(s) for each chapter, and the general monitoring of the preparation of each chapter. While the typical pattern is to have one chapter per research area in each volume, there will be occasions in which an area is not represented or is represented by more than one chapter. The twelve Associate Editors and the research area for which each is responsible are listed opposite the title page.

It is obvious that the preparation of the *Handbook* is a collaborative effort in the fullest and finest sense of the term, involving the concerted efforts of the contributing authors and Associate Editors. It is a pleasure to have this opportunity to express my deepest appreciation to them for their enthusiasm and expertise which have made possible the publication of this initial volume in an annual series. The weaknesses that are inherent in any such large scale collaborative effort are mine alone.

I wish to further express my appreciation to three individuals whose counsel was instrumental in the evolution and preparation of this initial volume. Paul B. Hoeber was President of Agathon Press, Inc. at the time this publication was initially conceived and during the early stages of its preparation. He is a trusted friend and respected publisher whose contributions shall not be forgotten. Burton Lasky is the current President of Agathon Press, Inc. and has provided invaluable guidance and support throughout the preparation of this initial volume. Dr. Charles F. Elton was my mentor throughout my doctoral training at the University of Kentucky and has remained a valued friend and trusted colleague in the intervening years. My indebtedness to him for all aspects of my professional career is profound and I hope that this publication satisfies his rigorous standards for scholarly efforts. Last, but certainly not least, I wish to acknowledge the steadfast love and support of my parents and family which pervades my total being and makes such ventures as this possible and meaningful.

Blacksburg, Virginia   John C. Smart
February 1985

Contributors

PHILIP G. ALTBACH is Professor and Director of the Comparative Education Center, Faculty of Educational Studies, State University of New York at Buffalo. He serves as editor of the *Comparative Education Review*. He is co-editor (with E. Barber and R. Myers) of *Bridges to Knowledge: Foreign Students in Comparative Perspective* (1984) and co-author of *Foreign Students and International Study* (1985).

ROBERT T. BLACKBURN is Professor of Higher Education at the University of Michigan's Center for the Study of Higher Education. His principal research interest is the academic career, a subject on which he has extensively published.

ELLEN EARLE CHAFFEE is Director of the Organizational Studies Division at the National Center for Higher Education Management Systems (NCHEMS). Her research interests include the processes by which organizations make decisions, strategic management, and leadership. She has written books on rational decisionmaking and case studies of strategic management, plus articles in higher education and management journals. She and Raymond F. Zammuto are writing a book on organizational adaptation.

CLIFTON F. CONRAD is Professor of Higher Education in the Center for the Study of Higher Education at the University of Arizona. He has written on liberal and general education, academic change, and college and university curriculum. He is editor of the forthcoming *ASHE Reader on Academic Programs in Colleges and Universities*.

CAMERON FINCHER is Regents Professor of Higher Education and Psychology, and Director of the Institute of Higher Education, at the University of Georgia. He has written on policy, administration, evaluation, and assessment in higher education and has been designated a Distinguished Member of the Association for Institutional Research. In 1982 he was the first recipient of the Ben W. Gibson Award given by the Southern Regional Council of the College Board for outstanding contributions to education.

MARY FRANK FOX is a research scientist at the University of Michigan's Center for Research on Social Organization. Her work focuses upon stratification processes in science and academia and sex stratification in occupations and organizations. She has published numerous articles on these subjects, and is author (with Sharlene Hesse Biber) of *Women at Work* (1984) and editor of *Scholarly Writing and Publishing: Issues, Problems, and Solutions* (1985).

BARBARA A. LEE is Assistant Professor of Industrial Relations at the Institute of Management and Labor Relations, Rutgers University. She has written extensively on faculty collective bargaining, academic employment issues, and legal issues in higher education employment. She is completing a book with George LaNoue on the consequences of academic discrimination litigation, funded by the Carnegie Corporation.

Y. G.-M. LULAT is a doctoral candidate in the Comparative Education Center, State University of New York at Buffalo. He is co-author of *Foreign Students and International Study* (1985).

ANDREW T. MASLAND is Senior Marketing Specialist with Digital Equipment Corporation. He wrote his chapter for the *Handbook* while Research Associate and Assistant Professor in the Center for the Study of Higher Education at the Pennsylvania State University. His research interests encompass the use and management of computers in higher education. He has published on this topic in *Research in Higher Education, Liberal Education*, and *The Educational Record*.

MICHAEL T. McCORD is Assistant Professor at the University of Georgia's Institute of Higher Education. His research activities include studies of administrative climate and planning processes, student retention, developmental influences upon teaching techniques and faculty use of CAI. Currently he is completing a monograph on means and procedures for academic managers to encourage and support instructional use of microcomputers.

BRAD L. MITCHELL is Assistant Professor at The Ohio State University. He served on the staff of the National Commission on Excellence in Education. His primary research and writing is in educational politics and policy analysis. Currently he is studying the relationship of educational research and policy in ad hoc policy advisory committees.

ANTHONY W. MORGAN is Executive Assistant to the President and Associate Professor of Educational Administration at the University of Utah. He is the author of journal articles or monographs on topics of planning, resource allocation and governance in higher education. This chapter in the *Handbook* stems from his involvement with David Gardner in the work of the National Commission on Excellence in Education.

STEVEN G. OLSWANG is Assistant Provost for Academic Affairs at the University of Washington and Affiliate Associate Professor of Policy, Governance and Administration in its College of Education. He has published articles on issues relating to faculty, including tenure, faculty governance, scientific misconduct, retrenchment, and due process. He has recently co-authored, with Barbara Lee, a research monograph entitled *Faculty Freedoms and Institutional Accountability: Interactions and Conflicts*.

ERNEST T. PASCARELLA is Professor of Urban Education Research at the University of Illinois at Chicago. His research interests include student persistence in postsecondary education and the impact of college on student development. He has written and published extensively in these areas over the past ten years.

JOHN R. THELIN is Associate Professor and Director of the Higher Education Doctoral Program at The College of William and Mary; he also is a member of the American Studies Program Faculty. His research interests include public policy, social history, and institutional imagery. He is the author of *The Cultivation of Ivy* (1976) and *Higher Education and Its Useful Past*. His works in progress include studies of intercollegiate athletics, campus architecture, and analysis of historical statistics.

MICHAEL L. TIERNEY is Associate Professor at the University of Pennsylvania's Graduate School of Education and Associate Director of the Higher Education Finance Research Institute. He is co-author, with J. Victor Baldridge, of *New Approaches to Management* and has published articles in the *Journal of Higher Education, Higher Education*, and the *Economics of Education Review*.

LEE M. WOLFLE is an Associate Professor of Educational Research at Virginia Polytechnic Institute and State University. He has written extensively on the structural modeling of social processes and the causes and consequences of the acquisition of postsecondary education. He has written "Strategies of Path Analysis" in the *American Educational Research Journal* and is co-author, with Corinna A. Ethington, of "A Structural Model of Mathematics Achievement for Men and Women" in the same journal.

COLLEGE ENVIRONMENTAL INFLUENCES ON LEARNING AND COGNITIVE DEVELOPMENT:
A Critical Review and Synthesis

Ernest T. Pascarella, *University of Illinois at Chicago*

While we can find a modest body of literature on the impact of college on students extending back to the 1930s, it is probably the case that the works of Philip Jacob (1957) and Everett Eddy (1959) represent benchmarks in the growth of college impact as an area of research. Both investigations looked at multi-institutional samples and both focused on important, though broad, outcomes of college. (Jacob focused on the impact of college on student values, while Eddy investigated the ways in which college attendance influenced student character.) Both concluded that the institutions did not differ markedly in their influence on students, and that not all the institutions were particularly effective in bringing about the fundamental changes in student values and character development commonly associated with liberal education.

Beyond these sobering conclusions, however, the "Jacob Report" in particular had a leavening effect on the scholarly community. By raising serious questions about the extent to which college attendance influenced students' development of values Jacob helped focus the attention of a wide range of social scientists (e.g., anthropologists, psychologists, sociologists, and social psychologists) on a very central question: In what ways and to what extent does college bring about change in students? Thus, despite certain methodological problems (e.g., Barton, 1968; Reisman, 1958; Smith, 1968) the "Jacob Report" was in

An earlier version of this paper was presented at the 1984 meeting of the Association for the Study of Higher Education, Chicago, March 12-14, 1984. Sincerest thanks are due to Carolyn Ellner, Jonathan Shapiro, Patrick Terenzini, and Linda Tusin for their excellent comments on earlier drafts of the manuscript.

no small way responsible for a sharp increase in published and unpublished investigation focusing on college impact. Much of this vast body of research was conducted during the late 1950s, 1960s, and 1970s, and evidence of the volume of work conducted is perhaps demonstrated by the number of existing literature reviews (e.g., Axelrod, 1969; Bowen, 1977; Chickering, 1969, 1981; Feldman and Newcomb, 1969; Lenning et al., 1974; Pascarella, 1980; Sanford, 1962, 1967; Tinto, 1975.).

Feldman and Newcomb's (1969) is, of course, a particularly noteworthy work, reviewing and synthesizing the results of over 1,500 studies. It is clear from Feldman and Newcomb, as well as from more recent reviews, that the major focus of this literature has been on the ways in which college influences such factors as values, attitudes, personality orientations, political and racial views, educational and occupational aspirations, income, life goals, etc. Only a relatively small percentage of the research has been concerned with the effects of college on learning and cognitive development. Yet enhancing student learning and cognitive development is clearly central to the mission of the university. The major purpose of this chapter is to review and synthesize the accumulated evidence pertaining to the influence of postsecondary education on undergraduate student learning and cognitive development. A key focus will be on identifying those elements of the college environment that are salient factors in fostering growth in these areas.

It comes as no surprise that nearly all of the investigations reviewed will be nonexperimental or, at best, quasi-experimental in nature. That is, few of the investigations involve a control group; or, if a control group is present, it will be the result of subject self-selection rather than controlled random assignment to comparison groups or conditions. There is ample evidence, for example, that students attending different postsecondary institutions vary markedly in such precollege or input characteristics as academic aptitude and occupational aspirations, family background, and personality dimensions (e.g., Astin, 1965, 1977). Similarly, individuals who choose to attend postsecondary institutions differ substantially along many important aptitude, achievement, and motivational dimensions from individuals who do not attend college (Wolfle, 1980).

Given such demographic realities, the issue of partitioning effects due to different postsecondary experiences or institutional exposures from those of potentially confounding individual differences is far from trivial. It is particularly true of the research on college impact that the nature and validity of our conclusions (i.e., what influence we attribute to college versus what we attribute to other factors) are substantially influenced by our methodological approaches (Astin, 1970a, 1970b; Feldman, 1969). Thus this paper will also discuss the methodological issues involved in estimating the effects of postsecondary education on learning and cognitive development and illustrate the potential implications of these issues for our interpretation of the findings. Based on this analysis, the paper will also suggest and discuss several alternative conceptual and methodological approaches for future research.

DEFINING THE CRITERION

Before undertaking a critical synthesis of studies, it is essential to define exactly what is meant by the dependent/criterion variable "learning and cognitive development." This is particularly important since the operational definitions used in many studies can be overlapping and, in several cases, unintentionally misleading. The same terms can sometimes stand for quite different constructs in different investigations. The terms "undergraduate achievement" and "student achievement" as used by Astin (1968) and Rock, Centra, and Linn (1970), for example, refer to scores on various forms of the Graduate Record Examination (GRE). As employed by Thistlethwaite (1959), however, the term "student achievement" represented the educational attainment of students graduating from a particular postsecondary institution. Thus, there is a clear need for specificity in operationally defining the dependent/criterion measure "learning and cognitive development."

One useful approach is a simple taxonomy of postsecondary outcomes developed by Astin (1973). Astin suggests that college outcomes can be conceptualized along three dimensions: type of outcome, type of data, and time span. The first two dimensions can be conceived in terms of a 2 × 2 matrix where type of outcome is either cognitive or affective and type of data is dichotomized into psychological and behavioral. (The temporal dimension makes less sense as a dichotomy and instead can be considered a continuous variable tapping the time span over which outcomes are assessed.) Cognitive outcomes refer to those measures having to do with the utilization of higher-order intellectual processes such as analysis, synthesis, reasoning, logic, and knowledge comprehension. As Astin points out, the cognitive learning outcomes of college are perhaps those most closely associated with the educational objectives not only of students, but also of faculty, administrators, trustees, parents, and other constituencies concerned with postsecondary education. Indeed, of all conceivable outcomes of college, those encompassing the cognitive dimension are probably the most central to the traditional mission of the university.

Affective or noncognitive outcomes refer to students' attitudes, values, self-concepts, aspirations, interpersonal relationships, and personality dispositions. While these are arguably less central to the mission of the university than learning and cognitive development, they have nevertheless been the focus of substantial research and writing (e.g., Feldman and Newcomb, 1969). Astin suggests that the techniques for measuring such outputs are not as far advanced psychometrically as those for measuring cognitive outputs.

The second dimension of Astin's taxonomy refers to the operations that are required to collect measurements or observations of the cognitive or affective outputs under consideration. This dimension is dichotomized into psychological data and behavioral data. Psychological data refer to the internal states or traits of the individual and are, therefore, typically assessed indirectly. The investigator, for example, infers that a student "thinks critically" or has a certain amount of "mathematics aptitude" judging by the student's scores on a particular test or examination. Thus the researcher is inferring an internal state of the individual based on responses to a set of questions. Behavioral measures, on the other hand, are based on direct observation of the individual in his or her environment. Consequently, there is little to infer.

Astin's 2 × 2 model of college outcomes, then, permits one to look at four distinct types of outcomes based on the intersection of the two dimensions: *cognitive-psychological* (e.g., knowledge, general intelligence, critical thinking ability, academic achievement); *cognitive-behavioral* (e.g., level of educational attainment, occupational attainment, income); *affective-psychological* (e.g., self-concept, values, attitudes, satisfaction with college); and *affective-behavioral* (e.g., choice of major, choice of career, interpersonal relations).

Since this paper reviews the accumulated evidence pertaining to the effects of postsecondary education on learning and cognitive development, it will be concerned primarily with the cognitive-psychological cell of Astin's taxonomy of college outcomes. Thus it will include measures of intellectual aptitude, general and specialized knowledge, academic achievement, and higher-order cognitive skills such as critical thinking ability. Excluded will be measures such as theoretical orientation and interest in ideas. While obviously important outcomes of postsecondary education, such measured personality traits fall more appropriately into the affective-psychological cell of the taxonomy.

REVIEW OF THE LITERATURE

Synthesizing the influence of postsecondary education on learning and cognitive development really entails asking four fundamental questions of the existing literature:

1. *What evidence do we have that learning and cognitive development increase during college?* This, of course, is the most fundamental question of all, and one on which hinges the importance of all subsequent questions we might ask concerning college impact. Unless there is some reason to believe that individuals increase their knowledge and reasoning skills during college, questions such as the effects of different colleges or of college versus non-college experiences become moot.

2. *What evidence do we have that differential increases in learning and cognitive development occur as the result of differential exposure to postsecondary education?* This question is more specific than the initial question in that it is not only concerned with change, but also focuses on the extent to which change can be attributed to college attendance.

3. *What evidence do we have that different postsecondary institutions have a differential influence on learning and cognitive development?* This question is essentially asking whether or not discernible differences in learning and cognitive development during college are attributable to the type of institution attended.

4. What evidence do we have that differences in learning and cognitive development are attributable to different college experiences within the same institution? This question is concerned with identifying different subenvironments within the institution that may differentially influence learning.

I. EVIDENCE PERTAINING TO GROWTH IN LEARNING AND COGNITIVE DEVELOPMENT DURING COLLEGE

As indicated in a review by Pace (1979), there is substantial evidence to suggest that students learn a considerable amount during college. He synthesizes the last fifty years of standardized testing on college populations (Educational Testing Service, 1954, 1976, 1978; Learner and Wood, 1938) and concludes that the longer one attends college, the more one knows in terms of general knowledge. Furthermore, the more one studies in a particular area of knowledge (e.g., majoring in humanities, social sciences, mathematics, physical sciences), the more one knows in terms of knowledge specific to that area. This is not particularly surprising, in that the longer one is exposed to an environment that emphasizes both general and specific knowledge comprehension, the more likely one is to internalize the normative values of that environment and to learn from it (Coleman, 1960).

Similar evidence is presented by Lenning, Munday, and Maxey (1969) in research conducted at five institutions: two state colleges, a private liberal arts college, a junior college, and a state university. The tests of the American College Testing Program were administered to samples of students at each institution prior to their freshman year and at the conclusion of their sophomore year. The ACT tests are designed to be generalized measures of educational development in the subject matter areas of English, mathematics, social studies, and natural sciences. (Only students on whom two scores were available were included in the analysis.) Pre-test to post-test gain scores were tested for significance. With the exception of the female sample at one institution, the gains on ACT composite scores for all samples were statistically reliable. On the subject matter scales students made the largest gains on the social studies and natural sciences subscores and less pronounced gains on the English and mathematics subscores.

A follow-up study to Lenning, Munday, and Maxey's was conducted by Dumont and Troelstrup (1981). Using essentially the same longitudinal design, Dumont and Troelstrup followed a small ($N = 112$) sample of students from one institution over a four-year period (1974–1978) to assess their gains on the ACT tests. The average freshman to senior gains on the ACT composite and the four subject matter areas were all statistically significant and ranged from .30 to .68 of the pre-test standard deviations. Compared to the sophomores at all five institutions in the Lenning, Munday, and Maxey study, the seniors in the Dumont and Troelstrup study showed greater gains in English and mathematics achievement. They also showed greater gains than the five-institution averages of the Lenning, Munday, and Maxey sophomores on the ACT composite and on the social studies and natural science subtests.

There is, in short, substantial consistent evidence in the literature to support the undramatic contention that students typically "know" more when they leave college as seniors than when they entered as freshmen. There is additional evidence, moreover, to suggest that the cognitive gains are not limited to increases in academic knowledge. It would appear that students also make substantial gains in their capacity for complex thought processes. This is particularly evident in a cluster of areas which can best be termed "critical or reflective thinking ability." This concept encompasses such intellectual capabilities as the formulation of concepts, the ability to analyze arguments and supporting data, and the ability to think abstractly and to discriminate among abstractions.

Perhaps the earliest comprehensive investigation in this area was conducted by Lehmann (1963). Lehmann used a longitudinal design which followed a cohort of 1,051 first-time freshmen entering Michigan State in 1958 over a four-year period. The American Council on Education's Test of Critical Thinking Ability was administered to the sample at entrance to college and again at the end of the freshman and subsequent years in college. The ACE Test of Critical Thinking Ability consists of 52 verbal, situational-type problems designed to tap five dimensions thought to be involved in critical thinking. These are the ability to (1) define a problem, (2) select information or data pertinent to the problem, (3) recognize stated and unstated assumptions, (4) formulate and select relevant hypotheses, and (5) draw valid conclusions. The composite score had a four-year test-retest reliability of .63 for men in the sample and .70 for women. Both male and female cohorts had significantly higher test scores as seniors than they did as freshmen. The greatest gains, however, appeared to occur sometime between the beginning and end of the freshman year. There was no significant differential change between sexes.

More recent evidence presented by Keeley, Browne, and Kreutzer (1982) tends to support Lehmann's findings. Using a cross-sectional design, Keeley, Browne, and Kreutzer administered open-ended and essay measures of critical thinking to 145 freshmen and 155 seniors at a large eastern state university. The two samples were each randomly divided into two halves, with one-half receiving general instructions and the other half receiving multiple specific instructions for writing critical evaluations of an essay. The resultant critical essays were scored for eight separate items and total score in the specific question condition and for various levels of criticism in the general question condition. Because of the cross-sectional nature of the design, analysis of covariance was employed to control freshman-senior differences in academic aptitude (the ACT composite score was the covariate). Adjusting for differences in initial aptitude, seniors scored significantly higher than freshmen on two questions (identifying the controversy and the conclusions of the essay, and identifying assumptions) and on total score in the specific question condition. In the general question condition seniors had significantly higher aptitude-adjusted scores on six of seven criticism categories: general criticism; specific criticisms; understanding of structure; logical consistency; explicit criticism strategy; and essay length. In the specific criticism subcategory seniors pointed out more ambiguities, logical flaws, and misuses of data than did freshmen.

The most recent research on the development of critical thinking during college is reported in a comprehensive evalution of a liberal arts program at Alverno College (Mentkowski and Strait, 1983). Over 700 freshman were assessed with a battery of instruments at entrance to college and at the end of their sophomore and senior years. Thus the design of the study was longitudinal and traced the same cohorts of students over time. The measure of critical thinking or reasoning was the Watson-Glaser Critical Thinking Appraisal (Watson and Glaser, 1964). This test measures critical thinking along three dimensions: inference (the ability to distinguish the degree of validity or invalidity of inferences drawn from data); recognition (ability to recognize unstated assumptions or presuppositions in given assertions); and deduction (deductive reasoning).

Mentkowski and Strait also employed a test of cognitive development which was essentially a measure of the extent to which an individual could reason abstractly, or at the Piagetian level termed "formal" reasoning. This test included two problems in proportionality, two problems in conservation of volume, and one problem on the separation of variables.

Repeated measures analyses of variance indicated statistically significant freshman to sophomore year increases on the inference and deduction scales of the critical thinking appraisal and significant sophomore to senior gains on the inference, recognition, and deduction scales. There was also a significant freshman to sophomore increase on the Piagetian measure of cognitive development. This latter finding is quite consistent with earlier research by Eisert and Tomlinson-Keasey (1978) on a somewhat smaller scale. They found that 22 freshman men and 33 freshman women showed significant increases during the freshman year on a specially devised test of formal operational reasoning.

As the above investigations indicate, most of the research on the development of critical thinking and reasoning during college has been conducted in single-institution settings. Winter and McClelland (1978) and Winter, McClelland, and Stewart (1981), however, have tried to estimate gains in critical thinking with multiple-institution samples of students drawn from three diverse institutions: an elite liberal arts college, a state teachers college, and a two-year community college. The design was cross-sectional at the teachers college and the community college, and both cross-sectional and longitudinal at the liberal arts college. The measure of critical thinking was the Test of Thematic Analysis (Winter and McClelland, 1978), an essay measure of critical thinking which assesses the "ability to form and articulate complex concepts and then the use of these concepts in drawing contrasts among examples and instances in the real world" (p. 9). As such it is a broad analytical measure of thinking or reasoning ability. The test presents a person with two different groups of Thematic Apperception Test stories. He or she is then asked to formulate and describe the differences between them in a thirty-minute essay. This essay is subsequently judged against nine criteria: parallel comparison; exceptions or qualifications; examples; overarching issues; redefinition; subsuming alternatives; nonparallel comparisons (e.g., "apples and oranges"); affective reaction; and subjective reactions.

A cohort of 80 students at the elite liberal arts college showed statistically significant freshman to senior year increases on the total Thematic Analysis score. In the cross-sectional comparisons of separate samples of freshmen and seniors at the the three institutions, seniors had significantly higher Thematic Analysis scores than freshmen at the elite liberal arts college. The freshman-senior differences at the teachers college and the freshman-sophomore differences at the community college, however, were small and not statistically reliable. Although no statistical control procedure was used to "covary out" possible differences between the freshman and senior samples, the various background and aptitude (SAT) differences noted between the freshman and senior samples at the same institution were not statistically significant. Thus it is unlikely that differences between the freshman and senior samples were simply the result of systematic differences in attrition or recruitment which might have produced a more selective senior-year population.

In addition to the concept of critical thinking ability, a considerable body of research has focused on another closely related concept which might be termed "intellectual flexibility." As suggested by Winter, McClelland, and Stewart (1981), disciplined flexibility in analytical thinking involves the ability to reason effectively and abstractly within relative value systems, that is, "it involves the ability to keep cool and see the elements of truth in all sides of a heated controversy, to analyze arguments and construct coherent ways of evaluating them" (p. 32). They sought to measure intellectual flexibility in analysis by means of the Analysis of Argument Test (Stewart, 1977). The test confronts subjects with a controversial statement (e.g., a statement defending abortion) and asks them to write both a defense and a critique of the statement. The two essays (one defending the statement and one attacking it) are scored along ten criteria (e.g., presence of a central organizing principle, focus on logic, proposing distinctions, and exposing contradictions).

Employing the same samples as in their previous analysis with the Thematic Analysis Test, Winter, McClelland, and Stewart (1981) found significant differences between freshmen and final-year students at all three institutions on the total score of the Analysis of Argument Test. A significant class × institution interaction, however, suggested that the freshman-final year differences were substantially greater at the liberal arts college than at either the teachers college or the community college.

A variation on the theme of intellectual flexibility is found in the body of work focusing on "reflective judgment." Reflective judgment, as developed by King (1977), Kitchener (1977), and Kitchener and King (1981), is a scheme to understand the development of complex reasoning and judgment skills, which draws heavily on the thinking of Perry (1970). As in the Perry scheme, reflective judgment can best be thought of as existing along a multilevel continuum (Schmidt and Davison, 1981). The positions (as summarized by Schmidt and Davison, undated) are: *dualism* (reasoning is simplistic and often illogical); *multiplicity* (reasoning is characterized by a recognition of alternative points of view); *relativism* (reasoning is characterized by the recognition that evidence is the basis of well-grounded opinions); *probalism* (reasoning is based on evidence and logic, views are subject to change based on new evidence).

Reflective judgment is measured by an interview which confronts the subject with four controversial dilemmas and a set of standardized questions designed to tap level of reasoning. Because the measurement of reflective judgment requires an interview, most research on the topic has been limited to small samples. At the same time there is a considerable body of research which links postsecondary education with increases in reflective judgment. Much of this research is summarized in an excellent review by Brabeck (1983).

Brabeck reviews the results of seven cross-sectional studies (Brabeck, forthcoming; King and Parker, 1978; Kitchener and King, 1981; Lawson, 1980; Mines, 1980; Strange and King, 1981; Welfel, 1982) and three longitudinal studies (Brabeck and Wood, 1983; King et al., forthcoming; Welfel and Davison, 1983) using the reflective judgment interview (RJI). The various cross-sectional studies compared high school students with college students, college freshmen with college seniors, undergraduate students with master's and doctoral students, and master's students with doctoral students. In all studies except one, students at higher levels of postsecondary education had significantly higher RJI scores than students at lower levels. Similarly, all three longitudinal studies showed statistically significant, though small, gains on the RJI from high school to college, from freshman to senior year, from undergraduate to graduate school, and from master's to doctoral degree. It would appear from these results that reasoning skills as measured by the reflective judgment interview follow a sequential development, and that this development is linked with one's extent of exposure to postsecondary education.

A final related aspect of intellectual or cognitive development studied in relation to postsecondary education is the concept of conceptual complexity. Conceptual or cognitive complexity is the extent to which a person is capable of attending to a large variety of cognitive stimuli and can organize his or her dealings with the external environment in complex and varied ways (Harvey, Hunt, and Schroder, 1961). Individuals with a high level of conceptual complexity "can generate their own criteria for organizing and evaluating their dichotomous distinctions, they can view more subtle relationships between elements in their environment, and can synthesize these elements more fully" (Khalili and Hood, 1983, p. 389).

Khalili and Hood (1983) investigated the link between postsecondary education and the development of conceptual complexity by means of a longitudinal investigation of 101 freshmen. In order to assess conceptual complexity the freshman sample was given the paragraph completion method (Hunt et al., 1978). (The paragraph completion method is a semi-projective measure designed to test conceptual level by having subjects complete six sentences. The responses are scored by independent judges, whose average ratings yield a conceptual level.) In order to assess gains in conceptual level the freshman sample was readministered the paragraph completion method during their senior year. The average freshman to senior gain in conceptual complexity was statistically significant and was approximately 1.33 standard deviations in magnitude.

Thus a rather substantial body of evidence suggests that exposure to postsecondary education is linked not only with gains in general, and to a somewhat lesser extent, specific knowledge, but also with increases in critical thinking (as assessed by a number of different methods), abstract or formal reasoning, intellectual and analytical flexibility, and conceptual or cognitive complexity. As compared to freshmen, seniors not only tend to know more but also to possess more highly developed reasoning and thinking skills.

Of course, saying that such increases in learning and cognitive development occur *during* college is quite a different matter from saying that they occur *as a result of* college. A number of fundamental design flaws in the studies reviewed above prevent the unequivocal attribution of the increases to the college experience. In cross-sectional designs (comparing separate samples of freshmen and seniors at the same time) differential institutional recruiting standards and the natural attrition of less capable students from the freshman to the senior year may yield a substantially more selective population of seniors than the population of freshmen with whom they are compared. Thus the differences noted could simply be the result of comparing samples from different populations rather than reflecting the effects of college. While longitudinal designs (e.g., following the same cohort of subjects from freshman to senior year) control for this threat to the internal validity of the study, the attrition of subjects may yield a sample which is unrepresentative of the population. Moreover, in the absence of a control group of similar individuals who do not attend college (a characteristic of all the above-reviewed studies), it is essentially impossible to separate the freshman to senior gains due to the college experience from those due to normal intellectual maturation in young adults.

II. ATTRIBUTING GROWTH IN LEARNING AND COGNITIVE DEVELOPMENT TO POSTSECONDARY EDUCATION

One rather direct method for determining the influence of college on learning and cognitive development is simply to ask those who attended college to estimate its impact retrospectively. This was the strategy of two large national surveys of college graduates during the late 1960s and early 1970s (Solomon, Bisconti, and Ochsner, 1977; Spaeth and Greely, 1970). Both studies report evidence suggesting that the majority of graduates attribute their undergraduate experience with having significantly increased both their knowledge and their ability to think clearly and effectively. Such evidence, of course, is encouraging. The possibility nevertheless exists that equally capable individuals who did not go to college would feel equally influenced by their own noncollegiate experiences.

This issue was addressed to some extent in a massive secondary analysis by Hyman, Wright, and Reed (1975). Using data from 72 Gallup, National Opinion Research Center, and Institute for Social Research samples covering more than 25 years, Hyman, Wright and Reed analyzed individuals' responses to a battery of factual questions on history, science, vocabulary, government, public affairs, etc. When age was taken into account the higher the subject's level of formal educational attainment, the more often correct responses were given. From this evidence the authors concluded that formal education produces "pervasive and enduring effects on knowledge" (p. 109). Of course, without controlling for potentially confounding background factors such as intelligence, motivation, and aspiration, attributing these effects to level of formal education is fraught with hazards. The results of the analyses may simply reflect systematic differences in background factors among those who seek varying levels of formal education.

Studies which attempt to determine if differential gains in learning and cognitive development are attributable to differences in exposure to postsecondary education are, by necessity, more complex in scope and design than investigations which show that students change during college. Typically, though not always, such studies are longitudinal and attempt to include control groups of subjects who do not attend college or who have less than four years' exposure to postsecondary education. Because it is nearly impossible to control individual differences among subjects by random assignment to different levels of exposure to postsecondary education, these studies often rely on various forms of statistical control (e.g., multiple regression, analysis of covariance) to identify the unique effects of college.

Much of the research on the influence of postsecondary education on learning has been conducted by Wolfle and colleagues (Robertshaw and Wolfle, 1982; Wolfle, 1980b, 1983). In an excellent combination of meticulous scholarship and empirical analysis, Wolfle (1980b) constructed a correlation matrix based on published evidence from eight different sources. From this correlation matrix he tested a causal model which postulated that verbal skills (as assessed by a 10-item measure of vocabulary) were a function of adult intelligence, formal education, age, sex, and father's education. Adult intelligence was a function of formal education, age, and childhood intelligence. Formal education (through the bachelor's degree level, mean = 12.29, standard deviation = 2.66) was a function of childhood intelligence, age, sex, father's education, and father's socioeconomic status. Wolfle solved each equation with ordinary least-squares multiple regression and found that amount of formal education had only a small (.03) direct influence on verbal skills when age, sex, father's education, and adult intelligence were controlled statistically. (The direct effect is the standardized regression, or beta, weight for a variable. It indicates the amount of change in the dependent measure for every unit standard deviation change in the predictor variable, holding constant the influence of all other variables in the equation.)

Although the direct effect of formal education on verbal achievement was small, education nevertheless had a moderate direct effect on adult intelligence (.19), which, in turn, had a strong direct effect (.80) on achievement. Thus amount of formal education also indirectly influenced achievement through its direct influence on adult intelligence. The indirect effect of education on achievement throught adult intelligence was .15 (the product of .19 × .80). This gave a total effect of education on verbal achievement of .18 (i.e., the direct effect, .03, plus the indirect effect, .15).

Additional evidence more directly related to the effects of college versus non-college is presented in Wolfle (1983) and Robertshaw and Wolfle (1982) using the 1979 follow-up of the National Longitudinal Study of the High School Class of 1972. The dependent measures in both studies were a 15-item vocabulary test and 25-item mathematics test administered in 1979. (The vocabulary test was designed *not* to have a "collegiate bias," and the math test required basic computational skills.) Wolfle controlled for ethnicity, parents' education, father's occupation, and 1972 scores on each 1979 outcome measure and found that amount of formal postsecondary education had statistically significant standardized regression coefficients with both 1979 vocabulary and 1979 mathematics scores. Using the metric (unstandardized) regression weight from Wolfle's data, each year of exposure to postsecondary education was worth a .355 point increase in vocabulary and a .487 point increase in mathematics. Thus, statistically controlling for all other variables in the equation, individuals who completed four years of college averaged 1.42 (out of 15) points higher in vocabulary and 1.95 (out of 25) points higher in mathematics than individuals who never attended college. No significant differences in the effects of postsecondary education were noted between black and white students.

Robertshaw and Wolfle reanalyzed the 1972 NLS data to determine the value of two-year colleges for black and white students. Amount of schooling was coded: 1 = high school only; 2 = non-college vocational school; 3 = two-year-college vocational; 4 = two-year-college academic; 5 = four-year college. Analysis of covariance was used to control for parents' education, father's occupation, and 1972 verbal and mathematics scores. Comparison of covariate-adjusted 1979 achievement scores for whites indicated significantly higher verbal and mathematics achievement for all groups with some education beyond high school (as compared to the high-school-only group). The greatest differences on both tests, however, were between the high-school-only group and the four-year-college group. Based on adjusted means, four years of college was worth 2.15 points (out of 15) on the verbal score and 2.66 points (out of 25) on the mathematics test.

For blacks the only significant mean achievement differences on both tests were between the four-year-college group and the high-school-only group. Four years of college was worth 2.08 points on the verbal test and 2.97 points on the mathematics test. Blacks having exposure to two years of college did have higher mathematics scores than those attending only high school; the differences, however, were nonsignificant. Thus, although both blacks and whites benefited significantly in verbal and mathematics achievement from four years of college, the cognitive value of two-year colleges was somewhat more pronounced for white students.

Robertshaw and Wolfle also report an additional finding of interest from their analyses. While verbal scores appeared to increase over the seven years from 1972 to 1979, mathematics scores tended to decline or remain constant, regardless of the amount or type of education completed. Thus the cognitive benefits in 1979 mathematics achievement derived from exposure to postsecondary education were more a matter of maintaining 1972 levels than of substantially increasing mathematics competencies. The significant differences found between those individuals attending four years of college and those attending high school only were largely a function of the first group's maintaining 1972 levels while the second group retrogressed. (Of course, it should be pointed out that for certain subgroups, e.g., those majoring in mathematics, science, or engineering in college, the mathematics gains are likely to be substantial.)

A final study using the same (NLS, 1972) data set was conducted by Owings and Fetters (1983). Owings and Fetters asked essentially the same questions of the data as Wolfle, with the exception that separate regression equations were solved for black and white males and females. Controlling for family socioeconomic status, employment experience and occupational level, marital status, number of children, and 1972 vocabulary and mathematics scores, amount of college education beyond high school had significant regression coefficients with 1979 vocabulary and mathematics scores for all groups except black males.

These recent analyses conducted on the National Longitudinal Study of the High School Class of 1972 are major contributions to our knowledge of the cognitive value of postsecondary education. Previous reviews (e.g., Bowen, 1977; Pace, 1979) have suggested that postsecondary education increases verbal achievement. The studies on which these conclusions were based, however, did not have control groups of non-college youth for comparative purposes, nor did they generally employ adequate statistical controls. Rather, they tended to be longitudinal or cross-sectional comparisons of different college samples (typified by those studies reviewed in the previous section of this paper). The recent work of Wolfle, Robertshaw and Wolfle, and Owings and Fetters adds increased credibility to the conclusions of Bowen and Pace by suggesting that exposure to postsecondary education has an influence on cognitive learning which is not simply the result of normal intellectual maturation processes. Individuals who completed four years of college demonstrate significantly greater gains in verbal achievement and are significantly more successful in maintaining levels of mathematics knowledge than individuals whose formal education ends with high school. (Unless one majors in mathematics or a related field, college may function essentially to prevent a drop in the level of mathematics with which one left secondary school.) There is some additional, modest evidence to suggest that attendance at various types of two-year colleges has greater cognitive benefit (in terms of verbal and mathematics knowledge) for white than for black students.

From the perspective of those interested in the cognitive "value added" of exposure to postsecondary education, the NLS study has been a particularly valuable and unique data base for secondary analysis. The results, while modest in magnitude, nevertheless tend to confirm the theoretical contentions of Bloom (1964); Horn and Donaldson (1976); McGinn, Viernstein, and Hogan (1980); and Willis, Blieszner, and Baltes (1981) that the intellectual environment to which one is exposed makes a measurable contribution to the development of verbal comprehension and numerical abilities through young adulthood. The measures used to assess verbal and mathematics achievement in the NLS data have the distinct advantage of being standardized across subjects and situations. One possible disadvantage, however, is that the measures are relatively short. As Robertshaw and Wolfle (1982) point out, more comprehensive tests designed to measure depth of knowledge may have shown greater sensitivity to the cognitive development fostered by college attendance.

While there is reasonably convincing evidence from the NLS data to suggest that college attendance positively influences verbal and quantitative learning, no comparable data base exists for assessing the influence of college on cognitive processes such as critical thinking or reflective judgment. This is unfortunate, but also understandable since many of the measures used to assess critical or reflective thinking processes require interviews or ratings of detailed essay responses. As a result we are forced to estimate the influence of postsecondary education on cognitive processes somewhat indirectly. The most useful study in this regard was conducted by Strange (1978).

Strange sought to determine if scores on the reflective judgment interview were more a function of education than of normal maturation (age). The research design employed a sex-balanced sample of 64 liberal arts college students in four groups: 16 traditionally aged freshmen (age = 18); 16 nontraditionally aged freshmen (age = 22); 16 traditionally aged seniors (age = 22); and 16 nontraditionally aged seniors (age = 26). For both the traditional and nontraditional age groups, seniors had significantly higher reflective judgment scores than did freshmen. Conversely, students who were four years apart in age but who were in the same college class (freshmen or seniors) did not differ significantly in reflective judgment scores.

Thus, although there was no control group of non-college subjects for comparative purposes, Strange's analyses nevertheless indicate that amount of postsecondary education may be a more salient factor than simple maturation in the development of reflective judgment. As such, there is at least indirect evidence to suggest that the development of intellectual flexibility (as measured by the reflective judgment interview) is attributable to the college experience itself and not just to the natural intellectual maturation process that occurs over a four-year period. This evidence, however, is somewhat less convincing than that pertaining to the influence of college on verbal and mathematics learning.

III. EVIDENCE PERTAINING TO THE DIFFERENTIAL EFFECTS OF DIFFERENT POSTSECONDARY INSTITUTIONS ON LEARNING AND COGNITIVE DEVELOPMENT

Since the early 1960s a substantial amount of research has been conducted on the effects of different postsecondary institutions on student learning. As with the investigations focusing on the unique effects of postsecondary education on student learning (reviewed in the previous section of this paper), this research is also hindered by the inability to assign individuals to different comparative conditions. In the previous section the problem involved the self-selection of individuals to the college and non-college groups. In this section the problem is manifest in the fact that students are not randomly distributed across different postsecondary institutions (Astin, 1965). Consequently, the achievement outcomes associated with different types of postsecondary institutions are likely to be confounded by differences in the aptitudes, motivations, and aspirations of entering students (Astin, 1970a, 1970b).

Attempting to separate these confounding influences from the effects of different institutional environments entails the use of rather complex statistical controls (e.g., regression analysis or analysis of covariance), as opposed to those more internally valid controls achieved by experimental designs. While there are a number of variations on the basic theme, the typical study uses some form of multiple regression analysis (or analysis of regression residuals) to statistically control for differences in student pre-college characteristics. With student pre-college characteristics controlled statistically, different measures of college characteristics or environmental dimensions are associated with various achievement outcomes. The studies vary in their use of the institution or the student as the unit of analysis. With the student as the unit of analysis, one is essentially asking if the college environment influences individual student behavior. When the institution is used as the unit of analysis, the question is whether the aggregate college environment influences the aggregate student outcome (Burstein, 1980). In the first type of analysis the outcome is individual student achievement, while in the second the outcome is the average student achievement for a particular institution.

Influences on Standardized Achievement Test Scores
Although a number of studies in the late 1950s and early 1960s focused on differences among institutions in their influence on educational aspirations and

status attainment (e.g., Astin, 1961, 1962; Thistlethwaite, 1959, 1960, 1962), the first study to really address the issue of differences in the achievement outcomes among various postsecondary institutions was conducted by Nichols (1964). Nichols used a sample of 356 National Merit Scholarship finalists attending 91 institutions to assess the effects of different colleges on the verbal and quantitative scores of the Graduate Record Examination (GRE). A large battery of student pre-college characteristics (e.g., Scholastic Aptitude Test scores, high school rank, National Merit Scholarship Qualifying Test scores, family characteristics) were controlled by multiple regression and partialling techniques. Partial correlations (controlling for pre-enrollment traits) were then computed between GRE scores and an extensive list of institutional structural/organizational characteristics and environmental measures. The structural/organizational characteristics included such factors as private versus public control, faculty-student ratio, enrollment, and library books per student. Environmental factors were measured using Astin's (1963) Environmental Assessment Technique (EAT). The EAT has six orientations derived from the distribution of major fields at the institution. Students were the unit of analysis.

Two general trends can be gleaned from Nichols' findings. First, the amount of variance in GRE scores associated with differences among colleges was quite small, relative to the amount associated with differences in the pre-college characteristics of students entering different institutions. In short, most of the output achievement differences among students at different institutions was explainable by differences in the pre-college characteristics of the students they enrolled four years earlier. The second major finding was that none of the college structural/organizational characteristics had significant partial correlations with verbal or mathematics achievement (when the influence of student pre-enrollment characteristics was held constant). The only significant (p less than .05) partial correlations were between the GRE verbal scores and three dimensions of the EAT: social orientation (proportion of students majoring in education, nursing, social sciences, etc., $r = .14$); enterprising orientation (proportion of students majoring in advertising, prelaw, etc., $r = .13$) and realistic orientation (proportion of students majoring in engineering, agriculture, etc., $r = -.13$). Such findings are not particularly encouraging, particularly when one considers the fact that, of some 116 partial correlations computed, at least 6 should be significant by chance at p less than .05. At the very best, then, Nichols' investigation presents only marginally suggestive evidence that environmental factors assessing the dominant intellectual orientation of the student culture on a campus have unique influences on learning.

Rather disappointing evidence with respect to differential institutional influence on achievement is also reported by Astin (1968) and Astin and Panos (1969). Using a design quite similar to Nichols' and a sample of 669 students from 38 institutions who had taken the National Merit Scholarship Qualifying Test in secondary school, they sought to determine if traditional indices of institutional quality (e.g., intelligence of student body, financial resources, library size, student-faculty ratio) facilitated the academic achievement of individual students. The dependent measures were scores on the humanities, social sciences, and natural sciences area tests of the Graduate Record Examination. Nearly all of the indices of institutional excellence had statistically significant zero-order correlations with the three GRE scores. When a battery of 103 student input variables (e.g., aspirations, secondary school achievement, aptitude, family background) was controlled statistically, however, nearly all of the partial correlations became trivial in size (average partial $r = .05$), with no single quality index consistently related to more than one of the three scores.

Additional analyses by Astin and Panos suggested that output achievement may be influenced by institutional characteristics other than quality indices. Considering only those factors having significant partial correlations with at least two of the GRE scores (controlling for student input characteristics), achievement was enhanced at institutions where students made frequent use of automobiles, and were undecided about their careers. It was also enhanced at institutions having a generally flexible curriculum with a realistic (technical) emphasis and a relatively large total enrollment. Achievement was negatively associated with student independence and verbal aggressiveness in the classroom, the severity of administrative controls over heterosexual and cheating behavior, and sectarian (Catholic) control. These partial correlations, however, were quite modest in magnitude (average partial $r = .10$). Indeed, when Astin (1968) held background characteristics constant in a hierarchical regression analysis, 69 measures of institutional characteristics and environment increased the explained variance in achievement only 3.3% for the social sciences score, 5.6% for the humanities score, and 3.4% for the natural sciences score. These are quite modest percentages compared to the corresponding percentages of 48.2%, 43.0%, and 49.6% explained by student input characteristics. Thus, consistent with Nichols' 1964 findings, Astin and Panos' analyses suggest that the influence of differences in institutional characteristics on student learning is quite small relative to the influence of differences in the pre-enrollment traits of students enrolled.

While Nichols, Astin, and Panos were concerned with the influence of institutional characteristics on individual student learning and thus used the student as the unit of analysis, more recent investigations by Rock, Centra, and Linn (1970) and Centra and Rock (1971) examined the relationship between college characteristics and student learning with the institution as the unit of analysis. Rock, Centra, and Linn analyzed data from 6,855 students attending 95 small, generally private colleges, 50% of which were church-related and 10 of which had enrollments in excess of 2,000. Their dependent measures were residual scores on the three area tests of the GRE. These residual scores were developed by first regressing the average GRE area score for each institution on the average Scholastic Aptitude Test verbal and mathematics scores for each institution and the proportion of students at each institution majoring in the three areas (humanities, social sciences, or natural sciences). The regression yielded predicted GRE scores for each institution, which when subtracted from the actual score produced the residual score.

Residual scores as used by Rock, Centra, and Linn have two properties. First, they are statistically independent of the predictor variables. Thus the investigators had a measure of institutional achievement which was statistically purged of the influence of the aptitude of the students. Second, despite problems in their reliability, residual scores can nevertheless be used as an estimate of institutional productivity or value added. Positive residual scores indicate institutional achievement higher than would be expected based on student aptitude, while negative residuals would indicate achievement lower than would be expected based on input aptitude.

Rock, Centra, and Linn then used a sophisticated grouping or clustering procedure to relate the three residual GRE scores to a battery of college characteristics traditionally associated with institutional quality (e.g., number of books in the library, proportion of faculty with doctoral degrees, faculty-student ratio). Only two institutional factors, college income per student and proportion of faculty with a doctorate, tended to consistently identify colleges with high residual achievement scores. This tendency was somewhat stronger for natural sciences and humanities than it was for social sciences achievement.

Centra and Rock used the same three dependent variables, and much the same analytical procedures, as Rock, Centra, and Linn, but focused on measures of the institutional environment rather than on traditional indices of institutional quality. Their sample was 1,064 students attending 27 small liberal arts colleges with enrollments of less than 1,500. Measures of the college environment were five factors derived from the Questionnaire on Student and College Characteristics completed by students in the sample: faculty-student interaction, curriculum flexibility, cultural facilities, student activism, and degree of academic challenge.

Each of the GRE scores was residualized on input SAT verbal and mathematics scores, plus major field of study. The residual GRE scores for each institution were then related to the five environmental factors. Faculty-student interaction tended to be linearly related to residual achievement in that colleges with high scores on this dimension tended to overachieve (i.e., have positive achievement residuals) on the humanities and natural science tests, while institutions with low levels of faculty-student interaction tended to underachieve (i.e., negative residuals) on all three GRE area tests. This finding is consistent with an ancillary finding reported by Astin [1968]). Using multiple regression to control salient student pre-enrollment characteristics, Astin found that a variable termed "familiarity with the instructor" had a significant (and positive) partial regression coefficient with the humanities score of the GRE. (The "familiarity with the instructor" scale was a measure of the degree of student-faculty informal interaction.)

Centra and Rock also found that curriculum flexibility was further related to higher than predicted institutional achievement on the natural sciences and social sciences tests. (This finding was also consistent with the positive partial correlations reported between flexibility of the curriculum and the GRE area tests by Astin [1968]). Colleges with relatively high scores on the cultural facilities scale tended to overachieve on the humanities test but to have lower than predicted scores on the natural sciences test. Finally, institutions with relatively high levels of challenge in their academic course work tended to overachieve on the humanities test.

Thus, based on the Centra and Rock findings, a college environment particularly effective in fostering learning is one with the following characteristics: frequent student-faculty interaction, with faculty perceived as being interested in teaching and treating students as individuals; a relatively flexible curriculum in which students have freedom in choosing courses and can experiment before selecting a major; an intellectually challenging academic program with a stress on intellectual rather than social matters; and strong cultural facilities (plays, concerts, lectures, etc.). This portrait of the academically productive college environment is strikingly similar to Jacob's (1957) and Heath's (1968) descriptions of institutions which are particularly effective in influencing student development in areas other than academic achievement (e.g., values, emotional maturity, interpersonal relations).

The most recent research focusing on institutional characteristics and achievement was conducted by Ayres and Bennett (1983) using a sample of 2,229 students from 15 public institutions in North Carolina, 10 predominantly white and five predominantly black. Institutions were the unit of analysis, which meant that the analyses conducted had relatively little statistical power to reject the null hypothesis because of the extremely small sample size. Unlike previous studies, which employed various forms of the Graduate Record Examination, the dependent variable used by Ayres and Bennett was the National Teacher Examination (NTE). The NTE is designed to measure college achievement in professional education, English expression, science, mathematics, social studies, literature, and fine arts. Thus the authors judged it to be a reasonable outcome estimate of a general undergraduate education program.

A regression equation which included the average SAT score of each institution, the average number of credit hours taken in general education, average educational attainment of the faculty, average faculty salary, institutional age, library size, and institutional size explained 88% of the variance in NTE achievement. With the influence of all other variables in the equation held constant statistically, the average educational attainment of faculty accounted for the largest percentage of unique variance in NTE achievement of all variables. (Using the statistics reported in the Ayres and Bennett paper, the unique variance explained by the faculty degree index was 4.8%, $p < .14$). No other institutional variable in the equation approached statistical significance.

Although the institutional sample size of the Ayres and Bennett study was quite small ($n = 15$), their study does have the advantage of a relatively large sample of individual students from each institution (222.9 students per campus). More important, perhaps, is the fact that the major finding of the study is consistent with the earlier results reported by Rock, Centra, and Linn (1970) that proportion of faculty with a doctorate tended to identify institutions that overachieved on the three area scores of the Graduate Record Examination.

Alternative Hypotheses and Methodological Issues

Generally speaking, the results of investigations designed to estimate the relationship between institutional characteristics and student achievement are somewhat disappointing. Regardless of whether individual students or institutions were the unit of analysis, when student input characteristics were held constant statistically, institutional structural or environmental characteristics accounted for a relatively minor percentage of the variance in standardized measures of post-college learning. Furthermore, if one considers only those findings consistent across at least two studies, only measures of student-faculty interaction, degree of curricular flexibility, and faculty formal education had significant partial associations (e.g., partial correlations, partial regression coefficients) with standardized measures of post-college learning. The magnitude of these associations was quite small, however, perhaps even trivial in terms of meaningful influence on learning or achievement.

One obvious interpretation of such findings is that, when statistical controls are made for the students enrolled, different kinds of postsecondary institutions appear to have essentially the same general influence on student learning. In one sense this interpretation of the literature tends to confirm Pace's (1974) findings of increasing homogeneity and conformity among American postsecondary institutions. If one assumes diminishing diversity and distinctiveness among the nation's postsecondary institutions, it follows logically that institutional effects on student learning will be essentially indistinguishable.

There is a certain appeal to this conclusion in that it agrees with existing evidence and provides a clearly parsimonious interpretation. On the other hand, given the fact that such a conclusion is based on only six studies carried out over a time period of nearly two decades, it is worth at least positing several alternative hypotheses to account for the results. Several of these alternative hypotheses are bound up in the methodological problems of existing investigations. One of the most obvious is the restricted range of the samples used. In the Nichols (1964) and the Astin and Panos (1969) investigations (both of which employed students as the unit of analysis), the sample was either National Merit finalists or students who took the Merit Scholarship Qualifying test in secondary school. Such a selective sample will typically attenuate the correlations in any analysis (Cohen and Cohen, 1975). Thus, even if these students attend very different kinds of institutions, environmental effects on individual outcomes are likely to be minimized by the relatively restrictive range of aptitude and achievement represented. In short, analyses of samples consisting largely of the most academically able incoming freshmen may mask important institutional effects that would be discernible in a sample representing a broader range of talent.

A similar problem exists in those studies which use the institution as the unit of analysis. The 95 institutions in the Rock, Centra, and Linn (1970) study were nearly all small, private liberal arts colleges, as were the 27 institutions employed by Centra and Rock (1971.) Restricting the range of institutions sampled may have the same masking tendency on environmental effects as does restricting the range of students sampled. A possible exception is the Ayres and Bennett (1983) study, which looked at a somewhat broader range of institutions. Given that the 15 institutions analyzed were public and in the same state, however, there is a certain lack of diversity even in this sample.

A second potential problem with existing research may be in the way we have operationally defined institutional characteristics. One of the hypotheses tested by existing research is that traditional measures of institutional quality (e.g., faculty-student ratio, library size, selectivity of the student body, formal education of the faculty) will influence student achievement. With minor exceptions, however, there has been little consistent evidence to suggest that differences in such structural/organizational characteristics of institutions have any real direct influence on student achievement.

The reason for this may lie in the fact that the structural characteristics of institutions are quite remote from the types of experiences which we might expect to directly influence learning (e.g., interactions with faculty and other students). Recent evidence presented by Lacy (1978), Pascarella and Terenzini (1980), and Pascarella (1984) has suggested that the structural/organizational characteristics of colleges have little, if any, direct influence on educational outcomes. Rather, their influence tends to be on the quality and frequency of interactions with major agents of socialization on campus (e.g., faculty and peers). It is these interactions with campus socializing agents which have significant direct effects on college outcomes. As such, the influence of institutional structural/organizational characteristics on educational outcomes tends to be indirect, being mediated by interactions with major socialization agents.

That being the case, the search for significant associations (direct effects) between structural indicants of institutional quality and student achievement is unlikely to yield meaningful results. A more fruitful approach may be to determine the ways in which structural measures of institutional quality affect students' formal and informal socialization experiences during college. The pattern of indirect effects can then be investigated by determining the magnitude of the associations between students' socialization experiences during college and achievement outcomes.

A third methodological issue concerns the level at which postsecondary effects are assessed. Most existing research has assumed that the effects of institutional characteristics or environmental factors on student learning are general in nature; that is, the influence of a particular institutional characteristic is esentially the same for all students. With minor exceptions (e.g., Astin, 1968) this assumption seems implicit in nearly all existing studies and certainly has the appeal of parsimony (i.e., other things being equal, the simplest explanation is usually the best). On the other hand, it can be argued that assuming general effects in one's analytical approach ignores individual differences among students attending the same institution. Such individual differences among students may interact with institutional characteristics to yield conditional rather than general effects. Thus the magnitude of the influence on achievement of a particular institutional characteristic may vary for different kinds of students (e.g., variations in aptitude, race, sex, aspirations, etc.). Conditional relationships of this sort are often masked in analyses which consider general effects only. Similarly, the effect on achievement of a particular institutional characteristic may depend to some extent on the time at which the outcome is assessed. Some institutions may have their most significant influence by the end of the freshman year, while for others the major influence may come substantially later. Thus assessing effects only at the end of college may mask significant patterns of institutional differences.

The concept of conditional effects in instructional research (often referred to as aptitude × treatment interactions) is dealt with in considerable detail by Cronbach and Snow (1977). Conditional effects, or aptitude × treatment interactions, typically attempt to determine if the effectiveness (or magnitude of effect) of a particular instructional treatment versus a control varies for students at different levels of the aptitude. Thus, for example, mastery learning may be most effective (in terms of achievement) for low-aptitude students, but least effective with high-aptitude students. Applications of the search for conditional effects with postsecondary samples are provided by Holland (1963) for career choice and grade point average; Pfeifer (1976) for race and grades; Buenz and Merrill (1968), Domino (1968), Pascarella (1978), Ross and Rakow (1981), and Stinard and Dolphin (1981) for different course instructional approaches; and Pascarella and Terenzini (1979) and Pascarella and Chapman (1983) in research on student attrition from college. Expanding this concept in an effort to determine how different institutional/environmental characteristics influence achievement for different kinds of students is a potentially important future research direction which has been largely ignored in existing investigations.

This sensitivity to conditional or interaction effects in college impact research has several important implications. The first is that it may be important to disaggregate institutional effects for different institutional constituencies. An important recent study of this type was conducted by Ayres (1983). Using the same sample as Ayres and Bennett (1983), but with the students ($N = 3,426$ from 15 institutions), rather than the institution, as the unit of analysis, Ayres sought to determine if the racial composition of an institution influenced black and white student achievement on the National Teacher Examination. Controlling for differences in entering aptitude (student SAT scores) with analysis of covariance, Ayres found that black graduates of predominantly white institutions tended to score higher on the NTE than black graduates of predominantly black institution. Here we have the suggestion of a potentially important and provocative institutional influence which may have been masked by failing to disaggregate institutional effects for different and specific racial groups.

A related issue concerns the level of organizational specificity on which we focus when we investigate the effects of institutional or environmental factors on student learning. Given evidence to suggest that a substantial number of distinguishable subenvironments exist within any institution (e.g., Lacy, 1978; Pascarella, 1976; Phelan, 1979; Weidman, 1979), one might legitimately question the sensitivity of existing studies which assess the effects of environmental dimensions or structural characteristics at the institutional level. This level of aggregation may simply be too gross to capture the more salient influence of differential subenvironments or subcultures in the institution. It seems reasonable that if students have more intensive exposure to these subenvironments or subcultures they are more likely to be influenced by them than they are by the global campus environment (Newcomb and Wilson, 1966). Indeed, at many institutions the "average" or "typical" environmental stimuli may have little to do with the reality impinging on students in different campus subenvironments (e.g., different academic majors or residential arrangements).

Thus one alternative explanation for the paucity of consistent institutional effects on student learning is that the institution is simply too general a level of aggregation. Evidence for this is offered by Hartnett and Centra (1977). Their study investigated the effects of academic departments (rather than entire colleges) and employed as a criterion standardized measures of achievement tests appropriate for individual departments. The criteria (dependent variables) were field test scores of the Educational Testing Service Undergraduate Program. The achievement tests for each department were residualized on SAT scores, and departments were the unit of analysis. The analysis revealed substantial between-department variation in educational effectiveness (i.e., residual achievement) within the same institution. For example, many institutions which had departments with achievement in the top 20% of positive residuals (i.e., better than predicted departmental achievement based on student SAT scores) also had departments in the lower 20% of negative residuals. It is likely that such substantive differences within institutions would have been masked in studies where mean institutional score on some structural characteristic or environmental dimension was employed as the unit of analysis.

Related to the issue of the level of organizational specificity at which we study the educational effects of postsecondary institutions is the issue of the specificity with which we measure environmental stimuli. In an important synthesis and critique of instruments which measure institutional environment, Baird (1974) has suggested that most instruments are simply too general or global to enlighten decision makers about the specific policies, practices, and interactions which foster student development. That is, the environmental dimensions assessed by most instruments are quite distal from the outcomes of college which they are assumed to eventually influence. If someone dropped a boulder in Lake Superior, he or she might theoretically anticipate a ripple in Lake Ontario. Whether the ripple would be noticeable, however, is extremely problematic. Instead of global measures of college environment, what may be needed are measures of student experiences more specific and proximal to the achievement outcomes expected. These might include, but not be limited to, the frequency and intensity of involvement in extracurricular and cultural activities, the quality and focus of interactions with peers, the extent and quality of informal interaction with faculty, and the quality of formal instruction received.

This emphasis on assessing students' specific college experiences, rather than their general perceptions of the college environment, has been developed in some detail in a model for college development outlined by Pace (1979). The Pace model suggests that the most important (and typically neglected) element in college impact may be the quality of effort expended by the student. (Certainly, student effort is an undeniably central element in academic learning.) An interesting extension of this argument is that we should probably not expect institutional environments to directly influence student learning with any appreciable degree of magnitude. Rather, certain environments or subenvironments present students with a set of challenging interpersonal, cultural, and intellectual/academic experiences. These environments encourage student involvement and effort, and it is the degree of involvement and quality of student effort which directly influences achievement.

From this perspective an important measurement concern becomes the specificity with which one measures the student's actual experiences, and both the level and quality of involvement in various activities (e.g., studying, reading, attending cultural events, interacting with faculty and peers) during college. To this end Pace (1984) has constructed an instrument termed the College Student Experiences Questionnaire. The instrument is essentially a series of scales which measure the amount, scope, and quality of effort students invest in using the salient facilities and opportunities provided by the institution. These salient facilities and opportunities include classrooms, laboratories, courses, libraries, residence units, cultural facilities, clubs and organizations, faculty and peer interactions, etc. The respondents are asked to indicate how often they have engaged in each activity during the school year. Since a number of the scales tap involvement in learning activities at different levels of cognitive development, the College Student Experiences Questionnaire is a potentially important new conceptualization in measuring those aspects of an institution which foster learning and knowledge acquisition.

Because of its recent development the College Student Experiences Questionnaire has had only limited research use. A report by Pace (1984), however, suggests not only that the various scales measuring quality of student effort have strong internal consistency reliability (ranging from .79 to .90), but also that they may be potentially quite useful in explaining different dimensions of achievement during college. Employing two large samples of students from 19 diverse postsecondary institutions, Pace attempted to predict a number of student self-reported gains in three areas: general education, literature, and arts (e.g., "gaining a broad general education about different fields of knowledge"); intellectual skills (e.g., "ability to think analytically and logically"); and understanding science (e.g., "understanding the nature of science and experimentation"). A series of hierarchical regression analyses was conducted in which Pace first entered student background characteristics (e.g., sex, ethnicity, family characteristics), college status (e.g., year in school, grades, residential status), and environmental factors (e.g., scholarly emphasis, occupational emphasis). With these variables in the equation, and thus controlled statistically, he then entered the quality of effort scales. This type of analysis permitted him to determine for each of the self-reported gain measures the unique variance increment attributable to the quality of effort scales.

In the six analyses conducted, the R^2 increments in self-reported gains attributable to the quality of effort scales ranged from 7% to 25%, all of which were statistically significant at $p < .01$ (by my own calculation). With the exception of college status measures, the quality of effort scales generally explained the largest increments of variance in the self-reported gains. Several of the quality of effort measures had the largest simple correlations of all predictors with the self-reported gains. For example, in both samples quality of effort in activities related to the arts, music, and theater was the best predictor of gains in general education, literature, and the arts. Similarly, quality of effort in science and technology and in science laboratories, had the largest correlations with gains in understanding science and technology. In terms of gains in intellectual skills, quality of effort in course learning experiences had the largest correlation in one sample and the second highest correlation (behind an environmental emphasis on criticism, evaluation, and analysis) in the other sample.

Clearly, the use of self-reported gains is a methodological problem with Pace's analyses. The ability of the quality of effort scales to predict less subjective measures of achievement and cognitive development waits upon additional analyses. At the same time, however, the findings reported are intriguing, and it is likely that considerations of the extent and quality of student effort will play an increasingly important role in future investigations of college impact.

A final measurement problem in existing research may stem from the instruments we have employed to assess the learning outcomes of college. Typically, these have been standardized measures of broad academic achievement (e.g., Graduate Record Examination verbal and quantitative tests, National Teachers Examination), or level of general knowledge in a somewhat more focused curricular area (e.g., Graduate Record Examination area tests in natural sciences, social sciences, and humanities). While such measures are quite strong in terms of their psychometric reliability and content validity, one might question whether they are sensitive or focused enough to capture those aspects of impact on cognitive development which may be unique to some institutions.

A GRE area test, for example, tends to measure commonly agreed-upon general information that characterizes the discipline. The emphasis tends to be on factual knowledge and discipline-centered skills rather than on higher-order cognitive processes such as critical thinking, the ability to form and articulate complex concepts, and the ability to analyze arguments. Of course, this is a matter of emphasis. The GRE area tests do have items which tap complex thinking processes, but this is not the central theme of the instrument. For example, in psychology the GRE would probably be quite interested in one's ability to identify and differentiate the developmental theories of Erikson and Piaget. Considerably less emphasis would be placed on one's ability to critically analyze these theories in light of logical development and evidence presented.

This emphasis on a common body of knowledge and skills is likely to mean that the material tested by the GRE in psychology (or any other area for that matter) is covered in most basic and advanced psychology courses in most institutions. Thus, in terms of performance on the GRE, being a psychology major at one institution may offer little consistent advantage over being a psychology major at another institution. In short, the GRE and related standardized achievement tests may be measuring a common body of knowledge in which there is not a great deal of variation among preparation programs at most institutions. This may, in part at least, account for the relative absence of substantial and consistent institutional differences in GRE performance when statistical controls are made for student pre-college characteristics. Existing studies may have simply focused on achievement outcomes in which we should expect only minimal differences among institutions.

An alternative hypothesis is that a more important difference among postsecondary institutions is in their impact on the development of thinking skills rather than in their impact on student acquisition of a common body of knowledge. Some modest evidence in support of this hypothesis has been reported by Winter and McClelland (1978) and Winter, McClelland, and Stewart (1981). Recall from Section I of this chapter that these researchers found that seniors at an elite liberal arts college had significantly higher scores on the Thematic Analysis Test (an essay measure of critical thinking) than did freshmen. The same cross-sectional comparison at a state teachers college showed much smaller differences which were not significant. Similarly, while seniors at both institutions had significantly higher scores than freshmen on the Analysis of Argument Test (an essay measure of intellectual flexibility in analysis), the magnitude of the difference was significantly greater at the liberal arts college than at the state teachers college. Since freshmen at the liberal arts college had somewhat higher scores on both measures, it is hazardous to attribute these scores to institutional effects. Some interaction of selection and maturation is quite possible (Campbell and Stanley, 1963), and the results would have been somewhat more convincing had freshman differences between institutions been controlled statistically. Nevertheless, the findings are promising and suggest that there may be important, though largely uninvestigated, differences among institutions in their effects on the development of complex cognitive processes and thinking skills. Additional findings supporting this notion have been reported by Pace (1984). In further analyses of student effort he found that small and highly selective liberal arts colleges, as compared to all other institutions, had substantially higher scores, not only on many of the quality of effort scales, but also on student self-reported gains in intellectual skills. Thus it may be that elite liberal arts institutions produce greater gains in cognitive development by fostering higher levels of involvement and effort in the academic and social life of the institution.

I have focused on these methodological and measurement problems not because existing research on the differential effects of college on learning and cognitive development is of particularly poor quality. Indeed, a number of the existing studies are clearly benchmark investigations. Rather, I would simply suggest that it is premature to seek closure on this body of research until a number of additional issues are adequately addressed in future investigations. These would include: analyses based on a broader range of samples at both the student and institutional levels; analyses of indirect and conditional (interaction) effects as well as direct and general effects; analyses which search for effects at a finer level of organizational specificity (e.g., departments) than the total institution; greater behavioral specificity in the assessment of environmental stimuli; and analyses which investigate institutional effects on thinking processes as well as academic achievement.

IV. EVIDENCE PERTAINING TO DIFFERENCES IN LEARNING AND COGNITIVE DEVELOPMENT ATTRIBUTABLE TO DIFFERENT COLLEGE EXPERIENCES WITHIN THE SAME INSTITUTION

In the body of research on the college environment conducted in the early and mid-1960s, the late Ralph Berdie (1967) made a particularly cogent point in a paper entitled "A University Is a Many Faceted Thing." He pointed out that most institutions are not monolithic organizations with a single uniform set of environmental stimuli impinging equally on all members. Rather, individuals are members of different subenvironments within the same institution which may have substantially different influences on growth and development. It would seem to follow, therefore, that considerable interest would focus on the question of whether exposure to different institutional subenvironments and experiences is associated with differences in student learning and cognitive development.

In developing a model of college impact on students Chickering (1969) has suggested that when student background traits and the structural/organizational characteristics of the institution are taken into account, interactions with the major agents of socialization on campus (i.e., faculty and peers) are a particularly important source of influence on student development. Indeed, much of the work which looks at the effects of different institutional experiences or sub-environments on student achievement defines the environment in interpersonal, social, or subcultural terms. From this perspective college is seen as a socializing organization in which individual student behavior is significantly influenced by the social/interpersonal context.

The idea that an individual's social or interpersonal milieu can substantially affect individual behavior is a concept with firm theoretical grounding and empirical support in social psychology (e.g., Asch, 1952; Katz and Kahn, 1978; Newcomb, 1943; Rossi, 1966; Sherif, 1952). Moos (1976) has argued that nearly every institution in our society attempts to provide social environments which maximize certain patterns and directions of personal growth and development. Moreover, as both Moos and Rossi point out, individuals who are members of (or attracted to) a particular social environment will tend to change in the direction of reducing differences between themselves and the normative attitudes, values, and behaviors of the environment.

This notion of "progressive conformity" (Moos, 1976) has an interesting set of potentials. It suggests, for example, that, other factors being equal, a student who is a member of a formal or informal peer group which places a relatively high value on studying hard to achieve good grades will himself also tend to value that behavior. Thus, as Coleman (1966) suggests, one important and immediate impact of student subcultures is on the distribution of the energies and efforts of its members. By influencing one's values or attitudes about the importance of studying behavior, the peer group may indirectly influence academic achievement.

Evidence supporting this notion is reasonably abundant in the study of adolescent subcultures in high school (e.g., Coleman, 1959, 1960; Epstein, 1978; McDill, Meyers, and Rigsby, 1967). The results of this body of evidence generally suggest that an individual student's academic behavior is influenced not only by ability, motivation, aspiration, and home environment, but also by the social pressures applied by other participants in the school setting. In schools, and in adolescent subcultures within schools, where academic competence and intellectual competition are valued and rewarded, individual students tend to conform to the reference-group norms and achieve at a higher level (i.e., receive better grades) than in environments where these behaviors are not valued as highly.

There is also substantial evidence to suggest that a similar social context or peer-culture influence on achievement holds in postsecondary institutions. To accept this conclusion, however, one has also to accept (at least tentatively) two assumptions: first, that academic aptitude is a reasonable proxy measure for academic motivation; and second, that cumulative grade point average is an acceptable, albeit imperfect, measure of academic learning or achievement during college. Given the rather substantial correlation between measures of academic ability and various measures of subsequent achievement in college (Astin, 1971), the first assumption seems reasonably acceptable. Other factors being equal, it seems likely that there would be a discernibly stronger contextual pressure for academic achievement in a group of high-ability students than in groups of more mixed or lesser aptitude (Newcomb, 1968). The second assumption may be somewhat less defensible. Clearly there are fundamental problems of reliability and content validity in the use of cumulative grades as a measure of learning. Despite these problems, however, cumulative grades represent perhaps our best *available* and commonly accepted measure of learning during college, with the exception of standardized tests such as the Graduate Record Exam.

Effects of Residential Environments on Achievement

Not surprisingly, perhaps, much of the research dealing with the influence of student subcultures on academic achievement has been conducted in university residence facilities. Residence halls provide a readily available laboratory setting for the purposeful structuring of student subcultures. Somewhat indirect evidence of subcultural influences is suggested in an early study by Hall and Willerman (1963). In two dormitories high-achieving students (above the median of secondary school class percentile rank) were randomly assigned to room either with another high-achieving student or with a low-achieving student (below the median secondary school class percentile rank). Similar room assignments were made for low-achieving students. Although the differences were not statistically significant (perhaps because of very small sample sizes), high-achieving students matched with other high achievers had higher fall-semester grade point averages than high achievers matched with low achievers. For low-achieving students the pattern was in reverse (i.e., "lows" did better when matched with other "lows" than when matched with "highs"). Again, however, the differences were not statistically significant. An additional set of analyses showed that regardless of their own prior achievement level, students living with high-achieving roommates reported their roommates as being more stimulating, providing a better example in study, and providing more praise and encouragement for studying than did students matched with low-achieving roommates.

DeCoster (1966, 1968) conducted two experiments in university residence facilities which more directly addressed the influence of student peer culture on achievement. The studies randomly assigned high-aptitude and average students to several different living arrangments. The 1966 experiment had four groups: (1) average students (i.e., not defined as high-aptitude) living with high-aptitude students (high ACT or SAT scores); (2) average students living with other average students; (3) high-aptitude students living in close proximity to one another; and (4) high-aptitude students randomly assigned to residence halls. The 1968 experiment randomly assigned high-aptitude students to high-aptitude residences or regular student residences.

In the 1966 study, high-aptitude students living in close proximity to each other in the residence hall had significantly higher cumulative achievement for the year than their high-aptitude counterparts randomly assigned to the residence halls. This effect only held, however, when high-aptitude students were at least 50% of the living unit. There was no significant achievement difference when high-aptitude students were only 25% of the living unit. Moreover, while high-aptitude students appeared to benefit, in terms of academic achievement, from being grouped with other high-aptitude students, the same effect did not hold for average students. Indeed, average students had significantly higher academic achievement when randomly assigned to the residence units than when living in proximity to a concentration of high-aptitude students. In the 1968 study, high-aptitude students in the high-aptitude residences had significantly higher cumulative achievement than their counterparts randomly assigned to the other student residences. The positive influence of homogeneous residence arrangements, however, was somewhat more pronounced for women than for men.

Evidence from the DeCoster experiments would tend to support the notion of peer-group influence on achievement. Indeed, in follow-up surveys the concentrated high-ability students reported that their living units were quite conducive to study, that informal talk sessions among peers had educational value, and that they were influenced by their fellow students to do better in their studies. (This evidence is quite consistent with that of Hall and Willerman, 1963.) The magnitude of this influence, however, would appear to depend upon at least two factors. First, the concentration of high-aptitude students forming the residence group needs to be fairly high (around 50% according to the 1966 experiment). Second, the most pronounced benefits of living with high-aptitude students appear to accrue to other high-aptitude students.

Additional studies by Blai (1971) and Duncan and Stoner (1977) have also investigated the effects on achievement of homogeneous residence grouping with high-ability students. In the Blai study, significantly higher levels of academic achievement were attained by average and below-average-aptitude students rooming with high-aptitude students than by average and below-average students rooming with other average and below-average students. This finding is somewhat at odds with the findings of the DeCoster experiments. Duncan and Stoner, however, found that high-aptitude (honors) students who were homogeneously grouped in a residence unit had higher (though not significant at p less than .05) cumulative achievement over three consecutive quarters than their counterparts randomly assigned to regular residence units.

A final, nonexperimental study conducted by Pascarella and Terenzini (1982) sought to determine if the peer context of a university residence influenced learning (freshman GPA) above and beyond the characteristics of the individual members of the residence unit. To do this they developed a regression equation which initially regressed freshman-year cumulative GPA on various individual measures such as academic aptitude and secondary school achievement and then on the aggregate or average level of these characteristics for seventeen residence facilities at a large private university. This method of multilevel regression modeling is known as contextual analysis (Firebaugh, 1980). Controlling for individual student characteristics, Pascarella and Terenzini found that the *average* secondary school achievement of the members of each residence had a significant positive influence on individual freshman-year academic achievement. Consistent with experimental research, these findings further suggest that a peer context of high achievement has a unique, positive influence on individual achievement.

Homogeneous peer grouping by aptitude or prior achievement is not the only way in which residence arrangement has been structured or investigated to determine its impact on student learning. Additional research has focused on grouping by similarities in personality and academic major. Ainsworth and Maynard (1976) studied the extent to which male roommate similarity on personality dimensions influenced academic achievement. Omnibus Personality Inventory scores were developed for five groups of roommate pairs who were identified as exhibiting similar cumulative achievement and ability patterns. These scores were then analyzed to provide an assessment of the degree of similarity or difference between individuals on the personality dimensions. The results suggest that personality similarity or dissimilarity may have a differential influence on cumulative achievement among students of different ability levels. The combination of a high-ability student (ACT composite one standard deviation or more above the university mean) rooming with an average-ability (ACT composite between plus or minus one standard deviation) or a low-ability student (ACT one standard deviation or more below the mean) whose personality profile is similar to his own may be beneficial to the achievement of the lower-ability student; by the same token it may not necessarily be deleterious to the achievement of the high-ability roommate. Conversely, a high-ability student's achievement appeared adversely affected if he roomed with a lower-ability student of dissimilar personality.

Elton and Bate (1966), Snead and Caple (1971), and Taylor and Hanson (1971) all studied the influence on achievement of grouping students by similar academic major. Snead and Caple found that the homogeneous residence unit grouping of students by Holland's (1963) six categories of academic major appeared to have a positive influence on male cumulative achievement, but not on female achievement. Similarly, Taylor and Hanson found that cumulative achievement was significantly higher for freshman engineering students living in a homogeneous (all-engineer) residence hall as compared with freshman engineers randomly assigned to the traditional residence halls. The magnitude of the effect, however, was most pronounced for students of average ability and least pronounced for high-ability students.

The Elton and Bate study was somewhat more specific in its focus, looking at the influence on achievement of similarity in roommate academic major. The first-semester achievement of roommates enrolled in similar academic programs was compared with that of roommates in different academic programs. Ability and personality factors accounted for nearly all of the variability in first-semester achievement. Matching freshman roommates by similarity of academic major had no significant influence on first-semester college achievement.

A related line of research, but with a somewhat different emphasis, has looked at the broad range of environmental dimensions of the residential experience which impact on student learning. Moos (1979) studied the effects of 52 residence groups on various student outcomes, including achievement. Students ($n = 868$) completed the University Residence Environment Scales (URES) early in the fall and again in the spring of one academic year. (The URES measures the student's residential environment along six dimensions.) End-of-year cumulative academic achievement was regressed on various student input measures (e.g., academic aptitude) to yield predicted achievement. Predicted achievement was then subtracted from actual achievement to produce a residual achievement measure which was statistically independent of input characteristics. Using living units as the unit of analysis, residual achievement was then correlated with the six URES scales.

Two of the URES scales had significant positive correlations with residual achievement: "supportive achievement oriented" ($r = .33$) and "independence oriented" ($r = .40$). The "supportive achievement oriented" focuses on the extent to which academic achievement and classroom competence are rewarded, but in a supportive, noncompetitive context. "Independence oriented" measures the extent to which the living unit encourages a wide diversity of student behaviors without social sanction, as opposed to socially proper conformist behavior being demanded. Two additional scales, "relationship oriented" ($r = -.39$) and "traditionally socially oriented" ($r = -.46$), were negatively associated with residual achievement. The "relationship oriented" scale assesses the extent to which the living unit values involvement and emotional support, while the "traditionally socially oriented" scale measures the degree to which the normative behavior in the living unit demands social order, organization, rules, schedules, and established procedures.

Winston, Hutson, and McCaffrey (1980) used the URES to study the residential environment of university fraternities. Fraternities having particularly high academic achievement were compared with those having particularly low achievement. No significant differences were found in academic aptitude (i.e., average fraternity SAT scores). There were, however, significant differences in the social environments of the fraternities, as measured by the URES. High-achieving fraternities were significantly lower on the "independence oriented" but significantly higher on the "academic achievement oriented" and "intellectuality oriented" scales than were low-achieving fraternities. (The "intellectuality" scale describes the amount of emphasis placed on cultural, artistic, and scholarly intellectual activities, as distinguished from strictly classroom, grade-producing activities.) Thus these results are consistent with those of Moos (1979) with respect to the positive influence on achievement of the living-unit social press for academic achievement. They are somewhat inconsistent with Moos, however, in terms of the influence of the unit environmental press for "independence."

Finally, a study by Blimling and Hample (1979) sought to determine if the total residential environment of a unit could be structured to increase concern with, and emphasis on, study. They reasoned that an increased concern with study would produce a concomitant increase in cumulative student achievement. The experimental condition was a study-floor concept which was expected to yield a structured and supportive study environment. Particular floors in a university residence hall were labeled as study floors. Quiet hours were maintained for study, and students agreed contractually to observe the study-floor rules. Additional support for the study-floor emphasis was anticipated through role modeling and peer conformity to the group norms. Using analysis of covariance to statistically control for sex, aptitude (ACT scores), and previous grade point averages, the study floors had significantly higher average cumulative GPA's than did regular (control) residence units.

Interactions with Faculty and Academic Achievement

Although the student peer culture (particularly as it functions in the residential experience) is a potentially significant influence on individual academic behavior, it is not the only agent of socialization on campus with implications for student achievement. Students, of course, have an extended series of interactions with faculty, in both formal classroom and informal, non-classroom settings. In a sense an institution's faculty, and the different subcultures which they constitute, are themselves important environmental stimuli. Classroom instructional experiences and their influence on specific course content learning constitute a large body of research and inquiry, which is beyond the scope of this paper. Nevertheless, students' interactions with faculty in less formalized, non-classroom situations appear to influence a wide range of outcomes (Clark et al., 1972; Pascarella, 1980; Wilson, Wood, and Gaff, 1974).

If one is willing to assume that faculty generally attach substantial value to student behaviors which increase academic achievement and learning (Wallace, 1963, 1967), and that faculty influence on student values and behaviors is enhanced through informal contact beyond the classroom, it would seem to follow that student-faculty interaction is a potentially important influence on achievement. A number of studies tend to confirm this notion, although the evidence is not unequivocal.

Pascarella and Terenzini (1978), Terenzini and Pascarella (1980), and Terenzini, Pascarella, and Lorang (1982) conducted a series of longitudinal studies of the freshman year at two institutions which sought to determine the influence of different measures of the frequency and quality of student-faculty interactions on a number of educational outcomes, including achievement. The

1978 study used a multiple regression model to control for the influence of fourteen student pre-enrollment characteristics, such as high school academic performance, academic aptitude, personality dimensions, and expectations of certain aspects of college. With these pre-enrollment characteristics controlled, eight measures of the frequency and quality of student-faculty non-classroom interaction accounted for a statistically significant increase in the variance in cumulative freshman-year academic performance of 9.3%. Controlling for the fourteen pre-enrollment characterstics and all other student-faculty interaction variables, two measures of the frequency of student informal interactions with faculty focusing on intellectual or course-related matters and career concerns had significant partial correlations with cumulative freshman-year academic achievement. The partial correlations, however, were quite modest (partial $r =$ .23 for interactions focusing on intellectual/course-related matters and .16 for interactions focusing on students' career concerns).

The Terenzini and Pascarella (1980) study is essentially an attempt to replicate Pascarella and Terenzini (1978) on a different sample of freshmen from the same institution. Using multiple regression to control for a similar set of input characterstics, as well as measures of extracurricular and peer involvement, a set of eight student-faculty interaction variables accounted for a significant increase in the variance in freshman-year GPA of 13.2%. The same two specific measures of the frequency of informal interaction with faculty had significant, positive regression weights with achievement (discussion of intellectual/course-related matters, $\beta = .27$; discussion of career concerns, $\beta = .15$).

The Terenzini, Pascarella, and Lorang study was carried out at a different institution with somewhat less convincing results. Controlling for a battery of pre-enrollment characteristics, and all other measures of student-faculty interaction, only the frequency of student informal interaction with faculty focusing on career concerns had a significant positive beta weight (.11) with freshman-year cumulative achievement. A measure of student perceptions of faculty concern for teaching and individual student development had a small (.09) but significant partial correlation with achievement, controlling for student pre-enrollment characteristics.

In general, the results of these three investigations tend to underscore the findings of Centra and Rock (1971) and Astin (1968) with respect to the importance of frequent student-faculty interaction as an influence on achievement and learning. (Recall that Centra and Rock found that institutions having particularly high Graduate Record Examination achievement had higher levels of faculty-student interaction than did the underachieving institutions.) A problem with the research predicting grade point average, however (which is not so serious a problem when GRE scores are the criterion), is that of causal direction. Do frequency and quality of informal interaction with faculty positively influence academic performance, or is it initial perceptions of academic success that eventually lead students to seek informal contact with faculty outside the classroom (Pascarella, 1980)?

A recent study by Bean and Kuh (1984) has addressed this issue. A causal model was developed which posited student-faculty interaction and freshman-year cumulative achievement as jointly dependent variables. Achievement was a function of high school performance, academic integration during college, and academic difficulty. Frequency of student-faculty informal contact was a function of academic integration, academic difficulty, membership in organizations, advisor contacts, and classroom verbal interaction. The data were analyzed by two-stage least-squares regression procedures (Anderson, 1978). This is a simultaneous equations regression procedure which permits one to determine the pattern of reciprocal influence in jointly dependent measures. For men there was no significant influence of faculty contact on GPA or vice versa. For freshman women, however, the frequency of faculty contact had a marginally significant ($p < .06$), positive effect on GPA (β weight $= .18$), while the influence of GPA on faculty contact was smaller ($\beta = .12$) and nonsignificant. Thus, although modest and not totally consistent, the results of the Bean and Kuh study lend at least weak support to the notion that the causal direction of influence is from frequency of informal contact to achievement.

The results of experimental research on student-faculty interaction and academic achievement are not nearly as positive as the correlational research. Rossman (1967, 1968) conducted two experiments which gave six faculty members in a small liberal arts college released time from teaching to devote to a special program of academic advising. Sixty men and 60 women from two successive freshman classes were assigned to the six special advisors, while the remaining members of the freshman class were assigned to faculty with regular teaching loads. These latter students constituted the control group. The experimental program participants engaged in a planned series of structured and unstructured group discussions with their advisors. In the spring of each year the experimental students (as compared to the controls) were found to be significantly more satisfied with their advisors and significantly more likely to have discussed course planning, career planning, and study problems with advisors. Despite a higher level of non-classroom interaction with faculty, however, the experimental groups did not have significantly higher freshman-year cumulative achievement than the control groups.

At first glance these results (particularly since they are based on experimental data) would seem to conflict with the results of correlational studies. The differences, however, may be accounted for by the fact that the correlational studies reviewed above look at the direct effects of specific types of non-classroom interaction on achievement. The Rossman experiments, on the other hand, look at the overall direct effects on achievement of a global, multidimensional intervention. It may well be, however, that the influence of this intervention is not, in fact, direct. Rather, the special advisor program would appear to positively influence the amount of non-classroom interaction participating students have with faculty. Increased interaction with faculty may, in turn, positively influence achievement (an association which was never really tested by

Rossman). Thus the Rossman experiments may indicate no significant overall direct effect of the experimental intervention on achievement since the discernible influence of the intervention is in reality only indirect, being transmitted through the increased levels of student-faculty non-classroom interaction which it fosters.

Some evidence to suggest that this may be the case is reported in a quasi experiment by Pascarella and Terenzini (1981) which investigated the educational effects of an experimental residence arrangement designed to increase student-faculty non-classroom interaction. Using multiple regression to control for aptitude, secondary school achievement, and a battery of other pre-college characteristics, they found that students living in the experimental residence had significantly more non-classroom interaction with faculty in five of six categories than did students in conventional residence units. (The only category where no differences occurred was "help in resolving a disturbing problem.") In turn, when the battery of pre-college characteristics was controlled statistically, frequency of interactions with faculty focusing on career plans and intellectual issues had significant, positive regression weights with freshman-year cumulative achievement. Thus the experimental intervention influenced student-faculty interaction, which, in turn, influenced student achievement.

Academic Achievement and Person × Environment Fit
By and large, the studies reviewed so far in this section have tended to look at the general impact on academic achievement of specific environments, social contexts, or socialization experiences within an institution. (A possible exception to this is the 1968 experiment by DeCoster.) An argument developed by Nasatir (1963), however, suggests that the academic motivation and success of students may depend not only on the specific social environments or experiences to which they are exposed, but also on the specific relationships of individuals to social environments and experiences. The influence of any particular environment or set of experiences depends on the student's degree of fit with the environment or experiences. (This is conceptually similar to the notion of conditional effects discussed in the previous section of the paper.)

The concept of person × environment fit has solid theoretical underpinnings in Lewin's (1936) social-psychological formula for explaining human behavior, $b = f(p,e)$. This formula posits that behavior (b) can be understood as a function (f) of the interaction or fit between the individual personality (p) and the environment (e). Person × environment fit has been an attractive concept for those interested in explaining various outcomes of college (e.g., Pace and Stern, 1958; Stern, 1970; Tinto, 1975). Relatively few studies, however, have operationally defined person × environment fit in an attempt to explain student learning.

Hayes (1974) investigated the ways in which the patterns of person × environment congruence were related to achievement for 138 minority students enrolled in a compensatory education program at a private institution. The students were administered Stern's (1970) College Characteristics Index (CCI) and Activities Index (AI). Each of 30 scales of the CCI measures the perceived external pressure in the environment for students to engage in particular types of behaviors and activities. The 30 corresponding AI scales, on the other hand, measure the amount of need felt by individual students to engage in these types of behaviors and activities. The 34 students with the most successful cumulative academic records were then compared with the 34 lowest achievers. For the high achievers the vast majority of corresponding scales on the AI and CCI tended to be positively associated, indicating a trend toward congruence between felt needs and perceived external pressures in both intellectual and nonintellectual aspects of their college experience. In contrast, the 34 least successful students had negative associations between several AI and CCI scales assessing felt needs and environmental pressure for various intellectual activities. For these students there was an indication of less needs-press congruence in intellectual activities than for the high achievers. Thus the results of the Hayes investigation suggest that, for minority students at least, achievement is positively associated with degree of congruence or fit between the individual student and environmental press.

Two additional studies by Holland (1963) and Pace and Baird (1966) also provide some evidence with multi-institutional samples to indicate that person × environment fit may influence student achievement. (I have included these two studies in this section of the paper because grade point average is the criterion variable, a criterion with which it is quite hazardous to make comparisons among institutions.) Holland conducted a four-year predictive study which attempted to explain vocational choice and academic achievement. A large sample of National Merit Scholarship finalists were polled during the senior year of secondary school to assess their plans for choosing a major, and again during their senior year of college to determine their actual choice and their cumulative college academic achievement. The Environmental Assessment Technique, which groups academic majors into six types (conventional, artistic, realistic, investigative, enterprising, and social), was used to categorize academic majors. The students attending a college dominated by EAT types similar to themselves were more likely to have high academic achievement than students in noncongruent EAT environments. For example, art majors in artistic-oriented environments displayed higher levels of achievement than their counterparts in schools dominated by other EAT orientations. (The EAT orientation of an institution is determined by the percentages of students in majors falling in each of the six categories.)

The Pace and Baird study also provides support for the notion of a relationship between person × environment congruence and student achievement during college. It offers additional evidence, however, to suggest that the relationship may be somewhat complex. Pace and Baird obtained environmental and personality measures on a sample of students from nine colleges. The College Characteristics Index was used to assess environmental press, while personality was assessed by a number of different measures (e.g., Allport-Vernon-Lindzey Study of Values, Heston Personal Adjustment Inventory, California Psychological Inventory, Activities Index). Pace and Baird then combined relevant CCI scales to form what they termed an Intellectual/Humanistic/Aesthetic (IHA) environmental press. They also aggregated personality scales to form a corresponding profile of personality orientations or needs. They found that students with above-average IHA needs in an above-average IHA environment were more likely to have above-average achievement than their above-average counterparts in below-average IHA environments. The academic achievement of students with below-average IHA needs, however, was essentially uninfluenced by the level of the IHA environment to which they were exposed.

Of course, a substantial part of these results may be explained by the likely covariation of academic aptitude with an intellectual/humanistic/aesthetic personality orientation. Academic aptitude was not statistically controlled in the study. Nevertheless, the results do suggest that, although needs-press congruence is related to academic achievement, the relationship is most pronounced for students with relatively high IHA needs to begin with. The cumulative achievement of students with relatively low IHA needs was relatively independent of their congruence with the environmental press. Thus the Pace and Baird results suggest a conditional relationship in which the magnitude of the association between needs-press congruence is moderated by level of individual personality needs.

Environmental Effects on Cognitive Development

Clearly the vast majority of investigations reviewed in this section of the paper have focused on the ways in which different social contexts, environmental pressures, and student interactions with faculty and peers influence academic achievement. In contrast, very little inquiry has been devoted to the ways in which these factors influence cognitive development and thinking skills. Perhaps the single most comprehensive and valid study of this type was that conducted by Winter, McClelland, and Stewart (1981).

As reported in Section III of this paper, Winter, McClelland, and Stewart found significantly greater changes in measures of critical thinking/broad analytical skill (Test of Thematic Analysis) and intellectual flexibility (Analysis of Argument) at a prestigious liberal arts college than at a state teachers college or a community college. In order to determine the institutional experiences which accounted for these changes, they conducted a series of intensive analyses of the liberal arts college sample. The dependent measures of interest were freshman-to-senior changes on the Test of Thematic Analysis and the Analysis of Argument, though the investigators also looked at other, noncognitive outcomes. The independent variables were seven scales derived from the factor analysis of a 70-item measure of college experiences. The scales were: academic involvement, extracurricular activity, dormitory-centered life, cultural participation, sports involvement, voluntary service, and science orientation. The raw change scores on the two measures of cognitive development were then regressed on the seven college experience scales. Separate regression equations were developed for the entire sample, men, women, and students graduating from public and private secondary schools.

For change scores on the Test of Thematic Analysis, significant positive regression weights were found for all students, men, and public school graduates on the sports involvement scale. Significant negative regression weights were found for public school graduates on the academic involvement scale, and for all students, men, and private school graduates on the dormitory-centered-life scale. For change scores on the Analysis of Argument, the only significant regression weight was a negative one for private school graduates on the science orientation scale. (Since this single significant regression weight had a reasonably good chance of being the result of fortuitous sampling error, I have chosen to interpret it as a chance finding.)

Clearly there are methodological problems with the Winter, McClelland, and Stewart analyses. Since the prediction equation did not include measures of aptitude or initial level of critical thinking, for example, it is impossible to determine the extent to which the contribution of each of the seven college experience variables to changes in critical thinking is merely the result of colinearity with student ability or initial level of critical thinking. Nevertheless, the results are interesting, if somewhat surprising. Of particular interest are the generally negative associations between dormitory-centered experiences and critical thinking (as measured by the Test of Thematic Analysis). Winter, McClelland, and Stewart suggest one explanation for this finding is that for both private and public school graduates the college's dormitories may be a constraining influence which prolongs an overly protective, quasi-familial living atmosphere (e.g., resident faculty and graduate students *in loco parentis*). Thus, rather than providing an intellectually challenging environment, many dormitory activities may simply provide an insulated, comfortable, and nonchallenging niche for students.

Another possible explanation for this finding is that the dormitory-centered-life scale did not appear to measure the specific amount and types of interactions students had with peers and resident faculty or graduate students in their living units. Such interactions have been shown to influence intellectual orientations and self-perceived intellectual growth, if not actual measures of cognitive development (e.g., Chickering, 1972; Chickering and McCormick, 1973; Pascarella et al., 1983; Terenzini and Pascarella, 1980; Terenzini, Pascarella, and Lorang, 1982).

The second, somewhat unexpected, finding of interest in the Winter, McClelland, and Stewart investigation was the positive influence of varsity sports participation (sports involvement scale) on critical thinking, particularly for men and public school graduates. This finding is explained as follows (1981, p. 134):

> Success in athletics [requires] at least two qualities of mind: disciplined, thorough practice and adaptability to complex and rapidly changing circumstances. Applied to

mental life, this practice and adaptability should enhance a person's ability to form and articulate abstract cognitive concepts to organize complex experience. (Thus coaches in many sports, for example, speak of a player's ability to diagnose or "read" the other team's intentions or the course of the game.)

This would seem to suggest that the student- or scholar-athlete has a set of experiences during college which are particularly rich in terms of their potential for impact on his adaptive and critical thinking processes. It should be pointed out, however, that the institutional ethos, particularly with respect to the importance of athletics in the total scheme of things, may be a significant moderator of this impact. At the particular institution in which these analyses were conducted the varsity athletes did not receive athletic scholarships, live in special dormitories, or take special academic programs. Indeed, they were a representative cross section of the entire student body and, as such, were likely to be active participants in the academic as well as the athletic life of the institution. Whether varsity sports participation would have a similar impact on the cognitive development of student-athletes at institutions where varsity athletics are emphasized at the price of the individual's academic life is quite problematic.

An additional problem with the Winter, McClelland, and Stewart analyses, which the authors themselves point out, is that they had little data on the specific curricular or instructional experiences of the students. The formal curriculum would seemingly be a natural place to look for the kinds of intellectual experiences which would foster critical thinking and general analytical skills. It is likely, however, that one would need to be quite specific in terms of the kinds of intellectual activities considered. Merely looking at differences in broad curricular programs, or even the courses taken, might reveal little without a more fine-grained analysis of such things as the content covered, the amount and type of writing required, the nature of the tests or other evaluations, and the level of intellectual discourse occurring in the classroom. A recent study by Welfel (undated, but supported by a 1979 grant from the National Institute of Education), for example, found no significant differences between liberal arts majors and engineers at the same university in freshman-senior differences on the reflective judgment interview. (Recall that the RJI measures the maturity of an individual's reasoning about complex issues.)

Curricular Effects on Cognitive Development

With respect to specific curricular experiences which positively influence cognitive development there is a small body of evidence to suggest that college classes can be designed to facilitate development along Perry's (1970) scheme of intellectual development (Knefelkamp, 1974; Stephenson and Hunt, 1977; Widick, Knefelkamp, and Parker, 1975; Widick and Simpson, 1978). The Perry scheme sees intellectual development moving through three basic stages: from a dualistic, right-versus-wrong stage, to a relativistic stage in which facts are seen in terms of their context, and finally to a commitment in relativisim stage in which the individual can make intellectual commitments within a context of relative knowledge.

Stephenson and Hunt (1977) report the results of a course-based quasi experiment founded on a theory of cognitive-developmental instruction which was designed to facilitate progress along the stages of the Perry continuum. Cognitive-developmental instruction assumes that intellectual development occurs as a result of "cognitive conflict or dissonance which forces individuals to alter the constructs they have used to reason about certain situations" (Widick, Knefelkamp, and Parker, 1975, p. 291). The experimental intervention was a freshman social science course called "Themes in Human Identity" which focused on human identity addressed within the context of literature and psychology (readings were from such authors as Edward Albee, James Baldwin, Arthur Miller, and Sylvia Plath). The method of instruction was specifically intended to move dualistic students toward the relativistic stage of the Perry continuum. As such, the instruction emphasized challenges to the students' values and cognitive constructs within a supportive teaching paradigm. The control groups were students in a humanities and an English class which focused on similar course content, but without the cognitive-developmental instructional approach.

Unfortunately, students self-selected themselves into both the experimental and control conditions, so the results may be confounded by different forms of selection bias and the interaction of selection and change. Nevertheless, the findings indicated substantially greater stage movement by the experimental students (mean change = +.85 stage) than the control groups (mean change = +.25 stage).

Similar results have been reported in a series of experimental course interventions reported by Knefelkamp (1974), Widick, Knefelkamp, and Parker (1975), and Widick and Simpson (1978). As with the Stephenson and Hunt study, the two interventions described sought to determine if cognitive-developmental course instruction matched to the student's stage on the Perry scheme could facilitate progress along the continuum. In the first study, two classes of freshmen and sophomores were the sample. In one class an instructional approach matched to students at a dualistic developmental level was used; in the other, the approach matched relativistic-thinking students. Students could choose which class to attend. As with the Stephenson and Hunt study, the course was interdisciplinary and included two basic content areas, literature and psychology, which were used to illustrate themes in human identity. The dualistic treatment used two general instructional approaches to provide learner challenges: emphasis on relativisim of viewpoint and experimental learning modes. The relativistic treatment used three general approaches to challenge students: demands for commitment in the face of relativistic, diverse content, indirect experimental learning, and a low level of structure in the instructional process. A projective measure assessing developmental status on the Perry scheme was used to assess pre-treatment to post-treatment change. In both instructional conditions there was a substantial pre- to post-treatment change of slightly more than three-quarters of a stage in the Perry scheme. Unfortunately, since there was an absence of a control group not exposed to one of the treatments, it is impossible to determine how much of this change was actually attributable to the treatments and how much was simply the result of maturation.

The content of the second study was a more traditional, discipline-based course in American history since the Civil War. One section of the course employed a dualistic-level instructional approach which had the following functional components: moderated diversity, experimental learning modes, a high degree of structure, and a "personal" atmosphere. Two control sections were taught in a more traditional discussion format. It is not clear from the study if students could choose the approach or if the intact sections were randomly assigned (the latter normally being a more internally valid design). Pre-treatment to post-treatment changes in Perry scheme developmental stages showed a somewhat greater percentage of the experimental group exhibiting stage progress (63%) than the average of the two control sections (51.5%). No significance test for the difference between these two percentages was reported, however, and my own reanalysis indicates that the difference was not significant at $p < .10$. Moreover, the design might have been more powerful had differences in initial stage level been controlled statistically (e.g., with analysis of covariance).

It also seems a reasonable hypothesis that the specific dynamics of classroom instruction might influence the development of thinking skills. This hypothesis was tested in a correlational investigation of the relationship between college classroom interactions and critical thinking by Smith (1977). The Flanders (1970) interaction analysis system was used to assess four dimensions of classroom behavior and interaction. Critical thinking was measured by the Watson and Glaser (1964) critical thinking appraisal and by Chickering's (1972) self-report index of critical thinking behavior. The classroom interaction measures were related to pre-course to post-course change scores on the critical thinking appraisal and post-course scores on the six dimensions of the self-report index of critical thinking behavior by means of canonical correlation (i.e., multiple regression analysis with more than one dependent variable). The sample was twelve classes (138 students) distributed across disciplines, with analyses conducted at both individual and classroom levels of aggregation. The results suggested that, at both levels of aggregation, three types of classroom interaction were consistently and positively related to gains in critical thinking and to the analysis and synthesis dimensions of critical thinking behavior. These were: the degree to which faculty encouraged, praised, or used student ideas; the degree to which students participated in class and the cognitive level of that participation; and the degree of peer-to-peer interaction in the class.

Clearly the Smith study has a number of methodological limitations (e.g., the lack of control for possible confounding differences in pre-course levels of critical thinking and the potential confounding influence of differences in faculty teaching effectiveness). Nevertheless, the results do suggest that student cognitive development is enhanced by instructional procedures which foster active student involvement in the learning process at a rather high level of intellectual interchange between student and teacher and between student and student. Considered along with the previous evidence from curricular interventions, these findings underscore the potential importance of courses and classroom instructional processes as an institutional mechanism for stimulating the cognitive development of students.

Summary

If one is willing to accept grade point average as a reasonable proxy measure of student learning and achievement during college, then there is modest but fairly consistent evidence to suggest that social contexts, residential environments, and specific types of experiences within an institution may differentially influence learning. The following general conclusions appear warranted.

1. High-aptitude students appear to benefit, in terms of achievement, from living with, or in close proximity to, other high-aptitude students. The evidence concerning the influence on low-aptitude students living with high-aptitude students, however, is mixed. Some studies have indicated a positive influence, while others have suggested a possible deleterious effect.

2. The evidence on homogeneous grouping in residence units by personality traits or academic major is somewhat mixed. Some studies have found no influence, while others report a conditional influence, with academic aptitude as the moderating variable. In two studies (Ainsworth and Maynard, 1976; Taylor and Hanson, 1971) similarity of roommate personality orientation and residence unit academic major had its most significant influence for average- or lower-ability students, particularly (in the Ainsworth and Maynard study) when the average- or lower-ability student was rooming with a higher-ability student.

3. Even when academic aptitude is taken into account, residence facilities (either dormitories or fraternities) in which there is a strong social press for study, academic activities, and academic competence appear to positively influence academic achievement. There is also evidence to suggest that it may be possible to structure a study environment in a living unit which has a positive impact on student achievement.

4. The weight of evidence suggests that when student pre-college characteristics, such as academic aptitude, secondary school achievement, and personality traits, are controlled statistically, the frequency and quality of student non-classroom interactions with faculty tend to be significantly and positively associated with student academic achievement. Such findings, however, are not totally consistent across the body of existing studies (e.g., Bean and Kuh, 1984). Furthermore, not all types of non-classroom interactions with faculty have an equivalent influence on student academic performance. The most salient interactions appear to be those focusing on student career concerns and intellectual issues. Evidence with respect to the direct influence on achievement of struc-

tured interventions designed to increase student-faculty interaction is weak. The reason for this, however, may be that the influence of such interventions on achievement is indirect, being mediated by the increased student-faculty interaction which they appear to foster.

5. The notion of student achievement as a function of person × environment fit has at least some modest support in the few studies in which it is addressed. Additional evidence, however, suggests that the association between student learning and person × environment fit is complex, the magnitude of the association being mediated by level of personality needs.

6. Considerably less attention has been paid to environmental factors or experiences which influence student cognitive development than to those which influence academic achievement. There is some evidence, nevertheless, to suggest that the protective, *in loco parentis* aspects of dormitories may negatively influence freshman-to-senior growth in critical thinking, while participation in varsity sports may have a positive influence. These results are from an elite liberal arts college, however, and the data analyses failed to control for potentially confounding influences such as academic aptitude or initial level of critical thinking. While broad curricular categorizations (e.g., liberal arts, engineering) do not appear to account for significant variations in the development of intellectual flexibility, certain specifically structured curricular interventions appear to be positively associated with gains in this trait. These curricular interventions focus on providing intellectual challenges and instructional supports appropriate for the student's particular level of cognitive development (i.e., person × instructional environment fit). The internal validity of experiments assessing the influence of these curricular interventions, however, is not particularly strong. Thus casual attribution is at best tenuous. Similarly, evidence exists to suggest that critical thinking may be positively influenced by instructional approaches which maximize student classroom involvement and participation at a relatively high level of cognitive activity. The research on which these findings are based, however, is correlational rather than experimental in nature.

V. DIRECTIONS FOR FUTURE RESEARCH

This final section is organized around the four basic questions addressed in the beginning of the chapter. It uses a brief summary of findings as a departure point for suggesting focal areas and methodological approaches to future inquiry on the effects of college on learning and cognitive development.

Increases in Learning and Cognitive Development During Postsecondary Education

There is sufficient evidence from a large number of studies to conclude that students make statistically reliable, and in some cases substantial, gains in general knowledge from freshman to senior year in college. Similarly, most investigations have shown significant freshman-to-senior gains on various measures of cognitive development or thinking skills; though the changes in these areas are not of the magnitude many educators would wish. This body of research has made valuable contributions to our knowledge of what happens to students during exposure to postsecondary education. On the other hand, due to inherent, and perhaps unavoidable, weaknesses, simple pre- and post-test designs make it extremely difficult to differentiate changes due to college from those resulting from normal maturation. Consequently, it is probably the case that we have already learned most of what there is to know from research of this genre. This should not be construed as a call for a moratorium on investigations with simple pre- and post-test designs, but as a contention that there are more important questions that need to be addressed. The answers to these questions will require substantially greater sophistication in both design and data analyses.

Attributing Growth in Learning and Cognitive Development to Exposure to Postsecondary Education
There is also substantial evidence, most of it comparatively recent, to suggest that exposure to postsecondary education may have a unique, positive influence on both verbal and mathematical knowledge. Moreover, given the designs and statistical analyses used in these studies, it would appear that this influence is not simply the result of initial aptitude differences between individuals who attend college and those who do not. This evidence, of course, is based on correlational data (the National Longitudinal Study of the High School Class of 1972) in which there is a clear problem of self-selection into comparison groups. Strictly speaking, causal inferences cannot be made from correlational data with the same degree of certitude as they can from experimental data, in which subjects are assigned to conditions. Nevertheless, the NLS 1972 data base is an important national resource that has permitted investigators to statistically control important confounding factors (e.g., aptitude, race, family background) in the study of college influences on achievement. Though falling short of the internal validity of controlled experiments, the statistical control of important pre-college differences (either through multiple regression or analysis of covariance) should be considered a minimum requirement for future research on college impact.

There is also some evidence to suggest that exposure to postsecondary education has a positive influence on cognitive development and thinking skills. This evidence, however, is not as convincing as that regarding college attendance and learning. An important direction for future research would be to conduct analyses similar to those predicting verbal and mathematical achievement with the NLS 1972 data, but with measures of cognitive development or thinking skills as the dependent variables. Unfortunately, while the NLS 1972 data contain measures of personality traits, such as locus of control, the study does not assess aspects of cognitive processes such as critical thinking ability or reflective judgment. The newly developed national data set ("High School and Beyond"), however, presents a unique opportunity to assess the influence of college on cognitive development as well as academic achievement. It is hoped that those who direct the structure and focus of "High School and Beyond" will make the effort to include measures of cognitive development in its various protocols. One can present a convincing argument that the development of cognitive processes and thinking skills is nearly equal to verbal and mathematical learning as a national education concern. In this regard, the College Outcome Measures Project Tests, recently developed by ACT, represent a potentially important set of additional tools for assessing the development of thinking skills and processes in a reasonably standardized format (Forrest, 1982).

Although there is reasonably clear evidence to suggest that exposure to post-secondary education does make a significant difference in an individual's verbal and mathematical knowledge, it is not clear why this is the case. Existing analyses typically indicate that a variable representing amount of exposure to postsecondary educational has a significant regression weight with various achievement measures, holding pre-enrollment characteristics constant. They do not, however, shed much light on the specific experiences which may underlie this influence. It may be, of course, that the influence which college has on learning is of the gestalt variety, something that derives from the total experience. On the other hand, college students have opportunities for a range of specific experiences and involvements which non-college youth typically do not (e.g., courses, interactions with faculty, cultural events, athletic participation, involvement in residential life). Are there specific experiences which college students have (and non-college youth do not) that account for the influence of exposure to post-secondary education on learning?

Answering this question is conceptually similar to treatment verification in experimental research. Operationally it would involve the development of a series of prediction equations which included measures of those experiences which tend to differentiate college from non-college subjects as well as a measure of differential college exposure. Examples of this procedure are detailed in Lacy (1978), Leinhardt (1980), Pascarella and Terenzini (1980), and White, Pascarella, and Pflaum (1981).

Another problem with existing research is that, while evidence suggests that college does have a unique influence on general verbal and mathematical learning, it is not clear that the influence is the same for all students. Robertshaw and Wolfle (1982), for example, found the cognitive benefits of two-year colleges to be somewhat more pronounced for white than for black students. Investigations which seek to determine if the magnitude of the learning and cognitive benefits of college varies for different kinds of students are an important direction for future research. Attributes such as ethnicity, gender, age, socioeconomic status, level of secondary school preparation, personality traits, and educational/occupational aspirations may be worth considering in terms of their moderating the influence of college on learning and cognitive development.

Differences Among Postsecondary Institutions in Their Effects on Learning and Cognitive Development

Evidence supporting the notion that different postsecondary institutions have a differential influence on learning is very modest, with few consistent findings across studies. Indeed, it may be the case that, when student inputs are controlled, postsecondary institutions have a very similar influence on basic content knowledge, at least as measured by standardized instruments such as the Graduate Record Examination. Such a conclusion, however, is based on the findings of only six studies covering a period of nearly twenty years. It may be premature, therefore, to declare closure on this area of inquiry.

Recent evidence has suggested that it may be possible to distinguish among institutions in terms of the extent to which they foster growth in cognitive processes and thinking skills. This category of outcomes has been largely neglected in multi-institutional studies which focus on differential college impacts. It is, nevertheless, an important area for future research. Cognitive development and thinking skills may constitute a cluster of outcomes on which institutions differ substantially in their impact.

Another area which has been largely ignored in studies of differential college impact on learning and cognitive development is that of conditional effects. One possible explanation for the general absence of consistently significant differences among institutions in achievement is that not all students may be influenced equally. Depending upon individual differences in such factors as ethnicity, gender, socioeconomic status, aptitude, and personal learning styles, the learning of some students may be fostered by a particular institutional environment while for others this same environment may have a less effective or perhaps even an inhibiting influence. It is unlikely that all students will benefit equally from the same institution, program, or instructional emphasis. Determining what kinds of institutional environments maximize learning and cognitive development outcomes for specific types of students is a research issue sorely in need of attention.

Two additional approaches have potential for improving multi-institutional research on the differential effects of colleges on student achievement: causal modeling and multilevel analysis. Causal modeling, which is essentially an attempt to fit a theoretical, explanatory model to data (in the form of a correlation matrix), is discussed in detail in another chapter in this volume. It is also the topic of numerous other discussions (e.g., Anderson and Evans, 1974; Heise, 1975; Kerlinger and Pedhazur, 1973; Maruyama and Walberg, 1982; Wolfle, 1980). An important purpose of causal modeling is to portray the system of direct and indirect influences in a causal system. Thus it is really an attempt to understand the pattern of causal influences leading to a particular criterion, rather than simply attempting to predict that criterion. It is important to understand that causal modeling is not a procedure designed to establish causality with nonexperimental data. This simply cannot be done with correlational evidence. Instead, causal modeling is a procedure which can be used to estimate the plausibility of a theoretical, causal structure.

Methodologically, causal modeling (often in the form of path analysis) offers two distinct advantages over past approaches to the analysis of college impact on learning. First, a causal structure forces the investigator to think theoretically when planning data analyses. One must specify not only the important variables to be included in the model, but also the causal ordering and the pattern of influences (causal paths) among variables through the development of structural equations. These structural equations, which are solved by ordinary least-squares multiple regression, specify how each variable (including the criterion) is a function of causally antecedent variables in the model. Establishing a sound theoretical structure to guide analyses not only makes the interpretation of findings easier but also provides a certain parsimony to the inquiry. One result of parsimony is to minimize colinearity (high intercorrelations) among independent variables in the model, thus better meeting the assumptions of linear regression. Several existing studies have included large numbers of variables in the prediction equations with little or no theoretical justification. The result was substantial multi-colinearity among predictors. This, in turn, produced results which were hazardous to interpret substantively (e.g., variables positively correlated with achievement having significant negative regression weights in the prediction equation).

In addition to conceptual parsimony and its attendant implications for regression analyses, causal modeling also has the advantage of allowing the investigator to estimate the magnitude of indirect as well as direct effects on the criterion measure. The investigation of indirect effects is almost completely absent from multi-institutional studies which look at the differential effects of colleges on learning and cognitive development. It is quite possible, however, that many college structural or environmental factors have important indirect effects on student achievement which have been masked by analytical approaches that consider direct effects only. For example, structural characteristics such as enrollment, student-faculty ratio, etc., may not directly influence college outcomes but may have an indirect effect through the kinds of interactions with major agents of socialization (e.g., faculty, peers) which they do influence. Similarly, Pace (1979) has suggested that the intensity of student effort is an often overlooked variable which may have an important influence on college outcomes (including perhaps levels of learning and cognitive development). It seems a reasonable hypothesis that certain environmental factors (e.g., the degree of study emphasis in the residential environment) might directly influence student effort. Thus a number of environmental factors that do not directly influence the learning and cognitive outcomes of college may nevertheless have important indirect effects through their influence on student effort.

These and similar questions are important topics for future research on the cognitive benefits of college. Sobel (1982) has developed a method for testing the statistical significance of indirect effects, and Wolfle and Ethington (1984) have developed a computer program for deriving standard errors of indirect effects, which can be used to calculate t-ratios. Thus the technical and statistical tools which support causal modeling are growing in both sophistication and usability.

Because it is concerned with understanding the actual dynamics of college impact, rather than merely predicting what happens, causal modeling is an important methodological approach which should find increased use by those interested in the cognitive and other outcomes of college. Indeed, it is likely that the most significant future analyses addressing this topic will be guided by a carefully developed, theoretical causal model.

One very general causal model which may be worth estimating in modified and more specific forms is portrayed in Figure 1. The model draws heavily on the work of Feldman (1971), Lacy (1978), Pace (1979), Pascarella (1980), Walberg (1982), Walberg et al. (1982), and Weidman (forthcoming). As the figure indicates, learning and cognitive development in college are seen as a function of the direct and indirect influences of five major blocks of variables. The dimensions of the institutional environment are directly influenced not only by the background or pre-college traits which matriculating students bring to the institution, but also by the institution's structural/organizational characteristics (e.g., size, admission requirements, faculty-student ratio, percent graduate students, percent residential students).[1] In turn, the college environment, structural characteristics, and student background traits are all seen as directly influencing the frequency and content of interactions with major socializing agents on campus (e.g., peers and faculty). The quality of student effort is posited as being directly affected not only by student background traits (e.g., aptitude, personality, and aspiration level), but also by the press of the dominant environment and the norms and values of the peer and faculty cultures with which the student is in contact. Finally, learning and cognitive development are directly influenced by student background characteristics, interactions with major agents of socialization, and quality of student effort. Interactions with faculty would, of course, also include classroom interactions and the quality and intellectual content of the instruction received. Structural/organizational characteristics and the college environment are not hypothesized by the model as directly influencing learning and cognitive outcomes. Their influence is hypothesized as indirect, being mediated by interactions with socializing agents and the quality of student effort.

It is worth reiterating that this general model is only suggestive of how causal modeling might be used to understand the pattern of influences involved in the impact of postsecondary education on learning and cognitive development. It is not intended to be prescriptive. Rather, its estimation should be expected to lead to more refined and accurate alternative models which better explain the causal structure in different contexts (see, for example, Pascarella, Duby, and Iverson, 1983; Pascarella and Terenzini, 1983).

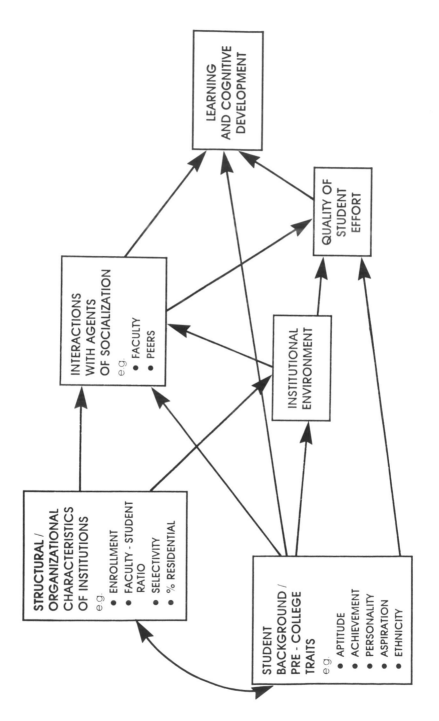

FIG. 1. A general causal model for assessing the effects of differential college environments on student learning and cognitive development.

The second potentially fruitful analytical tack, multilevel analysis, is essentially an approach to the issue of unit of analysis. In the existing multi-institutional research on the learning and cognitive outcomes of college, either the student or the institution has been the unit of analysis. Since these two levels of analysis are asking substantially different questions of the data (Burstein, 1980), differences in the unit of analysis may, at least partially, explain the lack of consistent results across studies. Neither unit of analysis (institutions or individuals) provides results which are inherently more valid than the other. One helpful direction for future research in this area would be to analyze data at both levels of aggregation whenever possible. Such a multilevel approach would permit a more valid and informative comparison of results across studies. It would also permit one to compare differences in the aggregate effects of college with the effects of college on individual student learning and cognitive development.

Most popular computer packages (e.g., Statistical Analysis System, Statistical Package for the Social Sciences) have aggregation routines which permit one to combine individual- and institutional-level data in a single file. Thus the data management problems involved with conducting parallel analyses at both the individual and institutional level are not overly cumbersome. Such combined data files present a convenient format not only for examining individual- and institutional-level effects on cognitive outcomes, but also for examining individual $\times$ institutional interactions (i.e., what institutional characteristics are most influential for students with different individual characteristics). Further, a combined data file also permits relatively convenient testing of hypotheses about the influence of person $\times$ environment fit on the cognitive outcomes of college. For example, what are the implications for the cognitive outcomes of an individual student with academic aptitude substantially above the institutional average versus a student closer to the average or a student substantially below the average? It is not particularly difficult to develop a regression equation to test this type of hypothesis by including theoretically relevant individual characteristics (most likely for control purposes) and a deviation term which subtracts each individual's score from the institutional average. (As a caution it should be noted that individual, institutional average, and institutional average minus individual deviation scores in the same equation create a linear dependency and the equation cannot be estimated [Burstein, 1980.]) An equation with any combination of two of the three vectors, however, can be estimated.

Different levels of analysis (e.g., individual, institutional average, institutional average – individual, and individual $\times$ institutional average) ask somewhat different questions of data. None, however, is inherently more valid than the others, and the question or questions asked should be the ultimate criterion for selecting the level (or unit) of analysis. It it time, perhaps, that we worried less about which level of analysis to use and focused more on testing different models with theoretically justifiable analyses at different levels of aggregation.

Of course, individuals and institutions are not the only important levels of aggregation worth consideration. In terms of impact on the cognitive outcomes of college, aggregates such as departments, classrooms, and even residential facilities may be significant units of analysis.

Effects of Differential Experiences Within the Same Institution on Learning and Cognitive Development

One can conclude from the evidence that there are different subenvironments within the same institution which have differential effects on academic achievement (grade point average) and cognitive development. Residential facilities appear to be a particularly potent social context for influencing student achievement. The academic aptitude of the dominant peer group and the extent to which the group norms of a residence unit function to reinforce a serious study environment are factors which tend to positively influence academic achievement. The protective, *in loco parentis* aspects of residential life, however, may have a negative influence on intellectual flexibility. Frequency of student informal, non-classroom interaction with faculty may also have a positive impact on achievement, particularly if it focuses on intellectual or career-related issues. Finally, there is some evidence to suggest that congruence between student intellectual needs/orientations and the intellectual press of the environment is positively associated with achievement. The relationship, however, appears complex and may be mediated by personality factors.

There is little evidence to suggest that broad curricular categorizations account for significant variations in the development of student intellectual flexibility. Certain specifically structured curricular interventions and instructional practices, however, appear to be positively associated with increases in this trait, as well as with critical thinking. The designs of these studies are not particularly strong, and more internally valid field experiments are needed.

One serious problem with research on the cognitive effects of different subenvironments and experiences within the same institution has been the nearly exclusive use of grade point average as a global measure of the learning that occurs during college. Clearly, an important line of future research would be to determine the direct and indirect effects of such factors as peer cultures, residence environments, and non-classroom interactions with faculty on standardized measures of learning (e.g., the area tests of the Graduate Record Examination). Additional research also needs to address the extent to which these and related institutional experiences influence the different dimensions of cognitive development. Grade point average has definite limitations as a measure of the learning and cognitive outcomes of college, and it is time that researchers considered more specific and valid indicators.

One advantage of single-institution studies is that they often present investigators with greater opportunities for controlled field experiements than are afforded by multi-institutional data. (Indeed, with many large multi-institutional samples researchers are essentially limited to secondary analysis.)

With the possible exception of research in residence facilities, field experiments (in which there is some control over those receiving the intervention and those not receiving it) have been comparatively rare in research on the cognitive outcomes of college. Field experiments, of course, have distinct advantages over correlational studies in terms of internal validity and the degree of confidence with which causal attributions can be made.

One particularly powerful investigative approach, which has seldom been employed, is a program of sequentially integrated correlational and experimental studies. Large-sample correlational investigations could be used to identify significant associations among environmental variables and cognitive outcomes which might be causal in nature. The results of these studies would then help direct the development of experimental interventions which would test the associations found in correlational research under conditions of greater internal validity. Thus correlational studies would be used primarily to formulate causal hypotheses about the direct and indirect effects of environmental factors on learning and cognitive outcomes. Experimental interventions would then be developed to test these hypotheses.

It would be important in analyzing the data from such field experiments to look not only at direct effects on learning and cognitive outcomes, but also at indirect effects. Many interventions which do not have a significant direct influence on cognitive outcomes may, nonetheless, foster experiences, interactions with major agents of socialization, or student efforts in ways that do directly influence these outcomes.

Similarly, it is also important to verify that such interventions are delivered as intended. This entails not only determining the effects of the intervention on the outcome, but also determining that there are intended behavioral, attitudinal, or perceptual differences between those exposed to the intervention and those not exposed to it. Students participating in an experimental program designed to foster critical thinking skills through increased interactions with faculty and peers focusing on discussions of pertinent ethical and philosophical issues, for example, should in fact report more such interactions than students not participating in the program. It is likely that experimental or quasi-experimental interventions designed to increase the cognitive outcomes of college will be multifaceted. Thus studies which relate measures of the various dimensions of an intervention to the criterion will increase the likelihood of understanding which particular dimensions have the most salient effect.

A FINAL THOUGHT

One of the more seductive dangers in the development of a body of knowledge is the temptation to seek premature closure, to think that we have learned enough. Clearly, a great deal has been done in terms of mapping the cognitive benefits of college. There is much of importance, however, that we do not know. We perhaps make more claims for the cognitive outcomes of postsecondary education than we can empirically substantiate. In the final analysis the major contribution of this paper is perhaps not so much as a summative, conclusion-oriented statement as it is a call for continued systematic inquiry in a particularly significant area of knowledge.

NOTES

1. The curvilinear path connecting background/pre-college traits with structural/organizational characteristics of an institution is considered noncausal. Clearly, student background characteristics do not influence such factors as institutional size. However, there is likely to be a noncausal association between student traits and the types of institutions attended.

REFERENCES

Ainsworth, C., and Maynard, D. The impact of roommate personality on achievement: An exploratory study and model of analysis. *Research in Higher Education*, 1976, *4*, 291-301.

Anderson, J. Causal models in educational research: Nonrecursive models. *American Educational Research Journal*, 1978, *15*, 81-97.

Anderson, J., and Evans, F. Causal models in educational research: Recursive models. *American Educational Research Journal*, 1974, *11*, 29-39.

Asch, S. *Social Psychology*. New York: Prentice-Hall, 1952.

Astin, A. A re-examination of college productivity. *Journal of Educational Psychology*. 1961, *52*, 173-178.

Astin, A. Influences on the student's motivation to seek advanced training: Another look. *Journal of Educational Psychology*, 1962, *53*, 303-309.

Astin, A. Further validation of the Environmental Assessment Technique. *Journal of Educational Psychology*, 1963, *54*, 217-226.

Astin, A. Who goes where to college? In A. Astin (ed.), *Who Goes Where to College?* Chicago: Science Research Associates, 1965.

Astin, A. Undergraduate achievement and institutional excellence. *Science*, 1968, *161*, 661-668.

Astin, A. The methodology of research on college impact. (I). *Sociology of Education*, 1970a, *43*, 223-254.

Astin, A. The metholodology of research on college impact. (II). *Sociology of Education*, 1970(b), *43*, 437-450.

Astin, A. *Predicting Academic Performance in College*. New York: Free Press, 1971.

Astin, A. Measurement and determinants of the outputs of higher education. In L. Solomon and Taubman (eds.), *Does College Matter?* New York: Academic Press, 1973.

Astin, A. *Four Critical Years: Effects of College on Beliefs, Attitudes, and Knowledge*. San Francisco: Jossey-Bass, 1977.

Astin, A., and Panos, R. *The Educational and Vocational Development of College Students*. Washington, D.C.: American Council on Education, 1969.

Axelrod, J. *Search for Relevance: The Campus in Crisis*. San Francisco: Jossey-Bass, 1969.

Ayres, Q. Student achievement at predominantly white and predominantly black universities. *American Educational Research Journal*, 1983, *20*, 291-304.

Ayres, Q., and Bennett, R. University characteristics and student achievement. *Journal of Higher Education*, 1983, *54*, 516–532.

Baird, L. The practical utility of measures of college environments. *Review of Educational Research*, 1974, *44*, 307–329.

Barton, A. Studying the effects of college education. In K. Yamamoto (ed.), *The Col-*

lege Student and His Culture: An Analysis. Boston: Houghton Mifflin, 1968.

Bean, J., and Kuh, G. The reciprocity between student-faculty informal contact and the undergraduate grade point average of university students. Paper presented at the annual meeting of the Association for the Study of Higher Education, Chicago, March 1984.

Berdie, R. A university is a many faceted thing. *Personnel and Guidance Journal*, 1967, *45*, 768-775.

Blai, B. *Roommate Impact upon Academic Performance*. Harcum Junior College, February 1971.

Blimling, G., and Hample, D. Structuring the peer environment in residence halls to increase performance in average-ability students. *Journal of College Student Personnel*, 1979, *20*, 310-316.

Bloom, B. *Stability and Change in Human Characteristics*, New York: Wiley, 1964.

Bowen, H. *Investment in Learning*. San Francisco: Jossey-Bass, 1977.

Brabeck, M. Intellectual development during the college years: How strong is the longitudinal evidence? Paper presented at the annual meeting of the American Educational Research Association, Montreal, April 1983.

Brabeck, M. Critical thinking skills and reflective judgment development: Redefining the aims of higher education. *Journal of Applied Developmental Psychology*, forthcoming.

Brabeck, M., and Wood, P. A longitudinal study of reflective judgment development, critical thinking skills and related life experiences. Unpublished manuscript, 1983.

Buenz, R., and Merrill, I. Effects of effort on retention and enjoyment. *Journal of Educational Psychology*, 1968, *59*, 154-158.

Burstein, L. The analysis of multilevel data in educational research and evaluation. In D. Berliner (ed.), *Review of Research in Education*, Vol. *8*. Washington, D.C.: American Educational Research Association, 1980.

Campbell, D., and Stanley, J. Experimental and quasi-experimental designs for research on teaching. In N. Gage (ed.), *Handbook of Research on Teaching*. Chicago: Rand McNally, 1963.

Centra, J. and Rock, D. College environments and student academic achievement. *American Educational Research Journal*, 1971, *8*, 623-634.

Chickering, A. *Education and Identity*. San Francisco: Jossey-Bass, 1969.

Chickering, A. Undergraduate academic experience. *Journal of Educational Psychology*, 1972, *63*, 134-143.

Chickering, A. *The Modern American College: Responding to the New Realities of Diverse Students and a Changing Society*. San Francisco; Jossey-Bass, 1981.

Chickering, A., and McCormick, J. Personality development and the college experience. *Research in Higher Education*, 1973, *1*, 43-70.

Clark, B., Heist, P., McConnell, T., Trow, M., and Yonge, G. *Students and Colleges: Interaction and Change*. Center for Research and Development in Higher Education, University of California, Berkeley, 1972.

Cohen, J., and Cohen, P. *Applied Multiple Regression/Correlation Analysis for the Behavioral Sciences*. Hillsdale, N.J.: Lawrence Erlbaum, 1975.

Coleman, J. Academic achievement and the structure of competition. *Harvard Educational Review*, 1959, *29*, 330-351.

Coleman, J. The adolescent subculture and academic achievement. *American Journal of Sociology*, 1960, *65*, 337-347.

Coleman, J. Peer cultures and education in modern society. In T. Newcomb and E. Wilson (eds.), *College Peer Groups*, Chicago: Aldine, 1966.

Cronbach, L. and Snow, R. *Aptitudes and Instructional Methods: A Handbook for Research on Interactions*. New York: Irvington, 1977.

DeCoster, D. Housing assignments for high ability students. *Journal of College Student*

Personnel, 1966, *7*, 19-22.

DeCoster, D. Effects of homogeneous housing assignments for high ability students. *Journal of College Student Personnel*, 1968, *8*, 75-78.

Domino, G. Differential prediction of academic achievement in conforming and independent settings. *Journal of Educational Psychology*, 1968, *59*, 256-260.

Dumont, R., and Troelstrup, R. Measures and predictors of educational growth with four years of college. *Research in Higher Education*, 1981, *14*, 31-47.

Duncan, C., and Stoner, K. The academic achievement of residents living in a scholar residence hall, *Journal of College and University Student Housing*. 1977, *6*, 7-9.

Eddy, E. *The College Influence on Student Character*. Washington, D.C.: American Council on Education, 1959.

Educational Testing Service, *Institutional Testing Program: Summary Statistics 1953-1954*. ETS Archives Microfiche No. 40, Princeton, N.J.: Educational Testing Service, 1954.

Educational Testing Service, *Undergraduate Assessment Program Guide*. Princeton, N.J.: Educational Testing Service, 1976.

Educational Testing Service, *Undergraduate Assessment Program Guide*. Princeton, N.J.: Educational Testing Service, 1978.

Eisert, D., and Tomlinson-Keasey, C. Cognitive and interpersonal growth during the college freshman year: A structural analysis. *Perceptual and Motor Skills*, 1978, *46*, 995-1005.

Elton, C., and Bate, W. The effect of housing policy on grade-point average. *Journal of College Student Personnel*, 1966, *7*, 73-77.

Epstein, J. *Friends in School: Patterns of Selection and Influence in Secondary Schools*. Report No. 266. Baltimore, Md.: Johns Hopkins University, Center for the Social Organization of Schools, 1978.

Feldman, K. Studying the impacts of college on students. *Sociology of Education*, 1969, *42*, 207-237.

Feldman, K. Measuring college environments: Some uses of path analysis. *American Educational Research Journal*, 1971, *8*, 51-70.

Feldman, K., and Newcomb, T. *The Impact of College on Students*. San Francisco: Jossey-Bass, 1969.

Firebaugh, G. Assessing group effects: A comparison of two methods. In E. Borgatta and D. Jackson (eds.), *Aggregate Data Analysis and Interpretation*. Beverly Hills, Calif.: Sage, 1980.

Flanders, N. *Analyzing Teaching Behavior*, Reading, Mass.: Addison-Wesley, 1970.

Forrest, A. *Increasing Student Competence and Persistence: The Best Case for General Education*. Iowa City, Iowa: American College Testing Program, 1982.

Hall, R., and Willerman, B. The educational influence of dormitory roommates. *Sociometry*, 1963, *26*, 294-318.

Hartnett, R., and Centra, J. The effects of academic departments on student learning. *Journal of Higher Education*, 1977, *48*, 491-507.

Harvey, O., Hunt, D., and Schroder, H. *Conceptual Systems and Personality Organization*. New York: Wiley, 1961.

Hayes, E. Environmental press and psychological need as related to academic success of minority group students. *Journal of Counseling Psychology*, 1974, *21*, 299-304.

Heath, D. *Growing Up in College*. San Francisco: Jossey-Bass, 1968.

Heise, D. *Causal Analysis*. New York: Wiley, 1975.

Holland, J. Explorations of a theory of vocational choice and achievement II: A four year predictive study. *Psychological Reports*, 1963, *12*, 547-594.

Horn, J., and Donaldson, G. On the myth of intellectual decline in adulthood. *American Psychologist*, 1976, *31*, 701-719.

Hunt, D., Butler, L., Noy, J., and Rosse, M. *Assessing Conceptual Level by the Para-*

graph Completion Method. Toronto: Ontario Institute for Studies in Education, 1978.

Hyman, H., Wright, C., and Reed, J. *The Enduring Effects of Education.* Chicago: University of Chicago Press, 1975.

Jacob, P. *Changing Values in College: An Exploratory Study of the Impact of College Teaching.* New York: Harper, 1957.

Katz, D., and Kahn, R. *The Social Psychology of Organizations.* 2nd ed. New York: Wiley, 1978.

Keeley, S., Browne, M., and Kreutzer, J. A comparison of freshmen and seniors on general and specific essay tests of critical thinking. *Research in Higher Education,* 1982, *17,* 139-154.

Kerlinger, F., and Pedhazur, E. *Multiple Regression in Behavioral Research.* New York: Holt, Rinehart and Winston, 1973.

Khalili, H., and Hood, A. A longitudinal study of change in conceptual level in college. *Journal of College Student Personnel,* 1983, *24,* 389-394.

King, P. The development of reflective judgment and formal operational thinking in adolescents and young adults. Unpublished doctoral dissertation, University of Minnesota, 1977.

King, P., and Parker, C. Assessing intellectual development in the college years: A report of the instructional improvement project, 1976-1977. Unpublished manuscript, University of Minnesota, 1978.

King, P., Kitchener, K., Davison, M., Parker, C., and Wood, P. A longitudinal study of reflective judgment and verbal aptitude in young adults. *Human Development,* forthcoming.

Kitchener, K. Intellectual development in late adolescents and young adults: Reflective judgment and verbal reasoning. Unpublished doctoral dissertation, University of Minnesota, 1977.

Kitchener, K., and King, P. Reflective judgment: Concepts of justification and their relationship to age and education. *Journal of Applied Developmental Psychology,* 1981, *2,* 89-116.

Knefelkamp, L. Developmental instruction: Fostering intellectual and personal growth. Unpublished doctoral dissertation, University of Minnesota, 1974.

Lacy, W. Interpersonal relationships as mediators of structural effects: College student socialization in a traditional and an experimental university environment. *Sociology of Education,* 1978, *51,* 201-211.

Lawson, J. The relationship between graduate education and the development of reflective judgement: A function of age or educational experience? Unpublished doctoral dissertation, University of Minnesota, 1980.

Learner, W., and Wood, B. *The Student and His Knowledge: A Report to the Carnegie Foundation on the Results of High School and College Examinations of 1928, 1930 and 1932.* Bulletin No. 29. New York: Carnegie Foundation for the Advancement of Teaching, 1938.

Lehmann, I. Changes in critical thinking, attitudes and values from freshman to senior years. *Journal of Educational Psychology,* 1963, *54,* 305-315.

Leinhardt, G. Modeling and measuring educational treatment in evaluation. *Review of Educational Research,* 1980, *50,* 393-420.

Lenning, O., Munday, L., Johnson, O., Vander Well, A., and Brue, E. *Nonintellective Correlates of Grades, Persistence and Academic Learning in College: The Published Literature Through the Decade of the Seventies.* Iowa City, Iowa: American College Testing Program, 1974.

Lenning, O., Munday, L., and Maxey, J. Student educational growth during the first two years of college. *College and University,* 1969, *44,* 145-153.

Lewin, K. *Principles of Topological Psychology.* New York: McGraw-Hill, 1936.

Maruyama, G., and Walberg, H. Causal modeling. In H. Mitzel (ed.), *Encyclopedia of Educational Research*, 5th ed., New York: Free Press, 1982.

McDill, E., Meyers, E., and Rigsby, L. Institutional effects on the academic behavior of high school students. *Sociology of Education*, 1967, *40*, 181-199.

McGinn, P., Viernstein, M., and Hogan, R. Fostering the intellectual development of verbally gifted adolescents. *Journal of Educational Psychology*, 1980, *72*, 494-498.

Mentkowski, M., and Strait, M. A longitudinal study of student change in cognitive development and generic abilities in an outcome-centered liberal arts curriculum. Paper presented at the annual meeting of the American Educational Research Association, Montreal, April 1983.

Mines, R. Levels of intellectual development and associated critical thinking skills in young adults. Unpublished doctoral dissertation, University of Minnesota, 1980.

Moos, R. *The Human Context: Environmental Determinants of Behavior.* New York: Wiley, 1976.

Moos, R. *Evaluating Educational Environments.* San Francisco: Jossey-Bass, 1979.

Nasatir, D. A contextual analysis of academic failure. *School Review*, 1963, *71*, 290-298.

Newcomb, T. *Personality and Social Change: Attitude Formation in a Student Community.* New York: Dryden, 1943.

Newcomb, T., The contribution of the interpersonal environment to students' learning. *NASPA Journal*, 1967, *5*, 175-178.

Newcomb, T. Student peer group influence. In K. Yamamoto (ed.), *The College Student and His Culture: An Analysis.* Boston: Houghton Mifflin, 1968.

Newcomb, T., and Wilson, E. *College Peer Groups.* Chicago: Aldine, 1966.

Nichols, R. Effects of various college characteristics on student aptitude test scores. *Journal of Educational Psychology*, 1964, *55*, 45-54.

Owings, M., and Fetters, W. An examination of the influence of different environmental factors on the postsecondary cognitive development of young adults. Paper presented at the annual meeting of the American Educational Research Association, Montreal, April 1983.

Pace, C. R. *The Demise of Diversity: A Comparative Profile of Eight Types of Institutions.* Berkeley, Calif.: The Carnegie Commission on Higher Education, 1974.

Pace, C. R. *Measuring Outcomes of College: Fifty Years of Findings and Recommendations for the Future.* San Francisco: Jossey-Bass, 1979.

Pace, C. R. *Measuring the Quality of College Student Experiences.* Higher Education Research Institute, Graduate School of Education, University of California, Los Angeles, 1984.

Pace, C. R., and Baird, L. Attainment patterns in the environmental press of college subcultures. In T. Newcomb and E. Wilson (eds.), *College Peer Groups*, Chicago: Aldine, 1966.

Pace, C. R., and Stern, G. An approach to the measurement of psychological characteristics of college environments. *Journal of Educational Psychology*, 1958, *49*, 269-277.

Pascarella, E. Perceptions of the college environment by students in different academic majors in two colleges of arts and science. *Research in Higher Education*, 1976, *4*, 165-176.

Pascarella, E. Interactive effects of prior mathematics preparation and level of instructional support in college calculus. *American Educational Research Journal*, 1978, *15*, 275-285.

Pascarella, E. Student-faculty informal contact and college outcomes. *Review of Educational Research*, 1980, *50*, 545-595.

Pascarella, E. Academic and interpersonal experiences as mediators of the structural influences of college on two measures of affective student development. Unpublished manuscript, 1984.

Pascarella, E., and Chapman, D. Validation of a theoretical model of college withdrawal: Interaction effects in a multi-institutional sample. *Research in Higher Education*, 1983, *19*, 25-48.

Pascarella, E., Duby, P., and Iverson, B. A test and reconceptualization of a theoretical model of college withdrawal in a commuter institution setting. *Sociology of Education*, 1983, *56*, 88-100.

Pascarella, E., Duby, P., Terenzini, P., and Iverson, B. Student-faculty relationships and freshman year intellectual and personal growth in a nonresidential setting. *Journal of College Student Personnel*, 1983, *24*, 395-402.

Pascarella, E., and Terenzini, P. Student-faculty informal relationships and freshman-year educational outcomes. *Journal of Educational Research*, 1978, *71*, 183-189.

Pascarella, E., and Terenzini, P. Interaction effects in Spady's and Tinto's conceptual models of college dropout. *Sociology of Education*, 1979, *52*, 197-210.

Pascarella, E., and Terenzini, P. Student-faculty and student-peer relationships as mediators of the structural effects of undergradate residence arrangement. *Journal of Educational Research*, 1980, *73*, 344-353.

Pascarella, E., and Terenzini, P. Residence arrangment, student/faculty relationships, and freshman-year educational outcomes. *Journal of College Student Personnel*, 1981, *22*, 147-156.

Pascarella, E., and Terenzini, P. Contextual analysis as a method for assessing residence group effects. *Journal of College Student Personnel*, 1982, *23*, 108-114.

Pascarella, E., and Terenzini, P. Predicting voluntary freshman year persistence/withdrawal behavior in a residential university: A path analytic validation of Tinto's model. *Journal of Educational Psychology*, 1983, *75*, 215-226.

Perry, W. *Forms of Intellectual and Ethical Development in the College Years*. New York: Holt, Rinehart and Winston, 1970.

Pfeifer, C. Relationship between scholastic aptitude, perception of university climate and college success for black and white students. *Journal of Applied Psychology*, 1976, *61*, 341-347.

Phelan, W. Undergraduate orientations toward scientific and scholarly careers. *American Educational Research Journal*, 1979, *16*, 411-422.

Reisman, D. The "Jacob Report." *American Sociological Review*, 1958, *23*, 732-738.

Robertshaw, D., and Wolfle, L. The cognitive value of two-year colleges for whites and blacks. *Integrated Education*, 1982, *19*, 68-71.

Rock, D., Centra, J., and Linn, R. Relationships between college characteristics and student achievement. *American Educational Research Journal*, 1970, *7*, 109-121.

Ross, S., and Rakow, E. Learner control versus program control as adaptive strategies for selection of instructional support on math rules. *Journal of Educational Psychology*, 1981, *73*, 745-753.

Rossi, P. Research strategies in measuring peer group influence. In T. Newcomb and E. Wilson (eds.), *College Peer Groups*. Chicago: Aldine, 1966.

Rossman, J. An experimental study of faculty advising. *Personnel and Guidance Journal*, 1967, *46*, 160-164.

Rossman, J. Released time for faculty advising: The impact upon freshmen. *Personnel and Guidance Journal*, 1968, *47*, 358-363.

Sanford, N. *The American College: A Psychological and Social Interpretation of the Higher Learning*. New York: Wiley, 1962.

Sanford, N. *Where Colleges Fail*. San Francisco: Jossey-Bass, 1967.

Schmidt, J., and Davison, M. Reflective judgment: How to tackle the tough questions. *Moral Education Forum*, 1981, *6*, 2-14.

Schmidt, J., and Davison, M. Does college matter? Reflective judgment: How students tackle the tough questions. Unpublished manuscript, University of Minnesota, undated.

Sherif, M. *The Psychology of Social Norms.* New York: Harper, 1952.

Shoff, S. The significance of age, sex, and type of education on the development of reasoning in adults. Unpublished doctoral dissertation, University of Utah, 1979.

Smith, D. College classroom interactions and critical thinking. *Journal of Educational Psychology*, 1977, *69*, 180-190.

Smith, J. Value convictions and higher education. In K. Yamamoto (ed.). *The College Student and His Culture: An Analysis.* Boston: Houghton Mifflin, 1968.

Snead, R., and Caple, R. Some effects of environmental press in university housing. *Journal of College Student Personnel*, 1971, *12*, 189-192.

Sobel, M. Asymptotic confidence intervals for indirect effects in structural equation models. In S. Leinhardt (ed.), *Sociological Methodology 1982*, San Francisco: Jossey-Bass, 1982.

Solomon, L., Bisconti, A., and Ochsner, N. *College as a Training Ground for Jobs.* New York: Praeger, 1977.

Spaeth, J., and Greely, A. *Recent Alumni and Higher Education: A Survey of College Graduates.* New York: McGraw-Hill, 1970.

Stephenson, B., and Hunt, C. Intellectual and ethical development: A dualistic curriculum intervention for college students. *Counseling Psychologist*, 1977, *6*, 39-42.

Stern, G. *People in Context: Measuring Person-Environment Congruence in Education and Industry.* New York: Wiley, 1970.

Stewart, A. *Analysis of Argument: An Empirically Derived Measure of Intellectual Flexibility.* Boston: McBer, 1977.

Stinard, T., and Dolphin, W. Which students benefit from self-paced mastery instruction and why. *Journal of Educational Psychology*, 1981, *73*, 754-763.

Strange, C. Intellectual development, motive for education and learning styles during the college years: A comparison of adult and traditional age college students. Unpublished doctoral dissertation, University of Iowa, 1978.

Strange, C., and King, P. Intellectual development and its relationship to maturation during the college years. *Journal of Applied Developmental Psychology*, 1981, *2*, 281-295.

Taylor, R., and Hanson, G. Environmental impact on achievement and study habits. *Journal of College Student Personnel*, 1971, *12*, 445-454.

Terenzini, P., and Pascarella, E. Student/faculty relationships and freshman year outcomes: A further investigation. *Journal of College Student Personnel*, 1980, *21*, 521-528.

Terenzini, P., Pascarella, E., and Lorang, W. An assessment of the academic and social influences on freshman year educational outcomes. *Review of Higher Education*, 1982, *5*, 86-109.

Thistlethwaite, D. College environments and the develpment of talent. *Science*, 1959, *130*, 71-76.

Thistlethwaite, D. College press and changes in study plans of talented students. *Journal of Educational Psychology*, 1960, *51*, 222-234.

Thistlethwaite, D. Fields of study and development of motivation to seek advanced training. *Journal of Educational Psychology*, 1962, *53*, 53-64.

Tinto, V. Dropout from higher education: A theoretical synthesis of recent research. *Review of Educational Research*, 1975, *45*, 89-125.

Walberg, H. A psychological theory of educational productivity. In F. Farley and N. Gordon (eds.), *Psychology and Education*, Berkeley, Calif.: McCutchan, 1982.

Walberg, H., Pascarella, E., Haertel, G., and Junker, L. Probing a model of educational productivity in high school science with national assessment samples. *Journal of Educational Psychology*, 1982, *74*, 295-307.

Wallace, W. *Peer Groups and Student Achievement: The College Campus and Its Stu-

dents. Report No. 91. Chicago: National Opinion Research Center, University of Chicago, 1963.

Wallace, W. Peer influences and undergraduates' aspirations for graduate study. *Sociology of Education*, 1965, *38*, 375-392.

Wallace, W. Faculty and fraternities: Organizational influence on student achievement. *Administrative Science Quarterly*, 1967, *11*, 643-670.

Watson, G., and Glaser, E. *Critical Thinking Appraisal.* New York: Harcourt Brace Jovanovich, 1964.

Weidman, J. Nonintellective undergraduate socialization in academic departments. *Journal of Higher Education*, 1979, *50*, 48-62.

Weidman, J. Impacts of campus experience and parental socialization on undergraduates' career choices. *Research in Higher Education*, (in press).

Welfel, E. Reflective judgment and its relationship to academic field. Project Report #3, Higher Education and Cognitive-Social Development Project, Department of Social, Psychological and Philosophical Foundations of Education, University of Minnesota, undated.

Welfel, E. The development of reflective judgment: Implications for career counseling of college students. *Personnel and Guidance Journal*, 1982, *61*, 17-21.

Welfel, E., and Davison, M. A longitudinal study of reflective judgment and scholastic aptitude. Unpublished manuscript, 1983.

White, C., Pascarella, E., and Pflaum, S. Effects of training in sentence construction on the comprehension of learning-disabled children. *Journal of Educational Psychology*, 1981, *73*, 697-704.

Widick, C., Knefelkamp, L., and Parker, C. The counselor as developmental instructor. *Counselor Education and Supervision*, 1975, *14*, 286-296.

Widick, C., and Simpson, D. Developmental concepts in college instruction. In C. Parker (ed.), *Encouraging Development in College Students*, Minneapolis: University of Minnesota Press, 1978.

Willis, S., Blieszner, R., and Baltes, P. Intellectual training research in aging: Modification of performance on the fluidability of figural relations. *Journal of Educational Psychology*, 1981, *73*, 41-50.

Wilson, R., Wood, L., and Gaff, J. Social psychological accessibility and faculty-student interaction beyond the classroom. *Sociology of Education*, 1974, *47*, 74-92.

Winston, R., Hutson, G., and McCaffrey, S. Environmental influences on fraternity academic achievement. *Journal of College Student Personnel*, 1980, *21*, 449-455.

Winter, D., and McClelland, D. Thematic analysis: An empirically derived measure of the effects of liberal arts education. *Journal of Educational Psychology*, 1978, *70*, 8-16.

Winter, D., McClelland, D., and Stewart, A. *A New Case for the Liberal Arts: Assessing Institutional Goals and Student Development.* San Francisco: Jossey-Bass, 1981.

Wolfle, L. Effects of higher education on ability for blacks and whites. *Research in Higher Education*, 1983, *19*, 3-10.

Wolfle, L. Strategies of path analysis. *American Educational Research Journal*, 1980(a), *17*, 183-209.

Wolfle, L. The enduring effects of education on verbal skills. *Sociology of Education*, 1980(b), *53*, 104-114.

Wolfle, L., and Ethington, C. A program for standard errors of indirect effects. Paper presented at the annual meeting of the American Educational Research Association, New Orleans, April 1984.

LEARNING THEORY AND RESEARCH
Cameron Fincher, *University of Georgia*

The relevance of learning theory and research for higher education is not a much discussed topic on college and university campuses. College instruction is not a research-based function, and much of what passes for classroom teaching cannot be derived from either learning or instructional theory. A preponderance of teaching methods and techniques, no doubt, is based on casual observation, conscious imitation, or intuitive guesswork and *not* on the uses and applications of sound learning principles. How students cope with academic tasks and demands is a subject that frequently surfaces in educational waters, but the emphasis on such matters seldom turns to learning as a psychological or educational explanation. Recent research in cognitive styles, the bilaterality of the human brain, and information-processing models of intelligence arouses interest in response acquisition and modification, but a varying use is made of learning and development as explanatory constructs.

The intent of this chapter is to review the tenuous relationship of learning theory and research with education beyond high school, and to suggest that the psychology of learning is by no means irrelevant to learning and teaching in institutions of higher education. The loss of popularity on the part of psychology, in general, may be attributed to an ascendancy of economics and sociology as those two disciplines became much concerned with distributive effects in education at all levels. There is also cause for the opinion that a psychology of individual differences, once regarded as the backbone of progressive education, has been displaced by a sociology of groups, as reflected in the many resolutions of group conflict that have taken place on college campuses. The reassertion of developmental psychology as a dominant force in education, however, suggests that economic and sociological determinism may have run their course of popularity and that a reaffirmation of the importance of teaching and learning in higher education is not only in order — but in the making!

WHAT IS LEARNING?
The uses and applications of learning theory and research in higher education are impeded, undoubtedly, by the difficulties of defining learning in terms that

are educationally relevant. There is an element of disservice in operational definitions that may serve experimental design and analysis well but push teachers and instructors into semantic quagmires. If we thus look for an authoritative definition of learning, we would hope to find one in the fifth edition of Ernest Hilgard's classic, *Theories of Learning.* Having instructed several generations of psychology students in learning theory and research, such a classic surely supplies a well-fashioned definition that would make sense to all who are interested in the psychology of learning. Much to our disappointment, we find that Bower (1981)—now the senior author—defines learning as follows (p. 11):

> Learning refers to the change in a subject's behavior or behavior potential to a given situation brought about by the subject's repeated experiences in that situation, provided that the behavior change cannot be explained on the basis of the subject's native responses tendencies, maturation, or temporary states (such as fatigue, drunkenness, drives, and so on).

Unfortunately for those who learn and teach in college, Bower's definition is much too utilitarian. Those of us who plan and organize five-hour courses and two-hour seminars will not think of our classrooms as "situations" in which "repeated experiences" are crucial. Furthermore, despite great pressure from enlightened deans and department heads to cast our instructional objectives in behavioral terms, we will not observe changes in either behavior or behavior potential as often as we would prefer. We will observe, of course, that on many occasions "temporary states" of our students are more influential than our lectures or group discussions.

The most significant weakness of Bower's definition for higher education, however, is the failure to link learning directly to instruction. College and university faculty are hard pressed to accept responsibility for the learning that takes place under conditions of classroom instruction, much less the learning that may result from "native response tendencies" and "maturation." And despite a great deal of speculation about the changes in behavior that would have taken place *without* college attendance, students apparently learn best when they are well instructed. Thus the uses and applications of learning theory and research on college and university campuses are dependent upon the conditions of instruction that prevail in academic settings. One effort to define learning in educational terms is as follows:

> [Learning is] a process of acquiring and integrating through a systemized process of instruction or organized experience varying forms of knowledge, skill, and understanding that the learner may use or apply in later situations and under conditions different from those of instruction. [Fincher, 1978, p. 420]

Such a definition is obviously an optimistic one. The intent is to specify that: (1) some learning can and does result from instruction but it can also result from other forms of organized experience; (2) the process of learning can and does include cognitive, behavioral, and experiential dimensions or components; (3) learning should be seen in relation to its future uses or applications and its transfer to other situations and conditions; and (4) learning and teaching are dual processes that must be treated systematically if they are to make educational sense. As a definition, it is quite compatible with Robert Gagne's (1977) more concise definition (p.3):

> Learning is a change in human disposition or capability, which persists over time, and which is not simply ascribable to processes of growth.

Both definitions should serve, furthermore, to specify that learning is something more than a change in performance. We infer that learning has taken place when we observe and/or record a change in performance, but we should never equate, as too many have done in recent years, learning with the performance we observe. In its broadest sense, learning can be defined as a process of progressive change from ignorance to knowledge, from inability to competence, and from indifference to understanding. In much the same manner, instruction—or education—can be defined as the means by which we systematize the situations, conditions, tasks, materials, and opportunities by which learners acquire new or different ways of thinking, feeling, and doing.

Learning and Development

If learning and teaching are complementary processes of which we should be mindful, learning and development are even more so. It is obvious that learning in infancy and early childhood is dependent upon the growth and maturation of the individual. Certain skills, such as walking and talking, cannot be learned until the child reaches some particular level of neuromuscular maturation. Growth and/or maturation are thus defined as changes that are not dependent upon learning, and parents are often advised to withhold various forms of training until their child is sufficiently mature. Whereas learning may occur as the result of direct stimulation and encouragement, maturation is viewed as a natural, unfolding process that cannot be accelerated without appreciable risk.

What is obvious in children is not so obvious in adolescents and adults. Stages of development are discernible throughout life, but the influence of developmental stages on student learning in college is a relationship but recently studied. Nevitt Sanford's (1962) classic, *The American College*, was most effective in calling attention to the importance of developmental processes in college students, but student development on most campuses continues as a responsibility of deans of students and not as an academic function. The recent reemergence of developmental psychology, nonetheless, suggests a robust interest in the changes that may be attributed to development instead of formal instruction. As the expected goals and outcomes of higher education have become more diverse and as many older, more mature students have taken advantage of educational opportunities, the need for a better understanding of learning *and* development has intensified. The popularity of adult development, in particular, is indicative of the need to study more systematically the continuing behavioral changes that occur in early adult years, mid-life, and old age.

Learning Conditions

The conditions under which learning occurs on college campuses are many and varied. The major factors within the learning situation may be identified as: (a) the individual differences of the learners themselves—their academic ability, their previous preparation at the secondary level, and the various motives or incentives that bring them to the college classroom; (b) the nature of the learning materials, tasks, and equipment that will be involved in academic course work—including the structure and content of the academic programs themselves; (c) the nature and quality of instruction the learner receives—the conditions of practice, guidance, mode of presentation, etc.; and (d) situational or environmental variables that may be both subtle and complex in their influence on learning outcomes.

Although there has been widespread interest in institutional characteristics, such as campus climate or environment, research has not been highly successful in demonstrating the impact of such characteristics on student learning *per se.* Cooley and Lohnes (1976), among many educational researchers, believe that the individual differences of learners will always account for the larger proportion of variance in learning outcomes. Institutional, as opposed to program, characteristics are too far removed from classroom instruction to have immediate and direct influence on what students learn and how well they learn. The influence of course organization and content, instructional methods, and teacher expectations can be appreciable, however, and the means by which student performance is evaluated can sometimes be a major determinant of learning.

Other variables, conditions, and situations affecting learning at the college level include those as simple as class size and those as complex as the various forms of reinforcement, feedback, or knowledge of results. Although the research supporting the influence of such variables is less than rigorous, the consistency with which some findings are reported and their compatibility with human expectations give them appreciable credence.

Class size is the perfect example. As one of the simplest classroom variables that might affect learning, class size is seldom dismissed as irrelevant. Small classes are consistently preferred to large classes by teaching faculty, and research, with all its faults, appears to support their good judgment in such matters. Glass and Smith (1979) recently brought the blessings of meta-analysis to bear on the topic and they readily conclude that small classes do indeed contribute to student learning. Suggested but not yet demonstrated is a point of diminishing returns for class smallness. For most college faculty, it is distinctly possible that some classes are too small to bring out the best of professorial behavior. In other words, there is no evidence that the best teaching-learning arrangement is a one-on-one confrontation between Mark Hopkins and a student on the other end of the log.

Order of presentation is a condition of instruction that joins many curricular debates. Whether the presentation of subject matter in a course is to be logical —proceeding from the general to the specific or building from the specific to the general—or chronological is often a matter of controversy that research cannot resolve without bringing in the nature and content of the subject matter. A random order is never advocated, but the manner in which some undergraduate courses are organized could have the same effects.

The extent to which college instructors can reinforce student learning is necessarily limited. Faculty members seldom have the influence that classmates, peers, and other groups have, but they do control academic credit and grades. The constructive use of course examinations or instructor-made tests for purposes of feedback or knowledge of results is only hinted at in research literature, but the negative aspects of irresponsible examining and grading practices have been documented (Milton and Edgerly, 1977). A direct implication is that course examinations have both motivational and informational properties that more college instructors would do well to exploit. In many classes, midterms and end-of-course examinations are the only opportunities students have for active participation. In virtually all classes, however, course examinations are a major determinant of final grades.

More than any other learning psychologist, Robert Gagne (1977) has tried to specify the conditions under which human learning occurs. In Gagne's view, learning takes place when external events in the form of stimuli and internal events in the form of memories affect the learner in such a way as to produce a change in performance. Instruction is defined as external events that are deliberately planned and arranged. The internal events that effect changes in performance are accounted for by information-processing models of learning and memory. The outcomes of learning are thus varied, but Gagne believes that most of them can be subsumed under five major capabilities: (1) intellectual skills, (2) cognitive strategies, (3) verbal information, (4) motor skills, and (5) attitudes. The events of learning *per se* are identified as: (a) sensory attending and selective perception, (b) storage in short-term memory, (c) encoding, (d) storage in long-term memory, (e) retrieval and response generation, and (f) feedback or reinforcement.

Much to his credit, Gagne has been directly concerned with the educational implications of his research. By defining instruction as the deliberate arrangement of the required conditions of learning, Gagne has given strong emphasis to instructional planning, design, management, and development. Many faculty members in higher education will see Gagne's views as being more relevant to industrial and/or military training and development than to college teaching, but there are many implications in his work that deserve attention. The most pertinent may be the emphasis that Gagne gives the structure or organization of instruction and the advantages of breaking down learning tasks into their less complex components. The inescapable message in all of Gagne's writing is that if instruction is to assist or enhance student learning, instruction must be designed for that specific purpose.

Methods of Instruction
Following the individual differences of learners, the most important condition of learning surely must be the methods of instruction that are employed for purposes of education, training, or development. Faith in methods of instruction is so pronounced in educational circles that Cross (1976) writes of an in-

structional revolution that has taken place as new or different methods of instruction have supplanted traditional or conventional methods in college classrooms. Technological change and innovation are forces that have spurred numerous efforts to instruct students in a better, easier, more efficient manner than lectures and classroom discussions. Many of these efforts have taken the form of individualized, self-paced modes of instruction in which the learner achieves a mastery of specific units and/or modules before proceeding to advanced or more specialized units (Baker, 1973; Frase, 1975).

The rubric of individualized instruction includes a host of alternative arrangements under which college students learn. Many of the assumptions built into individualized modes of instruction are variations on themes enunciated by an older generation of psychologists who took a functionalistic approach to learning and who worked within a context of human associative learning (see McGeoch and Irion, 1952). Others are the articulation of behaviorial principles that were either explicit or implied in the work of experimental psychologists working in the field of learning. Keller (1968), in the most dramatic example, turned behavioral psychology to good advantage by building into an instructional system such assumptions as: (a) self-pacing, according to the time that the learner has; (b) breaking the learning task down into more manageable units; (c) using classroom lectures primarily for motivational purposes; (d) detailed assignments that actively involved learners; and (e) frequent testing and immediate feedback.

In viewing the individualization of learning as an alternative to classroom lectures and group discussions, Cross (1976) points out that self-pacing, active participation, clear and explicit goals, small lesson units, and feedback are basic principles upon which all individualized education is based. The application of these principles can be found in programmed instruction, computer-assisted instruction, and individually prescribed instruction, (IPI) as well as Keller's personalized system of instruction (PSI). The ordering of learning sequences so that students will master each step as they proceed is a principle that is crucial to mastery learning, audio-tutorial methods, and various other learning systems. Effectiveness in the application of such a principle is contingent upon knowledge of results for the learner and implies either self-grading tests and examinations or other means of immediate and direct feedback. The assessment of learner performance and direct reporting of the results are instructional chores for which the computer is particularly well adapted.

As mentioned previously, technological applications are strong features of many efforts to provide alternatives to traditional methods of instruction. The uses of technology almost always imply, however, that learning tasks and materials must be analyzed in terms of the subgoals and subskills that learners may pursue and apply. Learning must be viewed as a process consisting of steps, stages, or phases that must be articulated, and the uses of technology must be seen as instrumental to particular parts of the process instead of the overall sequence of events. It is for this reason, as well as others, that technological innovations have not had the impact on teaching and learning that many of their early advocates anticipated.

Before leaving the subject of instructional methods, it is well to suggest that most of the instruction in most college classrooms continues along conventional lines. McKeachie and Kulik (1975) believe that each instructional advance has failed to meet the high expectations with which it was greeted. There is little doubt that Keller's PSI is an attractive mode of instruction for most students, that students will spend more time and effort working with the system, and that they will report learning more than they would have in lecture courses. Unfortunately, Keller's PSI and all other individualized learning require forms of self-management that many learners have not mastered. Kulik, Kulik, and Cohen (1979) report that the completion rate for PSI courses is as high as it is for conventional courses, but given the appreciable self-selection that is involved in PSI courses and the experience of high withdrawal rates on many campuses, it is best to conclude that alternative learning is *not* an alternative for all students.

TRENDS IN THEORY AND RESEARCH

Theory and research in learning have been dominated by the schools of psychology that gained ascendance in the early years of the 20th century and by the generation of psychologists who sought during the 1930s and 1940s to establish general theories of behavior based on learning. The influence of the early behaviorists, gestaltists, and associationists is still in evidence, and despite the hegemony of cognitive psychology in the past twenty years the theoretical and empirical questions raised by Edward L. Thorndike, John B. Watson, Edwin R. Guthrie, Clark L. Hull, Edward C. Tolman, Kurt Lewin, and B. F. Skinner are seldom ignored for long. Whether answered by their many productive students or by later generations of researchers, the questions posed early in learning research continue to provide either a point of departure or a critical background for theory and research. Some of the more crucial questions may be identified as follows:

1. How many kinds of learning are necessary to account for the behavior in which psychologists are interested? Distinctions were quickly made between classical conditioning, in which the conditioned response was autonomic, and instrumental conditional, in which the learned response was muscular. Skinner's respondent and operant behavior required a somewhat similar distinction, and Mowrer's (1960) work is an explicit two-factor theory of learning, with its distinctions between "sign learning" and "solution learning." Gagne's work implies that there are at least five kinds of learning that are relevant to education.

2. Are there basic processes of learning that can account for the acquired behavior of humans, apes, rats, pigeons, and other species not obviously governed by instinct? Watson apparently believed conditioning to be such a mechanism, and Hull contended that the same principle of reinforcement was involved in all learned behavior. Association has been accepted by many as a bas-

ic process underlying ideational or verbal learning. Other psychologists, such as Gagne, see a need for several basic forms of learning, such as learning to respond to signals, trial-and-error or stimulus-response learning, and associative or sequential learning. Related to this question are the nature and extent of learning that may be species-specific and whether or not there are processes of human learning that cannot be ascribed to other species or computers.

3. What is *it* that is learned? Do we learn specific responses and/or patterns of behavior, or do we learn to connect or associate responses to differential stimuli and/or situations? In learning, do we acquire habits and skills *or* cognitive structures, in the form of expectancies, schemata, or images? In learning to run a maze, does a rat learn to follow a path or to go to a particular place where food is waiting? This may be the basic question that separates behaviorists from cognitivists.

4. What are the necessary conditions of practice in response acquisition? Can learning occur without practice or some form of trial-and-error? Is a response acquired instantly as an insight into the inner relations of a problem? Guthrie is the foremost advocate of one-trial or all-or-none learning, while Hull best represents the view that learning proceeds in incremental stages. Thorndike believed most fervently in trial-and-error learning, while the gestalt psychologists, of course, are responsible for much of what we know about insight learning.

5. What is the nature of the reinforcement that presumably accounts for the fixation of a learned response? Is it drive reduction, as the S-R theorist so often contends, or is it confirmation of an expectancy, as Tolman so aptly proposed? Does contiguity of stimulus and response alone account for the acquisition of a response, as classical conditioning apparently implies, or is such further kind of feedback of knowledge of results necessary for a response to become part of a learner's repertoire? Reinforcement is apparently all-important to a good Skinnerian, while gestaltists make good use of their concept of closure.

6. To what extent are consciousness, memory, active attention, and other central states of the human nervous system involved in learning? Working with animals as laboratory subjects, behaviorists have preferred not to involve mental or unspecified brain states as explanatory constructs in learning. Skinner knowingly treats inner states or conditions as unknown and irrelevant variables. Cognitive theorists, needless to say, regard inner events, states, or conditions as crucial.

7. And finally, how can we account for the disappearance of acquired behavior after it has been well mastered? Do skills and habits dissipate for lack of reinforcement? Because we no longer use them frequently? Or because of interference from later learning? This question has been important to psychologists because the best evidence of experimental control might be the fashioning of a learned response, its extinction, and then its restoration. Such a feat can give solid credence to the psychologist's explanation of the particular response and the research methods employed.

The Status of Theory

Theories of learning should serve, as theories in other disciplines do, to define a field of inquiry in terms of its boundaries and its significant features. To serve well, a theory should incorporate the empirical or research findings that are accepted by active researchers and it should suggest new or different lines of inquiry and analysis that should be fruitful. The extent to which a theory implies application to professional or practical problems is a lesser criterion in the eyes of theorists and front-line researchers.

Judged by the research that has been stimulated over the past fifty years, behavioral theories of learning have been enormously successful. Although not successful in accomplishing its specific objective to generate a general theory of behavior, Clark Hull's hypothetico-deductive system has been most productive in stimulating experimental inquiry into the problems and issues of learning. Although avowedly atheoretical, B. F. Skinner's work has been quite provocative. In much the same manner, Kurt Lewin's writings have influenced at least two generations of researchers and theorists. E. R. Guthrie's work did not lead to a clustering of psychologists known as "Guthrienians," but his work does continue to be discussed and his influence is still evident. Much the same can be said for E. L. Thorndike and E. C. Tolman.

The theoretical issues of the 1930s and 1940s entered a new phase in the 1950s when the lines were rather clearly drawn between neo-behaviorists and cognitive theorists, a group strongly influenced by gestalt psychology. Unfortunately for the educational uses of learning theory, researchers sought better control of their experimental variables and resorted to explanatory constructs that would enable them to predict responses and/or acquired behavior that was highly specified. Such research was guided by miniature theories and models—not by grand systems or theories. The outcome in many instances was a careful experimental verification of acquired behavior that was less and less consequential for training, developmental, and educational purposes.

There is appreciable irony, therefore, in the possibility that as higher education encountered a need for systematic, verified knowledge about learning processes and their implications for education beyond high school, learning theory and research were quite remote. There was little that active researchers and learning theorists could tell college faculty about the learning that took place in their classrooms. There was almost nothing that learning researchers could say about what took place in libraries, laboratories, and computer centers.

Not the least failure of learning theory was the inability of researchers to agree on an acceptable typology for learning. Neither the neo-behaviorists nor the cognitive psychologists offered a taxonomy that made sense to college instructors who were as specialized in their research and teaching interests as the psychologists were in theirs.

A taxonomy with some promise did emerge in the 1950s when Bloom et al. (1956) published a taxonomy of educational objectives in the "cognitive domain.'' Cognitive objectives were divided into six major categories identified as: (1) knowledge, (2) comprehension, (3) application, (4) analysis, (5) synthesis, and (6) evaluation. A later volume (Krathwohl, Bloom, and Masia, 1964) dealt with the ''affective domain'' of educational outcomes and identified five categories as: (1) awareness, (2) responding, (3) valuing, (4) organizing, and (5) generalizing. A third volume, dealing with psychomotor skills, appeared much later, after interest in educational taxonomies was no longer apparent. For a while Bloom's taxonomy, as the first volume became known, was discussed among college and university faculty members, but interest was not sustained except for occasional research projects and a few planning efforts. Neither the affective nor the psychomotor ''domains'' had great appeal for college faculty, a fact that may be attributed to the reluctance of faculty members to find out what a ''domain'' was and to take seriously educational objectives expressed as gerunds.

A more direct application of learning theory may be seen in the efforts of some psychologists to translate theories of learning into a workable theory of instruction. Jerome Bruner (1960, 1966) set the pace for later psychologists by emphasizing the structure of knowledge as the content of what is taught and the scholar's methods of inquiry as the means by which students should learn. Bruner saw a theory of instruction as prescriptive insofar as it set forth rules for achieving knowledge or skills. A theory of instruction is also normative, as it establishes criteria for learning and states the conditions under which those criteria are met.

Atkinson (1972), Glaser (1976), and of course Gagne (1974) contributed significantly to developing theories of instruction by advocating, respectively, a decision-theoretic analysis of the instructional process, the systematic analysis of competent performance, and the implications of educational technology. In 1969 instructional psychology was officially recognized as an established area of inquiry and analysis when Gagne and Rohwer published the first review of related research in the *Annual Review of Psychology*.

Recent Research Trends

In reviewing the psychology of learning between 1960 and 1980, James Greeno (1980) sees a radical shift from studying changes in behavior to a concern with stochastic models that specify the probability of learned responses. The statistical analysis of rote memory, paired associates learning, and problem-solving protocols gives better insight into the structure and processes of memory. Learning, if that is what such researchers are studying, is viewed as structural networks of concepts and actions that link network components in schematic form. Although Greeno suggests that the time is now right for the analysis of learning as the acquisition of knowledge, his view of learning and knowledge is better comprehended as the analysis and/or processing of language.

Bower (1981) sees research on the learning process as accelerating and speculates that several thousand psychologists and scientists in related fields are now at work on the problems of learning. Unfortunately for those who seek some unity or coherence in learning theory, behavioral research is increasingly diversified and much better suited for identifying "subproblems" or subjects for further in-depth analysis than for arriving at working generalizations that might be applicable in training, development, and education. Only in the area of behavioral modification and biofeedback does there appear to be a concern for direct and immediate application.

Cognitive psychologists also appear to be overly concerned with model building and the networking of subroutines in cognition. Much of this research has resulted in a better comprehension of short-term memory, the functions of organization in long-term memory, and the different kinds of memory that may be utilized in information processing, but the educational implications of many suggestive leads are often ignored. In many cases where the educational implications of research might be discussed, there is a marvelous leap from minute research details to global and sweeping instructions for classroom teachers.

Glaser (1982, 1984) provides a welcome antidote to structural networking by suggesting that: (a) knowledge may be specific to the fields of study where that knowledge was acquired; and (b) the domain-specific knowledge we have acquired may influence appreciably the way in which we acquire new knowledge, solve problems, and comprehend or process information. Glaser is even more on target when he contends that a psychology of instruction should understand and facilitate the changes in cognition and performance that occur as each of us moves from status as a novice to status as an expert. A theory of instruction cannot be based on "artificial laboratory tasks" but must be related to the analysis of educational processes and outcomes.

GENERAL PRINCIPLES OF LEARNING

The advances of learning theory tell us little about the empirical findings, warranted generalizations, or laws of learning presumably established by learning research. There are many reasons why a general theory of behavior did not emerge from the confident efforts of theorists in the 1930s and 1940s, but something of a mystery is involved in the fate of lawlike hypotheses in which learning was the primary explanatory construct. The robustness of learning theory and research in the 1950s apparently convinced many psychologists that lawlike hypotheses or general principles of learning had been experimentally verified and thus the application of those hypotheses or principles to education was sufficiently warranted.

Granting the disappointments of theory construction in the 1950s and the increasing interest in model building, there were at that time a dozen or more empirical findings that many psychologists believed to be substantiated by the re-

search literature. These psychologists need not agree on the theoretical underpinnings or explanatory constructs involved in the establishment of empirical
findings, but they could acknowledge a creditable research basis for some well-
intended generalizations or working hypotheses. Among the most visible were
the following:

1. Learning is dependent upon the capacities of the learner.
2. Learning is a function of the conditions of practice and/or instruction
   imposed upon the learner.
3. Learning materials and tasks are more easily mastered when they are
   meaningful, i.e., when they are suitably organized, have a logically related
   part or components, and specify the conditions or circumstances under
   which they will be used or applied.
4. Learning is facilitated by knowledge of results—especially if that knowledge is immediate and specific.
5. The transfer of learning is dependent upon the similarities of the learning
   tasks and/or the similarities of principles and work methods that can be
   applied in the transfer situation.
6. Learning is related to the degree and quality of learner motivation, i.e.,
   learners apparently perform better when motivation is intrinsic (self-
   generated?) instead of extrinsic (imposed by others?) *and* reward is to be
   preferred over punishment.
7. Learning is also related to the learner's level of aspiration—and the
   learner's experiences with success or failure in striving to reach certain
   levels of aspiration.

The wording of these principles obviously cuts across several fields of research and a diversity of theoretical preferences. The principles are derived
from the work of earlier generations and reveal the influence of Hermann Eb-
binghaus and Ivan Pavlov. "Laws of association" are very much a part of
these tenets and date as far back as Aristotle's laws of similarity, contrast, and
contiguity. Their value as learning principles, however, may be seen in the research they stimulated. Derived from or implicit in such principles are the following corollaries and/or testable hypotheses:

1. Learning is an active process and not the passive reception of stimuli or
   information.
2. Motivation is a necessary condition of learning, but excessive motivation
   may not be conducive to learning effectiveness.
3. Intrinsic motivation may be preferable to extrinsic motivation but is seldom possible with human subjects—thus researchers must be satisfied to
   control incentives and not motives *per se.*
4. Some experience with success is necessary to develop a tolerance for
   failure.

5. Guidance in training can be effective if given early and in relatively small doses.
6. Transfer of training is facilitated by an understanding of relationships—*but* there is no substitute for repetitive practice in the acquisition and development of a skill.
7. Training methods must take into consideration not only the product of learning methods but the process as well, i.e., consideration must be given not only to "what to do" but "how to do it."

The Decline and Fall?

In his contribution to Sanford's *The American College,* Wilbert McKeachie (1962) provided a commendable overview of learning research as it then related to the problems of college instruction. If general principles and/or laws of learning were not firmly established, they still gave good instruction and guidance to college instructors who would but take the time to test their implications. Twelve years later in two articles, McKeachie (1974, 1974b) found the status of such principles of learning to be much in doubt. He pointed out that previously accepted principles or laws had been derived mostly from research involving animals, where better control of experimental variables was permissible but unlikely to produce assistance in classroom instruction. In studies with human subjects, who have greater ability to conceptualize and relate, the "laws of learning" were fading.

McKeachie believed that only two principles of learning held consistently. These were : (1) active participation is still better than passive learning, and (2) meaningful learning is still more effective than rote memory. Other principles apparently do not hold because education is an interactive situation in which the conditions, materials, and tasks of learning are different—and much more complex. The learning of students in school and college thus is an interaction of numerous complex variables over an extended period of time.

In 1966 Hilgard, in the third edition of his authoritative *Theories of Learning* (and coauthored for the first time with Gordon Bower), pointed out that learning might be better understood as a form of species-specific behavior and as theory-related constructs. Research had resulted in better analyses of learning tasks and the struggle for theoretical supremacy was no longer a private affair for behaviorists; the camps were now divided into behavioral and cognitive theorists. Under the former's banner, Hilgard and Bower found such principles as (a) active learning, (b) repetitive practice, (c) reinforcement, and (d) drive constructs as motivation. New or emerging principles located under behavioral banners were: (a) stimulus generalization and discrimination as a kind of *modus operandi,* (b) the acquisition of novel responses through the imitation of models, and (c) the necessity of dealing with conflicts and frustrations.

In the cognitive camp Hilgard and Bower found: (a) new implications for the perceptual features of the task, i.e., how it appeared to learners; (b) the organization of complex wholes out of simplified wholes instead of disjointed parts;

(c) the supremacy of learning with understanding; (d) feedback as correct information; (e) the relevance of goal setting; and (f) findings concerning divergent and convergent thinking. A third group of theorists, dealing with social/personal and motivational characteristics, evidently subscribed to principles related to: (a) the abilities of learners, (b) the cultural relativity of learning, (c) developmental concepts, (d) the motivational properties of internal states, (e) the organization of values and motives, and (f) group influences.

It is significant that where the second edition of Hilgard (1956) concludes with discussions of education and training—and research implications that would bridge the gap "from the laboratory to the classroom"—the concluding chapters of the 1966 edition cast the application of learning principles in a research and development mold. Hilgard saw at least six stages in a process ranging from basic research to developmental efforts leading to advocacy and adoption. The "era of great debates" was obviously over in 1966 and general theories were no longer advocated by great men—with the exception, of course, of B. F. Skinner.

Jumping the fourth edition of Hilgard and Bower (1975), we find in Bower's (1981) fifth revision a concluding chapter dealing with "Applications to Education." Principles of learning are reduced to "ideas from learning theory useful in education," and such recognition that can be given older concepts and principles is at the expense of Bower's cautious wording. The presence of behaviorists (or S-R theorists) and cognitivists, nonetheless, is much in evidence:

1. For the behaviorist, educational goals should be specified in concrete behavioral terms. This should only be done through careful analysis of learning tasks or skills — and it should permit a "shaping procedure" in which complex skills are acquired through a sequence of less complex tasks.
2. Active responding (manipulating, relating, reciting, etc.) is still advantageous to learning.
3. For academic skills like reading, writing, and arithmetic, there is still no substitute for recitation and repeated practice.
4. Prescribed study guides may indeed have a place in college. Rehearsal-and-review techniques, such as Frank Robinson's (1946) SQ3R method of study, can help!
5. Reinforcement can be effective if directed to "task-relevant behaviors." It will be more effective, however, if students learn to direct and reinforce their own study and learning tasks.
6. Counterconditioning might be effective in coping with test anxiety.
7. The learner's motives are best translated as goals and interests — and goal setting can be effective in motivating students.
8. Learning can be facilitated through the "perceptual structuring" of

learning tasks when "the essential features of the problem" are highlighted.
9. Understanding, as opposed to rote memorization, is still preferable.
10. Mnemonic devices and other memory aids can be effective when factual details must be remembered.

It is obvious from Bower's comprehensive survey of learning theory and research (577 pages, over 1,250 references) that the applications of learning theory and research to education have been directed primarily to the development of theories of instruction. One answer to questions about the status of learning theory and research thus must be that much of the interest and effect was channeled into the development of instructional theories and/or systems. The search for uniform, lawlike regularities in learning became, for many researchers, a process of developing systems and models that could account for highly specific behavioral patterns under conditions of instruction.

Of Time and Place
A more definite detouring of learning principles occurred in 1977 when Cronbach and Snow published *Aptitudes and Instructional Methods.* Summarized in that volume is a massive amount of research on aptitude/treatment interactions (ATI) and a convincing mass of evidence that generalizations from learning research are not easily warranted. Because the aptitudes, abilities, and interests of students interact in diverse ways with instructional conditions and methods, the inferences to be drawn from learning research may be confined to specific results on particular occasions. The relation of human differences to learning outcomes is thus reintroduced with detrimental impact on broad or sweeping generalities.

Unlike programmed instruction and mastery learning, the interactions of learner characteristics and instructional methods imply that time or learning rate is not the dominant variable affecting learning outcomes. Neither does the Cronbach-Snow volume suggest that systematic modes of instruction can greatly reduce individual differences in learning performance. To the contrary, there is ample evidence that individual differences influence both the amount of learning and the rate of learning under any given instructional conditions. Also implied is the possibility that instructional effectiveness may be facilitated or impeded by learner characteristics in subtle and unanticipated ways.

The direct implication of Cronbach and Snow's work is that in education, training, and development we must be satisfied with tentative conclusions, particular conjectures, or probabilistic truths instead of definitive research findings. Researchers should be reluctant to generalize their findings beyond their research subjects, their specific characteristics, the particular mode of instruction involved, and the peculiarities of the learning situation investigated. Learning principles thus become highly qualified and carry the full length of implication, they become statements about specific occurrences at a particular time and place. To wit: some students can learn some subjects better under some teachers than they can learn other subjects under other teachers.

Gagne and Dick (1983) reported six years later that interest in aptitude/treatment interactions remained high, with continuing study of learner characteristics such as anxiety, achievement via independence as opposed to achievement via conformity, and crystallized versus fluid or analytic intelligence. New learner attributes thus continue to be identified by researchers, and ATI research continues unabated.

LEARNING AND COGNITIVE PSYCHOLOGY

The influence of cognitive psychology is quite evident in the directions taken by learning theorists and researchers since 1960. Miller, Galanter, and Pribram (1960) introduced many psychologists to the seminal work of Herbert Simon and other researchers who were making excellent use of computers in simulating human decision-making and problem-solving behavior. In his presidential address to the American Psychological Association, D. O. Hebb (1960) spoke of behaviorism as only the first stage of a revolution in psychology and urged his colleagues to get on with the second stage—the study of mental and/or mediating processes. Other psychologists began to take seriously the work of Piaget (Berlyne, 1964), and of course, 1960 was the year in which Bruner's *Process of Education* was published with modest expectations by Harvard University Press.

The significance of cognitive theory is seen most quickly in its impact on verbal learning and memory. Anderson and Bower (1973) were among many researchers who reintroduced the study of memory as a valuable contribution to research on learning, convincing their readers in the meantime that the modeling of short-term and long-term memory gave good insight into the information-processing capabilities of learners. The investigation of mnemonic devices (Bower, 1970; Higbee, 1979) is again permissible and the study of mental imagery (Paivio, 1971; Shepard, 1978) is again shown to be fascinating, as well as worthwhile. And in 1980, Donald A. Norman could entitle an article "What Goes On in the Mind of the Learner" without fear of psychologic excommunication.

As the star of cognitive psychology rose, verbal learning could be interpreted as the encoding and retrieval of information that may be organized in many ways. The ease or efficiency with which information could be retrieved became a matter of its mode of representation and whether or not it was encoded for ready access. Bruner (1966) wrote convincingly of enactive, iconic, and symbolic forms of representation. Knowledge was at last recognized by psychologists as the encoding of propositions in which the basic unit of thought was a subject-predicate coupling. Human facility in recalling meaningful materials was thus clarified because such materials have a structure that is more than just its sequence.

For education, the impact of cognitive psychology has been stated best by Wittrock and Lumsdaine (1977) in contrasting cognitive and behavioristic models (p. 418):

> By contrast, a cognitive approach emphasizes the elaborations which the learner performs on information more than the features of instruction. Cognitive approaches emphasize that one can learn from observing others, by watching a model, by viewing a demonstration, by listening to a lecture, by being told, by reading a book, by constructing images, and by elaborating words into sentences.

Never have traditional modes of learning and teaching been given a stronger or more timely reprieve!

Cognitive Styles
Nowhere is the contrast between behaviorists and cognitivists more pronounced than in the cognitivists' enthusiasm for cognitive styles. Behaviorists can appreciate, perhaps, the importance of structure or organization in cognition and perceive some degree of similarity of such constructs with those of learning capacities or learning abilities that may, on occasion, appear to be general. The notion of individualized, habitual, or preferential modes of information processing may impress the behaviorist, nonetheless, as producing too loose a rack on which to hang explanatory constructs of learning. The extent to which cognitive styles are characteristic or typical, have adaptive value, or serve as organizational or controlling mechanisms is unknown to behaviorists; cognitivists are never in doubt about the existence of cognitive styles and find their study fascinating.

Messick (1976) has identified cognitive style as an individual's preferred way of organizing what he or she sees and remembers or thinks about. The test of a cognitive style is evidently in the consistency with which individuals organize and process information in a characteristic manner. Learning and other behavior thus are seen as functions of individual differences in cognitive and creative functioning. Other personal characteristics, or personality traits, are viewed in a context of the individual's "stylistic consistencies."

Tyler (1978) has written of the different styles of conceptualization and the patterning of activities that may be the most important characteristics of individuals. Although the term "structure" has too many architectural connotations to please Tyler, she believes the meaning of individuality to be found in the organized processes and activities that serve the individual's purposes in life.

Carefully distinguishing between cognitive styles and intellectual abilities, Messick defines over a dozen cognitive styles that he believes to be substantiated by research. Among these are conceptualizing styles, such as Tyler described. Children apparently form concepts by using functional relations, while adolescents are inclined to analyse the descriptive features of what they observe. Having gone though such previous stages, adults evidently rely more heavily on the inferences they can make from categories or classes.

Other cognitive styles identified by Messick are: (1) breadth of categorization, in which individuals show a preference for inclusive or exclusive categories; (2) compartmentalization, in which ideas and objects may be isolated in discrete, rigid categories; (3) conceptual complexity versus conceptual simplicity; (4) leveling versus sharpening in the recall of memories; (5) reflection versus impulsivity in thinking; and (6) risk taking versus cautiousness in judgment.

The cognitive style that has been most carefully studied, however, is that of field independence versus field dependence (Witkin, 1976). Research on this particular style began in the 1950s and has continued since that time. The polarized ends of the continuum appear to be analytical thinking and global thinking. One end suggests a pronounced tendency to articulate the separate figures and features of what is observed and to resist domination by the global or totalistic characteristics of one's perceptions. The other end is a preferred reaction to people, places, and events as an undifferentiated complex. As Witkin and other researchers make clear, there are no social or cultural criteria by which others can decide which mode of perception is the best for everyone.

The relevance of field dependence or independence for education has been underscored by Witkin (1976), Tyler (1978), Cross (1976), and others. Witkin views the application of cognitive styles to education as being in its beginning phase but thinks that tests emerging from the research on cognitive styles might eventually replace intelligence tests. He believes field independence to be particularly relevant to the decisions and choices that college students must make in their selection of a major field and subsequent career. Tyler points out that field-dependent teachers may prefer group discussion as a mode of teaching instead of lectures and individual projects. Field-dependent learners may prefer social forms of reinforcement for the studying they do, and they may be more easily attracted to careers that involve human services. Cross finds much about field dependancy that pertains to the New Students she describes in her book, *Beyond the Open Door.* Both groups are people-oriented, sensitive to the judgment of others, and somewhat deferential to authority. Neither group is noted for analytical problem solving, active participation in class discussions, or firm control of their individual destinies.

In their studies of aptitude/treatment interactions Cronbach and Snow (1977) gave good attention to cognitive styles. Cognitive skills, structures, and styles qualify as characteristics of learners that may forecast the probability of success and thus are included under the category of aptitude. Cronbach and Snow doubt, however, the cognitive styles and other such constructs can be measured so as to give information that is independent of general abilities. They conclude that studies on conceptual level, cognitive complexity, and field dependence are too inconsistent to permit generalizations.

Learning Strategies

If the distinctions among cognitive structures, skills, and styles are difficult to specify, they are even more difficult for cognitive styles and cognitive strategies. Messick (1976) assures us that (p. 6):

> . . . it is important to distinguish cognitive styles, which are high level heuristics that organize and control behavior across a wide variety of situations, from cognitive strategies, which are decision-making regularities in information processing that at least in part are a function of the conditions of particular situations.

As much as some of us may think that Messick and his cited authorities have confused cognitive strategies with cognitive tactics, there is a possibility that styles are generalized and unconsciously acquired while strategies are deliberately adopted. Cronbach and Snow (1977) place "style" midway between "ability" and "strategy" and more or less suggest that strategies are the operations of organizing and processing while styles are the consistent manner in which we do so. The extent to which strategies are a function of style is, nonetheless, an open question. Cognitive styles appear much more relevant for the study of perception and personality than they do for the investigation of learning. In the latter, there is better reason to believe that consciously employed strategies are more likely to be verified as a determinant of learning.

The ingenious manuevers of college students to obtain course credits and high grades are indicative of the great diversity of learning skills and strategies that they bring to the college classroom. Students may or may not recognize knowledge, competence, and personal development as the substantive and enduring values of higher education, but there can be no doubt that they see academic credits and grades as a means to academic credentials. The strategies and tactics that college students display in such quests are undoubtedly stylistic on many occasions, and the difference between styles and strategies, insofar as understanding learner behavior is concerned, may be meaningless. Both styles and strategies would seem closely tied to an incredible range of student sophistication concerning educational goals, learning outcomes, and instructional purposes.

Efforts to measure or assess learning styles and/or strategies have been made by Riechmann and Grasha (1974), Canfield (1976), and others. Riechmann and Grasha define six learning styles that they believe to be characteristic of students: (1) independent learning — by students who like to think for themselves and work on their own; (2) dependent learning — by students who learn only what is required; (3) collaborative learning — in which students cooperate and share ideas; (4) competitive learning — in which students seek to outperform each other; (5) participant learning — in which students may learn the most from class discussion and interaction; and (6) avoidant learning — as shown by uninterested or overwhelmed students.

Canfield views learning styles in terms of the conditions under which learning occurs, the content of what is learned, and the dominant mode by which students learn. Independence in learning, deference to authority, competitiveness, and peer relations, as conditions of learning, would appear to correspond to similar scales in Riechmann and Grasha's inventory. Learning content, however, is seen as basically numeric, qualitative, inanimate, or people-oriented. Dominant modes of learning are identified as listening, reading, iconic, and direct experience. Also germane to Canfield's view of learning are the expectations of learners, as reflected in predicted levels of student performance.

Unfortunately for those who would use inventories of learning styles or strategies in their instruction, the technical merits of such inventories are limited. The reliability of many of the scales must be suspect because of their brevity, and the construct validation of the inventories is by no means assured. It is significant, therefore, that Riechmann and Grasha speak of their efforts as a rational approach to developing and assessing the construct validity of an inventory.

The possibilities of matching learning styles or strategies with learning conditions and opportunities and with teaching styles has intrigued many researchers (for example, Andrews, 1981; Domino, 1971; and Salomon, 1972). The matching of learner characteristics with instructional treatment is based, of course, on expectations of interactions between learning and teaching efforts that will benefit learners. Cross (1976) points out that teachers, too, have cognitive styles and will teach by methods they find comfortable unless they consciously attempt teaching strategies that accommodate learner strategies. She concludes from her discussion that both teacher and students should gain insight into teaching and learning styles. She rejects any notion of "automatic matching" as counterproductive and rightly surmises that students and teachers will be happier and more productive if they are learning and teaching by methods that are compatible with personal preferences.

Messick (1976) has given attention to the problems of matching teaching and learning methods and suggests several models for matching. These include: (a) corrective matches, (b) compensatory matches, (c) capitalization matches, and (d) various combinations thereof. In combining corrective, compensatory, and capitalization models, Messick sees no reason why instruction treatments should not compensate for learner deficiencies at the same time that learner advantages or strengths are exploited.

Elsewhere in the same volume, Seymour Wapner (1976) expresses the belief that the matching of educational treatment and learner characteristics is beneficial only for subject-matter achievement. If the intent of education is to promote flexible and creative thinking, more might be gained through the mismatching of students and teachers. Wapner would seek a synergistic effect by putting learners in learning situations where opposition, contradiction, and obstacles were necessary conditions for the learner's development.

Irrespective of the difficulties in defining, assessing, and applying cognitive styles and/or learning strategies in college and university instruction, there are many reasons to believe that higher education is the beneficiary of cognitive theory and research. The greater bulk of research calls attention to teaching and learning as dual processes affecting learning outcomes and advocates a more serious effort to match teaching and learning efforts in an educationally relevant manner. Whether matched for their compatibility or their synergistic effect, the interaction of teaching styles and/or methods and learning strategies is a major challenge to undergraduate education.

LEARNING AND DEVELOPMENTAL PSYCHOLOGY

A historical view of learning suggests that in a more optimistic era there was an affinity between education and psychology that promised scientific status to both. At the time psychology was the most rapidly developing of the behavioral and social sciences, and the behavioral sciences were perceived as the basis for educational theory and practice. In a period of rapid social change, however, the relevance of behavioral psychology has often been submerged by developmental concepts and principles that explain more satisfactorily how change occurs. The same is true of differential psychology, or the psychology of individual differences.

If previously the variations of human behavior and learning were explained by individual capacities, aptitudes, abilities, interests, and preferences, there has been since the mid-1970s an appreciable inclination to explain changes in behavior by the differential development of learners. When individual A differs from individual B, the explanation might be that while each develops at his or her own pace, both are going through stages or phases of development that all are likely to go through. Individual differences in learning are thus a matter of timing — and patience presumably solves many personal problems, in the manner that Drs. Gesell and Spock once assured parents that problems of infancy and early childhood would be solved.

Leona Tyler (1978) suggests that the individual differences of learning cannot be explained without attention to the different schedules of development that learners undergo. Psychometricians who were once content to demonstrate the wide range of capacities and dispositions evident among individuals should now be dis-enamored with variation as such and become more attentive to the developmental progress individuals make as they grow and mature. Pace and phasing have their own regularities, and where once fatalism was associated with individual differences, a more realistic viewpoint implies that if individuals will continue to develop, they will eventually get to where they want to be. Such a change in viewpoints is not only optimistic, but is also constructive, with profound implications for whatever we try to learn and to teach.

Benjamin Bloom (1976) says much the same thing in quite a different manner. It is his contention that schooling need not result in accentuated learner differences but could result in a more similar or common outcome for everyone. Bloom proposes that the purpose of schooling is not to produce individual differences in learning but to reduce them. While he is obviously aware that individual differences in learners will persist, he is convinced that if instruction takes place in the right way, there will be less — not more — variation in the learning that students do. To accomplish this, the schools must offer something approaching a uniform curriculum and must agree on a finite set of learning and teaching objectives that they have not agreed upon in the past.

The arrival of pluralism and diversity in education has meant too frequently that any explanation of achievement or accomplishment in terms of individual capabilities is suspect. Differences in interests, motives, and cognitive styles are permissible, but differences in aptitudes, readiness, or predisposition are suspected of genetical or hereditarian biases that are unacceptable in an egalitarian society.

In their concern with pluralism and diversity, educators have permitted many psychological insights to slip by the wayside. Too often there has been a romanticism attached to student needs and interests with the result that curricular change sometimes has been predicated on the basis of some inexcusably faulty psychology. One need not be a psychologist or a cynic to suspect that much curricular reform has been advocated with unrealistic expectations about what students were capable of learning, willing to study and learn, and actually would learn. Open classrooms, alternative schools, and nontraditional programs have occasionally been advocated for populations of students that must surely be hypothetical. Reformers and advocates of change have indeed been able to see in students what neither the students nor their teachers could see without remarkable distortions of vision.

Personal Development

The extent to which personal development has been, can be, or should be a focal point of the undergraduate curriculum is a matter of debate. Concepts of student development have remained outside the undergraduate curriculum as such, and much that would seem to be a proper concern of a liberal or general education has been able to gain a quasi-curricular status only.

The campus function in which developmental concepts have been well received, however, is the area of student services. The concept of student development became quite relevant during the 1960s, and many professionals in student services now view student development as their primary function. Miller and Prince (1978) have provided a comprehensive student development model that fully integrates developmental thinking into all areas of student affairs. They believe a developmental view should permeate all education beyond high school, focusing directly on student goals and objectives, methods of assessing progress toward those goals, and managerial techniques for organizing a developmental environment in which academic programs and student affairs would be fully merged.

It is obvious that models and theories of student development have been influenced by the developmental stages, cycles, or phases described by Piaget, Erikson, and other developmental psychologists. Developmental stages or life cycles are progressive in the sense of representing qualitative changes with increasing age. The sequence of changes is expected to be uniform but may be accelerated or retarded by environmental or cultural events. Each stage or cycle represents a structured or organized experience for the individual and may take the form of an alternation of differentiation and integration as a basic growth process.

Developmental models for students in higher education have been influenced not only by the concepts and research findings presented in Sanford's *The American College* but also by Feldman and Newcomb's (1976) extensive survey of the developmental research on college students up to that time. Both volumes offered a positivistic view of developmental change within the college setting and suggested that higher education has a liberalizing effect on the attitudes and values of students. More noticeably, college students are believed to become more confident, less dogmatic, more oriented to intellectual values, less prejudiced, better able to handle personal impulses, and less conservative on political issues. An important conclusion of Feldman and Newcomb's work is that higher education is a means by which adolescents can become adults, and continued development should be one of the goals of a college education. Such conclusions about student development have been confirmed by the later work of Bowen (1977) and Astin (1978).

Chickering (1969) has also presented a view of education in which adolescents become adults by developing their competence, emotions, autonomy, identity, interpersonal relations, purpose, and integrity. Colleges can accelerate movements among the "vectors of change" and can set tasks and conditions that will provide a bridge from one status to the other — but they can also erect barriers and retard progress. Chickering concludes, much as Feldman and Newcomb, that the impact of education is dependent upon the developmental status of the student at entry.

Perry (1970), in another frequently cited study, has identified nine stages of intellectual and ethical development in a longitudinal study of Harvard and Radcliff students. Concepts and values apparently evolve from right-or-wrong, true-or-false distinctions through a phase of skepticism and relativism to an age of commitment where meaningful choices and decisions are made and a sense of personal style and identity achieved.

Developmental concepts are increasingly advocated by a number of specialists who see a need for both the secondary school and the college to provide education for human development. These advocates believe that cognitive skills, moral reasoning, and personal character develop by stages that have a logical and predictable sequence. Lawrence Kohlberg and his co-workers (1979) have described the phases or stages that the adolescent goes through in his or her moral development. Much like Piaget's stages of cognitive development, Kohlberg's stages of moral development proceed in something of an inexorable manner, unfolding as much from internal forces as by the stimulus of outside forces. Jane Loevinger (1979) has described similar stages for ego development. Parsons, Johnston, and Durham (1979) have offered a cognitive-developmental model for aesthetic experience, suggesting in turn that intellect, morals, aesthetic sensitivities, and emotions develop in much the same manner — i.e., stages can be delineated and a sequence for development through those stages can be expected.

The conflict between formal instruction and experiential learning, traditional and nontraditional study, conventional and alternative learning, has not lessened the difficulties of providing student services within a setting where instruction is sometimes perceived as the only legitimate function. Yet there does seem to be a trend toward either using the curriculum as a means of student development or devising curricular approaches to developmental objectives (Miller and Prince, 1978). The organization of student development laboratories, mini-courses, and other quasi-curricular approaches has introduced an instructional component that relies heavily on developmental concepts and principles. Many of these efforts have been in response to the new clientele in higher education, but the majority have been a response to new demands by students. Course and laboratory approaches have dealt with such popular and immediately relevant topics as human sexuality, human potential, group process, collegiate lifestyles, communication skills, nonverbal communication, race relations, and female potential. Other attempts have dealt more directly with leadership, self-awareness, assertiveness training, creativity, personal decision making, and academic development. Even more recently, workshops and seminars have been offered with the themes of inquiry development, inquiry strategies, developing higher-level thinking abilities, interpersonal influence, and facilitating inquiry. Such instructional efforts are said to place an emphasis on techniques, to be competency based, and to include practice in specific competencies.

The disadvantages of such quasi-curricular solutions are thought to be their excessively narrow focus on the student as subject matter, the caliber of professional training and experience on the part of course or lab leaders, and their unintended impact as a counterforce to academic and intellectual development. A more serious reservation may be the extent to which such concepts and techniques are teachable on a college campus. A contradiction may be involved in the sense that some forms of behavior are obviously developed and must be learnable but may not be teachable with the staff, resources, and situation at hand.

Quasi-curricular solutions in higher education are seldom successful in producing a lasting effect on problems and issues that may be perennial. A pattern for such curricular efforts may be seen in previous efforts to deal with critical thinking, personal adjustment, study skills, and speed reading. Each has known its moment of popularity in higher education, but each has failed to find a suitable place in the curriculum *per se*, and each has been subject to cycles of erosion and rediscovery. The need for direct instruction in reading and study skills was rediscovered on many campuses with the advent of disadvantaged students. Regardless of whether it was called remedial, developmental, or compensatory studies, the results often demonstrated the difficulties of short-term, quasi-curricular solutions to long-term, personal deficiencies.

Adult Development

The arrival of adult students on college campuses has left some student development specialists with their models outmoded. As Harrington (1977) has pointed out, adult students now outnumber their younger classmates, and higher education is not only expected to teach them but to help them solve their own developmental problems. The popularity of Gail Sheehy's (1976) book *Passages* suggests that adults do indeed have problems and that much of adult life is a matter of getting through its predictable crises.

Hodgkinson (1974) has discussed adult development in terms of its relevance for administrators and faculty members who must continue to cope with various crises in the college or university setting. Faculty members continue to make career choices for much of their professional lives. They may often consider options that open with experience and additional preparation, such as administration, and they must reconcile the conflicting demands of instruction, research, and service for purposes of career advancement. The crises of the thirties and forties do not appear radically different for faculty members and college administrators. Marital difficulties, divorce, career menopause, personal fears, social inadequacies, professional disappointment, and institutional frustrations are all part of the pattern for many faculty members. The necessities of coping with change may accompany new job opportunities, moving one's family, making community adjustments, and altering interpersonal relations. Identity crises may accompany professional growth and upward mobility as well as threaten personal aspirations that are inordinate.

The relevance of adult development for students in higher education has been delineated in good style by Cross (1981), Chickering (1981), Knox (1977), and Weathersby and Tarule (1980). No doubt is left about the presence of adult learners on college campuses and about the impact their presence has had or will have. Supporting evidence is provided by Aslanian and Brickell (1980), Peterson (1979), and Solmon and Gordon (1981). Antecedents for such interest in older or nontraditional students may be found in Knowles (1973) and others working in the field of adult or continuing education prior to the 1970s.

Cross does for adult learners what she did so well for the New Student. She introduces adult learners as new participants in organized learning activities and explains why they seek participation. Adult learners are likely to come from higher rather than lower socioeconomic classes and to have a higher level of educational attainment than the general population. A majority of them are women and, as a group, they are predominantly white. The reasons for seeking further learning are varied but can be described as personal and practical. They are not interested in knowledge "for knowledge's sake alone," but they do want to become better informed and they do have curiosities that they would satisfy by continuing their education. If barriers did not exist in the form of educational expenses, institutional regulations and requirements, and personal values or dispositions, there are reasons to believe adult learners would be more numerous and thus even more prominent on college campuses.

A lack of learning ability is not a barrier for most adult learners. Cross cites an abundance of evidence to suggest that learning is a function of age but only because of eventual declines in reaction time, vision, and hearing. Since each of these declines is characteristic of later rather than middle age and since there is no inevitable decline in intellectual functioning, rates of participation for adult learners could be increased significantly. A study in the University System of Georgia disclosed that performance on academic ability tests, such as the Scholastic Aptitude Test (SAT), need not be a barrier to most adult learners. When compared to entering freshmen of traditional age, older students entering college for the first time did less well only on the mathematics section of the SAT. Lower math scores are readily explained by time since high school graduation and by the subjects studied there; they do not imply a lack of quantitative ability or analytical capacities, as traditional users of the SAT have sometimes assumed (Fincher, 1983).

In brief, the impact of adult learners on teaching and learning is not felt in the learning abilities and accomplishments that typify adult learners but in the different demands and expectations they bring with them. Research gives good support to their expectation that they will be taught and evaluated differently. Adult learners are more likely to set their own learning pace, and they have definite preferences for the teaching styles that college faculty might use (Warren, 1974).

For many researchers, however, the significance of adult learners on college campuses is to be found in life-span development or the life-cycle stages. To recast institutional missions in such a manner would be to make development the heart and soul of college and university curricula. Other observers, less sanguine about adult development, see life-span development not as the content of college curricula but as a perspective that future faculty members and administrators will need (Fincher, 1981).

A PROVISIONAL CONSENSUS

Given the abundance of implications that learning theory and research have for higher education, does it make sense to look for signs of convergence? Granting the behaviorists and the cognitivists all their theoretical and methodological differences, what can we borrow and reconcile for purposes of improving learning and teaching in American colleges? In theoretical expositions there are surely insights and viewpoints that are useful, and in empirical research findings there must be some working generalizations that are worth applying. Field-dependent educators should concede to field-independent psychologists the limitations of time and place in theory construction and verification but listen again to Ralph Tyler (1976). It was his contention that we know a great

deal about stimulating and guiding learning and need not wait for final or conclusive answers from experimental research.

If, as some cognitivists suggest, we can learn from observation, we can see
much on college campuses that would signify behavioral, cognitive, and developmental dimensions in student learning. We do observe changes in student behavior and we attribute many of those changes to instruction. We do detect
changes in attitudes, beliefs, and values as students move from freshman
classes to senior seminars and we acknowledge that personal development is
difficult to program. And on many occasions, if we are observant, we can infer
that students do indeed "process" knowledge and information in interesting
and idiosyncratic ways. And if we reread what behavioral, cognitive, and developmental psychologists have written about the processes of learning and teaching, we might conclude that all of them are right.

The purposes of a college education have been much debated since the 1960s
but they have seldom been in doubt. Students still attend college for a mixture
of benefits and advantages they hope to gain. No one has contended since Cardinal Newman that higher education should serve a single, unitary purpose,
and the American university might well be the most utilitarian institution since
the medieval church. Yet there is reason to believe that both the objectives and
the outcomes of higher education can be distilled into three major, dominant
concerns: (1) knowledge, (2) competence, and (3) values.

The permissible variations are many. Howard Bowen (1977) has found more
than 1,500 educational goals in the literature of Western civilization but describes "a well-educated person" with eleven characteristics. In turn, his eleven
characteristics are easily sorted as either knowledge or information; skills, pro-
ficiencies, or competencies; or attitudes, beliefs, and values. All fit into the psy-
chologically primitive categories of knowing, doing, or feeling — as those
terms were once used.

If educators could agree that the behavioral, cognitive, and developmental
outcomes of education are knowledge, competence, and understanding, three
kinds of learning will suffice for an explanation of how those outcomes are attained. Learning theory and research suggest a form of conceptual/sym-
bolic/verbal learning that leads to knowledge as an organized structure of information. In much the same manner, theory and research imply a form of
skills/proficiency/competency learning that leads to competent or proficient
performance in such activities as arts and crafts, athletics, and professional
occupations.

Neither conceptual/symbolic/verbal learning nor skills/proficiency/com-
petency learning is strictly behavioral or cognitive in form and substance, but
no serious harm is done in viewing conceptual learning as primarily cognitive
and skills learning as mostly behavioral. Mastery might be a useful way of identifying the outcomes of both kinds of learning — as in mastering a body of
technical or specialized knowledge, or in mastering a complex skill that requires
timing and sensitive manipulation. Mastery should be easier to specify, how-

ever, for skills learning because it presumably would be more observable. Both knowledge and competence, nonetheless, must be inferred from performance because neither knowledge nor competence is overt.

The acquisition of attitudes, beliefs, and values calls for a third kind of learning that may be best identified as experiential learning. "Understanding" is the most accurate term to use in discussing the outcomes of experiential learning, and it is unfortunate that the term is used in conceptual/symbolic/verbal learning when "comprehension" would be more appropriate. As the end product of experiential learning, understanding should be used in the sense of Gordon Allport's (1961) apprehension of events and experiences in relation to a larger significance or context. Understanding thus is similar in many respects to the notion of realization, as used in "realizing" a desire or ambition. It is also similar to the concept of self-actualization as used by Maslow and other personality theorists. As the outcome of experiential learning, understanding is evidenced in the choices or decisions the learner makes and in observed lines of actions that the learner may follow. Krathwohl et al. (1964) describe similar outcomes in their taxonomy of learning objectives in the affective domain.

If educators do agree that the major outcomes of learning are knowledge, competence, and understanding, they could then agree that the psychological antecedents need not be the same. Conceptual/symbolic/verbal learning might be preceded by plans or intentions to learn particular concepts, principles, facts, details. Strategies might be effective in directing the acquisition of skills, and needs or expectations might be significant antecedents of experiential learning and the understanding that presumably follows.

The three kinds of learning identified here are not without intuitive appeal and each may be observed on college campuses, or inferred from student behavior. While learners are acquiring knowledge and competence, they may also be acquiring new or different attitudes, beliefs, and values that alter their understanding of particular events and activities. Students may be greatly influenced by personal-social experiences that may or may not affect the formal instruction they receive in class. Concurrently with instruction, students may undergo changes in tastes, preferences, viewpoints, sentiments, and other facets of personality and character. Quite often experiential change will begin with an awareness of discomfort or doubt that spurs the learner to attempt to relieve or improve the situation. Having made some effort to change his state of awareness, the learner might then step back or withdraw in an attempt to make sense of the experience. This might lead, in turn, to a second effort that will permit the learner to consolidate or internalize the experience and gain an understanding that was not possible previously.

Similar "stages of learning" can be inferred from conceptual and skills learning. Cognitive learning, in particular, begins with an initial stage of attending to or receiving information and makes some effort to order or arrange the information for further processing. Intermediate stages are inferred when the learner assimilates information, recalls and interprets it at a later date, or reorganizes and verifies the information so that it can be integrated with other information. Only when the information is integrated into a large body of information does it become knowledge.

The process of skills acquisition may be more observable, with more evidence of trial-and-error learning in its early stages. Most skills learning begins, nonetheless, with an attentive selection of movements, functions, and activities that are appropriate to the task. Suitable subskills may be encoded, stored, retained, retrieved, and applied in various stages and reinforced by their effects. Mastery of specific skills or competence will later be judged from the learner's performance and will be regarded as the competency, efficiency, or ease with which the learner does what he or she could not do in the beginning.

In brief, the behavioral, cognitive, and developmental dimensions of learning suggest three forms, channels, or levels through which knowledge, competence, and understanding are attained. Within each of the three kinds of learning, stages or phases can be described as initial, intermediate, and closing. For conceptual, skills, and experiential learning, the stages of progression are both similar and different. It all suggests that learning is complex, but it need not be mysterious.

SUMMARY AND CONCLUSIONS

Learning theory and research are often reviewed in the professional literature of psychologists and educational researchers. The intent of this review, however, has been specific. The relevance of learning theory and research for higher education has not been strongly emphasized in the past two decades, and there has been, some of us believe, a noticeable absence of psychological influence on curricula planning and development, instructional improvement, and the assessment or evaluation of learning. Neglect thus provides a harsh contrast with earlier periods in which the bonds of psychology and education were quite strong.

An effort has been made to define learning as the acquisition of knowledge, skill, and understanding under conditions of instruction and for later use or transfer. To serve well the purpose of education, a definition of learning should be descriptive of what actually takes place in education as well as specifying the crucial features of learning as a complex process.

The review of learning conditions and methods of instruction, as they relate to learning in higher education, has been somewhat perfunctory because both topics have either been covered more thoroughly elsewhere or are covered in other chapters of this volume. The comprehensive review of trends in theory and research is precluded by the highly specific focus of learning models and by the voluminous outpouring of research papers that address closely defined research topics or problems.

General principles of learning have been reviewed, however, with particular attention to their applicability in college instruction. Although eroded by later research, most general principles of learning would not seem disconfirmed as much as they appear to be forgotten. Where they have survived, they can be seen as a general condition of learning and not as a productive line of experimental inquiry. There are good reasons, nonetheless, to believe that efforts on the part of college instructors to adapt and to apply general principles of learning would be in the best interests of learners. Efforts to apply general principles would at least facilitate the organization of course objectives and requirements, and they should encourage a more systematic approach to instruction *per se.*

The influence of cognitive psychology and developmental psychology on learning theory and research is seen in the widespread use of cognitive and developmental concepts. Cognitive psychology has redirected many behavioristic trends, and developmental psychology has virtually replaced differential psychology. The implications for college instruction are quite pronounced, and both cognitive and developmental concepts bring a much-needed perspective to higher education in general. Information-processing models are relevant to student learning efforts, and personal development, as opposed to acquired knowledge and competence, is still a valid reason to attend college.

The attempt to synthesize cognitive, behavioral, and experiential concepts into a three-level, multiple-stage "schema" for learning is provisional only. The effort borrows generously from various researchers and theorists with no sense of liability for the misuse of constructs and insights. The schema does provide some economy of conceptualization, however, and it should suggest a better perspective on the multiple purposes and outcomes of a college education. There are many differences in what students study and learn in college, their reasons for attending, and the outcomes that are expected, but there are also many similarities. Furthermore, there are occasions when the similarities should be underscored and the differences should be reexamined. The remaining years of the twentieth century may be such a time.

REFERENCES

Allport, G. W. *Pattern and Growth in Personality.* New York: Holt, Rinehart and Winston, 1961.

Anderson, J. R., and Bower, G. H. *Human Associative Memory.* Washington, D.C.: V. H. Winston, 1973.

Andrews, J. D. W. Teaching format and student style: Their interactive effect on learning. *Research in Higher Education,* 1981, *14*, 161-178.

Aslanian, C. B., and Brickell, H. M. *Americans in Transition: Life Changes as Reasons of Adult Learning.* New York: The College Board, 1980.

Astin, A. W. *Four Critical Years.* San Francisco: Jossey-Bass, 1978.

Atkinson, R. C. Ingredients for a theory of instruction. *American Psychologist,* 1972, *27*, 921-931.

Baker, E. L. The technology of instructional development. In Robert M. W. Travers (ed.), *Second Handbook of Research on Teaching.* Chicago: Rand McNally, 1973.

Bandura, A. *Social Learning Theory.* Englewood Cliffs, N.J.: Prentice-Hall, 1976.

Bandura, A., and Walters, R. H. *Social Learning and Personality Development.* New York: Holt, Rinehart & Winston, 1963.

Berlyne, D. E. Recent developments in Piaget's work. Reprinted in R. J. C. Harper, C. C. Anderson, C. M. Christensen, and S. M. Hunka (eds.), *The Cognitive Processes: Readings.* Englewood Cliffs, N.J.: Prentice-Hall, 1964.

Bloom, B. S. *Human Characteristics and School Learning.* New York: McGraw-Hill, 1976.

Bloom, B. S., Englehart, M. C., Furst, E. J., Hill, W. H., and Krathwohl, D. R. *Taxonomy of Educational Objectives: Handbook I: Cognitive Domain.* New York: David McKay, 1956.

Bowen, H. R. *Investment in Learning: The Individual and Social Value of American Higher Education.* San Francisco: Jossey-Bass, 1977.

Bower, G. H. Analysis of a mnemonic device. *American Scientist,* 1970, *58,* 496-510.

Bower, G. H., and Hilgard, E. R. *Theories of Learning.* 5th ed. Englewood Cliffs, N.J.: Prentice-Hall, 1981.

Brown, A. L., Campione, J. C., and Day, J. D. Learning to learn: On training students to learn from texts. *Educational Researcher,* 1981, *10,* 14-21.

Bruner, J. *The Process of Education.* Cambridge, Mass.: Harvard University Press, 1960.

Bruner, J. S. *Toward a Theory of Instruction.* Cambridge, Mass.: Harvard University Press, 1966.

Canfield, A. A. Learning styles inventory manual. Ann Arbor, Mich.: Humanics Media, 1980.

Chickering, A. W. *Education and Identity.* San Francisco: Jossey-Bass, 1969.

Chickering, A. W. *Experience and Learning: An Introduction to Experiential Learning.* New Rochelle, N.Y.: Change Magazine Press, 1977.

Chickering, A. W., and Associates. *The Modern American College: Responding to the New Realities of Diverse Students and a Changing Society.* San Francisco: Jossey-Bass, 1981.

Cooley, W. W., and Lohnes, P. R. *Evaluation Research in Education: Theory, Principles, and Practice.* New York: Irvington, 1976.

Coombs, A. W. Fostering maximum development of the individual. In William Van Til (ed.), *Issues in Secondary Education.* Chicago: National Society for the Study of Education, 1976.

Cronbach, L. J., and Snow, R. E. *Aptitudes and Instructional Methods: A Handbook for Research on Interactions.* New York: Irvington, 1977.

Cross, K. P. *Beyond the Open Door: New Students to Higher Education.* San Francisco: Jossey-Bass, 1971.

Cross, K. P. *Accent on Learning: Improving Instruction and Reshaping the Curriculum.* San Francisco: Jossey-Bass, 1976.

Cross, K. P. *Adults as Learners.* San Francisco: Jossey-Bass, 1981.

Dirkes, M. A. The role of divergent production in the learning process. *American Psychologist,* 1978, *33,* 815-820.

Domino, G. Interactive effects of achievement orientation and teaching style on academic achievement. *Journal of Educational Psychology,* 1971, *62,* 427-431.

Feldman, K. A., and Newcomb, T. M. *The Impact of College on Students.* San Francisco: Jossey-Bass, 1976.

Fincher, C. What is learning? *Engineering Education,* 1978, *68,* 420-423.

Fincher, C. Higher education as a stage of transition. *Research in Higher Education,* 1981, *15,* 377-380.

Fincher, C. *Adult Learners and the SAT in the University System of Georgia.* Athens: Institute of Higher Education, University of Georgia, 1983.

Frase, L. T. Advances in research and theory in instructional technology. In Fred N. Kerlinger (ed.), *Review of Research in Education.* Vol. 3. Itasco, Ill.: Peacock, 1975.

Gagne, R. M. Educational technology and the learning process. *Educational Research-er*, 1974, *3*, 3-8.

Gagne, R. M. *The Conditions of Learning.* 3d ed. New York: Holt, Rinehart & Winston, 1977.

Gagne, R. M., and Briggs, L. J. *Principles of Instructional Design.* New York: Holt, Rinehart & Winston, 1974.

Gagne, R. M., and Dick, W. Instructional psychology. *Annual Review of Psychology,* 1983, *34*, 261-295.

Gagne, R. M., and Rohwer, W. D., Jr. Instructional psychology. *Annual Review of Psychology,* 1969, *20*, 318-418.

Glaser, R. Components of a psychology of instruction: Toward a science of design. *Review of Educational Research*, 1976, *46*, 1-24.

Glaser, R. Instructional psychology: Past, present, and future. *American Psychologist,* 1982, *37*, 307-318.

Glaser, R. Education and thinking: The role of knowledge. *American Psychologist.* 1982, *39*, 93-104.

Glass, G. V., and Smith, M. L. Meta-analysis of research on class size and achievement. *Educational Evaluation and Policy Analysis*, 1979, *1*, 2-16.

Goldstein, H., Krantz, D. L., and Rains, J. D. *Controversial Issues in Learning.* New York: Appleton-Century-Crofts, 1965.

Greeno, J. G. Psychology of learning, 1960-1980: One participant's observations. *American Psychologist*, 1980, *35*, 713-728.

Guthrie, E. R. *The Psychology of Learning.* Rev. ed. New York: Harper & Row, 1952.

Hansen, K. H. (ed.). *Learning: An Overview and Update.* Washington, D.C.: U.S. Office of Education, 1976.

Harlow, H. F. The formation of learning sets. *Psychological Review*, 1949, *56*, 51-65.

Harlow, H. F. The nature of love. *American Psychologist*, 1958, *18*, 673-685.

Harrington, F. H. *The Future of Adult Education: New Responsibilities of Colleges and Universities.* San Francisco: Jossey-Bass, 1979.

Hebb, D. O. The American revolution. *American Psychologist*, 1960, *15*, 735-745.

Higbee, K. L. Recent research on visual mnemonics: Historical roots and education fruits. *Review of Educational Research*, 1979, *49*, 611-629.

Hilgard, E. R. (ed.). *Theories of Learning and Instruction. Sixty-third Yearbook of the National Society for the Study of Education.* Chicago: University of Chicago Press, 1964.

Hill, W. F. *Learning: A Survey of Psychological Interpretations.* 3d ed. New York: Harper & Row, 1977.

Hodgkinson, H. L. Adult development: Implications for faculty and administrators. *Educational Record*, 1974, *55*, 263-264.

Hull, C. L. *Principles of Behavior.* New York: Appleton-Century-Crofts, 1943.

Jenkins, J. J. Remember that old theory of memory? Well, forget it. *American Psychologist*, 1974, *29*, 785-795.

Katona, G. *Organizing and Memorizing: Studies in the Psychology of Learning.* New York: Columbia University Press, 1940.

Keller, F. S. Good-bye, teacher . . . *Journal of Applied Behavior Analysis*, 1968, *1*, 79-89.

Knowles, M. S. *The Adult Learner.* Houston: Gulf, 1973.

Knox, A. B. *Adult Development and Learning.* San Francisco: Jossey-Bass, 1977.

Kohlberg, L., and Gilligan, C. The adolescent as philosopher: The discovery of the self in a postconventional world. In R. L. Mosher (ed.), *Adolescents' Development & Education: A Janus Knot.* Berkeley, Calif.: McCutchan, 1979.

Kohlberg, L., and Mayer, R. Development as the aim of education. In R. L. Mosher (ed.), *Adolescents' Development and Education: A Janus Knot.* Berkeley, Calif.: McCutchan, 1979.

Krathwohl, D. R., Bloom, Benjamin S., and Masia, B. B. *Taxonomy of Educational Objectives: Handbook II: Affective Domain.* New York: David McKay, 1964.

Kulik, J. A., Kulik, C. C., and Cohen, P. A. A meta-analysis of outcome studies of Keller's personalized system of instruction. *American Psychologist,* 1979, *34,* 307-318.

Lewin, K. *Principles of Topological Psychology.* New York: McGraw-Hill, 1936.

Loevinger, J. Stages of ego development. In R. L. Mosher (ed.), *Adolescents' Development & Education: A Janus Knot.* Berkeley, Calif.: McCutchan, 1979.

McGeoch, J. A., and Irion, A. L. *The Psychology of Human Learning.* New York: Longmans, Green, 1952.

McKeachie, W. J. The decline and fall of the laws of learning. *Educational Researcher,* 1974(a), *3,* 7-11.

McKeachie, W. J. Instructional psychology. *Annual Review of Psychology,* 1974(b), *25,* 161-193.

McKeachie, W. J. Implications of cognitive psychology for college teaching. In W. J. McKeachie (guest editor), *Learning, Cognition, and College Teaching.* New Directions for Teaching and Learning Series. San Francisco: Jossey-Bass, 1980(a).

McKeachie, W. J. (guest editor). *Learning, Cognition, and College Teaching.* New Directions for Teaching and Learning Series. San Francisco: Jossey-Bass, 1980(b).

McKeachie, W. J. Procedures and techniques of teaching: A survey of experimental efforts. In N. Sanford (ed.), *The American College.* New York: Wiley, 1962.

McKeachie, W. J., and Kulik, J. A. Effective college teaching. In F. N. Kerlinger (ed.), *Review of Research in Education.* Ithaca, Ill.: Peacock, 1975.

Messick, S., and Associates. *Individuality in Learning: Implications of Cognitive Styles and Creativity for Human Development.* San Francisco: Jossey-Bass, 1976.

Miller, G. A., Galanter, E., and Pribram, K. H. *Plans and the Structure of Behavior.* New York: Holt, Rinehart & Winston, 1960.

Miller, T. K., and Prince, J. S. *The Future of Student Affairs: A Guide to Student Development for Tomorrow's Higher Education.* San Francisco: Jossey-Bass, 1978.

Milton, O. *Alternatives to the Traditional: How Professors Teach and How Students Learn.* San Francisco: Jossey-Bass, 1972.

Milton, O., and Associates. *On College Teaching.* San Francisco: Jossey-Bass, 1978.

Milton, O., and Edgerly, J. W. *The Testing and Grading of Students.* New Rochelle, N.Y.: Change Magazine Press, 1977.

Mowrer, O. H. *Learning Theory and Behavior.* New York: Wiley, 1960.

Norman, D. A. What goes on in the mind of the learner. In W. J. McKeachie (guest editor), *Learning, Cognition, and College Teaching.* New Directions for Teaching and Learning Series. San Francisco: Jossey-Bass, 1980.

Paivio, A. *Imagery and Verbal Processes.* New York: Holt, Rinehart and Winston, 1971.

Parsons, M. J., Johnston, M. A., and Durham, R. F. A cognitive-development approach to aesthetic experience. In R. L. Mosher (ed.), *Adolescents' Development and Education: A Janus Knot.* Berkeley, Calif.: McCutchan, 1979.

Perry, W. G. *Forms of Intellectual and Ethical Development in the College Years.* New York: Holt, Rinehart & Winston, 1970.

Peterson, R. E., and Associates. *Lifelong Learning in America.* San Francisco: Jossey-Bass, 1979.

Posner, M. I., and Keele, S. W. Skill learning. In Robert M. W. Travers (ed.), *Second Handbook of Research on Teaching.* Chicago: Rand McNally, 1973.

Riechmann, S. W., and Grasha, A. F. A rational approach to developing and assessing the construct validity of a student learning style scales instrument. *Journal of Psychology,* 1974, *87,* 231-223.

Robinson, F. P. *Effective Study.* New York: Harper and Brothers, 1946.

Salomon, G. Heuristic models for the generation of aptitude-treatment interaction hypotheses. *Review of Educational Research,* 1972, *42,* 327-343.

Sanford, N. (ed.). *The American College: A Psychological and Social Interpretation of the Higher Learning.* New York: Wiley, 1962.

Sheehy, G. *Passages: Predictable Crises of Adult Life.* New York: E. P. Dutton, 1976.

Shepard, R. N. The mental image. *American Psychologist,* 1978, *33,* 125-137.

Skinner, B. F. *The Behavior of Organisms: An Experimental Analysis.* New York: Appleton-Century-Crofts, 1938.

Skinner, B. F. *Science and Human Behavior.* New York: Macmillan, 1953.

Skinner, B. F. *The Technology of Teaching. New York: Appleton-Century-Crofts, 1968.*

Snow, R. E. Individual differences and instructional theory. *Educational Researcher,* 1977, *6*(10), 11-15.

Solmon, L. C., and Gordon, J. J. *The Characteristics and Needs of Adults in Post-secondary Education.* Lexington, Mass.: Lexington Books, 1981.

Spady, W. G. Competency based education: A bandwagon in search of a definition. *Educational Researcher,* 1977, *6,* 9-14.

Spence, K. W. *Behavior Theory and Conditioning.* New Haven, Conn.: Yale University Press, 1956.

Thorndike, E. L. *The Psychology of Learning.* New York: Teachers College, 1913.

Tolman, E. C. *Purposive Behavior in Animals and Men.* New York: Appleton-Century-Crofts, 1932.

Travers, R. M. W. (ed.). *Second Handbook of Research on Teaching: A Project of the American Educational Research Association.* Chicago: Rand McNally, 1973.

Tyler, L. E. *Individuality: Human Possibilities and Personal Choice in the Psychological Development of Men and Women.* San Francisco: Jossey-Bass, 1978.

Tyler, R. W. What have we learned about learning: Overview and update. In Kenneth H. Hansen (ed.), *Learning: An Overview and Update.* A report of the Chief State School Officers 1976 Summer Institute. Washington, D.C.: USOE, 1976.

Wapner, S. Commentary: Process and context in the conception of cognitive style. In S. Messick and Associates, *Individuality in Learning.* San Francisco: Jossey-Bass, 1976.

Warren, J. R. Adapting instruction to styles of learning. *ETS Findings,* 1974, *1,* 1-5.

Watson, J. B. *Psychology From the Standpoint of a Behaviorist.* Philadelphia: Lipincott, 1919.

Weathersby, R. P., and Tarule, J. M. *Adult Development: Implications for Higher Education.* Washington, D.C.: American Association for Higher Education, 1980.

Wilson, J. D. *Student Learning in Higher Education.* New York: Halsted Press, 1981.

Witkin, H. A. Cognitive styles in academic performance and in teacher-student relations. In S. Messick and Associates, *Individuality in Learning.* San Francisco: Jossey-Bass, 1976.

Wittrock, M. C. The cognitive movement in instruction. *Educational Researcher,* 1979, *8,* 5-11.

Wittrock, M. C., and Lumsdaine, A. A. Instructional psychology. *Annual Review of Psychology,* 1977, *28,* 417-459.

METHODS AND THEORIES OF INSTRUCTION

Michael T. McCord, *University of Georgia*

Reviews of the published research on college teaching are seldom comprehensive. Numerous studies, of varying quality and research sophistication, have been published in various professional journals, conference proceedings, annals of professional societies, and *ad hoc* symposia. Many of these studies are in the "fugitive literature" of research centers, college colloquia, and government agencies, thus escaping many reviewers. No one in recent years has surpassed McKeachie's survey of experimental studies in *The American College* (Sanford, 1962), although McKeachie himself has continued to review the research on college teaching periodically since the early 1960s (McKeachie and Kulik, 1975; McKeachie, 1970). Trent and Cohen's (1973) review in the *Second Handbook of Research on Teaching* draws heavily from community and junior college studies without placing a similar emphasis on teaching at the senior college level and in graduate and professional education. Textbooks, of most uneven quality, give slight emphasis to research as such and often present new or innovative teaching methods as established practices (see Brown and Thornton, 1971; Davis, 1976).

The purpose of this chapter is to review methods and theories of instruction as they relate to teaching in American colleges and universities. Occasional use will be made of research at elementary and secondary school levels but only when such research is clearly related to instruction at higher levels. Although the review is not comprehensive, it should prove useful. The selected published literature that is incorporated into this review is based on working definitions of theory and method that are by no means rigorous. Instructional methods are regarded as the incredible diversity of techniques, procedures, and arrangements by which college faculty assist students in learning. Instructional theory is regarded as the varied attempts of theorists, researchers, and practitioners to bring system, order, or efficiency to the classroom behavior of teaching faculty. The criteria for inclusion in this review thus do not include rigorous experimental design, elaborate research methods, or intensive statistical analysis. The complexity of college instruction often defies the advantages of controlled observation, and there should be a great deal to learn about instruction that is not statistically significant at the .01 level of confidence.

As will be shown, a major weakness in many published studies is the lack of careful consideration of what constitutes "conventional" methods. In an age of wide exposure to a variety of ways of transmitting information and encouraging learning, an instructor is less likely to maintain one and only one instructional method during the life span of a teaching career. Even the traditional lecture is given an innovative flair with the interjection of a popular trend in societal communication such as punning. After all, if newscasters can do it in front of millions, why not the college professor in front of 30 students?

If there are principles of learning that apply to the acquisition of instructional behavior, it is most likely that of modeling or observational learning. What the instructor has witnessed or experienced as effective modes of instruction may significantly influence adoption and use. This type or principle of learning may be why reviewing a videotape of one's instruction often shows up in research studies as a significant effect upon efforts to improve instruction.

Other purposes of this chapter are to examine the major modes of instruction prevalent in higher education and to identify common features of instructional planning and organization that lead to a theory of instruction. A consideration of current theories of instruction should also yield concepts and principles that may be woven into the fabric of effective instruction. Additionally, an overview of other factors and conditions of instruction should denote trends and needs for future research efforts and hint at possibilities for a more comprehensive theory of instruction.

CONVENTIONAL MODES OF INSTRUCTION

Instruction in higher education has seen a variety of changes in techniques (Ellner and Barnes, 1983). During the 17th century the primary mode of learning was memorization and recitation. This eventually yielded to the methods of lecture which were introduced by teachers of science when this discipline obtained a place in the curriculum. The lecture in turn began to undergo changes as increased specialization and emphasis on "practical" learning influenced the curriculum. Several modes of instruction that constitute identifiable or distinct procedures used in college teaching today may be identified as: (a) lectures, (b) discussions, (c) seminars, and (d) independent study.

The Lecture

The lecture is probably the most widely used and the most frequently criticized instructional technique in higher education. The question is often raised as to why so many faculty members lecture, and the answer appears to be that lectures are traditional. They have served well in the past, so why not continue to use them? Most professors use lectures partially out of habit but probably more so because of certain assumptions they make about teaching methods. One assumption is that the lecture will facilitate the student's involvement in the process of reflective thinking which supposedly the teacher is demonstrating. Another assumption is that the presentation of facts to the learners will aid them in organizing those facts and understanding how they were derived, and will somehow enhance the learners' independent problem-solving ability. These assumptions may be valid to a limited degree, but they are questionable in many classroom situations. Unlike the medieval ages, when the limited number of books rendered the lecture the most efficient means to disseminate information, contemporary students have, or should have, access to adequately furnished libraries.

The lecture method varies according to whether the lecturer is imparting information or clarifying a particular problem. Lowman (1984) has delineated several types of lectures. At one end of the continuum is the formal oral essay, which is a tightly constructed, highly polished kind of lecture that presents information to support a particular point or conclusion. In this kind of lecture the professor has reviewed and selected information from a large and diverse body of knowledge that will support the major point. However, this is unlikely to be the most common kind of college lecture because the instructor must write down much of the information to be transmitted to the students. A more frequent variation is the expository lecture in which the lecturer defines and sets forth information. Again, the instructor does most of the talking, only occasionally allowing questions from students or asking questions of them.

A form of lecture closely related to the expository lecture is the provocative lecture. As with the previous two forms, the instructor does most of the talking but makes a conscious effort to provoke thought. The lecturer makes an assumption about the level and the type of existing knowledge that students have and then challenges this knowledge in order to stimulate a more complete and integrated perspective. While this type of lecture may be better suited for the humanities than for the sciences, lectures can challenge and question student assumptions in any discipline. Discussion that arises in this form of lecture stimulates students to question their personal values and attitudes.

Another variation of the lecture is the combination lecture and demonstration in which instructors use a variety of illustrations and examples. Yet another variation is to tack on a question period during which the teacher spends most of the class time responding to questions posed by students. The teacher may provoke questions from students and then launch into the presentation of detailed information previously prepared.

Considering the circumstances under which lectures might be preferred, Hoover (1980) presented the following:

1. When the needed background information is not readily accessible to students

2. When the facts or problems are conflicting or confusing in nature
3. When a unique experience of an individual will substantially contribute to the clarification of issues
4. When time is short and resources or data are widely scattered
5. When a change of pace is needed
6. When the best way to understand a topic is through oral presentation

The effectiveness of lectures has often been compared with that of class discussion and other conventional modes. McKeachie (1978) has presented a succinct consideration of the research on the lecture technique versus discussion and self-directing methods. However, very little recent research has focused on the major features of the lecture technique as an effective method of instruction in and of itself.

The literature is not without suggestions as to how to improve lectures. Several knowledgeable educators assert that lectures can be improved simply by organizing the course material, getting students to interact during the class hour, and supplementing the lecture with discussion (Bowman, 1979). Another suggestion for improving the lecture is to adopt a pausing principle (Brawer, 1980), which allows students the opportunity to gather their thoughts and think about what has just transpired. This technique is based on the supposition that students experience mental lapses when a lecturer suddenly makes an unobserved shift in the context, introduces an idea that the student fails to grasp, or stimulates an independent chain of thought. Pauses during the lecture also give students a chance to share notes and make comments.

Although the lecture has been criticized as an inefficient means of transferring knowledge that provides little feedback to either the student or the instructor and relies heavily on oral communication (Berquist and Phillips, 1977), others point out that the lecture can provide a framework for students, motivate them, introduce a new field, simplify complex subjects, and provide a host of material quickly (Cole, 1982). Kozma, Belle, and Williams, (1978) state that lectures can be modified to meet students' interest and level of ability. They note that experts maintain the effective lecturer is one who knows his audience and accommodates the message to the background and interest of the listeners. Since 1978 at least three books have included chapters specifically dealing with lecturing. *On College Teaching* (Milton and Associates, 1978) contains a lengthy chapter by John Satterfield in which the primary components of content and context, delivery and style, and form are given good coverage with several practical examples.

Hoover (1980) devotes a chapter to the lecture method in which he introduces the fundamental properties of the lecture and discusses them in relation to several critical issues, including the role of nonverbal feedback and the development of advanced organizers. Hoover's chapter ends with a brief listing of the values of the lecture method: (a) lecture methods are economical in terms of time and material; (b) lectures serve to channel thinking of all students in a given direction; (c) demonstrations enable class leaders to perform activities that would be too dangerous for students to perform themselves in the ordinary classroom; and (d) lectures are to some extent easier to prepare and are usually based on specialized knowledge. This list of values is followed by a consideration of the limitations of and problems with lecture methods: (a) information-giving methods encourage the retention of facts as ends in and of themselves; (b) lecture methods by themselves are inadequate for teaching certain types of concepts, i.e., attitudes and skills; (c) social learning is minimized during oral presentations; (d) lecture approaches tend to encourage acceptance of the teacher as the final authority; and (e) exposition processes are extremely difficult to adapt to individual differences among students.

Lowman (1984) includes a chapter on selecting and organizing materials for class presentation in which the lecture is emphasized almost exclusively as the mode of class presentation. While the above works may be useful resources and contain what seem to be rational ideas for conducting lectures, they still reflect a lack of recent research dealing with modifications of the lecture technique in detail. By default they are highly biased by the author's ideas, impressions, and subjective opinions about what is effective as a lecture. While such discussions do not reflect empirical evidence, they may be far more valuable for that very reason.

Discussion

Discussion is a creative process during which the instructor engages students by encouraging them to speak and listen in an orderly sequence so that relevant thinking can occur. If discussion techniques are employed properly, interaction is frequent and one contribution builds upon another. Overall there are generally three types of discussions: (a) leader-centered, (b) leader-guided, and (c) group-centered, which has no official leader (Hyman, 1980). Discussion is generally considered to be useful for: (a) utilizing the resources of class members; (b) giving students the opportunity to apply principles; (c) giving students timely feedback on course objectives; (d) allowing them practice in thinking; (e) developing motivation for further learning; and (f) allowing students to become aware of and to formulate problems, using the information that has been gained from readings or from previous lectures.

Discussions must be carefully planned and executed if they are to be an effective instructional method. Instructors should maintain a high degree of concentration, be able to improvise, and exhibit considerable patience. The most important advantage is that students become actively involved in learning. Wales and Stager (1978) have emphasized the use of a guided-design discussion method. In this procedure students work in groups of four to seven on open-ended questions. Each problem is broken down into a sequence of decision-making steps. The instructor moves among the groups facilitating the decision making. The intent is to develop in students a decision-making capability which can be applied to practical problems.

Eble (1980) speaks of another example of a discussion group, called the co-operative learning group, which is a permanent independent collection of eight to ten students. A faculty member sets goals for this group and acts as a resource consultant. The students engage in discussion oriented toward facilitating creativity, independence, and self-reliance. Some educators cautiously warn that, allowed free rein, students discussing anything and everything may well reduce class discussions to bull sessions instead of developing reflective thinking (Hoover, 1980). The limitations of class discussion thus can be identified as follows: (a) discussions presuppose adequate preparation; (b) the permissive characteristic of discussion tends to encourage digression; (c) even when carefully organized, discussion is unpredictable; (d) group agreement or consensus does not ensure accomplishment of goals.

Much of the literature that supports discussion as a teaching technique has evolved from the research into dynamics of group interactions. One of the strongest findings supporting the use of discussion groups points to the need for participant commitment and definition of decision and authority lines within the group (Barnes-McConnell, 1978). Although the involvement of class members is an important factor, a discussion must maintain focus on course objectives because even a lively and satisfying discussion can sometimes be counterproductive when contrary to factual information. Most of the research on discussion thus focuses on those methods and techniques which are primarily dependent upon student-centered emphasis. Instructor-centered variations of discussion techniques have not been vigorously investigated.

A summary of research spanning almost 50 years indicates that professor preference for either the lecture or the discussion method depends upon the instructional goals (McKeachie and Kulik, 1975). The influence of discussion on the acquisition of factual knowledge was found to be inconsistent, but in studies where ability, attitudes, or motivation were measured the results favored the discussion method. Determining the most effective method, therefore, depends upon the criteria by which they are compared. Combination lecture and discussion meetings resulted in no significant differences in achievement between groups, while the students in partial discussion classes persisted with more favorable attitudes over a two-year period. What appears to be valuable is the opportunity for student-student and student-teacher interaction.

Comparisons of student-centered versus teacher-centered instruction consistently point to a superiority of student-centered methods for higher-level cognitive goals and for motivational and attitudinal changes. Discussions can be instructor-centered, where student participation is in response to questions and encouragement to ask questions, or student-centered, where students are encouraged to interact with one another and thus reducing the authority role of the instructor. McKeachie and Kulik (1975) examined 31 reports of comparisons of these two discussion methods with findings similar to those obtained when comparing lecture with discussion. When effects upon tests of factual knowledge are examined, mixed results are obtained. However, on measures of attitude or motivation the student-centered classes were clearly superior to the instructor-centered classes. A variety of studies were cited which led to the general conclusion that instruction characterized by increased student activity and interaction with peers and faculty produces favorable learning outcomes.

The Seminar

The seminar is a mode of instruction that appears to be very similar to discussion. The difference, however, is that both atmosphere and topical focus are controlled by the instructor. In the seminar, conversation most likely occurs when the instructor extracts factual information from students or encourages discussion of the factual information he presents. For a seminar to be successful, lecturing should be avoided. Eble (1976) has pointed out that ideally a seminar should consist of a small number of intensely interested and knowledgeable individuals who let their minds play on a common topic. This would suggest uses of seminars in the upper-division and graduate-level courses only.

Eble listed three reasons for distrusting the seminar: (a) weakly supported yet strong assumptions often exist about the value of the seminar, (b) lack of definition results in unclear goals, and (c) a seminar often fails to consist of "intensely interested and knowing individuals." He later states that seminars are most appropriate for the upper-division and graduate courses.

The limitations of seminars as discussed by Hoover (1980) include: (a) seminars may disorient and confuse some students, (b) seminars are generally inappropriate for teaching an established body of knowledge, (c) instructors may have difficulty accepting their role as a facilitator, and (d) seminars are designed for small classes. When group size exceeds 20 students, the method becomes increasingly unwieldy.

A number of variations can be made in the seminar method in an effort to deal with these problems. The instructor may utilize a "round table" approach as a means to identify problems, develop small group or individual activities, and schedule presentations, thus providing a forum setting where all seminar members are responsible for some degree of participation. Written assignments can also facilitate the purpose of a seminar. Usually there are two types of seminar writing: (a) a brief summary of readings, and (b) a critique of the problem to be considered. This writing should be unencumbered and describe in concise, simple terms the points to be made. Occasionally, seminar writing may require members to take a position or evaluate the topic under consideration. A less structured approach to use for generating ideas on a specific problem is brainstorming. The instructor is responsible for identifying a specific problem for exploration, after which the seminar participants engage in discussion utilizing four rules: (1) criticism is not allowed, (2) imaginative ideas are welcomed, (3) quantity is desired, and (4) a combination of ideas is sought. While facilitating full participation of group members the instructor must judge when enough group cohesion exists to employ this technique.

The seminar may be enhanced by use of a symposium if the problem or topic can be readily divided into subtopics. The instructor invites guest speakers who make presentations in a predetermined order, ensuring that each presentation is related to the preceding one. The students are allotted discussion time with the guest speakers following their presentations. The instructor should monitor this discussion to keep the seminar within the topic and prevent unproductive digression from the main purpose.

These variations allow the seminar method to be adapted to a wide diversity of learning situations. Yet caution should be observed when application is attempted to topics where an organized and well-defined body of content already exists. Freshman-level seminars may be inappropriate due to the wide disparity in students' interest, competence, past experience, and information. However, skillfully employed with graduate students this method can greatly enhance group reflection on information and problems.

Independent Study

Reisman (1980) has described independent study as the academic work conducted on campus under the tutelage of a particular faculty member. While this definition emphasizes "on-campus teaching," independent study can also be accomplished elsewhere. Consider the definition of Duley (1978) of field study as being out-of-classroom learning activities sponsored by an institution or a faculty member in which the learner has the primary responsibility for the educational endeavor. This is similar to the definition of experiential learning used by Cole (1982). He emphasized that experiential learning takes place outside the classroom in the context of practical experience rather than through study alone.

Courses carrying the title of independent study are traditionally conducted on campus using the facilities of the institution. Students usually are involved in the selection of the problem or the course of study during the independent project. They then undertake the study, resolve the problem if there is one to be resolved, and report the results. Independent study uses the instructor as a facilitator and ultimately the evaluator, but there is little in the way of formal instruction. A major appeal of independent study to some educators is its affirmation of values such as freedom of choice, individualism, and democratic participation. Independent study gives students an increased capacity for generalization and transfer which enhances a sense of relevance and allows development of the ability to analyze, synthesize, and apply what is learned (Kozma, Belle, and Williams, 1978). McKeachie's survey (1978), however, led him to the conclusion that, as with other methods of teaching and instruction, few differences are found between the achievement of students working independently and those taught in conventional classes. If, nonetheless, research results have not shown independent study to be more effective than traditional methods of teaching, it appears that educators will continue to support it because it appeals to a sense of student responsibility for their own learning.

INNOVATIVE MODES OF INSTRUCTION

Since the early 1950s, various modifications or alternatives to instruction in higher education have emerged and received varying attention by college and university faculties. The most prominent innovations in college instruction are: (a) programmed instruction, (b) audio-tutorial systems, (c) personalized systems of instruction, and (d) computer-based instruction. As with any innovation, a variety of studies have been reported in which the results of innovative approaches are compared to those of conventional methods.

Programmed Instruction

Instruction presented by teaching machines came into existence in the 1950s and was a part of many college courses during the 1960s. The essential features of programmed instruction (PI) were the presentation of small amounts of information to students, requirements that students respond in some way, and immediate feedback. Students controlled the pace at which the material was handled and thus made self-pacing a primary component in individualizing instruction. In this manner PI offered instructors a means of "building in" a self-improvement procedure for students (Schiller and Markle, 1978). During the 1960s there were various efforts by instructors to create programs as supplements to conventional course work and on occasion to replace conventional textbooks. It was soon discovered that it was almost impossible to replace a course entirely with programmed instruction.

Some research findings did emerge about learning with programmed instruction. For instance, Moore, Smith, and Teevan (1965) discovered a higher degree of success in small-step programs than in large-step programs. Short programs requiring 30 minutes or less appeared to be more effective and less boring than longer programs which covered large blocks of material or an entire course (Beard, 1972). Although some advocates thought programmed materials might solve many problems of curriculum and course organization, the generating of high-quality programs required as much scholarship and skill as the writing of a good textbook (Krumboltz, 1964). The result was a very limited number of good programs for college use.

Numerous efforts were made to demonstrate the superiority of PI over conventional techniques. Silberman (1962), for example, reported the results from 15 comparisons of programmed and conventional instruction and found nine comparisons favoring PI and six reporting no major difference. Schramm (1964) reviewed evidence from another 36 studies and found that 18 reported no major difference in achievement obtained. However, 17 studies did show a significant superiority for students working with programs, and only one study showed a superiority for the students in a conventional class. Nash, Muczyk, and Vettori (1976) reviewed 138 studies, looking for the impact of PI on immediate learning. Forty-nine of these studies disclosed a significant difference in favor of PI, whereas 12 found significant differences in favor of conventional instruction. The remaining 71 reported no significant difference between the two methods. Cronbach and Snow (1977) examined 32 studies of the impact of PI on students at different ability levels. Of these 32 studies, 13 showed that the programmed group had a shallower slope of regression and only five studies reported that the conventional group had a shallower slope of regression. There was no evidence of interaction in the remaining studies. Overall, this led Cronbach and Snow to conclude that "programmed instruction often generates a lower attribute treatment regression slope but the opposite finding occurs often enough to discourage generalization" (p. 189).

Kulik, Cohen, and Ebeling (1980) studied the effectiveness of PI in higher education by conducting a meta-analytic study of selected studies. Meta-analysis applies the same objective methods that a researcher uses in analyzing results from an individual study, but these are applied across a collection of results. The meta-analyst is then able to draw reliable, reproducible, and general conclusions. From a pool of 5,000 studies, 624 were selected for closer examination but only 57 studies were identified as having sufficient data that could be used in a meta-analytic analysis. The results of this meta-analysis produced findings in five different areas relating to the effectiveness of programmed instruction: (1) student achievement, (2) aptitude-achievement correlation, (3) course completion, (4) student attitudes), and (5) instructional time. Table 1 presents a brief synopsis of their findings.

A clear majority of the studies favored PI effects on student achievement. The size of this effect was found to be small, raising student achievement only by one-quarter of a standard deviation. Nonetheless, this difference is statistically significant, indicating that PI does a better job of instruction when compared to conventional modes of instruction. This finding is given increased credibility when the effects of aptitude-achievement interaction are determined to be about the same for low-aptitude students as for high-aptitude students. Although the achievement gains of students taught by PI were significant, they were considered small by most standards. The potential for generalization of this finding is tempered by the large variations in effect size from study to study. Almost two-thirds of the studies reported small or trivial effects in favor of PI, but approximately one-third reported medium to large effects favoring PI.

The programmed instruction movement has been healthy for instruction in higher education because it has forced a clarification of educational objectives (McKeachie, 1978). At times, however, the emphasis has focused too heavily on writing objectives of a very specific nature such as is usually necessary for learning computer programming. All too often, the result has been trivial detailed objectives instead of broader significant objectives. The role that programmed instruction can play in higher education instruction thus has not been clearly defined. Clearer objectives for instructional materials are advantageous, but as a technique to complement the total instructional effort of an institution, are uncommon.

TABLE 1. Summary of Overall Effects Found in Meta-analysis of Studies on Programmed Instruction (PI)

Results/Effects	Major Findings
Student achievement	The PI class performed at a higher level than the conventional class in 40 of 56 studies. Twenty-one out of 25 reporting statistically significant differences favored PI.
	The "typical" student in a PI class performed at the 60th percentile on final examinations compared to the "typical" student in a control class achieving at the 50th percentile.
Aptitude-achievement correlation	"It seems safe to conclude that programmed instruction has, at best, a very small effect on aptitude-achievement correlations." Thus, effects of PI on achievement were about the same regardless of aptitude level of students.
Course completion	Typically the average withdrawal rate from PI classes was less than 1% higher than the average rate from the conventional classes. This resulted in a statistically trivial effect size.
Student attitudes/ratings	Very few (4) studies contained student rating data; examination of these provided no support for impressions that students will respond more favorably to programmed classes than to conventional classes.
Instructional/study time	" . . . PI makes no extra demand on student time and sometimes results in a significant time saving for students." Five hours for programmed approaches versus six hours per week required by the conventional approach.

Source. J.A. Kulik, P.A. Cohen, and B.J. Ebeling, "Effectiveness of Programmed Instruction in Higher Education: A Meta-analysis of Findings," *Educational Evaluation and Policy Analysis*, 1980, *2*, 51-64.

Audio-Tutorial Instruction

S. N. Postlethwait (1977) developed the audio-tutorial method at Purdue University. This system typically uses a multi-media approach with study guides provided by an audio tape rather than by a written text. It is a multi-faceted approach by which the student seeks to attain course objectives following the lines of instruction given by the professor on tape. Students proceed at their own pace, stopping when necessary to read or view films, conduct experiments, or consult with the instructor. There is usually a central study laboratory where students can view films and conduct simple experiments themselves and work on other instructional materials as they wish. Self-pacing and the ability to repeat lessons are the key characteristics of this method. However, in earlier versions examinations were scheduled at common times and the idea of mastery was not enforced prior to the assignment of grades. Later versions instituted the mastery requirement and invested heavily in the use of media. Students are able to move quickly through the system if they are already familiar with portions of the subject matter. This combined use of multi-media, printed matter, and a study laboratory, with a faculty member readily available, facilitates the students' use of consultation with an authoritative source of information (Cole, 1982).

In 1975, Mintz reviewed six studies which compared audio-tutorial and conventional approaches. Of these studies three favored audio-tutorial and one the conventional approach. In another study comparing audio-tutorial with conventional courses, Fisher and MacWhinney (1976) covered a diverse group of 44 comparisons. Included in their review were studies conducted at the college, high school, and elementary school levels. Many of the studies used final examination scores as a criterion of achievement, while others used instructor-assigned scores, weekly quiz scores, and a combination of these evaluations. Eighteen of these studies reported significantly higher student achievement in sections which used the audio-visual techniques. However, 25 reported no real significant differences and only one study favored a lecture method by a significant margin. The authors concluded that the affective response toward audio-tutorial instruction was more favorable than toward the conventional.

Kulik and Jaska (1977) reviewed the findings of 24 comparative studies of audio-tutorial and conventional instruction at the college level. Nine of these favored audio-tutorial approaches and two conventional instruction. The remaining 13 studies reported no significant difference in achievement between the two comparison groups. This led Kulik and Jaska to conclude that audio-tutorial instruction sometimes leads to improved student learning but on the average the improvements it produces are small.

Therefore, it could be concluded that audio-tutorial is at least as effective as traditional teaching in stimulating student achievement and in some cases leads to significant increases in student learning. Reviewing these reviews led McKeachie (1978) to promote the audio-tutorial approach as well worth instituting as a method in courses such as the sciences where visual, auditory, or laboratory experience is needed in order to achieve course goals.

While audio-tutorial instruction seems to be popular in the sciences, the expense involved in setting up and maintaining the system mitigates against its widespread adoption. Some studies indicate that students learn faster under this method and that conventional teaching methods are not as preferable when compared to audio-tutorial. Audio-tutorial instruction does place the major responsibility for learning with the student. Self-paced and conducted without proctors, this method may encourage, or at least allow for, more student procrastination in meeting obligations of the course.

TABLE 2. Summary of Overall Effects Found in Meta-analysis of Studies on Audio-Tutorial Instruction (A-T)

Results/Effects	Major Findings
Student achievement	A majority of studies (29 of 42) indicated examination performance at a higher level in A-T classes than in conventional classes.
	The "typical" student in an A-T class performed at the 58th percentile on final examinations compared to the "typical" student in the control class achieving at the 50th percentile.
Aptitude-achievement correlation	". . . ability has as much influence on student achievement in A-T classes as it has in conventional classes."
Course completion	No major influence. The average withdrawal rate in A-T classes was 19% whereas it was 17% for conventional classes. The average effect rate was trivial.
Student attitudes/ratings	The difference between A-T and conventional course ratings found in only six studies was not large enough to be considered statistically reliable. Again, a trivial average effect size.

Source. J.A. Kulik, C.-L. C. Kulik, and P.A. Cohen, "Research on Audio-Tutorial Instruction: A Meta-analysis of Comparative Studies," *Research in Higher Education*, 1979, *11*, 321-341.

A meta-analytic study of the research on audio-tutorial instruction has been reported by Kulik, Kulik, and Cohen (1979*b*). This study attempted to synthesize the results of previous studies in the following major areas: (a) student achievement, (b) course completion, (c) student course satisfaction expressed in student ratings, and (d) the relationship between aptitude and achievement. The results in these four areas are summarized in Table 2.

When considering the impact on student achievement, it initially appears that audio-tutorial classes have a much higher impact on achievement examination performance than does the conventional class. However, considering that the typical student performs at the 58th percentile on the final examination compared to the typical student in a controlled class achieving at the 50th percentile, this takes on a different perspective. Kulik, Kulik, and Cohen (1979*b*) conclude that the overall effect of audio-tutorial instruction on student achievement is significant but very small, which raises the question, Are the expense and time expended worth the difference?

Another major finding of this analysis concerns the correlation between aptitude and achievement. Contrary to what would be predicted in mastery learning, the individualized format of audio-tutorial does not seem to reduce the influence of aptitude on student achievement. Another concern about the efficiency of an innovative technique is the impact on course completion. Here again, there does not seem to be a major influence. The average withdrawal rate in audio-tutorial classes was 19% as compared to 17% in conventional classes. Finally, a comparison was made of the impact on student attitudes and ratings. The difference here between audio-tutorial instruction and conventional instruction was not large enough to be considered statistically reliable. The average effect size was considered to be trivial. These general findings bring into question McKeachie's (1978) conclusion as to the worthwhileness of instituting the audio-tutorial approach as a better method in courses such as the sciences, especially if a large outlay of funds for a small number of students is involved.

Personalized Instruction

Keller's personalized system of instruciton (PSI) has to be considered one of the recent major innovations in college instruction. Formally introduced by Keller (1968) in a classic paper entitled "Goodbye, Teacher . . ." it has become the central mode of instruction in hundreds of courses during the past decade. Researchers began publishing studies of the technique in numbers sufficient to support a journal (*The Journal of Personalized Instruction*) primarily dedicated to PSI.

Five primary characteristics of PSI differentiate it from conventional teaching. The PSI course is (1) mastery oriented, (2) student proctored, and (3) a self-paced course which uses (4) printed study guides to direct the student's learning and (5) occasional lectures to stimulate and motivate the students. This system allows the student to learn material and then be tested at his own speed. It emphasizes the written word to produce effective communication between instructor and student. The student's mastery of one unit must be attained before going on to the next, but it permits students to pace themselves. The lectures and demonstrations are voluntary, and their primary intent is to increase the student's motivation rather than to convey information. The proctors used in the course are normally previous students who performed at a superior level (Sherman and Ruskin, 1978). According to Bijou and Ruiz (1981), this process shifts the emphasis of education to a goal of teaching for accomplishment from that of merely selecting for achievement.

McKeachie (1978) states that the evaluative research on the PSI established five essential points: (1) PSI is an attractive teaching method to most students; in published reports students rated the Keller plan more favorably than teaching by lecture. (2) Self-pacing and interacting with tutors seemed to be the features favored by most students of the PSI courses. However, the feature which is supported most by research is that of frequent testing with immediate feedback. (3) Several investigators report higher than average withdrawal rates from PSI sections. (4) Content learning as measured by final examinations is good in PSI courses. The final examination performance in the PSI section equals or sometimes exceeds performance in lecture sections. In addition, superior performance is found in courses following the PSI course. (5) Courses initiating the use of PSI often drop it for noneducational reasons.

The major advantages of PSI appear to be that it allows students to progress at their own pace, requires them to accept responsibility for their own learning, focuses on mastery learning rather than formal instruction, and provides systematic feedback to students. Thus PSI instructors are free to devote their attention to students who need it most. Disadvantages include the fact that less motivated students will not find the system to their advantage. Some students find that the PSI educational experience is rather lonely and may be quite incompatible with scheduling and crediting procedures on some campuses (Berquist and Phillips, 1977; Davies, 1981). However, one of the greatest problems may be in the faculty adjustment to becoming course designers and course managers rather than performers as they have been traditionally in a lecture situation. This means that faculty must forgo the immediate gratification that is often a part of lecturing for the delayed gratification of improved student performance at the end of the course (Milton and Associates, 1978).

Another drawback to the PSI mode of instruction is the staffing and funding required of this system. It is usually expensive. Study centers are often desirable, and they add to the expense of running the system. Instructors may require special training and often do not have the opportunity to express their own creativity in the spontaneous setting of the traditional classroom.

One of the criticisms of PSI research stresses that the effectiveness of PSI has been no more than that which one would observe with a long-running Hawthorne effect. Kulik, Kulik, and Cohen (1979a) undertook a meta-analysis of selected research studies to bring the earlier findings into sharper focus. The meta-analysis consisted of three main parts. The first was a description of the outcomes of personalized instruction. The second part dealt with the question, Is PSI especially effective for certain types of students or on certain measures of instructional effectiveness? The third part explored the relation between PSI effects and design features of the study of PSI. A primary concern of this analysis was the effects of PSI which can be identified as unique and influential beyond the effects of conventional techniques and instruction. These findings have been summarized in one table (Table 3). The study results which are emphasized in this table are student achievement, final grades, aptitude-achievement correlation, course completion rate, student ratings, and instructional or study time. The results support the findings of earlier studies indicating an impact upon student achievement significantly greater than was observed in conventional courses. However, the meta-analysis serves to clarify the size of this effect. In other words, the meta-analysis examines whether or not PSI had a large effect or whether it had a significant but small effect.

Pertaining to student achievement, the PSI sections of courses produced superior final examination scores in 57 of the 61 studies which were included in the meta-analytic study. Forty-eight reported statistically significant results fa-

TABLE 3. Summary of Overall Effects Found in Meta-analysis of Studies on the Personalized System of Instruction (PSI)

Results/Effects	Major Findings
Student achievement	The PSI sections of courses produced superior final examination performance in 57 of 61 studies. Forty-eight reported statistically significant differences favoring PSI. No studies reported statistically significant differences favoring conventional instruction.
	The "typical" student in PSI class performed at the 70th percentile on final examinations compared to the "typical" student in the conventional class performing at the 50th percentile.
Final grades	Instructor-assigned grades in the PSI sections were higher than in conventional classes and this was found to be statistically reliable. The effect size was considered moderate.
Aptitude-achievement correlation	"The superiority of PSI to conventional instruction can be seen about as clearly with high-aptitude students as with low-aptitude students."
Course completion	Withdrawal rate was higher for the PSI section in 17 studies compared to being higher in 10 studies for the conventional section. However, the average effect size was considered "trivial by any standard."
Student attitudes/ratings	For each variable, quality, learning, enjoyment, and work load, PSI ratings by students were significantly higher than ratings in the conventional classes.
Instructional/study time	Time requirements for students in PSI are approximately equal to that of requirements for conventional students.

Source. J.A. Kulik, C.-L. C. Kulik, and P.A. Cohen, "A Meta-analysis of Outcome Studies of Keller's Personalized System of Instruction," *American Psychologist*, 1979, *34*, 307-318.

voring PSI while none reported statistically significant results in favor of conventional instruction. The final examination average in the typical PSI class was 73.6, whereas in the typical conventional class it was 65.9. When this finding was subjected to measures of effect size it was considered to be moderate in size, i.e., "large enough to be visible to the naked eye." This difference is similar to the difference that one would notice in the average height between 14- and 18-year-old girls. Thus, PSI raised the performance of a typical student with SAT scores of 500 to the level previously associated with above-average students having an SAT score of 600.

An even larger PSI effect was found when follow-up examinations were administered several months after the end of the course. Performance by students who had been in the controlled classes was about 14 percentage points lower than those who had been in PSI classes. As an additional indicator of student performance, the difference between essay and objective examination scores revealed that students in PSI had a slightly higher performance on essays. This latter finding could not, however, be considered statistically reliable due to the small sample of studies available which had included these data. The final grade distribution showed that the instructors of controlled classes assigned grades which were significantly lower than the grades assigned by the PSI instructors. On the average, PSI instructors assigned final grades that were .8 letter grade higher than grades in conventional classes. This magnitude of difference is consistent with the magnitude of difference found in the final examination scores in PSI and control classes.

The credibility of these results is strengthened upon finding that the influence of aptitude-achievement correlation is nullified. That is, the effect of PSI is about the same for students of low aptitude as it is for high-aptitude students. Another factor to be considered is course completion. PSI courses in a number of studies had been observed to have a high withdrawal rate. The meta-analysis study revealed that 17 studies indicated higher withdrawal rates for PSI courses, while the conventional classes had a high withdrawal rate in 10 studies. However, the average effect size calculated for this difference was considered to be trivial by any standard. This apparently does not confirm popular impressions that PSI completion rates are overall much lower than conventional classes. If considered in terms of the rate of successful course completion, it may be that there is a slightly higher rate in PSI classes because fewer students complete PSI classes with Ds and Fs.

Student attitudes and ratings toward the courses were judged on the basis of quality, learning, enjoyment, and work load variables. Students in the PSI classes turned in ratings in each of these four areas that were significantly higher than those of the students in conventional classes. A popular impression about personalized instruction which was not confirmed by the results of this meta-analysis concerns the amount of study time that the student has to spend in the PSI course. The time spent in PSI and conventional sections varies no more than an hour or two for a complete term. Of particular interest when looking further at the implications of the findings is the influence of study features. It was found that if the conventional class included a PSI feature or if the same teacher taught both PSI and conventional classes, the difference between PSI and the comparison course was reduced. There was also a relationship to the discipline in which the courses were offered. However, examining these relationships shows that when the control differences were smallest the PSI superiority was still statistically demonstrable, especially in the area of effects on student achievement.

Considering the total results of the meta-analysis, Kulik, Kulik, and Cohen (1979*a*) concluded that the superiority of personalized instruction is evident under a variety of conditions and with good and poor research design. The results of this analysis seemed to be in conflict with McKeachie's conclusions which followed a review of evaluative research, especially since the student ratings were found to be favorable in a number of areas, not just regarding the interaction with tutors. Since the average withdrawal rate was shown to be fairly trivial in terms of a generalizable effect, the objection to PSI as causing a large number of students to leave the course should be removed.

Computer-Based Instruction

Bork (1978) observed that, given the large number of educational institutions, few use computers as learning aids. There are many who would agree that this represents the situation regarding computer usage in educational institutions. However, there are many others who would take exception and point out that since 1978 the increase in the use of computers as learning aids has been dramatic. Of course, Bork followed his observation with the comment that "the computer will become a dominant device in teaching in higher education during the next 25 years." One wonders if Bork would be willing to revise his time estimate downward significantly in view of the reception which microcomputers have found in education during the past few years. Yet, for many, the possibility of computers fulfilling projected expectations is limited.

The teaching dialogues and conversations developed by Bork (1975) and Pask (1976) represent significant strides in making the computer an appropriate tool for teaching content, concept, and problem-solving skills. A variety of experiments have been conducted on computer-assisted college-level instruction showing a variety of benefits as a results of the students' interaction with the computer. For example, Schurdak (1965) and King (1977) have shown savings in time and improved performance compared to conventional instruction or even instruction with a programmed text. Additionally, the students enjoyed the studies with the computer, primarily because programs can maintain the motivational value of unexpected occurrences. Likewise, they can be adapted to students of different types.

Two reviews on research of computer-based instruction (CBI), Jamison, Suppes, and Wells (1974) and Edwards et al. (1975), came to the conclusion that it is about as effective as traditional instruction and usually saves time of both students and teachers. Two of the largest projects for CBI, the PLATO system (programmed logic for automated teaching operations) and the TICCIT system (time-shared interactive computer controlled information television), have been evaluated, but the results are contradictory. One study of both systems conducted by the Educational Testing Service revealed that the students and faculty reacted favorably to the PLATO system but that its use had no significant impact on student achievement. The evaluation of TICCIT revealed an improvement in student achievement, but students were more likely to drop out of the courses using TICCIT than those courses which were conventionally taught (Kulik, Kulik, and Cohen, 1980; Murphy and Appell, 1977). Notwithstanding the widespread use of these two systems, the implementation of computer-based instruction goes beyond the huge projects represented by PLATO and TICCIT.

A variety of studies have been conducted in institutions which did not have PLATO and TICCIT capabilities. Jamison, Suppes, and Wells (1974) reviewed almost a dozen small-scale studies of CBI in college classrooms. The results of the studies were difficult to summarize but Jamison and his colleagues came to a conservative conclusion that, at the college level, computer-assisted instruction is about as effective as traditional instruction when used as a replacement. They further pointed out that at the college level most alternative methods of instruction were equally effective. Thus a means by which computer-assisted instruction could be compared against conventional methods across a wide variety of research studies seems appropriate.

Kulik, Kulik, and Cohen (1980) applied the technique of meta-analysis to the results of studies of CBI. Their bibliographic search yielded over 500 titles, from which 180 were judged to be potentially useful documents. After reading these 180 documents, they determined that 59 of the reports contained data that were useful to the analysis. Five areas of results have been summarized in Table 4 at the risk of running afoul of cautions not to overgeneralize the findings of meta-analytic studies. When taken as a whole, the findings show that the computer has made a small but significant contribution to the effectiveness of college teaching.

In a large majority of the studies CBI examination performance was superior to examination performance of a conventional class. This was interpreted to show that the typical student in a CBI class performed at the 60th percentile, whereas one in a conventional class would perform at the 50th percentile. Thus the computer-based instruction raised examination scores about 3 percentage points, or about one-quarter of a standard deviation. Effects of this size are considered very small by Cohen (1977). However, this does not account for the wide variation of effect sizes from one study to another. According to Kulik, Kulik, and Cohen (1980), one-quarter of the studies reported a medium or large effect in favor of computer-based instruction. Nearly three-quarters of the studies found small or trivial effects. Very few studies (less than 5%) reported moderate or large effects favoring conventional classes.

What was the impact of aptitude-achievement correlation? The meta-analytic study found that CBI had only a small effect on the correlation between aptitude and achievement in college courses. In other words, the effectiveness for CBI on the high-aptitude student was about the same as it was on the low-aptitude student. Another outcome of the study concerns the rate of course completion. While only 13 of the 59 studies examined the effect of CBI on withdrawal rate, 7 indicated that the withdrawal rate was higher in the conventional classes. The average CBI withdrawal rate was 26.9%, whereas the

TABLE 4. Summary of Overall Effects Found in Meta-analysis of Studies on Computer-Based Instruction (CBI)

Results/Effects	Major Findings
Student achievement	In a clear majority of studies, CBI examination performance was superior to examination performance of a conventional class.
	The "typical" student in a CBI class performed at the 60th percentile, whereas the "typical" student in a conventional class performed at the 50th percentile.
Aptitude-achievement correlation	At best, CBI had only a small effect on the correlation between aptitude and achievement in college courses.
Course completion	No major influence. Average CBI withdrawal rate was 26.9%; average rate in the conventional class was 27.6%.
Student attitudes	Toward the instruction: CBI ratings were higher than conventional ratings but the overall difference was small.
	Toward the subject matter: 5 out of 7 studies reported CBI classes had more favorable attitudes; in general the CBI effects on subject matter attitudes were small.
Instructional time	" . . . the computer produced a substantial saving in instructional time." 2.25 hours for CBI versus 3.5 hours per week required by the conventional approach.

Source. J.A. Kulik, C.-L. C. Kulik, and P.A. Cohen, "Effectiveness of Computer-Based College Teaching: A Meta-analysis of Findings," *Review of Educational Research*, 1980, *50*, 525-544.

rate of withdrawal in the conventional class was 27.6%, pointing to the obvious conclusion that CBI did not influence withdrawal rate.

With regard to student attitudes toward the instruction, only 11 of the 59 studies contained data that could be used in this meta-analysis. CBI ratings were higher than conventional classes in 8 of the studies, and the remaining 3 studies were higher for conventional classes. Overall, while CBI ratings were higher than conventional ratings, the difference was very small in attitudes toward the instruction. With ratings of attitudes toward the subject matter, however, the CBI classes had more favorable effects in 5 out of 7 studies, but this again was considered to be a small and trivial effect. What the authors considered to be the most dramatic finding related to instructional time. The computer produced substantial savings in instructional time, indicating that it did its job quickly — on the average in about two-thirds the time required by conventional teaching methods.

While these findings appear to favor computer-based instruction methods, the overall effectiveness of CBI at the college level is still considered to be disappointingly small. By comparison, Keller's personalized system of instruction produces much more dramatic results in the college classroom. The findings regarding CBI are similar to those reported in the meta-analytic studies of programmed instruction and of Postlethwait's (1977) auto-tutorial approach to higher education instruction.

An additional interesting point relates to the design features of the studies. When the meta-analysis controls for instructor effects, it is found to be the only significant influence on the prediction of study outcomes. The implication of this seems to be that in studies where a single instructor teaches both experimental and controlled classes there are much smaller differences between the innovative course and the conventional course. This is similar to a relationship between the research design feature and experimental outcomes in the meta-analysis outcomes of Keller's personalized system of instruction. Thus, involving teachers in innovative approaches to instruction may well have a general effect on their quality of teaching. Particularly if these innovations are variations of behavioral instruction, the point is valid because instructors are required to outline objectives, construct lessons, and prepare evaluation materials. All of these things help teachers do a good job in their conventional teaching assignments. The next section is concerned with what developments have been made and what models are available for facilitating the teacher's preparation of instruction.

INSTRUCTIONAL PLANNING AND ORGANIZATION

If the primary purpose of instruction is the facilitation of learning, a theory of instruction should be based on what has been found effective or influential in the process of learning. By defining the conditions and other events of the environment in which the learning of college students occurs, steps can be taken to develop a theory of instruction. How learning occurs thus is the basic question to be addressed in the development of a conceptual framework that will help structure the environment in which learning occurs. There is considerable diversity among learning theories (see chapter by Fincher), but many have fallen by the wayside as support from research has waned. Some have seen moments of glory based upon popularity of philosophical and value trends embraced by segments of professional and social groups. The resulting evolutionary effect has produced a mixture of principles of learning which have diverged basically into two orientations, cognitive and behavioral.

The development of instructional theory is a way to relate instructional events to learning processes and learning outcomes, drawing upon systematic research into both learning and teaching. In contrast to descriptive theories of learning, instructional theories should be prescriptive in the sense that they attempt to identify conditions of instruction which will optimize learning, retention, and transfer (Gagne and Dick, 1983). In a classic reference, Jerome

Bruner (1966) identified four major features of a theory of instruction. A theory of instruction:

1. should specify experiences which effectively instill in an individual a predisposition to learn;
2. must specify ways in which a body of knowledge can be structured so that it can be readily grasped by the learner;
3. should specify the most effective sequence in which to present the materials to be learned; and
4. should specify the nature and pacing of rewards and punishments in the process of learning and teaching.

Many of these features are represented among efforts to define models of instructional design. Unlike instructional theory, however, models of instructional design are not required to specify causal relationships between instruction and learning.

Practitioners, psychologists, and educators have not waited for the resolution of conflicts to find means of employing the implications of learning theory. Efforts to establish procedures to construct effective instruction have been mandated more by the training needs of business and industry than by educators. Gagne (1977) states that knowledge of the learning process combined with analysis of the task to be learned finds direct application in the design of instruction. During the past decade the field of education has seen a variety of proposed strategies for developing instruction. The purpose of models for instructional design is to identify procedures by means of which instruction may be planned. It is not necessary for instructional strategies to be based on a rational account of causal relationships between the events of instruction and learning processes. However, these relationships will be implicit if they are not explicitly stated. Regardless, the point is that if the design of instruction results in effective learning, then there are elements within the strategies which could provide insight useful to efforts aimed at constructing a model of instruction based on practical if not empirical evidence. Thus the intent of this section of the chapter is to address the question, What components of instructional models and systems might be useful to designing effective instruction for higher education?

Basic Principles of Instructional Design
Gagne and Briggs (1979) describe a set of principles of instructional design primarily based on information-processing models of learning. The basic rationale for instructional design includes seven steps for the derivation of procedures to create instruction. The first of these steps is to consider the types of human capability which will be emphasized in the learning desired. This consists of describing a variety of human performances in the following categories: (a)

intellectual skills, (b) cognitive strategies, (c) verbal information skills, (d) attitudes, and (e) motor skills. Once the learned capability has been identified, the next step is to define the performance objectives. These are the planned outcomes of the events of learning. The identification of the performance objectives makes it possible to classify learner capabilities into useful categories. The next step is to describe the conditions which are necessary to bring about this learning with the greatest efficiency. Once the conditions for learning have been specified, it is possible to plan the sequence of instruction. Arranging the sequences of instruction is similar to creating a map for the student to follow in progressing from one level of capability to another.

After the course has been designed in terms of the sequence of performance objectives, the next step is to proceed in the detailed planning of the individual lesson. The focus of such planning is on the arranging of external conditions which will be most effective in bringing about the desired learning. These events together with sequencing constitute the components of instruction. What is then required for a complete instructional design is a means of assessment. The procedure for constructing assessment naturally follows from the performance objectives defined and stated in the beginning of the instructional design. Assessment is to be constructed as a direct measure of what students have learned as a result of instruction. Once lessons have been designed and compiled along with the procedures for assessing the learning outcomes, then there is the possibility of planning an entire system of instruction. Instructional systems have as their purpose the achievement of comprehensive goals. Finally, after the instructional system has been completed it is necessary to conduct an evaluation of the process. This final step of the instructional design is aimed at providing information which is needed for revision and refinement of the instructional events. Therefore, this is a formative evaluation process and not a summative evaluation procedure as would be employed if the effectiveness of this system were being compared to another.

Principles of instructional design thus can be viewed as providing the background for developing the appropriate instruction to address the learning desired. In 1977, Gagne presented a set of steps deemed necessary for learning to occur. The traits of an effective instructional event are as follows:

1. Gaining attention
2. Informing the learner of the objective
3. Stimulating the recall of prerequisite learning
4. Presenting the stimulus material
5. Providing learning guidance
6. Eliciting the performance
7. Providing feedback about performance correctness
8. Assessing the performance
9. Enhancing retention and transfer

Briggs (1977) indicated that the more sophisticated the learner, the more these events may be intrinsically a part of his or her study repertoire. Thus it is possible for these components of an instructional event to be present without the instructor actually creating activities explicitly for each. This does not mean that the instructor can ignore them. To the contrary, the instructor should make every effort to assure that those traits to be provided by the learner are identified and explicitly stated as expected of the learner. This would be especially true for students who are beginning their college experience. For instance, compare the expectations an instructor has of the graduate student versus those of the freshman student. With the graduate student it may only be necessary to agree upon the objectives to be learned. The student may then be expected to pursue his or her own line of instruction until some point of evaluation where feedback on performance is sufficient for the enhancement of retention and transfer. Rarely would the freshman student be allowed to pursue a self-directed line of instruction without some form of guidance. The important point in this consideration is the validity of each component of instructional design as distinct and necessary for effective instruction to occur — whether they are explicitly provided by the instructor or implicitly provided by the student. These could be considered as the building blocks of a model of instruction for higher education settings because of the global nature of applicability to a variety of instructional situations. The nature of the subject matter, desired learning outcomes, appropriate instructional events, and the sophistication of the learner are crucial to the formulation of these components into a model of instruction relevant to higher education.

One model of instruction, based on a model that was developed in the early 1960s (Carroll, 1963), is the mastery learning model described by Bloom in 1971 and again in 1981. The major variables included in the model are: (a) aptitude, which is the time required to learn; (b) the quality of instruction, or the ability to understand instruction; (c) perseverance, which is the time the learner is willing to spend in learning; and (d) opportunity, which is the time allowed for learning. Bloom (1976) has given primary emphasis to "alterable variables" for schooling. These alterable variables are (a) cognitive entry behaviors of students, (b) affective entry characteristics, and (c) a number of specific factors making up the quality of instruction. Among the specific factors of this latter component are the alterable variables of student participation and corrective feedback which follows the student participation.

The emphasis on the study of alterable variables is a unique, important feature of Bloom's model. It is opposed to the relatively stable variables often proposed in other models of instruction such as aptitudes and abilities. It is a component that is well developed and is documented with a good body of evidence (Bloom, 1976). Additional evidence has been assembled by a number of Bloom's students (MESA Seminar, 1980). Particular traits which have received recent research attention include the effects of cognitive prerequisites, distinctive cues, learner practice, and corrective feedback on learner achievement.

Another feature of Bloom's model is its basic hypothesis. He proposes that differences in achievement can be reduced over time *if* there are successive learning units. These reductions in the variation of achievement over time can occur as those students who were originally low achievers are given high-quality instruction and then permitted to take more time to reach mastery. When this procedure is carried out over a successive sequence of instruction, the lower-achieving students are more likely to exhibit performance behavior patterns similar to the higher-achieving students. In other words, it is possible that as achievement improves with quality instruction, there will be secondary effects from this improvement resulting in an overall improvement of performance. Programs of developmental studies in institutions of higher education provide an excellent opportunity for instructional psychologists or theorists to test this variation-reduction hypothesis.

The major weakness of Bloom's model is its lack of effort to explain the effect of instructional variables on learning transfer and retention. However, its proposition of alterable variables offers opportunities of investigation which should be considerably valuable through the promise it holds for designing high-quality instruction. These variables (derived from evidence concerning "what makes a difference" in the determination of instructional outcomes) constitute what may become the empirical base for Bloom's theory.

Collins (1977) has proposed a model, labeled Socratic Tutoring, which he considers to be capable of teaching new knowledge and also the skills necessary for applying that knowledge to new situations. Instruction employing this strategy can be best characterized as a blend of diagnosis and correction strategy. The instructor probes the student's understanding and uses his mistakes as clues to errors in the student's understanding. Applications of these ideas have been described by Stevens and Collins (1981).

Twenty-four rules are described by which various questions can be constructed to constitute a tutoring system. Fifteen of these rules are labeled formulation rules and the remainder are application rules. Their use in computerized tutoring dialogues has been analyzed to indicate that students learn new information, make inferences, and learn to reason about the problems presented in the tutoring situation. These rules would be particularly appropriate for the construction of computer-assisted instruction (CAI) routines. The Socratic Tutoring method would construct CAI capable of allowing students to carry out problem-solving exercises in areas of knowledge that are not familiar to them. Though this model appears to be very promising in the area of tutoring strategies for computer-assisted instruction, there are questions about the influence of student characteristics on learning outcomes and the transferability of the outcomes as a result of instruction via the Socratic Tutoring model.

The model of instructional elaboration promotes the idea of micro-strategies for organizing instruction. These are strategies that pertain to the sequencing and interrelating of topics within a course. The general conception of instruction is compared to viewing a scene with the use of a zoom lens beginning with the wide-angle lens and then gradually coming down to a more specific view in order to integrate the specific with the whole. Periodic review and testing are important aspects of this model and are considered to have the effect of enhancing learning retention and transfer. In addition to dealing with rote facts, this elaboration model also deals with concepts, principles, and procedures as the primary kinds of instructional content. The wide-angle view has the purpose of epitomizing the organizing content or teaching a small number of concepts by applying those concepts.

In the design of instructional sequences Reigeluth (1979) presents an "epitome" which is followed by the teaching of an operation, which in turn is followed by an expanded epitome. Reigeluth and Rodgers (1980) recommend the following steps be involved in designing an instructional sequence:

1. Select all the operations to be taught,
2. Decide which operation to teach first,
3. Sequence all the remaining operations,
4. Identify the supporting content,
5. Allocate all content to lessons and sequence time,
6. Sequence the instruction within each lesson,
7. Design instruction on each lesson and expanded epitome.

This model has a lot in common with other prescriptive teaching or instructional design techniques. It utilizes an information-processing task analysis and a learning hierarchy, both of which can be found in other models such as Gagne (1977). It also claims to use to advantage the ideas of subsumption, which comes from Ausubel, Novak, and Hanesion (1978). It accepts the procedures of micro-strategies for component lessons such as those involved in the theory of Merrill (1976). The most outstanding contribution of this particular theory appears to be the frequent "zooming" from the most general view of the content to be learned to selected specific details. This makes provision for the recall of prerequisites and returning to a general view once again, and for additional review and practice. Repeating this sequence makes it possible for the learner to acquire an increasingly elaborate view of the subject.

Merrill's prescriptive model of instruction emphasizes the importance of instructional quality to the outcomes of instruction. The central determinants of the quality of instruction are: (a) the consistency and adequacy with which the purpose of instruction is represented in objectives, (b) the consistency and adequacy with which these objectives are represented in tests, and (c) the consistency and adequacy with which the outcomes are represented in instructional presentation. The outcomes focused upon by this model are concepts, principles, and procedures. For each of these outcomes there are three levels of representing what has been acquired and what is to be tested: (1) remembering an instance, (2) remembering a generality, and (3) using a generality.

Various instructional strategies can be considered to be more or less adequate depending upon which is applied to obtain the desired outcome. For instance, the strategies that are considered relevant to concepts learning are as follows:

1. Providing immediate informative feedback
2. Isolating the presentation form by separating it from other material and clearly labeling it
3. Presenting help or learning aids such as attention-focusing points and algorithms
4. Providing an adequate sampling of instances
5. Indicating divergence of instances
6. Using a range of difficulty levels
7. Arranging instances so as to favor matching of common properties

Merrill and colleagues (1977, 1979) have listed a variety of strategies as applicable to the presentation of each category encompassed by this theory, its principles and procedures. A prominent feature of this model is actually an instructional design procedure. This is the insistence upon a precise consistency in the sequence of instructional derivation from goals to objectives to tests to instructional presentations. However, this model has received little empirical verification of the suggested strategies for the three categories of learning outcomes. The strategies do appear to provide a basis for a checklist of points to reference while designing instruction, but they await further research results before they can be soundly relied upon.

In brief, there are many ways in which research could facilitate useful instructional models. Just as theories of learning were popular in the 1950s, so theories, models, or systems of instruction appeared to have been in the 1970s. There are several criticisms, however, that can be raised of instructional models as they currently exist. One of the criticisms is the failure of these models of instruction to be stated in terms that are understandable to the instructor. The average college instructor will not be able to study most models of instruction and draw from them a meaningful conceptual framework to use in designing or planning an approach to instruction in the classroom. While it is obvious that instructional psychologists are more likely to be concerned with the immediate implications of research findings regarding underlying theoretical concepts, the impact "in the field" is worth their consideration and ultimately that application is the most appropriate end point for their research (Gagne and Dick, 1953).

Another drawback is the lack of studies or research in the area of higher education instruction based on various instructional models. Very few solid studies conducted in higher education instructional settings are based on the tenets of an instructional model. A notable exception to this criticism is the model of instruction by Gagne and Briggs (1979). A few other models may apply to specific instances within higher education instruction, such as Collins' Socratic Tutoring Theory, which has found its way into CAI.

CONCLUSIONS AND IMPLICATIONS

Studies of college teaching go back at least as far as 1923 (Kulik and Jaska, 1977). Since that time it has been obvious that the lecture method dominates college teaching, and researchers use it as a yardstick for comparing other methods. It is little wonder Trent and Cohen (1973) conclude that research on what happens in the college classroom was especially disappointing during the 1960s. Reviewers of research on college teaching which discussed alternatives to the lecture method have agreed that the relative effectiveness of the lecture when student achievement is used as an independent variable is somewhat inconclusive. Students seem to be more satisfied with discussion methods, but even this finding is not absolute (Costin, 1972; Dubin and Taveggia, 1968; McKeachie, 1970). McKeachie (1970) was one of the first reviewers to impose criteria other than general student achievement. He used the criteria of better retention, ability to apply, problem solving, attitude change, and motivation for further learning. Based on these outcomes, small classes seemed to be somewhat more effective than large ones, discussions were somewhat preferred over lectures, and student-centered instruction was preferable to teacher-centered instruction.

The current review of instructional methods reveals that the conventional/ traditional modes can no longer be considered uniform. There are variations which can be employed according to the instructor's assessment of the match between instructional objectives and type of instructional processes which will most effectively convey the topic or subject matter. The appropriateness of employing different conventional methods has also been shown to be related to the size of classes and the level of sophistication represented in the students and possibly the level of experience and expertise represented in the instructor (i.e., group dynamic leadership capability to manage discussions). The newer "innovative" methods seem to be at least as effective as the traditional modes (primarily lecture and discussion) on general measures of student achievement. Furthermore, these modes of instruction also have no deleterious impact on measures of student attitudes, and the aptitude-treatment interaction appears to be insignificant if measurable at all. Of the major innovative modes which have emerged during the past two decades one has obviously been more extensively utilized. The personalized system of instruction has enjoyed a greater degree of application, study, and apparent success in effectively and significantly enhancing student achievement. Computer-based instruction, while effectively enhancing student achievement, has the most beneficial impact upon reducing study/instructional time required to master the course content. The recent influx of the more portable and affordable microcomputers should influence the development of instructional strategies which will significantly enhance student achievement.

Individualized instruction techniques of recent years influence how, when, and how much students study on their own time. Barnes and Ellner (1983) point out that most investigations do not account for the fact that individual student study time may have an influence on achievement in college greater than classroom instruction. The effectiveness of PSI may well reside in three basic conditions: the frequent quizzing of student achievement, the immediate feedback from quizzes, and the requirement to restudy and repeat quizzes until a certain level of mastery is attained. These three conditions seem to increase student achievement in college courses. Cross (1976) supports the efficiency of the Keller plan as a means of achieving the goal for producing education for each as we have achieved making education available for all. The reason behavioral instruction will facilitate attaining this goal resides in the emphasis placed on the student's individual study time, not the classroom.

Computer-based instruction has not turned out to be the revolutionary answer that most expected when computers first made their entrance into higher education. Their impact gradually increased during the 1960s and 1970s, and the early 1980s saw another grand wave of computers. Microcomputers are proliferating and once again there is a recurrence of a phenomenon of the 1960s — hardware has outstripped the educational application of computers. While it can be demonstrated that computer instructional systems save substantial amounts of student time and that students learn as much from computer instruction as from traditional teaching methods, it remains a fact that development or even purchase of effective computer-based instruction is relatively expensive (Hamblen and Landis, 1980).

The majority of research studies comparing computer-assisted instruction with conventional techniques involved computer-based instruction on large mainframes which necessitated terminals fixed in one location. In the future it is expected that the research on CBI will increasingly reflect the involvement of microcomputers. According to a 1979 study, some institutions have already begun to employ microcomputers for offering instruction in amounts excessive to that provided by the centralized computers (Zinn, 1980). Others estimate microcomputers will be used by millions in the very near future to facilitate educational programs (Lewis and Tagg, 1980). While to some instructors the microcomputer and other computer-based instruction may pose a threat, there are others to whom it opens new potential for extending and improving instruction (Cole, 1982).

Articles in current periodicals reflect the debate that is arising about the impact of the computer on higher education. Some question whether this is a change for the better (McPherson, 1984). Others question whether or not it will lead to a new definition of education altogether (Tenner, 1984). Regardless of the ultimate response to these questions, the impact of computers on instruction in higher education will be felt noticeably more in the future than it has in the past simply because society in general will become more computer-literate. O'Neill (1981) believes the increasing technological sophistication of our society will require students to learn more complicated subject material and skills and perform those skills at higher standards of performance.

Barnes and Ellner (1983) point out several problems which persist in the research on college teaching. One problem is that what the teacher is becomes confused with what the teacher does. Studies that have emphasized effective teacher characteristics have resulted more in assemblages of virtues rather than descriptive data on what teachers actually do. Another problem that has plagued college teaching research is the tendency to look at global clusters of attributes. Gage (1961) pointed out that what few relationships between teaching and learning appear result from molecular and not molar approaches to the research. A third problem that has persisted in instructional research is the practice of viewing teaching as an act itself and not in relation to a particular topic or group of students. The situation is much more likely to be that there are skills which vary in effectiveness relative to course level and subject area. However, the task of analyzing teaching in relation to different learning situations remains untouched by investigations of college instruction.

Many benefits can be realized by systematic research of instruction in higher education. Not to be overlooked is the enhanced intellectual atmosphere resulting from the spirit of inquiry. Classrooms where attention is given to testing hypotheses about teacher and student behavior and interaction will enjoy the stimulation of shared exploration, which will in turn enhance the subject matter. The primary long-term influence will be the improvement of instruction at the institution. Various techniques have been profusely studied, but little has been done cooperatively and the results have sometimes been contradictory. Nevertheless, an increased understanding of instruction has occurred at least among those interested and motivated to inquire and strive to improve. Ellner (1983) has listed questions among which several are particularly crucial for significant instruction research to address:

What are the long-term effects of instructional behavior upon students?

How do faculty members' goals affect teaching behavior?

What behaviors do professors exhibit which tend to inhibit or foster student reponse?

Assuming students enter at different developmental levels, how does the professor bring them to higher levels of thinking?

How can a professor effectively increase higher-order verbal behavior?

Are different questioning patterns effective for different students?

Do effective questioning strategies differ across disciplines?

Are there more sensitive ways to measure the differences in instruction between colleges and universities of different types?

In order for these and a number of similar qustions to be addressed by future research on instruction in higher education, another dimension must become more evident. While much is known, most of what is known is of a descriptive nature. The next generation of instructional research is doomed to mediocrity unless significant strides are made to establish procedures for conducting experimentally designed studies of instruction. A better definition of the cause-and-effect relation between events of instruction and learning outcomes of students should be the purpose of studies conducted on instructional methods and models. To facilitate defining variables and controlling their influence, more sensitive measures of student and instructor interaction will be needed. The determination of what results from instruction will be dependent on more data concerning variables that are difficult to measure. Outcome measures should include tests of critical thinking ability, attitudes toward learning, and motivation to continue to learn, in addition to conventional standardized test results.

Levinson-Rose and Menges (1981) concluded their review of research on improving college teaching with four primary implications for the researcher:

1. Individual-difference variables deserve greater attention. Future research should note the specific traits of individuality both of students and teachers; otherwise significant interactions influencing the outcome of instruction will escape identification.

2. Dependent variables require comparable definition and operationalization across studies. Very few studies use the same instrumentation. Future research should be designed to facilitate comparability. This does not mean a forced uniformity; instead, what is sought is for studies to build upon one another.

3. Cross-campus collaboration should be encouraged. The majority of studies in the past have been isolated efforts of individual investigation on separate campuses. Establishing a cooperative intercampus research network would be a powerful means to coordinate efforts and yield more influential research.

4. Most data reflect only superficial levels of experience. Rarely does a study of instruction deal with cognitive, emotional, and developmental experiences. This is particularly evident when seeking information on the instructor. What are the cognitive processes of the instructor as she or he teaches? Are certain feelings aroused by various classroom activities? What is the influence of developmental tasks at particular stages of adult life on teaching problems and challenges?

While conventional research methods can be improved to address some aspects of the above questions and problems, the current quantitative methods which dominate research will result primarily in descriptive studies. Rigorous experimentation is necessary, but current hope for devising and implementing such studies is small in light of the difficulty of withholding a promising technique from the control group or of employing a potentially limited mode of instruction. Qualitative approaches appear to hold more promise. Involving faculty members as collaborators instead of the objects/subjects may result in disciplined case studies and sensitive clinical interviews. It may be time for quantitative and qualitative approaches to take a step closer to becoming intertwined and applied to the study of instruction.

A statement made a decade ago is appropriate today: "Progress has been slow not just because of our lack as theorists and researchers, but because education really *is* complicated" (McKeachie and Kulik, 1975, p. 199). Today, there are more insights to be gained from a study of the research on instruction in higher education. There also are more questions to answer and directions to explore with greater expectations of increasing the quality and effectiveness of higher education.

REFERENCES

Ausubel, D. P., Novak, J. D., and Hanesion, H. *Educational Psychology: A Cognitive View.* New York: Holt, Rinehart & Winston, 1978.

Barnes, C .P., and Ellner, C. L. The present perspective. In C. L. Ellner and C. P. Barnes (eds.), *Studies of College Teaching.* Lexington, Mass.: Heath, 1983.

Barnes-McConnell, P. W. Leading discussions. In O. Milton & Associates (eds.), *On College Teaching.* San Francisco: Jossey-Bass, 1978.

Beard, R. M. *Teaching and Learning in Higher Education.* Harmondsworth, England: Penguin Books, 1972.

Berquist, W. H., and Phillips, S. R. A. *A Handbook for Faculty Development.* Vol. 2 Washington, D.C.: Council for the Advancement of Small Colleges, 1977.

Bijou, Sidney W., and Ruiz, Roberto (eds.). *Behavior Modification: Contributions to Education.* Hillsdale, N.J.: Lawrence Erlbaum, 1981.

Bloom, B. S. Learning for mastery. In B. S. Bloom, J. J. Hastings, and G. F. Madaus (eds.), *Handbook on Formative and Summative Evaluation of Student Learning.* New York: McGraw-Hill, 1971.

Bloom, B. S. *Human Characteristics and School Learning.* New York: McGraw-Hill, 1976.

Bloom, B. S. *All Our Children Learning: A Primer for Parents, Teachers and Other Educators.* New York: McGraw-Hill, 1981.

Bork, A. The physics computer development project. Irvine: Department of Physics, University of California, 1975.

Bork, A. Computers in the classroom. In O. Milton & Associates (eds.), *On College Teaching.* San Francisco: Jossey-Bass, 1978.

Bowman, J. S. Lecture-discussion format revisited. *Improving College and University Teaching,* 1979, *27,* 25-27.

Brawer, F. B. Teaching the science. In F. B. Brawer (ed.) *New Directions for Community Colleges 31.* San Francisco: Jossey-Bass, 1980.

Briggs, L. J. (ed.). *Instructional Design: Principles and Applications.* Englewood Cliffs, N.J.: Educational Technology Publications, 1977.

Brown, J. W., and Thornton, J. W. *College Teaching: A Systematic Approach.* 2nd ed. New York: McGraw-Hill, 1971.

Bruner, J. S. *Toward a Theory of Instruction.* Cambridge, Mass.: Harvard University Press, 1966.

Carroll, J. B. A model of school learning. *Teaching College Record,* 1963, *64,* 723-33.

Cohen, J. *Statistical Power Analysis for the Behavioral Sciences.* Rev. ed. New York: Academic Press, 1977.

Cole, C. C., Jr. *Improving Instruction: Issues and Alternatives for Higher Education.* AAHE-ERIC/Higher Education Research Report No. 4. Washington, D.C.: AAHE, 1982.

Collins, A. Processes in acquiring knowledge. In R. C. Anderson, R. Spiro, and E. Montague (eds.), *Schooling and the Acquisition of Knowledge.* Hillsdale, N.J.: Lawrence Erlbaum, 1977.

Costin, F. Lecturing versus other methods of teaching. *British Journal of Teaching,* 1972, *3,* 4-30.

Cronbach, L. J., and Snow, R. E. *Aptitudes and Instructional Methods.* New York: Irvington, 1977.

Cross, K. P. *Accent on Learning: Improving Instruction and Reshaping the Curriculum.* San Francisco: Jossey-Bass, 1976.

Davies, Ivor K. *Instructional Technique.* New York: McGraw-Hill, 1981.

Davis, J. R. *Teaching Strategies for the College Classroom.* Boulder, Colo.: Westview Press, 1976.

Dubin, R., and Taveggia, T. C. *The Teaching-Learning Paradox.* Eugene, Ore.: Center for the Advanced Study of Educational Administration, 1968.

Duley, J. S. Learning through field experience. In O. Milton & Associates (eds.), *On College Teaching.* San Francisco: Jossey-Bass, 1978.

Eble, K. E. *The Craft of Teaching: A Guide to Mastering the Professor's Art.* San Francisco: Jossey-Bass, 1976.

Eble, K. E. (ed.) *Improving Teaching Styles. New Directions for Teaching and Learning, 1.* San Francisco: Jossey-Bass, 1980.

Edwards, J., Morton, S., Taylor, S., Weiss, M., and Dusseldorp, R. How effective is CAI? A review of the research. *Educational Leadership,* 1975, *33,* 147-153.

Ellner, C. L. Piercing the college veil. In C. L. Ellner and C. P. Barnes (eds.), *Studies of College Teaching.* Lexington, Mass.: Heath, 1983.

Ellner, C. L., and Barnes, C. P. (eds.). *Studies of College Teaching.* Lexington, Mass.: Heath, 1983.

Fisher, K. M., and MacWhinney, B. AV Auto-tutorial instruction: A review of evaluative research. *Audio-Visual Communications Review,* 1976, *24,* 229-261.

Gage, N. L. The appraisal of college teaching: An analysis of ends and means. *Journal of Higher Education,* 1961, *32,* 17-22.

Gagne, R. M. *The Conditions of Learning.* New York: Holt, Rinehart & Winston, 1977.

Gagne, R. M., and Briggs, L. J. *Principles of Instructional Design.* 2nd ed. New York: Holt, Rinehart & Winston, 1979.

Gagne, R. M., and Dick, W. Instructional psychology. In M. R. Rosenzweig and L. W. Porter (eds.), *Annual Review of Psychology.* Palo Alto, Calif.: Annual Reviews, 1983.

Hamblen, J. W., and Landis, C. P. (eds.). *The Fourth Inventory of Computers in Higher Education: An Interpretive Report.* Boulder, Colo.: Westview Press, 1980.

Herbert, J., and Attridge, C. A guide for developers and users of observational systems and manuals. *American Educational Research Journal,* 1975, *12,* 1-20.

Hoover, K. H. *College Teaching Today: A Handbook for Post-Secondary Instruction.* Boston: Allyn & Bacon, 1980.

Hyman, Ronald T. *Improving Discussion Leadership.* New York: Teachers College Press, 1980.

Jamison, C., Suppes, P., and Wells, S. The effectiveness of alternative instructional media: A survey. *Review of Educational Research,* 1974, *44,* 1-67.

Keller, F. S. Goodbye, teacher . . . *Journal of Applied Behavior Analysis,* 1968, *1,* 79-89.

King, P. G. Development and evaluation of CAI lessons for use in macro economic theory. *CLCA Faculty Newsletter,* April 30, 1977.

Kozma, R. B., Belle, L. W., and Williams, G. W. *Instructional Techniques in Higher Education.* Englewood Cliffs, N.J.: Educational Technology Publications, 1978.

Krumboltz, J. D. The nature and importance of the required response in programmed instruction. *AERA Journal,* 1964, *1,* 203-209.

Kulik, J. A., Cohen, P. A., and Ebeling, B. J. Effectiveness of programmed instruction in higher education: A meta-analysis of findings. *Educational Evaluation and Policy Analysis,* 1980, *2,* 51-64.

Kulik, J. A., and Jaska, P. A. *A Review of Research on PSI and Other Educational Technologies in College Teaching.* Report 10. Ann Arbor, Mich.: Center for Research on Learning and Teaching, 1977.

Kulik, J. A., Kulik, C.-L. C., and Cohen, P. A. A meta-analysis of outcome studies of Keller's personalized system of instruction. *American Psychologist,* 1979(a), *34,* 307-318.

Kulik, J. A., Kulik, C.-L. C., and Cohen, P. A. Research on audio-tutorial instruction: A meta-analysis of comparative studies. *Research in Higher Education,* 1979(b), *11,* 321-41.

Kulik, J. A., Kulik, C.-L. C., and Cohen, P. A. Effectiveness of computer-based college teaching: A meta-analysis of findings. *Review of Educational Research,* 1980, *50,* 525-544.

Levinson-Rose, J., and Menges, R. J. Improving college teaching: A critical review of research. *Review of Educational Research,* 1981, *51,* 403-434.

Lewis, R., and Tagg, E. E. (eds.). *Computer Assisted Learning.* Amsterdam, Holland: North Holland Publishing, 1980.

Lowman, J. *Mastering the Techniques of Teaching.* San Francisco: Jossey-Bass, 1984.

McKeachie, W. J. *Research on College Teaching: A Review.* Washington, D. C.: ERIC Clearinghouse on Higher Education, 1970.

McKeachie, W. J. *Teaching Tips.* 7th ed. Lexington, Mass.: Heath, 1978.

McKeachie, W. J., and Kulik, J. A. Effective college teaching. In F. N. Kerlinger (ed.), *Review of Research in Education.* Itasca, Ill.: Peacock, 1975.

McPherson, M. S. A change for the better? *Change,* April, 1984, 22-23 and 47-49.

Merrill, M. D., Reigeluth, C. M., and Faust, G. W. The instructional quality profile: A curriculum evaluation and design tool. In H. F. O'Neill, Jr. (ed.), *Procedures for Instructional Systems.* New York: Academic Press, 1979.

Merrill, M. D., Richards, R. E., Schmidt, R. V., and Wood, N. D. *The Instructional Strategy Diagnostic Profile Training Manual.* San Diego, Calif.: Courseware, 1977.

Merrill, P. F. Task analysis — an information processing approach. *NSPI Journal,* 1976, *15,* 7-11.

MESA Seminar. *The State of Research on Selected Alterable Variables in Education.* Chicago: Department of Education, University of Chicago, 1980.

Milton, O., & Associates (eds.) *On College Teaching: A Guide to Contemporary Practices.* San Francisco: Jossey-Bass, 1978.

Mintz, J. J. The A-T approach 14 years later: A review of the research. *Journal of College Science Teaching,* 1975, *4,* 247-252.

Moore, J. W., Smith, W. I., and Teevan, R. *Motivational Variables in Programmed Learning: The Role of Need Achievement, Fear of Failure, and Student Estimate of Achievement.* Lewisburg, Pa.: Bucknell University Press, 1965.

Murphy, R. T., and Appel, L. R. *Evaluation of the PLATO IV Computer-based Education System in the Community College.* Princeton, N. J.: Educational Testing Service, 1977.

Nash, A. N. Muczyk, J. P., and Vettori, F. L. The relative practical effectiveness of programmed instruction. *Personnel Psychology,* 1976, *24,* 397-418.

O'Neill, H. F., Jr. (ed.). *Computer-based Instruction: A State-of-the-Art Assessment.* New York: Academic Press, 1981.

Pask, G. Conversational techniques in the study and practice of education. *British Journal of Educational Psychology*, 1976, *46*, 12-25.

Postlethwait, S. N., and Associates (eds.). *Exploring Teaching Alternatives.* Minneapolis, Minn.: Burgess, 1977.

Reigeluth, C. M. In search of a better way to organize instruction: The elaboration theory. *Journal of Instructional Development*, 1979, *2*, 8-15.

Reigeluth, C. M., and Rodgers, C. A. The elaboration theory of instruction: Prescription for task analysis and design. *NSPI Journal*, 1980, *19*, 16-26.

Riesman, C. *On Higher Education: The Academic Enterprise in an Era of Rising Student Consumerism.* San Francisco: Jossey-Bass, 1980.

Sanford, N. (ed.). *The American College: A Psychological and Social Interpretation of the Higher Learning.* New York: Wiley, 1962.

Satterfield, J. Lecturing. In O. Milton and Associates (eds.), *On College Teaching.* San Francisco: Jossey-Bass, 1978.

Schiller, W. J., and Markle, S. M. Using the personalized system of instruction. In O. Milton and Associates (eds.), *On College Teaching.* San Francisco: Jossey-Bass, 1978.

Schramm, W. L. *The Research on Programmed Instruction.* Washington, D.C.: U. S. Government Printing Office, 1964.

Schurdak, J. J. *An Approach to the Use of Computers in the Instructional Process and an Evaluation.* Research Report RC-1432, IBM Watson Research Center, Yorktown Heights, N.Y., July 1965.

Sherman, J. G., and Ruskin, R. S. *The Personalized System of Instruction.* Englewood Cliff, N.J.: Educational Technology Publications, 1978.

Silberman, H. F. Characteristics of some more recent studies of instructional methods. In J. E. Coulson (ed.), *Programmed Learning and Computer Based Instruction.* New York: Wiley, 1962.

Stevens, A. L., and Collins, A. Multiple conceptual models of a complex system. In R. E. Snow, P. A. Frederico, and W. E. Montague (eds.), *Aptitude, Learning and Instruction.* Vol. 2, Arlington, Va.: Office of Naval Reserve, 1981.

Tenner, E. A new definition of education? *Change*, April 1984, 22-27.

Trent, J. W., and Cohen, A. M. Research on teaching in higher education. In R. M. W. Travers (ed.), *Second Handbook of Research on Teaching.* A project of the American Educational Research Association. Chicago: Rand McNally, 1973.

Wales, C. E., and Stager, R. *The Guided Design Approach.* Englewood Cliffs, N.J.: Educational Technology Publications, 1978.

Zinn, K. L. Instructional uses of computers in higher education. In J. Hamblen and C. P. Landis (eds.), *The Fourth Inventory of Computers in Higher Education: An Interpretive Report.* Boulder, Colo.: Westview Press, 1980.

THE CONCEPT OF STRATEGY:
From Business to Higher Education

Ellen Earle Chaffee, *National Center for Higher Education Management Systems*

The matter of transferring business practices to higher education is a touchy topic. Even when a particular system appeals to higher education administrators, they are likely to treat it with immediate disfavor if the suggestion comes from trustees or legislators. On the other hand, if they happen to pick a business system on their own, they may just as readily commit themselves to its usage with an equal, if opposite, zeal. In either case, intuition is likely to outweigh logic.

No matter how such a system comes into use — intuitively or logically — it will, nonetheless, tend to follow a set pattern. First, the system will be widely acclaimed in the higher education literature; institutions will eagerly ask how best to implement it. Next, the publication of a number of case studies will appear, coupled with testimonials to the system's effectiveness. Finally, both the term and the system will gradually disappear from view.

After the process has run its course, the effects of a borrowed system will probably be more residual than direct. When a higher education institution adopts a system, or even is just exposed to its concepts and practices, the institution is likely to discover subtle changes in its management processes. The net effect of borrowed systems on higher education during the past 15 years has presumably been to help administrators become more rational, more sensitive to the value of quantitative information, and more likely to define and act upon their priorities. Certainly this has been the case with two of the most widely discussed systems in the past two decades: planning-programming-budgeting systems (PPBS) and management by objectives (MBO).

The research reported here was supported by a contract (#400-83-0009) from the National Institute of Education. The section describing three models from the business literature is taken from "Three Models of Strategy," *Academy of Management Review*, 1985, *10*, 89-98. Used with permission.

Another new idea, too loosely structured to be called a system, has entered the higher education lexicon during the past five or six years. It is borrowed from the business literature, and most often it is called strategic planning. While the idea is still being developed, Baldridge (1983) claims that strategic planning is here to stay. The logic behind his assertion is shared by most authors today on strategic planning for higher education.

Before stepping further into the debate regarding whether this business-oriented concept of strategy ought to be applied to higher education settings, I would like to outline the context of the term "strategy" and the two associated terms "strategic planning" and "strategic management."

Strategy arose in the context of the military, and dates back as far as 550 B.C. (see Evered, 1983, for a brief review that compares strategy in military, business, and futures-research settings). Consistent with its military inceptions, strategy tends to require an advance plan, the resources necessary to implement this plan, and an ability to remain alert to signs that modification may be required. A few authors began using the term "strategic planning" in the late 1940s, but the work that is most often credited with provoking increased attention to strategic planning in the business literature during the 1960s and early 1970s was a book by Chandler (1962). Because the book was based on practice rather than theory, strategic planning evolved from an applied orientation and moved quickly into theoretical discussions and empirical research.

The term "strategic management" was brought into the lexicon with a landmark book edited by Ansoff and Hayes (1976), called *From Strategic Planning to Strategic Management*. In their introduction, Ansoff and Hayes recommended a shift away from strategic planning to compensate for several inherent deficiencies. They pointed out that strategic planning excluded certain variables that are critical for achieving preferred outcomes, as well as some dimensions that are important for maintaining a viable relationship between the organization and its environment — notably, psychological, political, and implementation factors. Ansoff, Declerck, and Hayes (1976) added in the book's first chapter that the outcome of strategic planning is simply a set of plans and intentions. By contrast, they suggested strategic management could include the operational management of the organization's competitive mode ("planning"), the entrepreneurial management of the organization's entrepreneurial mode ("adapting"), and the integrative management of both modes ("planned learning"). They referred to strategic management as a complex socio-dynamic process for strategic change.

Mintzberg, writing two years later, concurred with the implication that strategic planning was an inadequate concept, claiming that telling management to "state its goals precisely, assess its strengths and weaknesses, plan systematically on schedule, and make the resulting strategies explicit are at best overly general guidelines, at worst demonstrably misleading precepts to organizations that face a confusing reality" (1978, p. 948). Within five years of the Ansoff and Hayes book, the concept of strategic management had so thoroughly taken hold in the business literature that Jemison declared in a review that the concept of strategic planning was "all but obsolete" (1981, p. 637). And the point was reiterated in Ginter and White (1982, p. 253).

Since "strategy" is a broad, encompassing term, many authors have solved the definitional problem in individual articles by selecting a narrow component for close scrutiny, such as how strategic issues come to the attention of managers (Ansoff, 1980). Because this chapter attempts to review the state of the field as a whole, the option of selecting a narrow segment is not available. Moreover, a broad view of the strategy literature cannot adopt or create a specific definition without arbitrarily excluding a number of relevant and important works that adopt different definitions. It should be further noted that the literature includes many additional terms with "strategic" as a modifier. These authors, however, have achieved little or no consensus on their definitions (Bourgeois, 1980; Glueck, 1980; Hatten, 1979; Hofer and Schendel, 1978; Rumelt, 1979; Steiner, 1979).

The only feasible solution to this problem, and the one adopted here, is to include any work in which the author claims to be dealing with some aspect of strategy. This approach permits a broad view of the field, but understandably avoids analysis of the many narrower subtopics. The review will, however, organize other authors' general treatments of strategy into families of similar views. After examining the present discussion, the reader will have as clear an idea as is at present possible of what strategy, strategic planning, and strategic management mean in the literature.

Like many other concepts and practices, strategy, having shown its usefulness in business, was borrowed by higher education. And as is often true of borrowings, higher education's use of strategy lags behind that of business, both in scope and sophistication. To take but one obvious example, the higher education literature is based on strategic planning, not yet having caught up with the shift to strategic management (Myran, 1983, is an exception).

Despite such limitations, many authors point to the ways that strategic planning can provide the kind of thinking and action that higher education institutions desperately need to survive the lean years of the 1980s and 1990s. First, strategic planning encourages awareness of the organization's environment. Some authors believe that higher education organizations have exhibited an isolationist attitude for so long that they are in real danger of losing their constituencies and, therefore, their resources. Second, strategic planning encourages decision makers to recognize the fact that they need to anticipate or counter the moves of their competitors if they hope to attract students and funders. During the past 15 years, higher education has indeed stepped into a highly competitive marketplace, although many administrators would not admit it until quite recently. Finally, strategic planning encourages an approach that could be called "anticipatory adaptation." By scanning the environment, an organization can evaluate future possibilities and make changes to better equip itself for both the present and future marketplace.

If the idea of strategic planning does actually fade away, sensitivity to the environment, awareness of competition, and appropriate responses will likely be some of the major residual effects. A major reason that strategic planning might conceivably go the way of PPBS and MBO is that academic practitioners have had little to rely on in the way of empirically derived generalizations about either the comparability of business and higher education organizations or specific ways to define and use strategy in higher education. For example, any differences between profit and not-for-profit organizations that might relate to strategy have never been demonstrated empirically (Wortman, 1979).

Some authors actively advocate using business methods in general, and strategic planning in particular, in higher education, but little empirical evidence supports their assertions (Doyle and Lynch, 1976; Schendel and Hatten, 1972). Typically, they imply that strategic planning will have value for higher education institutions because: (1) it has value for businesses, and (2) higher education institutions are or should become similar to businesses. Other authors list similarities between businesses and universities, such as concern with the external environment; internal effects of demographic change; and some degree of external control from government, politics, consumers, unionism, and tenure (Wood and Wood, 1981).

A more general argument that favors the application of business concepts to not-for-profit organizations claims that either the specific characteristics of the organization in question or the nature of the organization's external environment is more relevant to transfer than is the profit or nonprofit distinction (Cameron, 1983; Newman and Wallender, 1978). Without a great deal of additional research, all such claims are subject to dispute.

It is not surprising, therefore, that many take the opposite point of view. Some of the distinctions claimed, again without conclusive evidence, for higher education organizations are:

1. Higher education organizations have multiple, often conflicting goals.
   a. Many important higher education outcomes are intangible.
   b. Leadership charisma tends to be important because there are fewer measures of effectiveness in education than in business.
2. Chief executives lack power.
   a. Employees are more committed to their profession than to the organization.
   b. Resource providers tend to intrude into organizational functioning.
   c. There are restraints on the reward and punishment options.
   d. Open debate, broad participation, and approval from representative bodies are expected.
3. Strategic options are constrained in higher education.
   a. The influence of clients (students) on some higher education institutions is weak.
   b. Higher education lacks opportunity to achieve economies of scale.

c. Geographic location is a significant determinant of success.

d. Functions tend to be integrated, not separable.

This list summarizes points made by several authors (Blyn and Zoerner, 1982; Corson, 1960; Cyert, 1978; Hambrick, 1976; Newman and Wallender, 1978; D. R. E. Thomas, 1978; R. Thomas, 1980). Each point is widely accepted, although some may be more true than others for a particular institution. In some contexts, these points are taken as intrinsic characteristics of higher education that invalidate the use of business-derived management practices; in others, they are construed as flaws that could be remedied by using business management practices. In others words, even if one admits that these are true and unique traits, this in itself does not determine the suitability of applying business techniques to colleges and universities.

Although this issue cannot be decided here or anywhere else without further research, it is nonetheless helpful to consider briefly its implications. Researchers, for example, confront perplexing situations when they attempt to apply business strategy ideas to higher education. If outcomes are intangible, how does one operationalize the concept of organizational success to develop normative prescriptions for strategy? Assuming that charisma matters, does it become an important aspect of strategy? And if so, then how does one get an empirical handle on charisma? Moreover, if functions are integrated and inseparable, how can strategic actions be defined so that they are relatively independent of one another? Finally, but certainly not least troublesome, if the process of making major decisions is complicated due to a lack of central authority and high levels of interest-group participation, can an institution of higher education be said to have a meaningful strategy at all? Unfortunately, researchers so far have not dealt with these issues. Implicitly, they assume that such issues are irrelevant. Although the assumption may have merit, the lack of explicit attention to it is troubling.

Practitioners' efforts to apply strategy in higher education are perhaps as perplexing as those of the researchers. Most important, as any seasoned president can avow, the list implies that a great deal of persuasion and negotiation will be inevitable in establishing an organizational strategy. Because strategy cannot be mandated from the top to the extent that it can in business, such changes become difficult. This point is confirmed in a study of five colleges that found, contrary to previous speculation, that the loosely coupled structures failed to promote organizational adaptability except under certain unlikely conditions (Rubin, 1979).

Furthermore, the range of strategic options is narrower in higher education than in business if the list of differences between the two is accepted. For example, dramatic changes in geographic location are likely to be more costly in higher education. Even without a physical move, major changes in services or markets are severely limited by the organization's dependence on professional employees with narrow specializations since they are not only entitled to participate in such decisions but they are also required — perhaps with some turn-over of individuals — to carry them out. Such changes are further limited by interdependence among services and markets.

In the absence of research findings, however, the validity of differentiating higher education strategy from business strategy is unknown. That void would be less troublesome if more research on strategy, as it occurs in higher educa-tion, existed. Then administrators' strategic decisions could at least be in-formed by a literature that describes what strategy is and how it works in col-leges and universities. But writers on higher education strategy have not yet looked deeply and widely into their own experience for a model that is inherent to their setting.

Instead, most writers have typically offered suggestions based on their own logic or experience as to how strategy may be modified to suit higher education settings. For example, Hatten (1982) suggested that when applying strategy to not-for-profit organizations, only one change was necessary: instead of identi-fying goals as the first step of the process, the organization should conduct an analysis of its current situation. Such a simple change may, in fact, have an enormously beneficial impact. But the literature is very short on analyses of how the nature and practice of strategy can procure what colleges and universi-ties need.

The following section presents an in-depth analysis of the evolution of stra-tegy that draws largely on the business literature. The review covers a great deal of material spanning two decades, but its organization into three models simpli-fies the presentation and provides a valuable springboard from which the high-er education version of strategy can be better understood. The section after that will describe related research, both in business and higher education, showing what is known empirically. This approach will show what and how we have borrowed from business and what we have missed. Finally, some of the missing links in both literatures are discussed.

Incorporating a great deal of the business literature understandably permits a fuller view of the concept of strategy than is possible from examining only the more limited higher education strategy. This approach not only permits looking at strategy in more advanced stages than currently exist in the higher education literature, but also allows higher education strategists to discover methods (theoretical, empirical, and practical) that might be borrowed from business. Furthermore, it allows higher education strategists the chance to learn from and avoid some mistakes made in the business literature.

EVOLUTION OF STRATEGY
Researchers and practitioners have referred to strategy freely — researchers have even measured it — for over two decades. Those who use the term gener-ally believe that they are all working with the same mental model.

An underlying problem, however, is that strategy is both multidimensional and situational, making any genuine consensus on definition difficult. Strategy also suffers from another, more fundamental problem; that is, the term "strategy" has been applied to three distinguishable models, rather than the supposed single model that most discussions assume. Beyond reflecting various authors' semantic preferences, the multiple definitions reflect three distinct, and in some ways conflicting, views.

This section seeks to analyze the ways strategy has been defined and operationalized in previous treatises and studies. First, it highlights those aspects of strategy where authors in the field appear to agree. Then it suggests three strategy models that are implicit in the literature.

A basic premise of strategy concerns the inseparability of organization and environment (Biggadike, 1981; Lenz, 1980). The organization uses strategy to deal with changing environments. Because this change brings novel combinations of circumstances to the organization, the substance of strategy remains unstructured, unprogrammed, nonroutine, or nonrepetitive (Mason and Mitroff, 1981; Mazzolini, 1981; Miles and Cameron, 1982; Narayanan and Fahey, 1982; Van Cauwenbergh and Cool, 1982). Not only are strategic decisions related to the environment and nonroutine, but they are also considered to be important enough to affect the overall welfare of the organization (Hambrick, 1980).

Theorists who segment the strategy construct agree on several dimensions. They implicitly agree that the study of strategy includes both the actions taken, or the content of strategy, and the processes by which actions are decided and implemented. They agree that intended (what we plan to do), emergent (what we did, although we hadn't planned it), and realized (what we did, planned or not) strategies may exist and differ from one another. Moreover, they agree that firms may have both corporate strategy ("What businesses shall we be in?") and business strategy ("How shall we compete in each business?"). Finally, they concur that the making of strategy involves conceptual as well as analytical exercises. Some authors stress the analytical dimension more than others, but most affirm that the heart of strategy-making is the conceptual work done by leaders of the organization.

Beyond these general factors, agreement breaks down. Yet the differences in point of view are rarely analyzed. Only the existence of multiple definitions of strategy is noted and, as in Mintzberg (1973), definitions are sometimes grouped by type. Analysis reveals that strategy definitions cluster into three distinct models, representing similar definitions in the literature.

This section briefly summarizes the three discernible strategy models. The name assigned to each model represents its primary focus. While these descriptions represent a collective version of similar views, each model also includes many variations of its central theme. Moreover, the three models are not necessarily independent. However, for present purposes, the three models will be treated according to their independent descriptions in the literature, and the theorists and researchers whose work exemplifies each model will be identified.

Model I: Linear Strategy

The first model to be widely adopted is linear and focuses on planning. The term "linear" was chosen because it connotes the methodical, direct, sequential action involved in planning. This model is inherent Chandler's (1962) strategy definition: "Strategy is the determination of the basic long-term goals of an enterprise, and the adoption of courses of action and the allocation of resources necessary for carrying out these goals" (p. 13).

According to the linear view, strategy consists of integrated decisions, actions, or plans that will set and achieve viable organizational goals. Both goals and the means of achieving them are subject to strategic decision. To reach these goals, organizations vary their links with the external environment by changing their products or markets, or else by performing other entrepreneurial actions. Terms associated with the linear model include "strategic planning," "strategy formulation," and "strategy implementation."

The linear model portrays top managers as having considerable capacity to change the organization. The environment is, implicitly, a necessary nuisance "out there" that is composed mainly of competitors. Top managers go through a prototypical rational decision-making process. They identify their goals, generate alternative methods of achieving them, weigh the likelihood that alternative methods will succeed, and then decide which ones to implement. In the course of this process managers capitalize on those future trends and events that are favorable while avoiding or counteracting those that are not. Since this model was developed primarily for profit-seeking businesses, two of its important measures of results are profit and productivity.

While several assumptions that underlie the linear model are not made explicit in most discussions, they nonetheless follow from the authors' tendency to emphasize planning and forecasting. For example: "Conceptually, the process [of strategic planning] is simple: managers at every level of a hierarchy must ultimately agree on a detailed, integrated plan of action for the upcoming year; they [start] with the delineation of corporate objectives and [conclude] with the preparation of a one- or two-year profit plan" (Lorange and Vancil, 1976, p. 75). If a sequential planning process is to succeed, the organization needs to be tightly coupled, so that all ramifications of decisions made at the top can be implemented throughout the organization. This tight coupling assumption enables intentions to become actions.

A second assumption arises from the fact that planning is time-consuming and forward-looking. In other words, while decisions made today are based on beliefs about future conditions, they may not be implemented until months, even years, from now. In order to believe that making such decisions is not a waste of time, one must assume either that the environment is relatively pre-

TABLE 1. Summary of Linear Strategy

Variable	Linear Strategy
Sample definition	" . . . determination of the basic long-term goals of an enterprise, and the adoption of courses of action and the allocation of resources necessary for carrying out these goals" (Chandler, 1962, p. 13)
Salient environment	Competitive forces
Nature of strategy	Planning
Focus for strategy	Goals and actions
Aim of strategy	Goal achievement
Strategic behaviors	Change markets, products
Associated terms	Strategic planning, strategy formulation and implementation
Associated measures	Formal planning, new products, configuration of products or businesses, market segmentation and focus, market share, merger/acquisition, product diversity
Associated authors[a]	Chandler 1962 Cannon 1968 Learned et al. 1969 Gilmore 1970 Andrews 1971 Child 1972 Drucker 1974 Paine and Naumes 1974 Glueck 1976 Lorange and Vancil 1976 Steiner and Miner 1977

[a]Classified by their *definitions* of strategy. Classification is not intended to imply that authors omit discussion of topics relevant to other models.

dictable or that the organization is well insulated from the environment. Also, most authors explicitly assume that organizations have goals and that accomplishing goals is the most important outcome of strategy.

Major characteristics of the linear model and the names of several authors whose definitions of strategy are consistent with this model are listed in Table 1. As the dates in these citations suggest, interest in the linear model waned in the mid-1970s. Ansoff and Hayes (1976) suggested that the reason for moving away from the linear model was that the strategic problem came to be seen as much more complex. Not only did it involve several dimensions of the managerial problem and the process, but also technical, economic, informational, psychological, and political variables as well. The model that arose next is labeled here the adaptive model of strategy.

Model II: Adaptive Strategy

Hofer's (1973) definition typifies the adaptive model of strategy, characterizing it as "concerned with the development of a viable match between the opportunities and risks present in the external environment and the organization's capabilities and resources for exploiting these opportunities" (p. 3). The organization is expected to continually assess external and internal conditions. Assessment then leads to adjustments in the organization or in its relevant environment that will create "satisfactory alignments of environmental opportunities and risks, on the one hand, and organizational capabilities and resources, on the other" (Miles and Cameron, 1982, p. 14).

The adaptive model differs from the linear model in several ways. First, monitoring the environment and making changes are simultaneous and continuous functions in the adaptive model. The time lag for planning that is implicit in the linear model is not present. For example, Miles and Snow (1978) portray strategic adaptation as recurring and overlapping cycles with three phases: the entrepreneurial phase (choice of domain), the engineering phase (choice of technology), and the administrative phase (rationalizing structure and process, and identifying areas for future innovation).

Second, the adaptive model does not deal as emphatically as the linear model with decisions about goals. Instead, it tends to focus the manager's attention on means, while the "goal" is represented by co-alignment of the organization with its environment.

Third, the adaptive model's definition of strategic behaviors goes beyond that of the linear model to incorporate not only major changes in products and markets, but also subtle changes in style, marketing, quality, and other nuances (Hofer, 1976a, and Shirley, 1982, list many such strategic behaviors).

A fourth difference follows from the fact that advance planning is relatively unimportant in the adaptive model, so, as might be expected, strategy is less centralized in top management, more multifaceted, and generally less integrated than in the linear model. However, top managers in the adaptive model still assume overall responsibility for guiding strategy development.

Finally, in the adaptive model the environment is considered to be a complex organizational life support system, consisting of trends, events, competitors, and stakeholders. The boundary between the organization and its environment is highly permeable, and the environment is a major focus of attention in determining organizational action. Whether taken proactively or reactively, this action is responsive to the nature and magnitude of perceived or anticipated environmental pressures.

In sum, the adaptive model borrows heavily on an evolutionary biological model of organizations. The analogy is made explicit in the following passage:

> As a descriptive tool, strategy is the analog of the biologist's method of "explaining" the structure and the behavior of organisms by pointing out the functionality of each attribute in a total system (or strategy) designed to cope with or inhabit a particular niche. The normative use of strategy has no counterpart in biology (as yet!), but might be thought of as the problem of designing a living creature . . . to exist within some environment . . . [Rumelt, 1979, pp. 197-198].

As interest in strategy as adaptation increased, so too did attention to the processes by which strategy arises and is carried out. Beginning with Mintzberg's (1973) modes of strategy making, a number of discussions have been presented to deal with the social, political, and interactive components of strategy (Fahey, 1981; Ginter and White, 1982; Greenwood and Thomas, 1981; Guth, 1976; Hofer, 1976b; E. A. Murray, 1978; J. A. Murray, 1978–79; Narayanan and Fahey, 1982; Tabatoni and Jarniou, 1976). Each of the authors dealt with organizational processes in the adaptive strategy model.

Adaptive strategy rests on several assumptions. The organization and its environment are assumed to be more open to each other than is implied in the linear model. The environment is more dynamic and less susceptible to prediction in the adaptive model. It consists of competitors, trends, and — of increasing importance — stakeholders. Rather than assuming that the organization must *deal with* the environment, the adaptive model assumes that the organization must *change with* the environment.

The adaptive model attempts to take more variables and more propensity for change into account than does the linear model. Table 2 lists terms that reflect this complexity, along with those authors whose strategy definitions fit the adaptive model. It also outlines the characteristics of the model. The number of authors using the adaptive model suggests that this strategy can successfully handle greater complexity and more variables than the linear model. However, opinion is mounting that the situation is complex in other ways. To meet this need, a third model of strategy is emerging.

Model III: Interpretive Strategy
Development of interpretive strategy parallels recent interest in corporate culture and symbolic management outside the strategy literature (for example, Dandridge, Mitroff, and Joyce, 1980; Deal and Kennedy, 1982; Feldman and March, 1981; Meyer and Rowan, 1977; Peters, 1978; Peters and Waterman, 1982; Pfeffer, 1981; Smircich and Morgan, 1982; Weick and Daft, 1983). While parameters of the emerging interpretive model of strategy are still unclear, a recurring theme suggests that the model is based on a social contract, rather than an organismic, view of organizations (Keeley, 1980). The organismic, or biological, view of the organization fits well with the adaptive model. The social

TABLE 2. Summary of Adaptive Strategy

Variable	Adaptive Strategy
Sample definition	" . . . concerned with the development of a viable match between the opportunities and risks present in the external environment and the organization's capabilities and resources for exploiting those opportunities" (Hofer, 1973, p. 3).
Salient environment	Consumer preferences
Nature of strategy	Achieving a "match"
Focus for strategy	Organizational change
Aim of strategy	Co-alignment with the environment
Strategic behaviors	Change style, marketing, quality
Associated terms	Strategic management, strategic choice, strategic predisposition, strategic design, strategic fit, strategic thrust, niche
Associated measures	Price, distribution policy, marketing expenditure and intensity, product differentiation, authority changes, proactiveness, risk taking, multiplexity, integration, futurity, adaptiveness, uniqueness
Associated authors[a]	Hofer 1973 Snow and Hambrick 1980 Guth 1976 Green and Jones 1981 Hofer and Schendel 1978 Hayman 1981 Litschert and Bonham 1978 Jauch and Osborn 1981 Miles et al. 1978 Kotler and Murphy 1981 Miller and Friesen 1978 Camillus 1982 Mintzberg 1978 Chakravarthy 1982 Dill 1979 Gluck, Kaufman, and Rumelt 1979 Walleck 1982 Steiner 1979 Hatten 1982 Bourgeois 1980 Miles and Cameron 1982 Hambrick 1980 Shirley 1982 Quinn 1980 Galbraith and Schendel 1983

[a]Classified by their *definitions* of strategy. Classification is not intended to imply that authors omit discussion of topics relevant to other models.

contract view, on the other hand, portrays the organization as a collection of cooperative agreements entered into by individuals with free will. The organization's existence relies on its ability to attract enough individuals to cooperate in a mutually beneficial exchange.

Interpretive strategy further assumes that reality is socially constructed (Berger and Luckmann, 1966). That is, reality is not something objective or external to the perceiver, that can be apprehended correctly or incorrectly. Rather, reality is defined through a process of social interchange in which perceptions are affirmed, modified, or replaced according to their apparent congruence with the perceptions of others.

Strategy in the interpretive model might be defined as orienting metaphors or frames of reference that allow the organization and its environment to be understood by organizational stakeholders. On this basis, stakeholders are motivated to believe and to act in ways that are expected to produce favorable results for the organization. "Metaphors" is plural in this definition because the maintenance of social ties in the organization precludes enforcing agreement on a single interpretation (Weick and Daft, 1983).

Pettigrew (1977) provided early signs of the interpretive model by defining strategy as the emerging product of the partial resolution of environmental and intra-organizational dilemmas. Although his emphasis on the political and processual nature of strategy might be considered compatible with the adaptive model, he offered several innovative contributions. Among them are: (1) his interest in the management of meaning and symbol construction as central components of strategy, and (2) his emphasis on legitimacy, rather than profit, productivity, or other typical goals of strategy.

Van Cauwenbergh and Cool (1982) defined strategy broadly as calculated behavior in nonprogrammed situations. They went on to posit middle management's central position in the strategy formulation process, as well as to point out that managing the organizational culture is a powerful tool in the hands of top management. The authors concluded by suggesting that their views differed from the traditional strategy literature in three ways: (1) organizational reality is incoherent in nature, not coherent; (2) strategy is an organization-wide activity, not just a matter of concern for top management; and (3) motivation, not information, is the critical factor in achieving adequate strategic behavior. Congruent with these authors' interest in organizational culture, Dirsmith and Covaleski (1983) dealt with what they called strategic norms, or "institutional level action postures . . . that serve to guide acceptable behavior. [S]trategic norms involve the establishment of maps of reality or images held of organizations and environments" (p. 137).

The new themes in these writings suggest a strategy model that depends heavily on symbols and norms. Hatten (1979) saw this change as moving from the goal orientation of the linear model to a focus on desired relationships, such as those involving sources of inputs or customers. He envisaged a new theory of strategy that was oriented toward managerial perceptions, conflict and consensus, as well as the importance of language. The relatively few entries in the model summary presented in Table 3 indicate the fact that the model is too new to have become well developed.

TABLE 3. Summary of Interpretive Strategy

Variable	Interpretive Strategy
Sample definition	Orienting metaphors to motivate behavior expected to produce favorable organizational results
Salient environment	Stakeholder perceptions
Nature of strategy	Symbolizing, attaching meaning
Focus for strategy	Communication, norms, relationships
Aim of strategy	Legitimacy
Strategic behaviors	Develop symbols, improve interactions and relationships
Associated terms	Strategic norms, social contract, social construction of reality
Associated measures	Measures must be derived from context, may require qualitative assessment
Associated authors[a]	Pettigrew 1977 Van Cauwenbergh and Cool 1982 Dirsmith and Covaleski 1983 Chaffee 1984

[a]Classified by their *definitions* of strategy. Classification is not intended to imply that authors omit discussion of topics relevant to other models.

Rather than emphasizing *changing with* the environment, as is true of the adaptive model, interpretive strategy mimics linear strategy in its emphasis on *dealing with* the environment. There is, however, an important difference. While the linear strategist deals with the environment by means of organizational actions that are intended to affect relationships instrumentally, the interpretive strategist deals with the environment through symbolic actions and communication.

Interpretive strategy, like adaptive strategy, assumes that the organization and its environment are an open system. But in interpretive strategy, the attitudes of participants and potential participants toward the organization and its outputs are shaped by the organization's leaders, who do not make physical changes in the outputs. This attitude change seeks to increase credibility for the organization or its output. In this regard, interpretive strategy overlaps with action that might be taken under the adaptive model. For example, when an adaptive strategist focuses on marketing to enhance product credibility, the strategist's behavior could be classified as interpretive. Since strategy is multi-faceted, examining the combination of this kind of marketing with other strategic moves permits classification into either adaptive or interpretive model.

A final noteworthy distinction between the adaptive and interpretive model relates to the ways in which each conceptualizes complexity. Adaptive strategy arose from (and attempts to deal with) structural complexity, notably conflicting and changing demands for organizational output. Interpretive strategy emphasizes attitudinal and cognitive complexity among diverse stakeholders in the organization.

Each one of the three models may be summarized briefly. In linear strategy, leaders of the organization plan how they will deal with competitors to achieve their organization's goals. In adaptive strategy, the organization and its parts change, proactively or reactively, in order to be aligned with consumer preferences. In interpretive strategy, organizational representatives convey meanings that are intended to motivate stakeholders in ways that favor the organization. Each model provides a way of describing a certain aspect of organizational functioning to which the term "strategy" has been applied.

By analogy, one would have three descriptions of a single phenomenon if a geologist, a climatologist, and a poet were to model the Grand Canyon. One value of diverse models, whether they relate to strategy or the Grand Canyon, is that they offer several options. For example, to promote tourism in Arizona, the poet's model of the canyon may be more apt than the other two.

STRATEGY IN THE HIGHER EDUCATION LITERATURE

With this analysis of the current state of the conceptual literature on strategy, it is helpful to examine specifically how the higher education literature relates to the concept of strategy. When writing about higher education, authors have dealt implicitly with strategy more often than explicitly. For example, Shirley, in an article published as recently as 1983, called strategic planning in the non-profit sector "a new and virtually untapped area for research and writing" (1983, p. 92).

A brief survey of the many treatises in the higher education literature that relate implicitly to strategy may prove helpful. For example, topics relevant to linear strategy could include organizational goals (Conrad, 1974; Fenske, 1980; Gross, 1968), rational planning (Dickmeyer, 1982; Flaig, 1979), program review and priority setting (Dougherty, 1981; Lenning, 1980; Shirley and Volkwein, 1978); master planning (Cosand, 1980; Millett, 1980), and forecasting (Curtis, 1983; Dede, 1983; Kirschling and Huckfeldt, 1980; Wing, 1980). Topics relevant to adaptive strategy could include organizational change (Bell, 1978; Bergquist and Shoemaker, 1976; Nordvall, 1982), marketing and market analysis (Krampf and Heinlein, 1981; Litten, 1979; Lucas, 1980; Muffo and Whipple, 1982; Zemsky, Shaman, and Berberich, 1980), and assessing the environment (Alfred, 1982; Baldridge, Kemerer, and Green, 1982; Barenbaum and Ricci, 1982; Huff and Ranney, 1981). Finally, higher education readings that relate to interpretive strategy include those on such topics as organizational saga (Clark, 1970), mission (Keeton, 1971; Mosely and Bucher, 1982; Tobias, 1982), and leadership (Dressel, 1981; Mayhew and Glenn, 1975; Pattillo, 1962; Peck, 1983; Simon, 1967).

Space prohibits reviewing the literature on all such topics, so the discussion that follows will focus on works that deal explicitly with strategy. These works are scattered among diverse periodicals and books. Some early pieces included articles by Orton and Derr (1975), Doyle and Lynch (1976), and Ellison (1977). Cope (1978) and Hosmer (1978) contributed the first books on strategy; Cope explained the concept and how it might be applied in higher education, and Hosmer discussed the ways strategy was used by three business schools. Summaries are available in Cope (1981), Peterson (1980), and Keller (1983).

Each of these works, as well as most of the others on strategy in higher education, expresses the adaptive model of strategy. For example, Peterson (1980) states that the primary purpose of strategic planning is to foster institutional adaptation; Keller (1983) states that the focus is on keeping the organization in step with the changing environment; and Cope (1981) states that the purpose is to achieve a synergistic match of program strengths with opportunities to serve society. Emphasis is on achieving a good fit between organizational activity and environmental demand (Baldridge, 1983; Baldridge and Okimi, 1982; Cameron, 1983).

Specifically, strategic actions are intended to increase the institution's share of the market for students or to make its product mix — the academic programs its offers — more attractive (Frances, 1980; Merson and Qualls, 1979; R. Thomas, 1980). To achieve such goals, institutions may seek new clientele types and change their geographic scope, mission, programs, and goals (Shirley, 1983). Perhaps the most obvious example of the use of the adaptive model in the higher education literature, and the one most likely to evoke controversy, is a statement by Kotler and Murphy that presidents should aim to make every faculty member see "his or her job as sensing, serving, and satisfying markets" (1981, p. 487). However vehemently some faculty members may disagree with that particular statement, adaptive-model views are shared by most higher education authors writing on strategy.

Two major differences prevail between treatments of strategy in higher education and the adaptive model in business. First, higher education authors who deal with adaptive strategy often approach it from a highly linear, strategic-planning orientation. They may suggest ways of tightly integrating strategy among institutional subunits (Shirley, 1983), list steps to be taken toward developing strategic plans (Groff, 1983), or state that strategy simply adds new dimensions to a familiar institutional planning process (Cope, 1981). Linear strategy is also apparent among those authors who present strategic planning in the tradition of the long-range planning literature (Dube and Brown, 1983; R. Thomas, 1980; Uhl, 1983).

Second, higher education authors hint at interpretive strategy. For example, one author emphasized tradition, politics, and myths in connection with higher education strategy, sounding much like an interpretive-model strategist (Toll, 1982). Another emphasized building relationships, both external and internal, as the foundation for strategic management (Myran, 1983). Many authors explicitly include a discussion of the mission or values of the institution. Such a discussion has been found less frequently in business, perhaps because the authors assumed that the mission was profit. Growing emphasis on corporate culture and interpretive strategy in the business literature has recently brought greater attention to mission and values in that context.

One might say, then, that the higher education literature also incorporates three models of strategy — linear, adaptive, and interpretive. Higher education authors seem to have sensed the importance of interpretive strategy before business authors did, and they seem to have clung to the linear model longer. The evolution of strategy was foreshortened in the higher education literature, probably because diverse elements, included in the long history of the business literature, were tapped almost simultaneously by various higher education authors. Nonetheless, the major emphasis in higher education is on adaptive strategy, with occasional entries of the linear-strategy approach, as well as traces of interpretive strategy.

The literature also includes many empirical studies of strategy as it relates to both business and higher education. Based on one or more of the three conceptual models, these studies cover topics ranging from the way strategic issues come to the attention of organizational leaders to the types of strategic actions that can help an organization recover from decline. The following assessment of empirical results gains importance given the potential value of research for improving strategy in higher education. Once again, the assessment is enriched by looking first at the research on business strategy to create a context for that on higher education strategy. Two central questions are considered for both business and higher education: Of what actions does strategy consist, and how is strategy related to organizational success?

EMPIRICAL STUDIES OF STRATEGY

This section focuses on two major issues in the empirical work on strategy — its content and its relationship to organizational success. Studies that categorize strategy content were selected because they provide critical tools for both the researcher and the practitioner. Such studies not only help the researcher understand the definition and meaning of strategy, but they also help the practitioner learn about the range of available strategic options, how they can be characterized, and ways to conceptualize what their organizations are doing and might do. In similar fashion, studies of strategic predictors of organizational success not only help researchers identify directions for further development, but they

TABLE 4. Business: Empirical Descriptions of the Content of Strategy

		N	Method	Types
Galbraith and Schendel	1983	1,200	Statistical	Strategic actions — in consumer organizations: harvest, build, continue, climb, niche, cashout; in industrial organizations: low commitment, maintenance, growth, niche Basis for typology — level of investment, product/market specialization
Hambrick, MacMillan, and Day	1982	1,028	Statistical	Strategic characteristics of four types of businesses: wildcats, dogs, cash cows, and stars (vary in market share and product life cycle) Basis for typology — prior conceptualization; and resource allocation patterns, domains, capital configuration, and others
Harrigan	1980	60	Cases	Business-level strategies: early exit, milk the investment, shrink selectively, hold present position, increase investment Basis for typology — amount and timing of change in product investment
Meyer	1982	19	Case/ statistical	Alternative responses to crisis: weather the storm, "what strike?", good experiment Basis for typology — attitude of leaders
Miles and Cameron	1982	6	Cases	Strategic adaptation: domain defense, domain offense, domain creation Basis for typology — product/market orientation, innovation
Miles and Snow	1978	84	Case/ statistical	Strategic predisposition: prospector, analyzer, defender, reactor Basis for typology — risk orientation
Miller and Friesen	1978	81	Statistical	Successful strategies: adaptive firm/moderate challange, adaptive firm/great challange, dominant firm, giant under fire, entrepreneurial conglomerate, innovator Basis for typology — product/market change and diversity, external pressure

150

TABLE 4. Business: Empirical Descriptions of the Content of Strategy (continued)

		N	Method	Types
Miller and Friesen	1980	135	Statistical	Archetypes of strategic transition: entrepreneurial revitalization, consolidation, toward stagnation, toward centralization, boldness and abandon, maturation, troubleshooting Basis for typology — initiative, organizational structure
Mintzberg	1978	2	Cases	Modes of strategy making: entrepreneurial, adaptive, planning
Mintzberg and Waters	1982	1	Case	Over 58 years of waves and cycles: formation, evolving global change, delay and diversion, resumption, shifting gears, the big push, consolidation and search for new options Basis for typology — entrepreneurship and planning
Paine and Anderson	1977	62	Statistical	Strategic types: adaptive planning, planning, adaptive entrepreneurial, entrepreneurial/stress Basis for typology — amount of change, control of change
Porter	1980	Review	Synthesis	Potentially successful generic strategies: cost leadership, differentiation, and focus Basis for typology — strategic target (industry-wide or particular segment) and strategic advantage (uniqueness or lowest cost)
Stevens and McGowan	1983	90	Statistical	Dimensions of management strategy: resource seeking, authority and financial issues, balance budget, more aid and authority, shift cost to others, cut safety and services Basis for typology — resource orientation, authority, domain choice flexibility

* In addition to the studies listed, many others have developed categories of strategy that apply primarily to specific business actions. For a review, see Bourgeois (1980).

151

also help practitioners understand how complex situations like their own have been handled successfully by others. Although all published studies that could be found on both content and its relationship to organizational success in the business literature are reviewed, many additional studies of strategy have been conducted.

All of the empirical studies to be reviewed in this section (Tables 4 through 7) were selected according to certain guidelines. First, because refereed, accessible works are most central to the field, virtually all studies included are available in published form. The two exceptions (Baker and Cullen, 1981; Cohen, 1982) were included because they relate directly to Table 7 and because so few published studies exist in this category. Secondly, studies were included if they related to a theoretical or conceptual frame of reference either in an exploratory or hypothesis-testing mode. Evaluations of single cases and works that used cases only to illustrate the author's point of view were excluded. For better or worse, a large proportion of works on higher education strategy fall into the excluded group.

Business Studies

Table 4 lists business studies on strategy content. Thirteen such studies in the past seven years have used empirical data to describe strategy types used by organizations. Nearly all of the studies focused on business organizations, but a few used hospitals, government agencies, or other organizations. Four of the thirteen studies dealt only with case studies; the other nine were partly or entirely based on statistical analysis. The range of sample sizes is from 1 to 1,200 organizations, with a mean of 231.

Six of the studies categorized ways in which organizations orient themselves toward environmental change (Meyer, 1982; Miles and Cameron, 1982; Miles and Snow, 1978; Miller and Friesen, 1980; Mintzberg, 1978; Paine and Anderson, 1977). These categories reflect the authors' observations that organizations will differ in their willingness to take risks, their levels of initiative, and their resistance to change. Other studies examined specific actions taken by organizations and grouped them into categories of related actions (Galbraith and Schendel, 1983; Harrigan, 1980; Miller and Friesen, 1978; Mintzberg and Waters, 1982; Stevens and McGowan, 1983).

The authors generally focused on adaptive strategy, although elements of the linear model are apparent in the attention paid by some to organizational planning. The adaptive model of strategy is apparent in the language researchers attach to their typologies (for example, four of the typologies use the word "adaptive" or "adaptation") and in the emphasis on organizations' changing with their environments as opposed to dealing instrumentally or symbolically with their environments.

Collectively, the studies provide many lenses for viewing organizational behavior. One dimension they differ on is that some emphasize the organization's attitudes while others emphasize its actions. Another dimension is the extent to which organizational leadership is seen as a pivotal strategic force. Still another is the relative emphasis on resource allocation or investment decisions. At this stage of research development, little guidance is available to evaluate the validity or utility of any of these typologies. Such guidance will evolve from the results of follow-on research and applied organizational analyses, some of which are under way. Examples of follow-on research will be shown in Table 5.

A few of the studies shown in Table 4 also appear in Table 5 because they categorized strategy and examined the relationship between strategy and organizational success (Hambrick, MacMillan, and Day, 1982; Harrigan, 1980; Miller and Friesen, 1978; Paine and Anderson, 1977). In addition, Hambrick (1983a) and Snow and Hrebiniak (1980) studied the typology that was developed by Miles and Snow (1978), and Hambrick (1983b) studied Porter's (1980) typology. Twenty-five studies of strategy and success conducted in the past ten years are reported in Table 5. All but one, a mathematical simulation, used statistical analysis. Sample size ranged from 13 to 1,200 firms, with a mean of 303.

Most of the measures of organizational success for these studies of profit-oriented businesses were financial. Many of the studies dealt with the context in which strategy occurs. Some of them took account of various environmental conditions, notably the organizations' levels of uncertainty, environmental dynamism, and hostility or scarcity of resources (Jauch, Osborn, and Glueck, 1980; Miller and Friesen, 1978, 1983; Paine and Anderson, 1977; Snow and Hrebiniak, 1980; Tuggle and Gerwin, 1980; Woo and Cooper, 1981). Two of the studies noted strategic differences between firms in different industries (Hambrick, 1983a; Harrigan, 1980). Three others dealt explicitly with discovering effective strategies for recovering from decline (Hall, 1980; Hambrick and Schechter, 1983; Schendel, Patton, and Riggs, 1976).

The very nature of the research question in all of these studies suggests that managerial and organizational actions affect organizational success. In other words, success is primarily due to controllable factors. Accordingly, one implicit conclusion in many of these studies is that managerial initiative and organizational proactivity are beneficial. However, a few studies suggest the value of more conservative management. For example, Snow and Hrebiniak (1980) found that prospectors (organizations that proactively initiated new activities) and defenders (organizations that attempted to protect the viability of their current activities) did equally well in similar environments. In addition, some recent studies have found that concern for efficiency and internal factors were central to success (Hambrick and Schechter, 1983; MacMillan, Hambrick, and Day, 1982; Pearce, 1983).

The clearest generalization that can be made about the findings reported in Table 5 is that the relationship between strategy and success is complex and dependent on numerous contingencies. The contingencies include the firm's size and diversification, perceived environmental uncertainty (dynamism, hostility, heterogeneity), perceived need for internal change, stage of product life cycle,

TABLE 5. Business: Empirical Descriptions of the Content of Strategy

		N	Method	Outcome	Strategic Predictors
Bettis and Hall	1982	80	Statistical	Return on assets and risk	Firms with related diversification do not outperform firms with unrelated diversification. Unrelated diversification does not yield superior risk-pooling characteristics.
Buzzell, Gale, and Sultan	1975	594	Statistical	Return on investment	Market share and its associated benefits
Buzzell and Wiersema	1981	1,200	Statistical	Market share	Beginning market share, new products, product quality, marketing budget, market segmentation
Hall	1980	64	Statistical	Financial return	Purposeful leadership, low cost, meaningful differentiation; do not diversify in order to recover from decline
Hambrick	1983a	850	Statistical	Profit, market share, cash flow	Defenders better than prospectors in profit and cash flow, regardless of environment; prospectors only gain market share in innovating industries
Hambrick	1983b	164	Statistical	Profit	Cost leadership differentiation and focus were associated with success. Multiple routes to profit exist within an industry type.
Hambrick, MacMillan, and Day	1982	1,028	Statistical	Return, risk, market share	"Cash cows" perform best (high market share, mature product life cycle stage).
Hambrick and Schecter	1983	260	Statistical	Profit, recovery from decline	In mature product business units, turnaround was due to efficiency moves, not entrepreneurial initiatives.
Harrigan	1980	60	Statistical	Recovery	Strategy depends on industry, firm's competitive posture, and timing of competitor's decisions. Some decline patterns are more favorable than others.

154

TABLE 5. Business: Empirical Descriptions of the Content of Strategy *(continued)*

		N	*Method*	*Outcome*	*Strategic Predictors*
Hatten, Schendel, and Cooper	1978	13	Statistical	Return on equity	Subgroups of firms within an industry follow similar strategies (patterns of investment in manufacturing, finance, and marketing). Each subgroup has its own pattern of relationships between strategies and performance.
Jauch, Osborn, and Glueck	1980	358	Statistical	*Fortune* rating, return on assets	No strategy-environment combination brings success on both outcome measures; financial actions and production efficiency decreased both measures.
Lenz	1980	80	Statistical	Return on assets	Low socioeconomic development of service area, high price/service, flat hierarchy
MacMillan, Hambrick, and Day	1982	1,011	Statistical	Profit	Capital intensity, value added, and manufacturing costs affect profit in four business types. Efficiency is profitable. Each of the four types showed certain additional strategy-performance relationships.
Miller and Friesen	1983	26, 36	Statistical	Sales growth, profitability	Environmental dynamism requires more analysis and innovation, hostility requires more analysis, heterogeneity requires more innovation — especially true of successful firms.
Miller and Friesen	1982	132	Statistical	Sales growth and profit	Concerted change in methods of reducing uncertainty, differentiating and integrating the organization is associated with success, piecemeal change is not.
Miller and Friesen	1978	81	Statistical	Achieved objectives	Certain archetypes succeeded (see listing in Table 4).
Paine and Anderson	1977	62	Statistical	Goal achievement	Four successful modes (adaptive planning, planning, adaptive entrepreneurial, and entrepreneurial/stress), depending on perceived uncertainty of environment and perceived need for internal change

155

TABLE 5. Business: Empirical Descriptions of the Content of Strategy *(continued)*

	Year	N	Method	Outcome	Strategic Predictors
Pearce	1983	137	Statistical	Profit and risk	High orientation of key individuals toward internal factors (e.g., cost control), not external factors (e.g., relations with government agencies), is associated with performance.
Robinson and Pearce	1983	50	Statistical	Four measures of financial performance	Formal and informal planners in small firms did equally well.
Schendel, Patton, and Riggs	1976	54	Statistical	Recovery	Upturn dominated by managerial action (better efficiency, strategies, processes); downturn dominated by inactivity and inefficiency
Schoeffler, Buzzell, and Heany	1974	620	Statistical	Profit	High market share and product quality, low investment intensity, certain size/diversification factors
Snow and Hrebiniak	1980	88	Statistical	Ratio of income to assets	Different strategies (prospector and defender) work in similar environments.
Tuggle and Gerwin	1980	N.A.	Simulation	Profit	Organization is better in munificent environment *if* it has resources to exploit it; sensitivity to environmental change is better *only if* environment has business cycles; unpredictable environment requires organizational slack and insensitivity to environmental changes.
Woo	1983	112	Statistical	Low return on investment among high market share firms	High market share is not always profitable. Market stability, certain demand characteristics, and competitive posture mediate relationship.
Woo and Cooper	1981	126	Statistical	High return on investment among low market-share firms	Stable environments, selective competitive focus, and standardized products enabled high profit despite low market share. Emphasis tended to be high quality, low price.

156

what industry the firm is in, its subgroup within the industry, the firm's competitive posture, the timing of competitors' decisions, and the firm's location. Furthermore, studies that used multiple measures of success tended to find that some strategies led to success on some measures, other strategies led to success on other measures.

Because of this, the studies do not provide general prescriptions for effective strategy. Instead, the strategist needs to understand the nature of the organization's environment, industry, and situation, and the performance measures that are of highest priority. On the basis of that assessment, the strategist may examine studies such as those in Table 5 to see whether one of them relates to the situation and therefore provides guidance regarding the best choice of strategy. Most likely, since so many contingency combinations are possible, no research will be available to guide the strategist.

Although there are no universal prescriptions discernible in the research, certain ideas emerge as general themes. As noted above, managerial initiative, organizational proactivity, and concern for efficiency are usually valuable. Obtaining a large share of the market is usually profitable, but having a small share is not necessarily a liability. Quality and cost are key strategic dimensions. Innovation and diversification are sometimes beneficial but not always, so their use should be carefully considered. An integrated set of strategic actions is probably more effective than isolated or disjointed strategic actions. Finally, the choice of a particular strategy may depend on so many contingencies that it is organization-specific.

The overall impression from these two sets of studies is that empirical strategy research has a relatively long history in the business literature. It tends to use large samples and to rely on statistical analyses. Some typologies in the first set of studies were analyzed further in the second set, suggesting that researchers read each others' work and are seeking to build common understandings. However, such synergy limits the scope of inquiry in that it reinforces the researchers' tendency to deal only with the adaptive-strategy model as it appears in multiple cases. The field lacks studies that compare linear or interpretive strategies across cases, and it lacks studies that examine interrelationships among the three kinds of strategies in individual cases. Suggested means to remedy such omissions will be presented after a look at the comparable research on higher education organizations.

Higher Education Studies

A reviewer once characterized research on higher education administration as consisting largely of historical studies and descriptive surveys, empirical descriptions rather than tests of theoretical hypotheses, and dealing with the present while rarely attempting to predict change or define norms (Olive, 1967). She concluded that higher education administration was virgin territory for research. If one excludes case studies that attempt to define norms by proposing the value of a particular institution's methods ("how we did it" is "how to do it''), Olive's conclusions need hardly be altered to describe the status of strategy research in higher education. However, since the kind of study that Olive found typical does not meet the guidelines for inclusion in this discussion, the studies that follow are exceptions to Olive's rule.

Five studies on strategy content in higher education have been reported in the past six years. They are listed in Table 6. The studies represent case and statistical methods equally, with sample sizes ranging from 14 to 40 organizations, with a mean of 22. Three of the studies developed categories of organizational attitudes toward environmental change, such as risk orientation and initiative. One such study (Anderson, 1978) set out explicitly to compare consequences of changing with the environment versus not changing. He found that although change led to larger enrollments, it also brought about a decline in campus climate. Another applied the Miles and Snow (1978) typology that was developed in business to a study of six colleges, five hospitals, and six life insurance companies (Hambrick, 1982). A third developed strategy types inductively, by comparing ten years of strategy in each of fourteen colleges (Chaffee, 1984).

TABLE 6. Higher Education: Empirical Descriptions of the Content of Strategy

	N	Method	Types
Anderson (1978)	40	Statistical	Strategy: maintain distinctiveness, broaden mission Basis for typology — scope and nature of mission
Chaffee (1984)	14	Case/statistical	Strategy: adaptive and interpretive Basis for typology — organizational actions
Finkelstein, Farrar, and Pfnister (1984)	17	Cases	Strategic states: presidential shakeup, shakeup and consolidation, change in competition, enrollment increase, planned expansion, student protest Basis for typology — organizational events
Hambrick (1982)	17	Statistical	Strategic predisposition: prospectors and defenders (differences between them are in internal analysis and politics, not in scanning the environment) Basis for typology — risk orientation
Mingle and Norris (1981)	20	Cases	Responses to decline: resist, adapt, reassess priorities, cut back Basis for typology — initiative, program change

The other two studies (Finkelstein, Farrar, and Pfnister. 1984; Mingle and Norris, 1981) developed strategic action categories by grouping related actions, such as program change or resource reallocation. The study by Finkelstein, Farrar, and Pfnister (1984) examined several cases longitudinally, as Mintzberg and Waters (1982) had done for a single case. Mingle and Norris (1981) categorized responses to decline, as had Harrigan (1980).

All the higher education studies assume the adaptive model of strategy, except that Chaffee (1984) began to outline the interpretive model. As was true in the business studies listed in Table 4, the adaptive model is apparent in the authors' emphasis on how the organization changes with its environment (changing/not changing its mission, shakeup, resisting or adapting), rather than examining how the organization deals with its environment either instrumentally or symbolically.

Seven studies in eight years have examined strategic predictors of success in higher education organizations, as listed in Table 7. Again, the studies are balanced between case and statistical methods. The sample size ranges from 1 to 245 organizations, with a mean of 75. Compared with the outcome measures for business studies in Table 5, the outcome measures for higher education are far more reputational and less financial. Nearly half of the higher education studies, but only one-seventh of the business studies, deal with strategies for recovering from decline.

TABLE 7. Higher Education: Strategic Predictors of Organizational Success

	N	Method	Outcome	Strategic Predictors
Anderson (1978)	40	Case/ statistical	Enrollment and financial growth	Broadened clientele increased enrollments but generally led to lower morale, poorer campus climate.
Baker and Cullen (1981)	199	Statistical	Survival	Growth becomes a liability in old age (no slack, saturated markets). High administrative ratio helped young colleges, hurt old colleges.
Chaffee (1984)	14	Case/ statistical	Recovery	Interpretive and adaptive strategies
Cohen (1982)	245	Statistical	Reverse enrollment decline	Key predictors were external, not subject to managerial control. Among management variables, only changing academic programs was effective.
Dube and Brown (1983)	1	Case	Enrollment and quality improvement	Formal version of adaptive strategy
Peck (1984)	19	Cases	Reputation for success	Informed judgment, dominant mission, highly innovative and opportunity-conscious
Smith and Finch (1975)	5	Cases	Recovery	Multiple approaches: new markets, professionalized management, retain mission

Higher education studies do not generally deal explicitly with the context in which strategy occurs. Unlike seven of the business studies, no study in Table 7 dealt with variations in the organizations' environments, such as dynamism, hostility, or uncertainty. The authors tended instead to control implicitly for environmental characteristics by selecting similar colleges for their samples — for example, assuming that a set of small private liberal arts colleges faced similar environments. Therefore, given that each study dealt with a single industry and with one type of organization at a time, contingencies did not play a role in these analyses as they did in the business studies. That is, the business studies' conclusions contained many qualifiers ("if the environment is hostile," "if the industry is highly innovative," and so forth) that described contingencies under which their findings are likely to obtain. The higher education studies do not lend themselves to that kind of conclusion.

Taken together, the studies in Table 7 suggest that a successful strategy is multifaceted, but requires that the institution retain its existing mission (Chaffee, 1984; Peck, 1984; Smith and Finch, 1975; and, depending on whether enrollment or climate matters most, Anderson, 1978). The results show some conflict, however, when it comes to assessing the role of innovation. Cohen (1982), Peck (1984), and Smith and Finch (1975) found positive results from innovation; Anderson (1978) and Chaffee (1984) found reason to be cautious about innovating.

Finally, Table 7 contains the only study in this review that casts doubt on management's ability to affect organizational destiny. The Cohen study (1982) used variables that managers could control and those they could not control, finding that the effects of the latter far outweighed nearly everything that managers could do. The issue is well worth testing far more extensively than either business or higher education researchers have yet attempted. Theoretically, it is at the heart of a fundamental controversy between those who assert the power of strategic choice (Child, 1972) and the population ecologists, who assert that environmental forces are more powerful than anything management can do (Hannan and Freeman, 1977). To the extent that one accepts the arguments of the population ecologists, strategists can hope at best to make only a marginal difference. Cohen's findings in Table 7 are a sobering reminder of the point.

The higher education studies number only half as many as those in business. The gap is due to the shorter time and the relatively slow production rate of studies on strategy in higher education. Higher education research uses far more case studies relative to statistical studies, which helps account for the fact that sample size in higher education is, on average, less than one-fourth that in business.

Most higher education researchers (both those reviewed here and those whose studies did not meet the selection criteria) prefer case study research. The choice is valid and useful inasmuch as case studies permit longitudinal analysis and determination of cause-and-effect relationships, both of which are crucial issues in understanding how strategy works in an organization. Ironically and unfortunately, very few higher education studies have specified independent and dependent variables, except in the small number of studies in Table 7, so they cannot examine the causal structures underlying strategy. Thus, there is a good deal of room for more and better strategy research both in business and in higher education, as the final section will discuss.

ASSESSING THE STATE OF THE FIELD

As noted earlier, theoretical business literature began with a linear model of strategy, then moved to an adaptive model, and is now formulating an interpretive model. Conceptual work on linear strategy is extensive, both in the literature on business strategy and in the literature on long-range planning in higher education. However, virtually no empirical research that fits the guidelines for inclusion in this review has adopted the linear definition of strategy. This gap, however, may be more semantic than real. At the time linear strategy was developed, much research that may be related to strategy used other terminology — such as "planning," "long-range planning," or "formal planning." Some early studies that dealt with long-range planning examined the relative value of using a formal planning system, and produced conflicting results (see Hofer, 1976b, pp. 262-264, or Lorange, 1979, for a review). But by the time the concept of strategy became sufficiently well developed to foster empirical studies, its leading authors had moved into the adaptive model.

Adaptive strategy is the subject of most conceptual work, as well as all empirical work reviewed here for the business literature. Presumably the model will continue to play a significant role in business studies. If one focuses only on works dealing explicitly with strategy, adaptive strategy serves as the only model with any following in the higher education literature. More broadly, however, higher education authors have also contributed many conceptual papers relating to linear and interpretive strategies. Treatments of strategy *per se* in higher education have been neither as comprehensive nor as frequent as those in business, due in part to approximately fifteen years' lead time in concept development for business. Higher education authors have just begun empirical studies to explore the nature of adaptive strategy and its links to higher education performance.

Because interpretive strategy is an underdeveloped newcomer in the conceptual business literature, it is not yet available in the empirical business strategy literature. Moreover, higher education authors have only touched lightly on the interpretive model in the strategy literature. As might be expected, most of the work related to interpretive strategy in both business and higher education has been done outside the area of strategy.

Coverage of the three models, then, is similar in business and higher education, but the latter falls behind in quantity and, arguably, in sophistication of contributions. The conceptual strategy literature in business is broad in scope, precisely detailed, and highly differentiated. The conceptual literature in higher education — in fact in all nonprofit areas — is fragmented, repetitious, and relatively sparse. Most of it is applications-oriented and expository.

The business studies deal with complex sets of contingencies (including numerous dimensions of the organization's environment and multiple industry characteristics) as they affect diverse organizations. Business studies make capable use of an array of research techniques, such as survey development, analysis from large-scale data bases, secondary case analysis, interviews, and identification of quantifiable proxy variables for complex concepts. They use the data in a variety of sophisticated statistical analyses. Because these methods can accommodate large sample sizes, the studies have considerable credibility in terms of the generalizability of their findings. The higher education studies do not deal with contingencies. Instead, they use narrowly defined samples to minimize the likely effects of unmeasured contingencies. For early works in the field, however, this is an acceptable approach because it simplifies the research agenda.

The relatively heavy emphasis on higher education case studies is potentially valuable, but few higher education authors have exploited such opportunities, as indicated in Tables 6 and 7. Case studies permit a deeper examination of the variables, their longitudinal behavior, and their apparent causal relationships than is feasible with statistical analysis. However, most case studies in higher education are not reported here because they are used for normative, not analytical, purposes. Used analytically, the case method affords a promising avenue for understanding strategy in higher education.

At this early research stage, the only conclusion one may draw confidently from the higher education studies is that radical departure from the organization's mission is probably an unwise strategy — a conclusion many observers have drawn without the benefit of research. If Wortman is right in saying that "not-for-profit organizations can be helped more through rigorous, empirical studies in strategic management than can profit-making organizations" (1979, p. 353), then a great deal more work will be needed. Furthermore, the results should be reported in journals that are widely read, to promote the kind of complementary and synergistic development that business strategists have achieved. Suggestions for further strategy research in nonprofit organizations may be found in Cope (1981), Schendel and Hofer (1979), and Wortman (1979).

Five topics for further research arise from the present discussion. First, the critical factors differentiating higher education organizations from other organizations, such as those listed previously, have not been studied. By better understanding the extent to which such factors are present and relevant in higher education, researchers and administrators can identify which research on business organizations, if any, may be useful for colleges and universities. If these differences prove to be minimal, those in higher education can gain immensely from the extensive business literature. If, instead, they clearly indicate colleges are unique, proper precautions can be taken.

Second, and regardless of the outcome in the first area, higher education strategists can learn from the business literature. For example, some of the bases on which business typologies have been built, such as risk orientation, initiative, and leader attitude (see Table 4), may be helpful. Typologies that describe higher education organizational strategies could be used in hypothesis-testing research, perhaps using hypotheses borrowed from analogous business studies. Moreover, the business literature exhibits properties that the higher education literature needs, including grounding in theoretical frameworks, attending to conceptual as well as operational functions, and comparisons of multiple cases and their achievement of desired organizational outcomes.

A third research area concerns the applicability of the three models to higher education. One possibility is that the interpretive model provides a way to accommodate the unique characteristics of higher education organizations through its emphasis on perception, constituencies, motivation, and legitimacy. Numerous questions arise from this perspective. Is one model more applicable to higher education than others? If so, does the primacy of one model over the others vary according to the type of institution, the nature of the institution's circumstances, or other factors? Are behaviors in all three models mutually consistent? If so, is consistency more productive than inconsistency? Through what media and on what bases do constituents perceive and judge a strategy? What criteria do they use for granting legitimacy to a higher education organization? Shifting to the individual level of analysis, how do top executives form perceptions of the organization and of the environment? How do they translate those perceptions into decisions and symbolic representations? How do they rate and choose among alternative possible interpretations?

A fourth research area, related largely to adaptive strategy, is organizational change. To what degree do boundaries in higher education restrict change? Are there limits on the type or amount of change colleges and universities can make without jeopardizing their legitimacy? Business studies focus on changes in products, markets, and geography. Do higher education organizations have more subtle options for change that constitute potentially valuable strategies? For example, what about changes in key personnel, governance structure, physical facilities, marketing, extracurricular activities, or cultural activities?

A final research area that this review could not cover in the space available concerns the processes by which strategic decisions arise and are made. Fredrickson (1983) describes where research is needed in this area for the business literature. Despite widespread availability of business literature on that topic, higher education strategy literature — both conceptual and empirical — has hardly broached the topic except in normative exhortations that are based either on "how we did it" or on a formal, perhaps unrealistic, version of rationalism and logic. Is strategy formulated in higher education organizations, or is it a by-product of interest-group negotiations? How does strategy move from the idea stage to implementation? Does implemented strategy bear any resemblance to intended strategy?

Regarding needed research methods, Schendel and Hofer (1979, p. 530) placed the following recommendation for business studies of strategic management at the top of their list:

An understanding of the philosophy of science and the power of scientific method must be developed and appreciated by researchers in the field. There is a need for empiricism that goes beyond mere subjective description and interpretation. The field needs to accept and develop more rigorous research methodologies to continue its advancement. In particular, training of young researchers must be given careful attention.

Given the proportionately large body of strategy literature in higher education that is expository, illustrative, or atheoretical (and therefore did not meet the criteria for inclusion in this review), Schendel and Hofer's point is even more applicable to higher education than to business. Another general rule that would benefit the development of strategy for higher education is to encourage researchers to build a coherent body of literature, based on one another's conceptual and empirical works.

In addition, empirical studies at this early developmental stage of higher education strategy need to concentrate more on generating hypotheses than on testing hypotheses. Studies should develop comparative and normative descriptions of institutional strategy that are based on concepts rather than on functional attributes. Such studies would serve two important purposes. First, they would ground the concept of strategy in the experience of higher education institutions themselves. Second, they would yield suggestions about how the concept of strategy in higher education could be operationalized in statistical studies. The measures used in business studies often have no counterparts in higher education.

Higher education researchers should more fully exploit the opportunities offered by the case study method, while also developing more and better quantitative, statistical, large-sample projects. In both cases, longitudinal research is needed. And similarly, these studies should occasionally include diverse types of institutions and, in some instances, compare business organizations with colleges, as Hambrick (1981a, 1981b, and 1982) has done. When such a study does indeed focus on a single type of institution, researchers should recognize that most existing studies have dealt with private liberal arts colleges and, if appropriate, select a less-studied type.

To study strategic management is to begin to understand the nature of the organization itself, how it creates and responds to myriad and shifting external forces, and what it needs to accomplish if it is to survive and prosper. The course of higher education in times of change and scarcity will be determined largely by how well administrators and faculties understand strategic management. Fortunately, many administrators and faculty members are remarkably skilled in strategic management. But they need the kind of guidance that can arise from a strong basic and applied research program. The best of them want it; the others may sink without it. We have a model in the business literature, albeit an imperfect one, of how that program can be built. We need to become more aware of that literature and to develop the necessary sophistication to address the topic profoundly.

REFERENCES

Alfred, R. L. An enterprise in need of investment. *Community and Junior College Journal*, 1982, *52*, 43-45.

Anderson, R. E. A financial and environmental analysis of strategic policy change at small private colleges. *Journal of Higher Education*, 1978, *49*, 30-46.

Andrews, K. R. *The Concept of Corporate Strategy*. Homewood, Ill.: Richard D. Irwin, 1971.

Ansoff, H. I. Strategic issue management. *Strategic Management Journal*, 1980, *1*, 131-148.

Ansoff, H. I., Declerck, R. P., and Hayes, R. L. (eds.). *From Strategic Planning to Strategic Management*. New York: Wiley, 1976.

Ansoff, H. I., and Hayes, R. L. Introduction. In H. I. Ansoff, R. P. Declerck, and R. L. Hayes (eds.), *From Strategic Planning to Strategic Management*, New York: Wiley, 1976.

Baker, D. D., and Cullen, J. B. The moderating effect of growth, decline, and age on organization structure and survival. Paper presented at the annual Academy of Management meetings, San Diego, August 1981.

Baldridge, J. V. Strategic planning in higher education: Does the emperor have any clothes? In J. V. Baldridge and T. Deal (eds.), *The Dynamics of Organizational Change in Education*. Berkeley, Calif.: McCutchan, 1983.

Baldridge, J. V., Kemerer, F. R., and Green, K. C. *The Enrollment Crisis: Factors, Actors, and Impacts*. AAHE-ERIC/Higher Education Research Report No. 3. Washington, D.C.: AAHE, 1982.

Baldridge, J. V., and Okimi, P. H. Strategic planning in higher education: New tool — or gimmick? *AAHE Bulletin*, 1982, *35*, 6-18.

Barenbaum, L., and Ricci, R. Forecasting enrollment: An extrapolative approach. *College and University*, 1982, *57*, 135-142.

Bell, E. Administrative planning: Science or art? *Planning for Higher Education*, 1978, *7*, 12-15.

Berger, P., and Luckmann, T. *The Social Construction of Reality*. New York: Doubleday, 1966.

Bergquist, W. H., and Shoemaker, W. A. *A Comprehensive Approach to Institutional Development*. Number 15 in New Directions for Higher Education series. San Francisco: Jossey-Bass, 1976.

Bettis, R. A., and Hall, W. K. Diversification strategy, accounting determined risk, and accounting determined return. *Academy of Management Journal*, 1982, *25*, 254-264.

Biggadike, E. R. The contributions of marketing to strategic management. *Academy of Management Review*, 1981, *6*, 621-632.

Blyn, M. R., and Zoerner, C. E., Jr. The academic string-pushers: The origins of the up-coming crisis in the management of academia. *Change*, 1982, *14*, 21-25, 60.

Bourgeois, L. J., III. Strategy and environment: A conceptual integration. *Academy of Management Review*, 1980, *5*, 25-39.

Buzzell, R. D., Gale, B., and Sultan, R. Market share — a key to profitability. *Harvard Business Review*, 1975, *53*, 97-106.

Buzzell, R. D., and Wiersema, F. D. Successful share-building strategies. *Harvard Business Review*, 1981, *59*, 135-144.

Cameron, K. S. Strategic responses to conditions of decline: Higher education and the private sector. *Journal of Higher Education*, 1983, *54*, 359-380.

Camillus, J. C. Reconciling logical incrementalism and synoptic formalism: An integrated approach to designing strategy planning processes. *Strategic Management Journal*, 1982, *3*, 277-283.

Cannon, J. T. *Business Strategy and Policy*. New York, Harcourt Brace Jovanovich, 1968.

Chaffee, E. E. Successful strategic management in small private colleges. *Journal of Higher Education*, 1984, *55*, 212-241.

Chakravarthy, B. S. Adaptation: A promising metaphor for strategic management. *Academy of Management Review*, 1982, *7*, 35-44.

Chandler, A. D., Jr. *Strategy and Structure*. Cambridge, Mass.: MIT Press, 1962.

Child, J. Organizational structure, environment, and performance: The role of strategic choice. *Sociology*, 1972, *6*, 1-22.

Clark, B. R. *The Distinctive College: Antioch, Reed, and Swarthmore*. Chicago: Aldine, 1970.

Cohen, B. G. An analysis of institutional response and environmental constraints with respect to patterns of institutional enrollment decline in American higher education. Paper presented at the Association for the Study of Higher Education Conference, Washington, D.C., March 1982.

Conrad, C. University goals. *Journal of Higher Education*, 1974, *7*, 504-516.

Cope, R. G. *Strategic Policy Planning: A Guide for College and University Administrators*. Littleton, Colo.: Ireland Educational Corporation, 1978.

Cope, R. G. *Strategic Planning, Management, and Decision Making*. Washington, D.C.: American Association of Higher Education, 1981.

Corson, J. J. The university — a contrast in administrative process. *Public Administration Review*, 1960, *20*, 2-9.

Cosand, J. P. Developing an institutional master plan. In P. Jedamus and M. W. Peterson and Associates (eds.), *Improving Academic Management*. San Francisco: Jossey-Bass, 1980.

Curtis, R. K. Retrojective planning: Fifteen scenarios for Indiana University. *World Future Society Bulletin*, 1983, *17*, 15-23.

Cyert, R. M. The management of universities of constant or decreasing size. *Public Administration Review*, 1978, *38*, 344-349.

Dandridge, T. C., Mitroff, I., Joyce, W. F. Organizational symbolism: A topic to expand organizational analysis. *Academy of Management Review*, 1980, *5*, 77-82.

Deal, T. E., and Kennedy, A. A. *Corporate Cultures: The Rites and Rituals of Corporate Life*. Reading, Mass.: Addison-Wesley, 1982.

Dede, C. The future of higher education. Paper presented at the American Educational Research Assocation Meeting, Montreal, April 1983.

Dickmeyer, N. Financial management and strategic planning. In C. Frances (ed.), *New Directions for Higher Education: Successful Responses to Financial Difficulty*. San Francisco: Jossey-Bass, 1982.

Dill, W. R. Commentary. In D. E. Schendel and C. W. Hofer (eds.), *Strategic Management: A New View of Business Policy and Planning*. Boston: Little, Brown, 1979.

Dirsmith, M. W., and Covaleski, M. A. Strategy, external communication and environmental context. *Strategic Management Journal*, 1983, *4*, 137-151.

Dougherty, E. A. Evaluating and discontinuing programs. In J. R. Mingle and Associates (eds), *Challenges of Retrenchment*. San Francisco: Jossey-Bass, 1981.

Doyle, P., and Lynch, J. E. Long-range planning for universities. *Long Range Planning*, 1976, *9*, 39-46.

Dressel, P. L. *Administrative Leadership*. San Francisco: Jossey-Bass, 1981.

Drucker, P. F. *Management: Tasks, Responsibilities, Practices*. New York: Harper & Row, 1974.

Dube, C. S., II, and Brown, A. W. Strategic assessment — a rational response to university cutbacks. *Long Range Planning*, 1983, *16*, 105-113.

Ellison, N. Strategic planning. *Community and Junior College Journal*, 1977, *48*, 32-35.

Evered, R. So what is strategy? *Long Range Planning*, 1983, *16*, 57-72.

Fahey, L. On strategic management decision processes. *Strategic Managment Journal*, 1981, *2*, 43-60.

Feldman, M., and March, J. G. Information in organizations as signal and symbol. *Administrative Science Quarterly*, 1981, *26*, 171-186.

Fenske, R. H. Setting institutional goals and objectives. In P. Jedamus and M. W. Peterson and Associates (eds.), *Improving Academic Management*. San Francisco: Jossey-Bass, 1980.

Finkelstein, M, Farrar, D., Pfnister, A. O. The adaptation of liberal arts colleges to the 1970s: An analysis of critical events. *Journal of Higher Education*, 1984, *55*, 242-268.

Flaig, H. The budgetary and planning options for higher education in a period of contraction. *Planning for Higher Education*, 1979, *8*, 20-27.

Frances, C. Apocalyptic vs. strategic planning. *Change*, 1980, *12*, 19-44.

Fredrickson, J. W. Strategic process research: Questions and recommendations. *Academy of Management Review*, 1983, *8*, 565-575.

Galbraith, C., and Schendel, D. An empirical analysis of strategy types. *Strategic Management Journal*, 1983, *4*, 153-173.

Gilmore, F. F. Formulating strategy in smaller companies. *Harvard Business Review*, 1970, *49*, 71-81.

Ginter, P. M., and White, D. D. A social learning approach to strategic management: Toward a theoretical foundation. *Academy of Management Review*, 1982, *7*, 253-261.

Gluck, F., Kaufman, S., and Walleck, A. S. The four phases of strategic management. *Journal of Business Strategy*, 1982, *2*, 9-21.

Glueck, W. F. *Business Policy: Strategy Formation and Management Action*. New York: McGraw-Hill, 1976.

Glueck, W. F. *Strategic Management and Business Policy*. New York: McGraw-Hill, 1980.

Green, J., and Jones, T. Strategic development as a means of organizational change: Four case histories. *Long Range Planning*, 1981, *14*, 58-67.

Greenwood, P., and Thomas, H. A review of analytical models in strategic planning. *Omega*, 1981, *9*, 397-417.

Groff, W. H. Strategic planning. In G. A. Myran (ed.), *Strategic Management in the Community College*. Number 44 in New Directions for Community Colleges series. San Francisco: Jossey-Bass, 1983.

Gross, E. Universities as organizations: A study of goals. *American Sociological Review*, 1968, *33*, 518-544.

Guth, W. D. Toward a social system theory of corporate strategy. *Journal of Business*, 1976, *49*, 374-388.

Hall, W. K. Survival strategies in a hostile environment. *Harvard Business Review*, September-October 1980, *59*, 75-85.

Hambrick, D. C. The university as an organization: How is it different from a business? In G. L. Anderson and Associates (eds.), *Reflections on University Values and the American Scholar*. University Park, Pa.: Pennsylvania State University Center for the Study of Higher Education, 1976.

Hambrick, D. C. Operationalizing the concept of business-level strategy in research. *Academy of Management Review*, 1980, *5*, 567-575.

Hambrick, D. C. Environment, strategy, and power within top management teams. *Administrative Science Quarterly*, 1981(a), *26*, 253-276.

Hambrick, D. C. Strategic awareness within top management teams. *Strategic Management Journal*, 1981(b), *2*, 263-279.

Hambrick, D. C. Environmental scanning and organizational strategy. *Strategic Management Journal*, 1982, *3*, 159-174.

Hambrick, D. C. Some tests of the effectiveness and functional attributes of Miles and Snow's strategic types. *Academy of Management Journal*, 1983(a), *26*, 5-25.

Hambrick, D. C. High profit strategies in mature capital goods industries: A contingency approach. *Academy of Management Journal*, 1983(b), *26*, 687-707.

Hambrick, D. C., MacMillan, I. C., and Day, D. L. Strategic attributes and performance in the BCG Matrix — a PIMS-based analysis of industrial product businesses. *Academy of Management Journal*, 1982, *25*, 510-531.

Hambrick, D. C., and Schechter, S. M. Turnaround strategies for mature industrial-product business units. *Academy of Management Journal*, 1983, *26*, 231-248.

Hannan, M. T., and Freeman, J. H. The population ecology of organizations. *American Journal of Sociology*, 1977, *82*, 929-964.

Harrigan, K. R. Strategies for declining industries. *Journal of Business Strategy*, 1980, *2*, 20-34.

Hatten, K. J. Quantitative research methods in strategic management. In D. E. Schendel and C. W. Hofer (eds.), *Strategic Management*. Boston: Little, Brown, 1979.

Hatten, K. J., Schendel, D. E., and Cooper, A. A strategic model of the U.S. brewing industry: 1952-1971. *Academy of Management Journal*, 1978, *21*, 592-610.

Hatten, M. L. Strategic management in not-for-profit organizations. *Strategic Management Journal*, 1982, *3*, 89-104.

Hayman, J. Relationship of strategic planning and future methodologies. Paper presented at the 1981 Annual Convention of the AERA, Los Angeles, April 1981.

Hofer, C. W. Some preliminary research on patterns of strategic behavior. *Academy of Management Proceedings*, 1973, 46-59.

Hofer, C. W. *Conceptual Scheme for Formulating a Total Business Strategy*. Boston: HBS Case Services, 1976(a).

Hofer, C. W. Research on strategic planning: A survey of past studies and suggestions for future efforts. *Journal of Economics and Business*, 1976(b), *28*, 261-286.

Hofer, C. W., and Schendel, D. E. *Strategy Formulation: Analytical Concepts*. St. Paul, Minn.: West, 1978.

Hosmer, L. T. *Academic Strategy*. Ann Arbor: Division of Research, Graduate School of Business Administration, University of Michigan, 1978.

Huff, A. S., and Ranney, J. M. Assessing the environment for an educational institution. *Long Range Planning*, 1981, *14*, 107-115.

Jauch, L. R., and Osborn, R. N. Toward an integrated theory of strategy. *Academy of Management Review*, 1981, *6*, 491-498.

Jauch, L. R., Osborn, R. N., and Glueck, W. F. Short term financial success in large business organizations: The environment-strategy connection. *Strategic Management Journal*, 1980, *1*, 49-64.

Jemison, D. B. The contributions of administrative behavior to strategic management. *Academy of Management Review*, 1981, *6*, 633-642.

Keeley, M. Organizational analogy: A comparison of organismic and social contract models. *Administrative Science Quarterly*, 1980, *25*, 337-362.

Keeton, M. T. *Models and Mavericks: A Profile of Private Liberal Arts Colleges*. New York: McGraw-Hill, 1971.

Keller, G. *Academic Strategy: The Management Revolution in American Higher Education*. Baltimore: Johns Hopkins University Press, 1983.

Kirschling, W. R., and Huckfeldt, V. E. Projecting alternative futures. In P. Jedamus and M. W. Peterson and Associates (eds.), *Improving Academic Management*. San Francisco: Jossey-Bass, 1980.

Kotler, P., and Murphy, P. E. Strategic planning for higher education. *Journal of Higher Education*, 1981, *52*, 470-489.

Krampf, R. F., and Heinlein, A. C. Developing marketing strategies and tactics in higher education through target market research. *Decision Sciences*, 1981, *12*, 175-192.

Learned, E. P., Christensen, C. R., Andrews, K. R., and Guth, W. R. *Business Policy*. Homewood, Ill.: Richard D. Irwin, 1969.

Lenning, O. T. Assessing student program needs. In P. Jedamus and M. W. Peterson and Associates (eds.), *Improving Academic Management*. San Francisco: Jossey-Bass, 1980.

Lenz, R. T. Environment, strategy, organization structure and performance: Patterns in one industry. *Strategic Management Journal*, 1980, *1*, 209-226.

Litschert, R. J., and Bonham, T. W. Conceptual models of strategy formulation. *Academy of Management Review*, 1978, *3*, 211-219.

Litten, L. H. Market structure and institutional position in geographic market segments. *Research in Higher Education*, 1979, *11*, 59-83.

Lorange, P. Formal planning systems: Their role in strategy formulation and implementation. In D. E. Schendel and C. W. Hofer (eds.), *Strategic Management: A New View of Business Policy and Planning*. Boston: Little, Brown, 1979.

Lorange, P., and Vancil, R. F. How to design a strategic planning system. *Harvard Business Review*, 1976, *54*, 75-81.

Lucas, J. A. Identifying regional and community markets. In P. Jedamus and M. W. Peterson and Associates (eds.), *Improving Academic Management*. San Francisco: Jossey-Bass, 1980.

MacMillan, I. C., Hambrick, D. C., and Day, D. L. The product portfolio and profitability — a PIMS-based analysis of industrial product businesses. *Academy of Management Journal*, 1982, *25*, 733-755.

Mason, R. O., and Mitroff, I. I. *Challenging Strategic Planning Assumptions*. New York: Wiley, 1981.

Mayhew, L. B., and Glenn, J. R., Jr. College and university presidents: Roles in transition. *Liberal Education*, 1975, *6*, 299-308.

Mazzolini, R. How strategic decisions are made. *Long Range Planning*, 1981, *14*, 85-96.

Merson, J. C., and Qualls, R. L. *Strategic Planning for Colleges and Universities: A Systems Approach to Planning and Resource Allocation*. San Antonio: Trinity University Press, 1979.

Meyer, A. D. Adapting to environmental jolts. *Administrative Science Quarterly*, 1982, *27*, 515-537.

Meyer, J. W., and Rowan, B. Institutionalized organizations: Formal structure as myth and ceremony. *American Journal of Sociology*, 1977, *83*, 340-363.

Miles, R. E., and Snow, C. C. *Organizational Strategy, Structure, and Process*. New York: McGraw-Hill, 1978.

Miles, R. E., Snow, C. C., Meyer, A. D., and Coleman, H. J., Jr. Organizational strategy, structure, and process. *Academy of Management Review*, 1978, *3*, 546-563.

Miles, R. H., and Cameron, K. S. *Coffin Nails and Corporate Strategies*. Englewood Cliffs, N.J.: Prentice-Hall, 1982.

Miller, D., and Friesen, P. Archetypes of strategy formulation. *Management Science*, 1978, *24*, 253-280.

Miller, D., and Friesen, P. Archetypes of organizational transition. *Administrative Science Quarterly*, 1980, *25*, 268-299.

Miller, D., and Friesen, P. Structural change and performance: Quantum vs. piecemeal-incremental approaches. *Academy of Management Journal*, 1982, *25*, 867-892.

Miller, D., and Friesen, P. Strategy making and environment: The third link. *Strategic Management Journal*, 1983, *4*, 221-236.

Millett, J. D. Relating to governance and leadership. In P. Jedamus and M. W. Peterson and Associates (eds.), *Improving Academic Management*. San Francisco: Jossey-Bass, 1980.

Mingle, J. R., and Norris, D. M. Institutional strategies for responding to decline. In J. Mingle and Associates (ed.), *Challenges of Retrenchment*. San Francisco: Jossey-Bass, 1981.

Mintzberg, H. Strategy-making in three modes. *California Management Review*, 1973, *16*, 44-53.

Mintzberg, H. Patterns in strategy formation. *Management Science*, 1978, *24*, 934-948.
Mintzberg, H., and Waters, J. A. Tracking strategy in an entrepreneurial firm. *Academy of Management Journal*, 1982, *25*, 465-499.
Moseley, J. D., and Bucher, G. R. Church-related colleges in a changing context. *Educational Record*, 1982, *63*, 46-51.
Muffo, J. A., and Whipple, T. W. The use of an expectancy-value model in studying a university's image. Paper presented at the Annual Forum of the Association for Institutional Research, Denver, May 1982.
Murray, E. A. Strategic change as a negotiated outcome. *Management Science*, 1978, *24*, 960-972.
Murray, J. A. Toward a contingency model of strategic decision. *International Studies of Management and Organization*, 1978-79, *8*, 7-34.
Myran, G. A. (ed.). *Strategic Management in the Community College*. In New Directions for Community Colleges series, No. 44. San Francisco: Jossey-Bass, 1983.
Narayanan, V. K., and Fahey, L. The micro-politics of strategy formulation. *Academy of Management Review*, 1982, *7*, 25-34.
Newman, W. H., and Wallender, H. W. Managing not-for-profit enterprises. *Academy of Management Review*, 1978, *3*, 24-31.
Nordvall, R. C. *The Process of Change in Higher Education Institutions*. AAHE-ERIC/Higher Education Research Report No. 7. Washington, D.C.: AAHE, 1982.
Olive, B. A. The administration of higher education: A bibliographical survey. *Administrative Science Quarterly*, 1967, *4*, 671-677.
Orton, D. A., and Derr, C. B. Crisis and contingencies for the small private college. *Teachers College Record*, 1975, *77*, 231-245.
Paine, F. T., and Anderson, C. R. Contingencies affecting strategy formulation and effectiveness: An empirical study. *Journal of Management Studies*, 1977, *14*, 147-158.
Paine, F. T., and Naumes, W. *Strategy and Policy Formulation: An Integrative Approach*. Philadelphia: Saunders, 1974.
Pattillo, M. M. The role of administration in the development of academic excellence. *AAUP Bulletin*, 1962, *48*, 359-363.
Pearce, J. A., II. The relationships of internal versus external orientations to financial measures of strategic performance. *Strategic Management Journal*, 1983, *4*, 297-306.
Peck, R. D. The entrepreneurial college presidency. *Educational Record*, 1983, *64*, 18-25.
Peck, R. D. Entrepreneurship as a significant factor in successful adaptation. *Journal of Higher Education*, 1984, *55*, 269-285.
Peters, T. J. Symbols, patterns, and settings: An optimistic case for getting things done. *Organizational Dynamics*, 1978, *7*, 3-23.
Peters, T. J., and Waterman, R. H. *In Search of Excellence*. New York: Harper and Row, 1982.
Peterson, M. W. Analyzing alternative approaches to planning. In P. Jedamus and M. W. Peterson and Associates (eds.), *Improving Academic Management*. San Francisco: Jossey-Bass, 1980.
Pettigrew, A. M. Strategy formulation as a political process. *International Studies of Management and Organization*, 1977, *7*, 78-87.
Pfeffer, J. Management as symbolic action: The creation and maintenance of organizational paradigms. In L. L. Cummings and B. M. Staw (eds.), *Research in Organizational Behavior*. Greenwood, Conn.: JAI Press. 1981.
Porter, M. *Competitive Strategy*. New York: Free Press, 1980.
Quinn, J. B. *Strategies for Change: Logical Incrementalism*. Homewood, Ill.: Richard D. Irwin, 1980.
Robinson, R. B., Jr., and Pearce, J. A., II. The impact of formalized strategic planning on financial performance in small organizations. *Strategic Management Journal*, 1983, *4*, 197-208.

Rubin, I. Loose structure, retrenchment, and adaptability. *Sociology of Education*, 1979, *52*, 211-222.

Rumelt, R. P. Evaluation of strategy: Theory and models. In D. E. Schendel and C. W. Hofer (eds.), *Strategic Management: A New View of Business Policy and Planning.* Boston: Little, Brown, 1979.

Schendel, D. E., and Hatten, K. J. Strategic planning and higher education: Some concepts, problems, and opportunities. Reprint # 442. Lafayette, Ind.: Institute for Research in the Behavioral, Economic, and Management Sciences, Purdue University, 1972.

Schendel, D. E., and Hofer, C. W. *Strategic Management: A New View of Business Policy and Planning.* Boston: Little, Brown, 1979.

Schendel, D. E., Patton, R., and Riggs, J. Corporate turnaround strategies: A study of profit, decline, and recovery. *Journal of General Management*, 1976, *3*, 3-11.

Schoeffler, S., Buzzell, R. D., and Heany, D. F. Impact of strategic planning on profit performance. *Harvard Business Review*, 1974, *52*, 137-145.

Shirley, R. C. Limiting the scope of strategy: A decision-based approach. *Academy of Management Review*, 1982, *7*, 262-268.

Shirley, R. C. Identifying the levels of strategy for a college or university. *Long Range Planning*, 1983, *16*, 92-98.

Shirley, R. C., and Volkwein, J. F. Establishing academic program priorities. *Journal of Higher Education*, 1978, *49*, 472-488.

Simon, H. A. The job of a college president. *Educational Record*, 1967, *48*, 68-78.

Smircich, L., and Morgan, G. Leadership: The management of meaning. *Journal of Applied Behavioral Science*, 1982, *18*, 257-273.

Smith, J., and Finch, H. L. Private colleges: Strategies for change. *Planning for Higher Education*, 1975, *4*, 3-4.

Snow, C. C., and Hambrick, D. C. Measuring organizational strategies: Some theoretical and methodological problems. *Academy of Management Review*, 1980, *5*, 527-538.

Snow, C. C., and Hrebiniak, L. G. Strategy, distinctive competence, and organizational performance. *Administrative Science Quarterly*, 1980, *25*, 317-335.

Steiner, G. A. *Strategic Planning.* New York: Free Press, 1979.

Steiner, G. A., and Miner, J. B. *Management Policy and Strategy.* New York: Macmillan, 1977.

Stevens, J. M., and McGowan, R. P. Managerial strategies in municipal government organizations. *Academy of Management Journal*, 1983, *26*, 527-534.

Tabatoni, P., and Jarniou, P. The dynamics of norms in strategic management. In H. I. Ansoff, R. P. Declerck, and R. L. Hayes (eds.), *From Strategic Planning to Strategic Management.* New York: Wiley, 1976.

Thomas, D. R. E. Strategy is different in service businesses. *Harvard Business Review*, 1978, *56*, 158-165.

Thomas, R. Corporate strategic planning in a university. *Long Range Planning*, 1980, *13*, 70-78.

Tobias, S. Can we afford to improve liberal education? And can we afford not to improve it? *Liberal Education*, 1982, *68*, 87-113.

Toll, J. S. Strategic planning: An increasing priority for colleges and universities. *Change*, 1982, *14*, 36-37.

Tuggle, F. D., and Gerwin, D. An information processing model of organizational perception, strategy and choice. *Management Science*, 1980, *26*, 575-592.

Uhl, N. P. Editor's introduction: Institutional research and strategic planning. In *Using Research for Strategic Planning*. Number 37 in New Directions for Institutional Research series. San Francisco: Jossey-Bass, 1983.

Van Cauwenbergh, A., and Cool, K. Strategic management in a new framework. *Strategic Management Journal*, 1982, *3*, 245-265.

Weick, K. E., and Daft, R. L. The effectiveness of interpretation system. In K. S. Cameron and D. A. Whetten (eds.), *Organizational Effectiveness: A Comparison of Multiple Models*. New York: Academic Press, 1983.

Wing, P. Forecasting economic and demographic conditions. In P. Jedamus and M. W. Peterson and Associates (eds.), *Improving Academic Management*. San Francisco: Jossey-Bass, 1980.

Woo, C. Y. Evaluation of the strategies and performance of low ROI market share leaders. *Strategic Management Journal*, 1983, *4*, 123-135.

Woo, C. Y., and Cooper, A. C. Strategies of effective low share businesses. *Strategic Management Journal*, 1981, *2*, 301-318.

Wood, K. L., and Wood, S. H. Are corporate strategic planning techniques useful in public higher education? Paper presented at the joint conference of the Southern Association for Institutional Research and the North Carolina Association for Institutional Research, Charlotte, North Carolina, October 1981.

Wortman, M. S. Strategic planning: Not-for-profit organizations. In D. E. Schendel and C. W. Hofer (eds.), *Strategic Management*. Boston: Little, Brown, 1979.

Zemsky, R., Shaman, S., and Berberich, M. A. Toward an understanding of collegiate enrollments: A first test of the market segment model. *Journal of Educational Finance*, 1980, *5*, 355-374.

ADMINISTRATIVE COMPUTING IN HIGHER EDUCATION

Andrew T. Masland, *Digital Equipment Corporation*

Computers have been present on college and university campuses for several decades. Yet the intensity of the current debate and interest in computing might lead one to think that computers are a new arrival in academia. In some ways this is true because computer technology has changed drastically and rapidly in the past few years. The computer of today hardly resembles its predecessors in many respects. Microcomputers are now commonplace or soon will be on many campuses. "Computer literacy" is a topic that finds its way into the press regularly. And administrators at every level find that computers are affecting their daily activities. It seems appropriate, therefore, to look at what we know about administrative computing in higher education, to summarize the available literature, and then to ask what we still do not know and what questions we need to ask. That is the purpose of this chapter. It provides a perspective on how computing influences administrators' work and decisions. It describes the current state of knowledge about administrative computing as a basis for further research.

Specifically, the chapter begins with a discussion of the evolution of computing as it affects its use on campuses. The second section describes the wide variety of administrative uses for computers and how these have changed over the past 15 to 20 years. This section also reviews evaluations of administrative computing to assess the success and influence of such applications. The third section summarizes what is known about managing computer resources and how management policy influences computer use. Fourth, the chapter looks at the implications of administrative computing. Finally, the chapter probes what we

This chapter was written while the author was Research Associate and Assistant Professor, Center for the Study of Higher Education, The Pennsylvania State University.

still do not know about administrative computing and its influence on college and university decision makers and their work.

The chapter deals with academic computing — the use of computer technology for instruction and research — only to the extent it interacts and impinges upon administrative computing. Limitations of space simply do not allow research on academic computing to be included in this discussion. This does not mean that these topics are any less important than administrative computing. In fact, they may fundamentally alter the nature of students' educational experiences.

The literature reviewed comes from a wide variety of sources and varies greatly in its quality and scholarly orientation. There are research pieces that evaluate the effectiveness of administrative computing and question how decision makers use technology. As Adams (1977) noted, however, this body of literature is of limited scope. A large percentage of the literature is descriptive, often telling the story of one campus's experience with administrative computing. While this is not research in the formal sense, it can be used as evidence when many such accounts find the same relationships and influences. Another segment can be labeled the "wise-old-man school" because it draws upon the personal experience of those who have been closely involved with administrative computing. This normative approach is useful and supports the research findings, but does not replace research. The chapter occasionally draws upon research conducted in noneducational organizations because their experiences often parallel those of administrative computing.

Professional associations and nonprofit organizations whose interests are computer related also provide a great deal of information on computing and higher education. Two key examples are EDUCOM, the Interuniversity Communications Council, based in Princeton, New Jersey, and CAUSE, the Professional Association for Development, Use, and Management of Information Systems in Higher Education, located in Boulder, Colorado. Both organizations publish bulletins and monographs. While they provide valuable information, they tend to reflect their respective memberships and so may not represent the higher education community as a whole.

I. THE EVOLUTION OF ADMINISTRATIVE COMPUTING

Administrative computing has evolved over the past few decades. Before discussing the details of administrative computing and its management, it is helpful to highlight two aspects of the evolutionary process. The section begins with technological evolution which drives many other changes. Next it examines several stage theories of computing which explain the evolution of computing in "developmental" terms. The stage concept is a useful means of understanding administrative computing, so the chapter returns to this theme periodically.

Technological Change

Computer technology has evolved in a series of generations (Swoyer, 1980a). Vacuum tube technology characterized first-generation machines of the 1950s.

The second generation, starting about 1960, utilized transistors and sold-state engineering. The third generation began with integrated circuits, and the fourth with very large scale integration (VLSI). Since 1955 these developments have lowered the cost of computers in current dollars by 200% and have increased their processing speed by 400%. The cost of electronic circuits continues to decrease by about one-third each year (Emery, 1978). For long-term disk storage, capacity per square inch has increased 600 times since 1957, while cost has declined 150 times (Branscomb, 1983).

Technological change is evident in a number of ways: a decrease in the size of components and an increase in the number of elements per unit size; an increase in speed and a decline in power consumption of the circuitry; an improvement in reliability of the components; an improving ease of use of the machinery; and a widespread availability of computers (Gwynn, 1979; Resnikoff, 1982). All of these elements are closely related. Decreasing size, for example, improves speed and reliability while lowering power consumption. In more practical terms these advances appear as improvements in microcomputers, telecommunications, data-base technology, interactive systems, graphics, security, and networking ("How to Use Advanced Technology," 1979; Orcutt, 1981; Staman, 1981).

All of the past technological trends are expected to continue into the future. Computers of 1993 are likely to be twenty times as powerful as those of 1983 (Branscomb, 1983). Electromechanical devices such as printers and disk drives are likely to remain more stable in terms of cost and performance than purely electronic components such as memory. As advances continue, technology will take an increasingly distant role and human factors will become more important (Resnikoff, 1982). Computers have already become more powerful, compact, and reliable and relatively less expensive than in the past.

Stage Theories

Several researchers have described institutional use and management of computer resources in terms of a "stage theory" in which the organization passes through particular applications, management methods, and crises. The literature reports stages for all types of organizations. The stage theories, some more formal that others, are informative because they provide a useful framework against which to observe administrative computing. The stages reflect increasingly sophisticated and extensive use of computing for both administrative and academic tasks. They sometimes appear to be quite distinct, and it is not possible to jump from an early stage to a later stage without first passing through those in the middle ("Educating Executives in New Technology," 1980).

Wise (1979) described four stages of development in common administrative computer-based applications. A campus begins to use the computer for its brute force ability to do current activities more rapidly and accurately than is possible by hand. In the second stage the institution moves to problem-solving applications in less highly routinized tasks. Third is an information-system phase in which a more highly integrated system is built from the many small systems developed in the previous stages. Fourth is a simulation phase in which administrators use computer software to guide them to better decisions in a wide variety of areas. In the fourth stage computing is structurally integrated in and perceived as a fundamental element of the organization (Gillespie and Dicaro, 1981).

Mann (1982) found the same progression in the control of computer resources. In the first stage computers are used on an individual and somewhat fragmented basis as they are applied to specific problems and situations. In the second stage there are experimental combinations of efforts and shared activities. In the third stage control of the resource becomes much more important as administrators attempt to avoid duplication and incompatibilities among different systems. In the fourth stage, as users and administrators become more familiar with the resource, there is heavy investment in computer resources and widespread use of them.

The stages reported for college and university administrative computing applications are similar to those found in the more extensive research on stages of computer use in business. Gibson and Nolan (1974) observed four stages in large businesses' computer applications, personnel, budgets, and management techniques. Each stage had its own rewards, traumas, and managerial problems. Gibson and Nolan labeled the stages initiation, expansion, formalization, and maturity. As an organization progresses through the stages, applications move from simple cost reduction to complex data-base applications. Personnel for computing and management techniques reflect the same shift from efficiency and control to data-base technology. In the fourth stage a top-level manager oversees computing operations.

Nolan (1979) proposed a more complex scheme with six stages that supplant but do not invalidate his four-stage theory. The six stages are initiation, contagion, control, integration, data administration, and maturity. He noted that there may be more advanced stages but that the 38 large businesses he studied had not yet reached them. Nolan provided benchmarks to help administrators place their organization along the six-stage continuum. These include changes in expenditures, technology, applications, computer resource management, planning and control, and user awareness. Placing an institution along the continuum provides administrators with evidence of what applications and problems they are likely to encounter as computer use continues to evolve on their campus.

One important observation about all of the stage theories is that there is a shift in orientation as an organization passes through them. In the early stages there is an emphasis on data processing and the management of computer resources. In the later stages there is a transition to the management of information and how the organization uses it. Computers are first used to do tasks better, then they are used for new tasks, and finally they change the way an organization does its work (McCarter, 1978). While this shift is implicit in several of the stage theories discussed above, Nolan (1979) made it explicit. The stages of evolutionary computer use provide a valuable framework for understanding administrative computing. This important theme is apparent in the later discussions of administrative applications, the management of computer resources, and the implications of administrative computing.

II. ADMINISTRATIVE APPLICATIONS

Thirty years ago computers had only a limited influence on college and university campuses. They were large, awkward machines that were costly to operate and limited in their applications. Fifteen years ago conversational time sharing became available and some administrators used computers in an interactive problem-solving environment. Using computers as simple record-keeping devices for personnel records and payroll was much more common. In the past ten years there has been a fairly rapid spread of computer technology to every area of higher education (McCredie, 1983).

Larger expenditures on administrative computing are one indication of the growing use of computers. Between 1966–67 and 1976–77 total expenditures on computing increased an average of 35% a year (Alcorn, 1980). In 1969–70 administrative computing consumed $161 million (34% of higher education's computing expenses). By 1980–81 this figure had increased to $650 million (50% of college and university computing expenditures). Most institutions spend roughly 1% of their budgets for administrative computing (Gillespie and Dicaro, 1981).

Colleges and universities are also spending more of their own money on computing. Funding sources for computing have shifted over the years, in part because of changes in federal legislation and support (Masat, 1981). In 1966–67 the federal government funded 28% of computing expenses and institutions funded 56%. By 1976–77 federal support had decreased to 7% and institutions funded 82% of computer-related expenses (Alcorn, 1980). While hardware and facilities consumed most of the expenditures for early computing efforts, computer personnel cost nearly as much as hardware and software in 1980 (Nyman, 1980).

Expenditures have increased in part because colleges and universities use computing in more administrative tasks. Thomas (1981) reported on administrative computer use at CAUSE member institutions. These colleges and universities represent only 10% of all institutions in the nation and the sample underrepresents small institutions, but the survey results are indicative of the wide variety of current administrative applications. The average institution used computers in 51 administrative areas, a figure which is twice that reported in a 1976–77 survey (Thomas, 1980, 1981). Administrative uses reflect both internal information needs and the imposition of data requirements from external

TABLE 1. Administrative Computing Applications as a Percentage of Total Applications

Application	Percentage of All Administrative Computing
Admissions and records	33
Financial management	22
Planning and institutional research	11
General administration	7
Auxilary services	5
Logistics	5
Financial aid	4
Library	4
Physical plant	2
Hospital	1
Other administrative	6
Total	100

Source. Reproduced with permission from CAUSE, the Professional Association for Development, Use, and Management of Information Systems in Higher Education (Thomas, 1981, p. 126).

sources such as the federal government. Table 1 displays the percentage of administrative applications in various functional areas reported in the CAUSE survey (Thomas, 1981).

Administrative computing is often part of a management system or an "interrelated collection of information, decision procedures, and people who direct the operation of an organization" (Schroeder, 1977, p. 99). Colleges and universities use these systems in the belief that they will improve management and the decision-making process. As this chapter notes, research does not always support this belief. Thorough evaluation of management systems remains crucial. Many administrative and managerial functions, however, can benefit from computer support (Skarulis and Thomas, 1980; Wise, 1979). Specific benefits cited in the literature include obtaining higher-quality information, coordinating information among offices, reducing "information float" or the time between requesting and receiving information, and reaching more effective decisons (Bailey, 1982). In addition, the process of building and using a management system may help a decision maker better understand the problems he or she faces and so improve decisions in an indirect manner (Bloomfield and Updegrove, 1981). Management systems often produce such unintended consequences (Baldridge and Tierney, 1979).

But use of administrative computing and management systems is not without its hazards. Deardon (1972) stated that it is impossible to build a "total" system for managers because the task is too complex. It may also be easy to be lulled into a false sense of security by a computerized management system that seems to provide all of the necessary answers (McCorkle, 1977). Enarson (1975) noted:

> "How could one resist the 'systems approach' or deny its purity and compelling logic? It's almost as if we warded off the sense of engulfing chaos by ritual incantation of magic words." (p. 171)

The literature on administrative computing falls into five broad categories: data processing, management information systems, models, decision support systems, and office automation. These five categories represent an increasing sophistication in administrative computing. As the discussion demonstrates, these categories reflect the evolution the stage theories suggest. There is a change from a technology and data management orientation to a more highly developed use of information and data resources. Each category is reviewed below, including descriptive accounts of such systems, evaluations of their success, and suggestions for improving these applications in the future. The section concludes with a discussion on improving administrative applications.

Data Processing

Data processing was the first administative application of computer technology in higher education. During this initial period computers replaced older equipment that was used for record keeping and tasks such as payroll. Such use is now commonplace, although there are small colleges that have yet to adopt these systems. Data processing focuses on operational tasks that are prestructured and prescheduled (Chachra and Heterick, 1982). Although such systems remain crucial to many administrative functions such as personnel, finance, and student records, their implementation is not without problems. Despite this they have received little attention in the scholarly literature. As institutions search for greater economies and efficiencies these systems deserve greater attention. Colleges and universities must learn to use them successfully.

Management Information Systems

The primary purpose of a management information system (MIS) is to make current and accurate data available to campus decision makers. Administrators use these systems for routine, predetermined reports and data. Colleges and universities began using MIS soon after data-processing applications. Discussion about them in the literature began in the middle to late 1960s. Minter and Lawrence (1969) provided a good summary of the applications of MIS in college administration during this period. Recent publications continue the tradition of describing MIS applications at various institutions which meet both common and specialized administrative needs. In general, however, the applications described are only implemented on one campus. This makes transferring the implications of system development and use to other institutions problematic because administrative systems and methods are often institution-specific.

Although descriptive literature abounds, there is much less research evaluating the success of MIS or judging its impact on administrators and their ability to manage complex organizations. Wyatt and Zeckhauser (1975) conducted an early evaluation of computer-based information systems in higher education. They studied six diverse institutions to determine the effectiveness of MIS for executives and discovered similar problems with the system at each institution. They reported that expectations for MIS were too high in comparison to achieved results. The isolation of executives from system design decreased the use of computer-based information systems. Administrators tended to use their system through an intermediary rather than directly. In fact, they were more disposed to use information from other sources. Parallel systems developed to meet local information needs. Finally, implementation touched upon sensitive political and bureaucratic issues.

Baldridge and Tierney (1979) investigated the effect of implementing management information systems, management by objectives (MBO), or both at 34 colleges and universities that participated in the Exxon Education Foundation's Resource Allocation Management Project in the early 1970s. Of the 34 institutions, 11 had successful MIS projects, 6 combined MIS with MBO, 8 had not yet had enough experience with their new systems to warrant evaluation, and 9 were not successful in implementing a new management system. Successful projects were considered to be those which improved significantly the quality and quantity of data available to decision makers. In those institutions with successful MIS, data quality improved, the speed of problem solving increased, "hot-spot analysis" was facilitated, and general sophistication about administrative problems increased. The systems did not provide new information in many cases, but they corrected misinformation and allowed administrators to manipulate and compare data in ways that were impossible before installation of the systems. At the 11 successful MIS institutions, however, only 39% of administrators felt that the costs of the project were reasonable for the benefits received and slightly less than 50% felt the systems had become an integral part of institutional management. Thus some of the institutions were successful with their MIS, but not all institutions enjoyed success.

Adams (1975) investigated managers' perceptions of MIS in ten major corporations. In general the managers he interviewed were satisfied with MIS; they felt the systems were accurate, precise, and provided relevant information. When asked about possible improvements in MIS, the managers wanted improved quality instead of greater quantity. More recently, Cheney and Dickson (1982) found that computer-based information systems increase the level of satisfaction with information and job satisfaction among managers.

There are several possible explanations for the differences among these studies. The more recent studies conducted in businesses may reflect improvements in the design of information systems. It is also likely that businesses use data differently or rely on different types of data in decision making. It is important to note, however, that studies in both environments show that users prefer improved quality to greater quantity. Part of the evaluation problem arises because it is difficult to separate a management system from its user. The questions a decision maker asks often determine the effectiveness of a system. At the same time, however, if a system does not provide accurate and useful information it will be of little value. While answers may be elusive, the basic evaluation questions are relatively straightforward. First, does a system encompass all necessary functions and information needs? Second, does it support the institution's decision-making structures? And third, does it support management (Baughman, 1969; Gwynn, 1969)? These questions should become part of the implementation of any administrative computer application.

Modeling Systems

Modeling systems in higher education move from a data orientation to one in which the computer is used to simulate an organization or a decision process (Alter, 1980). A model is a mathematical representation of an organization or some organizational process. The model's user can ask "what if" questions by substituting new values for key policy variables. Thus the model is intended to help an administrator compare alternatives and improve the decision-making process (Weathersby and Weinstein, 1970). An administrator can also use a model to better understand the current situation. This often develops through the process of defining and building a model. As the stage theories suggest, models appeared on the administrative scene after management information systems and represent a more sophisticated use of organizational data.

There are a variety of ways in which to classify models in higher education. One possibility is to describe them in terms of the mathematical methods they use (Gray, 1977; Johnstone, 1974). Such a scheme includes difference equations, Markov Chains, and regression equations. Another means is to describe models as algorithmic or heuristic (Hudson, 1977). Algorithmic models produce one solution. Heuristic models depict logical relationships among variables and can calculate outcomes, but they depend on the user's guidance to determine a solution. A third means of classification, more helpful to the nonmathematically inclined administrator, is to describe models in terms of function and availability. Since the late 1960s the most popular and widely studied models have been those used in resource allocation, financial trend projection, faculty planning, and enrollment analysis. Colleges and universities have also used a variety of lesser-known models for other functions.

The well-known, early models were cost simulation or resource-planning models. These were built in and reflected a period of expanding resources and enrollments. Their basic objective was to divide resources among competing programs and departments (Gray, 1977; Hopkins, 1971; Schroeder and Adams, 1976). The Comprehensive Analytical Model for Planning in the University

Sphere (CAMPUS) was the first example of such models (Judy and Levine, 1965; Mowbray and Levine, 1971). Originally developed for the University of Toronto in 1964, CAMPUS used enrollment projections and estimates of departmental course variables to predict space requirements and budgets. The National Center for Higher Education Management Systems (NCHEMS) built the Resource Requirements Preduction Model (RRPM), a second well-known cost simulation model (Clark et al., 1973; Gaunt and Haight, 1977; Gamso, 1977; Gulko and Hussain, 1971). Like CAMPUS, RRPM used projected enrollments and historical data on course enrollment patterns (in an induced course load matrix) to project the resources required to support a given level of activity. An institution could purchase either CAMPUS or RRPM and install the model on its own computer system. Two less widely used models of this type were SEARCH and HELP/PLANTRAN (Hussain, 1976).

Institutions had mixed success with both CAMPUS (Andrew and Alexander, 1974; Farmer et al., 1978; Foreman, 1974) and RRPM (Plourde, 1976; Rodgers and Rhodes, 1978; Schroeder and Adams, 1976; Wartgow, 1973). Colleges and universities found that they had difficulty realizing the models' predicted potential. CAMPUS and RRPM both required large amounts of data in a particular format. Often historical data available on the campus did not fit the model's requirements. Users viewed the models as too technical, complex, and costly in comparison to perceived benefits. Plourde (1976) reported that only 32.4% of surveyed institutions had met all or a considerable number of their original objectives for using one of the resource allocation models.

A second major type of model is the trend projection model. These models reflect a period of projected enrollment decline and financial difficulties. In their initial application they projected current budgets and predictions of financial conditions to show administrators the institution's financial future. Administrators at Stanford University developed the first of these models, TRADES, that received widespread attention (Dickmeyer, 1979; Hopkins and Massy, 1981). Stanford had great success in using the model to help formulate a plan to reduce its deficit. EDUCOM, with a grant from the Lilly Endowment, built EDUCOM's financial planning model (EFPM), a generalized version of TRADES for use by other institutions. Technically EFPM is a modeling system instead of a model because each user defines his or her own model depending on institutional needs. Users build their models through a question-and-answer dialogue with EFPM. Because institutions now use EFPM for a variety of purposes, EDUCOM no longer refers to it as a financial planning model (Updegrove, 1978, 1982).

EFPM has enjoyed greater success than the earlier models, in part because EFPM's builders learned from the limitations of the first models. Currently 95 institutions use EFPM for applications that include finance, athletics, dining, housing, and student financial aid (Updegrove, 1982). A number of users have reported on their applications of EFPM (Hopkins et al., 1982; Knodel et al., 1979; Ottervik, 1979). These reports are small case studies that describe successful applications of modeling and illustrate how different institutions used EFPM. Thus they demonstrate potential applications for new users. They do not, however, formally evaluate EFPM.

A third popular use for models in higher education is examining faculty demographics (Bleau, 1982; Bloomfield, 1977; Bottomley, 1978; Hopkins, 1974; Nevison, 1980). Interest in faculty flow models reflects current conditions of steady-state staffing at many institutions. Administrators can use these models, for example, to determine the effects of changes in retirement, tenure, and promotion policies. While the resource and trend projection models have been widely used by many institutions, the faculty models have tended to be institution-specific. This has allowed users to tailor the model to institutional needs and characteristics. It typically means, however, that the user must be fairly sophisticated in modeling techniques.

A fourth use for models is in the area of admissions and enrollment (Averill and Suttle, 1975; Bailey, 1980; Bradley, Fargo, and Shettle, 1981; Kieft, 1977; Ottervik, 1979; Suslow, 1977). Like the faculty models, these models tend to be institution-specific and use a variety of mathematical techniques. Published reports describe their use at one institution but do not evaluate it. Similar accounts have been published in the areas of course scheduling (Dyer and Mulvey, 1977) and departmental budgeting (Masters and Munsterman, 1975).

Modeling has not been without criticism. Kirschling (1976) summarized many of the shortcomings of models while also describing their benefits. Models can create the illusion of certainty, their builders may make unrealistic claims, they can be too technically oriented for most users, and model builders and users can have trouble communicating, thus aggravating other problems. Despite all of these problems, however, many believe that successful models are possible (Porter, Zemsky, and Oedel, 1979).

The literature on models demonstrates that model builders and users have made progress recently. Model builders have learned that the decision process is not the same at all colleges and universities and that models need to be institution-specific (Wiseman, 1979). Institutions, for example, may use unique budgeting processes, have unusual personnel policies, have different state funding formulas, or offer special academic programs. Factors such as these can limit the utility of standardized models. There currently is a shift from the large comprehensive models to smaller interactive models and modeling systems, such as EFPM and microcomputer spreadsheet software, that allow decision makers to custom-build models for particular problems (McNeish, 1982; Mayo and Kallio, 1983; Sandin, 1977). Because the decision maker often builds the model or is part of a team that builds it, modeling is more successful. Changes in computer technology are partly responsible for this trend. Increasing sophistication among administrative computer users is also responsible.

Decision Support Systems

A decision support system (DSS) is an evolutionary step from MIS and modeling (Alter, 1976, 1980; Keen and Scott Morton, 1978). A DSS focuses on unstructured tasks in which the user guides the system through analytic questions. It is used on an *ad hoc* basis as the need arises rather than on a routine or predetermined schedule. It reflects the personal needs and style of the decision maker. A DSS is built from the administrator's perspective to support, not replace judgment (Alter, 1980; Chachra and Heterick, 1982; Keen, 1982; Keen and Scott Morton, 1978). Such systems can include sophisticated analytic techniques and may tap large organizational data bases. But their personal nature makes them less remote to the user. Because of its expanded uses and user-defined capabilities, EFPM crosses the boundary between a model and a DSS. Thus a DSS is a logical step from the small personal modeling systems discussed in the previous section and reflects the evolutionary trend toward the use of institutional data resources.

There has been little written to date about DSS use on the college and university campus. Like the early literature on MIS and models, what has appeared usually recounts one campus's experience with a DSS. Examples include using DSS for enrollment forecasting (Pope and Cross, 1982), as a generalized tool for administrators (Doty and Krumrey, 1982), and for institutional research (Sheehan, 1982). Each of these applications might have been called MIS or modeling a few years ago and illustrates the trend toward the latest in administrative computing techniques. There is a subtle distinction, however, between evolving techniques and changes in terminology. Some institutions may adopt new terminology without any accompanying changes in technique.

In a study of 56 business organizations using DSS, Alter (1976) found that managers use the systems to improve their effectiveness. But defining the impact of a DSS is a difficult task. Alter reported that users valued the systems for benefits other than those they originally expected. Managers used their DSS as tools of persuasion or as aids to communication, for example. Other possible benefits may become apparent as DSS is more widely used and evaluated. Keen and Scott Morton (1978) listed several other areas where benefits might be observed, including decision outputs, changes in the decision process, changes in managers' concepts of the decision situation, and procedural changes. Keen (1980, 1982) has also suggested, however, that DSS benefits may be qualitative in nature and thus difficult to measure. The systems may facilitate better decisions, yet not cause improvements in efficiency or effectiveness directly. Those trying to save dollars or replace staff through a DSS may not see such explicit benefits. Identifying the influence of DSS implementation is a clear research need. Administrators should know what to expect of these systems before beginning the implementation process.

Two studies (Masland, 1984; Welsch, 1980) defined DSS success in terms of two elements: the degree to which administrators had internalized the system or regarded it as an integral part of the decision-making process, and whether or not they had institutionalized it or regarded it as a permanent fixture in the organization. Masland (1984) found that, using this definition, EFPM was successful on many campuses. Administrators judged it useful and effective at 64% of the campuses, 76% felt it improved the decision-making process, and 43% agreed that their institution relied on EFPM. While success is evident, it is not certain at every institution using administrative tools such as a DSS.

Office Automation
A fifth administrative application is in the area of office automation. This is a much more diffuse set of applications than those previously discussed. As Staman (1981) stated, "Office automation has become a euphemism for many requirements and functions, some unique to the office environment" (p. 2). In general, office automation refers to any task in the administrator's office environment that can be or has been computerized. Tasks commonly included are electronic preparation, editing, filing, and distribution of text and mail. In a report for Harvard University, the consulting firm of Arthur D. Little predicted that by 1990 administrative offices would have display telephones, document creation and retrieval terminals, communicating copiers, teleconferencing facilities, minicomputers connected to central data bases, and intra-building and intra-university networks as standard equipment. These changes should lead to increased effectiveness (Withington, 1981). But office automation is more than a list of possible tasks and equipment. It is "an attitude, a commitment to a new way of thinking about the office and its processes. It is dynamic and ongoing, a continued re-evaluation process which governs the cost-effective and productive use of human resources and equipment" (Ganus and Sherron, 1983).

Because office automation is a relatively new area of computer application on many campuses, relatively little literature describes or evaluates it. Carlson (1980), for example, described one institution's pilot project in office automation. The article does not discuss the outcome of the project, however. Boynton (1982) outlined the process of automating one department.

The Terminals for Managers program at Stanford University is an exception which serves as a valuable example of combining administrative computer applications with a research agenda. Stanford designed the program to educate executives in information technology and to provide useful management-oriented tools for those executives (Bennet, 1983). The program was also based on four premises: (1) it was more important to provide many users with basic capabilities than provide complex capabilities to a few users, (2) the entry price should be relatively low, (3) the expected useful life of the system should be five to six years, and (4) writing and communicating by messages had the broadest application (Sandelin, 1981). CONTACT/EMS, the first major project, is the system Stanford developed to meet these objectives (Bennett, 1983).

As part of the project Stanford is evaluating the Terminals for Managers program (Bennett, 1983; Rice and Case, 1983). Approximately 100 managers were involved in the initial stages of the project. They averaged 4.5 messages a day on the system, although 25% of the users sent over 10 messages a day. Asked to evaluate the system after two to five months of use, the managers clearly felt the system was more useful for some tasks than others. Table 2 shows the percentage of users who felt the system was useful for different tasks. Using the system reduced the number of phone calls made and received for about three-quarters of the managers and reduced the paper produced and received for about half of the managers. Approximately 45% thought the quantity of their work increased, and about 30% reported an increase in the quality of their work. Finally, slightly over 40% thought that their work would be difficult or very difficult to do without the system (Rice and Case, 1983). Thus many of the administrators using the system at Stanford felt there were benefits after only short exposure to the system. Because the Stanford program is a pilot project, however, the results may not be generalized to other campuses.

TABLE 2. Percentage of Administrators Who Feel Electronic Mail Is Appropriate for Different Tasks

Tasks	Percentage of Administrators
Exchanging information	100
Asking questions	95
Exchanging opinions	81
Staying in touch	84
Generating ideas	73
Decision making	47
Exchanging confidential information	30
Bargaining or negotiating	18
Resolving disagreements	15
Getting to know someone	15

Source. Rice and Case, 1983, p. 138.

Office automation promises to be a major thrust of administrative computing in the near future. It is part of the move from distant computing applications to those that are user-specific and useful in nonroutine tasks. Office automation illustrates the trend toward the management of data resources for top administrators. It also reflects the ongoing concern with developing and improving systems so that they are as useful as possible to administrators. The question is not whether colleges and universities will address the issues of technology but when they will do so.

Improving Administrative Applications

In addition to the descriptive and evaluative discussions in the literature, researchers and administrators have compiled numerous suggestions on how to improve the implementation of administrative systems. This literature reflects a perceived dichotomy between systems and users (McKenney and Keen, 1974). The systems approach in the literature suggests how to improve administrative computing software and facilitate its implementation. While occasionally based on formal evaluations, these suggestions more often arise from personal experience in designing, implementing, or using administrative systems. Another approach studies administrators and their behavior so that administrative systems can more directly meet decision makers' real needs.

The literature from the systems approach discusses either technical or organizational issues (Masland, 1983). Early models, for example, often suffered from technical problems such as a lack of accurate and complete data upon which to base their projections (Johnstone, 1974). Applications based on historical data built past inaccuracies into their solutions (Hopkins, 1971). Wartgow (1973) also noted that access to accurate data increased reliance on resource allocation models. Some system designers tended to apply the same solution to every administrative problem whether or not it was appropriate (Enarson, 1975). And structurally rigid systems did not meet the individual needs of decision makers (Adams, Kellogg, and Schroeder, 1976). Early administrative systems tended to be complex "black boxes" that users did not understand. This too decreased the success of the systems (Updegrove, 1982). Finally, many administrators still do not have the knowledge and skills necessary to use administrative systems (Byrne and Kardonsky, 1983).

As experience with models expanded, more technically accurate administrative systems became available to decision makers but the systems still did not have a significant impact on higher education (Gray, 1977). In addition to the technical issues, there were a number of organizational and behavioral problems. As Keen (1978) stated, "Technical competence . . . in no way compensates for resolution of behavioral issues" (p. 38). One of the most basic organizational problems, for example, was a lack of communication and trust between system builders and users (Kirschling, 1976).

A number of authors advocated improving the implementation process by using the principles of organizational change (Alter, 1976; Gaunt and Haight, 1977; Zund and Sorensen, 1975). Two studies (Masland, 1984; Welsh, 1980) applied the concept of organizational change to the implementation of DSS and found that the active presence of a change agent improved the likelihood of successful implementation. Such an individual both facilitated use of the DSS and interpreted the technical aspects of the system.

Evaluation is another crucial aspect of improving the success of administrative computing applications, yet it is often lacking. Keen (1975) suggested that evaluation should be part of the implementation process so that appropriate changes can be made in the model. Schroeder (1977) took this one step further with his suggestion for a "life cycle" approach to management systems design. Schroeder proposed that the design process should include six steps: (1) develop the project plan, (2) study present subsystems, (3) recommend improved subsystems, (4) develop subsystems, (5) implement the subsystems, and (6) evaluate the subsystems during their operation. The sixth step leads directly back to the first stage in a continuous process of development and improvement.

Recently the concept of prototyping has encompassed the suggestions discussed above. In prototyping, system builders quickly produce a working model of an administrative system without extensive analysis of requirements. Decision makers can then work with the system to determine if it meets their needs. The process is iterative, with builders modifying the prototype until administrators are satisfied with it. This method replaces efficiency in system design with effectiveness. A prototyped system should be more successful in practice because users have actively directed its construction (Alter, 1976; Henderson and Ingraham, 1982). Prototyping meets the need for tailor-made systems which overcome technical problems and many of the behavioral issues (Adams, Kellogg, and Schroeder, 1976). While not labeled prototyping, Teeter and Stolz (1981) described the benefits of involving administrators in the process of first building simple interactive models before building complex models. A simpler technique is to let executives identify those pieces of information that are critical to the organization's success and their work. Then the information system should be built around these "critical success factors" (Rockhart, 1979).

Many of the observations about improving administrative systems are easily translated into practical suggestions for increasing the likelihood of success. Some of these come from formal research and evaluation efforts while others are found in descriptive or normative literature. Yet the similarity of the suggestions from many sources increases their validity. Table 3 lists many common recommendations found in the literature. They reflect both the technical and organizational observations discussed above.

The second major approach to improving administrative applications is to better comprehend the role and function of administrative personnel who use the system. According to this perspective, understanding decision making should lead to administrative systems that are more congruent with administrators' real needs. This approach is quite different from that of an early model builder who stated: "Few university administrators are accustomed to using the type and volume of information that can be provided by a good systems analysis group. Certain changes in managerial style of thinking are necessary before this information can be used to best advantage" (Levine, 1969, p. 65).

The first task for this approach is to understand the functions of administrators. Quite often their duties do not fit the classic model of planning, organizing, staffing, directing, coordinating, reporting, and budgeting (Mintzberg, 1972). Instead of performing these typically assumed duties, many managers spend their days in brief, discontinuous tasks that are action oriented. They have frequent exceptions to normal duties. They favor verbal media and spend 78% of their time communicating with others (Mintzberg, 1975). This is quite different from the image of administrators who spend a majority of their time in planning activities that can benefit from administrative systems (Adams, 1975).

TABLE 3. Recommendations for Model Implementation

1. Define the model's goals explicitly.
2. Use accurate data representative of the institution.
3. Express input and output in familiar format.
4. Build a model that readily displays the effects of policy alternatives.
5. Learn to use the model effectively.
6. Develop the expertise to manage and update the model.
7. Involve potential users in the development process.
8. Gain a broad base of support.
9. Start simple and keep it simple.
10. Put a manager, not a modeler, in charge.
11. Define roles clearly.
12. In the early stages use established organizational procedures.
13. View model development as a process, not a product.
14. Use knowledge of organizational change to facilitate organizational issues.
15. Find an executive "Godfather" to support the process.
16. Use training and in-service education.

Source. Arns, 1978; Baldridge and Tierney, 1979; Hammond, 1974; Keen, 1978; Wartgow, 1973; Wyatt, Emery, and Landis, 1979.

From this perspective there are a number of questions to answer: What do administrators actually do with data (Schroeder, 1973)? What level of detail is necessary for them? And when do data become useful information for the decision maker (McCorkle, 1977; Schmidtlein, 1977)? Answers to these questions are not straightforward, but without accurate answers administrators may have to use ineffective systems. System designers may forget that administrators are sophisticated information processors themselves and that getting information rapidly may be more important than absolute accuracy. Current information is vital (Mintzberg, 1972). These characteristics conflict with formal management systems and may reduce reliance on them.

About 20% to 30% of administrators' information comes from informal sources and cannot be placed in computer systems (Adams, 1975). Current systems do not take these information needs into account. While it may be an impossible task to do so, Mitroff, Nelson, and Mason (1974) suggested that administrators need a Myth-MIS which would present information in an informal story form. Presentation of information in this format might increase its usefulness.

There is also evidence that administrators do not follow rational decision-making models. Leavitt (1975) suggested that analytic methods, particularly those of management science, should not necessarily be equated with good thinking. Lindblom (1959) and Rowe (1974) went beyond this to suggest managers do not apply the rational decision-making process in their work. If managers do not practice the rational analytic method, administrative systems designed around it will not be successful (Masland, 1983).

Another part of the literature examines individual characteristics and how they affect the evaluation of MIS (Zmud, 1979). The literature shows that individual differences among managers in cognitive style, personality traits, demographics, and situational factors influence MIS success. In the area of cognitive style, for example, field-independent subjects seek more detailed, aggregated, and quantitative information. Decision makers with an internal locus of control, low degree of dogmatism, and high risk-taking propensity undertake greater information search activities. Unfortunately, however, the specific relationships among these factors remain unclear and more research is necessary. Zmud's review highlights the problems inherent in evaluating MIS. A system and its success are situation- and decision-maker-specific. It is difficult to make broad generalizations about the success of MIS when there are so many intervening factors.

Rice and Case (1983) reported that individual "media styles" influenced administrators' use and evaluation of an electric mail and text system. Media style is a measure of an individual's preference of various communication media such as writing, telephoning, personal contact, and electronic mail. Some offices and departments at Stanford made greater use of electronic mail, most likely because of the nature of their job and communication requirements (Business and Finance had the highest level of use). The media style which made greatest use of the system also included not preferring writing, not preferring the telephone, and indifference to personal contact or using the electronic system. These results suggest that system builders should consider the individual characteristics of managers when building and evaluating administrative applications. Researchers must continue to discover those factors and how they influence administrative computing.

A Myth-MIS may be an extreme reaction, but the fact remains that administrators will not use systems that do not reflect their needs. As systems become more personal, as reflected in DSS and office automation, it is likely that success will improve. But even the best technical support systems cannot make good managers; they can simply help good administrators function more effectively (Lyon, 1981).

III. MANAGING ADMINISTRATIVE COMPUTING

A small body of literature describes approaches to managing administrative computing. This material is of interest for several reasons: administrators must manage their computer resources; managerial policy influences computer use; and changes in managerial policy often reflect the evolution of administrative applications. Once again, much of the literature describes one campus's method of organizing and controlling computer resources. Another approach includes normative discussions of which method is best. There are also surveys of current managerial practices at a number of institutions. Throughout this literature three key elements of managerial practice and policy emerge: personnel, facilities, and resource allocation. They are described below. (This discussion is largely taken from Masland, 1982.) While presented as distinct options, the elements are used in many combinations to suit individual needs. As noted in the conclusion of this section, most of the literature was written before the widespread introduction of microcomputers. The proliferation of personal computing dramatically changes some of the issues of managing computer resources.

Personnel

Personnel structure is one element of managing computer resources. The literature discusses who manages the computer and where the manager fits within the institution. One option is a computer-center director (Robbins, Dorn, and Skelton, 1975). Such an individual, both a technician and manager, is responsible for day-to-day operation of the computer center. The director often serves as the administration's technical adviser for policy decisions. He or she can report to a number of positions, including the president and either the chief academic or administrative officer.

At a higher organizational level responsibility can lie with a "computer czar" (Mosmann, 1973). Such an individual is an academic officer who understands technical issues but who is not a technician. The czar coordinates and controls all computer operations on a campus through control of computer policy and budgets. A vice-presidential title is possible, but even without the title a czar may report to the president. The primary distinction between a computer czar and a computer-center director is that the former is usually placed higher in the administrative structure and has less involvement in the daily operation of the computer center. A czar is an administrator for computing and other technologies, while a computer-center director manages the resource, runs the computer, and advises decision makers. A czar is more typically found at larger institutions but appears to becoming more popular as technology's role on the campus expands. This reflects the move toward top management representation of computer resources that stage theories suggest.

Management by committee is another alternative (Robbins, Dorn, and Skelton, 1975). The committee's members can include individuals from all segments of the institution. While a committee may appoint a manager to handle the day-to-day operation, ultimate responsibility lies with the committee. In this sense the committee is equivalent to the computer czar because it is responsible for policy and control but not actual operation. The committee approach may prove burdensome because of problems inherent in the committee process: reaching a consensus may be difficult, decision making may be slow, and one or two knowledgeable individuals may exert a powerful influence over the committee.

Committees are more commonly used in an advisory capacity. Two types exist (Cloward, 1971; Mosmann, 1973). The first, which advises a computer czar, consists of high-level administrators and representatives of users. Its role is to review policy and planning. The committee can provide powerful support for a czar. The second type of committee is a users' committee which meets with a director of computing to discuss common problems and needs. It is a means of two-way communication between the computer-center director and users.

Two additional personnel structures are less common (Robbins, Dorn, and Skelton, 1975). An institution can hire an outside professional team to manage equipment owned by the institution. Or it can create a separate corporate identity to provide computer resources. These approaches place the burden of day-to-day management elsewhere and may resolve some internal conflicts over computing. But both approaches also present some new problems. Long-term commitments may limit flexibility and remove incentives for meeting institutional needs.

In addition to managerial personnel, successful management of computer resources depends on support personnel (Gellman, 1975). The cost of the staff often exceeds the expense of computer hardware and software (Mann, 1979). The availability and accessibility of computer-center support staff influence the use of computing (Masland, 1982). User-oriented computer-center personnel actively encourage computer use among campus groups that otherwise might not use the resource. A major problem, however, is retention of capable staff. In the data-processing industry, the annual turnover rate is about 29% (LeDuc, 1981). In addition to the loss of personnel, a high turnover rate causes problems with retraining, missed deadlines, and low morale.

Facilities

There are several traditional approaches for organizing computer facilities. The first technical structure is the centralized computer facility, in which one computer is available for all users on campus. Such arrangements were common for second-generation computers because of their size and expense (Robbins, Dorn, and Skelton, 1975; Swoyer, 1980b). Centralized systems are still found at many schools, but today they may also support remote terminals or more than one computer. The major argument for centralized systems has always been that one system is more efficient to operate. Historically, computing power followed Grosch's Law: the unit cost of computational power varied inversely with system costs (Mosmann, 1973). Roughly speaking, if system A cost twice as much as System B, it was four times as powerful. Thus economy of scale was one of the key arguments for centralized operations. A centralized system has also traditionally provided greater personnel support for users. System programmers, analysts, and user support staffs tended to be more efficiently managed when centralized (Ralston, 1971).

As computers have become smaller and cheaper there is a growing tendency toward decentralized facilities (Staman, 1979; Swoyer, 1980b). Under such an arrangement more than one computer center is available on the campus. Critics have felt that there is no real advantage in the economy-of-scale argument (Roberts, 1971). Some faculty members with research grants have also wanted to purchase their own computers. Lower cost and increased capabilities of microcomputers have promoted even greater decentralization of computer resources. Proliferation rather than decentralization is often a more accurate term (Withington, 1980). Personnel in centralized facilities, however, may oppose proliferation if they view it as a threat to their position (Patton, 1981). Centralized facilities may find, however, that demand on their services increases as new users want greater capabilities than are possible on microcomputers. There are also a number of tasks, such as large computational programs, database storage, and high-speed printing, for which a centralized facility is best suited (Emery, 1978; Masat, 1981).

Another reason for decentralized facilities arises from the disparate needs of computer users. When administrative and academic users share one facility, the computer center often becomes the focal point for hostilities between the two groups. While technical problems do not preclude combining administrative and academic tasks on one system, they remain separate at many institutions. Each user group distrusts the other and often believes it is not receiving its "fair share" of computer resources. The merit of combining administrative and academic functions is still an issue of debate (Mann, 1979; Masat, 1981). There is evidence, however, that it is less of a problem than it once was. In a recent survey (Thomas, 1981), 69% of the responding institutions reported combined administrative and academic central facilities. Separate operations were more commonly reported at large institutions.

A third technical structure is networking. This term is used in many ways, but here it means the use of telecommunications to access a computer facility that is geographically removed from the user's institution. Under a networking relationship one user or institution uses computer services provided by another institution, association, or commercial vendor (Cornew and Morse, 1975; McCredie and Timlake, 1983; Miller, 1979; Mosmann, 1980). This has become increasingly feasible in recent years through advances in telecommunications (Heller, 1981). In many parts of the country, users may now gain access to a multitude of computers through a local telephone number. Edunet is one example of a provider of such services.

For some institutions networking is a low-cost means of providing basic computer services. It also can meet specialized needs (Miller, 1979; Mosmann,

1980). Institutions might use networking, for example, to take advantage of specialized software such as EFPM. Thus networking often supplements an institution's own computing resources. For many specialized users this is more cost-effective than purchasing a machine or software package.

Networking and telecommunications have recently received increased attention. Institutions have realized that in addition to linking decentralized computers or tying into national computer networks, they must plan for other communication needs. Several authors have described how institutions have dealt with the problem of combining voice, data, and video communication (Gillespie, 1983; McCredie, 1983; Tucker, 1983; Welling, 1983). This issue is often raised because of changing telephone needs and the divestiture of AT&T. Campuses now realize that telecommunication is a major expense and deserves close attention. These factors focus attention on the management of computer facilities and how data communication needs relate to other communication problems. Unfortunately, the need for adequate planning and attention is not recognized by some campuses, especially those with more immediate crises. Other than the brief discussions in the few case studies mentioned above, there has been little written in the area of telecommunications and the relationship between computing and other campus needs. The area deserves further attention.

Facilities management includes more than the hardware configuration. Users also need software resources for their work. One issue in this area is whether or not an institution should purchase software from vendors or develop its own software in-house. As discussed in the section on administrative applications, some early users of models found it was difficult to adapt standard modeling packages to their individual needs (Farmer et al., 1978). Unfortunately, software development is expensive and time-consuming. Recently there has been a greater choice in commercial software available for administrative tasks. This is particularly true for microcomputers where the packages designed for business management are transferable to the college or university environment. The problem then becomes selecting the proper software to meet local administrative needs (McNeish, 1982). There have not been any recent evaluations of user satisfaction comparing commercial software products to software designed in-house. With the greater availability of commercial software more institutions may choose that approach. It would be useful to know how their experiences compare to those who develop their own software.

Allocation Policy

A third issue in the managerial literature is allocation of computer resources among competing users. When there is an abundance of computer power available, allocation is not a problem: enough slack exists to meet the needs of all users (Nolan, 1979). When slack is not present, a more common situation, control of the resource becomes important, and allocation is one means of exerting control. Allocation policy is also a means of recovering the costs of operating the computer facility by charging users for the resources they consume.

These two factors, control and cost recovery, are the driving forces behind allocation policy. But a stable allocation policy also is the user's guarantee of the availability and cost of computer resources (Mosmann, 1973).

Before describing various allocation methods, it is helpful to briefly review the computer resources they control: (1) central system resources, including central processing unit (CPU) time, memory, and time required for input/output requests; (2) unit record peripherals, such as card readers, punches, and printers; (3) data storage devices, including disks and tapes; (4) terminals or ports (terminal connections); (5) personnel resources, such as operator requests for tape mounts and printer paper changes, or analyst and programmer support; and (6) supplies (Bernard et al., 1977).

Three basic methods of allocating computer resources are free access, restrictions on use, and chargeback. Free access is the simplest: its philosophy is that all users should have as much computing as they need. The institution carries the cost of computing and overhead. A free-access policy is often justified by comparison to libraries, which do not charge users according to the number of books they check out or the number of requests they make of the reference desk. Others have argued that the incremental cost of one library user is insignificant, while one computer user could monopolize the system (Ohio Board of Regents, 1973). Free access, however, removes a possible obstacle to computer use. Because users may not know in advance the value of computer resources in their work, they are unable to determine if charges for computer resources are reasonable. Hence they may not use the computer (Luehrmann, 1973).

As users realize the power of computing, they consume more of the resource (Diehr, 1976). This problem leads to ever increasing demands which can be met only through additional or more powerful equipment. If resources remain constant, demand will outstrip supply and users will not be satisfied. Once slack resources disappear, allocation policy becomes "first come, first served" and free access is not a fair method of allocation. Users have no way of knowing what they can reasonably expect of the system, and managers have no means of controlling the resource. The loss of slack resources may also slow the evolutionary growth of administrative applications because computing becomes less reliable and more expensive.

Restricting or rationing use, a second allocation policy, resolves some of the problems associated with free access. Under a system of restrictions, users still receive computer resources free of charge but their access is limited in one or more ways. Users may be restricted to one or two hours of connect time, for example. Other common illustrations are limiting each user's disk storage or the amount of memory used during execution of a program. Another type of limitation is the use of priority categories. Under this scheme computer personnel can delineate various classes of users. High-priority users might receive a greater share of CPU time, while low-priority jobs might run overnight or on weekends. Restrictions are on a continuum from less restrictive, such as limited disk storage space, to more restrictive, such as limited connect time. A reasonable rationing policy which is not too restrictive gives users a better idea of the availability of the resources while at the same time slowing the growth of demand.

A third basic allocation policy is chargeback, or making users pay for the resources they consume. Varying the cost of using different system resources controls demand: raising the price lowers demand (Nielsen, 1970). A chargeback system must meet several objectives if it is to serve its purpose well. The user must respond to it. Chargeback systems can become so complicated that the user cannot understand how costs are derived (Hootman, 1969; Khtaian, 1976; Nolan, 1977). The user should only pay for the resources that are under his or her control. And the cost of running a particular job should not depend on characteristics of other programs that are running at the same time. Complex chargeback systems also make demands on system accounting programs, and thus may consume substantial portions of computer resources themselves. Government regulations concerning sponsored research may further complicate pricing structures (Kanter, Moore, and Singer, 1968).

Chargeback structures also vary according to the specific methods of charging users. Charges can be in actual dollars. Each user, class, or department can budget a given dollar value to spend on computing. The user pays for the resources consumed. Such a scheme puts computing on a par with other budgeted items. Administrative policy may limit spending to on-campus computing. Or it may permit users to spend funds for on-campus resources, off-campus service bureaus, or computer purchases. Budgeting in real dollars may be difficult for the computer-center director, however. Most computer costs are fixed. Under such a scheme, the computer center's income depends on demand and thus may be unpredictable.

An alternative to budgeting in real dollars is to budget in another "resource unit." Under this scheme users receive internal dollars or a number of resource units used for accounting and control. Users cannot trade "funny money," as such units are often called, for real budget dollars or noncomputing resources. This method may not be effective if users treat funny money differently from other types of resources. But it still reminds them of the value of the scarce resource that they are consuming (Brink, 1971). Under this scheme the institution may calculate the computing budget separately, solving the problem of uncertain income for the computer-center director.

Administrators may combine the different allocation policies mentioned above. Priority classes may restrict access, or they can be part of the pricing structure, with users deciding to pay more for higher-priority service. Restrictions may control access, and a simple pricing scheme, such as charging for connect hours, may recover costs. Different organizational levels may operate under different allocation policies. An institution that participates in a network, for example, may pay for connect hours and include that item in the institutional budget, but individual users may never see the connect-hour charge and behave as if it were a free-access system.

The final aspect of allocation policy is the question of who decides which allocation method an institution should follow. While allocation may appear to be a purely technical problem, there are policy implications (Gellman, 1975; Mosmann, 1973). When viewed as part of the institution's educational philosophy, decision making at a high administrative level is appropriate (Mosmann and Stefferud, 1971). The global view allows consideration of overall organizational goals. But top administrators often lack the detailed technical knowledge necessary for such decisions. Users might like to make the allocation decisions, but they typically lack the necessary objectivity. And the computer-center director, who has both the technical knowledge and a sense of user needs, may lack perspective on organizational goals. Consultation among these groups or the use of an advisory committee often is the best solution (Nielsen, 1970).

Other Management Issues
The proliferation of microcomputers changes some of the management issues and problems that past research raised. While technology has placed the computer in the user's office, questions about needed central facilities remain. New problems arise about networks and communication needs. Administrators must decide if one office should try to coordinate purchases so that all institutional equipment is compatible. And centralized service contracts may be cost-effective for maintenance. Personnel needs may also shift. Users may need access to local experts who can quickly answer questions and solve problems. This may involve training a large number of individuals. As office personnel learn to use new equipment they may ask for compensation commensurate with new skills. Allocation may now mean adjusting budgets to allow individual units or departments to purchase microcomputers just as they would purchase other types of office equipment. At the local level, however, questions of access and scheduling may remain if demand exceeds the capacity of available computer resources. Thus, while proliferation of microcomputers may solve some management problems, it introduces new one. This may be one reason for the apparent increase in the number of computer czars.

The competing needs of computer users further complicates the management issue. In most cases users need services rather than specific types of equipment or facilities (Masat, 1981; Mosmann, 1973). These include the capability to perform required tasks, special software, access to facilities, reasonable response time, reliability and predictability of service, security or protection of stored data and programs, and personnel support. Users' needs may be mutually exclusive. Increasing access, for example, may decrease security. For data-processing tasks that are prescheduled, such as payroll, reliability and maintaining a schedule are critical. Office automation requires quick and local access if users are to rely on it. Management information systems present conflicting needs of data access and security. Managing computer resources often means reaching compromises on issues such as these. Typically the only evidence on how different management solutions affect administrative use are the observations of computer-center directors reflecting upon their own operation. There is little information which would permit comparison of various methods.

Evaluation and planning are common problems in managing computer resources, regardless of personnel, facilities, and allocation policy. The fact that evaluation and planning often involve both technical matters and policy issues complicates their resolution. But effective evaluation does not have to be complex. Measuring how long users must wait to get on the system or how many jobs can run at one time are simple evaluation techniques. Monitoring performance to determine bottlenecks in the existing system configuration is an example of a more technical evaluation (Enger, 1976).

Planning is closely related to evaluation. It is difficult to plan for future needs without first understanding current system performance. Today planning for computer resources frequently involves many technologies as diverse as video and telephone systems (Adams, 1982). Evaluation and planning are technical in nature, but they also involve basic policy issues. The institution must decide what level of performance is acceptable and if expansion is within financial means or exceeds desired service levels.

In sum, institutions must attend to the problems and issues of managing their computer resources. In addition to adequate facilities, they must ensure that there are personnel to support administrative computing and an allocation policy compatible with institutional goals. Computer resources must mesh closely with other technologies on the campus, particularly in the area of telecommunications. Because of the rapid changes in technology and the proliferation of microcomputers, past managerial policies may no longer be effective. Further investigation of this area is crucial, especially in light of the institutional resources, both time and money, it consumes.

IV. IMPLICATIONS OF ADMINISTRATIVE APPLICATIONS

As discussed in the first section of this chapter, a number of researchers have proposed stage theories to describe the evolution of computer use and management in organizations. Introducing computing seems to set in motion a process that moves a college or university from primitive and limited uses in data processing to more advanced applications such as modeling, decision support systems, and office automation. There is an underlying trend in all of the proposed stage theories from a data and control orientation to an information perspective where the emphasis shifts to what the computer can do for the users. This section reviews the changes in organizational structure and decision making related to increasingly sophisticated computer use. It also notes the influence of changing technology and how this may affect colleges and universities in the foreseeable future. Finally, the section suggests some of the problems that may arise from the apparent trends.

Organizational Changes

There is some evidence that smaller colleges are more resistant to technological change than larger institutions (Davis and Emery, 1978). It is also apparent, however, that the changes technology produces will eventually affect organizations of every size ("How to Use Advanced Technology," 1979; Mann, 1982). All organizations are likely to benefit from advances in administrative computing. It is only a question of when this occurs. Strange (1983) has predicted that the organizational changes accompanying technological advances will be the most profound changes on the campus — more than those in academic areas. What will these changes entail? On a basic level there are apt to be shifts in organizational structure and the alignments among different groups on the campus. The geographic location of organizational units will become less important. Travel will also diminish as information needs change and data sharing becomes easier ("How to Use Advanced Technology," 1979; Mann, 1982; Withington, 1980).

Of more interest, however, are trends in decision making and the campus power structure. Researchers and administrators have long recognized that information translates into power, and administrative computing systems can provide new information or better information to decision makers (Foreman, 1974). Introduction of administrative systems thus redirects the flow of information in an organization and may threaten the status and power of decision makers (Strassman, 1980).

A fundamental change is possible, for example, in the degree of centralization or decentralization in an organization. In the early 1970s the literature predicted that computerized data bases would produce an increase in centralization. The implicit hypothesis was that centralized and accurate data would lead to centralized decision making. As a campus ties together separate administrative systems there is a tendency to build a strong centralized data base to ensure that all decision makers share common data definitions and elements (Wise, 1979). In a 1974 survey of 442 institutions using computer-based information systems, 41% of the respondents thought there was an increased degree of centralization of decisions by top administrators (Mann et al., 1975). Baldridge (1979) reported centralization of decision making in colleges and universities which used management information systems. He found that the systems put information into the hands of administrators who could devote the time to studying and using it. Baldridge also found, however, that the degree of centralization was not as strong as expected.

Subsequent investigations reported that administrative systems bring a better balance between centralization and decentralization ("How to Use Advanced Technology," 1979; Mann, 1982). As data become an organizational resource there can be a breakdown of traditional functional divisions if information is shared among those who can use it. Administrative systems can also enhance information sharing in policy discussions. Ottervik (1979) reported that public access to a modeling system and data increased participation in the decision-making process. It allowed various campus constituencies to understand how and why administrators made decisions.

The most recent predictions are that administrative systems will result in de-centralization of power and decision making (Strange, 1983). This is a logical continuation of the trend in the research literature. It reflects the stage theories, which predict that more advanced systems will focus on use rather than control of information. Decentralization is apparent, for example, in sophisticated decision support systems that take advantage of individual use of centralized data bases. It reflects more personalized computer technology that can use central-ized data resources through communication abilities. Thus organizational changes may be tied to technological changes. As campuses expand their ad-ministrative computing facilities, possible shifts in organizational structure and function deserve further attention.

Technological Changes

While the chapter's introduction summarized the technological changes which have occurred on the campus since the introduction of computing in the 1950s, recent developments have a direct influence on the implications of administra-tive computing and so are worth discussing here. The key to the new technology is its distributed nature. Microcomputers and personal workstations have put advanced computer power on many executives' desks. An administrator can now retrieve information, for example, instead of relying on assistants or a data-processing department to provide reports ("How to Use Advanced Tech-nology," 1979; McCredie, 1983; Withington, 1980). Frequently personal com-puters are tied to central facilities through a network on the campus and to other universities through regional or national networks. Networks have ex-panded at a tremendous rate in the past few years to meet administrators' needs. They now permit administrators to communicate by electronic mail and to share institutional data ("Data Sharing Funded by Exxon," 1983; "Mailnet Service Launched," 1983; McCredie and Timlake, 1983). It is not yet clear how data sharing will influence administrative actions and effectiveness.

The stage theories predict these trends, although perhaps not the actual de-tails of the changes. There is greater interest in what administrative systems can do for decision makers rather than how they work. This is apparent in DSS and office automation applications. The systems are useful in daily activities and there is more interest in evaluating the success of the systems in terms of how administrators interact with them.

Recent technical changes also affect the management of computer resources on the campus. This is obvious in the shift toward more decentralized facilities. Other management changes are also likely and are already observable in colleges and universities known for their exemplary use of computer resources (McCredie, 1983). These trends include having a single individual coordinate computing on the campus (a computer czar); planning to integrate microcomputers into existing computer resources; developing local and national networks; automating library functions; studying the needs and requirements for computer literacy among various campus constituencies; viewing text processing as an integral part of administrative computing needs; and building electronic mail systems.

Advances in computer technology, however, are not without side effects. A fundamental problem is the cost of technology. Although hardware costs continue to decline, personnel and software consume an increasing proportion of computer budgets, and this constrains an institution's options (Swoyer, 1980a). Another battle is for the scarce computer resources on campuses. Most institutions cannot afford an infinite supply of computing. Because changing current technology is costly, many colleges and universities take an incremental approach. But integrating the successive waves of technological change is expensive (Mann, 1982). Some campuses may find that coordinating each office's purchases is a nearly impossible task or that proliferation means incompatibility among different systems on the campus (Mann, 1982).

Centralized data bases and networking also raise new questions and issues (McCredie and Timlake, 1983). One example is security. Institutions must take steps to ensure that sensitive systems are secure from either intentional or unintentional damage. If more decision makers maintain their own personal data bases, the accuracy of the information they use may decline. Separate data bases may also mean unique definitions of data elements and lack of comparibility among each administrator's or department's information.

Thus a few implications of new technolgoy and administrative systems are clear. Administrative applications are becoming more personal and more flexible in nature. They still access institutional data but they do it in a greater number of ways permitting individual analyses of information. Administrative systems are less remote in another sense because they are available for more common administrative tasks such as communication through electronic mail and text-processing applications. It is not yet clear how these new applications will affect the office. There could be major shifts in the duties and employment of office support staff, for example. The process is difficult to control, and the major question becomes when and how an institution will participate in changing use of administrative systems, not whether it will do so.

V. A FUTURE AGENDA

There is a substantial body of literature about administrative computing written in the past two decades. As the previous discussion demonstrates, the literature has a practical orientation. It is also apparent that in many areas the current state of administrative computing has not advanced very far. Many questions and issues remain. This section first briefly summarizes the characteristics of the current literature and examines its orientation. It then outlines some of the major issues that are not yet understood. Finally, it highlights several vital questions for researchers and administrators to answer as they continue to explore and use administrative computing systems.

Current Knowlege

What is known about administrative computing comes from the accumulated knowledge found in many descriptive accounts of using and managing computer resources. There are also normative discussions of how a college or university ought to use and manage computers. And there is a substantial set of recommendations for improving the likelihood of successful implementation of administrative systems. This literature is useful to those who want to learn what is happening on other campuses or how they might use the latest administrative applications.

Because most of the literature is practice-based, it pays little attention to theoretical perspectives. Those pieces that are grounded in theory tend to use an organizational approach. A number of articles, for example, discuss organizational change and how the change process affects implementation. There is some discussion of the decision-making process and how administrators use information. But even these discussions are biased toward practical problems such as improving the implementation process (Arns, 1978; Hammond, 1974; Masland, 1983).

The literature often assumes the benefits of using computer-based systems and does not formally evaluate the success of new systems. The limited number of evaluations typically ask simple questions about the uses of the system, if users feel its cost is worth perceived benefits, or what obstacles hinder implementation. In addition, most evaluations are case studies at one or at most a few institutions. There are only a small number of studies that examined success across many campuses, and most of these analyzed older administrative systems such as resource allocation models (Plourde, 1976; Rodgers and Rhodes, 1978; Wartgow, 1973). This may be in part because it is difficult to define and measure the influence of computer-based systems. As an ongoing part of campus administration it may also seem inappropriate or too time-consuming to conduct extensive evaluations.

Despite these limitations, the literature on administrative computing forms a fairly coherent whole. There are connections among the descriptive accounts, normative suggestions, theoretical approaches, and evaluations. They produce a picture of expanding use and understanding of administrative computing. Applications have advanced and become more useful to campus decision makers. As the stage theories suggest, computer use and management are evolving as administrators learn about current applications and apply new technology. Yet a variety of important questions remain. As administrators continue to use computer-based systems, these questions deserve serious attention.

Remaining Questions

Rapidly changing technology and concurrent shifts in the context of administrative computing raise once again a number of questions examined in the past. For example, how does the new technolgoy change the problems of managing computer resources? How will colleges and universities fund the growth of microcomputer use? How will administrators and their staffs learn to use the resources? How will campuses control, if necessary, the proliferation of types of equipment? These are practical questions, but they must be addressed nevertheless. As technology advances and institutions evolve toward more sophisticated administrative applications, some of these old questions need new answers.

There are also a number of vital questions that have never received adequate answers. Primary among them is the influence of administrative systems on the campus. Institutions often assume the value of new administrative systems. They do not study the influence of such systems on institutional structure and function. More important, they do not examine institutional policy to determine if it coherently supports the evolutionary stages of computing. There are several elements which are part of the potential influence of administrative computing. The most important are highlighted below.

Defining the success of computer-based systems is the first area of importance. While administrators may hope to increase the speed with which they can make decisions or their efficiency, many administrative applications should instead improve effectiveness. This is difficult to measure. On a practical level, applications may bring changes in manager's actions, more complete understanding of their tasks, increasing their use of computer resources, or redefinition or extension of their tasks. In too many cases computer applications are used because administrators think that they will be beneficial. Frequently, no one actually examines how a system is used and how it affects the user's work. It may not be possible to know in advance all of the possible effects of implementing a new administrative application, but users should ask themselves how a new system influences their activities, how benefits can be measured, and if they are worth the cost.

In addition to better definitions of success, it would be informative to look at those institutions that are commonly perceived as leaders in the area of administrative computing systems. Are there certain characteristics of successful campuses? If so, are these related to the institution itself, its administrators, or some other set of variables? An investigation of this type would have to move beyond the standard listing of factors contributing to successful implementation. It would have to better define the elements of success and relate them to a conceptual approach such as the stage theories or the process of organizational change which would explain why such elements were important.

A second important area is the influence of adminstrative applications on the organization and its functions. For example, do computer-based systems influence the degree of centralization or decentralization in the organization? Do the systems affect patterns of governance? Do administrators address different issues and questions when new information becomes available or old information appears in a new form? How do the new, more personal forms of computer technology affect the answers to these questions? While researchers have examined the structure of decision making, the influence of faculty collective bargaining, the reduction of resources and enrollment, and other similar issues, the increasing use of computer-based systems, greater information flow, and readily available technological aids have not been examined.

A third and perhaps more basic question is whether use of administrative computing systems leads to a different type of administrator. Will those who through personal interest or academic training understand and feel comfortable with administrative computing systems become successful administrators while those without skills in these areas fall behind? Several institutions that are known, at least in the popular literature, for their advanced uses of administrative computing have top administrators with backgrounds in management science, quantitative fields, or computing. Such individuals may be in the forefront of administrative applications, but it is not clear if individuals of this type are the only ones who will make use of such systems.

As noted above, most of the scholarly literature in the area of administrative computing is practice-based. Future work should be better grounded conceptually. An organizational perspective has proved useful in past research efforts. This should be extended to future work in the area. For example, how will technology affect the structure and function of administrative organization, and would organizational theory predict these changes? Issues surrounding implementation and change continue to exist. Other possible avenues are to look at the theory behind technological innovation. This body of literature is closely related to organizational change but may add a new persepctive on the issues of administrative computing. Researchers might use communication theory to examine the influence of new technologies such as electronic mail. A psychological perspective might illuminate the decision-making process and the use of information. Researchers might also apply it to further the study of how differences among individuals affect the use and perceptions of administrative systems. A number of such theoretical approaches might provide new insights into administrative computing. Before this can happen, however, additional research is necessary.

To answer the important research and policy issues raised above, an explicit research agenda could become part of a campus's efforts in the area of administrative systems. This must be more than a simple descriptive account of the system and administrators' experience with it. It could be a formal evaluation. The research on Stanford University's electronic mail system is an example of this approach. Many institutions have considerable faculty research expertise which they could apply toward evaluation of administrative systems. Because outcomes are not always predictable, the methodology must allow for unexpected results. A successful study would likely include both quantitative analysis of data on system use and a qualitative investigation of users' reactions to and perceptions of the technology. While limited to one institution, a number of studies of this type would begin to expand the base of knowledge useful to researchers and practitioners alike.

These important issues and questions could also be studied across a number of institutions. A representative survey would provide more up-to-date information on administrative applications. While this would necessarily be descriptive in nature, it could provide more current information on topics such as specific applications, patterns of funding, methods of managing the process of proliferation, or characteristics of users. Of more interest would be questions relating to the perceived successes of administrative applications, the effect of such systems on governance, or changes in decision-making techniques. A large-scale survey might reveal connections between important variables which are not found in more limited case studies.

This discussion has demonstrated that there is a broad base of knowledge about administrative computing applications and the management of such systems. Researchers and practitioners have both contributed to the literature on administrative computing and undoubtedly will continue to do so. Each brings a valuable perspective, and the two groups need not be distinct. It is equally apparent, however, that greater understanding of the area would benefit those who want to use these systems to improve the management of institutions of higher education. Applying new theoretical approaches to the study of administrative applications would add a useful perspective missing in much of the past literature in the field. Using administrative computing as an area of inquiry for various theoretical approaches could also advance knowledge in those fields. Thus the area remains one of vital interest to the higher education community and one which holds the promise of being increasingly productive as the issues and questions of technological change and evolving computer use continue to emerge on college and university campuses.

REFERENCES

Adams, C. R. How management uses new information systems. *Decision Sciences*, 1975, *6*, 337-345.

Adams, C. R. (ed.). Appraising information needs of decision makers. *New Directions for Institutional Research*, 1977, *15*, 79-88.

Adams, C. R. Information technology and impacts on planning issues and processes. *New Directions for Institutional Research*, 1982, *35*, 59-72.

Adams, C. R., Kellogg, T. E., and Schroeder, R. G. Decision-making and information systems in colleges: An exploratory study. *Journal of Higher Education*, 1976, *47*, 33-49.

Alcorn, B. K. Institutional resources for computing. In J. W. Hamblen and C. P. Landis (eds.), *The Fourth Inventory of Computers in Higher Education: An Interpretive Report*. Boulder, Colo.: Westview Press, 1980.

Alter, S. L. How effective managers use information systems. *Harvard Business Review*, November-December 1976, pp. 97-104.

Alter, S. L. *DSS: Current Practice and Continuing Challenges*. Reading, Mass.: Addison-Wesley, 1980.

Andrew, G. M., and Alexander, M. D. The Minnesota and Colorado experiences with the CAMPUS planning system. In A. C. Heinlein (ed.), *Decision Models in Academic Administration*. Kent, Ohio: Kent State University Press, 1974.

Arns, R. G. Organizational characteristics of an university: Implications for design and use of informant systems. In M. E. Schouest and C. R. Thomas (eds.), *Development, Uses, and Management of Information Systems in Higher Education*. Proceedings of the 1978 CAUSE national conference, Boulder, Colo.

Averill, R. F., and Suttle, J. L. A model for university enrollment planning. *Socio-Economic Planning Sciences*, 1975, *9*, 257-261.

Bailey, R. L. Managing the office of tomorrow — people, people, people. *College and University*, Fall 1980, *56*, 20-31.

Bailey, R. L. *Information Systems and Technological Decisions: A Guide for the Non-technical Administrator*. AAHE-ERIC/Higher Education Research Report No. 8. Washington, D.C.: American Association for Higher Education, 1982.

Baldridge, J. V. Impacts on college administration: Management information systems and management by objective systems. *Research in Higher Education*, 1979, *10*, 263-282.

Baldridge, J. V., and Tierney, M. L. *New Approaches to Management: Creating Practical Systems of Management Information and Management Objectives*. San Francisco: Jossey-Bass, 1979.

Baughman, G. W. Evaluating the performance and effectiveness of university management systems. In J. Minter and B. Lawrence (eds.), *Management Information Systems: Their Development and Use in the Administration of Higher Education*. Boulder, Colo.: WICHE, 1969.

Bennett, C. S. Stanford's terminals for managers program: two years later. Paper presented at the CAUSE 1982 national conference. Boulder, Colo., 1983.

Bernard, D. J., Emery, J. C., Nolan, R. L., and Scott, R. H. *Charging for Computer Services: Principles and Guidelines*. New York: Petrocelli Books, 1977.

Bleau, B. L. Faculty planning models: A review of the literature. *Journal of Higher Education*, 1982, *53*, 195-206.

Bloomfield, S. D. Comprehensive faculty flow analysis. *New Directions for Institutional Research*, 1977, *13*, 1-18.

Bloomfield, S. D., and Updegrove, D. A. Modeling for insight, not numbers. *New Directions for Higher Education*, 1981, *35*, 93-104.

Bottomley, W. N. The USC faculty planning model. USC Faculty Planning Services, University of Southern California, 1978.

Boynton, G. R. Computing in universities: Setting up a computerized department. *EDUCOM Bulletin*, 1982, *17*, 22-24.

Bradley, D. W., Fargo, P. T., and Shettle, C. F. A computer model for long-range enrollment planning. Paper presented at the 1981 Northeast Association for Institutional Research Conference.

Branscomb, L. M. The computer's debt to science. *Perspectives in Computing*, 1983, *3*, 4-19.

Brink, V. Z. *Computers and Management*. Englewood Cliffs, N.J.: Prentice-Hall, 1971.

Brown, J. W., and Service, A. L. Enrollment decline and institutional size: Using management information to ask the right questions. In M. E. Schouest and C. R. Thomas (eds.), *Development, Uses, and Management of Information Systems in Higher Education*. Proceedings of the 1978 CAUSE National Conference, Boulder, Colo.

Byrne, M. M., and Kardonsky, S. Preparing administrators for automated information technologies. Paper presented at the 1982 CAUSE National Conference. Boulder, Colo., 1983.

Carlson, B. Office automation pilot: A popular office at the College of Dupage. Paper presented at the 1980 CAUSE National Conference. Boulder, Colo., 1980.

Carnegie Commission on Higher Education. *The Fourth Revolution: Instructional Technology in Higher Education.* New York: McGraw-Hill, 1972.

Chachra, V., and Heterick, R. C. Anatomy of a decision support system. *CAUSE/ EFFECT*, September 1982, pp. 6-11.

Cheney, P. H., and Dickson, G. W. Organizational characteristics and information systems: An exploratory investigation. *Academy of Management Journal*, 1982, *25*, 170-184.

Clark, D. G., Huff, R. A., Haight, M. J., and Collard, W. J. *Introduction to the Resource Requirements Prediction Model 1.6. Technical Report No. 34A.* Boulder, Colo.: NCHEMS, 1973.

Cloward, S. J. Who runs your computer center? *Educational Technology*, 1971, *11*, 45-47.

Cornew, R. W., and Morse, P. M. Distributive computer networking: Making it work on a regular basis. *Science*, 1975, *189*, 523-531.

"Data Sharing Funded by Exxon." *EDUCOM Bulletin*, 1983, *18*, 21-22.

Davis, D. L., and Emery, J. C. Computing for the liberal arts college. *EDUCOM Bulletin*, Winter 1978, pp. 16-22.

Deardon, J. MIS is a mirage. *Harvard Business Review*, January-February 1972, pp. 90-99.

Dickmeyer, N. Computer-aided university budget policy making. Unpublished doctoral dissertation, Stanford University, 1979.

Diehr, D. M. Putting a price on EDP services. In E. O. Joslin and R. A. Bassler (eds.), *Managing Data Processing.* Alexandria, Va.: College Readings, 1976.

Doty, K. E., and Krumrey, A. J. Administrators build their own systems at Loyola University. *CAUSE/EFFECT*, September 1982, pp. 20-23.

Dyer, J. S., and Mulvey, J. M. Computerized scheduling and planning. *New Directions for Institutional Research*, 1977, *13*, 67-86.

"Educating Executives in New Technology." *EDP Analyzer*, 1980, *18*.

EDUCOM. Policies, strategies, and plans for computing in higher education. Paper presented at EDUCOM Fall Conference, 1975.

Emery, J. C. The coming challenges of campus computation. *EDUCOM Bulletin*, 1978, *13*, 20-23.

Enarson, H. L. The art of planning. *Educational Record*, 1975, *56*, 170-174.

Enger, N. C. Computer performance evaluation In E. O. Joslin and R. A. Bassler (eds.), *Managing Data Processing.* Alexandria, Va.: College Readings, 1976.

Farmer, C. H., Frame, K. H., Priest, R. A., and Ozment, J. Management information systems and simulation models: To buy or not to buy? In R. H. Penshe and P. J. Stashey (eds.), *Proceedings of Annual Forum of the Assocation for Institutional Research*, 1978, pp. 157-160.

Foreman, L. Impact of the CAMPUS model in decision processes in the Ontario community colleges. In A. C. Heinlein (ed.), *Decision Models in Academic Administration.* Kent, Ohio: Kent State University Press, 1974.

Gamso, G. *The RRPM Guide: A Primer for Using the NCHEMS Resource Requirements Prediction Model (RRPM1.6). Technical Report 104.* Boulder, Colo.: NCHEMS, 1977.

Ganus, S., and Sherron, G. T. Management tips for office automation. Paper presented at the CAUSE 1982 National Conference. Boulder, Colo.: 1983.

Gaunt, R. N., and Haight, M. J. Planning models in higher education administration. *Journal of Education Finance*, 1977, *2*, 305-323.

Gellman, H. S. Managing computer services. *Business Quarterly*, 1975, *4*, 43-47.

Gibson, C. F., and Nolan, R. L. Managing the four stages of EDP growth. *Harvard Business Review*, January-February 1974, pp. 76-88.

Gillespie, R. G. How computers are transforming higher education. *New Directions for Higher Education*, 1983, *44*, 53-68.

Gillespie, R. G., with Dicaro, D. A. *Computing and Higher Education: An Accidental Revolution*. Seattle: University of Washington, 1981.

Gray, P. *University Planning Models: A Survey and Bibliography*. Exchange Bibliography No. 1279. Chicago: Council of Planning Libraries, 1977.

Gulko, W. W., and Hussain, K. *A Resource Prediction Model (RRPM-1): An Introduction to the Model. Technical Report 19*. Boulder, Colo.: NCHEMS, 1971.

Gwynn, J. The data-base approach to a management information system. In J. Minter and B. Lawrence (eds.), *Management Information Systems: Their Development and Use in the Administration of Higher Education*. Boulder, Colo.: WICHE, 1969.

Gwynn, J. W. The new technology means power to the people. *New Directions for Institutional Research*, 1979, *22*, 1-24.

Hammond, J. S. Do's and don'ts of computer models for planning. *Harvard Business Review*, March-April 1974, pp. 110-123.

Heller, P. S. Applications and economics of value-added networks. *EDUCOM Bulletin*, 1981, *16*, 12-17.

Henderson, J. C., and Ingraham, R. S. Prototyping for DSS: A critical appraisal. In M. J. Ginzberg, W. Reitman, and E. A. Stohr (eds.), *Decision Support Systems*. New York: North Holland Publishing Company, 1982.

Hootman, J. T. The pricing dilemma. *Datamation*, 1969, *15*, 61-66.

Hopkins, D. S. P. On the use of large-scale simulation models for university planning. *Review of Educational Research*, 1971, *41*, 467-478.

Hopkins, D. S. P. Analysis of faculty appointment, promotion, and retirement policies. *Higher Education*, 1974, *3*, 397-418.

Hopkins, D. S. P., Landry, L. L., Sonenstein, B., and Tschectelin, J. D. Financial Modeling: Four success stories. *EDUCOM Bulletin*, Fall 1982, pp. 11-15.

Hopkins, D. S. P., and Massy, W. F. *Planning Models for College and Universities*. Stanford, Calif.: Stanford University Press, 1981.

"How to Use Advanced Technology." *EDP Analyzer*, 1979, *17*.

Hudson, B. M. Educational planning: Notes on the state of the art. University of California at Los Angeles, Urban Planning Program, 1977.

Hussain, K. M. Comprehensive planning models in North American and Europe. *New Directions for Institutional Research*, 1976, *9*, 87-103.

Johnstone, J. N. Mathematical models developed for use in educational planning: A Review. *Review of Educational Research*, 1974, *44*, 177-201.

Judy, R. W., and Levine, J. B. *A New Tool for Educational Administration*. Toronto: University of Toronto Press, 1965.

Kanter, H., Moore, A., and Singer, N. The allocation of computer time by university computing centers. *Journal of Business*, 1968, *41*, 375-384.

Keen, P. G. W. Computer-based decision aids: The evaluation problem. *Sloan Management Review*, 1975, *16*, 17-29.

Keen, P. G. W. The California school finance simulation: A case study of effective implementation. Research Paper No. 467, Graduate School of Business, Stanford University, January 1978.

Keen, P. G. W. Decision support systems: Translating analytic techniques into useful tools. *Sloan Management Review*, Spring 1980, pp. 33-44.

Keen, P. G. W. Decision support systems: Lessons for the 80s. *EDUCOM Bulletin*, Fall 1982, pp. 17-21.

Keen, P. G. W., and Scott Morton, S. *DSS: An Organizational Perspective*. Reading, Mass.: Addison-Wesley, 1978.

Khtaian, G. A. Costing of data processing services. In E. O. Josslin and R. A. Bassler (eds.), *Managing Data Processing*. Alexandria, Va.: College Readings, 1976.

Kieft, R. N. Enrollment planning using student registration information and an induced course load matrix. *College and University*, 1977, *52*, 187-194.

Kirschling, W. R. Models: Caveats, reflections, and suggestions. *New Directions for Institutional Research*, 1976, *9*, 1-15.

Knodle, L. L., Noval, L., Powell, J., Rogers, F., and Updegrove, D. EFPM: Users' experiences at Purdue University, Oberlin College, and Carnegie-Mellon University. *EDUCOM Bulletin*, 1979, *14*, 5-11.

Leavitt, H. J. Beyond the analytic manager. *California Management Review*, 1975, *17*, 5-12.

LeDuc, A. L. Personnel retention in the college and university information systems environment. *CAUSE/EFFECT*, May 1981, pp. 4-9.

Levine, J. B. The implementation of CAMPUS simulation models for university planning. In J. Minter and B. Lawrence (eds.), *Management Information Systems*. Boulder, Colo.: WICHE, 1969.

Lindblom, C. The science of muddling through. *Public Administration Review*, 1959, *19*, 79-88.

Luehrmann, A. W. Free-access computing at Dartmouth. In *Facts and Futures*, proceedings of the EDUCOM Fall Conference, 1973, pp. 193-197.

Lyon, H. S. What decisions can be better made using technology? In D. D. Mebane (ed.), *Solving College and University Problems Through Technology*. Princeton, N.J.: EDUCOM, 1981.

McCarter, P. M. Where is the industry going? *Datamation*, 1978, *24*, 99-109.

McCorkle, C. O. Information for institutional decision making. *New Directions for Institutional Research*, 1977, *17*, 1-9.

McCredie, J. W. Office automation in the university: Administrative issues. In J. C. Emery (ed.), *Closing the Gap Between Technology and Application*. Princeton, N.J.: EDUCOM, 1978.

McCredie, J. W. (ed.). *Campus Computing Strategies*. Bedford, Mass.: Digital Press, 1983.

McCredie, J. W., and Timlake, W. P. Evolving computer networks in American higher education. *EDUCOM Bulletin*, 1983, *18*, 5-10.

McKenney, J. L., and Keen, P. G. W. How managers' minds work. *Harvard Business Review*, 1974, *54*, 79-90.

McNeish, M. F. Selecting a modeling system. *EDUCOM Bulletin*, Fall 1982, pp 37-41.

"Mailnet Service Launched." *EDUCOM Bulletin*, 1983, *18*, 20.

Mann, R. L. The people problem. *New Directions for Institutional Research*, 1979, *22*, 59-75.

Mann, R. L. Institutional applications of new information technology. *New Directions for Institutional Research*, 1982, *35*, 25-39.

Mann, R. L., Thomas, C. R., Williams, R. C., and Wallhaus, R. A. An overview of two recent surveys of administrative computer operations in higher education. Boulder, Colo.: NCHEMS, 1975.

Masat, F. E. *Computer Literacy in Higher Education*. AAHE-ERIC/Higher Education Research Report No. 6. Washington, D.C.: American Association for Higher Education, 1981.

Masland, A. T. Organizational influences on computer use in higher education. Unpublished doctoral dissertation, Harvard University, 1982.

Masland, A. T. Simulators, myth, and ritual in higher education. *Research in Higher Education*, 1983, *18*, 161-178.

Masland, A. T. Integrators and decision support system success in higher education. *Research in Higher Education*, 1984, *20*, 211-233.

Masters, R. J., and Munsterman, R. E. Departmental planning-budgeting system (DPBS). *Journal of Educational Data Processing*, 1975, *12*, 1-9.

Mayo, M., and Kallio, R. E. Effective use of models in the decision process: Theory grounded in three case studies. *The AIR Professional File*, Spring-Summer 1983, *15*.

Mebane, D. D. (ed.). *Solving College and University Problems Through Technology*. Princeton, N.J.: EDUCOM, 1981.

Miller, W. F. The role of national networking in a changing computing environment. In J. C. Emery (ed.), *The Reality of National Computer Networking for Higher Education*. Princeton, N.J.: EDUCOM, 1979.

Minter, J., and Lawrence, B. (eds.). *Management Information Systems: Their Development and Use in the Administration of Higher Education*. Boulder, Colo.: WICHE, 1969.

Mintzberg, H. The myths of MIS. *California Management Review*, 1972, *15*, 92-97.

Mintzberg, H. The manager's job: Folklore and fact. *Harvard Business Review*, July-August 1975, pp. 49-61.

Mitroff, I. I., Nelson, J., and Mason, R. O. On management myth-information systems. *Management Science*, 1974, *21*, 371-382.

Mosmann, C. *Academic Computers in Service*. San Francisco: Jossey-Bass, 1973.

Mosmann, C. Networks and special service organizations. In J. W. Hamblen and C. P. Landis (eds.), *The Fourth Inventory of Computers in Higher Education: An Interpretive Report*. Boulder, Colo.: Westview Press, 1980.

Mosmann, C., and Stefferud, E. Campus computer management. *Datamation*, 1971, *17*, 20-23.

Mowbray, G., and Levine, J. B. The development and implementation of CAMPUS: A computer-based planning and budgeting system for universities and colleges. *Educational Technology*, 1971, *11*, 27-32.

Nevison, C. H. Effects of tenure and retirement policies on the college faculty. *Journal of Higher Education*, 1980, *51*, 150-166.

Nielsen, N. R. The allocation of computer resources—is pricing the answer? *Communications of the ACM*, 1970, *13*, 467-474.

Nolan, R. L. Controlling the costs of data services. *Harvard Business Review*, July-August 1977, pp. 114-124.

Nolan, R. L. Managing the crisis in data processing. *Harvard Business Review*, March-April 1979, pp. 115-126.

Nyman, D. Financing computing. In J. W. Hamblen and C. P. Landis (eds.), *The Fourth Inventory of Computers in Higher Education: An Interpretive Report*. Boulder, Colo.: Westview Press, 1980.

Ohio Board of Regents. Computer services: universities. Management Improvement Program, Ohio Board of Regents, 1973.

Orcutt, R. L. Microcomputers: A revolution of awareness. Paper presented at the 1981 Northeast Assocation for Institutional Research Conference.

Ottervik, E. V. Modeling the budget at Lehigh University. In J. B. Wyatt, J. C. Emery, and C. P. Landis (eds.), *Financial Planning Models: Concepts and Case Studies in Colleges and Universities*. Princeton, N.J.: EDUCOM, 1979.

Patton, P. L. Planning for microcomputers in higher education. *EDUCOM Bulletin*, 1981, *16*, 2-8.

Plourde, P. J. Institutional use of models: Hope or continued frustration? *New Directions for Institutional Research*, 1976, *9*, 17-33.

Pope, J. A., and Cross, E. M. An admissions DSS for forecasting and simulating college enrollment. *CAUSE/EFFECT*, September 1982, pp. 24-29.

Porter, R., Zemsky, R., and Oedel, P. Adaptive planning: The role of institution-specific models. *Journal of Higher Education*, 1979, *50*, 586-601.

Ralston, A. University EDP: Get it all together. *Datamation*, 1971, *17*, 24-26.

Resnikoff, H. L. Developments and trends in information technology. *New Directions for Institutional Research*, 1982, *35*, 5-23.

Rice, R. E., and Case, D. Electronic message systems in the university: A description of use and utility. *Journal of Communication*, 1983, *33*, 131-152.

Robbins, M. D., Dorn, W. W., and Skelton, J. E. *Who Runs the Computer?* Boulder, Colo.: Westview Press, 1975.

Roberts, M. M. A separatist's view of university EDP. *Datamation*, 1971, *17*, 28-30.

Rockhart, J. F. Chief executives define their own data needs. *Harvard Business Review*, March-April 1979, pp. 81-93.

Rodgers, K. W., and Rhodes, I. N. A study of the impacts of selected products developed by NCHEMS. Cambridge, Mass.: A. D. Little, 1978.

Rowe, A. J. The myth of the rational decision maker. *International Management*, August 1974, pp. 38-40.

Sandelin, J. Planning electronic office systems in a university. In D. D. Mebane (ed.), *Solving College and University Problems Through Technology*, Princeton, N.J.: EDUCOM, 1981.

Sandin, R. T. Information systems and educational judgment. *New Directions for Institutional Research*, 1977, *17*, 19-28.

Schmidtlein, F. A. Information systems and concepts of higher education governance. *New Directions for Institutional Research*, 1977, *17*, 29-42.

Schouest, M. E., and Thomas, C. R. (eds.). *Development, Uses, and Management of Information Systems in Higher Education*. Proceedings of the 1978 CAUSE National Conference, Boulder, Colo.

Schroeder, R. G. A survey of MS in university operations. *Management Science*, 1973, *19*, 895-906.

Schroeder, R. G. Management system design: A critical appraisal. *New Directions for Institutional Research*, 1977, *13*, 39-113.

Schroeder, R. G., and Adams, C. R. The effective use of management science in university administration. *Review of Educational Research*, 1976, *46*, 117-131.

Sheehan, B. S. Decision support systems: An institutional research perspective. Association for Institutional Research Forum paper, 1982.

Skarulis, P. C., and Thomas, C. R. (eds.). *Productivity: A Key to Survival in the 80s*. Proceedings of the 1980 CAUSE National Conference, Boulder, Colo.

Society for College and University Planning. *Let's End the Confusion about Simulation Models*, Proceedings of the 1973 Spring Conference.

Staman, E. M. Trends in administrative computing. *New Directions for Institutional Research*, 1979, *22*, 95-104.

Staman, E. M. Computing and office automation — changing variables. *The AIR Professional File*, Summer/Fall 1981, *10*.

Strange, J. H. Preparing for today and tomorrow: Training for the new technologies. *AAHE Bulletin*, *36*, 10-14.

Strassman, P. A. The office of the future: Information management for the new age. *Technology Review*, December/January 1980, pp. 54-65.

Suslow, S. Benefits of a cohort survival projection model. *New Directions for Institutional Research*, 1977, *13*, 19-42.

Swoyer, V. H. Computer system changes. In J. W. Hamblen and C. P. Landis (eds.), *The Fourth Inventory of Computers in Higher Education: An Interpretive Report*, Boulder, Colo.: Westview Press, 1980*a*.

Swoyer, V. H. Computing center organization. In J. W. Hamblen and C. P. Landis (eds.), *The Fourth Inventory of Computers in Education: An Interpretive Report*, Boulder, Colo.: Westview Press, 1980*b*.

Taylor, R. P. (ed.). *The Computer in the School: Tutor, Tool, Tutee*. New York: Teachers College Press, 1980.

Teeter, D. J., and Stolz, R. K. Promoting and planning dialog: A role for resource models. Association for Institutional Research Forum paper, 1981.

Thomas, C. R. Administrative uses of computing in higher education. In J. W. Hamblen, and C. P. Landis (eds.), *The Fourth Inventory of Computers in Higher Education: An Interpretive Report*. Boulder, Colo.: Westview Press, 1980.

Thomas, C. R. *Administrative Information Systems: The 1980 Profile*. Boulder, Colo.: CAUSE Publications, 1981.

Tucker, M. S. The turning point: Telecommunications and higher education. *Journal of Communication*, 1983, *33*, 118-130.

Updegrove, D. A. EFPM — the EDUCOM financial planning model. *EDUCOM Bulletin*, Winter 1978, pp. 6-11.

Updegrove, D. A. EFPM: A two-year progress report. In D. D. Mebane (ed.), *Solving College and University Problems Through Technology*, Princeton, N.J.: EDUCOM, 1981.

Updegrove, D. A. Computer modeling for comparative financial assessment. *New Directions for Higher Education*, 1982, *38*, 45-98.

Wartgow, J. F. Computerized institutional planning models: An objective analysis. Paper presented at the North Central Association Annual Meeting, Chicago, 1973.

Weathersby, G. B., and Weinstein, M. C. A structural comparison of analytical models for university planning. Paper P-12, University of California Ford Foundation Program for Research in University Administration, 1970.

Welling, J. A management perspective. *New Directions for Higher Education*, 1983, *44*, 33-51.

Welsch, G. M. Successful implementation of decision support systems: Pre-installation factors, service characteristics, and the role of the information transfer specialist. Unpublished doctoral dissertation, Northwestern University, 1980.

Wise, F. H. Implications of computers for the administration and management of higher education. *New Directions for Institutional Research*, 1979, *22*, 77-94.

Wiseman, C. New foundations for planning models. *Journal of Higher Education*, 1979, *50*, 726-744.

Withington, F. G. Coping with computer proliferation. *Harvard Business Review*, May-June 1980, pp. 152-164.

Withington, F. G. The promise of future technology. In D. D. Mebane (ed.), *Solving College and University Problems Through Technology*, Princeton, N.J.: EDUCOM, 1981.

Wyatt, J. B., and Zeckhauser, S. University executives and management information: A tenuous relationship. *Educational Record*, 1975, *56*, 175-189.

Watt, J. B., Emery, J. C., and Landis, C. P. *Financial Planning Models: Concepts and Case Studies in Colleges and Universities*. Princeton, N.J.: EDUCOM, 1979.

Zinn, K. L. Instructional uses and computing in higher education. In J. W. Hamblen and C. P. Landis (eds.), *The Fourth Inventory of Computers in Higher Education: An Interpretive Report*, Boulder, Colo.: Westview Press, 1980.

Zmud, R. W. Individual differences and MIS success: A review of the empirical literature. *Management Sciences*, 1979, *25*, 966-979.

Zund, D. E., and Sorensen, R. E. Theory of change and the effective use of management science. *Administrative Science Quarterly*, 1975, *20*, 532-545.

LEGAL PARAMETERS OF THE
FACULTY EMPLOYMENT RELATIONSHIP

Barbara A. Lee, *Rutgers University*, and Steven
G. Olswang, *University of Washington*

Tracing the employment relationship between college faculty and their employing institutions reveals numerous paradoxes, which make such an exercise at once both fascinating and frustrating. Academic norms place a high value on collegial governance of colleges and universities, yet faculty are also employees of the institution and have interests as employees which may differ from the interests of the institution. Employment decisions, especially concerning tenure, may result in a lifetime commitment to an individual faculty member, and potential colleagues are understandably anxious to tenure only those who "fit" the personality and values of the academic unit. Yet state and federal laws prohibit employment decisions being made on the basis of an individual's personal attributes, such as gender, race, or national origin. Furthermore, the concept of "academic freedom" raises questions of academic autonomy, both to conduct one's teaching and research free of interference and to make decisions about the future of the institution and the faculty within it. How, in this potential clash between academic norms and the requirements of the law, have the parameters of the faculty's employment relationship with a college or university been established? In what respects is the employment relationship between faculty and an institution of higher education like that of any other employee and employer? Conversely, how does the system of academic norms modify the faculty employment relationship? Is there evidence of dysfunction between the legal system which enforces employee rights and the academic norm system which protects academic autonomy?

This chapter explores the employment relationship between faculty and their institutions. It examines case law and scholarly analysis of the legal system on faculty employment matters, and focuses in particular upon real or potential conflicts between legal and economic requirements and academic values. The chapter concentrates on several areas of employment disputes in academe which have had special salience in the recent past and will likely continue to do so: reductions of faculty based on economic crises or programmatic shifts within a college, the aging faculty population and institutional attempts to shape its faculty to fit new curricular emphases, employment discrimination and faculty evaluation, and issues of salary equity.

The parameters of the faculty employment relationship have provided substantial grist for the litigation mill over the last quarter of a century. While litigation against colleges in the 1960s focused primarily upon issues of access to higher education, the economic woes of higher education in the 1970s engendered litigation over employment discrimination, reductions in force, and the scope of faculty academic freedom. Litigation in the present decade has so far focused upon the legality of rising standards for promotion and tenure, continued reductions or eliminations of programs as institutions reorganize and reassess their missions, and equity in employment decisions, as well as attempts to maintain and increase faculty professionalism and productivity (such as post-tenure review). As the enrollment declines predicted for the 1980s increase in severity (Carnegie Council, 1980), it is likely that litigation will increase and the issues involved in the faculty employment relationship will become more complex.

BASIC FACULTY EMPLOYMENT RIGHTS

The employment rights of faculty have been the subject of lively debate for centuries, but the most interesting, and the most consequential, writing has focused on tenure and academic freedom protections. Professional norms regarding academic freedom and tenure began to crystallize early in the twentieth century when a group of faculty members created the American Association of University Professors and drafted the 1915 "Report of the Committeee on Academic Freedom and Tenure" (Hofstadter and Metzger, 1955). These early principles, and other policy statements developed subsequent to the 1915 Report, represented a set of aspirations rather than a codification of academic practice, and focused primarily on procedural protections for faculty who found themselves threatened with discharge because their beliefs were unpopular with trustees, administrators, or benefactors (p. 481). Much later in the twentieth century, AAUP statements of professional standards won judicial recognition as statements of "academic common law" (McKee, 1980) and even as legally binding contractual terms ("The Role of Academic Freedom in Defining the Faculty Employment Contract," 1981).

However, many of the employment rights of college faculty are determined not by legal analyses peculiar to academe, but by basic contract law applicable to all employees. Just as is the usual case with employees of nonacademic organizations, faculty members generally enter some form of contractual arrangement with the employing college or university. Despite the apparent simplicity of the concept of an "employment contract," however, contractual practices in higher education vary greatly, and a court may find that at one college a one-paragraph letter to a faculty member constitutes the employment contract, while at another institution the "contract" may include a negotiated collective bargaining agreement, a faculty handbook, various policy documents, previous practices of the institution heretofore uncodified, and the writings of external groups such as those in the AAUP policy statements (Kaplin, 1978, p. 88).

Whatever the complexity of the contract, it is a series of promises, by both the employer and the employee, which are enforceable in court (Corbin, 1968). For untenured faculty, contracts generally are in effect for a specific period of time: an academic year, a calendar year, three years, etc. Generally, a college may not terminate a contract which is still in effect unless the faculty member has refused to perform his or her duties, has abandoned the job, or has failed to live up to the terms of the contract in some other way (Brown, 1977).

Tenure, when it exists, is based upon the employment contract in private institutions, and upon either a state statute or rule, or a contract of employment in public institutions (Edwards and Nordin, 1979, p. 223). Tenured status generally protects a faculty member against dismissal except for reasons of financial exigency, unprofessional conduct, or other "just cause" (Commission on Academic Tenure, 1973), with the specific reasons justifying dismissal spelled out in either the statute or the contract (Lovain, 1983–84).

Employment Rights of Untenured Faculty

The employment rights of untenured faculty are limited by the terms of the employment contract. The U.S. Supreme Court has ruled that a faculty member whose contract is not renewed at its expiration has no "legitimate expectation of continued employment," and thus no legal recourse to reverse the nonrenewal decision (*Board of Regents v. Roth*, 1972). As long as that decision not to renew is made in accordance with both the specific terms of the contract and all applicable state and federal laws, if any, a college or university may refuse to renew a faculty member's employment for virtually any reason, even though based on subjective evaluation (*Hetrick v. Martin*, 1973), and absent a showing of "gross abuse" in making the decision (such as discrimination), a court will not review the merits of the nonrenewal (*Stebbins v. Weaver*, 1976). In fact, according to the Supreme Court, a college need not even give an untenured faculty member reasons for a negative employment decision (O'Brien, 1974, p. 184), although Van Alstyne (1976) has argued that refusal to give the reasons on the college's part probably causes more litigation than would otherwise occur (p. 286).

Faculty members employed by public institutions enjoy special protections against arbitrary termination because of the requirements of the Fourteenth Amendment of the U.S. Constitution. Simply put, the Fourteenth Amendment forbids state officials or agencies to deprive individuals of property or liberty without "due process of law," which has been interpreted by the courts to include a series of procedural steps designed to ensure that government decisions which deprive individuals of certain rights are made fairly and for adequate reasons (Van Alstyne, 1970). The U.S. Supreme Court has ruled that an individual who has a "legitimate expectation" of the continuance of a public entitlement (such as welfare, Social Security, or a public job) has a property interest in that expectation and, in order to terminate that entitlement, the public agency must afford the individual procedural due process (*Mathews v. Eldridge*, 1976). In addition, if the acts of a public agent call into question the reputation or character of an individual (such as publicly stating that an individual was terminated for incompetence), a constitutionally protected liberty interest attaches. However, absent some clear statement to the contrary by the college, the Supreme Court has ruled that untenured faculty at public colleges and universities who do not have their appointments renewed do not have a "legitimate expectation" of reemployment and thus do not have a property right adversely affected so as to entitle them to procedural due process. Nor do nonrenewed faculty, as a result of nonrenewal, have a liberty interest at stake, unless the college or university makes a "charge against [the faculty member] that might seriously damage his standing and associations in his community" or that could jeopardize that individual's ability to secure another job (*Board of Regents v. Roth*, 1972, pp. 2704, 2707).

Some scholars have criticized the Court for this ruling, citing the widespread practice in higher education of nearly automatic contract renewal for untenured faculty up to the time the tenure and/or promotion decision is to be made. Van Alstyne (1972) noted that nonrenewal at the University of Wisconsin was quite unusual, and that Professor Roth had at least an informal expectation of reemployment, based on the past practice of the institution. Despite the criticism, courts in subsequent cases have followed *Roth* and have refused to require colleges to offer reasons for nonrenewal or to provide even rudimentary due process protections to untenured faculty (see, for example, *Ortwein v. Mackey*, 1975, and *Johnson v. Christian Brothers College*, 1978). Indeed, courts have even held that inconsequential violations of institutional procedures will not prevent an institution from denying faculty tenure or not renewing contracts (*Goodisman v. Lytle*, 1984).

Courts will review nonrenewal cases, however, when faculty members allege that the negative decision was made solely in response to conduct protected by the First Amendment. The First Amendment to the U.S. Constitution forbids any state official or agency from abridging the free speech and association rights of any individual; this protection is especially important for public employees, who might otherwise be fired for exercising their free speech rights in opposition to the policies or views of the public employer. First Amendment rights of teachers have received strong protection from the U.S. Supreme Court, although these rights are not unlimited, and are counterbalanced by the interest of the public employer in efficient operation and harmonious employee relations (Hirsch and Kemerer, 1982).

Generally, a public employer may not discontinue an employee solely because that employee exercised his or her First Amendment rights (Hodges,

1982-83). For example, an untenured college professor was denied tenure, although she had previously been evaluated as an excellent instructor, because she wrote an editorial critical of a member of the board of trustees (*Endress v. Brookdale Community College*, 1976). The court required that she be reinstated with back pay and with tenure, holding that, absent the protected conduct of publishing the editorial, she would have received tenure at the institution.

The First Amendment does not, however, protect faculty members unequivocally against negative employment decisions, for the court will examine the motivation for the decision, and will not allow an exercise of First Amendment rights by a faculty member to overturn what otherwise would have been a permissible decision not to rehire a faculty member (Hodges, 1982-83). The Supreme Court has ruled that if conduct protected by the First Amendment was the "motivating factor" behind the decision to terminate the faculty member's employment, then the decision was made upon unconstitutional grounds and must be reversed. However, if the employer could demonstrate that it would have reached the same decision not to rehire the faculty member, irrespective of the occurrence of the protected conduct, then the nonrenewal was permissible (*Mt. Healthy v. Doyle*, 1977, p. 576). In such cases, the assertion by a faculty member that protected speech or conduct motivated the negative employment decision does not necessarily result in reinstatement, but rather merely requires the college or university to conduct a hearing to determine the motivating factors behind that decision. Should the finding be that the termination was motivated by the exercise of protected conduct, courts may order reinstatement (*Goss v. San Jacinto Junior College*, 1979), back pay (compensatory damages), and even punitive damages (*Aumiller v. University of Delaware*, 1977).

However, courts exercise caution in applying the First Amendment to certain types of faculty conduct. A federal court refused to use the First Amendment to protect what it characterized as "bickering and running disputes" between faculty and a department chair, stating that "a college has a right to expect a teacher to follow instructions and to work cooperatively and harmoniously with the head of the department" (*Chitwood v. Feaster*, 1972, p. 361). At another college, a nontenured faculty member was dismissed because the administration disapproved of her "pedagogical style and philosophy." The court upheld the dismissal in this instance, noting that "a university has a right to require some conformity with whatever teaching methods are acceptable to it" (*Hetrick v. Martin*, 1973, p. 709).

A second exception to the general rule that untenured faculty members are not entitled to due process is when the faculty member has been accused of some form of misconduct and a constitutionally protected liberty interest arises. For example, a college decided not to renew the contract of an untenured faculty member who had been accused of racial bias against students, and gave the faculty member neither reasons for the decision nor a hearing. The faculty member argued that the public allegations of racial bias against him triggered a liberty interest, and the college was required to conduct a hearing to help him refute these charges. The reviewing court agreed and ordered the college to conduct the hearing (*Wellner v. Minnesota State Junior College Board*, 1973). However, the charges against a faculty member must have been made public before a liberty interest will attach (Kaplin, 1978, p. 139). It is also important to note that all that was required was a hearing to allow the faculty member to clear his name; reinstatement was not required.

Untenured faculty members are, of course, to be afforded procedural due process in nonrenewal decisions in public institutions where a state law or institutional policy requires that such procedures be provided (*Kilcoyne v. Morgan*, 1981) or where the college's own policies "bestow a property interest sufficient to require a procedural due process hearing" (*State ex rel. McLendon v. Morton*, 1978). Beyond these exceptions, courts generally do not impose due process procedures or grant other forms of relief to untenured faculty members who challenge negative employment decisions, except in the rare instance where the faculty member can demonstrate that the sole reason motivating the termination was the exercise of First Amendment rights.

Employment Rights of Tenured Faculty

In contrast to the limited protections for untenured faculty, faculty who have been awarded tenure enjoy an array of procedural protections which the courts have recognized and enforced. Whether tenure has been awarded under a state statute or under a contract between the faculty member and the institution, courts require colleges and universities to adhere to the statutory protections or the contractual conditions in their decisions to terminate the employment of tenured faculty. In the case of private institutions, the terms of the contract generally determine the breadth of the protections afforded tenured faculty, and most contracts state that the individual has the right to continued or permanent employment, subject to dismissal for "cause" (Commission on Academic Tenure, 1973). If the contract is silent on the definition of "cause," or if there is no explicit description of the procedural protections afforded tenured faculty dismissed for cause, courts have incorporated the protections developed in procedural statements promulgated by the American Association of University Professors into the employment contract (*Greene v. Howard University*, 1969).

In the case of tenured faculty employed by public institutions, procedural protections have been developed through case law and are now viewed as constitutional entitlements of tenured faculty. If a faculty member has either been awarded tenure explicitly, or can demonstrate the existence of "rules and understandings, promulgated and fostered by state officials, that . . . justify [the faculty member's] legitimate claim of entitlement to continued employment," the college is obligated to "grant a hearing at [the faculty member's] request where he [can] be informed of the grounds for his nonretention and challenge their sufficiency" (*Perry v. Sindermann*, 1972, p. 603).

Although tenured faculty at public institutions are guaranteed procedural due process in termination decisions, the amount and nature of these guarantees have not been formalized. Courts have been unwilling to require colleges to hold trial-type hearings, with counsel, cross-examination of witnesses, and a written transcript, but have ruled that informal proceedings, as long as they were run fairly and permitted the faculty member an opportunity to be informed of and answer the charges, were sufficient for constitutional purposes. With regard to this issue, a federal court stated that

> it is not essential in all circumstances to a fair and adequate hearing that it be conducted in a trial-like atmosphere, complete with attorneys to challenge offered evidence and legally trained hearing officers to rule on evidentiary questions . . . . A proceeding may provide a fair and adequate opportunity for the grievant to present his side of the issues without either the legal technicalities of the hearing rule or the presence of counsel. [*Toney v. Reagan*, 1972, p. 1001]

This court made evident its lack of sympathy for tenured faculty facing dismissal, saying "welfare recipients dealing with state officials are a class far more likely to be in need of the services of counsel than college professors dealing with their peers" (*Toney*, p. 958).

Another federal court explained that the procedural safeguards afforded terminated public employees must be "adapted to the particular characteristics of the interests involved and the limited nature of the controversy." The court listed safeguards which could apply, but which were not necessarily required in each case: (1) written notice of the grounds for the termination; (2) disclosure of the evidence supporting termination; (3) the right to confront and cross-examine adverse witnesses; (4) an opportunity to be heard in person and to present witnesses and documentary evidence; (5) a neutral and detached hearing body; (6) a written statement by the fact finders as to the evidence relied upon (*Chung v. Park*, 1975, p. 386). In general, if the college has afforded the faculty member in question a fair chance to challenge the basis upon which the decision to terminate rests, the courts will not attempt to decide whether the final decision reached by the college was correct. If the hearing produced evidence sufficient to permit a reasonable group of individuals to conclude that the faculty member should be terminated, the courts will generally not second-guess that decision, for "due process should not be employed to insure that this (decision) is 'wise' but only that it is not unreasonable, arbitrary or capricious" (*Chung*, p. 387).

De Facto Tenure

In a small number of cases, faculty have alleged that they have received "tenure by default," or *de facto* tenure, because the institution continued to employ them beyond the normal probationary period. In a few cases, courts have agreed that, at institutions without a formal tenure system, practices and policies of the institution have created a legitimate expectation of reemployment, and that certain faculty members are in a *de facto* tenure status (McKee, 1980).

The U.S. Supreme Court described the circumstances under which a faculty member might be able to prove that he or she held *de facto* tenure:

> A teacher . . . who has held his position for a number of years, might be able to show from the circumstances of this service — and from other relevant facts — that he has a legitimate claim of entitlement to job tenure. Just as this court has found there to be a "common law of a particular industry or of a particular plant" that may supplement a collective bargaining agreement . . . so there may be an unwritten "common law" in a particular university that certain employees shall have the equivalent of tenure. This is particularly likely in a college or university . . . that has no explicit tenure system even for senior members of its faculty, but that nonetheless may have created such a system in practice. [*Perry v. Sindermann*, 1972, p. 602]

Courts have cited statements in faculty handbooks regarding an expected continuation of the employment relationship as evidence of a *de facto* tenure system (*Zimmerer v. Spencer*, 1973). In other cases, state laws bestowing tenure after a certain number of years of continuous and satisfactory employment have been used to grant "automatic" tenure to faculty who were not notified of their nonrenewal in accordance with the statutory requirements (McKee, 1980, pp. 38-39). In still other cases, an institution's failure to follow its own procedures regarding proper notification of nonrenewal may afford a faculty member *de facto* tenure (*Sawyer v. Mercer*, 1980).

In most cases, however, faculty allegations of tenure by default are unsuccessful. If institutional policy documents state that the president or the board of trustees awards tenure, courts generally will not find that tenure has accrued by default, even if department chairs, deans, or other administrators have repeatedly assured the faculty member that tenure is "automatic" or "guaranteed" or have made other representations upon which the faculty member relied (*Haimowitz v. University of Nevada*, 1978). The prevailing rule of law requires an affirmative act by the authorized and designated officials at the institution for tenure to be granted, and tenure by default is granted only in exceptional circumstances.

Dismissal of Tenured Faculty for "Cause"

Although the reasons for which a faculty member may be terminated would usually appear either in the employment contract (and related policy documents) or in the state statute or rule which established tenure, a general definition of "cause" for termination includes the following: (1) demonstrated incompetence or dishonesty in teaching or research; (2) substantial and manifest neglect of duty; (3) personal conduct which substantially impairs the individual's fulfillment of his institutional responsibilities (Commission on Academic Tenure, 1973, p. 75). The AAUP's "1976 Recommended Institutional Regulations on Academic Freedom and Tenure" state that "adequate cause for a dismissal will be related, directly and substantially, to the fitness of the faculty member in his professional capacity as a teacher or researcher. Dismissal will not be used to restrain faculty members in their exercise of academic freedom or other rights of American citizens" (AAUP, 1977b, p. 19). Further, both the courts and AAUP policies permit termination for reasons of financial exigency or program discontinuance (Olswang, 1982–83).

Most of the cases in which faculty challenged terminations for cause have involved allegations of immoral conduct, insubordination, failure to follow institutional rules, or incompetence. Institutions which have been able to substantiate that tenured faculty members committed "immoral" acts with students (for example, *Board of Trustees of Mount San Antonio Junior College v. Hartman*, 1966, and *Board of Trustees v. Stubblefield*, 1971) have prevailed even though the students were adults and the conduct occurred off campus. Lax supervision of minor students has also been found sufficient cause for termination of a faculty member (*White v. Board of Trustees of Western Wyoming Community College*, 1982).

Courts have also affirmed administrative decisions to terminate the employment of tenured faculty who refuse to comply with institutional rules or policies. In *Shaw v. Board of Trustees* (1976), faculty who refused to perform their required professional duties in protest over proposed changes in tenure policies were dismissed for breaching their employment contracts. A tenured faculty member whose antiwar protest disrupted an official university ceremony was found guilty by a faculty committee of violating the university code, and the court upheld his subsequent dismissal (*Adamian v. Jacobsen*, 1975). Verbal attacks made by faculty against the administration were characterized as "insubordination" and served as a justification for dismissal according to one court (*Roseman v. Indiana University of Pennsylvania*, 1975), while taking a leave of absence against the express direction of a dean constituted "insubordination" and justified termination in another case (*Statsny v. Central Washington University*, 1982). However, a Nevada court asserted that criticism of college administrators was protected by the First Amendment, unless that criticism was actually an "attack" upon either the university or its administration (*State ex rel. Richardson v. Board of Regents, University of Nevada*, 1954).

While courts have heightened their scrutiny of personnel decisions in recent years — protecting academic freedom and free speech and recognizing the due process rights related to tenure — courts have also "consistently affirmed that colleges and universities may terminate tenured faculty for adequate cause if proper procedures are followed" (Lovain, 1983–84, p. 432). The courts have given substantial latitude to institutions to make such judgments. Yet, courts will look at institutional rules to insure they were adhered to and will not hesitate to protect faculty against administrators violating their own rules or making arbitrary or capricious decisions.

Incorporation of AAUP Standards

Since its creation in the first part of the twentieth century, the American Association of University Professors has attempted to safeguard academic freedom and professional autonomy for faculty in colleges and universities (Tucker and

Mautz, 1982). From time to time, the AAUP issues policy statements, developed by groups of faculty members and circulated widely among the profession for comment and modification. In particular, the "1940 Statement of Principles" on academic freedom and tenure (AAUP, 1977*a*, pp. 1-4) and the "1976 Recommended Institutional Regulations on Academic Freedom and Tenure" (1977*b*, pp. 15-21) have influenced institutional practice in decision making regarding promotion, tenure, nonrenewal, and reductions in force.

Although many institutions have explicitly incorporated the AAUP standards into faculty handbooks, employment contracts, or other policy documents, other institutions have not done so, and may have few or no written standards for the procedures to be used in making decisions about faculty employment. In some circumstances, courts have incorporated AAUP standards into employment contracts which are otherwise silent, unless the institution has adopted policies which explicitly reject or differ from the AAUP standards. For example, in *Greene v. Howard University* (1969), a federal appeals courts required the university to honor the AAUP standards for notice and reappointment, even though a statement in the faculty handbook expressly exempted the university from the AAUP standards; the court noted that the faculty handbook "purports to accept as guiding principles the policy of the American Association of University Professors on matters of academic tenure" (*Greene*, pp. 1133-34). In a case involving the termination of a professor for unprofessional conduct, the faculty member complained that the university regulations governing dismissal of faculty for inappropriate "external utterances" were vague and overbroad, and thus unconstitutional. The reviewing court noted, however, that the university regulation was identical to the AAUP's 1940 Statement, and that the AAUP had published an interpretation of that policy statement which sufficiently delimited the scope of the regulation and eliminated the problem of potential overbreadth. By accepting the AAUP definitions, the court found the institution's rules to be clear and acceptable (*Adamian v. Jacobsen*, 1975, pp. 934-35). Furthermore, courts reviewing challenges to terminations of tenured faculty in cases where the college or university had asserted that financial exigency justified the terminations have held institutions to the standards and procedures promulgated by the AAUP related to such terminations (*AAUP v. Bloomfield College*, 1975).

The willingness of courts to accept AAUP standards as norms of the profession has benefited faculty, because these standards have provided legitimate sources of "industry practice," a concept which courts have honored in nonacademic settings as unwritten but permissible supplements to employment contracts.

> Courts know that academic employment contracts are usually facially simple and incomplete documents, making it necessary for the courts to assimilate ancillary materials into the agreements to integrate the contracts. . . . AAUP policy also can provide insight, direction, and support to courts grappling with ambiguous terms, such as "financial exigency" and "academic freedom," in an attempt to discern accepted customary and usual practice at the academic institution. . . . Because it is

difficult to codify clear, precise, and acceptable standards of behavior, dismissals based on conduct or speech pose the most dangerous threat to academic freedom. If the boundaries of protected sppech and action are not demarcated clearly, academic freedom will become an empty privilege. The . . . AAUP policy documents, however, provide clarity and substance to the typical academic employment contract. Without such clarity in employment contracts, faculty members will continue to be victimized by vague contracts and indeterminate personnel regulations . . . ["The Role of Academic Freedom in Defining the Faculty Employment Contract," 1981, pp. 630-31]

Review of the case law and the literature demonstrates that, while faculty members not only enjoy all the employment protections afforded employees in nonacademic organizations, they also have the additional employment protections of academic freedom and tenure. Although faculty employed at private colleges and universities are not generally protected by the Fourteenth Amendment's due process provisions, explicit contractual protections and AAUP procedural standards, which may be incorporated into employment contracts, provide substantial protections to these faculty as well.

FINANCIAL EXIGENCY AND PROGRAM ELIMINATION

The traditional due process requirements which attach to faculty contracts and tenure and which are applicable in causal termination situations are not directly transferable to situations where an institution terminates a faculty member because of financial exigency or program elimination. Under circumstances where financial problems prohibit an institution from continuing an appointment, the courts have been very generous in allowing institutions to terminate faculty, including those with tenure, with little due process.

In recent years, higher education has encountered, and will continue to be confronted with, declines in enrollment and state and private support (Carnegie Council, 1980; Glenny and Bowen, 1981). Further, shifts in student demand from liberal arts or other disciplines to business, engineering, and the professions have forced institutions to reassess the makeup and distribution of their faculty bodies. And while "no excuse exists for higher educaiton institutions or state agencies to have failed to replace temporary expedients with well developed plans and procedures for reduction" (Glenny, 1982, p. 34), few institutions have done appropriate advanced planning (Dolan-Greene, 1981; Dougherty, 1981; Olswang, 1982-83). Indeed, the recent literature is replete with guidelines (Melchiori, 1982; Mingle, 1981; Mortimer and Tierney, 1979) and recommendations for choosing reduction scenarios (Boulding, 1975; Bowen, 1982; Newman, 1982). However, the courts and the AAUP have played the major role in defining the legal rights of faculty impacted by termination actions prompted by financial crises or program reorganization.

The AAUP, in its "1940 Statement on Academic Freedom and Tenure," has stated that a faculty member's appointment and tenure may be terminated because of "bona fide" financial exigency. The AAUP has defined a financial exigency as "an imminent financial crisis which threatens the survival of the institution as a whole and cannot be alleviated by less drastic means" than terminating tenured faculty (1977*b*, p. 17). In *AAUP v. Bloomfield College* (1975), the college claimed it was close to bankruptcy, and had given notice to 13 tenured faculty members that they would be terminated, while placing all remaining faculty on one-year terminal contracts. The college itself had adopted the 1940 AAUP Statement, including the requirement that terminations "because of financial exigency must be demonstrably bona fide." When the terminated faculty members challenged the bona fides of the Bloomfield College trustees' declaration of exigency, the trial court determined that indeed the declaration was not bona fide since other institutional assets existed (a golf course) which, if sold, could cover operating expenses. Further, the court decided that the action of hiring replacement faculty while placing the other continuing faculty on one-year contracts made the entire action of the institution questionable and therefore in bad faith.

However, on appeal, the court determined that the authority over the proper management of the assets was properly within the administrative discretion of the college board and that the trial court had gone outside of its authority when it substituted its judgment with respect to how the assets of the college should be used (p. 617). It clarified that the existence of a financial exigency should be based on the adequacy of the college's operating assets rather than its capital assets (see also *Scheuer v. Creighton University*, 1977). Nonetheless, though finding the financial exigency was *per se* bona fide, the Appellate Court struck down the termination of the faculty members as not being motivated by the financial crisis.

The essence of the *AAUP v. Bloomfield College* case is that a decision on whether a financial exigency exists normally will rest with the governing board. The cases which have followed *Bloomfield* have unanimously held that the decision on the financial welfare of the institution and what action should be taken to preserve it rest with the governing board.

> When there is a showing that the administrative body, in its exercising its judgment acts from honest convictions, based upon the facts which it believes are for the best interests of the School, and there is no showing that the acts are arbitrary or generated by ill-will, fraud, collusion, or other such motives, it is not the province of the court to interfere and substitute its judgment for that of the administrative body. [*Levitt v. Board of Trustees of Nebraska State College*, 1974, p. 950]

Though a deficit in the institution's operating budget may be present, this alone may not require the declaration of financial exigency when other, less drastic, options are available. One such option is the elimination of a program of study. Just as the AAUP recognizes the validity of faculty removals as a result of financial exigencies, so too does it recognize the validity of removal of faculty due to program elimination. The AAUP states that the "termination of an appointment with continuous tenure or a probationary or specified appointment before the end of the specified term may occur as a result of a bona fide formal discontinuance of a program or department of instruction" (1977*b*, p.

18). Thus a program or an entire department could be eliminated, with the faculty therein terminated, without affecting the tenure rights of faculty in other departments (Olswang, 1982-83).

In the best of all worlds, a tenure contract would specify the bases for termination. However, where financial or programmatic reasons have not been so specified, the courts have gone so far as to find that financial exigency is an "implicit" term of the tenure contract (see *Krotkoff v. Goucher College*, 1978, p. 678) justifying termination, just as is a program elimination.

> American courts and secondary authorities uniformly recognize that, unless otherwise provided in the agreement of the parties, or in the regulations of the institution, or in a statute, an institution of higher education has an implied contractual right to make in good faith an unavoidable termination of right to the employment of a tenured faculty member when his position is being eliminated as part of a change in an academic program. [*Jiminez v. Almodovar*, 1981, p. 368; see also Clague, 1982]

Thus both public and private institutions may terminate faculty for financial or programmatic reasons, whether such terms are explicitly stated in the contract or the university rules, or not stated at all ("Dismissal of Tenured Faculty for Reasons of Financial Exigency," 1976; Mix, 1978; Tucker, 1974, in conjunction with Wilson, 1977). With this institutional right to terminate tenured appointments clearly in place, the issues revolving around faculty terminations focus primarily on how faculty are identified, and what their rights are after being so identified.

In a complete program elimination situation it is relatively easy to identify which faculty members should be selected for layoff. All of the faculty members with their primary affiliation in the eliminated program would be subject to termination. However, in a financial exigency situation where a policy decision is made to eliminate faculty not on a program-specific basis, the question of what criteria may be valid as a basis of selection is often the most critical. This becomes even more problematic in that program reductions — the scaling down of an area of instruction by eliminating selected individuals from a program while retaining others — is not directly recognized by the AAUP as acceptable.

The AAUP does not give guidance on what criteria an institution should use in selecting faculty for termination in program reduction situations. It does, however, clearly state a preference for retaining tenured faculty over nontenured faculty in all faculty reduction situations it does accept. "The appointment of a faculty member with tenure will not be terminated in favor of retaining a faculty member without tenure except in extraordinary circumstances where serious distortion of the academic program would otherwise result" (1977b, p. 17). Also the AAUP states, "As particular reductions are considered, rights under academic tenure should be protected. The service of a tenured professor should not be terminated in favor of retaining someone without tenure who may at a particular moment seem more productive" (1977c, p. 48). The national organizations believe that when financial reasons require faculty terminations, tenured faculty must be given a preference over nontenured faculty. However, no court has formally stated that tenured faculty must be given preference over nontenured faculty in such situations. Indeed, courts have always found that tenured faculty may themselves be removed in such situations for financial reasons. "No case indicates that tenure creates a right to exemption from dismissal for financial exigency reasons" (*Krotkoff v. Goucher College*, 1978, p. 679, note 11).

If tenured faculty are not given an absolute preference, what criteria have been accepted for selecting among faculty for removal? In *Krotkoff v. Goucher College*, both tenured and nontenured faculty members were selected for removal. "These professors were selected largely on the basis of a dean's study of enrollment projections and necessary changes in curriculum" (1978, p. 675). The court found this to be a valid procedure. In *Levitt v. Board of Trustees of Nebraska State College* (1974), the administration, faced with a legislatively mandated budget reduction, prepared a list of criteria which would be used to evaluate and select faculty members for removal. This list was created "in order to verify the judgment made in deciding which faculty members would be terminated" with the objective of maintaining the most necessary programs and retaining individual faculty "necessary to carry on these programs" (p. 949). This procedure was upheld by the court though both tenured and nontenured faculty were selected and terminated. In *Bignall v. North Idaho College* (1976), the court was squarely faced with the question of whether junior faculty could be retained over more senior tenured faculty. In upholding the removal of a tenured faculty member while a more junior faculty member in the same unit was retained, the court found that the college had formulated guidelines which were applied equally to all members of the faculty in the college. The court further found that "while there was some perhaps unavoidable flexibility in the selection process, the district court was not clearly erroneous in concluding that the college did not act discriminatorily" (p. 250).

Thus the present state of the law allows an institution, provided that it can justify on financial grounds the declaration of financial exigency or on either financial or academic grounds the elimination of a program, substantial flexibility as to how it may identify faculty for termination. Indeed, in this area, it seems clear from judicial decisions that institutions can remove both tenured and nontenured faculty as long as adequate guidelines for selection are developed, equally applied, and arguably in the best interests of the institution.

Of course, the fact that faculty may be identified for removal does not vacate their due process rights to challenge the bona fides of the exigency or the validity or application of the criteria used in their selection. However, because terminations of faculty for financial exigency or program elimination do not fall within the standard concept of termination for cause, different due process requirements attach. In *Johnson v. Board of Regents of the University of Wisconsin System* (1975), the court outlined the minimal due process elements institutions are required to make available to faculty who appeal their layoffs.

These rights include

> furnishing each [faculty member] with a reasonably adequate written statement of the basis for the initial decision to lay off; furnishing each with a reasonably adequate description of the manner in which the initial decision had been arrived at; making a reasonably adequate disclosure to each of the information and data upon which the decision-makers had relied; and providing each the opportunity to respond. [p. 240]

Hearing procedures normally associated with terminations of tenured faculty are not generally available in program elimination or financial exigency terminations. Further, in terminations for cause, faculty members are entitled to pretermination hearings before adverse consequences attach, while in removals for financial reasons, due process procedures may be afforded after the termination is implemented (*Klein v. Board of Higher Education of City University of New York*, 1977). Finally, while the AAUP recommends faculty receive at least 12 months notice or equivalent compensation when being removed for financial reasons (1977*b*, p. 18), reality shows that institutions faced with financial crises are often unable to provide such lengthy notice periods. Courts, when confronted with such situations, have approved financial exigency removals of tenured faculty with notice as short as 30 days (*Klein*, p. 1113).

But even though the due process procedures to be afforded faculty are truncated in such situations, other faculty rights do attach. In the situation where a faculty member is removed primarily because of program elimination, it may be that positions exist elsewhere in the institution for which the faculty member could qualify. Of course, in a financial exigency, it is less likely that this would happen since it is a requirement of financial exigency that all other options to reduce a budget, including freezing of all vacant positions, should first have been exhausted. "If an institution because of financial exigency terminates appointments it will not at the same time make new appointments except in extraordinary circumstances where a serious distortion of academic program would otherwise result" (AAUP, 1977*b*, p. 17). But there exists the obligation to try to place a faculty member in a suitable vacancy in the institution should one exist. Indeed, one court has found that it is the "national academic community's understanding" that tenure includes the requirement that the university make a good-faith effort to find another position for released faculty members (*Krotkoff v. Goucher College*, 1978, p. 769).

It may also happen that positions in other programs for which the terminated faculty member is not now trained or skilled would be available. Indeed, program reductions and eliminations can come about because a program, in light of shifting student demands, is overstaffed, requiring that one program have its size reduced while other programs expand to meet the growing student demand. The AAUP in its financial exigency guidelines states that a tenured faculty member should be given the opportunity to "readapt within a department or elsewhere within the institution. Institutional resources should be available for assistance in readaptation" (1977*c*, pp. 48-49). Though the AAUP policies provide for the consideration of retraining, courts have not required this where it was not an explicit part of the institutional contract (*Browzin v.*

Catholic University, 1975; *Krotkoff v. Goucher College,* 1978).

It should be recognized that even though courts approve faculty removals in financial exigency and program reduction situations, negative outcomes occur from such actions. Removals of faculty inevitably result in declining faculty morale (Williams, Olswang, and Hargett, forthcoming). Further, censure by the AAUP is always a possible outcome, particularly where program reduction strategies are utilized, the validity of the exigency is challenged, or questions are raised as to underlying motives for the faculty removals.

It is abundantly clear that the potential for abuse of financial bases for removal of tenured faculty members exists (see Mortimer, 1981; Richards, 1983–84). Indeed, the courts themselves have recognized the potential for misuse. "The obvious danger remains that financial exigency can become too easy an excuse for dismissing a teacher who is merely unpopular or controversial or misunderstood — a way for the university to rid itself of an unwanted teacher but without, according to him, his important procedural rights" (*Browzin v. Catholic University,* 1975, p. 847). Despite this potential for abuse, courts have consistently upheld such terminations as consistent with the principles of academic freedom and tenure. "Dismissals based on financial exigency, unlike those for cause or disability, are impersonal; they are unrelated to the views of the dismissed teacher. . . . Hence bona fide dismissals based on financial exigency do not threaten the values protected by tenure" (*Krotkoff v. Goucher College,* 1978, p. 680). And even if the economic conditions for higher education should stabilize, reducing the need to use financial reasons for faculty removals, educational necessity — forced by shifts in student demand for business or high-technology programs — may increase pressures on institutions to reallocate resources internally, requiring faculty reductions in certain no-longer-essential areas. Thus courts are going to be further pressed to provide institutions the latitude they need to handle institutional reallocation decisions. Since faculty rights and employment contracts will be held in the balance, other institutional structures are being examined to relieve the growing use of financial or programmatic terminations.

RETIREMENTS: VOLUNTARY AND INVOLUNTARY

In recent years, concern has risen about the impact created by faculty's choosing to stay at their institutions longer, slowing down the ability of institutions to hire new faculty for academic areas in more demand. The trend toward faculty's delaying retirement has been caused by two primary factors, the first being faculty fear that the increasing rate of inflation would cut heavily into retirement income, and the second being the adoption of federal and state legislation raising the mandatory retirement age from 65 to 70 years (Felicetti, 1982). This trend toward the graying of the professoriate has prompted much attention to incentive retirement plans and other alternatives to make second careers attractive to faculty (Furniss, 1981; Patton, 1979).

One of the critical factors prompting attention to alternative strategies to buy out older faculty in order to make room for newer or different faculty, or to just reduce overall university expenditures, was the passage in 1978 of the Age Discrimination in Employment Act Amendments. This law provides that it is unlawful for an employer

> to fail or refuse to hire or to discharge any individual with respect to his compensation terms, conditions, or privileges of employment because of such individual's age; or to limit, segregate, or classify his employees in any way which would deprive or tend to deprive an individual of employment opportunities or otherwise adversely affect the status of an employee because of an individual's age. [29 U.S.C. § 623(a)]

When passed, after substantial lobbying from the higher education community, the amendment included a special four-year exemption for tenured faculty. "Nothing in this chapter shall be construed to prohibit compulsory retirement of any employee who has attained 65 years of age but not 70 years of age and who is serving under contract of unlimited tenure or similar arrangement providing for unlimited tenure at an institution of higher education" (29 U.S.C. 631(d)). This exemption expired on July 1, 1982, and thus after that date the age 70 mandatory retirement provision applied to tenured faculty in institutions of higher education as well. The essence of this provision is that a faculty member may not be compelled to retire against his or her will prior to age 70. Thus the use of age in making decisions on staffing patterns was prohibited, and remains prohibited, if the faculty members are between the ages of 40 and 70.

During the four-year period of the exemption, numerous faculty were indeed mandatorily retired and their tenure severed. However, many of the retirees were hired back by their institutions, prompting the interesting question of such retirees' recoverage by the Age Discrimination Act's protections. In the literature this issue is commonly called "decoupling." In other words, a faculty member is retired at age 65 and tenure is decoupled from the new reemployment status occurring between ages 65 and 70. Since the exemption applied only to tenured faculty, do the protections then apply to the now nontenured faculty member until age 70? The Equal Employment Opportunity Commission's final interpretation on this subject reads:

> An employee within the exemption can lawfully be forced to retire on account of age, age 65 or above. In addition, the employer is free to retain such employee either in the same position or status or in a different position or status, provided that the employee voluntarily accepts this new status. . . . An employee who accepts a nontenured position or part-time employment, however, may not be treated any less favorably on account of age than a similarly situated younger employee. [29 C.F.R. § 1625.11(g), 1981]

In *Levine v. Fairleigh Dickinson University* (1981), the court held that the university "could not avoid its obligations under the ADEA" to a faculty member who was indeed retired at age 65 and thereafter reemployed (p. 829). Thus the courts and administrative interpretations held that once tenure was decoupled from a faculty member between ages 65 and 70, the faculty member was once again protected from age discrimination (see Barnes and Schlottman, 1982–83; Bompey, 1981–82). Of course, since July 1, 1982, the age 70 requirement applies to faculty with tenure, as well as without tenure, making the decoupling issue, in the sense of exemption, no longer applicable. Nonetheless, the question "Can tenure be separated from employment without violating the Age Discrimination Act?" is still relevant, particularly if mandatory retirements are to be prohibited entirely, as some states have already done.

The question of tenure as a barrier to institutional flexibility, while always a subject of debate, is one that is more evident than ever. In *Beyond Traditional Tenure* (Chait and Ford, 1982), the authors examined various existing structures, including unusual contract plans, that provide additional institutional flexibility. Some argue, however, that these alternatives to tenure have substantial institutional and personnel consequences (Finkin, 1983–84). But assuming that tenure systems are to continue, institutions are examining mechanisms to induce retirements or faculty career changes.

Retirement inducement programs can be classified into three primary schemes. The normal early retirement structure usually contains financial or other incentives to encourage faculty and administrators to fully retire prior to mandatory retirement age. The partial retirement structure, or full retirement with vested reemployment rights, permits academic personnel to maintain partial employment status, usually less than one-third time, while receiving full retirement benefits. The phased retirement program usually permits faculty and administrators to gradually reduce their employment percentage over a period of years, with the institution maintaining a full level of contribution into the retirement program (Todd, 1983).

In addition to retirement plans themselves, institutions are encouraging faculty to consider mid-career changes (Patton, 1979). Institutions are entering into consortia with business to make outside employment options available to faculty (Shulman, 1979). Institutions are providing career counseling (Bouchard, 1980; Centra, 1976) and acting as brokers between faculty and outside organizations (Felicetti, 1982). And, of course, institutions are offering cash buy-out incentives.

While early studies questioned the cost savings realized from alternative retirement or other incentive plans (Palmer and Patton, 1978), it is clear that institutions have gotten more involved in them. They are a humane way to reduce institutional costs and provide flexibility in staffing requirements. Yet they are not a panacea for resolving the concerns many still harbor about the employment structures in academe, and particularly about tenure.

EMPLOYMENT DISCRIMINATION AND COLLEGIALITY

Ever since the protection of the civil rights employment laws was extended to higher education faculty in 1972, faculty employment discrimination litigation has mushroomed. College faculty have taken their employing institutions to court in over 150 cases since 1972, and it is likely that even more cases have been settled out of court (Lee, forthcoming).[1] Many of the questions raised in faculty discrimination cases strike at the very essence of the academic enterprise. What is the role of peer review in academic employment decisions? Is it appropriate to conduct peer review and employment decision making in confidence to encourage honest evaluations, or does confidentiality permit discrimination or arbitrariness to occur with impunity? Does a department have the right to raise its standards for faculty performance, or to shift its emphasis to a different area of research, or to make adjustments to its curriculum if such changes have negative employment implications for women or members of ethnic and racial minority groups? Can a peer review group take into consideration the quality of collegiality displayed by a candidate for promotion or tenure? The responses of the courts to these issues need to be examined closely for their effect upon traditional methods of evaluating faculty for hiring, promotion, tenure, and merit salary increases.

Before reviewing the research on the impact of courts on faculty employment practices, it is useful to summarize the type of evidence and the kinds of proof required in academic discrimination cases. A faculty member challenging an employment decision as discriminatory (usually a denial of promotion, tenure, hiring, renewal, or a claim that salary discrimination has occurred) must first establish that he or she is a member of a "protected class" under the law, was qualified for the position, was not hired (or promoted, etc.), and that either an individual with similar or lesser qualifications was hired, or, in the case of promotion or tenure, other individuals possessing similar qualifications as the faculty member in question received more favorable treatment. The burden then shifts to the college to "articulate some legitimate, nondiscriminatory reason" for the negative decision concerning the faculty member. At that point, the faculty member must demonstrate that the college's stated reason was, in fact, a pretext for discrimination (Lee, 1982–83, p. 288; *Texas Dept. of Community Affairs v. Burdine*, 1981).

The legal standards for proving an academic employment discrimination case require the plaintiff faculty member to prove that he or she was well qualified for the position (promotion, etc.) and concomitantly require the institution to show that the faculty member was, in some important respect, unqualified. In most academic discrimination cases, colleges attempt to demonstrate that the faculty member was inadequate in either scholarship, teaching, service, or colleagueship, and it is this segment of the litigation which has raised the many troublesome issues referred to earlier.

One issue of special importance to higher education is the question of "judicial intervention" in the employment practices of colleges and universities. Because an allegation of discrimination requires the court to examine the reasons for the negative decision and evaluate their fairness, such cases have the potential to force changes in criteria, standards, and procedures for peer review and evaluations of faculty.

In early academic discrimination cases, the written opinions demonstrated the discomfort of trial judges faced with complicated issues of faculty evaluation and peer review. Researchers have noted a trend in these early cases to keep "hands off" the subjective evaluations of faculty concerning their colleagues, and defer to the judgments of academics rather than scrutinizing them for evidence of discrimination (Mazia and de Ita, 1978-79; Shanor and Shanor, 1981; Vladeck and Young, 1978; "Civil Rights: Academic Freedom, Secrecy and Subjectivity," 1982). However, toward the end of the 1970s, opinions in academic discrimination cases began to demonstrate an awareness that allegations of employment discrimination in higher education should receive the same kind of scrutiny that alleged discrimination in nonacademic organizations received from the courts, and that "Congress did not intend that these institutions which employ persons who work primarily with their mental facilities should enjoy a different status . . . than those which employ persons who work primarily with their hands" (*Kunda v. Muhlenberg College*, 1980, p. 550). The federal courts made it clear in several important academic discrimination cases that they rejected the " 'hands off,' 'anti-interventionist,' 'extraordinary deference,' or 'different status' approach to higher education [discrimination] cases" (Flygare, 1980–81, p. 108).

Despite the exhortations of the courts, both to themselves and to other courts, to treat colleges and universities like any other organization accused of discrimination, some researchers are unconvinced that academic discrimination cases receive the same kind of judicial scrutiny that similar cases in nonacademic organizations receive. One team of researchers has identified three causes of what they believe to be the continuing disinclination of courts to scrutinize academic employment decisions:

> First, the courts are unfamiliar with academic employment practices. Second, a negative attitude generally exists toward sex discrimination cases. Third, less clear but more difficult to overcome, there is the sense that the decisions of employers are based on a desire for excellence and are made by individuals with extensive expertise. These decisions are therefore immunized from challenge under law. [Vladeck and Young, 1978, p. 62.]

Other researchers have noted the courts' reluctance to "second guess" faculty expertise in evaluating the qualifications of their colleagues ("Academic Freedom Versus Title VII," 1981; Shanor and Shanor, 1981, p. 146). But researchers analyzing discrimination litigation brought by white-collar and professional employees against nonacademic employers have concluded that the courts are reluctant to intervene in *any* employment decision which requires the application of subjective standards, as is required in evaluating professionals, managers, and other individuals performing high-level, responsible jobs. (Bartholet, 1982; Waintroob, 1979–80).

The apparent reluctance of the courts to scrutinize decisions made using subjective evaluation criteria suggests, then, that courts would be loath to overturn peer review determinations by departmental or institutional faculty colleagues. Although one researcher warned that increased judicial scrutiny of academic discrimination cases could result in the destruction of peer review (Flygare,

1980–81, p. 108), others have concluded that over a decade of academic discrimination litigation has not weakened peer review but, in fact, has legitimated peer review as the appropriate method for reaching academic employment decisions (Lee, forthcoming.).

A second area of considerable concern to academics has been the implications of litigation for the maintenance of confidentiality in peer review deliberations. The issue was dramatized when a professor from the University of Georgia was jailed for 90 days and fined for refusing to disclose his vote in a tenure-denial case (Middleton, 1980, p. 1, col. 10), but the issue of a faculty plaintiff's access to personnel files, to the reasons for the negative employment decision, and to other evidence necessary to conduct a legal challenge to an academic employment decision has troubled courts for over a decade. Two important interests clash when a plaintiff seeks information about the employment decision, and the courts have been less than successful in establishing a balance between the plaintiff's legitimate need for evidence and the college's interest in preserving an atmosphere in which faculty may evaluate their colleagues in confidence (Lee, 1982–83, pp. 302-307).

Proponents of preserving confidentiality in the peer review process argue that disclosure of such information would chill the entire process, and would result in evaluations which were overcautious or noncommittal (Bunzel, 1975; "Preventing Unnecessary Intrusions on University Autonomy," 1981; "Report of the Committee on Confidentiality," 1979). Opponents of confidentiality, on the other hand, argue that the public policy interests in eliminating employment discrimination overcome institutional or faculty interests in preserving the confidentiality of peer review deliberations, and that academic tradition should not be preserved at the expense of civil rights ("Academic Freedom Privilege," 1982; Lee, 1982–83, pp. 303-34).

One response to this debate has been an attempt on the part of institutions and faculty peer reviewers to secure judicial creation of an "academic freedom privilege" which would protect peer review deliberations from disclosure in court. To date, three academic discrimination cases have addressed the issue of (1) whether an academic freedom privilege should be created by the courts and (2) if such a privilege is appropriate, whether it should be applied to the particular case at hand. Whether federal courts will be inclined to approve an "academic freedom privilege" is not clear, for only one court has created an academic freedom privilege, one court has approved the concept of such a privilege but declined to apply it to a specific case, and one court rejected the concept altogether. In the *Dinnan* case, the court said that an academic freedom privilege would "give an institution of higher learning *carte blanche* to practice discrimination of all types," and that the privilege would not be in the interest of public policy because "society has no strong interest in encouraging timid faculty members to serve on tenure committees" (*In re: Dinnan*, 1981, pp. 431-432). Despite the approval of the privilege by the Court of Appeals for the Second Circuit in the *Gray* case, the court ordered that the information requested by the plaintiff be given to him. However, in a later case, the Court of

Appeals for the Seventh Circuit protected the identities of external reviewers with an academic freedom privilege because it believed that maintaining their anonymity was more important than the plaintiff's interest in knowing their identity (*Gray v. Board of Higher Education, CUNY*, 1982; *EEOC v. University of Notre Dame*, 1983). Thus the debate over the propriety of the "academic freedom privilege" will continue, and the question of how to balance the interests of confidentiality and disclosure remains unresolved.

Other related disputes over access to confidential peer review records have arisen in the context of investigations by federal and state regulatory agencies. Probably the most widely publicized dispute was between the University of California at Berkeley and the U.S. Department of Labor. The Labor Department, in conducting a compliance review prior to awarding the university a federal contract, attempted to copy several hundred confidential peer review records. The university refused to release the records to an off-site location, although it permitted investigators to use the records, but not to copy them, on campus. After lengthy administrative litigation, the university and DOL entered into a consent decree in which the government provided greater protection for the secrecy of peer review evaluations, but was allowed to copy those which were essential to its investigation (Smith, 1981–82).

The confidentiality of peer review records may be controlled by state public laws as well. For example, laws in Pennsylvania and Indiana give faculty employed at public institutions the right of access to letters of recommendation and other "confidential" evaluative material. These laws would not affect the confidentiality of peer review records at private insitutions, however.

Other litigants alleging that denials of promotion or tenure were discriminatory have claimed that rising performance standards have unfairly burdened women and minority group members. Little research has been conducted on the issue of whether departmental or institutional attempts to "raise standards" are legally permissible if such actions have a disproportionately negative effect upon members of protected classes. This dearth of research may be a result of the courts' overwhelming rejection of claims that increased hiring, promotion, or tenure standards were a pretext for discrimination, asserting that a college or university has a legitimate interest in improving the quality of its faculty (*Akhtar v. Van de Wetering*, 1982). Similarly, the courts have rejected arguments that institutions should not be permitted to apply higher standards to candidates for promotion than were in existence when the individual was hired (*Banerjee v. Board of Trustees*, 1980), and have also rejected assertions that institutions should "grandfather" faculty, using the criteria in effect at the time of hiring to evaluate the faculty member at the time of promotion (*Randolph v. Regents of Oklahoma Colleges*, 1982). Nor have researchers examined the reaction of the courts to the legality of a college's assertion that, while the faculty member performed adequately in the areas of research, teaching, and service, the research or curricular focus of the department had shifted and the services of that particular faculty member were no longer needed. To the arguments of plaintiffs that such "shifts" in research or curricular emphasis were merely pretexts for discrimination, the courts have replied that colleges and their collective faculty have the right to use managerial discretion in reaching decisions about how resources will be deployed, and that such changes are legitimate reasons for negative employment decisions (see, for example, *Johnson v. University of Pittsburgh*, 1977; *Smith v. University of North Carolina*, 1980; *Timper v. Board of Regents, University of Wisconson*, 1981).

A final area of interest in academic discrimination litigation is the courts' willingness to accept lack of collegiality as a legitimate reason for reaching a negative employment decision. The issue of collegiality is especially important in tenure decisions, for the award of tenure means that the faculty member may be one's colleague for the remainder of his or her professional career. Courts have recognized this special concern of academics, and have permitted peer review committees to use poor collegiality or personal incompatibility between the candidate and his or her colleagues as a rationale for denying a faculty member tenure (Lee, 1982–83, pp. 292-293). Zirkel (1983) has warned that allegations of poor collegiality may be pretenses for attempts by colleagues who dislike the candidate's views to deny him or her the academic freedom rights protected by both the First Amendment and academic norms. Nevertheless, courts appear to view this issue in the same way that other courts have viewed claims of "freedom of association," and have deferred to institutional decision makers in challenges of this sort (Yurko, 1980).

Reviewing the research on the impact of academic discrimination litigation suggests that the impact has not been as substantial, nor as detrimental, as early writers had predicted (Lee, forthcoming). However, the research focuses primarily on the written opinions themselves, and only a few articles have been published which describe the impact of an academic discrimination case on the institution that was sued (see, for example, Clark, 1977). Further research is needed which investigates the impact, either direct or indirect, of such litigation on peer review and institutional criteria and procedures for faculty employment decisions.

SALARY EQUITY

Although the issue of salary equity in academe has generated less litigation than discrimination in hiring and promotion decisions, the issue has received much attention from researchers. Faculty members alleging salary inequities may sue under several state and federal laws, though under each similar legal and policy issues are raised.[2] Researchers have focused on three broad areas relating to salary inequity in academe: studies which document the existence of salary discrimination, studies which attempt to explain (and occasionally to justify) salary inequities, and analyses of various methodological tools used to prove, or disprove, the existence of salary discrimination on a particular campus.

A number of studies have collected data on faculty salaries and have analyzed the relationship between certain faculty characteristics, including race and gender, and salary levels. For example, Gordon, Morton, and Braden (1974) analyzed the faculty salary levels by sex, race, and discipline, while other researchers have limited their analyses to the effect of gender on salary levels (Bayer and Astin, 1975; Carnegie Commission on Higher Education, 1973). Data collected in a 1982 national survey indicated that, on the average, female faculty members were earning approximately 81% of the average male salary, and differences by sex within every faculty rank were also found (Evangelhauf, 1984, p. 20).

Other researchers have concentrated on the explanations, economic, social, or otherwise, for salary inequities in academe (Lester, 1980; Sowell, 1976). The limited geographic mobility of women faculty has been studied and cited as one cause of depressed salaries for female academics (Maxwell, Rosenfeld, and Spilerman, 1979), as well as societal expectations for women's responsibilities for the home and children, which may result in lower productivity and fewer promotions for women faculty members (Lester, 1980).

With regard to the issue of "proving" academic salary inequities, a threshold issue must be addressed: that of the equality or comparability of faculty jobs. Courts have struggled with this issue, but it has received little attention from researchers. The question is whether faculty positions are equal at all, or whether departmental and individual differences are too substantial to permit comparisons, for example, between an assistant professor of biochemistry and an assistant professor of physical education.

> Professors at major universities divide their time among a bewildering array of tasks — classroom teaching, counseling students, supervising dissertations, working on committees, engaging in administrative duties, writing books and articles, directing research laboratories, giving seminars and public lectures, recruiting, and part-time consulting for private industry or government. Many devote substantial energy to vying for research grants. Furthermore, a department itself may encourage diversity by hiring a mix of outstanding teachers, well-known scholars, and diligent writers who can crank out their quota of articles. It may even create positions for unique "headliners" who are renowned scholars in residence, unburdened by teaching duties. Even within a relatively homogeneous department, each professor is likely to branch out and strive for expertise in a particular speciality . . . [Greenfield, 1977, p. 47]

Greenfield noted that such diversity makes it nearly impossible to create uniform salary levels for faculty and, as a result, salary decisions are often made subjectively and on an *ad hoc* basis (p. 47).

Lester (1975) argued that attempts to apply equal pay principles to academe are inappropriate because job *content* is not the basis for salary distinctions, but job *performance* is the criterion used. He explained that faculty at all ranks perform essentially the same tasks, and that the contributions of the faculty members are, and should be, the basis for differential salary levels (p. 30). Lester's argument assumes, however, that some fair and uniform method of evaluating faculty "contributions," which is free of race or gender bias, is used to make salary decisions in academe; data from studies of academic salaries suggest that disparities are too widely distributed to be accounted for solely by the "contributions" theory (Pezzulo and Brittingham, 1979, pp. 8-9).

Although early judicial decisions appeared to sympathize with the arguments that traditional equal pay analyses were inappropriate in academic organizations (Koch, 1982), courts in several recent cases have operated on the assumption that faculty members of the same rank and qualifications are entitled to the same salary, unless a market rationale (e.g., a scarce specialization) or differences in productivity are evident (Hendrickson and Lee, 1983). For this reason, several class-action plaintiffs have won major victories. Although the results over the past several years have been mixed, plaintiffs suing Montana State University received over $350,000 in salary adjustments, and the University of Minnesota entered a consent decreee with a group of women faculty plaintiffs that could result in $60 million in financial awards (Wehrwein, 1981), in addition to the $1.5 million the university has already been ordered to pay in attorney fees ("University of Minnesota Will Pay $1.5 Million in Legal Fees," 1983). Furthermore, a federal trial judge recently ruled against the City University of New York in a class-action salary discrimination case, and the potential compensatory damages could exceed $60 million (McFadden, 1983, p. 27). Clearly, academic salary discrimination cases have overwhelming financial consequences for colleges and universities, and the methods by which such cases are proven has become a fertile area for research.

Recent academic salary discrimination cases have been class-action suits, that is, several faculty members sue the college or university on behalf of all similarly situated faculty members (in most cases, women faculty). Should the class plaintiffs prevail in court, the defendant college or university must provide the required relief to all members of the class, not just those individuals who initiated the suit. Two methods of proving institutionwide discrimination have been used in these cases: a method called "pairing," and multiple regression.

In pairing, individual female faculty members are matched with male faculty members on the basis of the similarity of their qualifications. Typical pairing criteria include "educational level attained, years at the given institution, field of employment, present rank, and any license held" (Greenfield, 1977, p. 49). Although pairing may be attractive because it is "an intuitively reasonable way to prove equal skill, effort and responsibility [and] . . . is especially useful if a department is too small to permit overall statistical comparisons" (p. 49), it is often difficult to find a male faculty member whose qualifications match those of a particular female faculty member (p. 48). An unreported case in which Memphis State University was found guilty of salary discrimination demonstrates the difficulties presented by the pairing technique, for the judge "found himself considering the relative value of a Medieval English specialist versus other specialists in an English department, whether teaching public administration involved the same skill, effort and responsibility as teaching political science" (LaNoue, 1982, p. 24). One researcher has characterized the problems posed by pairing as "almost insurmountable," explaining that the major problem with pairwise analysis of salary differences is that often one cannot prove the necessary assumption: that all other relevant factors are equal when comparing two faculty members. What does an analyst do when one faculty member is identical to another except that the first published a book with a reputable university press? When the second won a "teacher of the year" award? When the first faculty member is a computer scientist and the second a musician? [Koch, 1982, p. 12]

Furthermore, Pezzulo and Brittingham (1979) point out that the pairing method can show the existence of salary inequity, but cannot demonstrate the extent of the salary inequity because it is limited to the actual comparisons made. Fortunately for the parties and the judges alike, subsequent cases used a more sophisticated, although still imperfect, statistical technique which eliminated some of the weaknesses of the pairing method, but which introduced new difficulties which appear equally troublesome.

Regression analysis is a "statistical device for making precise and quantitative estimates of the effects of different factors on some variable of interest" (Fisher, 1980, p. 702). This technique is useful in analyses of salary inequities because it permits the researcher to predict the salaries of individuals based upon the overall effect of each of their qualifications. In regression analysis, the effect of a group of independent, or "predictor," variables upon the dependent variable, salary, is measured by calculating the effect of the predictor variables upon the salaries of male faculty, and then developing predicted salaries for female faculty using the regression equation developed from the male salaries. The actual salaries of female faculty members are then compared with their predicted salaries, and statistically significant differences may be indicative of discrimination (Greenfield, 1977, pp. 51-56). While this description of regression analysis is oversimplified and incomplete, it demonstrates the importance of identifying *all* of the variables which actually influence salary decisions, for the regression technique assumes that salary differences which are not explained by some predictor variable are attributable to sex discrimination.

Although regression analysis is a useful tool in salary discrimination litigation, researchers have cautioned that several factors may confound analyses of academic salary inequities which use the regression model. First, presumably "unbiased" predictor variables, such as rank, discipline, years in the profession, or other variables, may have been "tainted" by unlawful practices at the time of hiring or promotion, bias in graduate program admissions and mentorship, or other, often subtle forms of discrimination (Bodner, 1983–84; Pezzulo and Brittingham, 1979, p. 5). In fact, plaintiffs' statistical experts in academic salary discrimination cases have often argued that rank is a tainted variable and should not be entered into the regression equation for that reason; this argument was successful in a few cases (*Mecklenberg v. Board of Regents, Montana State University*, 1976; *Melani v. Board of Higher Education, City of New York*, 1983). The argument, however, has not been universally accepted by judges in other academic salary equity cases, probably because of the naturally high correlation between rank and salary (Finkelstein, 1980, pp. 741-742).

A second area which confounds regression analyses in academic salary disputes is the relative status and economic value of various academic disciplines. It may be difficult to separate institutional perceptions from market variables in determining salaries for nursing or home economics faculty on the one hand, and chemistry and engineering faculty on the other (Pezzulo and Brittingham, 1979, p. 5). Women also tend to be overrepresented in traditional disciplines (such as education, the humanities, and the social sciences) and underrepresented in disciplines such as business or computer science (see, for example, Koch, 1982, p. 8).

A further problem in using the regression model to discern academic salary inequity is its inability to account for qualitative differences among faculty. For example, the quality of a faculty member's research is often cited as an important determinant of faculty salaries (Lester, 1975); yet regression analysis uses quantified variables (such as number of publications) to predict salaries. Nor has the quality of the journal in which a faculty member's articles been published normally been taken into consideration in a regression analysis (Tuckman, 1979, p. 22), although one study of faculty in one discipline at one institution did measure the effect of journal quality on faculty salaries (Katz, 1973). Furthermore, neither teaching ability nor quality of professional service can be adequately quantified (Finkelstein, 1980, p. 744). Judicial reaction to the lack of qualitative data in academic salary litigation has been mixed: in *Mecklenberg* (1976) the judge believed quantitative evidence to be sufficient proof of salary discrimination, while in *Sobel v. Yeshiva University* (1983) the judge viewed productivity differences among faculty as a critical component of salary decisions, and refused to rule that salaries were inequitable in the absence of such qualitative data (see Bompey and Saltzman, 1982–83).

As might be expected, researchers have given a considerable amount of attention to the merits and disadvantages of particular regression models, the treatment of various predictor variables, and the interpretation of the outcomes of the statistical analysis. The literature is replete with articles touting a new model, followed by articles criticizing the model, and other articles describing how a certain college evaluated salary practices and remedied identified inequities. (See Pezzulo and Brittingham, 1979, for a collection of writings on these issues.) Related literature includes analyses of how faculty performance is evaluated and rewarded (Blackburn and Clark, 1975; Buzan and Hunt, 1976; Katz, 1973), and certain methods of evaluating the quality of faculty research (citation analysis, for example) are explored (Garfield, 1972).

A new type of salary discrimination litigation is developing which may complicate even more the courts' attempts to ensure equitable salary practices in academe. In 1981 the U.S. Supreme Court ruled that it was not necessary for a plaintiff alleging salary discrimination to prove that she performed work equal to that of the men with whom she was comparing herself (*County of Washington v. Gunther*, 1981). Although this case was heralded as a victory for the doctrine of "comparable worth" (a doctrine in which the intrinsic worth of a job is compared with that of other, higher-paying jobs), the Court's ruling was, in fact, made on narrow procedural grounds.

However, the concept of comparable worth has significance for the faculty employment relationship because of the disparities in the salaries paid by different disciplines. As mentioned earlier, faculty salaries in disciplines in which women have tended to cluster (such as nursing, home economics, education, and languages) tend to be lower than salaries of faculty in the hard sciences, business, and the professions. The comparable worth doctrine would require an assessment of the relative values of faculty trained in various disciplines.

Recent comparable worth litigation in nonacademic organizations suggests that this legal theory may prove to be a popular one for women seeking salary parity with males performing work of comparable value to the organization. In *Washington State Federation of State Employees v. State of Washington* (1983), a federal trial judge ruled that the state had discriminated against its female employees by paying them approximately 25% less than males in comparable jobs. The comparability of the jobs was established by a study commissioned by the state itself; the study assigned points to jobs that required similar knowledge and skills. While this case may be *sui generis* because of the existence of the state's study (whose recommendations the state only partially followed), the potential for litigation against colleges by plaintiffs using this legal theory is worth some attention. For example, women faculty in Oregon have sued the state higher education system; their litigation raises comparable worth issues similar to those in the Washington case (Farrell, 1984, p. 21). The Oregon case and similar cases have important consequences for higher education. Until more comparable worth cases have completed the litigation process, however, it will be difficult to predict the implications of this legal theory for faculty employment rights.

The perplexing methodological problems and the enormity of a college's potential liability if faculty salary discrimination claims are successful suggest that salary equity will continue to be an active area of scholarly inquiry. To date, however, judicial reactions to the particular regression model used, the absence of qualitative data, and the appropriate population to be used in the analysis have been inconsistent (Hendrickson and Lee, 1983; LaNoue, 1982), and the uncertainty as to how judges will respond to certain methodological issues makes it especially difficult for the parties to select an appropriate regression model or to predict the outcome of these cases. The litigation itself is enormously expensive and lengthy, for the size of the potential damage payments to succesful plaintiffs would justify, at least in economic terms, an institution's decision to appeal an unfavorable ruling as far as the U.S. Supreme Court. It would seem that further research on the factors confounding regression analyses of academic salary inequities, and continued attempts to refine and improve the validity of the variables used in the model, would not only provide valuable information to researchers but would assist the parties and the judges in these cases, who now must endure a "battle of the experts" in their efforts to win the methodological case so that they can prevail in their legal claims as well.

FACULTY EMPLOYMENT AND ACADEMIC NORMS

Over the last quarter of a century, the parameters of faculty employment status have been shaped by a large number of judicial opinions. Of particular concern to many academics observing this process has been the potential of the judiciary to weaken or destroy academic norms of collegiality, peer review, and academic autonomy. Numerous legal developments coalesced over the last few decades which modified many traditional academic practices regarding faculty employment decisions: collective bargaining, arbitration and mediation, civil rights laws regulating employment, federal regulatory control of institutional employment practices, and affirmative action, to name a few. These legal developments have unquestionably affected the way in which employment decisions are made in virtually all kinds of organizations, both academic and nonacademic. But have academic norms and autonomy been destroyed by judicial scrutiny, or have the courts attempted to protect these norms as they enforced the employment laws? Judicial review of academic employment decisions has implications for at least two areas of concern to academics: institutional self-determination (or administrative discretion) and faculty collegial relationships (and, more specifically, peer review).

Institutional self-determination has been of concern since the Dartmouth College litigation of 1819, where the state of New Hampshire attempted to regulate Dartmouth by amending its corporate charter (*Trustees of Dartmouth College v. Woodward*, 1819). Courts were initially reluctant to intervene in the internal affairs of colleges and universities, viewing attendance at college as a privilege revocable virtually at will (Kaplin, 1978, pp. 4-7). Until the early 1960s, when increased state and federal regulation brought closer judicial scrutiny of institutional practices, courts had tended to give colleges "wide discretion to run their own affairs, free from external restraints" and "finally accountable to no one" (Russell, 1978, p. 517).

A sizable body of literature exists which describes the impact of state and federal regulation upon institutional autonomy (e.g., Berdahl, 1971; Hobbs, 1978; McGuiness, 1981; Millett, 1981). Within the framework of this regulation, however, the courts have frequently stressed the importance of administrative flexibility in the area of employment decisions, especially decisions on tenure. The courts have recognized, and have frequently reiterated, the relationship between tenure, institutional flexibility, and long-range planning (see, for example, *Lieberman v. Gant*, 1980), and are reluctant to intercede in such decisions unless the institution's "tenure procedures are irreparably tainted and further recourse to them would be futile, rendering a fair consideration impossible" (*New York Institute of Technology v. State Division of Human Rights*, 1976, p. 602). This reluctance of the judiciary to intervene in the in-

ternal management of colleges and universities is known as "academic abstention," and the concept means, in legal terms, that courts defer to the academic
decision-making process and will not review the merits of the decision (Edwards and Nordin, 1979, p. 14).

The courts have been especially solicitous of a college administration's need
for flexibility in making staffing and resource allocation decisions. For example, courts' refusals to overturn dismissals of tenured faculty during times of
financial exigency or program reduction/elimination (assuming that good faith
and proper procedures were utilized by the institution) have been grounded on
the courts' unwillingness to enforce tenure contracts at the expense of institutional vitality (Olswang, 1982-83). Judicial approval of raising evaluation standards, even if such an act has a disproportionately negative effect upon members of protected classes, is another example of judicial concern for the integrity of the academic process (*Campbell v. Ramsey*, 1980; *Scott v. University of
Delaware*, 1979). And an especially interesting and important example of judicial concern for institutional autonomy is the degree to which courts will permit
administrators to use reasons *other* than teaching, scholarship, and institutional
service to justify denial of promotion or tenure, if the institution has determined that "its best educational interests will not be served by a conferral of
tenure, however capable and collegial the candidate may be" (*Mayberry v.
Dees*, 1981, p. 509). Similarly, courts have condoned tenure denials because a
faculty member did not "fit" well with departmental colleagues, because a
professor failed to attend meetings, or because the faculty member was simply
incompatible with colleagues (Hendrickson and Lee, 1983).

The courts have also applied the academic abstention doctrine to peer review
deliberations. As noted earlier, judicial review of academic discrimination cases
has actually strengthened the legal effect of a peer determination, and the fledgling "academic freedom privilege" may further remove peer review deliberations from judicial "interference" (Lee, forthcoming). While judicial deference to subjective evaluations of professionals is not unique to higher education
(Bartholet, 1982; Waintroob, 1979-80), the courts have stated emphatically
that judgments made by a faculty member's colleagues (including administrators), as long as those judgments are based upon reasonable, lawful criteria,
are beyond the expertise of the court to evaluate (*Keddie v. Pennsylvania State
University*, 1976). And, furthermore, the courts' willingness to protect the confidentiality of individual votes and written evaluations of peer reviewers, absent
convincing evidence of bias in the evaluation process, tends to elevate further
the protection afforded by the judiciary system to peer judgments and academic autonomy.

This is not to say, however, that courts give academics a license to behave un-
lawfully. Where objective criteria are used to make decisions, they must be applied fairly and consistently (for example, *Mecklenberg*, 1976). There must be a
rational relationship between the evaluation criteria and the responsibilities of
and expectations for the faculty member (*EEOC v. Tufts*, 1975). And the capri-

cious application of shifting evaluative standards to certain faculty members, but not to others, is not tolerated (*Acosta v. University of the District of Columbia*, 1981; *Kunda v. Muhlenberg College*, 1980). If the court finds that the institution has behaved in accordance with these requirements, the doctrine of academic abstention is normally invoked and it will not attempt to substitute its judgment for the institution's.

It seems evident, therefore, that the courts have protected academic autonomy where appropriate (Brubacher, 1973; Edwards, 1980), and that judicial review has not had a devastating effect upon academic norms or institutional self-determination. This is not to suggest, however, that employment decision making in higher education has not changed as a result of the interaction of state/federal regulation and judicial review. Clearly such a change is reflected in the process of reviews and the care toward record keeping. But quantitative research on such change is scarce, and its scarcity leaves gaps in any attempt to identify the parameters of the faculty employment relationship.

CONCLUSIONS
The employment relationship between faculty and their institutions has been a central theme in higher education literature and litigation in recent years. It should not be surprising that in times of stress, issues of rights and security are foremost in the minds of faculty. What conclusions can be drawn from these judicial interventions to prevent further external impositions into the faculty employment structure?

One essential fact can be drawn from the majority of the employment cases involving faculty, and that is the better, clearer, and more equally applied the procedures that institutions have, the more likely that their employment relationship with faculty will go unchallenged, or if challenged, will be left unscathed. Central to the rule courts have applied in reviewing employment-related faculty complaints is the proposition that the court generally will not examine the merits of employment decisions, provided that arbitrary or capricious action cannot be demonstrated. Stated another way, when procedures exist within an institution which can be shown to have been followed, the likelihood of a court intervening in the substantive decision is remote.

What this means for the institution is that it should clarify its employment relationship with faculty. This is not to say that each individual faculty member within the institution should sign a contract. Indeed, such a process goes against the principle of collegial governance and the fact that many rules applicable at institutions are promulgated by the faculty themselves, or developed jointly through negotiation. But institutional handbooks or other faculty-related documents ought to be clear and concise, with ambiguities minimized. Yet at the same time such specification of procedures does not have to infringe on the substantive considerations to be made by peers.

However, even with clearly written and concise procedures regarding the process of tenure, promotion, and merit salary increases, the matter of the substantive evaluative criteria used by institutions and faculty will continue to be an area of vagueness and ripe for judicial intervention. Much has been written about the evaluative process (Centra, 1979; Miller, 1972; Seldin, 1980; Smith, 1976) and the need to use some kind of objective evidence in making tenure, promotion, and salary decisions (Gilmore, 1983–84). Much research can yet be done in this area to clarify the evaluative process so as to preserve the legitimacy of its usage.

Another area which will continue to be of concern revolves around the fact that institutional flexibility and faculty tenure will always seemingly be incompatible. As long as tenure is interpreted as giving faculty the absolute right to continued employment until retirement, institutions will be compelled to use non-causal termination structures, such as a financial exigency and program elimination, in order to gain the flexibility they need to operate. The use of causal termination bases, such as incompetence, is consistently avoided because of the political dynamics between faculty and administration, and the consequences of pitting faculty against their colleagues. Indeed, this avoidance was one of the reasons the four-year exemption for tenured faculty to the ADEA was enacted.

> Many colleges and universities maintain for the foreseeable future the number of available faculty positions will be closely related to the number of retirements, thereby making it difficult to employ younger professors, particularly women and minorities. Moreover, the financial burden on already hardpressed institutions of higher learning may be increased by this legislation, because it may require the retention of highly paid senior employees for additional years.
>
> Concerns were expressed by the committee that although it is theoretically possible to discharge tenured faculty for cause, the difficulty of objectively evaluating the job performance of such employees makes such good cause discharges difficult. [Committee on Human Resources, 1978, pp. 511-512]

One answer to the dilemma of trying to maintain appropriately focused and highly productive faculty is to institute a program of systematic post-tenure review. Of course, the subject of post-tenure review is highly volatile. Both the challengers to tenure (O'Toole, 1979) and the champions of tenure (Commission on Academic Tenure, 1973) agree that tenure has inherent problems, but cannot agree as to the mechanics to improve it. Various alternative tenure structures have been proposed but none that incorporate systematic structures for evaluating faculty while preserving its traditional form (Chait and Ford, 1982). Yet legally, post-tenure review is compatible with tenure and the due process principles which attach (Olswang and Fantel, 1980–81). But faculty evaluation structures and development programs must be created to make such a plan fair and effective.

Evaluation ambiguities also relate to issues of sex discrimination and salary equity. If clear evaluation standards were developed and equally applied, it would provide the documentation individuals need to judge their performance as well as the documentation institutions can rely upon to combat allegations of discrimination or unfair salary level.

It is of course unrealistic to assume that litigation by faculty will go away no matter what clarifications or improvements are made in faculty employment contracts. However, without internal action to preserve the best parts of this relationship while improving its weaknesses, outside judicial intervention, on the theory of fairness, may not be as sensitive to separating the good from the bad. Higher education faces the potential of having the baby thrown out with the bathwater.

POLICY DILEMMAS AND SUGGESTIONS FOR FURTHER RESEARCH
The literature and litigation related to the faculty employment relationship answers many questions about the basic rights of faculty and the ways in which courts protect those rights. But other questions emerge from this analysis of the faculty employment relationship. Some of these questions are being investigated, while others have not yet been addressed.

The courts have explicitly upheld the right of college trustees and administrators to reshape institutional missions and priorities by terminating programs and faculty. Yet little is known about how institutions have gone about the reshaping process. A research project now in progress is studying institutional practices in reallocating "people, programs, and resources" (Mortimer, 1982, p. 6). Further research on this important issue is necessary to describe and evaluate models of resource allocation and their impact upon faculty employment.

Similarly, research is needed to collect and analyze information on institutional attempts to reshape their faculty by early retirements, contract buy-outs, etc. Models developed and used in academe will assist other higher education institutions to redirect their personnel resources while complying with the laws protecting faculty tenure and prohibiting decisions made on the basis of age.

A further area of research is suggested by the frustrating problems faced by individuals seeking to prove (or disprove) salary discrimination in academe. Research in faculty evaluation methods should be linked more directly to establishing measurable variables which can be used in statistical tests for salary inequity. Researchers focusing on the improvement of regression models might consider how to translate qualitative evaluations of productivity and scholarly competence into statistically manipulable variables. And scholars of higher education management might consider conducting research on the relationship between productivity, competence, and institutional rewards for college faculty, including systems for monitoring faculty productivity after tenure is obtained.

Finally, the research literature and the litigation suggest that research should be conducted on the methods used by institutions to encourage professional ethics and accountability on the part of the faculty. State-level governing and coordinating boards, as well as legislatures and other funding sources, are pressuring colleges and universities to develop and enforce accountability measures. We know very little about how accountability is fostered, nor about how institutional self-regulation may be used to facilitate professional self-regulation. Researchers need to identify and study those institutions or systems where faculty and administrators are working cooperatively to increase the institution's accountability and to reinforce the professional ethics of the faculty.

It bears repeating that the judiciary defers to academic autonomy when academe conducts its affairs responsibly and with integrity. What is not well understood, however, is how, or whether, the members of academic organizations enforce responsible professional conduct and accountability, either through the peer governance process or through administrative action. In the final analysis, the parameters of the faculty employment relationship are merely sketched out by the courts, but they are refined and given meaning by the academic community.

NOTES

1. While numerous state and federal laws may be invoked in an employment discrimination case, the laws used most frequently in academic cases are Title VII of the Civil Rights Act of 1964 and Section 1983 of the Civil Rights Acts of 1866, 1970, and 1971. (For further information on these laws, see Kaplin, 1978).

   A recent opinion by the U.S. Supreme Court (*Grove City v. Bell*, 1984) suggests that Title IX of the Education Amendments of 1972, heretofore used by women faculty to sue their employing colleges for sex discrimination, will be available only to those women employed in programs that are direct recipients of federal funds, such as financial aid offices or grant projects funded by a federal agency. The Court ruled that Title IX prohibits sex discrimination only in programs that receive federal funds; women employed in other units of a college or university have no cause of action under Title IX but may sue under Title VII or Section 1983.

2. Two federal statutes provide remedies for salary discrimination. Title VII of the Civil Rights Act prohibits salary discrimination on the basis of race, sex, national origin, religion, or color. The Equal Pay Act prohibits sex discrimination in salaries. While the Equal Pay Act requires "equal skill, effort, and responsibility," Title VII has been interpreted as requiring comparable, but not equal work. (For additional information on these laws, see Hendrickson and Lee, 1983.)

REFERENCES

Books and Periodicals

AAUP. Academic freedom and tenure, 1940 statement of principles and 1970 interpretive comments. *AAUP Policy Documents and Reports*. Washington, D.C.: AAUP, 1977(a).

AAUP. 1976 recommended institutional regulations on academic freedom and tenure. *AAUP Policy Documents and Reports*. Washington, D.C.: AAUP, 1977(b).

AAUP. On institutional problems resulting from financial exigency: Some operating guidelines. *AAUP Policy Documents and Reports*. Washington, D.C.: AAUP, 1977(c).

AAUP. Report of the Investigating Committee on Academic Freedom and Tenure: The State University of New York. *AAUP Bulletin*, 1977(d), *63*, 237-260.

"Academic Freedom Privilege: An Excessive Solution to the Problem of Protecting

Confidentiality." *University of Cincinnati Law Review*, 1982, *51*, 326-352.

"Academic Freedom Versus Title VII: Will Equal Employment Opportunity Be Denied on Campus?" *Ohio State Law Journal*, 1981, *42*, 989-1004.

Barnes, M. V., and Schlottman, B. A. After "decoupling": Further thoughts. *Journal of College and University Law*, 1982–83, *9*, 315-323.

Bartholet, E. Application of Title VII to jobs in high places. *Harvard Law Review*, 1982, *95*, 945-1027.

Bayer, A. E., and Astin, H. S. Sex differentials in the academic reward system. *Science*, 1975, *88*, 796-802.

Berdahl, R. O. *Statewide Coordination of Higher Education*. Washington, D.C.: American Council on Education, 1971.

"Beyond the Prima Facie Case in Employment Discrimination Law: Statistical Proof and Rebuttal." *Harvard Law Review*, 1975, *89*, 387-422.

Blackburn, R. J., and Clark, M. J. An assessment of faculty performance: Some correlates between administrator, colleague, student, and self ratings. *Sociology of Education*, 1975, *48*, 242-256.

Bloom, D., and Killingsworth, M. R. Pay discrimination research and litigation: The use of regression. *Industrial Relations*, 1982, *21*, 318-339.

Bodner, G. A. Analyzing faculty salaries in class action sex discrimination cases. *Journal of College and University Law*, 1983–84, *10*, 305-323.

Bompey, S. H. Decoupling tenure and employment under the 1978 Amendments to the Age Discrimination Employment Act. *Journal of College and University Law*, 1981–82, *8*, 425-432.

Bompey, S. H., and Saltzman, B. N. The role of statistics in employment discrimination litigation — a university perspective. *Journal of College and University Law*, 1982–83, *9*, 263-278.

Bouchard, D. R. Experience with Proposition 13 and other retrenchment conditions. *Journal of College and University Personnel Association*, 1980, *31*(1), 61-65.

Boulding, K. E. The management of decline. *Change*, 1975, *7*(8-9), 64.

Bowen, H. R. Sharing the effects: The art of retrenchment. *American Association for Higher Education Bulletin*, 1982, *10*, 12-13.

Brown, R. C. Tenure rights in contractual and constitutional context. *Journal of Law and Education*, 1977, *6*, 279-318.

Brubacher, J. The impact of the courts on higher education. *Journal of Law and Education*, 1973, *2*, 267-282.

Bunzel, J. H. The eclipse of confidentiality. *Change*, 1975, *7*(9), 30-35.

Buzan, B. C., and Hunt, L. Y. Evaluating faculty performance under the equal pay for equal work doctrine. *Research in Higher Education*, 1976, *4*, 113-123.

Carnegie Commission on Higher Education. *Opportunities for Women in Higher Education*. New York: McGraw-Hill, 1973.

Carnegie Council on Policy Studies in Higher Education. *Three Thousand Futures*. San Francisco: Jossey-Bass, 1980.

Centra, J. A. *Faculty Development Practices in U.S. Colleges and Universities*. Princeton, N.J.: Educational Testing Service, 1976.

Centra, J. A. *Determining Faculty Effectiveness: Assessing Teaching, Research, and Service for Personnel Decisions and Improvement*. San Francisco: Jossey-Bass, 1979.

Chait, R. P., and Ford, A. T. *Beyond Traditional Tenure*. San Francisco: Jossey-Bass, 1982.

"Civil Rights: Academic Freedom, Secrecy and Subjectivity as Obstacles to Proving a Title VII Sex Discrimination Suit in Academia." *North Carolina Law Review*, 1982, *60*, 438-450.

Clague, M. W. *Jiminez v. Almovodar*: Program discontinuance as a cause for termination of tenured faculty in public institutions. *Education Law Reporter*, 1982, *9*, 805-821.

Clark, D. L. Discrimination suits: A unique settlement. *Educational Record*, 1977, *58*, 233-240.

Commission on Academic Tenure in Higher Education. *Faculty Tenure*. San Francisco: Jossey-Bass, 1973.

Committee on Human Resources, United States Senate. *U.S. Code Congressional and Administrative News*, 1978, pp. 511-512.

Corbin, A. L. *Corbin on Contracts*. St. Paul: West, 1968.

"Dismissal of Tenured Faculty for Reasons of Financial Exigency." *Indiana Law Journal*, 1976, *51*, 417-431.

Dolan-Greene, C. What if the faculty member to be laid off is the governor's brother? In S. R. Hample (ed.), *New Directions for Institutional Research*, vol. 8, no. 2: *Coping with Faculty Reduction*. San Francisco: Jossey-Bass, 1981.

Dougherty. E. A. Should you starve all programs or eliminate a few? In S. R. Hample (ed.), *New Directions for Institutional Research*, vol. 8, no. 2: *Coping with Faculty Reduction*. San Francisco: Jossey-Bass, 1981.

Edwards, H. *Higher Education and the Unholy Crusade Against Government Regulation*. Cambridge, Mass.: Institute for Educational Management, Harvard University, 1980.

Edwards, H. T., and Nordin, V. D. *Higher Education and the Law*. Cambridge, Mass.: Institute for Educational Management, Harvard University, 1979.

Evangelauf, J. Women's average pay trails men's by 19 per cent in three top professional ranks. *Chronicle of Higher Education*, Jan. 18, 1984, p. 20.

Farrell, C. S. Comparable worth ruling by U.S. Court prompts widespread interest on campuses. *Chronicle of Higher Education*, Jan. 11, 1984, p. 21.

Felicetti, E. A. Retirement options to offer college faculty. *Educational Record*, 1982, *63*, 22-26.

Finkelstein, M. O. The judicial reception of multiple regression studies in race and sex discrimination cases. *Columbia Law Review*, 1980, *80*, 737-754.

Finkin, M. W. Review of *Beyond Traditional Tenure*. *Journal of College and University Law*, 1983–84, *10*, 105-112.

Fisher, F. M. Multiple regression in legal proceedings. *Columbia Law Review*, 1980, *80*, 702-736.

Flygare, T. J. *Board of Trustees of Keene State College v. Sweeney*: Implications for the future of peer review in faculty personnel decisions. *Journal of College and University Law*, 1980–81, *8*, 100-110.

Furniss, W. T. New opportunities for faculty members. *Educational Record*, 1981, *6*, 8-15.

Garfield, E. Citation analysis as a tool in journal evaluation. *Science*, 1972, *178*, 471-479.

Gilmore, G. M. Student ratings as a factor in faculty employment decisions and periodic review. *Journal of College and University Law*, 1983–84, *10*, 557-576.

Glenny, L. A. Concept of short-run decision making. In R. A. Wilson (ed.), *Responses to Fiscal Stress*. Tucson: University of Arizona Center for the Study of Higher Education, 1982.

Glenny, L. A., and Bowen, F. M. Warning signals of distress. In J. R. Mingle and Associates (eds.), *Challenges of Retrenchment*. San Francisco: Jossey-Bass, 1981.

Gordon, N. M., Morton, T. E., and Braden, I. C. Faculty salaries: Is there discrimination by sex, race, and discipline? *American Economic Review*, 1974, *64*, 419-427.

Green, D. H. An application of the equal pay act to higher education. *Journal of College and University Law*, 1980–81, *8*, 203-218.

Greenfield, E. From equal to equivalent pay: Salary discrimination in academe. *Journal of Law and Education*, 1977, *6*, 41-62.

Hendrickson, R. M., and Lee, B. A. *ASHE-ERIC Higher Education Research Report No. 8. Academic Employment and Retrenchment: Judicial Implications and Administrative Action.* Washington, D.C.: Association for the Study of Higher Education, 1983.

Hirsh, A., and Kemerer, F. R. Academic freedom in the classroom. *Educational Leadership*, 1982, *39*, 375-377.

Hobbs, W. C. *Government Regulation of Higher Education.* Cambridge, Mass.: Ballinger, 1978.

Hodges, D. K. Postsecondary faculty members' rights of free speech. *Journal of College and University Law*, 1982-83, *9*, 85-99.

Hofstadter, R., and Metzger, W. P. *The Development of Academic Freedom in the United States.* New York: Columbia University Press, 1955.

Kaplin, W. A. *The Law of Higher Education.* San Francisco: Jossey-Bass, 1978.

Katz, D. A. Faculty salaries, promotions, and productivity at a large university. *American Economic Review*, 1973, *63*, 469-477.

Koch, J. V. Salary equity issues in higher education: Where do we stand? *AAHE Bulletin*, 1982, *35*(2), 7-14.

La Noue, G. R. Judicial responses to academic salary discrimination. Paper presented at the annual conference of the Association for the Study of Higher Education. Washington, D.C., March 1982.

Lee, B. A. Balancing confidentiality and disclosure in faculty peer review. *Journal of College and University Law*, 1982-83, *9*, 279-314.

Lee, B. A. Federal court involvement in academic decision-making: Impact on peer review. *Journal of Higher Education*, forthcoming.

Lester, R. A. The equal pay boondoggle. *Change*, 1975, *7*, pp. 38-43.

Lester, R. A. *Reasoning about Discrimination.* Princeton, N.J.: Princeton University Press, 1980.

Lovain, T. B. Grounds for dismissing tenured postsecondary faculty for cause. *Journal of College and University Law*, 1983-84, *10*, 419-433.

McFadden, R. D. U.S. court rules against City University in sex bias suit. *New York Times*, March 19, 1983, p. 1, 27.

McGuiness, A. C., Jr. The federal government and postsecondary education. In P. G. Altbach and R. O. Berdahl (eds.), *Higher Education in American Society.* Buffalo, N.Y.: Prometheus Books, 1981.

McKee, P. W. Tenure by default: The non-formal acquisition of academic tenure. *Journal of College and University Law*, 1980, *7*, 31-56.

Maxwell, G., Rosenfeld, R., and Spilerman, S. Geographic constraints on women's careers in academia. *Science*, 1979, *205*, 1225-1231.

Mazia, J. A., and de Ita, N. Sex discrimination in academia: Representing the female faculty plaintiff. *Golden State University Law Review*, 1978-79, *9*, 481-505.

Melchiori, G. S. *AAHE-ERIC Higher Education Research Report No. 5. Planning for Program Discontinuance: From Default to Design.* Washington, D.C.: American Association for Higher Education, 1982.

Middleton, L. Academic freedom vs. affirmative action: Georgia professor jailed in tenure dispute. *Chronicle of Higher Education*, Sept. 2, 1980, p. 1.

Miller, R. I. *Evaluating Faculty Performance.* San Francisco: Jossey-Bass. 1972.

Millett, J. D. State government. In P. G. Altbach and R. O. Berdahl (eds.), *Higher Education in American Society.* Buffalo, N.Y.: Prometheus Books, 1981.

Mingle, J. P., and Associates (eds.), *Challenges of Retrenchment.* San Francisco: Jossey-Bass, 1981.

Mix, M. C. *AAHE-ERIC Higher Education Research Report No. 3. Tenure and Termination in Financial Exigency.* Washington, D.C.: American Association for Higher Education, 1978.

Mortimer, K. P. Procedures and criteria for faculty retrenchment. In J. P. Mingle and Associates (eds.), *Challenges of Retrenchment*. San Francisco: Jossey-Bass, 1981.

Mortimer, K. P. Governance and planning. *Postsecondary Education Newsletter*, October, 1982, pp. 4-6.

Mortimer, K. P., and Tierney, M. L. *AAHE-ERIC Higher Education Research Report No. 4. The Three R's of the Eighties: Reduction, Reallocation, and Retrenchment*. Washington, D.C.: American Association for Higher Education, 1979.

Newman, F. Selecting the effects: The priorities of retrenchment. *AAHE Bulletin*, 1982, *35*, p. 11.

O'Brien, F. W. Due process for the nontenured in private schools. *Journal of Law and Education*, 1974, *3*, 175-202.

Olswang, S. G. Planning the unthinkable: Issues in institutional reorganization and faculty reductions. *Journal of College and University Law*, 1982-83, *9*, 431-449.

Olswang, S. G., and Fantel, J. I. Tenure and periodic performance review: Compatible legal and administrative principles. *Journal of College and University Law*, 1980-81, *7*, 1-30.

O'Toole, J. "A conscientious objection." In *Tenure*. New Rochelle, N.Y.: Change Magazine Press, 1979.

Palmer, D. D., and Patton, C. V. Academia's attitudes toward and experience with incentive early retirement schemes. In *Changing Retirement Policies: Current Issues in Higher Education*. Washington, D.C.: American Association for Higher Education, 1978.

Patton, C. V. *Academia in Transition: Mid-Career Change or Early Retirement*. Cambridge, Mass.: Abt Books, 1979.

Pezzulo, T. R., and Brittingham, B. E. *Salary Equity: Detecting Sex Bias in Salary Among College and University Professors*. Lexington, Mass.: Lexington Books, 1979.

"Preventing Unnecessary Intrusions on University Autonomy: A Proposed Academic Freedom Privilege." *California Law Review*, 1981, *69*, 1538-1568.

"Report of the Committee on Confidentiality in Matters of Faculty Appointment." *University of Chicago Record*, May 22, 1979.

Richards, M. S. "Financial emergency" and the faculty furlough: A breach of contract? *Journal of College and University Law*, 1983-84, *10*, 225-242.

"The Role of Academic Freedom in Defining the Faculty Employment Contract." *Case Western Law Review*, 1981, *31*, 608-655.

Russell, D. W. Goal accountability in higher education: Towards a comprehensive legal conception of the university. *Journal of Law and Education*, 1978, *7*, 507-522.

Seldin, P. *Successful Faculty Evaluation Programs*. Creigers, N.Y.: Coventry Press, 1980.

Shanor, C. O., and Shanor, G. J. The practical labor lawyer: Title VII and university tenure decisions. *Employment Relations Law Journal*, 1981, *7*, 145-154.

Shulman, C. H. *AAHE-ERIC Higher Education Research Report No. 2. Old Expectations, New Realities: The Academic Profession Revisited*. Washington, D.C.: American Association for Higher Education, 1979.

Smith, A. B. *AAHE-ERIC Higher Education Research Report No. 8. Faculty Development and Evaluation in Higher Education*. Washington, D.C.: American Association for Higher Education, 1976.

Smith, M. R. Protecting the confidentiality of faculty peer review records: Department of Labor v. The University of California. *Journal of College and University Law*, 1981-82, *8*, 20-53.

Sowell, T. Affirmative action reconsidered. *The Public Record*, 1976, *42*, 47-65.

Todd, J. E. *Survey of Early, Partial and/or Phased Retirement Programs: State Supported *Colleges and Universities with Enrollments of 7,500 or More*. Portland, Ore.: Portland State University, 1983.

Tucker, A., and Mautz, R. B. Academic freedom, tenure, and incompetence. *Educational Record*, 1982, *63*, 22-25.

Tucker, J. C. Financial exigency: Rights, responsibilities and recent decisions. *Journal of College and University Law*, 1974, *2*, 103-113.

Tuckman, B. H. Salary differences among university faculty and their implications for the future. In T. R. Pezzulo and B. E. Brittingham (eds.), *Salary Equity*. Lexington, Mass.: Lexington Books, 1979.

"University of Minnesota will pay $1.5 million in legal fees." *Chronicle of Higher Education*, Feb. 9, 1983, p. 2.

Van Alstyne, W. The constitutional rights of teachers and professors. *Duke Law Journal*, 1970, *1970*, pp. 841-879.

Van Alstyne, W. The Supreme Court speaks to the untenured: A comment on Board of Regents v. Roth and Perry v. Sindermann. *AAUP Bulletin*, 1972, *58*, 267-270.

Van Alstyne, W. Furnishing reasons for a decision against reappointment: Legal considerations. *AAUP Bulletin*, 1976, *62*, 285-286.

Vladeck, J. P., and Young, M. M. Sex discrimination in higher education: It's not academic. *Women's Rights Law Reporter*, 1978, *4*, 59-78.

Waintroob, A. The developing law of equal employment opportunity at the white collar and professional level. *William and Mary Law Review*, 1979-80, *21*, 45-119.

Wehrwein, A. C. Sex bias claims filed in Minnesota. *Chronicle of Higher Education*, Feb. 9, 1981, p. 21.

Williams, D. T., Olswang, S. G., and Hargett, G. R. A matter of degree: Faculty morale as a function of involvement in institutional decisions during times of financial distress. *Review of Higher Education*, forthcoming.

Wilson, J. B. Financial exigency: Examination of recent cases involving layoff of tenured faculty. *Journal of College and University Law*, 1977, *4*, 187-197.

Yurko, R. J. Judicial recognition of academic collective interests: A new approach to faculty Title VII litigation. *Boston University Law Review*, 1980, *60*, 473-541.

Zirkel, P. A. *Mayberry v. Dees*: Collegiality as a criterioin for faculty tenure. *Educational Law Reporter*, 1983, *12*, 1053-1059.

Cases

AAUP v. Bloomfield College, 129 N.J. Super 249, 332 A. 2d 846 (1974); Aff'd, 136 N . J .
Super. 442, 346 A. 2d 615 (1975).

Acosta v. University of the District of Columbia, 528 F. Supp. 1215 (D.D.C. 1981).

Adamian v. Jacobsen, 523 F. 2d 929 (9th Cir. 1975).

Akhtar v. Van de Wetering, 642 P. 2d 149 (Mont. 1982).

Aumiller v. University of Delaware, 434 F. Supp. 1273 (D. Del. 1977).

Banerjee v. Board of Trustees, 495 F. Supp. 1148 (D. Mass. 1980), Aff'd, 648 F. 2d 61 (1st Cir.) *cert. denied*, 102 S. Ct. 671 (1981).

Bignall v. North Idaho College, 538 F. 2d 243 (9th Cir. 1976).

Board of Regents v. Roth, 408 U.S. 564 (1972).

Board of Trustees v. Stubblefield, 16 Cal. App. 3rd 820, 94 Cal. Rptr. 318 (1971).

Board of Trustees of Mount San Antonio Junior College v. Hartman, 55 Cal. Rptr. 144 (Ct. App. 1966).

Browzin v. Catholic University, 527 F. 2d 843 (D.C. Cir. 1975).

Campbell v. Ramsey, 22 Fair Empl. Prac. Cas. 83 (E.D. Ark. 1980).

Chitwood v. Feaster, 468 F. 2d 359 (4th Cir. 1972).

Chung v. Park, 514 F. 2d 382 (3rd Cir. 1975).

County of Washington v. Gunther, 452 U.S. 161 (1981).

EEOC v. Tufts, 421 F. Supp. 152 (D. Mass. 1975).

EEOC v. University of Notre Dame, 715 F. 2d 331 (7th Cir. 1983).

Endress v. Brookdale Community College, 364 A. 2d 1080 (N.J. Super., A.D., 1976).

Goodisman v. Lytle, 724 F. 2d 818 (8th Cir. 1984).

Goss v. San Jacinto Junior College, 588 F. 2d 96 (5th Cir. 1979).

Gray v. Board of Higher Education, CUNY, 692 F. 2d 901 (2d Cir. 1982).

Greene v. Howard University, 412 F. 2d 1128 (D.C. Cir. 1969).

Grove City v. Bell, 104 S.Ct. 1211 (1984).

Haimowitz v. University of Nevada, 579 F. 2d 526 (9th Cir. 1978).

Hetrick v. Martin, 480 F. 2d 705 (6th Cir. 1973).

In re. Dinnan, 661 F. 2d 426 (5th Cir. 1981), *cert. denied,* 102 S. Ct. 2904 (1982).

Jiminez v. Almodovar, 650 F. 2d 363 (1st Cir. 1981).

Johnson v. Board of Regents of the University of Wisconsin System, 377 F. Supp. 227 (W.D. Wis. 1974) Aff'd, 510 F. 2d (7th Cir. 1975).

Johnson v. Christian Brothers College, 565 S.W. 2d 872 (Tenn. 1978).

Johnson v. University of Pittsburgh, 435 F. Supp. 1328 (W.D. Pa. 1977).

Keddie v. Pennsylvania State University, 412 F. Supp. 1264 (M.D. Pa. 1976).

Kilcoyne v. Morgan, 664 F. 2d 940 (4th Cir. 1981).

Klein v. Board of Higher Education of City University of New York, 434 F. Supp. 1113 (S.D.N.Y. 1977).

Krotkoff v. Goucher College, 585 F. 2d 675 (4th Cir. 1978).

Kunda v. Muhlenberg College, 621 F. 2d 532 (3rd Cir. 1980).

Levine v. Fairleigh Dickinson University, 646 F. 2d 825 (3rd Cir. 1981).

Levitt v. Board of Trustees of Nebraska State College, 376 F. Supp. 945 (D. Neb. 1974).

Lieberman v. Gant, 630 F. 2d 60 (2d Cir. 1980).

Mathews v. Eldridge, 424 U.S. 319 (1976).

Mayberry v. Dees, 663 F. 2d 502 (4th Cir. 1981).

Mecklenberg v. Board of Regents, Montana State University, 13 Emp. Prac. Dec. ¶ 11,438 (D. Mont. 1976).

Melani v. Board of Higher Education, City of New York, 561 F. Supp. 769 (S.D.N.Y. 1983).

Mt. Healthy City School District Board of Education v. Doyle, 429 U.S. 274 (1977).

New York Institute of Technology v. State Division of Human Rights, 353 N.E. 2d 598 (N.Y. 1976).

Ortwein v. Mackey, 511 F. 2d 696 (5th Cir. 1975).

Perry v. Sindermann, 408 U.S. 593 (1972).

Randolph v. Regents of Oklahoma Colleges, 648 P. 2d 825 (Ok. 1982).

Roseman v. Indiana University of Pennsylvania, 520 F. 2d 1364 (3d Cir. 1975), *cert. denied,* 424 U.S. 921 (1976).

Sawyer v. Mercer, 594 S.W. 2d 696 (Tenn. 1980).

Scheuer v. Creighton University, 260 N.W. 2d 595 (Neb. 1977).

Scott v. University of Delaware, 601 F. 2d 76 (3d Cir. 1979).

Shaw v. Board of Trustees of Frederick Community College, 549 F. 2d 929 (4th Cir. 1976).

Smith v. University of North Carolina, 632 F. 2d 316 (4th Cir. 1980).

Sobel v. Yeshiva University, 566 F. Supp. 1166 (S.D.N.Y. 1983).

State *ex rel.* McLendon v. Morton 249 S.E. 2d 919 (Sup. Ct. of App., W.Va. 1978).

State *ex rel.* Richardson v. Board of Regents, University of Nevada, 269 P. 2d 265 (Nev. 1954).

Statsny v. Board of Trustees of Central Washington University, 32 Wash. App. 239, 647 P. 2d 496 (1982) *cert. denied,* 103 S. Ct. 1528 (1983).

Stebbins v. Weaver, 537 F. 2d 939 (7th Cir. 1976).

Texas Dept. of Community Affairs v. Burdine, 450 U.S. 248 (1981).

Timper v. Board of Regents, University of Wisconsin, 512 F. Supp. 384 (W.D. Wisc. 1981).

Toney v. Reagan, 467 F. 2d 953 (9th Cir. 1972).

Trustees of Dartmouth College v. Woodward, 4 Wheat. (U.S.) 518 (1819).

Washington State Federation of State Employees v. State of Washington, 23 Empl. Prac. Cas ¶ 33,976 (1983).

Wellner v. Minnesota State Junior College Board, 487 F. 2d 153 (8th Cir. 1973).

White v. Board of Trustees of Western Wyoming Community College, 648 P. 2d 528 (Wyo. 1982).

Zimmerer v. Spencer, 485 F. 2d 176 (5th Cir. 1973).

Statutes and Regulations

Amendment to the Age Discrimination in Employment Act Amendments (1978) 29 U.S.C. 621-634.

Equal Employment Opportunity Commission, Final Interpretation on ADEA Amendments, (1981) 29 C.F.R. § 1625.11(g).

PUBLICATION, PERFORMANCE, AND REWARD IN SCIENCE AND SCHOLARSHIP

Mary Frank Fox, *University of Michigan*

The reward structure of any social system centers upon the relationship between the performance of roles and the return on that performance. In science and scholarship, the central activity, performance, and social processes involve the communication of findings of research (Allison, 1980; Merton, 1973*b*; Price, 1963). The social structure of scholarship (disciplines, specialties, and networks) is organized around communication, and publication is the principal means of that communication (Mullins, 1973).[1] Through publication, scholars keep abreast of a field, verify information, obtain critical response to work, and redirect research interests.

Publication is, in turn, the primary basis of scholarly recognition and esteem (Cole and Cole, 1973; Gaston, 1978; Price, 1963; Storer, 1966). And recognition — symbolized in awards, citations, editorial appointments, and board and panel memberships — is the prime reward for scholarly performance (J. Cole, 1979; Merton, 1973*a*; Storer, 1973; Zuckerman, 1977). In economic analogy, scholarly recognition has been called the equivalent of property (Cole and Cole, 1973) — the "coin of the realm" of scholarship (Storer, 1973).

Scholars and scientists sometimes maintain that the research process is its own reward and that they require no further compensation (Hagstrom, 1965). One problem with this claim is that that the "significance" and "importance" of research depend upon the response and evaluation of the relevant social — collegial — group (Mulkay, 1977). The link between research, recognition, and reward is highlighted further in the priority disputes that have raged throughout the history of science (Merton, 1961, 1973*a*). Being the first, or the second, or the simultaneous party to a discovery does not diminish the quality of the work process or the satisfaction of research. But it does determine recognition derived.

For his detailed and thoughtful comments on an earlier draft of this chapter, I am grateful especially to Alan Bayer.

Beyond recognition, other, more extrinsic, rewards such as salary and promotion also result from publication.[2] Across fields and institutions, Tuckman (1976) shows an increasing probability of promotion to associate professor with increasing publication of articles. In salary also, Tuckman (1976) and Tuckman and Hagemann (1976) report that those who publish are rewarded more highly than those who do not, with higher returns accruing over the lifetime from articles than from books; with greatest incremental returns from the first compared to subsequent articles; and with diminishing returns with increased output. In analysis of data from a large university, Katz (1973) found that number of publications was paramount in determining salary, while public service and committee work gave some returns, and teaching inconsequential returns. Using data from a national sample of academics across fields and institutions however, Gregorio, Lewis, and Wanner (1982) caution that the publication of books and articles is related to salary but that the effects are not as great as those of high rank or experience (seniority).

Beyond seniority, the relation of publication to salary is also determined by functionally irrelevant characteristics — especially sex. In an analysis of data from a national survey of faculty, Bayer and Astin (1975) show much higher correlations between publication and salary levels for men than for women. David (1971) reports that while 70% of the male scientists who had published were in in the highest salary group, only 29% of the women who had published were in this group. However, data from faculty in twenty-two disciplines (Tuckman, 1976, Table 6-1) suggest that sex-specific salary returns may vary by *level* of publication. Specifically, for a single article, salary returns are twice as great for men compared to women; for five articles, returns are also higher for men. But at the highest levels of productivity — 15, 20, or 25 articles — salary returns are more equitable for the sexes. One must note, on the other hand, that few academics are in the highest producing groups, and thus for the vast majority, male returns to productivity are much higher.

Salary returns relative to publication also vary by discipline and institutional location (Johnson and Kasten, 1983; Smart and McLaughlin, 1978; Tuckman and Hagemann, 1976). For example, economists show a stronger relation between salary and publication than do faculty in education (Tuckman and Hagemann, 1976). Further, within a given university, Marshall and Perrucci (1982) show that publication is more critical in determining salaries within high-consensus compared to low-consensus fields.[3] In addition, at major research universities compared to more minor universities, the association between publication and salary is especially strong (see Katz, 1973; Koch and Chizmar, 1973).

These variations suggest institutional diversity in academic reward structures. Yet diversity in salary and promotional criteria at an institutional level coexists with a national (and international) reward structure that is monolithic rather than plural.[4]

> The aspiring academic may draw his paycheck locally, but the most valued kudos of recognition and reward are often conferred elsewhere as a consequence of the judgments made by members of the larger community of scholars and scientists who are "referees" and "gatekeepers" of merit symbols. The most widely publicized estimates of scholarly and scientific worth — special fellowships, distinguished lectureships, major awards, listings in citation indexes, honorary degrees, editorial appointments, board and panel memberships, memberships in the National Academy of Sciences, and so on — are all symbols of visibility and esteem. [Wilson, 1979, p. 141]

In this larger scholarly community, research productivity and recognition are the central aspects of the reward structure.

Teaching is a significant activity for many academics, but it does not bring national recognition and esteem. Those academics who define themselves primarily as researchers rather than teachers get more outside funding, have more opportunities for paid consulting, and report higher job satisfaction (Astin, 1984). This lower recognition accorded to teaching is due to several factors. First, teaching has limited visibility. A reputation for outstanding teaching rarely extends beyond a given institution. As Lewis (1975, p. 27) says: "Who in the chemistry department at the University of Minnesota can name the superior teachers in the state university in neighboring Wisconson? Who in the multiuniversity in Bloomington, Indiana, knows the master teachers at her sister school, Purdue?" Second, compared to publication output, the products of teaching are difficult to measure and success is difficult to quantify (Tuckman, 1976). Third, standards of judgment about effective teaching differ from one campus to another, while standards of excellence in research are much the same nationally (and at the upper reaches as in Nobel science awards, internationally) (Wilson, 1979). Finally, since World War II the needs for productive technology in industry and commerce have become increasingly dependent upon research and the institutions that do research (see Shils, 1975). As this occurred, the teaching role has lost esteem (Altbach, 1980).[5] For these reasons, accomplishment in teaching "lacks universal currency" (Wilson, 1979, p. 140) in the scholarly community.

Along with research and teaching, professional service is a third — and catchall — component of academic performance. Professional service includes activities ranging from local committee work and guest lectures to the refereeing of papers for national journals, reviewing of grant proposals, and holding of offices in professional associations. In the latter cases, the service is a recognition in itself, and in fact it correlates with publication productivity (see Jauch and Glueck, 1975).

FUNCTIONS OF REWARDS OF PUBLICATION

The central rewards of publication act as both a "stimulus" and a "control" in academia (Wilson, 1979). Recognition and esteem validate past performance by bringing attention to accomplishments judged to be of high quality. The rewards also provide motivation for future performance by encouraging successful scholars to continue to be productive (Cole and Cole, 1973; Zuckerman, 1970). These mechanisms in turn reinforce standards of performance by focusing attention upon work that helps set the pace of scholarly achievement. If, in fact, honor follows excellence, then the most visible rewards can evoke performance in others by conveying research standards of a high order (see Merton, 1973*b*). In this way, recognition and reputation both reflect and generate productivity (Gaston, 1978). Fame may be a reward that few will attain, but its elusive promise serves as an incentive for many others (Blau, 1973).

On the flip side of these purposes are more subtle functions of the scholarly reward system. By reinforcing standards of success, the reward structure can serve to perpetuate intellectual hegemony and obstruct innovative paradigms that threaten established intellectual traditions. It can function to control junior members of the academy, disguise power struggles, and justify decisions that are, in fact, particularistic (see Lewis, 1975; Martindale, 1976). Beyond this, by focusing upon publication and recognition, the academic reward structure helps support faculty control of the university. Because research originates with and is governed by faculty, it provides for peer review and evaluation, and thus increased faculty authority in the university (Skiff, 1980).

PERFORMANCE LEVELS IN PUBLICATION

Despite the centrality of publication to science and scholarship, average levels of performance are low. In a sample of academics from both natural and social sciences, J. Cole (1979) found that one or two years after the doctorate, 53% had failed to publish a single paper and 34% had published just one. In most years, 70% of these academics published nothing. With a national sample of faculty across fields, Ladd and Lipset (1975) also document astonishingly low levels of publication: over half of the full-time academics had never written or edited any sort of book; more than one-third had never published an article; and more than one-quarter had never published a scholarly work of any kind over the course of their careers.

Within-discipline analyses show variations by field, but at the same time confirm the global pattern of low productivity. In a study of academics in three discipline areas, Wanner, Lewis, and Gregorio (1981) show that natural scientists publish almost two and a half times as many articles as humanists, and 40% more than social scientists. In publication of books, the social scientists lead, followed by the humanists, and then the scientists (the mean rates are 1.80, 1.44, and .89, respectively). The differences can be partly accounted for by different styles of reporting research. In the natural sciences, articles are shorter — frequently just research notes — and in the social sciences, and especially the humanities, articles are longer essays. In addition, large-scale laboratory projects, requiring diverse specialists and expensive equipment, have led increasingly to team work in the sciences. In many cases, the name of the principal investigator appears — together with names of the others working on the project — on publications coming out of the lab. This also influences rates of publications between disciplines.

Yet even in the more prolific scientific disciplines, publication rates are low. For example, in a random sample of chemists Reskin (1977) reported that in any given year 60% of the chemists had not published a single article. Likewise, among physical scientists in colleges and universities, Ladd and Lipset (1977) reported that 29% had published nothing while another 24% had published one or two articles.

While average levels of publication are low, the variation between academics is very high. Whether one considers publication over the past two years, past five years, or professional lifetime, publication varies enormously. Since Lotka's (1926) analysis of articles published in physics journals, it has been known that productivity is strongly skewed, with a small group producing the bulk of publications and the vast majority publishing little or nothing.

In an analysis of long-term patterns, Price (1963) estimated that 10% of scientists contributed over one-third of the papers in print, and that only 3% of all scientists were "highly prolific, major contributors." Other studies between and within fields confirm Price's general conclusion about the concentration of publication. In a sample of academics in the social and natural sciences, J. Cole (1979) reports that 15% of the group accounted for half of all papers published. Reskin (1977), likewise, found that 15% of chemists contributed half of the papers published in a sixteen-year period. Allison and Stewart (1974) similarly show high concentration of publication among physicists and mathematicians, as well as chemists.

Thus the data on publication show conclusively that (1) the average level of performance is low, and (2) it is highly variable. But beyond these two facts, agreement splinters and explanation of the determinants of these patterns is a central problem in the study of science and scholarship.

EXPLAINING DIFFERENTIAL PUBLICATION

Explanations of productivity in publication fall broadly into three categories.[6] The first emphasizes the role of personal or individual characteristics, such as psychological traits, work habits, and demographic factors. The second perspective emphasizes aspects of the work environment, especially prestige of department. A third perspective of "cumulative advantage" and "reinforcement" focuses upon feedback processes of the environment and its presumed resources and rewards.

Personal Characteristics

Among the studies of personal characteristics, the largest number have focused on psychological factors. One version of this perspective has been termed the "sacred spark" theory because it attributes productivity to "inner compulsion" which persists even in the absence of external rewards (Cole and Cole,

1973). A second variant of this perspective focuses not so much on motivation and attitude as on "stamina" or the capacity to work hard, tolerate frustration, and persist in the pursuit of long-range goals (Merton, 1973b; Zuckerman, 1970). A third variety of the psychological perspective is represented by clinical investigations of (1) the emotional styles (Cattell and Drevdahl, 1955; Knapp, 1963; Roe, 1953, 1964); (2) the biographical backgrounds — early childhood experiences, sources of satisfactions and dissatisfactions, attitudes, values, and interests (Chambers, 1964; Roe, 1952; Stein, 1962; Taylor and Barron, 1963; Taylor and Ellison, 1967); and (3) the cognitive structure of productive scientists (Cropley and Field, 1969; Eiduson, 1962; Gordon and Morse, 1970; Selye, 1964; Wilkes, 1980).

From the above studies, we find that certain psychological and attitudinal factors do correlate with publication. The biographical studies, especially, show that autonomy or self-direction is characteristic of the most productive. This is apparent in their early preferences for teachers who let them alone, in attitudes toward religion, and in personal relations. Productive scientists and scholars tend to be detached from their immediate families and wider social relations and attached, instead, to the inanimate objects and abstract ideas of their work (Chambers, 1964; Stein, 1962; Taylor and Ellison, 1967).

Further, data suggest the superior stamina of the high producers, revealing them as absorbed, involved, and indefatigable workers (Bernard, 1964; Eiduson, 1962; Pelz and Andrews, 1976; Zuckerman, 1970). Driven by curiosity, ambition, or need for achievement, high producers tend to organize their lives around their work.

In cognitive and perceptual styles, productive scholars and scientists also show certain modes of perceiving and thinking, including a capacity to play with ideas, stave off intellectual closure, and tolerate ambiguity and abstraction (Eiduson, 1962; Gordon and Morse, 1970; Selye, 1964). The emphasis here is upon *style* rather than level of ability. Measured ability level, in fact, correlates very weakly with productivity and achievement in science (Cole and Cole, 1973). Although high IQ may be a prerequisite for doctoral training, once the degree is obtained, differences in measured ability do not predict subsequent levels of performance (Cole and Cole, 1973). Rather, persons with equal ability differ markedly in the ways in which they deploy intellectual resources (see Cropley and Field, 1969).

The fundamental problem of the psychological perspective is that personality traits and attributes do not exist in a vacuum (Andrews, 1976). These individual traits and dispositions are strongly affected by the social and organizational context in which they exist. Andrews shows that measured creativity, for example, does not result in productivity unless scientists have strong motivation, diverse activities, and the capacity to exercise power and influence over decisions. Likewise, other studies fail to show a direct relationship between measured creativity and measured performance (Connor, 1974; Gordon and Morse, 1970), and suggest the "interface of psychological capability and organizational requisite'' (Gordon and Morse, 1970) as the nexus of research performance. However, unlike Andrews' investigation, these others do not actually test the extent to which organizational context mediates psychological characteristics and productivity. Thus the link between individual attributes and environment remains a critical area for investigation.

Compared to the large number of psychological studies, those on work habits are few, and the commentary on the subject tends to be speculative (see, for example, Stinchcombe, 1966). Exceptions include Hargens' (1978) study, which focuses upon disciplinary context, and Simon's (1974) study of the work practices of eminent scholars. Hargens' work reports that habits relate to productivity according to the level of "routine" or "predictability" in the work. Thus in chemistry, a more routinized discipline, time spent in research and engagement in multiple projects are associated with productivity, while in less routinized fields such as mathematics these work practices have weak to nonexistent impact upon output. Simon's study reports that, as a group, eminent scholars have certain work patterns: they devote enormous time to research (some working 365 days of the year); they work on several projects at once; they tend to devote mornings to writing.

While studies of work habits are few, they are suggestive, and strongly appealing for further research — because work routines (unlike factors such as "insight" or "imagination") are more adaptive strategies available to aspiring scholars.

Finally, among investigations of individual characteristics and productivity are studies of demographic characteristics: age and, more recently, gender. Almost fifty years ago, Lehman (1936, 1944, 1953) began presenting evidence that major contributions occur in scientists' late thirties and early forties and decline thereafter. In subsequent work (1958, 1960), he elaborated that the age peaks occur earlier in more abstract fields (such as mathematics) and later in more empirically based fields (such as biology). He also observed that the age peak is sharper for major contributions and flatter for more minor contributions.

Although Lehman's conclusions have gained wide acceptance in scientific lore, his work is methodologically flawed (see S. Cole, 1979; Reskin, 1979b). Instead of determining the proportion of scientists in each age group who had made important discoveries, Lehman simply compared the proportion of all important discoveries made by scientists of different ages. In failing to take into consideration the number of scientists in each age group, he assumed equal proportions in each group. However, because science has been growing exponentially over the past two centuries, scientists are disproportionately young and thus discoveries — both important and unimportant — will have been made disproportionately by younger persons.

Other investigations have modified Lehman's findings, and shown that the association between age and productivity is neither linear nor monotonic. Pelz and Andrews (1976) report a productivity peak in scientists' late thirties and early forties — but also a second peak ten to fifteen years later at age fifty. In analyses of data from academics in seven fields, Bayer and Dutton (1977) obtain results similar to Pelz and Andrews'. In five of the fields, Bayer and Dutton observe a "spurt-obsolescence" function between age and articles published in the past two years, with the first productivity peak reached about the tenth year of career age followed by a second peak near retirement age. However, the reported relationships are weak in all fields, and age accounts for little variation in publication levels.

For a cross section of academics in six fields, S. Cole (1979), on the other hand, reports a slightly curvilinear relationship between age and quantity of publication. Publication rates rise gradually with age, peak in the late thirties and early forties, and then drop off. Additional longitudinal data from mathematics, and cohort effects, show the same curvilinear pattern. Yet despite these variations, productivity does not differ significantly with age.

Most studies of age and productivity, however, have been cross-sectional. As such, they are unable to distinguish between the effects of generational differences in socialization, training, and access to resources which might be responsible for the lower productivity of older scholars (Reskin, 1979b). A recent and intriguing exception to this cross-sectional work is Hammel's (1980) longitudinal study of chemists in the University of California system.

Challenging the notion of productivity declines with age, Hammel reports that "productivity increases strongly with age and decreases strongly with the square of age, so that the pattern is one of gradually decelerating increase" (p. 5).[7] In other words, he finds that productivity increases with age — with some flattening but not necessarily decline. Further, he reports that these increases are more dramatic for recent cohorts, and that declines apparent in a mean rate across persons are "attributable to 'shooting stars' — the high producers who climb to a peak and then decline" (pp. 4-5).

Other studies may have failed to capture a pattern of decelerating increase with age because they do not separate behavior by birth cohort. Hammel's analyses, which do separate by cohort, show that only the very oldest cohort (over age 61) manifests a decline in mean productivity over age 40, and that the two cohorts prior to it (age 51-55 and age 56-60) exhibit only a leveling off of productivity with increasing age.

Along with the problems of cross-sectional analyses, studies of age and productivity are flawed in other ways (see Reskin, 1979b). First, the predominant bivariate analyses (analyses limited simply to measures of age and productivity) fail to control for factors such as early experience, institutional location, primary work activity, and availability of resources. Further, failure to report the *magnitude* of the association between age and productivity can be misleading. Studies that have reported the strength of the association (Bayer and Dutton, 1977) have shown a weak impact of age upon productivity. This strongly cautions against any educational policy on the basis of age and productivity relationship *per se*.

The most recent studies of individual characteristics have focused on gender. These studies converge on one point: as a group, academic women publish less than men. Although the data vary somewhat, they indicate that, within a given period, women publish about half as many articles as men. Thus, among academics in the fields of chemistry, biology, psychology, and sociology, J. Cole (1979) found that over a twelve-year period the median publication was 8 papers for men and 3 for women. Likewise, among a sample of male and female scientists in six fields, who were "matched" for year of Ph.D. and doctoral department, Cole and Zuckerman (1984) report that men had published 11.2 papers compared to 6.4 for women.

Analyses within fields also show sex differentials in publication. Over a three-year period male psychologists were significantly more productive than women, publishing an average 1.7 papers compared to women's .7 (Helmreich et al., 1980). Among educational researchers — two-thirds of whom were in education and one-third in other social science fields — Persell (1983) found that throughout their careers the average number of articles published by men was 12.6 and the average for women 7.6. For chemists, however, Reskin (1978a) reports slighter differences, which suggest "a true but small sex difference between the populations" in this field (p. 1236).

The data above show the central tendencies — means and medians — in the publication of women compared to men. In variability, on the other hand, there are smaller proportions of women than men among the prolific (Astin, 1978; Bayer, 1973; Cole and Zuckerman, 1984; Ladd and Lipset, 1976), but women's publication is as skewed, or more so, than that of men. This indicates that among both gender groups most of the work is published by a few persons, while the majority publish little or nothing. Specifically, in J. Cole's (1979) sample of academics in both social and physical sciences, 15% account for about 50% of the total papers published by each gender group. Further, in their sample of male and female scientists, Cole and Zuckerman (1984) found that the most prolific women account for an even larger proportion of all papers published by women than do their counterparts among men.

Documenting sex-differential productivity is one thing, and accounting for it quite another. While the sex differential is certain, the explanations are not. In accounting for sex-differential productivity, studies have controlled for variables such as institutional location, family status, years of experience, and age at Ph.D.

Some studies (Astin, 1978; Persell, 1983) show that controls for institutional location and marital status do reduce the differential — although not always in the expected direction. Astin's work shows that married women publish more than single women, rather than the other way around. This she attributes in part to the marriage of academic women to other academics, which, she argues, puts these women into contact with male colleagues and collegial networks (Astin and Davis, 1985). Other studies, however, have found that significant sex differences in publication remain even after controlling for family status or institutional affiliation (see J. Cole 1979; Helmreich et al., 1980). On the other hand, within a particular occupational location — the most distinguished research universities — Helmreich et al. report minimal sex differences in the productivity of psychologists.

In assessment of sex-differential productivity, a major shortcoming of the studies is their failure to assess organizational variables as they affect the productivity of men and women. These variables include level and type of teaching (undergraduate versus graduate, lecture versus seminar), collegial interaction, mentoring and support, research assistance, and funding information and networks — factors that are discussed in the following sections.

Environmental Location

The second major category of productivity studies focuses on the structural context often overlooked in investigations of individual characteristics. These studies emphasize the importance of early academic environment (i.e., graduate school background) and characteristics of subsequent environment, particularly prestige of location.

Graduate school background is important not only because it develops knowledge, skills, and competencies, but also because it cultivates norms, values, and opportunities. Graduate education shapes conceptions of the scholarly role, styles of work, and standards of performance (Zuckerman, 1977). In fact, most academics do not significantly alter their ideas and approaches following graduate school (Kuhn, 1970; Mullins, 1973). Given the salience of this socialization, investigators have looked to graduate school background to explain publication levels. Despite variation in the findings, prestige of doctoral program, along with predoctoral productivity, emerge as predictors of productivity.

In an early study of academics in three fields — biology, political science, and psychology — at universities of varying prestige levels, Crane (1965) reported that the setting in which an academic receives training is more decisive for productivity than the setting in which one works after obtaining the degree. More specifically, Crane reports that academics with degrees from a major university are more likely to be productive independent of present location, while academics trained at minor universities are unlikely to be productive unless currently located at a major university. Crane attributes the stronger effect of current environment for graduates of minor universities to two factors — motivation and judgment in selecting research topics.

Subsequent studies of graduate school background and productivity have extended the investigation by differentiating training processes, refining the measures, and further specifying the effect of graduate school upon publication productivity. With data from chemists, Reskin (1979a) analyzes the effect upon both pre- and postdoctoral publication and citation of three different aspects of graduate school background: caliber of doctoral program, training with a productive sponsor, and collaborative publication with a sponsor. Reskin's findings indicate that sponsorship may be important in launching early — pre-doctoral — publication, but once the degree is obtained, the quality of the doctoral program as a whole is more critical in facilitating sustained — postdoctoral — publication.

Long, Allison, and McGinnis (1979) challenge these findings. Analyzing data from biochemists, they report that while prestige of doctoral department and sponsor's eminence are positive in their effects on productivity, the associations are weak. Instead, they find that the strong and direct determinant of productivity is predoctoral publication, and that the effects of doctoral program are indirect, influencing productivity by way of prestige of first appointment.

Another group of researchers, Chubin, Porter, and Boeckman (1981), question the generalizability of these findings to fields beyond chemistry. Replicating aspects of Long et al.'s work on doctorates in engineering, physics, psychology, sociology, and zoology, as well as biochemistry, they support Long's contention that early publication influences later publication. But they also maintain that prestige of doctoral program is critical.

Beyond studies of graduate school background, the strongest and most consistent of all correlates of publication is the prestige of institutional affiliation (see Blackburn, Behymer, and Hall, 1978; Blau, 1973; Long, 1978; Long and McGinnis, 1981; Wiley, Crittenden, and Birg, 1981), suggesting that more prestigious locations foster, and less prestigious hinder, the research orientation and activity of their members. Of course, the causal relationship between productivity and location might operate in the effect of productivity upon location as well as the other way around — so that more prestigious departments are selecting more productive scholars. However, recent longitudinal studies, which have actually monitored the publication histories of scientists between locations and over time, indicate a stronger causal effect of location upon publication rather than vice versa.

Among these studies, Long (1978) reports that while the effect of publication upon prestige of location is weak, the effect of location upon publication is strong. For academics moving into first position, publication is not immediately affected by location; rather, it is affected by early, predoctoral publication levels. However, after the third year in the job, productivity is more strongly related to prestige of department than to previous predoctoral publication. Specifically, those in prestigious departments increase their publication, and those in less prestigious settings begin to publish less. Among those who switch institutions, the change in publication level after the move is more clearly related to the prestige of the new department that to that of the old department. Long's findings suggest a process of cumulative advantage: even if later job mobility is based upon more objective criteria, the prestige of first appointment, which is independent of earlier productivity, has an impact upon subsequent productivity and, in turn, prestige of second appointment.

In a subsequent study, Long and McGinnis (1981) extend these analyses beyond the prestige of academic department to the effects of larger organizational contexts — the research university, non-research university or four-year college, and nonacademic or industrial sectors. They report that the chance of obtaining employment in a given context is unrelated initially to publication level. However, once in the job, publication comes to conform to the context. Location in four-year colleges and in industrial settings depresses publication, while location in research universities fosters publication. Moreover, when changes occur in context, the new location takes hold as the determinant of publication — but only after three years in the new job. The fact that it takes some time for new location to take effect suggests that productivity levels are not simply a result of changes in individuals' goals or of global barriers to publication in some settings.

A major gap in these investigations, however, lies in their failure to explain how environment fosters or impedes publication. Specifically, the research has failed to determine the extent to which institutional location promotes productivity through the cultivation of individual habits or dispositions, or through the influence of institutional factors such as research facilities, graduate assistance, or a favorable reward structure. Among the environmental factors which might mediate productivity levels, however, one variable — collegial exchange and communication — does emerge with some consistency.

Data indicate that collegial exchange stimulates research involvement by testing ideas, activating interests, and reinforcing work (Blau, 1973; Reskin, 1978b; Pelz and Andrews, 1976). Explaining the collegial process, Blau (1973, p. 113), argues:

> Whether a faculty member's interests are stimulated or stifled in an academic institution depends on his colleagues. The discussions of such colleagues about their research experiences — the problems encountered and the exciting discoveries made — with those who share research interests, and primarily with them, are incentives likely to activate any latent interest in research a person may have. To become a genuine member of a colleague group of this kind, one must be involved in research and thus be able to participate fully in discussions about research. These processes of social exchange are a continual source of rewards for scholarly endeavor and create group pressure to engage in scholarly research by depriving those failing to do so of social rewards.

The prestigious academic departments which are said to provide a context favoring productivity are also reported to have stronger patterns of scholarly exchange (see Parsons and Platt, 1968). Further, certain accounts (Blau, 1973; Mandell, 1977; Martindale, 1980) suggest that the collegial atmosphere in minor institutions may actually discourage research and publication by belittling or beleaguering its significance. Martindale's (1980, p. 238) account is chilling:

> When one does write and publish extensively in the teaching universities, a new ambivalent situation develops between an individual and his colleagues. One's achievement then becomes a source of envy and fear — lest the administration demand this in addition to its teaching and service requirements. The individual also becomes a source of mixed pride and anxiety to the administration — lest it lead productive writers and scholars to demand salary increases and free time to pursue their research.

Because the scholarly community — and it central reward structure — is national rather than local, collegial networks clearly transcend immediate environment. Attachments, loyalties, and reference groups outside the institution constitute a "cosmopolitan" compared to "local" professional orientation (Gouldner, 1957, 1958; Merton, 1942). "Locals" identify with their employing institution, its organization and rewards. "Cosmopolitans" are committed to achievement and recognition within the discipline as a whole. The cosmopolitan orientation is associated with research productivity among scientists and scholars; further, while it is possible to score high on both local and cosmopolitan dimensions, the interaction of both dimensions is not more strongly associated with productivity than is the cosmopolitan orientation alone (Jauch, Glueck, and Osborn, 1978; Stahl, McNichols, and Manley, 1979).

However, collegial exchange (as opposed to local identification or loyalty) within the unit or department does appear to facilitate productivity. Ongoing, face-to-face contact helps provide ideas, catch errors, and stimulate development (see Pelz and Andrews, 1976). In a particular study of theoretical high-energy physicists, J. Blau (1976) concludes that for this group the best departmental environment is one in which the physicists have a *few* colleagues working in the same specialized environment but *many* who share the general theoretical orientation. Such departmental heterogeneity promotes both collective emphasis upon research and stimulating cosmopolitan contacts outside the deparment.

Beyond collegial exchange, certain organizational and management studies have reported that higher levels of organizational freedom support publication productivity. But these investigations focus on levels of freedom as they operate in industrial and nonacademic labs rather than in academic settings (see Box and Cotgrove, 1968; Stahl and Stevens, 1977; Vollmer, 1970). Related studies focus on factors such as group coordination or style of leadership as they influence productivity of the research aggregate (e.g., lab unit or team) rather than the individual, or they focus on productivity through patents, reports, and other products in primarily nonacademic settings (Jitendra, 1974; Kowalewska, 1979; Smith, 1971; Visart, 1979). Although these studies suggest the general importance of organizational climate, they tell us little about particular processes of environment as they affect publication in academic settings, specifically.

Feedback Processes: Cumulative Advantage and Reinforcement
While the psychological theories assume a simple additive relationship between publication and individual characteristics, the environmental perspective begins to suggest feedback processes — whereby initial appointment affects productivity and, in turn, subsequent employment and productivity patterns. These reciprocal processes of environment, resources, and reward are the very focus of the cumulative advantage perspective.

From this perspective, scholars who experience early success are able to command increased time, facilities, and support for continued research. Once these rewards are obtained, they have an independent effect upon the acquisition of further resources and rewards. Thus the accumulation of advantage involves "getting ahead initially and moving further and further out front" (Zuckerman, 1977, p. 61).

One variation of cumulative advantage has been called the "Matthew effect" (after the Gospel of St. Matthew).[8] This effect consists of the accrual of greater recognition to contributions of those with considerable repute and lesser recognition to those with limited repute (Merton, 1973b). Heightened recognition can then be converted to resources for further performance. This effect applies especially in cases of collaboration and independent multiple discoveries by those of unequal rank (Merton, 1973b). In both instances, the already eminent get disproportionate credit.

Although the perspective of cumulative advantage is well developed, tests of the hypotheses are difficult, since they require data on the research resources of scholars. Lacking these data, findings have supported the perspective only indirectly. Showing almost perfect linearity between career age and productivity differences, Gaston's (1978) longitudinal data, for example, indirectly suggest a pattern whereby productivity differences become ever larger between those initially advantaged and those not so advantaged. Allison and Stewart's (1974) data, which are merely cross-sectional, also show strong linear increases in publication differences with increasing career age.

The cumulative advantage and reinforcement perspectives are frequently lumped together. However, the reinforcement perspective focuses not on how productivity is advanced, but rather on why it is sustained. The perspective derives from the fundamental behaviorist principle that behavior which is reinforced continues to be emitted, and that which is not rewarded tends to be extinguished. Applied to productivity, early publication and citation should result in continued performance, while failure to produce early on should result in continued nonproductivity.

The problem with the reinforcement perspective is that the social context of scholarly productivity is much more complex than the laboratory settings and animal experiments (Skinner, 1938, 1953, 1969) from which the reinforcement principle derives. Further, while reinforcement and cumulative advantage are conceptually distinct, the processes are related in ways that make it difficult to untangle the effects analytically. Positive reinforcement alone will not account for much productivity unless it is accompanied by the cumulation of resources for research. Cumulative advantage, on the other hand, does not exist without some prior reinforcement; thus reinforcement almost always accompanies the enabling resources of advantage.

Despite the difficulties in assessing reinforcement, certain studies have attempted to do so, and the data lend support to the perspective. For example, with data on the publication records of 83 sociologists, Lightfield (1971) found that among those who published and received citations to their work in the first five years following the doctorate, the majority (73%) continued to publish and to be cited in the second five-year period. In contrast, only 6% of those who published and were cited dropped out in the second period. Most critically, of the 21 sociologists who published but did not receive citation to their work during the first period, only one received citation during the second period. With these data, Lightfield concludes that "unless a person achieves a qualitative piece of research during the first five years, it seems unlikely that he will do so during the next five years — if at any time during his career" (p. 133).

Data from other fields also support the reinforcement principle of publication. Among physicists, Cole and Cole (1973) report those whose work is uncited are much less likely to continue publishing than those whose work is cited. With a sample of men and women in six scientific fields — astronomy, biochemistry, chemistry, earth sciences, mathematics, and physics — Cole and Zuckerman (1984) also found that later productivity relates strongly to early publication and its citation. Specifically, 29% of those who had published four or fewer papers in an earlier period, but who receive citation, were prolific publishers in a later period. However, only 9% of those who published fewer than five papers, but went uncited, were prolific later on. Correspondingly, two-thirds of those who both published five or more papers and were comparably cited in an earlier period continued to be as productive later, while less than one-half of those who were equally productive but uncited continued to be productive.

Among chemists, likewise, Reskin (1977) found that early publication and citation support productivity in the following decade. However, she adds an important qualification: the strength of the effects varies by type of first employment. For those employed in research universities, early publication in itself is important for continued productivity. But for those in settings with less emphasis on research, citation is particularly important. These patterns suggest that for those in research universities the informal and immediate response of colleagues may be more important than the formal but delayed reinforcement of citation. However, in settings with less emphasis on research, the formal acknowledgment of citation may be especially important, because it can symbolize ties to the research community and its norms and activity.

These findings highlight the role of organizational context in the operation of reinforcement. They also point to the limitations of the studies in their reliance on citation as the sole measure of reinforcement. We do not know the extent to which scholars are aware that they are being cited, nor do we know whether a few citations from prominent researchers are more sustaining than numerous citations from the rank and file (Cole and Zuckerman, 1984). Further, it may be the awards, honors, and grants — associated with citation — that actually support and sustain publication.

AGENDA FOR FUTURE RESEARCH

In studies of productivity, the major problem of the psychological perspective is that personal traits and dispositions do not exist in a vacuum. By themselves, psychological factors do not necessarily translate to productivity. Studies show no direct relationship between measured creativity or intelligence, for example, and research performance, and suggest that social and organizational variables interact with, and affect, the manifestation of these characteristics. Yet only one study (Andrews, 1976) actually tests and demonstrates a social process — that creativity results in research productivity only with motivation, diverse activities, and the capacity to influence the organizational environment. Although ability, creativity, and other characteristics are undoubtedly important in research activity, studies need to specify the way in which these factors translate to productivity and the organizational and environmental processes involved.

Another underdeveloped area of inquiry is that of work habits and productivity. The relationship between work habits and productivity is intriguing because work routines and practices (unlike insight and imagination) are more adaptive strategies available to individual scholars. Practices such as when one works, with whom, for how long, and on how many projects may be pertinent to productivity. Another pertinent factor is the proportion of time spent in research compared to nonresearch activities. In an unpublished paper (reported in Pelz and Andrews, 1976), Meltzer found that full-time researchers published less than those spending three-quarters of their time on research. Likewise, Pelz and Andrews and Knorr et al. (1979) found that some mixture of research and teaching or administration is associated with higher productivity. But a confounding factor — and one worthy of future research — is the causal relationship between habits and productivity. Thus practices such as simultaneous work on several projects or diverse activities of research and administration can either be the cause *or* the result of productivity. We need to untangle the ordering of the variables.

Studies of the age and productivity relationship also need fine tuning — with controls for mediating and moderating factors. The study of age and productivity has a long research tradition stemming back some 50 years to Lehman's investigations of productivity declines with increasing age. While subsequent studies have modified Lehman's work and showed curvilinear and bimodal relationships between age and productivity, most of the studies have been cross-sectional. Thus they have failed to distinguish the effects of generational differences in socialization, training, and access to resources that might be responsible for lower productivity of older scientists. Since the growth of science and scholarship is leveling off and the age of the participants is increasing as fewer positions are available for the young, the age and productivity relationship becomes more important. Studies need to get beyond simple, cross-sectional bivariate analyses and begin to assess how factors such as generational differences, environmental location, primary work activity, and availability of resources figure into the age and productivity relationship. At present, the methodological shortcomings of current studies plus the weak association between age and productivity, reported in one of the few studies showing magnitude of relationship, provide little basis for any standard policy such as "early retirement" (Bayer and Dutton, 1977).

Likewise, the study of sex and productivity suffers from failure to consider organizational factors. First, we need to determine how factors such as type of teaching, inclusion or exclusion from collegial networks, research assistance, and funding opportunities affect the productivity — and productivity differences — of men and women. Second — and this is more subtle — we must consider whether the same type of institutional setting (major research university, minor university, or liberal arts college) may, in fact, offer different organizational opportunities and constraints for one sex compared to the other. Thus, although research opportunities are frequently more limited in liberal arts colleges than in universities, such an environment does not necessarily operate uniformly. The women may have patterns of heavier teaching loads, less access to released time, fewer claims on in-house grants, limited opportunities for collaboration, and fewer administrative favors for travel funds and the like.

Moving yet more broadly to the relationship between environment and productivity, fundamental questions are left unanswered. First, we lack adequate data about the ways in which "group climate" vary in academic institutions and the way it relates to productivity. From studies of nonacademic (industrial, government, and agency) research settings, we know that higher levels of freedom support publication productivity. When scientists are free to select, initiate, and terminate their own research projects or influence the process, publication productivity is higher (Box and Cotgrove, 1968; Pelz and Andrews, 1976; Vollmer, 1970). Further, in scientists' own subjective impressions about group climate and productivity, they stress the importance of organizational freedom and autonomy (see Parmerter and Garber, 1971). In nonacademic settings, the more creative researchers value a "loose rein" and "minimal structure" in their work (Gantz, Stephenson, and Erickson, 1969).

Academic settings generally do permit more academic freedom and autonomy for researchers than do nonacademic organizations in which goals of profit and direct application frequently conflict with individual research initiative. Yet within the academic setting work climates differ, and we need to specify (1) how factors such as organizational freedom, as well as style of administrative leadership, degree of group coordination, and lines of communication, vary in academia, and (2) how they affect the productivity of its faculty.

Freedom and independence are certainly strong precepts in science and scholarship, and as a correlate to these structural norms, scholarship tends to attract the "solitary mind." Yet the solitary dispositions and independent norms of science and scholarship are contravened by the communalism of the work (see Fox and Faver, 1984). The communalism and exchange of research engender cooperation and interdependence. Correspondingly, collegial exchange emerges with some consistency in the literature as an environmental correlate of productivity. However, we need to know much more about the way in which collegiality operates. For example, what constitutes collegial exchange —

group colloquia and the interchange of papers and written work, as well as interpersonal communication? How do such types of exchange vary in their relationship with productivity? What is the optimal frequency of collegial communication? For productive outcomes, is collegiality best as a "monogamous" or "polygamous" arrangement — that is, to support productivity, is it better to have one significant colleague or a more diverse but less intensive circle? In collegial exchange, are parallel or divergent intellectual approaches, skills, and perspectives more effective for research productivity? How do factors of colleagues' academic rank and gender affect collegiality and productivity — what are the relative costs and benefits of peer compared to junior-senior alliances and cross-sex relationships compared to same-sex ones? Further, how do each of these issues of collegiality and productivity vary (1) by discipline, (2) by inter- versus intradepartmental (and university) exchange, and (3) for formal collaboration and team work compared to informal exchange?

Better data on organizational processes and productivity would also increase understanding of feedback processes of cumulative advantage. So far, studies showing that productivity differences become greater with career age have offered only indirect support for the cumulative advantage perspective. To make an adequate test of the perspective that the initially advantaged move further and further ahead and those not so advantaged further behind, we need data on scholars' productivity and organizational resources — time, assistance, funding, networks — as they vary over time.

We also need better tests of the reinforcement perspective. While data do indicate that early publication and citation support continued performance, Reskin's (1977) work suggests that the effects vary by type of first employment. For those in settings with less emphasis on research, the formal citation is important; for those in research universities, the informal and immediate acknowledgment of colleagues may be more important than formal but delayed citation. This points again to the importance of organizational context and collegial exchange. In doing so, it also indicates once more the need for future work that further specifies how collegiality varies between contexts and does, or does not, reinforce productivity in research. Future work also needs to assess the extent to which scholars are aware that they are being cited, and the extent to which it is other awards, honors, and grants — associated with citation — that actually reinforce performance.

IMPLICATIONS AND RECOMMENDATIONS FOR EQUITY AND PERFORMANCE

Achievement — along with objectivity and rationality — are the manifest values that guide and control the behavior of scientists and scholars (Cole and Cole, 1973; Merton, 1949). In academia, achievement is not merely a criterion for reward. Rather, it has intrinsic value for the very activity and goals of the institution:

> In the university, the achievement ideology explains and justifies reward and supports and maintains inequality, as does ideology everywhere. But, as part of the scientific work ethos, the university's achievement and performance standards justify the presence, the purpose, and the activity, itself. [Fox, 1981, p. 81]

Manifest values notwithstanding, academia is hardly immune from particularistic processes. As Max Weber said years ago: "Academic life is a mad hazard. If the young scholar asks for my advice with regard to habilitation, the responsibility of encouraging him can hardly be borne" (Weber, [1919] 1946, p. 133). Politicking, committeeing, and power-wooing continue to beset academic life — to the particular disadvantage of women and other marginal members (Fox, 1984; Reskin, 1978b). Still, as a standard of activity and reward, the academic achievement value persists. Scholarship (along with organized sports) is said to offer an approximation to structured situations in which individual rewards stem from performance (Goode, 1967).

But while a meritocratic standard helps to provide normative pressure for rewards to follow performance, it does not guarantee equal opportunity to acquire the credentials and produce performance. We have seen that achievement through publication is not a simple function of motivation and ability. It is the result also of organizational background, environment, and access to the means of performance — training, resources, and support.

Structural barriers, however, restrict the access to performance and reward in academia. At the onset, a small and select group of students derives advantages from contact with eminent scholars. These scholars selectively provide students the opportunity to pose important questions, solve problems, and set goals. Moreover, for these favored groups of students, elite scholars provide access to informal communication networks and fashionable, emergent areas of research (Crane, 1972; Hagstrom, 1965; Mulkay, 1976). These opportunities to enter a growing field — when the chances for making a significant contribution are greater — may be a major determinant of early and continued success in scholarship (Mulkay, 1976). Accordingly, 50% of American Nobel laureates were themselves students of laureates (Zuckerman, 1970). While this may be due to "an extremely efficient albeit uncoordinated process of selective recruitment," it is also attributable, in large part, to selective patronage, support, and opportunity (Mulkay, 1976).[9]

Such patterns of selection help create and maintain a class structure in science and scholarship by providing stratified chances for performance and reward. To point to a high correlation between citation and other types of awards as evidence of meritocracy begs the question. The correlations merely show that both kinds of rewards go to the same group of persons (Mulkay, 1980) without explaining how a select group gains access to the ways and means of performance and reward, and without explaining how opportunity is affected by structural access.

For some academics, research and publication may be a questionable aspiration. Bayer (1973) found that only about a third of American faculty would want lighter teaching loads to pursue research. It would be a mistake, then, to impute to the vast group of academics the motivations of the most productive. But at the same time, we must recognize that aspirations tend to reflect levels of available opportunity (Kanter, 1977). Academics, like other groups, limit and modify their choices in favor of socially realistic and attainable options. Although there may be little that can be done to raise the performance of the least productive, and least motivated, academics (Hammel, 1980), organizational resources and a facilitating environment are potentially important for a large group of academics who have not benefited from the cumulative advantage — elite scholarship, prestigious appointments, early performance, and recognition — that supports productivity. Resources and a favorable environment are also important to sustain the performance of the already productive. What, specifically, can universities do to activate and sustain the productivity of their faculty?

First, despite the shortcomings of the psychological studies, data do point to tendencies of the "research mind and personality," and administrators would be wise to take heed. Biographical and clinical studies show that productive scientists and scholars are independent, self-sufficient, and self-directed persons. As a group, they tend to be detached from personal relations, adverse to personally toned controversy, and attached to abstractions and ideas rather than people (see Chambers, 1964; Roe, 1952; Stein, 1962; Taylor and Ellison, 1967). If administrators want to encourage such researchers, they should minimize both the pressures and the rewards for social — "gadabout" — behavior. Productive, creative researchers are apt to be frustrated by an interpersonally centered climate and resentful about deflections from their work.

At the same time, the solitary disposition of scholars is to some extent contravened by communal norms of the work. Collegiality facilitates productivity. It is wise, then, to encourage colloquia and professional meetings on site, with an aim to create collegiality such that one can gain significant membership and rewards by active involvement in research. The aim is to foster not simply collegiality but *research-based* collegiality, with interaction and exchange centering on scholarly inquiry. In departmental groups without interests and rewards based on research performance, opposite normative pressures can stifle research, and berate it with criticisms of "careerism" and "publish or perish."

Furthermore, since productivity is associated with "cosmopolitan" rather than "local" orientations, academic institutions can help activate productivity by subsidizing travel to meetings where faculty may gain wider recognition and reinforcement for research by participation in panels and symposia. Moreover, these meetings impose external deadlines for completion of papers that can be subsequently prepared for publication.

Access to funding is also important to support research, which is increasingly technical, large-scale, and costly. Thus intramural seed money can be useful in developing the research productivity of faculty with potential, but without the external funding advantages of the academic superstars (Hammel, 1980).

Colleges and universities can affect work behavior through the manipulation of the reward structure for promotion, salary, honors, and awards.[10] To foster achievement and equity and minimize bias and particularism, institutions need to standardize the criteria for evaluation. Schools have resisted this, however, and defended shifting criteria as a "flexible" standard. "Flexibility" may be a favored organizational word, but the problem is that "it keeps other things from being equal" (Huber, 1973), especially for women and minorities. Studies indicate that the more loosely defined the criteria, the more likely that white males will be perceived as the superior candidates and the more likely that bias will operate (see Deux and Emsmiller, 1974; Nieva and Gutek, 1980; Pheterson, Kiesler, and Goldberg, 1981; Rosen and Jerdee, 1974).

To counter these tendencies and promote both equity and performance, schools should take steps to standardize criteria for evaluation — with research productivity as a principal component. In an effort to distribute merit increases fairly, Bowling Green University recently developed one criterion-based point system (see Partin, 1984). In the interests of publication productivity, I would argue with the weights assigned — since more peripheral activities such as presentation of a paper earns 14 points, preparation of an in-house report 8 points, reviewing a book for a publisher 5 points, and editing a newsletter 7 points, while publication of an article in a refereed journal returns, in comparison, only 20 points.[11]

Nonetheless, as a tool for objectivity and accountability — and as a potential device for relating rewards to productivity — a standardized instrument for evaluation would be a valuable step. Without objective standards, functionally irrelevant attributes can govern evaluation to an appalling degree. In a survey of deans of liberal arts colleges, Seldin (1984) found that "personal attributes" — one's dress, politics, and friends — were a "major factor" in overall evaluation of faculty among 38% of the deans in 1978 and 28% in 1983. Publication, by contrast, was a major consideration for only 19% in 1978 and 29% in 1983.

While standardized criteria can promote equity and performance, administrators must be careful to avoid applying a single standard of productivity across disciplines. As discussed earlier, short research reports and patterns of team collaboration account in part for a higher rate of publication in the natural sciences; in the social sciences, and especially in the humanities, longer essays and books are more frequent and account in part for fewer publications in these fields.

Efforts to activate and sustain faculty research performance can and should be a central institutional concern. The Ph.D. is, after all, a degree in research, and all doctorate holders have been trained to design, carry out, and report research projects. Further, academic research is critical, since 90% of all discoveries come out of institutions of higher learning (Kolstoe, 1975). Thus, when the dissertation is the single and last rather than the first of one's scholarly works — as it is for almost half of American academics (Mandell, 1977) — the loss is considerable to the nation, to the colleges and universities, and to the academics themselves.

NOTES

1. In some fields, particularly those in rapidly changing, technical areas, research findings are communicated with preprints. The preprints tend to be circulated, however, to a limited group of researchers working on closely related problems. Wider communication comes with publication, and publication legitimizes authorship of the work.
2. As Smelser and Content (1980) argue, however, in academia monetary rewards simply act as a kind of "floor" for comfortable existence and moreover as a symbolic reflection of prestige and esteem for the productive. In this way, "monetary rewards should be regarded not as inducements proffered to secure specific performance, but rather as a symbolic recognition of past, present, or promised performance" (p. 6).
3. "Consensus" (also called "paradigm development" or "codification") refers to level of agreement within a field on prevailing theory, methods, and significant areas of research. In this sense, fields such as physics and mathematics have high consensus and fields such as sociology and psychology have low consensus.
4. The "nationalization" of the scholarly reward structure occurred especially after World War II — with increased speed of modern communication, concentration of research efforts, and mobility of students and faculty (see Altbach, 1980).
5. Of course, in certain cases, most notably in the supervision of doctoral work, the research and teaching roles are integrated.
6. This section draws upon the author's "Publication Productivity Among Scientists: A Critical Review," *Social Studies of Science*, 1983, *13* 285-305.
7. Hammel's productivity index includes measures of teaching and service performance as well as publication. However, publication measures correlate very strongly with the other two — suggesting that those who do a lot in one area do a lot in the other areas as well. When publication measures are separated, they show the same age and productivity patterns as the combined measures.
8. "For whosoever hath, to him shall be given, and he shall have more abundance: but whosoever hath not, from him shall be taken away even that he hath." Matthew 13:12.
9. Even when procedures are formally open and universalistic, they can produce the same consequences — in elite formation and cumulation of advantage — as do informal patterns of exclusion. In a sobering account of "open" hiring at Berkeley, Smelser and Content (1980, p. 175-176) conclude:

   Though we advertised widely and we encouraged the application of minorities and women, the final results of the search — in terms of persons invited for interviews and in terms of persons actually appointed — was much the same as it would have been if we had simply written letters to colleagues in the dozen leading departments and asked them to name their best students. We were aware of this at the time of the search. Toward the end, when we knew generally who the successful candidates were going to be, we developed a somewhat bitter joke that the whole thing could have been done for the cost of two 13-cent stamps to send letters to a colleague at Chicago and a colleague at Harvard.

10. When collective bargaining schedules fix salary increments, merit increases may not be possible. Faculty collective bargaining can, however, provide better assurances of objectivity and accountability.
11. Thus with these weights, one can accumulate more points, more readily, through peripheral activities than through the central activity of doing research and publishing the results.

REFERENCES

Allison, P. D. *Processes of Stratification in Science*. New York: Arno Press, 1980.

Allison, P. D., and Stewart, J. A. Productivity differences among scientists: Evidence for accumulative advantage. *American Sociological Review*, 1974, *39*, 596-606.

Altbach, P. The crisis of the professoriate. *Annals of the American Academy of Political and Social Science*, 1980, *448*, 1-14.

Andrews, F. Creative process. In D. Pelz and F. Andrews (eds.), *Scientists in Organizations*. Rev. ed. Ann Arbor, Mich.: Institute for Social Research, 1976.

Astin, H. S. Factors affecting women's scholarly productivity. In H. Astin and W. S. Hirsch (eds.), *The Higher Education of Women*, New York: Praeger, 1978.

Astin, H. S. Academic scholarship and its rewards. In M. W. Steinkamp and P. Maehr (eds.), *Advances in Motivation and Achievement*, vol. 2. Greenwich, Conn.: JAI Press, 1984.

Astin, H. S., and Davis, D. E. Research productivity across the life and career cycles: Facilitations and barriers for women. In M. F. Fox (ed.), *Scholarly Writing and Publishing: Issues, Problems, and Solutions*. Boulder, Colorado: Westview Press, 1985.

Bayer, A. E. Teaching faculty in academe: 1972-73. *ACE Research Report* 8, 1973.

Bayer, A. E., and Astin, H. S. Sex differentials in the academic reward system. *Science*, 1975, *188*, 796-802.

Bayer, A. E., and Dutton, J. E. Career age and research-professional activities of academic scientists. *Journal of Higher Education*, 1977, *48*, 259-282.

Bernard, J. *Academic Women*. University Park, Pa.: Pennsylvania State University Press, 1964.

Blackburn, R. T., Behymer, C. E., and Hall, D. E. Research note: Correlates of faculty publications. *Sociology of Education*, 1978, *51*, 132-141.

Blau, J. R. Scientific recognition: Academic context and professional role. *Social Studies of Science*, 1976, *6*, 533-545.

Blau, P. *The Organization of Academic Work*. New York: Wiley, 1973.

Box, S., and Cotgrove, S. The productivity of scientists in modern industrial research laboratories. *Sociology*, 1968, *2*, 163-172.

Cattell, R. B., and Drevdahl, J. E. A comparison of the personality profile of eminent researchers with that of eminent teachers and administrators, and that of the general population. *British Journal of Psychology*, 1955, *46*, 248-261.

Chambers, J. Creative scientists of today. *Science*, 1964, *145*, 1203-1205.

Chubin, D. E., Porter, A. L., and Boeckman, M. Career patterns of scientists. *American Sociological Review*, 1981, *46*, 488-496.

Cole, J. R. *Fair Science: Women in the Scientific Community*. New York: Free Press, 1979.

Cole, J. R., and Cole, S. *Social Stratification in Science*. Chicago: University of Chicago Press, 1973.

Cole, J. R., and Zuckerman, H. The productivity puzzle: Persistence and change in patterns of publication among men and women scientists. In M. W. Steinkamp and M.

Maehr (eds.), *Advances in Motivation and Achievement*, vol. 2. Greenwich, Conn.: JAI Press, 1984.

Cole, S. Age and scientific performance. *American Journal of Sociology*, 1978, *84*, 958-977.

Connor, P. E. Scientific research competence as a function of creative ability. *IEEE Transactions on Engineering Management*, 1974, *EM-21*, 2-9.

Crane, D. Scientists at major and minor universities: A study of productivity and recognition. *American Sociological Review*, 1965, *30*, 699-715.

Crane, D. *Invisible Colleges*. Chicago: University of Chicago Press, 1972.

Cropley, A. J., and Field, T. W. Achievement in science and intellectual style. *Journal of Applied Psychology*, 1969, *53*, 132-135.

David, D. *Career Patterns and Values: A Study of Men and Women in Science and Engineering*. Columbia University, Bureau of Social Science Research, 1971.

Deux, K., and Emsmiller, T. Explanations of successful performance in sex-linked traits. *Journal of Personality and Social Psychology*, 1974, *22*, 80-85.

Eiduson, B. T. *Scientists: Their Psychological World*. New York: Basic Books, 1962.

Fisch, R. Psychology of science. In I. Spiegel-Rosing and D. Price (eds.), *Scientific Technology and Society*, London: Sage, 1977.

Fox, M. F. Sex, salary, and achievement: Reward-dualism in academia. *Sociology of Education*, 1981, *54*, 71-84.

Fox, M. F. Women and higher education: Sex differentials in the status of students and scholars. In J. Freeman (ed.), *Women: A Feminist Perspective*, Palo Alto, Calif.: Mayfield, 1984.

Fox, M. F., and Faver, C. A. Independence and cooperation in research: The advantages and costs of collaboration. *Journal of Higher Education*, 1984, *55*, 347-359.

Gantz, B., Stephenson, R., and Erickson, C. Ideal research and development climate as seen by more creative and less creative research scientists. *American Psychological Association Proceedings*, 1969, 605-606.

Gaston, J. *The Reward System in British and American Science*. New York: Wiley, 1978.

Goode, W. The protection of the inept. *American Sociological Review*, 1967, *32*, 5-19.

Gordon, G., and Morse, E. V. Creative potential and organizational structure. In M. J. Cetron and J. D. Goldhar (eds.), *The Science of Managing Organized Technology*, Vol. II, New York: Gordon and Breach, 1970.

Gouldner, A. W. Cosmopolitans and locals: Toward an analysis of latent social roles — I. *Administrative Science Quarterly*, 1957, *62*, 281-306.

Gouldner, A. W. Cosmopolitans and locals: Toward an analysis of latent social roles — II. *Administrative Science Quarterly*, 1958, *62*, 444-480.

Gregorio, D., Lewis, L., and Wanner, R. Assessing merit and need: Distributive justice and salary attainment in academia. *Social Science Quarterly*, 1982, *63*, 492-505.

Hagstrom, W. *The Scientific Community*. New York: Basic Books, 1965.

Hammel, E. Report on the task force on faculty renewal. Berkeley, Calif.: University of California, Program in Population Research, January 1980.

Hargens, L. L. *Patterns of Scientific Research: A Comparative Analysis of Research in Three Scientific Fields*. Washington, D.C.: American Sociological Association, 1975.

Hargens, L. L. Relations between work habits, research technologies, and eminence in science. *Sociology of Work and Occupations*, 1978, *5*, 97-112.

Helmreich, R., Spence, J., Beane, W., Lucker, G. W., and Matthews, K. Making it in academic psychology: Demographic and personality correlates of attainment. *Journal of Personality and Social Psychology*, 1980, *39*, 896-908.

Huber, J. Criteria for hiring, promotion, and tenure. *ASA Footnotes*, March 1973, p. 3.

Jauch, L., and Glueck, W. Evaluation of university professors' research performance. *Management Science*, 1975, *22*, 66-75.

Jauch, L., Glueck, W., and Osborn, R. Organizational loyalty, professional commitment, and academic research productivity. *Academy of Management Journal*, 1978, *21*, 84-92.

Jitendra, S. *Management of Scientific Research*. New York: International Publications, 1974.

Johnson, M., and Kasten, K. Meritorious work and faculty rewards: An empirical test of the relationship. *Research in Higher Education*, 1983, *19*, 49-71.

Kanter, R. M. *Men and Women of the Corporation*. New York: Basic Books, 1977.

Katz, D. A. Faculty salaries, promotions, and productivity at a large university. *American Economic Review*, 1973, *63*, 469-477.

Knapp, R. Demographic, cultural, and personality attributes of scientists. In C. Taylor and F. Barron (eds.), *Scientific Creativity: Its Recognition and Development*. New York: Wiley, 1963.

Knorr, K., Mittermeir, G., Aichholzer, G., and Waller, G. Individual publication productivity as a social position effect in academic and industrial research units. In F. Andrews (ed.), *Scientific Productivity: The Effectiveness of Research Groups in Six Countries*, Cambridge, England: Cambridge University Press, 1979.

Koch, J. V., and Chizmar, J. F. The influence of teaching and other factors upon absolute salaries and salary increments at Illinois State University. *Journal of Economic Education*, 1973, *5*, 27 34.

Kolstoe, O. P. *College Professoring*. Carbondale, Ill.: Southern Illinois University Press, 1975.

Kowalewska, S. Patterns of influence and the performance of research units. In F. Andrews (ed.), *Scientific Productivity: The Effectiveness of Research Groups in Six Countries*, Cambridge, England: Cambridge University Press, 1979.

Kuhn, T. *The Structure of Scientific Revolutions*. Chicago: University of Chicago Press, 1970.

Ladd, E. C., and Lipset, S. M. How professors spend their time. *Chronicle of Higher Education*, October 14, 1975, p. 2.

Ladd, E. C., and Lipset, S. M. Sex differences in academe. *Chronicle of Higher Education*, May 10, 1976, p. 18.

Ladd, E. C., and Lipset, S. M. Survey of 4,400 faculty members at 161 colleges and universities. *Chronicle of Higher Education*, November 21, 1977, p. 12, and November 28, 1977, p. 2.

Lightfield, E. T. Output and recognition of sociologists. *American Sociologist*, 1971, *6*, 128-133.

Lehman, H. C. The creative years in science and literature. *Scientific Monthly*, 1936, *43*, 162.

Lehman, H. C. Man's most creative years: Quality v. quantity of output. *Scientific Monthly*, 1944, *59*, 384-398.

Lehman, H. C. *Age and Achievement*. Princeton, N.J.: Princeton University Press, 1953.

Lehman, H. C. The chemist's most creative years. *Science*, 1958, *127*, 1213-1222.

Lehman, H. C. The age decrement in scientific creativity. *American Psychologist*, 1960, *15*, 128-134.

Lewis, L. *Scaling the Ivory Tower: Merit and Its Limits in Academic Careers*. Baltimore: Johns Hopkins University Press, 1975.

Long, J. S. Productivity and academic position in the scientific career. *American Sociological Review*, 1978, *43*, 899-908.

Long, J. S., Allison, P. D., and McGinnis, R. Entrance into the academic career. *American Sociological Review*, 1979, *44*, 816-830.

Long, J. S., and McGinnis, R. Organizational context and scientific productivity. *American Sociological Review*, 1981, *46*, 422-442.

Lotka, A. J. The frequency distribution of scientific productivity. *Journal of the Washington Academy of Sciences*, 1926, *26*, 317.

Mandell, R. D. *The Professor Game*. New York: Doubleday, 1977.

Marshall, H., and Perrucci, R. The structure of academic fields and rewards in academia. *Sociology and Social Research*, 1982, *66*, 127-147.

Martindale, D. *The Romance of a Profession: A Case History in the Sociology of Sociology*. St. Paul, Minn.: Wildflower, 1976.

Martindale, D. King of the hoboes: Portrait of an international cultural workman. In D. Martindale and R. Mohan (eds.), *Ideals and Realities: Some Problem Areas of Professional Social Science*, Ghaziabad, India: Intercontinental Press, 1980.

Merton, R. Science and technology in a democratic order. *Journal of Legal and Political Sociology*, 1942, *1*, 115-126.

Merton, R. Science and democratic social structure. In *Social Theory and Social Structure*, Glencoe, Ill.: Free Press, 1949.

Merton, R. Singletons and multiples in scientific discoveries. *Proceedings of the American Philosophic Society*, 1961, *105*, 470-486.

Merton, R. Priorities in scientific discovery. In *The Sociology of Science*. Chicago: University of Chicago Press, 1973(a).

Merton, R. The Matthew effect in science. In *The Sociology of Science*, Chicago: University of Chicago Press, 1973(b).

Mulkay, M. The mediating role of the scientific elite. *Social Studies of Science*, 1976, *6*, 445-470.

Mulkay, M. Sociology of the scientific research community. In I Spiegel-Rosing and D. Price (eds.), *Scientific Technology and Society*, London: Sage, 1977.

Mulkay, M. Sociology of science in the West. *Current Sociology*, 1980, *28*, 1-184.

Mullins, N. C. *Science: Some Sociological Perspectives*. Indianapolis: Bobbs-Merrill, 1973.

Nieva, V., and Gutek, B. Sex effects on evaluation. *Academy of Management Review*, 1980, *5*, 267-276.

Parmerter, S. M., and Garber, J. D. Creative scientists rate creativity factors. *Research Management*, 1971, *14*, 65-70.

Parsons, T., and Platt, G. M. Considerations of the American academic system. *Minerva*, 1968, *5*, 497-523.

Partin, R. A case study: Evaluating faculty at Bowling Green State University. *Change*, 1984, *16*, 31ff.

Pelz, D. C., and Andrews, F. M. *Scientists in Organizations: Productive Climates for Research and Development*. Ann Arbor, Mich.: Institute for Social Research, 1976.

Persell, C. H. Gender, rewards, and research in education. *Psychology of Women Quarterly*, 1983, *8*, 33-47.

Pheterson, G. T., Kiesler, S. G., and Goldberg, P. A. Evaluation of women as a function of their sex, achievement, and personal history. *Journal of Personality and Social Psychology*, 1971, *19*, 110-114.

Price, D. *Little Science, Big Science*. New York: Columbia University Press, 1963.

Reskin, B. F. Scientific productivity and the reward structure of science. *American Sociological Review*, 1977, *42*, 491-504.

Reskin, B. F. Scientific productivity, sex, and location in the institution of science. *American Journal of Sociology*, 1978(a), *83*, 1235-1243.

Reskin, B. F. Social differentiation and the social organization of science. *Sociological Inquiry*, 1978(b), *48*, 6-37.

Reskin, B. F. Academic sponsorship and scientists' careers. *Sociology of Education*, 1979(a), *52*, 129-146.

Reskin, B. Age and scientific productivity. In M. McPherson (ed.) *The Demand for New Faculty in Science and Engineering*, Washington, D.C.: National Research Council, 1979(b).

Roe, A. A psychologist examines 64 eminent scientists. *Scientific American*, December 1952, pp. 21-25.

Roe, A. *The Making of a Scientist*. New York: Dodd, Mead, 1953.

Roe, A. The psychology of scientists. In K. Hill (ed.), *The Management of Scientists*. Boston: Beacon Press, 1964.

Rosen, B., and Jerdee, T. H. Influence of sex-role stereotypes on personnel decisions. *Journal of Applied Psychology*, 1974, *59*, 9-14.

Seldin, P. Faculty evaluation: Surveying policy and practices. *Change*, 1984, *16*, 29-33.

Selye, H. *From Dream to Discovery: On Being a Scientist*. New York: McGraw Hill, 1964.

Shils, E. The academic ethos under strain. *Minerva*, 1975, *13*, 1-37.

Simon, R. J. The work habits of eminent scientists. *Sociology of Work and Occupations*, 1974, *1*, 327-335.

Skiff, A. Toward a theory of publishing or perishing. *American Sociologist*, 1980, *15*, 175-183.

Skinner, B. F. *The Behavior of Organisms*. New York: Appleton-Century, 1938.

Skinner, B. F. *Science and Human Behavior*. New York: Macmillan, 1953.

Skinner, B. F. *Contingencies of Reinforcement*. New York: Appleton-Century-Crofts, 1969.

Smart, J. C., and McLaughlin, G. W. Reward structures of academic disciplines. *Research in Higher Education*, 1978, *8*, 39-55.

Smelser, N. J., and Content, R. *The Changing Academic Market: General Trends and a Berkeley Case Study*. Berkeley: University of California Press, 1980.

Smith, C. G. Scientific performance and the composition of research teams. *Administrative Science Quarterly*, 1971, *16*, 486-495.

Stahl, M., McNichols, C., and Manley, R. Cosmopolitan-local orientations as predictors of scientific productivity, organizational productivity, and job satisfaction for scientists and engineers. *IEEE Transactions on Engineering Management*, 1979, *E-M26*, 39-43.

Stahl, M. J., and Stevens, A. E. Reward contingencies and productivity in a government research and development laboratory. Paper presented at the Joint National TIMS/ORSA Meeting, San Francisco, May 9, 1977.

Stein, M. I. Creativity in the scientist. In B. Barber and W. Hirsch (eds.), *The Sociology of Science*, New York: Free Press, 1962.

Stinchcombe, A. L. On getting "hung up" and other assorted illnesses. *Johns Hopkins Magazine*, 1966, 25-30.

Storer, N. W. *The Social System of Science*. New York: Holt, Rinehart and Winston, 1966.

Storer, N. W. *The Sociology of Science*. Chicago: University of Chicago Press, 1973.

Taylor, C. W., and Barron, F. *Scientific Creativity: Its Recognition and Development*. New York: Wiley, 1963.

Taylor, C. W., and Ellison, R. L. Biographical predictors of scientific performance. *Science*, 1967, *155*, 1075-1080.

Tuckman, H. P. *Publication, Teaching, and the Academic Reward Structure*. Lexington, Mass.: Lexington Books, 1976.

Tuckman, H. P., and Hagemann, R. P. An analysis of the reward structure in two disciplines. *Journal of Higher Education*, 1976, *47*, 447-464.

Visart, N. Communication between and within units. In F. Andrews (ed.), *Scientific Productivity: The Effectiveness of Research in Six Countries*, Cambridge, England: Cambridge University Press, 1979.

Vollmer, H. M. Evaluating two aspects of quality in research program effectiveness. In M. J. Cetron and J. D. Goldhar (eds.), *The Science of Managing Organized Technology*, Vol. IV, New York: Gordon and Breach, 1970.

Wanner, R., Lewis, L., and Gregorio, D. Research productivity in academia: A comparative study of the sciences, social sciences, and humanities. *Sociology of Education*, 1981, *54*, 238-253.

Weber, M. Science as a vocation. In H. H. Gerth and C. Wright Mills (eds.), *From Max Weber: Essays in Sociology*, New York: Oxford University Press, 1946.

Wiley, M. G., Crittenden, K. S., and Birg, L. D. Becoming an academic: Early vs. later professional experience. *Sociological Focus*, 1981, *14*, 139-145.

Wilkes, J. M. Styles of thought, styles of research, and the development of science. Worcester, Mass.: Worcester Polytechnic Institute, 1980.

Wilson, L. *American Academics: Then and Now*. New York: Oxford University Press, 1979.

Zuckerman, H. Stratification in American science. In E. O. Laumann (ed.), *Social Stratification: Research and Theory for the 1970s*, New York: Bobbs-Merrill, 1970.

Zuckerman, H. *Scientific Elite: Nobel Laureates in the United States*. New York: Free Press, 1977.

PROGRAM QUALITY IN HIGHER EDUCATION:
A Review and Critique of Literature and Research

Clifton F. Conrad, *University of Arizona,* and
Robert T. Blackburn, *University of Michigan*

Program quality in higher education — what it is, how to identify it, and how to foster it — has been an enduring concern among educators since the founding of Harvard College in 1636. Today, a variety of social forces has made program quality perhaps the single most important issue in higher education. Public disenchantment with educational institutions, pressures for accountability, and declining resources are but three factors that have precipitated a renewed interest in quality. State systems of higher education often must decide which programs to retain in the face of declining enrollments and limited resources. Many private liberal arts colleges must demonstrate for their very survival that their high costs are linked to a quality education. Local tax revolts are forcing many community colleges to decide which programs to eliminate. The federal government and private foundations need to identify quality programs before investing their limited resources.

Much recent literature has focused on the assessment of program quality. Aside from program evaluations at individual institutions, which are not reviewed here, program evaluation research has been aimed primarily at assessing and ranking departments, professional schools, and sometimes entire colleges and universities. In these evaluation studies, quality has been assessed either through a "reputational" approach or through an approach based on "objective" indicators of quality. More recently, there has emerged a third approach to research on program quality. Instead of evaluating program quality, this line of research has focused on the identification of quantifiable program characteristics associated with programs considered to be of high quality.

The major purpose of this article is to review and critique these lines of research and to examine the implications of each for future research. The paper is divided into four major sections. In order to provide a context for examining the three areas of research, the first section looks at the multiple meanings of quality. The second section examines the program evaluation research that is based on a "reputational" approach; the third reviews the program evaluation research based on "objective" indicators; and the fourth looks at research on the quantitative correlates of program quality. In each section the pertinent literature and major findings are reviewed, the major criteria and methodological procedures examined, and a critique of the limitations and strengths of the approach provides the foundation for some recommendations for future research.

THE MEANINGS OF QUALITY

Quality . . . you know what it is, yet you don't know what it is. But that's self-contradictory. But some things are better than others. That is they have more quality. But when you try to say what that quality is, apart from the things that have it, it all goes poof! There's nothing to talk about. But if you can't say what quality is, how do you know that it even exists? If no one knows what it is, then for all practical purposes it doesn't exist at all. But for all practial purposes it does exist. What else are the grades based upon? Why else would people pay fortunes for some things and throw others in the trash pile? Obviously, some things are better than others . . . but what's the "betterness"? . . . So round and round you go, spinning mental wheels and nowhere finding any place to get traction. What the hell is Quality? What is it? [Pirsig, 1974, p. 179]

As Pirsig concluded, the concept of quality is as elusive as it is pervasive. The difficulty of definition makes it not unlike obtaining general consensus on what is pornographic. When Justice Potter Stewart remarked, "I can't define it, but I know it when I see it," he in part was admitting that it would be impossible to obtain universal agreement on the concept.

While universal agreement on the concept of quality is impossible, we can illuminate the concept even while acknowledging that quality has multiple meanings and that no single definition will be acceptable to all people. It is particularly useful to examine the ways the term is used in different cultures and in different contexts. Such an examination brings to the fore the often unstated assumptions about the meaning of quality that underpin studies of program quality in American higher education.[1]

As a point of departure, we can say that quality seems to have a national (cultural) dimension to it. While there are many cultural similarities between our country and other nations, we tend to set the term within the context of our own cultural growth and development. Our belief in democracy contains within it the goal of equality, as Bonham (1977, p. 6) has noted:

We still tend to believe that we can be equal and superior [highest quality] at the same time, that the potential for human growth is bounded only by the given opportunity and of course access thereto. . . . We cannot all hit home runs, but we all deserve a chance at bat. . . . When we seek excellence [quality] it must be in the context of a concern for all.

The American concern for excellence (highest quality) is also associated with the process of achievement, the effort the individual makes to accomplish goals. Furthermore, the scope of excellence is large. Rogers (1981) puts it this way:

There is the excellence of a beautifully crafted silver bas-relief on a delicate drinking vessel — and there is the excellence of a well crafted critical essay on the structure and meaning of a great work of literature.

There is the excellence of a master training a wild horse and eventually riding in precise dressage. And there is the excellence of mastery of rules of evidence by which an intelligent and interesting argument can be made both truthful and convincing.

There is the excellence of a finely tuned instrument played with both technical competence and deep feeling. And there is the excellence of an elegantly constructed research design in mathematics or the sciences.

In every case there are those hard-won elements of discipline, refinement, quest for constant improvement, extension to the limit — the final blending of attention to every detail and to the attainment of beauty in the whole.

McClelland (1961, p. 144) also places excellence in a national context:

Our national problem is that we have tended to focus increasingly on encouraging one type of excellence, and a practical, measurable action oriented type of excellence at that. Other types of human excellence exist, particularly those involving character, and inner life, and the world of the imagination and human sensitivity.

As these quotations suggest, the concept of quality in this country clearly has multiple dimensions and can be seen in many contexts. As we develop this dialectic on "quality" and focus more sharply on its meaning in higher education, it will be well to remember that even within this limited sphere the term is likely to have different meanings within college and university subcultures. Program quality is not likely to be the same in a highly rated research university as it is in a state college or a selective liberal arts college or an open-admissions four-year institution or an urban community college.

Before illuminating the meanings of quality by contrasting it with excellence — and other concepts such as goal accomplishment, efficiency, accountability, and effectiveness — it is useful to examine some of the major elements or ingredients of quality as it is commonly defined in our colleges and universities. By itself, no single dimension will be a sufficient condition of quality, and none will even be a necessary condition in all people's eyes and in all contexts. Each, however, appears at one time or another in someone's meaning of quality.

Quality programs are almost always related to characteristics of the faculty responsible for the implementation of the curriculum. In fact, as will be seen below, studies of program quality frequently seem to be little more than efforts to ascertain *faculty* quality. Others, including ourselves — especially as one moves from highly rated research universities to consider other types of colleges and universities — consider facilities, support, the curriculum, and student attributes as dimensions of quality. A program of high quality is presumed to have the facilities necessary for its success such as well-equipped laboratories, appropriate library holdings, computers, and all the material things needed for the desired learning to take place. A quality program is one with adequate support — the resources to maintain the operation, provide for faculty travel, and attract and retain outstanding faculty. The curriculum of a high-quality program is one that has all of the essential ingredients — such as variety and depth of courses. And last, the students exist in sufficient numbers so that there is an adequate mix to foster students' learning from one another and yet not so many students that individualized attention is lost.

In addition to these frequently appearing elements of quality, some individuals identify other, less quantifiable attributes of a quality program: leadership, esprit, morale, clarity of purpose, and a healthy organizational climate. For many people a quality program cannot be reduced to a set of quantitative indicators, and is more like a living organism than a collection of component parts.

While individuals will nod their heads affirmatively when such words as "esprit" are introduced into a discussion of program quality, it is usually not clear that all participants attach the same meaning to the terms. Seldom are such concepts operationalized, indicators for them agreed upon, and evidence collected so as to ascertain the extent of their existence and their degree of relationship to the more common ingredients of quality. This is not to say that such components as morale and leadership are not a part of quality; rather, one finds that as yet they have not been especially helpful in attempts to determine the relative quality of programs.

Another set of terms sometimes advanced in discussions of quality are similar to the above terms in their nebulousness, but they are somewhat different in kind. They tend to address more personal dimensions, like achievement, persistence, purpose, worth, beauty, meritoriousness, and character. These terms are implied in the introductory quotations. They carry distinct values related to American ideals. No doubt they are a part of many people's notion of quality. That they also introduce complications when it comes to their assessment does not mean that they are not important. In fact, it is because of this richness of the concept of quality that Kuh (1981) argues for taking a holistic approach to the assessment of quality. He believes that breaking out components that are measurable vitiates the essence of the concept itself.

The meaning of quality can also be illuminated by comparing it with other concepts that are used in discussions of programs. Four frequently employed terms are accountability, efficiency, effectiveness, and excellence. "Accountable" implies that a program is at least adequate: a program that meets some minimum set of standards and achieves its goals is said to be an accountable one. "Quality," on the other hand, suggests that essentially complete goal fulfillment is attained, not just an acceptable amount. Thus quality encompasses accountability. In addition, demonstrating the accountability of a program frequently implies legitimizing its existence for others: if a program can do so, then it has justified itself.

"Efficiency," like "accountability," carries an economic overtone. Once goals to be achieved are established, alternative programs for attaining them are advanced. The superior program is the one which is most efficient. The efficient program is one which will accomplish the same ends as another program but with less cost or in less time, or both. A quality program will more likely be efficient than inefficient. In fact, parsimony is an attribute of high value for those who strive for quality. Persons advocating quality will place efficiency farther down on their list of critical elements for judging what is best. They expect efficiency, but they ask for more than that when they insist on quality.

As Cameron and Whetten (1983) make clear, investigators of organizational effectiveness do not agree as to the meaning of the term in the large body of studies that have been conducted under its name. The reasons for the differences are many, just as they are for the meaning of quality. And because they are multiple, it is all but impossible to contrast each of the meanings of effectiveness with each of the meanings of quality. But some contrasts can be made. In judging program effectiveness in contrast to its quality, the former is likely to concentrate on how well the outcomes are achieved.[2] Those assessing relative quality, while paying attention to outcomes, will look beyond the structure of a program; they will also be examining process. For example, one would look at the environment and the amount and kind of student/faculty interaction. Pace (1980) describes the day-to-day operation of an academic program along a number of scales called "quality of student effort" and means by this phrase something more than effectiveness. Effectiveness assumes efficiency but does not include all that is meant by quality.

When it comes to the concepts of excellence and quality, the line of demarcation becomes more blurred. While John Gardner (1961) was not the first person to address excellence, his book set a tone that is still felt today. Our opening quotations found the two terms essentially interchangeable. Like quality, excellence carries with it a dimension of style, not just an outstanding accomplishment but the manner in which the accomplishment is achieved. Both excellence and quality imply the highest standards and an unwillingness to settle for anything less than that which could be achieved. "Excellence" may even be the more egalitarian term, for frequently — mistakenly, we believe — "quality" is identified with a snobbish elitism, especially in higher education. (Writers in the field invariably talk about the top-ranked graduate schools as the elite, the institutions with "high quality" programs, as if quality does not exist in other settings.)

Nonetheless, a minor distinction can be noted between the two terms. In current usage "excellence" is used more frequently in connection with the acts of an individual, whereas "quality" is the label that is placed on the collectivity, such as an organization or a program. Still, the ingredients for both are essentially identical. We have opted for the term "quality" because it pervades the literature reviewed below. In addition, despite its ambiguities, the term is not likely to fall from usage. "Quality" carries too great an emotional charge or subjective overtone to be grounded by our dialectical analysis. That said, we proceed with a review of the literature on program quality in higher education.

REPUTATIONAL STUDIES
Reputational studies have long dominated research on program quality in higher education. Built upon a foundation of peer evalutation in which experts in the field are considered to be the best judges of program quality, these studies have been criticized as severely by some as they have been advanced by others. Notwithstanding the controversy surrounding the approach, much of the best-known research on program quality has been in this tradition.

The most salient characteristic of reputational studies is the emphasis placed on peer evaluation, in which judgments of program quality are made by faculty raters or by other experts such as department chairpersons and deans. In general, reputational studies follow a similar procedure: the researcher selects one or more criteria (such as faculty quality) to serve as a basis for evaluation, employes a panel of experts to rate individual programs in terms of those criteria, and then combines individual panelists' responses in order to generate a ranking of programs by institution. Since most reputational studies have evaluated programs at the doctoral level, we turn first to a review of studies at the graduate level before examining the literature on professional schools and undergraduate programs.

The first major reputational study of graduate programs was conducted by Hughes in 1924. Using panels of scholars in each discipline to identify top scholars in the field, Hughes (1925) ranked 38 universities in 20 graduate fields according to the number of top scholars they employed. A second Hughes (1934) study rated 59 universities in 35 fields according to judgments of staff and facilities made by faculty experts. The two studies by Hughes established important precedents for later studies of program quality: a focus on the graduate (doctoral) level, reliance on ratings by academics rather than outside observers, and an emphasis on the nation's most visible institutions (Lawrence and Green, 1980, p. 4). No less important, Hughes's studies set the precedent that the major criterion for evaluating quality should be the quality of the faculty.

A quarter of a century after the second Hughes study, Keniston (1959) selected department chairmen from institutional members of the American Association of Universities to rank 24 graduate programs at the 25 institutions leading in doctorate production. In addition to ranking programs by institution, Keniston rank-ordered the top 20 institutions. His study, as well as the two earlier Hughes studies, was severely criticized by researchers on methodological grounds. These criticisms, which included complaints about geographical and rater bias, led to subsequent reputational studies aimed at updating and improving ratings of graduate programs.

The most methodologically sophisticated of the reputational studies were designed under the auspices of the American Council of Education (ACE), which sponsored ratings of the doctoral programs in the arts and sciences in 1964 and 1969 (Cartter, 1966; Roose and Anderson, 1970). The Cartter study yielded institutional rankings in 29 disciplines at a total of 106 universities, while the Roose-Anderson study ranked programs in 36 disciplines at 130 universities.

In both ACE surveys, ratings within each discipline were made by department chairpersons, distinguished senior scholars, and selected junior scholars. Each respondent rated doctoral programs in his or her own field in terms of two criteria: quality of the graduate faculty and effectiveness of the graduate program. The individual ratings were then averaged, and the leading programs in each field were rank-ordered in two separate lists, one based on faculty quality and the other on program effectiveness. The two sets of rankings in both the Cartter and Roose-Anderson studies corresponded closely.

Several scholars have rightly noted that the methodological procedures in the ACE studies gave careful attention to the statistical validity and reliability of the ratings (Clark, 1976; Lawrence and Green, 1980). Cartter (1966) used detailed analyses to show that the rankings were similar whether respondents were separated by rank, institution of employment, degree, or geographical region. Moreover, he showed consistency between the ACE ratings and ratings by smaller and more select panels in several fields.

Since 1970, three major reputational studies of doctoral program quality have been published. One study, conducted under the joint sponsorship of the Council of Graduate Schools (CGS) and the Educational Testing Service (ETS), used faculty raters to assess and rank graduate programs (Hartnett, Clark, and Baird, 1978). As in the ACE ratings, programs were rated in terms of faculty quality and program effectiveness. Another study, by Ladd and Lipset, asked more than 4,000 faculty members at four-year colleges and universities to name the five departments nationally in their disciplines that had the most distinguished faculties (Scully, 1979). Ladd and Lipset then ranked the departments that were rated among the top five by at least 10% of the respondents in each of 19 fields.

The most recent reputational study was sponsored by the Conference Board of Associated Research Councils (1982) and compared the quality of research-doctorate programs in 32 disciplines from 228 universities. The multidimensional approach used to assess graduate programs employed 16 separate measures "related to quality," including a reputational survey in which faculty raters were asked to rate faculty scholarly competence, program effectiveness, and program improvement over the last five years. The results were presented in raw scores and standardized scores showing how far above or below the mean each program was ranked; no single composite measure of the quality of graduate programs was developed. While there were few surprises in most of the ratings, the ratings of programs that had improved in quality over the past five years identified institutions that had not been ranked in previous reputational studies.

Comparison of the rankings of graduate programs across all of the studies discussed above reveals a consistent pattern of findings: although there are minor variations in the absolute rankings of programs, reputational assessments of graduate program quality have consistently identified the same graduate programs at the top of the rankings.[3] In terms of departments with middle and lower rankings, the absolute rankings vary considerably but still show a high degree of stability across broad groups of departments.

Although most reputational researchers discourage the aggregation of departmental rankings into institutional rankings, many have felt compelled to make such aggregations (American Council on Education, 1971; Magoun, 1966; Morgan, Kearney, and Regens, 1976; National Science Board, 1969; Petrowski, Brown, and Duffy, 1973). When universities with high overall standings in the Ladd-Lipset and ACE surveys are compared with the overall rankings of Hughes (1925) and Keniston (1959), the stability of university reputations is clearly seen: all but one of the top 20 institutions are still at the top, and less than a handful of new ones has been added. The remarkable stability in the rankings is supported by the fact that six institutions (California-Berkeley, Chicago, Harvard, Michigan, Princeton, and Yale) have been ranked among the top ten institutions in all six of the major reputational studies of graduate education (Cartter, 1966; Conference Board of Associated Research Councils, 1982; Hughes, 1925; Keniston, 1959; Ladd and Lipset in Scully, 1979; Roose and Anderson, 1970).

In summary, the reputational method has served as the major way of evaluating program quality at the graduate level. Reputational studies, which place major emphasis on faculty quality as judged primarily by faculty raters, have yielded highly stable ratings of top-ranked graduate programs and institutions.

While most studies of program quality have examined graduate departments in the arts and sciences, recent interest in professional programs has led a few researchers to apply the reputational method to assessing professional program quality. Two fairly recent studies evaluated programs in at least three professional fields, and several other studies (conducted both by academics and by the professions themselves) have focused on a single field.

In a widely publicized study of professional education, Margulies and Blau (1973) rated programs in 17 professional fields. Deans of professional schools served as raters and were asked to identify the top five programs in their field. The responses were then aggregated and programs were ranked, by institution, for all 17 fields. Criticized for the low overall response rate to their survey, Blau and Margulies (1974–1975) subsequently completed a replication study using the same fields plus one more. Even though the response rate increased dramatically in their follow-up study, the rankings remained about the same in all fields.

Another study of professional programs rated programs in law, education, and business (Cartter and Solmon, 1977). Unlike the earlier study by Blau and Margulies, Cartter and Solmon used faculty members as well as deans as raters, had raters evaluate faculty and program attractiveness on Likert-type scales rather than simply select the top five programs, and provided raters with a list of institutions to evaluate rather than asking them to name, by recall, top programs in their field. Despite these methodological differences, comparisons between the Blau-Margulies and Cartter-Solmon rankings in law, education, and business reveal many similarities. There are, however, some notable differences, which may be due primarily to differences in sample size and selection and in the survey instruments used (Munson and Nelson, 1977).

Other reputational studies of professional education have ranked programs in a single field. For example, Cole and Lipton (1977) ranked top medical schools; Carpenter and Carpenter (1970) ranked library science programs; *MBA* magazine ("The 15 Top-Ranked," 1974; "The Top 15," 1975) ranked the top 15 business programs in two reputational studies; and *Juris Doctor* magazine ("The Popular Vote," 1976) ranked the top 20 law schools.

Two important observations can be made about reputational studies of professional programs. First, while they have been influenced by earlier reputational studies at the graduate level (particularly the methodology of the 1966 Cartter study), they often have utilized more diverse groups of raters and more diverse rating criteria. Second, as Lawrence and Green (1980, p. 22) have reported, most reputational rankings have consistently identified the same professional schools at the top, though there is some variance in the rankings of institutions across studies. Three rankings of law schools (Blau and Margulies, 1974–1975; Cartter and Solmon, 1977; "The Popular Vote," 1976) have in common seven institutions among those at the top of the rankings; three rankings of business schools (Blau and Margulies, 1974–1975; Cartter and Solmon, 1977; "The Top 15," 1975) share six institutions at the top; and two rankings of medical schools (Blau and Margulies, 1974–1975; Cole and Lipton, 1977) have eight institutions in common among those at the top.

In the last few years, there have been only two reputational studies of program quality at the undergraduate level. One study, sponsored by *Change* magazine, identified ten "leading" institutions in terms of national influence (Johnson, 1978). The list of ten institutions is very similar to the top-rated institutions as identified in the aforementioned reputational studies of graduate programs (see Petrowski, Brown, and Duffy, 1973).

A second, more recent study (Solmon and Astin, 1981; Astin and Solmon, 1981) also rated undergraduate programs using a reputational approach. Solmon and Astin asked faculty raters to rank departments in their field of specialization (from a list of about 100 institutions) on the basis of six rating criteria. After faculty in seven departmental specializations had ranked departments according to each of the six rating criteria, the researchers identified the ten top-ranked institutions on each list. The final list of top-ranked undergraduate departments in each of the seven fields included those departments which had been ranked in the top ten according to at least one criterion.

While the Solmon and Astin lists of top-ranked institutions included most of the institutions identified in earlier reputational studies of graduate education, the researchers identified a fairly large number of institutions that had not appeared in those studies. This finding may be especially significant, for it suggests that broadening the rating criteria to include dimensions such as "faculty commitment to undergraduate teaching" leads to the identification of programs of excellence which are otherwise ignored when the traditional criterion of faculty quality is the main criterion for evaluation.

Astin and Solmon (1981) admit that their reputational study is only preliminary, given the relatively small samples of departments and institutions. Still, they have extended the assessment of quality beyond faculty quality and found that diversifying rating criteria can lead to the identification of "quality" programs that would otherwise be overlooked.

Critique

Given the visibility of most of the reputational studies, it is hardly surprising that they have received a stream of criticism. Most of this criticism has been on methodological rather than substantive issues, and some of it has been unfounded.[4] Our intent here is to examine the most valid criticisms and major strengths of reputational studies, as well as to make some suggestions regarding future research. We begin by discussing two methodological weaknesses of reputational studies.

First, reputational studies can be justly criticized for rater bias, which can take several forms. For example, the overall reputation of an institution may influence raters' assessments of a particular department, especially when raters are not well informed. Such "halo effects" have been found by researchers at both the undergraduate and graduate level (see Solmon and Astin, 1981, p. 27). Also, departmental or institutional reputation may lag several years behind current quality, thereby introducing another source of rater bias (Hughes, 1925; Cox and Catt, 1977). In addition, scholars from the highly ranked universities often are overrepresented as raters and may tend to rate higher those departments with similar emphases as their own (Webster, 1981, p. 21). Other sources of rater bias — such as "alumni effects" (the tendency of raters to highly rate their alma maters) and the influence of an institution's age or size on raters' perceptions of quality — have been noted in the literature (Lawrence and Green, 1980, p. 10). However, there is insufficient evidence to conclude that these sources affect raters' assessments of program quality.

A second, and related, methodological criticism of reputational studies is that many raters are not sufficiently well informed to make judgments about the quality of programs at other institutions, particularly when the evaluative criteria extend beyond faculty quality. Since most reputational studies have ranked programs presumably on the criterion of faculty scholarly achievement, this criticism often has been rejected on the grounds that who but faculty are most competent to judge their peers (Blackburn and Lingenfelter, 1973, p. 24). While this rejoinder has some merit, it overlooks the fact that many faculty are relatively uninformed about faculty at other institutions, particularly at less visible universities. Moveover, if reputational studies are to evaluate something more than faculty quality, raters should be selected who are well informed about programs in terms of all the criteria serving as the basis for evaluation.

At least five other criticisms can be directed against most reputational studies. First, because the primary emphasis is on ranking programs rather than evaluating them against a normative standard of quality, reputational studies do not inform us whether a particular program is of high, medium, or low quality; they tell us only its relative quality vis-à-vis those programs to which it is compared.

Second, the criteria used to assess quality in most reputational studies are severely limited. Most studies at the graduate level have relied on a single yard-stick to assess quality: faculty quality.[5] As a consequence, most reputational studies are peer judgments of departmental faculty quality, presumably based almost entirely on scholarly publication. Given the use of a single criterion, it is hardly surprising that the same institutions are consistently ranked at the top. By reifying the criterion of faculty quality, most reputational studies have ignored a number of other potential evaluative criteria, most notably teaching and program effectiveness. As stated in one review of reputational studies at the graduate level: "They say little or nothing about the quality of instruction, the degree of civility or humaneness, the degree to which scholarly excitement is nurtured by student-faculty interactions, and so on" (Hartnett, Clark, and Baird, 1978, p. 1311). Faculty quality alone is an insufficient criterion for assessing overall program effectiveness — whether at the graduate, professional, or undergraduate level.[6]

Third, because most reputational studies have used the department as the unit of analysis, the institutional environment outside of the department is rarely considered in the evaluation. Especially at the undergraduate level, where students are exposed to a variety of fields and extracurricular influences, quality assessment should take the institutional environment into account. Indeed, the argument has been forcefully made in terms of the graduate level: "Quality is a property of the total institution . . . [and] a component of high quality can be expected to flourish best within an environment of high quality" (National Science Board, 1969, p. 50).

Fourth, since they have focused exclusively on ranking the "top" 20 to 150 institutions, all of the major reputational studies have failed to consider programs at most of the postsecondary institutions in the nation. Graduate, professional, and undergraduate programs in state and regional colleges and universities have been ignored.

Fifth, while reputational studies at the graduate level have received considerable attention, relatively little attention has been given to professional schools and undergraduate programs. To be sure, there have been a fair number of studies of professional schools in recent years, but with only two exceptions (Blau and Margulies, 1974-1975; Cartter and Solmon, 1977) all of these studies have been limited to a single field. At the undergraduate level, there have been only two major studies of program quality.

Notwithstanding these criticisms, reputational studies have contributed to the understanding of program quality in American higher education. Reputational studies at the graduate level have provided defensible ratings of "leading" departments in terms of faculty scholarship (Blackburn and Lingenfelter, 1973, p. 25). At the professional school level, reputational studies have consistently identified most of the same "top" programs while using multiple criteria for evaluation. And at the undergraduate level, some progress has been made in assessing program quality based on multiple criteria.

Over a decade ago, the controversy over the last of the ACE-sponsored graduate-level studies (Roose and Anderson, 1970) prompted the American Council on Education to discontinue sole sponsorship of any further reputational studies. Since then, with the exception of the recent study sponsored by the Conference Board of Associated Research Councils (1982), most reputational studies have been conducted at the professional school and undergraduate level. In our view, controversy over reputational studies should not deter researchers from conducting such studies in the future. If reputational studies are designed to respond to the criticisms raised here, they can make a more important contribution to evaluating quality in higher education. Especially if methodological refinements are made, if quality is evaluated through multiple criteria, if normative standards are used, and if quality is evaluated not just at "leading" schools, then future reputational studies may help to shed further light on program quality at the undergraduate and professional as well as the graduate level.

STUDIES BASED ON OBJECTIVE INDICATORS OF QUALITY

Although reputational studies have dominated research on program quality, criticism of the reputational approach has prompted some researchers to explore more "objective," quantifiable procedures for assessing program quality in higher education. These researchers have sought to "quantify" quality in order to measure it empirically.

Quantitative studies of program quality generally follow a straightforward format: the evaluator selects criteria (such as faculty scholarship) along with objective indicators (such as average number of articles per faculty member for each of the last five years) on an *a priori* basis, develops an index of those indicators, and then rates programs on the basis of that index. With regard to the identification of evaluative criteria and objective indicators, a few researchers have designed systematic studies to identify criteria and indicators by surveying selected respondents (Barak, 1976; Clark, Hartnett, and Baird, 1976; Clewell, 1980; Fotheringham, 1978; Longanecker, 1978; Lynd, 1976). Most researchers, however, seem to have relied on their own insight and judgment to develop quality indicators or have borrowed indicators from accreditation or fugitive institutional or statewide reports on program quality.

Owing to the lack of agreement among researchers regarding appropriate indicators, a wide range of criteria and indicators have been used to assess and rank graduate programs and undergraduate colleges and, in a few cases, provide composite institutional rankings (Adams and Krislov, 1978; Bowker, 1964; Calvert, Pitts, and Dorion, 1971; Clemente and Sturgis, 1974; Conference Board of Associated Research Councils, 1982; Cox and Catt, 1977; Eells, 1960; Glenn and Villemez, 1970; Hurlbert, 1976, Knudsen and Vaughan, 1969; Krause and Krause, 1970; Lewis, 1968; Siebring, 1969; Somit and Tanenhaus, 1964). In some studies only one or two indicators have been used to assess quality, but in the majority, multiple criteria and multiple indicators have been used.

One of the first major quantitative studies of program quality at the graduate level, conducted by Bowker (1964) two decades ago, illustrates the general procedure followed by researchers using this approach to examining program quality. In order to develop a ranking of U.S. graduate schools in the social sciences–humanities and the sciences, Bowker developed a quantitative index which included objective indicators in each of the two major fields. In the social sciences–humanities, for example, he used four quantifiable indicators of quality: number of former Woodrow Wilson fellows on the faculty, number of Woodrow Wilson fellows choosing to attend the institution, number of American Council of Learned Societies Award winners on the faculty, and the number of Guggenheim Memorial fellows on the faculty.

Since Bowker's study, most of the research based on objective indicators of quality has focused on the evaluation and ranking of graduate programs in particular disciplines, with graduate programs in sociology and psychology receiving the most attention. Numerous rankings of graduate departmental quality have been published, but many of these rank different programs and thus are not comparable to one another. In those cases where rankings can be compared, there is a pattern: although the absolute ranks of graduate programs vary (some considerably, others hardly at all) from one study to the next, objective assessments have consistently identified the same graduate programs at the top of the rankings. To be sure, the high degree of consensus may be attributed to heavy reliance on the criterion of faculty research productivity and research-oriented indicators, and the fact that researchers have been concerned only with the ranking of a relatively small number of institutions (usually 20 to 80). Still, the relatively high agreement among the rankings is noteworthy, since most of the studies have been based on more than one criterion and multiple, frequently different, indicators of quality.

The debate over rankings of graduate programs and institutions has prompted some scholars to compare reputational rankings with rankings based on objective indicators of quality. After ranking graduate programs and institutions based on objective measures, these researchers have compared their rankings with the ACE-sponsored rankings by Cartter (1966) and Roose-Anderson (1970). A consistent pattern emerges across these comparisons: there is a close correspondence between objective and reputational rankings, although the absolute ranks of particular programs usually vary modestly (Adams and Krislov, 1978; Clemente and Sturgis, 1974; Cox and Catt, 1977; Glenn and Villemez, 1970; Hurlbert, 1976; Knudsen and Vaughan, 1969; Lewis, 1968; Siebring, 1969). In other words, the research so far suggests that for graduate programs the same institutions will be ranked at the top whether or not departments are evaluated "objectively" through quantifiable indicators or "subjectively" through peer ratings.

With the exception of a study which ranked law schools on the basis of a "resource index" (Kelso, 1975), there has been little published research evaluating and ranking professional schools on the basis of objective indicators of quality. However, the evaluation and the ranking of undergraduate colleges have received a modest amount of attention in the last several decades.

Studies of undergraduate colleges tend to utilize one criterion — student achievement — as the basis for rating the institutions. Using this criterion, Bowker (1964) ranked the top 20 institutions on the basis of the number of baccalaureate recipients who received Woodrow Wilson fellowships and the number of baccalaureate recipients who eventually earned a doctorate; Krause and Krause (1970) ranked colleges according to the number of their baccalaureate graduates who contributed articles to *Scientific American*; Dube (1974) ranked 100 undergraduate colleges according to the number of their alumni who entered medical school; Tidball and Kristiakowski (1976) ranked institutions according to the proportions of their baccalaureate graduates who went on to earn doctorates; and Astin and Solmon (1979) ranked institutions according to a selectivity index based on an estimate of the average academic ability of an institution's entering freshmen (Astin and Henson, 1977).

Several other studies have used multiple criteria and multiple indicators as a basis for ranking undergraduate colleges (Brown, 1967; Gourman, 1967; Jordan, 1963). By way of illustration, Brown (1967) grouped colleges on the basis of eight indicators: (1) proportion of faculty with a doctorate, (2) average faculty compensation (salary and fringe benefits), (3) proportion of students going on to graduate school, (4) proportion of graduate students, (5) number of library volumes per full-time student, (6) total number of full-time faculty, (7) student-faculty ratio, and (8) total current income per student.

Comparisons of the published rankings of undergraduate colleges, whether the rankings are based on single or multiple criteria and indicators, reveal substantial disparities. Although many of the same colleges appear in all or most of the rankings, studies using objective assessments have not consistently identified the same colleges at the top of the rankings. Moreover, even in those studies where many of the same institutions have been ranked, there is wide variation in the absolute ranks of colleges. In short, research aimed at ranking undergraduate institutions has not resulted in the high degree of agreement across studies that has characterized research on graduate programs.

Critique

Since studies based on objective indicators have been viewed more as a check on reputational studies than as an independent method of rating programs, there has been relatively little scholarly criticism of this line of research, and most criticism has been confined to objections about specific indicators. Nevertheless, several overall criticisms — both methodological and substantive — should be raised about evaluation studies based on objective indicators.

Most important, serious methodological questions can be asked about the appropriateness of many of the indicators or measures that have been employed in these studies. Instead of establishing the appropriateness of their measures, either through conducting independent surveys of professionals or by selecting indicators from the literature, most researchers apparently have selected indicators on the basis of their personal preferences and, presumably, data availability. As a consequence many, if not most, of the indices used to assess various evaluative criteria may not be good indicators of program quality.

As a result of the rather haphazard approach to selecting indicators, there is little consensus in the literature concerning the most appropriate measures for evaluating program quality. For example, there is little agreement among researchers regarding the best measures of undergraduate student quality. Is it the proportion of graduates going on to graduate school? Proportion of graduates who earn doctorates? Academic ability of freshmen as measured by standardized tests? Of course, differences over the appropriateness of any measure or index are to be expected in any area of investigation. But when there is such little agreement among researchers regarding the best measures, it must be concluded that more attention needs to be given to establishing appropriate indicators.

In the search for measures of program quality, researchers may be well advised to seek quality indicators that assess adequacy as well as frequency or volume. Most of the existing research is based on indicators that assess easily quantifiable program characteristics (such as number of volumes in the library) rather than adequacy (such as comprehensiveness and accessibility of the library). To be sure, some researchers have attempted to measure the adequacy of certain program characteristics. In the area of scholarly productivity, for example, some investigators have sought to separate quantity of publication from quality of publication. Instead of simply measuring scholarly publication using frequency tabulations, they have constructed "citation indexes" as a measure of the quality of scholarship (Smith and Fiedler, 1971). While citation indexes represent an honest attempt to improve quality measurement, they have — like other indices that attempt to measure quality — come under attack from various scholars (Webster, 1981, pp. 22-23). The debate over most indicators of quality serves to underscore the more telling point: the search for appropriate indicators of program quality is only in its infancy. Put another way, researchers need to improve upon their "objective" assessments of the valuative, subjective concept of quality.

Questions about the appropriateness of indicators are linked to a second major criticism that can be made about most studies based on objective indicators, namely, that they are in fact highly subjective. Since research is infrequently based on "objective" measures that have been established through research, most studies reflect the researchers' biases in the selection of indicators. Ironically, much of the research in this tradition can be fairly criticized for its failure both to acknowledge and reduce the "subjectivism" that is intended to be reduced or eliminated in this approach to evaluation research.

Third, studies at the graduate level have been heavily based on the single criterion of faculty research productivity. Although a range of research-oriented indicators have been used to measure that criterion, the reliance on a single criterion has doubtless contributed to the marked similarity in rankings of programs across comparable studies. Most studies at the graduate level have neglected other evaluative criteria, especially teaching and program effectiveness.

Fourth, most of the indicators used to assess quality are useful only for ranking schools at the very top (Webster, 1981, p. 22). For example, the number of Guggenheim Memorial fellows on the faculty or the number of students contributing articles to *Scientific American* may be good indicators of faculty and student quality at leading institutions. But for the vast majority of postsecondary institutions, their utility, relevance, and appropriateness are highly doubtful.

Fifth, none of the studies using objective indicators has assessed programs in terms of contributions to bringing about changes in students — presumably the major purpose of education at the graduate and professional levels as well as the undergradauate level. This "value added" concept has been advanced by many scholars in the higher education literature (Astin, 1977; Bowen, 1977; Blackburn and Lingenfelter, 1973; Clark, Hartnett, and Baird, 1976; Lawrence and Green, 1980), but such an approach has not been used in any large-scale study of program quality in higher education.

Finally, several criticisms made earlier about reputational studies also can be applied to research based on objective indicators. First, most studies have focused on the department as the unit of analysis and thus have failed to use indicators of quality that take the institutional environment into account. Second, because almost all studies have been concerned with ranking programs, they have identified a rank order of excellence rather than evaluated programs in terms of a normative standard of quality. Third, by making the questionable assumption that programs have identical goals, objective indicator studies have assessed all programs against the same yardstick. Fourth, they have consistently focused on ranking only the "top" institutions, thereby ignoring programs in the vast majority of postsecondary institutions.

Despite these criticisms, studies based on objective indicators have already made a contribution to evaluating program quality in higher education. In terms of methodological sophistication, many studies have gone beyond reputational studies not only in using a more "objective" approach but, perhaps more significantly, in employing a multidimensional approach to evaluating programs. Especially at the undergraduate level, a range of criteria — and multiple indicators of those criteria — have been used to assess program quality. Moreover, studies at the graduate level have yielded defensible rankings of "leading" departments in terms of faculty scholarly achievement — rankings which generally have a close correspondence to those in the most recent ACE-sponsored reputational studies (Cartter, 1966; Roose and Anderson, 1970). At the undergraduate level, "top" programs have been identified — though the wide difference in rankings across studies indicates considerable disagreement over the top-ranked programs.

In summary, this overall approach to program evaluation holds considerable promise. If researchers can more effectively respond to the methodological and substantive criticisms raised here, and above all seek to anchor their criteria in theory and relate them to program goals, then research in this tradition can truly become more "objective."

STUDIES OF THE QUANTITATIVE CORRELATES OF QUALITY

In the last few years, a growing number of researchers have searched for quantitative correlates of quality. These researchers have attempted to identify objective characteristics, or "correlates of quality," associated with programs that are taken to be of high quality.

Most of the studies on the quantitative correlates of quality have followed a similar format. The researcher first selects one or more fields that have been evaluated and ranked in a reputational study (in some studies, more than one field is examined so that comparisons can be made across fields). Then, by either comparing simple (bivariate) correlations of one or more variables, or by using multiple regression or multiple discriminate function analysis to estimate the relationship between groups of variables and those programs having high ratings, the researcher distills a cluster of objective traits associated with program quality.

Most studies in this tradition have examined the correlates of program quality as measured in the reputational studies by Cartter (1966) and Roose-Anderson (1970). Since the two ACE studies focused exclusively on evaluating graduate program quality, most researchers have examined the correlates of program quality solely at the graduate level. However, one major study has been completed at the undergraduate level (Astin and Solmon, 1981; Solmon and Astin, 1981), which will be discussed after a review of the literature on the correlates of graduate program quality.

Cartter (1966, pp. 112-114) was the first to find strong relationships between several objective correlates — including faculty compensation and library resources — and institutional rankings. Shortly thereafter, a number of other researchers followed his lead, examining the relationship between a range of potential correlates of quality and the Cartter and Roose-Anderson rankings in specific disciplines.

Many early studies focused on graduate programs in sociology. For example, Lewis (1968) found some correspondence between measures of faculty and student publication and the Cartter rankings of sociology departments. Other investigators found relationships between the Cartter rankings of sociology departments and various indicators of quality, including individual prestige (Lightfield, 1971), research productivity (Knudsen and Vaughan, 1969; Glenn and Villemez, 1970), student-faculty ratios (Janes, 1969; Lavendar, Mathers, and Pease, 1971), and hiring patterns (Gross, 1970; Schichor, 1970). Studies conducted later, both in sociology and other single disciplines, identified such correlates as size (Elton and Rogers, 1971; Elton and Rose, 1972) and research productivity (Drew, 1975; Guba and Clark, 1978) as well as a number of other correlates (Abbott, 1972; Solmon, 1972; Solmon and Walters, 1975).

In the last decade, several other researchers have worked with subsets of the ACE-rated departments. Hagstrom (1971), for example, sampled 125 departments in four scientific fields: physics, chemistry, mathematics, and biology. He found large, significant correlations between departmental prestige (Cartter ratings of the quality of graduate faculty) and department size, research production, research opportunities, faculty background, student characteristics (including undergraduate selectivity), and faculty awards and offices. Subsequent studies which sampled at least four major fields also found relationships between the ACE ratings and other quality indicators: a National Science Board (1969) study found 14 correlates of quality; Beyer and Snipper (1974) identified fourteen independent variables; Morgan, Kearney, and Regens (1976) found four predictor variables; and Drew and Karpf (1981) identified a powerful single predictor variable — departmental rate of publication in highly cited journals.

While the search for empirical correlates of graduate program quality has yielded some impressive findings, several caveats are in order. First, many of the correlates that researchers have identified are highly interrelated with one another, and the independent effects of specific correlates have not always been isolated. Second, the magnitude of correlations varies somewhat across comparable studies, owing at least in part to the particular correlates and measures of those correlates that researchers have used. Third, some researchers have found some noteworthy differences among the relative importance of some key correlates across different fields (Hagstrom, 1971; Beyer and Snipper, 1974).

Although the magnitude of correlations varies somewhat across studies and disciplines, the correlations have been generally high enough to conclude that researchers have been quite successful in identifying quantitative correlates of departmental quality at the graduate level (as indicated in the ACE reputational studies). As Hagstrom (1971, p. 389) stated a decade ago: "Unless it is possible to devise some systematic causal theory, it will make little sense to seek additional predictors of departmental prestige or productivity. More refined measurements will permit only slight improvements in the proportion of variance explained."

While research on the quantitative correlates of quality has focused almost exclusively on the graduate level, a recent study by Astin and Solmon (1981) examined objective correlates of reputational quality ratings in seven undergraduate fields. In brief, Astin and Solmon wanted to know if it was possible to estimate undergraduate quality by examining objective, quantifiable information about an institution.

While the researchers found some differences across fields, they identified a number of factors that correlated quite highly with their reputational ratings of "overall quality of undergraduate education" (Solmon and Astin, 1981). The major correlates they identified include size, prestige, selectivity, financial expenditures per student (such as expenditures for educational and general purposes), and measures of curricular concentration (for example, higher quality was associated with relatively large concentration of bachelor's degrees in the natural sciences and engineering). They found that a combination of prestige (weighted positively) and size (weighted negatively) provided a highly accurate estimate of overall quality ratings in each of the seven fields.

The study by Astin and Solmon is an important piece of research for a number of substantive and methodological reasons, not least of which is that it focuses attention on quality at the undergraduate level. Yet as Astin and Solmon themselves suggest, more research is needed on the correlates or quality at the undergraduate level. In particular, research is needed which is based on assessments of quality other than the Solmon and Astin (1981) ratings and which uses quality ratings from a larger sample of institutions and undergraduate fields.

Critique

Based on this review of the research on quantitative correlates, it is tempting to conclude that this approach has been highly successful — at least in the graduate domain. After all, researchers seem to have reached considerable agreement on the major correlates of quality at the graduate level, and some scholars have concluded that further research at the graduate level is unlikely to make much of a contribution. In our view, however, this conclusion is premature, and we begin our critique with a discussion of the major limitation of research in this tradition.

First, almost all of the research has examined correlates of quality as measured by the ACE-sponsored reputational studies of graduate programs at leading institutions (Cartter, 1966; Roose and Anderson, 1970), now more than a decade old. Significantly, researchers have not searched for correlates of program quality as measured by objective indicators or through such studies as accreditation reports and statewide reviews of program quality. As a consequence of being completely dependent on the ACE ratings of program quality, research on the quantitative correlates of quality is, in turn, subject to all of the limitations associated with these reputational studies of program quality.

Because of the dependency of correlational studies on the ACE-sponsored reputational studies, the main limitations of those studies bear repeating: they have methodological limitations (such as rater bias), they focus exclusively on the graduate (doctoral) level, they measure program quality based largely on faculty reputation, and they focus only on highly visible institutions. Even if the methodological limitations are minimized, the singular fact remains that quality has been identified only at the "top" institutions, at one level (doctoral), using one major criterion (faculty quality).

Further research is needed which overcomes the limitations associated with exclusive reliance on reputational ratings to identify program quality. More specifically, researchers should identify high-quality programs at institutions which have been rated on criteria in addition to faculty quality and which are not limited to the "top-ranked" ACE institutions. Either by conducting their own studies or by relying on various independent assessments of program quality, researchers should use ratings of program quality that are not as limited in scope and generalizability as the ACE studies.

Second, most studies have used an "atheoretical" approach in identifying quantitative correlates of quality. Instead of identifying potential correlates on the basis of a theory of quality (which, in turn, would suggest specific variables that may be associated with quality), many investigators seem to have rummaged through their data in search of any factors that might conceivably be linked empirically to program quality (exceptions include Drew and Karpf, 1981, and Solmon and Astin, 1981). Thus, even though research has yielded considerable agreement on the major correlates of program quality at the graduate level, there are few explanations as to why particular correlates make theoretical sense. If we are to move toward the development of theory about quality, the selection of correlates must be linked to some emerging theory of quality. Otherwise, we are left with only a series of empirical correlates that lack any theoretical foundation.

Third, many of the correlates of quality that have been identified are highly interrelated with one another (for example, size and prestige), and many researchers have failed to isolate the independent effects of individual correlates. In some cases, this omission is due to limitations associated with the research design. For example, studies that rely on bivariate correlations cannot, by definition, isolate the independent effects of individual correlates. In other cases, researchers using multivariate approaches (such as regression analysis) have not examined the interrelationships of variables.

Finally, studies of the objective correlates of quality have focused almost exclusively on the graduate domain. Aside from the recent study discussed above (Solmon and Astin, 1981), little attention has been given to the undergraduate level, and no studies have been conducted using professional schools.

Despite these criticisms, there have been some impressive findings regarding the quantitative correlates of graduate program quality. Although researchers may be justly criticized for often failing to link their findings to any theoretical scaffolding, the fact remains that a number of correlates have been identified that seem to have a strong association with program quality. Thus this approach to studying program quality has rich possibilities. At the undergraduate and professional levels, as well as the graduate level, further research is needed which addresses the methodological criticisms raised above and, equally important, is based on evaluations of program quality that are not encumbered by the limitations of the ACE reputational studies. The ACE studies have been a convenient measure of program quality, but other assessments are needed if the major correlates identified are to be linked with a more multifaceted conception of quality.

SUGGESTIONS FOR FUTURE RESEARCH

There is a pressing need to assess program quality not just in the nation's most visible universities but also in programs that are scattered across nearly 3,000 other institutions. Our search of the literature uncovered few such studies, and those efforts, for the most part, were not successful. In short, there are practical and theoretical needs to expand the level of program assessment, for what has been done so far is limited primarily to the Ph.D. and professional-degree levels.

Our own efforts to move beyond the elite institutions are beginning to bear some fruit (Conrad and Blackburn, 1985). In brief, we have collected extensive data on all public four-year colleges and universities in two states. The data include institutional self-studies and reports, public documents from the states, HEGIS reports, data collected from site visits, vita on all faculty in departments of biology, chemistry, education, history, and mathematics, and, most important of all, the evaluation reports of outside teams of peers who reviewed the programs. None of the institutions are in the Carnegie Research University–I classification; most are regional colleges. The departments studied were principally at the master's level.

One of our most important findings has been that faculty scholarship accounts for only 28% of the variance in departmental quality in these colleges and universities, not the 50% to 80% that is usually found when leading Ph.D. programs are examined. Hagstrom concluded (1971, p. 385) that there is little need to extend the number of measures when several will account for over 70% of the variation. But we have had to introduce other variables, conceptually as well as operationally, in order to predict program quality in regional colleges and universities.

In addition to collecting information on faculty attributes, we systematically obtained data on program characteristics (curriculum), facilities, students, and support. Future research is needed along the dimensions just indicated, and on other aspects as well. For example, Pace (1980) has instruments for estimating the quality of student effort in a program, a series of scales that rest on the assumption that the quality of a student's education depends in part on how well she or he makes use of what the institution has available. Pace's findings show variation across institutions, but as yet there have been no systematic studies which link his scales to an independent assessment of program quality.

In a similar vein, Clark, Hartnett, and Baird (1976) developed for the Educational Testing Service a set of instruments which contain a variety of dimensions expected to be related to program quality. (These exist at both the master's and doctoral level.) In addition to the typical faculty indicators, Clark and her colleagues have included student assessment of instruction and general satisfaction with a program. Her scales also include data collected from alumni. As yet, however, there have been no large-scale studies of program quality against an independent measure. They, too, should be on an agenda of future research.

In our own studies in progress, we noted the mention of leadership in connection with program quality in more than one peer assessment report. A department often would be considered "weak," i.e., of lower quality, when the department chair was judged ineffective or if there was not imaginative leadership at the dean or vice-presidential level, and conversely.

In addition to leadership, many of the peer assessment reports in our study mentioned esprit, morale, clarity of purpose, and a healthy organizational climate as factors contributing to program quality. While there are few readily available quantifiable indicators for these variables, that does not mean that they cannot be created. A profitable area of research would be to develop ways of estimating such variables and then relating them to program quality.

Finally, as attempts are made to assess the quality of programs at other levels — for example, at the bachelor's level and in remedial English programs in community colleges — we believe ever increasing attention must be paid to the environment in which a program resides. Indicators of the environment need to be included to assess quality. For example, the quality of a biology department may be highly dependent on the quality of the chemistry department.

In conclusion, there will doubtless continue to be controversy surrounding any approach to studying program quality. For no matter how it is approached, "quality" is ultimately based on subjective judgments. Nevertheless, this review and critique of the literature suggests that researchers can improve their designs for studying quality. Given the concern over quality in the nation's colleges and universities by the public and the profession, we invite researchers to address with alacrity the research agenda on program quality.

NOTES

1. We are indebted to A. Richardson Love for many of our reflections on the dimensions of quality. His analysis exists in an unpublished paper (Ph.D. preliminary examination), "The Assessment of Quality in a Selected Liberal Arts College," Center for the Study of Higher Education, University of Michigan, 1982.
2. For example, Young's (1983, p. 461) editorial in *Science* states: "Yokagawa-Hewlett-Packard (YHP) was honored last year with the Deming Prize, Japan's highest prize for overall *quality*. The award recognized a 5-year program that reduced the production costs by one-third and inventory by two-thirds, and warranty failure rates by

more than half. During the 5-year period, YHP almost tripled its market penetration" (emphasis added). The use of the term "quality" here makes it essentially equivalent to effectiveness.

3. Although the CGS-ETS study does not identify institutions, the authors report that their rankings are very similar to the 1966 and 1970 ACE lists (Hartnett, Clark, and Baird, 1978).

4. For example, one argument advanced against reputational studies is that they are intrinsically "subjective." This criticism is unfair, for it ignores the fact that reputational studies are purposively based on "subjective" peer evaluations. Moreover, subjectivity cannot be completely avoided in evaluation studies, regardless of the evaluation technique used. As Cartter noted, even so-called objective measures (such as number of Nobel laureates on the faculty) are, for the most part, " 'subjective' measures once removed" (1966, p. 4).

5. While several of the reputational studies have used more than one criterion, faculty quality has been the major criterion in all studies at the graduate level. For example, though the Cartter (1966) study of doctoral programs used "effectiveness of the doctoral program" as well as "quality of the faculty," the high correlation between the two sets of rankings in the study suggests that raters probably chose to emphasize what they knew best (i.e., quality of the faculty) when evaluating "effectiveness" (Blackburn and Lingenfelter, 1973, p. 24). In effect, faculty quality was the major criterion.

6. It should be noted that expanding evaluative criteria beyond faculty quality may lead to different rankings of programs. Several evaluation studies, one conducted at the graduate level, found that when independent assessments of commitment to teaching/program effectiveness and faculty quality are made, programs are ranked quite differently (Astin and Solmon, 1981; Hartnett, Clark, and Baird, 1978).

REFERENCES

Abbot, W. F. University and departmental determinants of the prestige of sociology departments. *American Sociologist*, 1972, *7*, 14-15.

Adams, A. V., and Krislov, J. Evaluating the quality of American universities: A new approach. *Research in Higher Education*, 1978, *8*, 97-109.

American Council on Education. Survey of 37 academic fields and 130 schools in U.S. finds graduate facilities have improved substantially between '64 and '69 at most schools. *New York Times*, January 3, 1971, p. 54.

Astin, A. W., *Four Critical Years*. San Francisco: Jossey-Bass, 1977.

Astin, A. W., and Henson, J. W. New measures of college selectivity. *Research in Higher Education*, 1977, *6*, 1-8.

Astin, A. W., and Solmon, L. C. Measuring academic quality: An interim report. *Change*, 1979, *11*, 48-51.

Astin, A. W., and Solmon, L. C. Are reputational ratings needed to measure quality? *Change*, 1981, *13*, 14-19.

Barak, R. J. A survey and analysis of state-level academic program review in higher education. Unpublished doctoral dissertation, State University of New York at Buffalo, 1976.

Beyer, J. M., and Snipper, R. Objective versus subjective indicators of quality. *Sociology of Education*, 1974, *47*, 541-557.

Blackburn, R. T., and Lingenfelter, P. E. *Assessing Quality in Doctoral Programs: Criteria and Correlates of Excellence*. Ann Arbor, Mich.: Center for the Study of Higher Education, University of Michigan, 1973.

Blau, P. M., and Margulies, R. Z. The reputations of American professional schools. *Change*, 1974-1975, *6*, 42-47.

Bonham, W. The maintenance of academic quality in a time of uncertainty. Paper presented to a Seminar of State Leaders of Postsecondary Education, Keystone, Colo., July 1977.

Bowen, H. R. *Investment in Learning*. San Francisco: Jossey-Bass, 1977.

Bowker, A. H. Quality and quantity in higher education. *Journal of the American Statistical Association*, 1964, *60*, 1-15.

Brown, D. G. *The Mobile Professors*. Washington, D.C.: American Council on Education, 1967.

Calvert, J. G., Pitts, J. N., Jr., and Dorion, G. H. *Graduate School in the Sciences: Entrance, Survival, and Careers*. New York: Wiley-Interscience, 1971.

Cameron, K. S., and Whetten, D. A. *Organizational Effectiveness: A Comparison of Multiple Models*. New York: Academic Press, 1983.

Carpenter, R. L., and Carpenter, P. A. The doctorate in librarianship and an assessment of graduate library education. *Journal of Education for Librarianship*, 1970, *11*, 3-45.

Cartter, A. A. *An Assessment of Quality in Graduate Education*. Washington, D.C.: American Council on Education, 1966.

Cartter, A. A., and Solmon, L. C. The Cartter report on the leading schools of education, law, and business. *Change*, 1977, *9*, 44-48.

Clark, M. J. The meaning of quality in graduate and professional education. In J. Katz and R. T. Hartnett (eds.), *Scholars in the Making: The Development of Professional Students*. Cambridge, Mass.: Ballinger, 1976.

Clark, M. J., Hartnett, R. T., and Baird, L. L. *Assessing Dimensions of Quality in Doctoral Education: A Technical Report of a National Study in Three Fields*. Princeton, N.J.: Educational Testing Service, 1976.

Clemente, F., and Sturgis, R. B. Quality of department of doctoral training and research productivity. *Sociology of Education*, 1974, *47*, 287-299.

Clewell, B. C. Assessing educational quality in higher education. Unpublished doctoral dissertation, Florida State University, 1980.

Cole, J. R., and Lipton, J. A. The reputation of American medical schools. *Social Forces*, 1977, *55*, 662-684.

The Conference Board of Associated Research Councils. *An Assessment of Research-Doctorate Programs in the United States*. 5 vols. Washington, D.C.: National Academy Press, 1982.

Conrad, C. F., and Blackburn, R. T. Correlates of departmental quality in regional colleges and universities. *American Educational Research Journal*, forthcoming.

Conrad, C. F., and Blackburn, R. T. Current views of departmental quality: An empirical examination. *Review of Higher Education*, forthcoming.

Cox, W. M., and Catt, V. Productivity ratings of graduate programs in psychology based on publication in the journals of the American Psychological Association. *American Psychologist*, 1977, *32*, 793-813.

Drew, D. E. *Science Development: An Evaluation Study*. Washington, D.C.: National Academy of Sciences, 1975.

Drew, D. E., and Karpf, R. Ranking academic departments: Empirical findings and a theoretical perspective. *Research in Higher Education*, 1981, *14*, 305-320.

Dube, W. F. Undergraduate origins of U.S. medical students. *Journal of Medical Education*, 1974, *49*, 1005-1010.

Eells, W. C. Leading American graduate schools 1948-1958. *Liberal Education*, 1960, *46*, 16-20.

Elton, C. F., and Rogers, S. A. Physics department ratings: Another evaluation. *Science*, 1971, *174*, 565-568.

Elton, C. F., and Rose, H. A. What are ratings rating? *American Psychologist*, 1972, *27*, 197-201.

"The 15 Top-Ranked Business Schools in the United States." *MBA*, 1974, *8*, 21-25.

Fotheringham, D. J. Quality indicators in undergraduate education as viewed by selected respondents in selected colleges and universities. Unpublished doctoral dissertation, State University of New York at Albany, 1978.

Gardner, J. *Excellence*. New York: Harper & Row, 1961.

Glenn, N. D., and Villemez, W. The productivity of sociologists at 45 American universities. *American Sociologist*, 1970, *5*, 224-252.

Gourman, J. *The Gourman Report: Ratings of American Colleges*. Phoenix: Continuing Research Institute, 1967.

Gross, G. R. The organization set: A study of sociology departments. *American Sociologist*, 1970, *5*, 25-29.

Guba, E. G., and Clark, D. L. Levels of R&D productivity in schools of education. *Educational Researcher*, 1978, *7*, 3-9.

Hagstrom, W. O. Inputs, outputs and the prestige of university science departments. *Sociology of Education*, 1971, *44*, 375-397.

Hartnett, R. T., Clark, M. J., and Baird, L. L. Reputational ratings of doctoral programs. *Science*, 1978, *199*, 1310-1314.

Hughes, R. M. *A Study of the Graduate Schools in America*. Oxford, Ohio: Miami University Press, 1925.

Hughes, R. M. Report of the committee on graduate instruction. *Educational Record*, 1934, *15*, 192-234.

Hurlbert, B. M. Status and exchange in the profession of anthropology. *American Anthropologist*, 1976, *78*, 272-284.

Janes, R. W. The student-faculty ratio in graduate programs of selected departments of sociology. *American Sociologist*, 1969, *4*, 123-127.

Johnson, R. R. Leadership among American colleges. *Change*, 1978, *10*, 50-51.

Jordan, R. T. Library characteristics of colleges ranking high in academic excellence. *College and Research Libraries*, 1963, *24*, 369-376.

Kelso, C. D. How does your law school measure up? *Student Lawyer*, 1975, *4*, 20-24.

Keniston, H. *Graduate Study and Research in the Arts and Sciences at the University of Pennsylvania*. Philadelphia: University of Pennsylvania Press, 1959.

Knudsen, D. C., and Vaughan, T. R. Quality in graduate education: A re-evaluation of the rankings of sociology departments in the Cartter report. *American Sociologist*, 1969, *4*, 12-19.

Krause, E. D., and Krause, L. The colleges that produce our best scientists: A study of the academic training grounds of a large group of distinguished American scientists. *Science Education*, 1970, *54*, 133-140.

Kuh, D. *Indices of Quality in the Undergraduate Experience*. Washington, D.C.: American Association for Higher Education, AAHE-ERIC Research Report No. 4, 1981.

Lavendar, A. D., Mathers, R. A., and Pease, J. The student-faculty ratio in graduate programs of selected departments of sociology: A supplement to the Janes report. *American Sociologist*, 1971, *6*, 29-30.

Lawrence, J. K., and Green, K. C. *A Question of Quality: The Higher Education Ratings Game*. Washington, D.C.: American Association for Higher Education, AAHE-ERIC Research Report No. 5, 1980.

Lewis, L. S. On subjective and objective rankings of sociology departments. *American Sociologist*, 1968, *3*, 129-131.

Lightfield, T. E. Output and recognition of sociologists. *American Sociologist*, 1971, *6*, 128-133.

Longanecker, D. A. Assessing quality in graduate education: A multivariate approach. Unpublished doctoral dissertation, Stanford University, 1978.

Lynd, A. G. The identification of criteria for evaluating graduate programs in higher education at Big Ten institutions. Unpublished doctoral dissertation, Michigan State University, 1976.

Magoun, H. W. The Cartter report on quality in graduate education. *Journal of Higher Education*, 1966, *37*, 481-492.

Margulies, R. Z., and Blau, P. America's leading professional schools. *Change*, 1973, *5*, 21-27.

McClelland, C. Encouraging excellence. In S. R. Graubard and G. Holton (eds.), *Excellence and Leadership in a Democracy*. New York: Columbia University Press, 1962.

Morgan, D. R., Kearney, R. C., and Regens, J. L. Assessing quality among graduate institutions of higher education in the United States. *Social Science Quarterly*, 1976, *57*, 671-679.

Munson, C. E., and Nelson, P. Measuring the quality of professional schools. *UCLA Educator*, 1977, *19*, 41-52.

National Science Board. *Graduate Education: Parameters for Public Policy*. Washington, D.C.: National Science Foundation, 1969.

Pace, C. R. Measuring the quality of student effort. *Current Issues in Higher Education*. Washington, D.C.: American Association for Higher Education, 1980.

Petrowski, W. R., Brown, E. L., and Duffy, J. A. National universities and the ACE ratings. *Journal of Higher Education*, 1973, *44*, 495-513.

Pirsig, R. *Zen and the Art of Motorcycle Maintenance*. New York: William Morrow, 1974.

"The Popular Vote: Rankings of Top Schools." *Juris Doctor*, 1976, *6*, 17-18, 21.

Rogers, W. R. Inaugural address of the president of Guilford College, Greensboro, N.C., July 31, 1981.

Roose, K. D., and Anderson, C. J. *A Rating of Graduate Programs*. Washington, D.C.: American Council on Education, 1970.

Scully, M. G. The well-known universities lead in rating of faculties' reputations. *Chronicle of Higher Education*, January 15, 1979, pp. 6-7.

Shichor, D. Prestige of sociology departments and the placing of new Ph.D.'s. *American Sociologist*, 1970, *5*, 157-160.

Siebring, B. R. The American Council on Education rankings of quality in graduate education and membership in the National Academy of Science. *Science Education*, 1969, *53*, 75-77.

Smith, R., and Fiedler, F. E. The measurement of scholarly work: A critical review of the literature. *Educational Record*, 1971, *52*, 225-232.

Solmon, L. C., and Astin, A. W. Departments without distinguished graduate programs. *Change*, 1981, *13*, 23-28.

Solmon, W. E. Correlates of prestige rankings of graduate programs in sociology departments. *American Sociologist*, 1972, *7*, 13-14.

Solmon, W. E., and Walters, A. T. The relationship between productivity and prestige of graduate sociology departments: Fact or artifact? *American Sociologist*, 1975, *10*, 229-236.

Somit, A., and Tanenhaus, J. *American Political Science: A Profile of a Discipline*. New York: Atherton Press, 1964.

Tidball, M. E., and Kristiakowski, V. Baccalaureate origins of American scientists and scholars. *Science*, 1976, *193*, 646-652.

"The Top 15: The MBA Survey of Graduate Business Schools." *MBA*, 1975, *9*, 33-35.

Webster, D. S. Advantages and disadvantages of methods of assessing quality. *Change*, 1981, *13*, 20-24.

Young, A. Quality: The competitive strategy. *Science*, 1983, *222*, 461.

THE QUEST FOR EXCELLENCE:
Underlying Policy Issues

Anthony W. Morgan, *The University of Utah*
and Brad L. Mitchell, *The Ohio State University*

Each generation must confront the problem of defining educational excellence. Over the past century the quality of American education has been questioned and debated many times. Educational historians have chronicled this quest for excellence through such benchmarks as the Committee of Ten's report of 1892, the Cardinal Principles of 1918, the launching of Sputnik in 1957, and many points in between. We are in the throes of yet another struggle to define educational excellence, and the resurgence of education as an important matter of public policy has indeed been dramatic.

Education as a political issue has gained prominence in the 1980s because of the widening gap between expectations and perceived performance of the schools. Gallup polls from 1973 to 1982 confirm the Jeffersonian belief that schools are essential to individual and societal success. Over this period, responses to the question "How important are schools to one's future success?" were as follows (Elam, 1983):

	1973	1980	1982
Extremely important	76%	82%	80%
Fairly important	19	15	18
Not too important	4	2	1
No opinion	1	1	1

A similar question was asked about college education in 1978 and again in 1982. Belief that college is "extremely important" to success grew from 36% in 1978 to 58% in 1982.

Despite the overwhelming expectation that education is vital to one's success, perceived performance of the schools has been diminishing. Each year between 1974 and 1980, fewer Gallup Poll respondents gave their schools a rating of "A" or "B." Grade deflation was slow but inexorable. Whereas 18% gave an A rating in 1974, only 8% did so in 1979. Then the ratings seemed to stabilize over the next three years. In 1983, 31% gave the schools an A or a B, whereas in

1974 a respectable 48% had done so. By contrast, the percentage giving D's and F's has grown from 11% in 1974 to an average of 20% over the past three years (Elam, 1983, p. 32). More significant, perhaps, is the rating given their local public schools by parents with children attending the schools. In 1974, 64% of the parents gave the schools an A or B rating. By 1983 the figure was 42%.

An equally ominous sign of the decline of schools as positive environments is the response of parents asked the question "Would you like to have a child of yours take up teaching in the public schools as a career?" The responses over the past 14 years were as follows (Elam, 1983):

	1969	1972	1980	1983
Yes	75%	67%	48%	45%
No	15	22	40	33
Don't know/No answer	10	11	12	22

The rising tide of rumblings among parents, educators, and politicians did not go unheard. The discontent expressed in these Gallup polls has made itself manifest in policy changes in local school districts, colleges, and state legislatures. For example, since the mid-1970s more than half the states have adopted new testing requirements for teacher certification and high school graduation. A 1982 report of the National Association of Secondary School Principals found that 13 major state universities had already increased entrance requirements and that another 15 were considering doing so. An Education Commission of the States report indicated that at least 38 states had enacted some form of minimal competency testing in their public schools (Samuelson, 1983).

Building on this rise in public concern, major national studies of secondary education were undertaken by various foundations, commissions, and independent researchers. In 1982 the Johnson Foundation identified 25 national studies under way on the American high school and called a "summit conference" of those involved to discuss issues of common concern. The reports these groups produced did not so much identify new issues as reflect the growing popular discontent and endorse policies already under development and implementation. Yet focusing national attention on the problems of education and setting an agenda of reform proposals are important functions in translating popular concerns into concrete public policies.

The excellence reports reviewed for purposes of this chapter include the following:

Academic Preparation for College, Report of the College Board, 1983

Action for Excellence, Report of the Task Force on Education for Economic Growth, Education Commission of the States, 1983

America's Competitive Challenge, Report of the Business–Higher Education Forum, 1983

The Condition of Teaching, Emily Feistritzer, Carnegie Foundation for the Advancement of Teaching, 1983

Educating Americans for the 21st Century, National Science Board, Commission on Precollege Education in Mathematics, Science and Technology, 1983

High School: A Report on Secondary Education in America, Ernest Boyer, Carnegie Foundation for the Advancement of Teaching, 1983

Horace's Compromise, Theodore Sizer, 1984

Making the Grade, Report of the Task Force on Federal Elementary and Secondary Education Policy, Twentieth Century Fund, 1983

Meeting the Needs for Quality in the South, Southern Regional Education Board, 1981.

A Nation at Risk, Report of the National Commission on Excellence in Education, 1983

The Paideia Proposal, Mortimer Adler, 1982

A Place Called School, John Goodlad, 1984

To Strengthen Quality in Higher Education, National Commission on Higher Education Issues, 1982

We have not attempted to summarize here the principal recommendations of each report; others have provided such reviews (Davies and Slevin, 1983–1984; Gross, 1983; Harvard Educational Review, 1984). Our intent is to select policy issues common to most of the reports and to assess the contributions the reports bring to long-standing policy debates on several basic issues.

Drawing upon the excellence reports identified and a host of supporting literature, this chapter looks at differing views of educational excellence. Following an overview of the various perspectives, five policy themes are discussed: (1) the crisis of purpose in American education; (2) the tie between education and economic growth; (3) higher education's relationships to the high schools; (4) governance; and (5) the setting of strategic priorities for attainment of quality education.

The excellence reports of 1983 focus largely on secondary education. The National Commission on Higher Education Issues, established by the American Council on Education, is an exception. In most of the excellence reports, higher education is implicated in issues of teacher preparation programs, strengthening the high school–college connection, raising college admissions standards, and producing more technically trained people. To some extent, then, this chapter deals with the literature of secondary education — a literature relatively unfamiliar to many scholars in higher education. Unfamiliarity with secondary education issues is a criticism of our field, and not one without foundation. The separate worlds of secondary education and higher education are being drawn closer together, however, by the debates over the purposes and quality of education at all levels.

SIX PERSPECTIVES ON EDUCATIONAL EXCELLENCE

The vast majority of recent educational reform reports place heavy emphasis on the word "excellence." However, the spectrum of reform jargon also includes terms like innovation, competitiveness, revitalization, prosperity, productivity, and integration. Do all of these concepts fit under the rubric of educational excellence? Can prosperity be gained through innovation, or must productivity come first? Will the integration of educational functions among various social institutions make America more competitive in the international marketplace? Is educational excellence the cure for economic stagnation?

A comparison of the excellence reports suggests that there are at least six distinct approaches to defining excellence in education. Table 1 outlines these various viewpoints and lists the reform reports most closely tied with each perspective. The perspectives are obviously not mutually exclusive. Various reports contain elements of each, some emphasizing one or the other. The important point is one of emphasis in communicating a notion of excellence to a wide public with diverse and sometimes conflicting notions of its own.

Political Economy Approach
Zald and Wamsley (1973) define political economy as the interrelation between a political system and an economy. The key dimension of this relationship is the influence political and economic forces have on the formulation and implementation of individual, institutional, and social objectives. Educational organizations, like any formalized collective, must constantly try to assimilate these objectives in order to sustain societal and political support.

A political economy approach to defining excellence in education focuses on the connection between educational organizations and their political and economic environments. Academic quality is measured by how well schools, colleges, and universities support and enhance the political and economic strength of the country. Almost all of the reform reports emphasize the importance of using education as a cornerstone in pursuing political and economic imperatives. The Business–Higher Education Forum (1983, p. iii) concludes that "unless we rebuild the American economy and strengthen our educational system, it will be increasingly difficult — if not impossible — to maintain a just society, a high standard of living for all Americans, and a strong national defense."

The Task Force on Education for Economic Growth (1983) consistently refers to political and economic themes in its report, *Action for Excellence*. The National Science Board Commission (1983, p. 5) claims that all their recommendations are founded upon one basic objective:

> The improvement and support of elementary and secondary school systems throughout America so that, by the year 1995, they will provide all the nation's youth with a level of education in mathematics, science and technology, as measured by achievement scores and participation levels (as well as other non-subjective criteria), that is not only the highest quality attained anywhere in the world but also reflects the particular and peculiar needs of our nation.

Other reports (Boyer, 1983; Sizer, 1984) identify the political economy perspective as just one of several yardsticks that should be used to judge American education. These latter reports place less emphasis on a political economy view, maintaining instead that "education is an end in itself."

TABLE 1. Six Perspectives on Educational Excellence

Perspective	Short Definition	Representative Excellence Reports
Political economy approach	Excellence is measured by how well schools and colleges support and enhance the political and economic strength of the nation.	Business – Higher Education Forum, *America's Competitive Challenge* Task Force on Education for Economic Growth, *Action for Excellence*
Productivity approach	Excellence is measured by how efficiently schools and colleges convert inputs into outputs.	National Science Board Commission on Precollege Education, *Educating Americans for the 21st Century*
Value-added approach	Excellence in measured by how well schools and colleges enhance individual development.	Southern Regional Education Board, *Meeting the Needs for Quality in the South*
Producer-consumer quality approach	Excellence is determined by the quality of producers (teachers) and consumers (students).	John Goodlad, *A Place Called School* Theodore Sizer, *Horace's Compromise*
Content approach	Excellence is judged by the quality and scope of the curriculum.	Mortimer Adler, *The Paideia Proposal* John Goodlad, *A Place Called School* The College Board, *Academic Preparation for College*
Eclectic approach	Excellence is evaluated on a variety of dimensions, including efficiency, effectiveness, and characteristics of participants.	Ernest Boyer, *High School: A Report on Secondary Education* National Commission on Excellence in Education, *A Nation at Risk*

313

Linking educational excellence with political and economic outputs dictates the direction and content of reform. What is perceived as needed to bolster economic and political weaknesses becomes the agenda for school reform. If economic productivity is perceived as a function of a high proportion of engineers and other technically trained people, then educational institutions must respond accordingly. The political economy perspective places high expectations on our educational institutions and assumes a direct, tightly coupled link between education and the economy.

Productivity Approach

In 1983 over $220 billion was spent on education in the United States. Many advocates of school reform are demanding substantially increased levels of expenditure in the future. The high cost of education invites strong pressures from various groups to fund only those educational practices which provide a favorable ratio of benefits to costs. School productivity is thus regarded as a measure of excellence.

Lindsay (1982) identifies two overarching problems in applying the productivity concept to education. Essentially these problems are the same as those involved in defining excellence. The first concerns the "difficulties of capturing in a set of measurements the intangibility of the multiple objectives and outputs in education and the different values placed on them by people with differing perspectives" (p. 179). The second problem relates to the inability of some educational administrators and policymakers to recognize the limitations of such productivity measures as student-teacher ratios and per-student costs.

State legislatures are not adopting a "free spending" policy toward educational reform. Schools, colleges, and universities must demonstrate their worth in return for additional dollars. The National Science Board Commission (1983, p. 64) states:

> It is mandatory that a search for all such savings and the elimination of unnecessary expenditures be undertaken at each level of government (with help from the private sector). The public will not tolerate waste if, at the same time, it is called upon to increase significantly its support for education. Any perception of waste, whether well founded or not, will reduce the public zeal for changes which require additional governmental outlays.

Productivity as a measure of excellence brings a focus on rationalization of the educational process and regulation or control over components of the production function. Wise (1983) characterizes such a focus as "hyper-rationalization" of education and maintains that significant educational reform will not occur until policymakers exchange their excessively rational view of the educational process for a more humanistic one. The desire to establish measurable means-ends relationships in education may unduly inhibit the development of "less than rational" but highly creative reform efforts.

The productivity approach can be viewed as the operational version of the political economy approach to academic excellence. Thomas (1969, p. 31), for example, adopts the political economy perspective when he observes, "Education is a matter of national concern because adequate supplies of high quality schooling are essential for the achievement of national objectives." He then ties this perspective to that of productivity: "Education must be produced in the quantity and quality required, at a cost which is within the nation's capabilities. In other words, education must be efficient." A paraphrasing of John Gardner's famous inquiry comes to mind: "Can we be excellent and efficient too?" The tack taken by several of the excellence reports is to convince policymakers to fund educational programs based on the premise "Excellence costs. But in the long run mediocrity costs far more" (National Commission on Excellence in Education, 1983, p. 33).

Value-Added Approach
Is excellence an absolute or relative measure of performance? The answer largely determines how schools, colleges, and universities are evaluated. For example, an absolute version of excellence will demand that all the comprehensive high schools in a school district or colleges in a state be judged by the same standard. Proponents of the value-added approach to educational excellence consider this interpretation as unrealistic and unfair. According to their perspective, educational excellence should be calibrated on a scale which recognizes contextual constraints, opportunities, and improvements in performance.

Willie (1982) argues that absolute standards of academic excellence may provide an excuse to exclude students "who are not good enough." An alternative approach is to judge institutions according to how well they have added to the student's realization of his or her potential. This type of thinking recognizes the diversity in the American educational system and considers this diversity a key factor in the successful pursuit of excellence. As Willie observes, "A higher education system that has a Harvard without a Hampton is incomplete, meaning that neither Harvard nor Hampton can be the best. They are different; both are necessary and essential in the development and cultivation of human talent for the survival of our society" (p. 18).

Educational opportunity, academic quality, and institutional diversity are common goals of American education. The underlying assumption for each of these objectives is a belief that schools do make a difference in determining student achievement. The value-added approach to defining excellence is constructed upon a commitment to high expectations, but also supports equal access to education. The Southern Regional Education Board Task Force (1981, p. 3) concluded that:

> Our schools and postsecondary institutions serve a student population with a wide span of abilities and needs that require programs with varying objectives. Yet each set of needs — whether for basic literacy, for vocational education, or for college preparation — demands focused and unwavering attention to quality. Diversity should not be used as an alibi for failure to challenge the highest potential in each student.

Producer-Consumer Quality Approach

Who is responsible for how much a student learns? Many argue that prior to the 1960s the primary responsibility for acquiring knowledge rested with the individual student, the "consumer." Tomlinson (1981, p. 373) notes how this way of thinking has shifted:

> To borrow an industrial analogy, children, as workers, were the locus of production; their ability and effort were the machine that determined their performance. The quality and quantity of the teacher's input was fixed; they supplied the raw material. The children then treated the material with their ability and effort . . . . Things have turned about in recent times. The ability and labor of teachers have replaced the ability and labor of students as the putative determinants of academic production. According to current reports, the student is the constant, and it is the variable ability and motivation of teachers, along with the variable quality of educational resources, that now determine student performance.

Most current excellence reports place a greater burden of responsibility on the teachers as the "producers" of the educational product. Several state legislatures (e.g., Florida, Alabama, Tennessee, and Utah) are focusing on producer variables, such as teacher evaluation and compensation, as the core strategy of their educational reform efforts. Similarly, the educational research community in recent years has focused on the issue of "school effectiveness" (Brookover, et al., 1978; Edmonds, 1982; Rutter et al., 1979). The main features of the school effectiveness model include the ability of teachers to instill high expectations in students, the strength of principals to serve as instructional leaders, and the importance of school characteristics, curricular requirements, and classroom climate (Cohen, 1981).

A producer emphasis applies a factory metaphor to educational institutions. Product quality is determined by the clarity of expectations and goals of the producers and the characteristics of the production process. The strengths of this emphasis are in its ability to communicate clearly the complexity of the educational process, to designate responsible parties, and to simplify political remedies. Focusing solely on producer quality does not, however, provide an adequate conceptual framework for identifying the range of educational purposes, the complexity of the production function, and the role that other societal institutions play in education.

Some of the excellence reports (Goodlad, 1983*b*; National Commission on Excellence in Education, 1983; Sizer, 1984) argue for a more balanced view of producer and consumer responsibility. Goodlad, for example, notes (1983*b*, p. 557): "A significant component of my recommendations pertains to the roles of students . . . . Students are relegated to a passive stance in the vital business of their own school-based learning; classes and teachers are not, to them, the most important part of the school environment." The National Commission on Excellence in Education, despite all the publicity surrounding its recommendations on courses, time, and teachers, closes its report by placing a good share of the responsibility for excellence in education on parents and students.

Content Approach

The decade of the 1980s may be remembered as the era of secondary-school curricular reform in the computer age. Nearly all of the reform reports express dissatisfaction with the scope and rigor of the high school curriculum. The content approach to excellence critically examines schools according to what is being taught. In other words, high-quality education is dependent fundamentally on a high-quality curriculum. John Goodlad's study (1983a) examined the teaching process and the curriculum. On the latter issue, he concludes (p. 467):

> The most striking discovery to emerge from the data is what might be called a sameness of form in the substance and design of the curriculum . . . . Moreover, the form and substance of the curriculum appeared to call for and make appropriate only some ways of knowing and learning, not others . . . . Students rarely planned or initiated anything, read or wrote anything of some length, or created their own products. They scarcely ever speculated on meanings, and most of the time they listened or worked alone . . . . Why this curricular sterility?

In addition to its homogenization, the secondary curriculum is being criticized for several other reasons. First, there is general agreement that more course requirements are needed for math and science education. Second, the "blandness" of the curriculum is viewed as inhibiting the development of higher-order thinking skills. Third, many of the reports suggest that schools fail to inculcate a "core of common learning" to all students (Boyer, 1983).

Suggestions for rectifying these deficiencies call for a tighter core curriculum with more course requirements in math, science, English, social studies, and computer science. Increasing the core curriculum requirements may not by itself ensure academic excellence, however. Other factors in the educational process (i.e., teaching, performance expectations, and learning time) significantly influence how well content is transmitted to each student.

Eclectic Approach

Many politicians and ideologues, dismissing the ambiguity and complexity of education, prefer to adopt one perspective as a basis of advocating a clear line of reform. Most of the excellence studies are more temperate and eclectic in their analyses, but many do have an overriding emphasis on one perspective. The National Commission on Excellence in Education (1983, pp. 12-13) exemplifies the eclectic approach:

> We define excellence to mean several related things. At the level of the individual learner, it means performing on the boundary of individual ability in ways that test and push back personal limits, in school and in the workplace. Excellence characterizes a school or college that sets high expectations and goals for all learners, then tries in every way possible to help students reach them. Excellence characterizes a society that has adopted these policies, for it will then be prepared through the education and skill of its people to respond to the challenges of a rapidly changing world.

This definition of excellence contains slices of the other five approaches. It clarifies the need to identify and articulate the central purpose of schools (political economy approach); recognizes the political and practical imperatives of applying efficiency measures to education (productivity approach); reflects the dynamic tensions along the equity-excellence axis and the need to produce an educational system that reflects and cultivates both values (value-added approach); attempts to show that school quality, teacher quality, and student quality are dependent upon one another (producer-consumer approach); and, finally, considers the curriculum as the anchor at the end of a chain of crucial educational processes (teaching, use of instructional time, articulation of expectations, and establishment of standards).

At the heart of all these definitions of excellence is a question of purpose. Inevitably, schools and colleges are judged by how well they fulfill some prescribed objective or set of objectives. Our review of these perspectives on educational excellence suggests that the productive alignment of these various objectives will be a difficult task for policymakers at all levels of educational governance.

CRISIS OF PURPOSE: TENSIONS ALONG THE EQUALITY-EXCELLENCE AXIS

Crisis of purpose is a continuing saga in American education. Is the purpose of education to develop the intellect? Inculcate moral principles and build character? Provide training for jobs? Provide custodial services for working parents? Socialize youth into adult society? Or simply to provide more education to more people? The contemporary answer seems to be "all of the above," or as the title of one of Ernest Boyer's chapters asserts, "We want it all" (Boyer, 1983). After reviewing national public opinion surveys and studies of the purposes of American schools and colleges, the National Commission on Excellence in Education (1983, pp. 5-6) concludes:

> Our society and its educational institutions seem to have lost sight of the basic purposes of schooling . . . . That we have compromised this commitment is . . . hardly surprising, given the multitude of often conflicting demands we have placed on our schools and colleges. They are routinely called on to provide solutions to personal, social, and political problems that the home and other institutions either will not or cannot resolve. We must understand that these demands . . . often exact an educational cost as well as a financial one.

The Ebb and Flow of Predominant Values

Underlying present as well as past crises of purpose is a fundamental tension, not unique to but perhaps more visible in American society, between egalitarianism and elitism. American schools, rooted in an egalitarian society, were initially elitist at primary, secondary, and higher education levels. Public elementary schools spread rapidly in the 19th century, but secondary education remained for the relatively few and was dominated by private academies. Educational reformers denounced these academies as exclusive, aristocratic, and un-American. Aided by the emergence of compulsory attendance laws, public secondary education began to take hold and gradually transformed the high school into a mass-education institution. The transition altered the character of high schools much as the movement to mass higher education decades later would alter the character and purposes of colleges. In the late 19th century, the relatively small clientele of public high schools was composed of highly selected students. While these students were not necessarily college bound (only 29% of high school graduates in 1891 were described as "prepared" to enter college as opposed to 49% by 1910), they and their parents were relatively homogeneous in the expectations they held for the high school experience (Hofstadter, 1962, p. 326).

In 1892 the National Council on Education's prestigious Committee of Ten reflected a consensus of purpose in the secondary schools when it stressed the centrality of "mental discipline." The committee argued that the curriculum ought to be academic, with college preparatory subjects — Greek, Latin, mathematics, English, foreign languages, natural history, physical science, geography, history, civil government, and political economy — as its core. Furthermore, the committee argued that such a curriculum was the best preparation for life, irrespective of one's life ambitions (Passow, 1976). These arguments are strikingly similar to those made almost a century later by the National Commission on Excellence in Education, the Task Force on Education for Economic Growth, the Paideia Group, and others.

Two decades later, however, the demographics of public secondary schools were changing rapidly and so were the purposes of education. The essentially academic content of the 1890s curriculum was being modified to fit the demographic realities of the 1910s. The National Education Association's Commission on the Reorganization of Secondary Education (1918) expanded the purposes of secondary education to include health, citizenship, and worthy home-membership. As the percentage of high school graduates (as a proportion of the 17-year-old population) grew from 8.6% in 1910 to 28.8% in 1930 to 50.8% in 1940 (Boyer, 1983, p. 55), the "progressive" or "life adjustment" movement in education came into full bloom. The purposes of education were expanded and modified to fit the changing clientele. Hofstadter devotes an entire chapter in his book *Anti-intellectualism in American Life* to what he refers to as the "silly season in education writing" where every imaginable societal need was justified as educationally sound.

The "silly season" evoked a response from the educational "essentialists," as reflected in the 1936 report of the Essentialist Committee, which advocated a return to more demanding studies that would build mental discipline (Boyer, 1983). But the essentialists, who counted Mortimer Adler among their number, were building sand dikes against a tidal wave of public opinion favoring universal access to secondary education and a concurrent rise in the expectation that the schools would solve a wide range of social needs.

By 1930 high schools were enrolling 47% of the age group, and by 1950, 67%. The rise in percentage of high school graduates is similarly striking and demonstrates that increasing proportions of youth were able to persist, or that the curriculum was adjusted to enable greater numbers to pass successfully through America's high schools. Shortly after World War II, seven out of ten young people entered high school but fewer than four out of them remained to graduate (Hofstadter, 1962, p. 343). By 1965 high school graduation rates had risen to over 75% (Boyer, 1983).

The Impact of Egalitarianism on Schools

Cusick (1983) argues that dominance of the egalitarian ideal in American secondary schools accounts for the current structure of the schools and permeates their explicit and implicit purposes. That is, trying to meet the educational needs of everyone, irrespective of inclinations or abilities, has led to diverse curricula where courses are given equal weight, where teachers are free to develop their own curriculum, and where the maintenance of order pervades the system.

> Simply stated, in the schools I studied, the diversity and disparity of the curriculum and the accompanying autonomy of teachers to create and implement their private versions of the curriculum can be viewed as a retreat by the school from taking any posture or stance which might have interfered with the taking, retaining and instructing of everyone. Were the schools to assume a position requiring a uniformity of curriculum, standards of achievement, or consensus among the staff on how to conduct themselves and their classes, it is inevitable that they have had [sic] to make judgments about and take actions against students which might have damaged those students' opportunity for equality. [Cusick, 1983, p. 111]

Yet the excellence reports are virtually unanimous in their call for more uniformity of curriculum and for higher standards of achievement. The age-old education debate then ensues: "Will a required core of academically oriented subjects and higher standards adversely affect the egalitarian ideal?" The dilemmas of this debate are being aired explicitly in discussions surrounding *The Paideia Proposal* (Adler, 1982; Harvard Educational Review, 1983). *The Paideia Proposal* and most of the excellence reports deal with the tension between egalitarianism and elitism by asserting that better-quality education for all serves the interests of both excellence and true equality. As Ravitch (1983a) points out, Adler has wisely connected the two values and has attempted to win the hearts of egalitarians who reject tracking and sorting schemes that differentiate among students. Similarly, the National Commission on Excellence in Education recommends that all students be required to take a core of "New Basics," which appears to some critics as a rigid college-preparatory curriculum reminiscent of the 1892 Committee of Ten report. The National Commission takes a middle ground, however, in that it provides for differentiation within the core and allows almost half of all course work to be elective (1983, p. 24):

> We must emphasize that the variety of student aspirations, abilities, and preparation requires that appropriate content be available to satisfy diverse needs. Attention must be directed to both the nature of the content available and to the needs of the particular learners . . . . Nevertheless, there remains a common expectation: We must demand the best effort and performance from all students . . . . Our recommendations are based on the beliefs that everyone can learn, that everyone is born with an urge to learn which can be nurtured, that a solid high school education is within the reach of virtually all.

In some states differentiation among schools is gaining renewed public policy support. Royster (1983, pp. 200-201) describes the shift that is occurring in North Carolina:

> Mediocrity is mediocrity wherever you find it. Now . . . I sense a change of direction, a swing of the pendulum. In my own state, North Carolina, we are abandoning the idea that mere attendance at high school entitles one to a diploma . . . . A high school diploma in North Carolina, at least, will cease to be a meaningless document. The state has also established within the public school system special schools for those who are exceptionally talented in the arts, in mathematics, or in other fields. It is even in the process of establishing a publicly supported boarding school to prepare students of ability for college. In one sense this is a return to elitism in education, but it will be an individually earned elitism, not one based on family fortune or racial or other background.

None of the excellence reports, however, rejects the notion of comprehensive secondary education or open access to higher education. In fact, each report reaffirms a commitment to those ideals. Two of the reports cite evidence that the American strategy of broad-based investment in educational opportunity, as opposed to selective investment by means of early selection tests, is the best educational strategy. In a study sponsored by the National Commission on Excellence in Education, Thorsten Husén (1982, p. 48; see also Husén, 1983) concludes:

> . . . the comprehensive system, by its openness, lack of selective examinations during the primary and initial secondary school period and its high retention rate, is a more effective strategy in taking care of all the talent of a nation. By casting the net as widely as possible an attempt is made to "catch" an optimum number of fish. A selective system with early separation of students who are rated to have academic potential is destined to produce good end products. But this advantage is bought at the high price of excluding a sizeable number of students from lower class homes from further education and of limiting the opportunities for the great mass of students to get access to quality education.

Similarly, the Task Force on Education for Economic Growth (1983) cites evidence from Japan that the American model is not only working for others but that it has been used successfully against us in producing a better-educated work force. "The great accomplishment of the Japanese primary and secondary education lies not in its creation of a brilliant elite . . . but in its generation of such a high average level of capability" (p. 20). The Japanese have apparently succeeded in achieving America's twin ideals of egalitarianism and excellence. Excellence in this context, however, is clearly measured by the existence of a highly skilled and productive work force.

Most of the excellence reports of the 1980s point to the development of a highly trained work force as the primary purpose of education. Emphasis on this purpose attempts to subordinate the egalitarian-elitism tension to higher values of national economic well-being. Yet several of the reports — for example, Boyer (1983), Goodlad (1984), Sarason (1982), and Sizer (1984) — give greater emphasis to the process of education as a means of developing the intellect irrespective of future economic gains. The tie between education and the economy, a subject treated at greater length in a subsequent section of this chapter, is an appealing goal to a nation characteristically pragmatic and currently worried about its economic competitiveness.

Is Consensus Possible?

Both public and higher education institutions are often characterized by an accumulation of multiple, and sometimes conflicting, purposes. The accumulation process is not dissimilar to an omnibus piece of legislation where the demands of various interest groups are accommodated by adding provisions rather than discriminating or prioritizing on the basis of a clear hierarchy of goals. While not as neat, the accumulation strategy is politically less risky. Is it likely, therefore, that the clarion call of various excellence reports for more focus of purpose in our schools and colleges will lead to any narrowing of multiple purposes? A narrowing of purposes would require legislatures, school boards, and governing boards to make judgments about the relative value of educational programs designed to advance scientific and technological progress, prevent traffic accidents, raise health standards, refine moral character, overcome differences among ethnic groups, lower the crime rate, eliminate poverty, enrich the common culture, reduce unemployment, ease the assimilation of immigrants, guide young people into useful occupations, retrain displaced workers, etc. (Jencks, 1981; Ravitch, 1983).

We have successfully avoided making hard choices among such competing values largely because we have been willing and able to afford accommodation through accumulation. We have also tended to repress or ignore possible conflict by concentrating instead on overarching goals or purposes around which we could unite or by focusing on the process of education (i.e., universal access) instead of purposes or product (i.e., performance).

One of the most important of these consensus-generating strategies at both public and higher education levels has been to focus on educating increasing proportions of the relevant age groups — quantitative goals of more education for more people. Michael Bakalis (1983), commenting on the rising dissatisfaction with education evident in the various excellence reports, notes the conspicuous absence of serious concern with the intellectual content or the intellectual processes of education. Echoing Hofstadter's laments over the dominance of egalitarianism and the deep-rooted anti-intellectualism in America, Bakalis argues that Americans have translated the goal of quality education into goals for quantity of education. Educational historian Diane Ravitch (1981, p. 337) corroborates this view: "In recent years the policymakers have sought to equalize educational attainment (years of schooling) without regard to the quality of education. This is like putting people on a diet of eighteen hundred calories a day without caring whether they are consuming junk food or nutritious food."

We have proved to be very successful in fulfilling quantitative purposes; perhaps we have been too successful. Drawing on historian Daniel Boorstin's (1974) notion of "self-liquidating ideals," Bakalis (1983) posits that the goals of universal access and mass education have been met with such success that this long-standing ideal has now been "liquidated" and we are now left without an overarching national consensus about the purpose of education. The education battle against limited access has been won, and we now find ourselves in a paradoxical state characterized by de Tocqueville as "the strange unrest of Happy Men."

Yet others, such as Chester Finn (1983), see promising signs of movement toward a new national consensus. Finn cites evidence of a populist movement among parents, employers, and elected officials to focus on qualitative goals in education at all levels, e.g., raising standards for student achievement and admission to colleges, and improving the quality of teachers. Finn further suggests that we are witnessing the beginnings of a "major shift" in society's ideas and values about education. This shift, Finn believes, holds the likelihood of a new consensus forming to effect higher standards, the acquisition of higher levels of skills, and the strengthening of character through education.

The focal point of an emerging consensus of purpose centers, Finn and others believe, on the notion of a core curriculum. In a presentation before the National Commission on Excellence in Education, Resnick and Resnick (1982) cite evidence from their studies of American education that lends support to the thesis of an American ideal of extending the years of education and rising concern over a core curriculum:

1. The increasing variety of students in attendance has tended to press the schools toward differentiated curricula as a way of interesting and holding students in school.
2. America's effort to expand educational opportunity over the past century can be viewed as the purchase of democratic access at the price of longer years of schooling.
3. We have not really eliminated selectivity in education; we have only delayed it — until college or beyond.
4. The notion of a high-level, academically oriented curriculum is a radical idea because it takes seriously the goal of a fully educated citizenry — not just a long-schooled one.

Whether current interest over qualitative issues such as a core curriculum and higher standards persists and emerges as a major purpose of education remains to be seen. In the annual Gallup polls on education, a small minority of respondents cite poor curriculum and poor standards as major problems. Discipline wins out every time.

EDUCATION AND THE ECONOMY: THE TIE THAT BINDS

The utilitarian character of education runs deep in America. While colleges were initially intended for the privileged few, dominated by training for the clergy and funded largely by private means, the rise of public colleges and universities was rooted in more instrumental values of preparation for a wider range of professions and application of scientific knowledge to practical problems in agriculture and engineering. The Morrill Acts and many subsequent federal statutes underwriting higher education reflect explicit assumptions about the instrumental value of higher education to the nation's economic well-being. The agricultural research and extension model became the prototype link between higher education and economic progress.

"Human capital," another model more general in nature, was espoused by some economists in the late 1950s and 1960s. While the roots of human capital theory go back to Adam Smith's interest in the economic value of education, it wasn't until the 1960s that Schultz, Becker, and others brought it to the forefront of public policy. Schultz (1971) maintained that traditional analyses of economic growth concentrated almost solely on the contributions made by capital and land to the exclusion of education, on-the-job training, health improvements, and mobility of the labor force. Becker (1964) attempted to demonstrate that the social rate of return on educational investment was comparable with private rates of return (from 10% to 15% at the time of his studies), and may even be higher since his methods did not pretend to capture the full range of returns. Juster (1975) and other contributors to the Carnegie Commission's volume on the relationship between higher education and the labor market confirm the finding that investment in education yields a "profit" both to the individual being educated (private rate of return) and to society as a whole, even after accounting for the influence of ability and family background on earnings. Another major Carnegie Commission report (June 1973) concluded that the division of private and societal benefits of higher education was roughly equivalent to the proportion of total economic costs (including forgone income) borne privately (about two-thirds) and borne publicly (about one-third).

Studies of private and social rates of return tend to concentrate on increased earnings to individuals and the tax "earnings" to society. Favorable private rates of return and the extension of these benefits to more people were prominent arguments in public policy discussions of the late 1960s (Carnegie Commission, 1968) and in the debates over major changes in student aid programs (Carnegie Council, 1979). The Educational Amendments of 1972 incorporated an entitlement program (the Basic Educational Opportunity Grant) designed in part to bring these private benefits to those who historically had not benefited from the luxury of such investment opportunities.

Emphasis on the individual benefits of higher education lured increasing proportions of youth to invest by enrolling and led public policy discussions toward equalizing the opportunities to invest. In the 1970s, however, some economists found declining rates of return on investment in college (Freeman, 1971; Freeman and Holloman, 1975). Investors equivocated and participation rates, particularly among white males, dropped. The well-publicized tie between higher education and economic benefits loosened.

Revitalized Human Capital
By the late 1970s the slack began to be taken up by the reemergence and re-formulation of the more general argument that education and economic growth are causally linked. The various excellence reports clearly reflect this strategic argument. The Task Force on Education for Economic Growth (1983, p. 14) is very straightforward on the point: "It is the thesis of this report that our future success as a nation — our national defense, our social stability and well-being and our national prosperity — will depend on our ability to improve education and training for millions of individual citizens." Similarly, the National Commission on Excellence in Education (1983, p. 7) notes that "knowledge, learning, information and skilled intelligence are the new raw materials of international commerce. . . . Learning is the indispensable investment required for success in the information age we are entering."

Arguments for a positive relationship between education and economic growth are hardly new. Denison (1962) and Schultz (1971) both found that about 20% of the U.S. economic growth rate in the twentieth century was due to increases in the educational level of the labor force. Denison's more recent study (1974) found that education per worker accounted for 14.1% of total economic growth over the period 1929–1969. Bowen (1977) assumes that one-fourth of this economic growth is due to higher educaiton and then calculates the very favorable dollar return on investment in higher education (excluding returns on research and public service).

Yet as Bowen notes, the specific linkages between education and economic productivity are not precisely known and are subject to some controversy. The excellence reports offer little concrete evidence to support the thesis of added investment in education to achieve economic growth. But virtually every report either assumes or asserts the connection. *Action for Excellence* (Task Force on Education for Economic Growth, 1983, pp. 18-20), one of the most detailed reports in terms of its citation of evidence, refers to three principal sources: (1) common sense and observation; (2) Denison's 1974 study cited above; and (3) Rohlen's 1983 study of Japanese high schools. The conclusion cited in Rohlen's study is more assertive than empirical: that the relatively high average level of education lies at the heart of Japan's economic achievements. Other reports tend to refer more generally to the connection between education, industrial competitiveness on an international scale, and our social and economic well-being.

Many more difficult questions as to relative levels of investment and the possibility of declining marginal utility, or differential investments at different levels of education or in different fields, are not raised.

Connections Between Higher Education and the Economy
Edgerton (1983) has attempted to categorize the nature of the connections between higher education and the economy as fivefold: (1) the "R&D connection," wherein universities transform research into new technologies

which in turn increase economic productivity; (2) the "supplier of experts" connection, exemplified in such books as *Global Stakes* (Bodkin, Dimancescu, and Stata, 1982), which argues that colleges and universities should produce increased numbers of engineers, scientists, and other technically trained persons; (3) the "expertise/talent pool" connection, a corollary of the second category, which includes efforts of colleges and universities to shore up their own, as well as secondary education's, programs in basic math and science; (4) the "worker retraining" connection, in which higher education takes an active role in the training of workers displaced by technological and other structural shifts in the economy; and (5) the "changing nature of work" connection, which harks back to the general human capital notion that more education is needed for a more complex, information-based economy.

Some of the most important policy themes of the excellence reports are rooted in these connections between higher education and the economy. The various reports underscore their importance by prominently asserting the general connection and referring to issues included in Edgerton's categories, thereby setting the agenda for public debate. As Carnevale (1983, p. 9) observes, the single driving force justifying national resource commitments to any institution in the 1980s will be "the prospective impact on the nation's overall economy." The argument is being made nationally, regionally, and at the state level.

The New England Board of Higher Education has perhaps been the most aggressive in promoting a regional industrial and education strategy (Hoy and Bernstein, 1981, 1982*b*). New England has suffered greater losses of jobs than other regions in recent years, and yet many of its industries that have grown, such as electronic and computer-related companies, are closely related to university research and development. Many states have taken up the challenge and are competing to attract high-technology firms, believing that such firms generate unusually high multiplier effects for the state economy, that they attract a desirable work force, and that this growing sector of the economy is the wave of the future. Major state initiatives to provide incentives for high-technology growth have been spawned in Massachusetts, North Carolina, Florida, Arizona, Colorado, California, Minnesota, and other states.

Yet as many observers have pointed out, the high-tech bandwagon is a rather narrow view of the much larger problem of higher education's relationship to the nation's economy. Fundamental relationships between education and work (Levin, 1982) and basic demographic patterns (Carnevale, 1983) lie at the heart of longer-term strategies for national, regional, and state policy bodies and for institutions of higher education. Some of the issues emerging from analyses of these data include:

1. The coming "baby bust" will mean a shortage of work force entrants in years to come and the need to recruit more women, minorities, and immigrants into the work force (Hoy and Bernstein, 1982*a*).

2. The aging baby boom, when combined with the baby bust, will mean unusually large numbers of middle-aged workers having to cope with changing

technologies and job displacement (McPherson and Schapiro, 1983).

3. The demographic shifts will require a major new emphasis on lateral rather than vertical job mobility and further require employees to become more involved in lifelong or recurrent education for work (Butler, 1983; Lynton, 1983).

These emerging issues have profound implications for institutions of higher education, although the demographics will not be the same for all regions or states. But to the extent the workplace changes, higher education will have to shift its preoccupation from preemployment, formative education and adapt to emerging patterns in which education is provided on a continuing and intermittent basis (Lynton, 1983). Concurrently, different segments of higher education will need to re-evaluate their respective roles. Community colleges might focus on retraining strategies for the labor force and preparing new work force entrants such as older women. Universities might focus their efforts on further developing their R&D and "supplier of experts" connections.

Many are now arguing that higher education ought to position itself strategically as the cornerstone of national policy in an increasingly information-based economy. Furthermore, it is argued, leadership in higher education should be actively involved in the formulation of new national industrial policies, which would give higher education a renewed place of prominence with a resulting rise in public confidence and commitment. Others, however, caution against tying higher education too closely to the economy. One cautionary note is that the case for closer ties will be made too narrowly or will be oversold. The "high-tech hype," as it has come to be known in some circles, is fraught with the possibility of unrealistically high expectations being dashed by the reality of labor market demographics (Levin and Rumberger, 1983). Another cautionary note is that a tight education-economy tie will only reinforce what some consider to be overly pragmatic and utilitarian tendencies in American higher education. Harold Howe (1975), for example, warns against overplaying the economic arguments because they rest on only one measure of judging value — a cost-benefit calculus — to the exclusion of other values which may in the long run have more important contributions to make in our personal and civic lives.

HIGHER EDUCATION AND THE HIGH SCHOOL
Traditionally American high schools and colleges have maintained a casual and somewhat distant relationship. There have been exceptions (Harvard Committee, 1945). Where such relations do exist, those in the public schools often view the higher education institution as paternalistic rather than cooperative. The primary binding function between the two sectors has been the education of teachers and school administrators. In recent years, this and other linkages between secondary and postsecondary education have received considerable attention. The diversification of the high school curriculum in the 1960s and 1970s, the decline in the level of preparation of college-bound students, and the corresponding increase in college-based remedial education have added several dimensions to the school-college connection.

Questions regarding teacher quality, curriculum strength, articulation of performance expectations, and educational program duplication are addressed in several of the national and regional studies of American schooling. While the connections between high schools and higher education are multifaceted, three principal linkages are treated here: college admission standards, coordination of secondary and postsecondary curricula, and the professional preparation of teachers and principals.

Linkage 1: College Admission Standards

One of the more commonly expressed views in the current drive for excellence is that college admission standards strongly influence the quality of high schools by establishing low, average, or high expectations for academic achievement. Bartlett Giamatti (Barry, 1982, p. 7) states:

> The high schools in this country are always at the mercy of the colleges. The colleges change their requirements and their admissions criteria, and the high schools, by which I mean public and private parochial schools, are constantly trying to catch up with what the colleges are thinking. When the colleges don't seem to know what they think over a period of time, it's no wonder that this oscillation takes place all the way through the system.

Do different admission criteria have differing effects on students' behavior in high school? Many colleges and universities have come to rely principally on an admission formula, developed in part to handle large numbers of applicants and to ensure an air of objectivity, that relies heavily on high school grade point average or its counterpart, class rank. Studies by the University of California indicate that under such admission criteria students tend to take less challenging courses in a given subject field so as not to jeopardize their grade point average. It is not surprising, therefore, that an institution such as the University of California has expended large sums for remedial education even though it admits only the top 12.5% of graduating seniors. Given this type of evidence on unintended incentives, many institutions, including the University of California, are beginning to specify the courses that must be taken and to award additional points in their admission formulas to students who have taken more demanding courses (such as advanced placement).

An alternative approach to an admission formula based on grade point, class rank, and/or test scores is to rely more heavily on an individual assessment of academic preparation in high school. Stanford University employs this approach, which admittedly is more expensive, by evaluating a variety of admission criteria and conducting personal interviews. What have they found to be the most reliable criterion for successful performance at Stanford? Stanford's dean of admissions, Fred Hargadon (1982, p. 7) reports the following:

> Contrary to popular myth, test scores and grades, in and of themselves, while not insignificant, are nevertheless secondary. In short, an applicant with a high level of achievement in a first-rate academic program and only modest test scores fares better in our process than a student with high test scores and high grades but only a modest academic program.

How selective are U.S. colleges and universities? The answer is important in gauging the strength of the link between the high schools and higher education. Two recent research studies (Hargadon, 1981; Harnett and Feldmesser, 1980) suggest that with the exception of a very small number of competitive colleges and universities, the degree to which college admissions can be characterized as "highly selective" is greatly exaggerated. The 1979 American Association of Collegiate Registrars and Admission Officers survey (Hargadon, 1981) reported that 34% of collges and universities admit virtually all who wish to enroll without reviewing conventional academic qualifications. Another 56% admit all applicants who meet some academic qualifications, such as completion of certain subject in high school or attainment of a particular grade point average or class rank. Only 8% of institutions surveyed are classified as "competitive" in that candidates who meet specified requirements do not necessarily secure admission.

What is remarkable about the rising concern for educational excellence is that many of these essentially open-door colleges and universities are raising admission requirements — and doing it at a time when many face stable or even declining enrollments.

Colleges have long assumed, of course, that the secondary schools will dutifully provide whatever academic courses are required in order to ensure that their students will have a reasonable chance of gaining admission. Hargadon (1982, p. 14) questions the assumption that secondary school quality can be improved by making admission standards more rigorous:

> External forces in an educational sequence constitute less than an ideal foundation upon which to build and maintain educational programs of high quality, whether such forces be the influence of college admission requirements on secondary school programs or professional school requirements upon college programs. Such forces invariably invite educational hypocrisy, if not outright dishonesty; inflated grades, teaching to tests and course titles and descriptions leaving little resemblance to actual content. While I am not unaware that students, like the rest of us, may achieve a fine education for the wrong reasons, to motivate students largely by dangling passage to the next level in front of them invites many of them to miss a good education along the way.

Another frequently stated objection to the use of more rigorous college admission standards as an incentive for improving academic quality in the secondary schools is the danger of handicapping high-ability students who attend high schools which do not adequately respond to the challenge of higher admission standards.

Despite these concerns, admission requirements were examined and/or changed by 27 states in 1982 (National Association of Secondary School Principals, 1982). Several of the national reports on education call for the adoption of more stringent admission standards (National Commission on Excellence in Education, 1983; National Science Board Commission on Precollege Education, 1983), in addition to raising requirements for high school graduation. One of the purposes of these actions is to diminish the finger-pointing between colleges and high schools. The message from these reports is clear: both levels of education must bear some of the blame for the weakening of the high school core curriculum.

Linkage II: Curricular Coordination

The academic abilities of high school seniors is a fundamental concern for every institution of higher learning. There is substantial evidence to demonstrate that today's entering college students are not as academically prepared as their college-bound counterparts of a generation ago (Astin, 1982*a*). Many colleges and universities find themselves having to instruct growing numbers of freshman students in the basic skills of thinking and writing clearly. Maeroff (1982, p. 130) concludes that "the need for such courses has altered the character of the university, giving it the role of high school as well as postsecondary institution and making the teaching of basic skills almost as important a mission as the pursuit of advanced knowledge."

Remedial education is not the only negative product of the loose school-college curricular connection. Some observers argue that there is a widening gap between the last course given in high school in a particular subject area and the corresponding introductory course in college. Subjects like math and science are frequently cited as victims of this curricular gap. Project Equality is an attempt by the College Board to identify what student competencies are needed by the twelfth grade in order to ensure a successful and productive transition to postsecondary education. A Carnegie Foundation Special Report on higher education and the high school (Maeroff, 1983, p. 14) recommends:

> Clearly all states should establish a school-college panel to permit educators at both levels to agree upon the core of education and develop a school-college curriculum that provides both continuity and coherence. . . . High schools are usually in the dark about how their students perform when they go off to college. The colleges pass along general complaints — or praise — but there is no specific information to let high schools know how their students measure up. Every summer, North Carolina State University at Raleigh provides a student performance summary to each of the nearly 800 high schools from which the previous year's freshmen came. The performance of each student is reported relative to the entire freshman class. The report includes information such as SAT scores, mean high school grade point average, freshman year grade point average and performance on freshman English, mathematics and science courses. With concrete information such as this, the high school administrator knows how the school measures up.

These recommendations demand extensive cooperation involving integration of previously separated institutional performance information and mutual acceptance of the burdens of curricular integration. Colleges and universities will participate in such a collaboration if they think it will substantially diminish their remedial education efforts. High schools will support such a partnership if they are given some influence on the formulation and development of such collaborative efforts and have the resources and flexibility to respond appropriately.

Linkage 3: Educating Principals and Teachers

Higher education is the provider of formal preparation programs for school-teachers and administrators. In recent years, the status of these education programs has floundered near the bottom of the informal academic hierarchy in most colleges and universities (Judge, 1982). This condescending attitude toward schools of education is not in higher education's best interest. Astin (1982*b*, pp. 9-10) observes:

> Bright students who want to become school teachers are frequently encouraged to switch into some other, more "demanding" field. Thus, it is not surprising that, of all undergraduate majors, education attracts the most poorly prepared students. These students in turn go out to teach and administer to elementary and secondary students. Those in the most lofty reaches of the education system are fond of criticizing the secondary schools, but could it be that the chickens are coming home to roost? Are the declining educational competencies of today's freshmen directly attributable to the poor quality of the teachers that are sent out to educate them?

Are colleges and universities ignoring their role in forging the link between teacher quality and education quality? The simple but ambiguous answer is yes and no. A number of school-college cooperative ventures have developed across the country in the last five years (Maeroff, 1982, 1983). The nature of these joint projects ranges from raising teacher education admission requirements (e.g., Pennsylvania State University, University of South Dakota, University of Pittsburgh, University of Cincinnati, University of Georgia, California State College at Bakersfield, University of Tennessee, and the University of Wisconson) to the development of continuing teacher education programs (e.g., Yale-New Haven Teachers Institute, New England Studies Institute at Dartmouth, and the Middle School Math and Science Program at the University of North Carolina at Chapel Hill). The *ad hoc* nature of many of these programs is not always suited to developing permanent and coordinated school-college partnerships. The important point, however, is that there is an exciting mood of experimentation and cooperation on many high school and college campuses. Unfortunately, there is also limited evidence to suggest that some of the nation's universities are withdrawing from teacher preparation activities due to declining enrollments and financial constraints (Ambach, 1982). The development of a strong school-college connection in teacher preparation requires a commitment of resources as well as an expansion of such joint programs from more than just a handful of colleges and universities.

Maeroff (1983) has identified several diverse approaches to the issue of joint school-college responsibility for the preparation of teachers. One approach is to influence the quality of teachers by improving the selection of students to be trained to teach. Raising admission requirements and requiring teacher candidate examinations are two commonly suggested means of making schools of education more selective. Opponents of these measures argue that the pool of qualified candidates would be so few that the demand for new teachers could not be adequately fulfilled. Further, it is asserted that tests may make it more difficult for disadvantaged students to get into the teaching profession. Advocates of this approach recognize these problems but feel that entrance requirements can be raised if there is more effort expended on recruiting good teacher candidates from a variety of academic and cultural backgrounds.

Another vehicle for merging school and college teacher-preparation interests is the laboratory school. Maeroff (1983, p. 32) observes:

All laboratory schools . . . have not been the center of research and development that their sponsors would like to believe. Sometimes such institutions have been little more than low-cost preparatory schools for the precocious children of faculty members and the relationship with the sponsoring college has produced little interaction between professors and teachers. Nevertheless, at their best, laboratory schools have been places where models of elementary or secondary education could be implemented, places where those who work in higher education have been able to join forces with their colleagues at the precollegiate level to perfect the process of schooling.

The "lab" school is not a new idea. In fact, laboratory schools have been the traditional link between higher education and the schools. The renaissance of lab schools shifts the activity from the college campus to the school district. "Mini" lab schools are being developed within regular schools to provide an opportunity for classroom teachers to interact with prospective teachers and professors of education.

The continuing education of teachers is also a topic of mutual school-college concern. The decline in number and quality of secondary and elementary math and science teachers has spurred the development of numerous teacher in-service training programs in these subject areas. Overall school improvement will, however, require strong continuing teacher education projects across the curriculum. Maeroff (1983, p. 33) maintains the quality of schools will increase by "bolstering the skills and morale of those who are already on the job." He warns against falling into the traditional trap of using in-service training as a means of expanding university coffers as well as a quick and easy way for teachers to gain academic credit and quickly move up the salary scale.

Development of the elementary and secondary curriculum is another product of the emerging school-college partnership. The mere act of bringing together schoolteachers and professors in similar subject areas raises important questions on what students should know as they travel from one level of schooling to the next. The Paideia Proposal (Adler, 1982) is a good example of how school and university people can tackle questions regarding academic standards and expectations.

There are some teacher quality issues that have not been adequately addressed by a combined school-college perspective. For example, there is a gap between university research and school practice on the multifaceted relationship between teacher compensation and performance evaluation. Reform proposals pertaining to merit pay, incentive pay, differential pay, and career ladders are being debated in many parts of the country. Unfortunately, there is little evidence to suggest that these issues are being defined and examined through an integrated effort of school districts and schools of education. Another teacher quality issue that deserves multilevel attention is the development of teacher education accreditation programs that measure both quantitative and qualitative aspects of teacher training efforts (Watts, 1983).

A strong connection between schools and colleges is still far from a reality despite heightened interest and a variety of collaborative efforts under way in almost every state. There is a pressing need to develop an inventory of these various cooperative ventures in order to learn from notable successes as well as noble failures. The Carnegie Foundation for the Advancement of Teaching has made a start, by identifying joint projects now in progress. The coordinator of this study, Gene Maeroff (1983, pp. 3-5), has identified five principles that "must be followed if collaborative projects are to succeed." A synthesized list of these principles is as follows:

1. Effective school-college cooperation requires agreement on the existence of common problems by educators at all levels of schooling.
2. Meaningful collaboration requires that the traditional academic "pecking order" be overcome.
3. Joint projects must be sharply focused.
4. Participants in cooperative ventures must be recognized and rewarded.
5. The focus of the projects must be on activities, not machinery.

Perhaps the single most important rule of thumb is the first one. Participants must acknowledge that problems exist and agree on an agenda. A failure to accomplish this task will perpetuate institutional isolation.

EXCELLENCE IN GOVERNANCE

Does the new quest for educational excellence call for different forms of governance? The excellence reports have surprising little to say about governance, but one theme is present to some extent in several reports: that more power and leadership should be exerted by lower levels in the organizational hierarchy. Some reports, such as *Making the Grade* and *Educating Americans for the 21st Century*, call for significant leadership and fiscal initiatives at the national level. No report, however, calls for a basic restructuring of governance in terms of federal, state, and local roles. The National Commission on Excellence in Education (1983), for example, essentially calls for a continuation of the present roles for these respective levels.

Sizer's (1984) report and recommendations on the secondary school level stand out as an indictment of the present organizational structure of the American high school. The predominant hierarchical management model is reinforced, Sizer maintains, by our infatuation with "systems." While he recognizes some virtues of the "hierarchical bureaucracy" model, he concludes (p. 206):

> . . . it has its costs, and these are today paralyzing American education. The structure is getting in the way of children's learning . . . .
> The trend today is toward greater centralization . . . . As state governments be-

come more involved in the regulation of the schools (the inevitable result of their increased assumption of educational costs), the distance between the directors and the directed has become greater, and standardization more pervasive.

Building-Level Leadership

The effective school research over the past several years has identified the pivotal role of the principal as an instructional leader and in setting the tone and climate of the school (Rutter, 1979; Bossert et al., 1982; Edmonds, 1982). In some cases the superintendent is identified as having a significant impact on school improvement (Crim, 1981; Lightfoot, 1981). Boyer's (1983) field studies confirmed these findings and led him to recommend that principals and teachers need far more authority to carry out their responsibilities. "Heavy doses of bureaucracy are stifling creativity in too many schools, and preventing principals and their staffs from exercising their best professional judgment on decisions that properly should be made at the local level" (p. 227). Boyer further recommends that principals be given authority for the selection of teachers for their schools. These types of reforms may seem elementary to those in higher education, where far more local autonomy exists. But at the elementary and secondary levels there is a renewed push for what is termed "school-based governance" where the basic premise is that the school site or building is the most manageable unit for school decision making (Davies, 1981).

Corporate America is also rediscovering the importance of autonomy at the operating level. Peters and Waterman's (1982) review of successful companies concludes (pp. 310-313):

> Regardless of industry or apparent scale needs, virtually all of the companies we talked to placed high value on pushing authority far down the line, and on preserving and maximizing practical autonomy for large numbers of people. . . . Virtually every function in the excellent companies is radically decentralized, down to the division level, at least. . . . We believe that if the manager of a business can control all aspects of his business it will be run a lot better. And we believe that a lot of the efficiencies you are supposed to get from economies of scale are not real at all.

The National Commission on Higher Education Issues (November 1982) voices a "healthy skepticism" over centralization of authority in higher education and expresses its belief that "quality is jeopardized when decisions about academic programs are made by agencies remote from institutions" (p. 2). Their conclusion is strikingly similar to Peters and Waterman's findings as to the best route to corporate success. The commission recommends that governors and legislators review their state-level coordinating or governing mechanisms "to determine whether evolution of the coordinating machinery has led toward lower-common-denominator policies" and "has destroyed the institutional flexibility" required to build excellent programs. The message of this national commission as well as of Sizer (1984), Goodlad (1983a, b), and Boyer (1983) is clear: a greater degree of decentralization will contribute to institutional responsiveness, to quality of people attracted to such working conditions, and to a more meaningful educational environment.

Kerr's 1982 retrospective view of the importance of governance structures in higher education is that "forms of governance make some difference" but not so much as he had once supposed (pp. 175-176). Kerr cites a study financed by the Carnegie Commission which showed no significant variation of performance under different forms of state coordination. Yet Kerr is not unconcerned with issues of governance and its roles in revitalizing higher education. He cites participatory decision modes, where all voices are not only heard but possess veto power, and weakened campus leadership as two serious obstacles to revitalization of higher education.

Blurring of Traditional Boundaries

Many of the excellence reports call for new ties between education and business. School partnerships, businesses' sponsoring of schools, and personnel exchanges are a few of the increasingly common phenomena designed to do several things (Boyer, 1983, pp. 270-278): (1) work with students who are educationally disadvantaged; (2) help gifted students, especially with new technologies; (3) provide opportunities for teacher renewal (e.g., periodic workplace experiences) and for corporate employees to teach; (4) help students take the step from school to work; and (5) aid schools in securing better equipment and other important resources. Yet, Boyer cautions, such help should enrich the school program, not control it. "Business can benefit from aiding education, but this alone should not be the motivation. Larger social purpose should be sensed and the watchword should be learning, not training. . . . Businesses and schools should do what each can do best" (p. 279).

In higher education closer ties between institutions and the corporate world are being sought for a variety of reasons including more industry input into the design of curricula, securing modern equipment, increasing cooperative education opportunities, and obtaining more corporate financial underwriting. Universities and their increasingly important research activities are the focus of attention of several of the excellence reports. The Business–Higher Education Forum identifies improved transfer of technology developed by universities to U.S. industry as critically important to the nation's competitive position. The General Accounting Office has issued a report on the federal government's role in fostering university-industry cooperation (U.S. General Accounting Office, 1983). Such calls for closer university-industry ties, along with the well-publicized research agreements between major universities and leading research-oriented industries, have raised new concerns about institutional autonomy and independence (Bok, 1982b). While these fears have not as yet focused on governance structures of higher education, other than raising difficult questions of governing bodies, the future may bring the issues of business ties and governance closer together. University foundations and other organizational entities established for a variety of purposes, including the fostering of business ties, may acquire greater resources and become more heavily involved in entrepreneurial ventures that raise important issues of control for governing and legislative bodies.

To the extent the excellence reports deal directly with issues of governance, they tend to support the notion of enabling leaders at the lower levels to assume greater levels of responsibility. Yet the call for educational reforms, like any attempt to induce change in organizations, carries with it a tendency for those outside the system not only to prod but also control. The problems cited by many of the reports — incompetency, variability in outputs, poor coordination among educational institutions, etc. — are ready-made targets for those who see as a solution increased managerial controls exerted at higher levels.

Bardach's (1977) description of policy implementation as a process centered on competition for policy control and acted out through a series of "games" is hauntingly familiar to those working at policy levels in higher education institutions and agencies. Bardach maintains that many people possess the mistaken notion that problems such as incompetence, variability, and poor coordination can be solved by designing better management tools and procedures and by giving more power to agencies specializing in such management functions. The result is a "management game" where the players on the "better management" side, such as central budget authorities, auditors, and fiscal committees of the legislature, make demands for better information systems, more audits, more detailed policies and procedures, and so forth. Conservatives and liberals alike view favorably such centralizing tendencies when they believe such means will aid their causes.

One's view of what constitutes excellence influences one's view of appropriate governing structures and prerogatives. Proponents of a productivity perspective, for example, tend to value efficiency and to be sympathetic to a range of internally and externally imposed control systems at central levels. Alternatively, those such as Boyer, Goodlad, and Sizer, who tend to emphasize excellence as a delicate balance of motivating consumers (students) and producers (teachers), stress the importance of governing mechanisms that place responsibility and decision prerogatives at the building or institutional level.

Herein lies the danger in implementing the excellence reports. Will the control structures enacted by legislatures, school boards, and governing bodies prod institutions in constructive ways, or will they inhibit positive responses on the part of operating-level administrators and faculty? Most commentators urge erring on the side of fewer controls and positive incentives. But many central authorities are inherently suspicious of incentives.

STRATEGIC PRIORITIES FOR EXCELLENCE

Noting the array of enrollment and fiscal uncertainties that colleges and universities face, the National Commission on Higher Education Issues (1982) takes the position that quality will attract support — both externally and internally. Furthermore, the commission asserts that "across-the-board" cuts in college and university budgets pose the most important threat to academic quality over the next decade. As the commission notes, the pressures for across-the-board budget cuts are intense in both public and private sectors: "Administrators who take a little from all programs will run into less resistance than will those who try to establish priorities. Yet even over a relatively short period, the practices of the former are far more likely than the latter to threaten the quality of the enterprise" (Chronicle of Higher Education, 1983, p. 10).

The warning is a long-standing and oft-repeated one. Clark Kerr (1982, pp. 160-161), in commenting on the future of the multiuniversity and which institutions will emerge as leaders by the year 2000, cites as one major factor "the extent to which individual institutions make difficult selective changes in academic programs, building on strengths and eliminating weakenesses, or just act 'across-the-board,' as is comparatively easy to do." The same warning can be sounded at a higher level of aggregation, e.g., all universities in the nation. Kerr notes that federal research funds for academic science have been spread more evenly around the country. In 1963 the top twenty universities received 50% of these funds, while today they receive only 40%. Kerr believes that the more even allocation of 60% of these funds among the top forty research universities is reflective of legitimate growth in the scientific talent pool but questions whether the remaining 40% spread among some 900 institutions is reflective of "excellence" or "balance." His concern is that a shift toward balance may continue with consequent erosion of funds available for excellence.

Kerr also calls attention to the fact that in 1963, 75% of new Ph.D.'s came from the 50 leading research universities. By 1982 only 50% of Ph.D.'s were coming from this category. While Kerr does not draw any explicit conclusions from these data, the clear inference is that lesser-quality programs have been producing a greater proportion of Ph.D.'s while higher-quality programs have been trimming back.

The pressures for across-the-board decreases in budgeting practices generally are well documented (Wildavsky, 1975). Recession-driven budget cuts of the 1970s in higher education confirmed these strong tendencies (Bowen and Glenny, 1976; Morgan, 1982). Yet there are exceptions to these practices. In 1981, Great Britain's University Grants Committee allocated highly publicized differential cuts that were based largely on judgments of program quality (Berdahl, 1982). While anecdotal in nature, informal evidence at the institutional level in this country suggests that differential allocations may be far more prevalent than reported in formal studies.

Strategic Choice
The excellence reports, in general, clearly advocate decisions that result in differential allocations rather than "fair shares" practices. This sense of strategic choice is evident in discussions of remedies to declining levels of excellence at both national and institutional levels. The Business–Higher Education Forum, in its report *America's Competitive Challenge* (1983), epitomizes the national strategic-choice argument. The Forum outlines a series of strategic choices that they believe must be made to improve our competitive position in a fast-moving world economy. Those choices involve targeted capital and human investment plans.

Unless the United States improves its ability to compete, unless we develop a comprehensive, coherent, long-term approach, and unless we address our problems from a broad perspective — we fear that dramatic economic revitalization will remain an elusive goal . . . . We are convinced that previous efforts have failed for two principal reasons — an unwillingness to face the true nature and seriousness of the competitive challenge, and an inability to integrate the multitude of specific short-term solutions into a multifaceted, long-term response. [p. iii]

The long-term, planned view of strengthening the economy by improving education has gathered support in circles other than those of national commissions. Ellen Chaffee's insightful review of the strategy literature in various academic fields (page 133 herein) portrays a hierarchical view of strategy. The first level, "linear" strategy, suggests a classically rational view of a relatively closed system, a focus on goals and means, and concentration on internal organizational mechanisims to meet those goals. A second level, "adaptive" strategy, focuses less on goals and more on means and alignment of the organization with the environment. The third level, "interpretive" strategy, focuses on the symbolic interpretation of an organization's relation to its environment. In this concept of strategy, legitimacy and organizational commitment are secured through orienting metaphors and strategic norms.

Colleges, particularly community and comprehensive four-year colleges, tend to adopt the "adaptive" model of strategy — responding to the changing demands or preferences of customers. Marketing approaches to strategy development (Kotler and Murphy, 1981) are characteristically adaptive. Research universities, while adaptive in important respects, tend to adopt interpretive strategies in securing the commitment of top researchers and in attracting students and scholars.

An overall national strategy, and higher education's role in that strategy, as articulated by the Business–Higher Education Forum, is highly linear or rational. Given a national goal of economic competitiveness, the role of higher education is viewed as that of producer of the requisite human resources to drive the economic machine.

Yet strategic choice, whether linear, adaptive, or interpretive, implies some degree of differentiation within and among institutions. Institutional diversity has characterized American higher education and is still hailed as a desirable virtue in its own right irrespective of strategic choice. But persistent pressures for uniformity exist, ranging from legislative and coordinating or governing board tendencies to treat all constituents alike to more subtle but powerful forces of "academic drift." Declining numbers of students and economic hard times have also tended to push many institutions to adopt comprehensive strategies and overlapping missions, offering a wide array of programs to attract as many students as possible (Morgan and Newell, 1981).

In the National Commission on Higher Education Issues report (September 1982), the following recommendation, reflecting the need for strategic choice and differentiation, appeared (pp. 13-14):

Higher education must take affirmative steps to ensure that differences among institutional categories are more precisely articulated. . . . In the past, higher education leaders have often paid lip service to diversity, all the while homogenization among institutions moved apace as if a single educational ideal existed. Diversity in the future must be strengthened, built around distinctly differentiated missions of doctoral granting research universities, comprehensive colleges and universities, liberal arts colleges, community colleges, and specialized institutions . . . . Every category of institution must strive for quality within the bounds of its categorical mission and individual institutions must not attempt to emulate other categories.

Kerr (1982) concludes that universities have not changed much since the 1870s when the beginnings of their multiple purposes were established. The training of a highly skilled elite in a wide range of professions and the production of research and new knowledge have remained the central purposes of "multiuniversities." Comprehensive four-year colleges and regional universities, on the other hand, have been caught in transition. Hodgkinson's (1971) study of over 1,200 institutions reported significant increases in state-controlled colleges and universities offering the M.A. and Ph.D. between 1949 and 1966. Dunham's (1969) study of state colleges and regional universities characterized this same period as one of astounding growth and rapid change in function. As Dunham points out, one of the ironies of this period of transition is that a first-class teachers college may have become a third-class university.

The slowed growth and fiscal stresses of the 1970s, followed by an uncertain enrollment and fiscal outlook in the 1980s, have caught many institutions in midstream in their development. Some comprehensive four-year institutions are moving heavily into vocational training programs in response to shifting markets. Yet they retain earlier cores of teacher training and partially developed graduate or graduate-preparatory disciplines in the arts and sciences. Should the fledgling university that inherited program growth across a wide variety of academic fronts in the 1960s and early 1970s attempt to maintain its breadth? Or should strategic choices be made to focus its resources? Are regional universities primarily regional in nature and therefore obligated to offer program breadth and access?

Similar dilemmas are now a prominent focus of debate in community college circles. Gleazer (1980) has argued for community colleges providing an even broader range of services to their communities. Cohen and Brawer (1982), on the other hand, argue for a more focused mission centered on general education. Strategic choice of mission has become the issue of the 1980s for community colleges as they struggle for a clear sense of identity (McCartan, 1984).

The excellence reports, particularly those of the National Commission on Higher Education Issues and the National Commission on Excellence in Education, suggest that a focusing and narrowing of purpose is needed in American higher education. This view suggests the difficulty, if not impossibility, of achieving excellence in everything we undertake. In fact, the more we are willing to take on, at least after a certain point, the less likely are our chances of achieving excellence in selected areas or across the board. This assessment is similar to Porter's (1981) findings in identifying successful strategies of competitive winners in business: "differentiation," or providing a distinctive product, and "focus," or securing a segment of the market.

What is the likelihood of colleges and universities concentrating more resources on fewer areas? Several authors suggest that fiscal and enrollment crises increase the likelihood of radical surgery in academia. Keller (1983), citing examples of the University of Washington and the University of Minnesota, argues that such conditions compel reevaluations as never before. Wildavsky (1982) is in agreement, citing four decisive arguments employed to make or prohibit major changes: (1) there is not time; (2) it is unnatural; (3) God prohibits it; and (4) there is no money. Kerchner and Schuster (1982), reviewing six cases of response to organizational adversity, argue that astute leadership can transform "opaque" crises into "manifest" crises and widen latitude to make changes that would otherwise encounter overwhelming resistance.

Keller (1983) suggests that the stimulants for change in colleges and universities derive from three sources: (1) a crisis in finances, enrollments, or quality; (2) strong pressure from outside the organization; and (3) vigorous institutional leadership. Many institutions have been experiencing the first source for some time, and many others are facing such prospects. The second source is gathering momentum in part as a result of the excellence reports and public pressures for change. The third source, leadership, is often cited as being in short supply. Kerr (1982, pp. 177-181) cites the weakened position of institutional leadership and the increasing level of frustration leaders experience in working through all of the checks and balances as detrimental to positive changes in higher education. Kerr asserts that leadership does matter and that most of the successful new policies in higher education have come from the efforts of top leadership. The research on effective schools, a prominent movement in the public school literature, repeatedly identifies the role of building-level leadership as critical (Mackenzie, 1983). The elusive and slippery variable of leadership and its role in educational change seems to be emerging, once again, as a prominent policy issue of the 1980s.

CONCLUSIONS
Reading the excellence reports of the 1980s provides more frustration than fulfillment in the pursuit of an operational definition of educational excellence. Despite the absence of definition, the ideal of excellence most likely will govern local, state, and national education policy for the remainder of this decade. Throughout this chapter, we have tried to show how the theme of excellence is currently influencing decisions involving educational purposes, institutional governance, secondary-postsecondary linkages, and the allocation of public resources. At least three other questions deserve some attention First, what significant issues are being overlooked in the current educational reform movement? Second, what are some of the possible long-term policy trends evolving

from the excellence reports of the 1980s? Third, what are the implications for future research?

Overlooked Issues

In reference to the first question, our attention immediately turns to the relationship between excellence in education and in institutional staff. Many of the excellence reports stress the need to attract and retain high-quality teachers and administrators. Raising salaries and providing financial incentives for good instructional performance are the two most commonly proposed solutions to this problem. Monetary incentives alone, however, will not induce the desired performance changes. Underlying the good teacher–good education theory is a belief that genuine excellence depends upon people who are committed to improving education (Sizer, 1984). Thus teachers' compensation is just one aspect of employment relations that needs to be modified. Peters and Waterman (1982) identify the "productivity through people" concept as one of eight key factors in the development of successful corporations. Surprisingly, they hardly mention the use of monetary incentives to improve individual worker quality. Instead, they emphasize the need to create working conditions which communicate a philosophy that says "respect the individual, make people winners, let them stand out, treat people as adults" (p. 277). However, Peters and Waterman recognize that management cannot magically enrich and stimulate the worker's world solely by changing employment rules and policies (p. 242):

> As there is no easy way that just a few programs will hold and bring about fundamental change, so also there is no reason to expect any particular technique to have an effective life of more than a few years. Most of the excellent companies do have MBO systems, and they do have quality circles, and they probably have tried team building, and maybe they still use all of these. But they have lots more. We were astounded, as we did our research, by the sheer numbers of people programs we encountered and the frequency with which they were replenished or refurbished. And these programs are neither lip service nor gimmickry. We found rich systems of monetary incentives; but we expected that. We also discovered an incredible array of nonmonetary incentives and an amazing variety of experimental or newly introduced programs. No one device — even in the best institutions — is likely to be effective indefinitely.

Changing the working conditions of teachers involves a wide range of issues, including career ladders, differentiated staffing, in-service training, and instructional technology as well as societal attitudes toward teaching as a profession and the level of professionalism accorded teachers. The work of teaching needs to be viewed in this comprehensive framework. The works of Sizer, Goodlad, and Boyer emphasize this broader framework, yet their reports have received less attention than those reports prescribing a narrower range of remedies. There is also a need for more experimentation in teacher compensation and evaluation systems, along with other "people programs."

Another critical issue largely ignored in the excellence reports is the school-college connection as it pertains to college admission standards, curricular coordination, and teacher training. Yet higher education's most powerful contribution to the pursuit of excellence might be that of "inculcating in the minds of future doctors, engineers, lawyers, scientists, clergy, social workers, business executives, economists, politicians, journalists and reformers that they, not just graduates of schools of education, have the obligation and opportunity to be lifelong teachers. For if education is a ubiquitous need, all of us must partici-pate in the process of learning and teaching" (Bailey, 1976, p. 111). The Nation-al Commission on Excellence in Education echoes this thought in its plea for the cultivation of a "learning society." Unfortunately, this aspect of education-al excellence is receiving less serious attention. Most reform proposals focus on institutions that are primarily responsible for delivering education, not on such an amorphous target as a "learning society."

Long-Term Policy Trends

Three of the policy trends emerging from the excellence reports of the early 1980s have gathered considerable support and seem destined to remain near the top of the education policy agenda indefinitely. First, the school-college con-nection will continue to tighten, owing to common financial interests and the growing recognition that the relative success or failure of each sector is de-pendent on the other. Second, education-business collaborative efforts will be pursued for the same reasons. Third, education will continue to be a labor-in-tensive enterprise; but traditional concepts about the "work" of teaching will be reshaped as emerging information-technology breakthroughs continue and as career ladder and other workplace policies are pursued.

Implications for Further Research

The agenda for future research will vary somewhat depending upon which per-spective of educational excellence is emphasized. For example, a productivity approach generally will seek conceptual models and methodological tools to quantify input-output relations in the educational process. The most common type of research on educational input-output relationships has been the use of productivity techniques to determine costs per student. These measures have a tendency to be unidimensional and inappropriate for the multiproduct nature of educational institutions. As Gold (1971, p. 36) observes: "Juxtaposing the comparative magnitudes of specified inputs and outputs reveals nothing more than the level of, or changes in, the given ratio. To evaluate such quantitative findings, the variables should be derived from an analytical framework which encompasses all of the inputs and outputs of the system and provides a theory of how it functions."

Underlying "strategic priority" decision making is the need for fine-tuned measures of institutional performance. More research is needed to develop ana-lytical techniques which assess a variety of institutional performance dimen-sions and can be incorporated effectively into present management information systems (Lindsay, 1982).

There are other research issues which transcend several of the previously identified perspectives on educational excellence. Research pertinent to the effects of instructional time on educational outcomes, for example, has implications for curriculum development (content approach), teacher training (producer-consumer quality approach), and school staffing (productivity approach). The nature of the educational process is so complex that an eclectic approach to researching excellence is virtually mandatory.

We see three other highly fertile areas for further research. First, research is needed to establish more precisely the connection between education policy and educational outcomes. Coombs (1983, p. 608) notes:

> For basic research to be policy-relevant, it is necessary to identify variables that are alterable through policy change and that will also bring about the kinds of educational outcomes we seek. Until we have a much better idea of how interventions are going to affect such areas as academic achievement, student conduct, school learning, or access to continued schooling, policy analysis is likely to continue to be a sometimes futile exercise.

This type of policy research is particularly relevant for the study of such issues as raising college admission standards, promoting business-education partnerships, and changing teacher training and certification requirements. McLaughlin and Berman's (1978) study of change and innovation in education organizations is a step in this direction.

Research on employment policy in education needs to be intensified and expanded. Reform proposals like master teacher plans, career ladders, and merit pay rely fundamentally on the construction and implementation of a sound performance appraisal system. Historical and comparative studies of performance-based teacher compensation and evaluation systems need to be conducted and widely disseminated. A significant amount of state and local experimentation in this area is already under way. The transferability of faculty evaluation systems in colleges and universities to secondary schools also needs greater research attention.

Finally, a renewed concentration of research on leadership in schools and colleges seems inevitable. At the elementary and secondary levels, the "school effectiveness" research places a great deal of importance on the principal's ability to manage an orderly climate with clear educational goals and high performance expectations. The next logical step in this research is to determine how principals effectively accomplish this feat. At the postsecondary level, calls for strategic definitions and "better" leadership must take into account the ambiguous world that college presidents face. Cohen and March's (1974) call for the development of a "new theory of management" which reflects the uncertainties, ambiguities, and complexity that presidents face is now a decade old. Research has begun to identify such complexities but has not given the practitioner much help to date, other than sympathy.

REFERENCES

Adler, M. J. *The Paideia Proposal: An Educational Manifesto.* New York: Macmillan, 1982.

Ambach, G. The high school/college connection: A state perspective. *Change,* 1982, *14,* 22-25, 53.

Astin, A. W. Contradictions in American higher education. *Proceedings of the American Philosophic Society,* 1982(a), *126,* 6-10.

Astin, A. W. The American freshman, 1966-1981: Some implications for educational policy and practice. Paper prepared for the National Commission on Excellence in Education, May 1982(b).

Bailey, S. *The Purposes of Education.* Bloomington, Ind.: Phi Delta Kappa, 1976.

Bakalis, M. J. Power and purpose in American education. *Phi Delta Kappan,* 1983, *65,* 7-13.

Bardach, E. *The Implementation Game.* Cambridge, Mass.: MIT Press, 1977.

Barry, P. Interview: A talk with A. Bartlett Giamatti. *College Board Review,* 1982, No. 123, 2-7.

Becker, G. S. *Human Capital: A Theoretical and Empirical Analysis with Special Reference to Education.* National Bureau of Economic Research, General Series No. 80. New York: Columbia University Press, 1964.

Berdahl, R. Great Britain: Cutting the budget, resetting the priorities. *Change,* 1982, *14,* 38-43.

Bodkin, J., Dimancescu, D., and Stata, R. *Global Stakes: The Future of High Technology in America,* Cambridge, Mass.: Ballinger Press, 1982.

Bok, D. Balancing responsibility and innovation. *Change,* 1982(a), *14,* 16-25.

Bok, D. *Beyond the Ivory Tower: Social Responsibilities of the Modern University.* Cambridge, Mass.: Harvard University Press, 1982(b).

Boorstin, D. J. *Democracy and Its Discontents.* New York: Vintage Books, 1974.

Bossert, S. T., Dwyer, D. C., Rowan, B., and Lee, G. V. The instructional management role of the principal. *Educational Administration Quarterly,* 1982, *18,* 34-64.

Bowen, F. M., and Glenny, L. A. *State Budgeting for Higher Education: State Fiscal Stringency and Public Higher Education.* Berkeley: University of California, Center for Research and Development in Higher Education, 1976.

Bowen, H. R. *Investment in Learning: The Individual and Social Value of American Higher Education.* San Francisco: Jossey-Bass, 1977.

Boyer, E. L. *High School: A Report on Secondary Education in America.* The Carnegie Foundation for the Advancement of Teaching. New York: Harper & Row, 1983.

Brookover, W. D., Schweitzer, J. H., Schneider, J. M., Beady, C. H., Flood, P. K., Wisenbaker, J. M. Elementary school social climate and student achievement. *American Educational Research Journal,* 1978, *15,* 301-18.

Business-Higher Education Forum. *America's Competitive Challenge: The Need for a National Response,* Washington, D.C., April 1983.

Butler, E. P. Higher education's role in revitalizing America's work force. *Educational Record,* 1983, *64,* 26-33.

Carnegie Commission on Higher Education. *Quality and Equality: New Levels of Federal Responsibility for Higher Education,* New York: McGraw-Hill, December 1968.

Carnegie Commission on Higher Education. *Higher Education: Who Pays? Who Benefits? Who Should Pay?* New York: McGraw-Hill, June 1973.

Carnegie Council on Policy Studies in Higher Education. *Next Steps for the 1980s in Student Financial Aid.* San Francisco: Jossey-Bass, 1979.

Carnevale, A. P. Higher education's role in the American economy. *Education Record,* 1983, *64,* 6-17.

Chaffee, E. E. The concept of strategy. Page 133, herein.

Chronicle of Higher Education. Panel assails across-the-board budget cuts. *Chronicle of Higher Education*, January 5, 1983.

Cohen, A. M., and Brawer, F. B. *The American Community College*. San Francisco: Jossey-Bass, 1982.

Cohen, M. Effective schools: What the research says. *Today's Education*, 1981, *70*, 466-496.

Cohen, M. D., and March, J. G. *Leadership and Ambiguity: The American College President*. New York: McGraw-Hill, 1974.

The College Board. *Academic Preparation for College: What Students Need to Know and Be Able to Do*. New York: College Board, 1983.

Commission on the Reorganization of Secondary Education. *Cardinal Principles of Education*. Bulletin 1918, No. 35. Washington, D.C.: Government Printing Office, 1918.

Coombs, F. Educaition policy. In Stuart S. Nagel (ed.), *Encyclopedia of Policy Studies*. New York: Marcel Dekker, 1983.

Crim, A. A. A community of believers. *Daedalus*, 1981, *110*, 145-162.

Cusick, P. A. *The Egalitarian Ideal and the American High School*. New York: Longman, 1983.

David, E. E., Jr. The corporation on campus: Supporting research with a commercial mission. *Change*, 1982, *14*, 26-29.

Davies, D. Citizen participation in decision making in the schools. In D. Davies (ed.), *Communities and Their Schools*. New York: McGraw-Hill, 1981.

Davies, G. K., and Slevin, K. F. Babel or opportunity: Recent reports on education. *The College Board Review*, No. 130 (Winter 1983-84), 18-21.

Denison, E. F. *Accounting for United States Economic Growth, 1929-1969*. Washington, D.C.: Brookings Institution, 1974.

Denison, E. F. *Sources of Economic Growth in the U.S. and the Alternatives Before Us*. New York: Committee on Economic Development, 1962.

Dunham, E. A. *Colleges of the Forgotten Americas: A Profile of State Colleges and Regional Universities*. The Carnegie Commission on Higher Education. New York: McGraw-Hill, 1969.

Edgerton, R. A college education up to beating the Japanese. *Bulletin of the American Association for Higher Education*, 1983, *35*, 3-7.

Edmonds, R. R. Programs for school improvement: An overview. *Educational Leadership*, 1982, *40*, 4-11.

Education Forum. *America's Competitive Challenge: The Need for a National Response*. Washington, D.C.: Business–Higher Education Forum, April 1983.

Elam, S. M. The Gallup education surveys: Impressions of a poll watcher. *Phi Delta Kappan*, 1983, *64*, 26-32.

Feistritzer, C. E. *The Condition of Teaching: A State by State Analysis*. Princeton, N.J.: Carnegie Foundation for the Advancement of Teaching, 1983.

Finn, C. E., Jr. The drive for educational excellence: Moving toward a public consensus. *Change*, 1983, *15*, 14-22.

Freeman, R. B. *The Market for College-Training Manpower*. Cambridge, Mass.: Harvard University Press, 1971.

Freeman, R. B., and Holloman, J. H. The declining value of college going. *Change*, 1975, *7*, 24-31.

Gardner, J. W. *Excellence: Can We Be Equal and Excellent Too?* New York: Harper & Row, 1961.

Gleazer, E. J., Jr. *The Community College: Values, Vision and Vitality*. Washington, D.C.: American Association of Community and Junior Colleges, 1980.

Gold, B. *Explorations in Managerial Economics*. New York: Basic Books, 1971.

Goodlad, J. I. A study of schooling: Some findings and hypotheses. *Phi Delta Kappan*,

1983(a), *64*, 465-70.

Goodlad, J. I. A study of schooling: Some implications for school improvement. *Phi Delta Kappan*, 1983(b), *64*, 552-558.

Goodlad, J. I. *A Place Called School: Prospects for the Future*. New York: McGraw-Hill, 1984.

Gross, T. Reviewing the reports: Finding a blueprint for quality education. *Change*, 1983, *15*, 34-37.

Hargadon, F. Tests and college admissions. *American Psychologist*, 1981, *36*, 1112-1119.

Hargadon, F. From school to college. Testimony for the National Commission on Excellence in Education, Chicago, June 23, 1982.

Hartnett, R., and Feldmesser, D. College admissions testing and the myth of selectivity. *AAHE Bulletin*, 1980, *32*, 7.

Harvard Committee. *General Education in a Free Society*. Cambridge, Mass.: Harvard University Press, 1945.

Harvard Educational Review. Symposium: The Paideia proposal. *Harvard Educational Review*, 1983, *53*, 377-411.

Harvard Educational Review. Symposium on the year of the reports: Responses from the educational community. *Harvard Educational Review*, 1984, *54*, 1-31.

Hodgkinson, H. L. *Institutions in Transition*. New York: McGraw-Hill, 1971.

Hofstadter, R. *Anti-intellectualism in American Life*. New York: Vintage Books, 1962.

Howe, H. II *The Value of College: A Non-Economist's View*. New York: Ford Foundation, 1975.

Hoy, J. C., and Bernstein, M. H. (eds.). *Business and Academia: Partners in New England's Economic Revival*. Hanover, N.H.: University Press of New England, 1981.

Hoy, J. C., and Bernstein, M. H. (eds.). *Financing Higher Education: The Public Investment*. Boston: Auburn House, 1982(a).

Hoy, J. C., and Bernstein, M. H. (eds.). *New England's Vital Resource: The Labor Force*. Washington, D.C.: American Council on Educatio, 1982(b).

Husén, T. A cross-national perspective on assessing quality of learning. Paper presented to the National Commission on Excellence in Education, February 25, 1982.

Husén, T. Are standards in U.S. schools really lagging behind those in other countries? *Phi Delta Kappan*, 1983, *64*, 445-461.

Jencks, C. L. Foreword to *Quality Education: Achievement and Equity*. Proceedings of the Regional Forum, San Francisco, December 1981.

Judge, H. *American Graduate Schools of Education: A View from Abroad*. New York: Ford Foundation, 1982.

Juster, F. T. (ed.). *Education, Income and Human Behavior*. New York: McGraw-Hill, 1975.

Keller, G. *Academic Strategy: The Management Revolution in American Higher Education*. Baltimore: Johns Hopkins Press, 1983.

Kerchner, C. T., and Schuster, J. H. The uses of crisis: Taking the tide at the flood. *Review of Higher Education*, 1982, *5*, 121-141.

Kerr, C. *The Uses of the University*. 3d ed. Cambridge, Mass.: Harvard University Press, 1982.

Kotler, P., and Murphy, R. Strategic planning for higher education. *Journal of Higher Education*, 1981, *52*, 470-489.

Levin, H., and Rumberger, R. The low-skill future of high tech. *Technology Review*, 1983, *86*, 18-21.

Levin, H. M. *Education and Work*. Program Report No. 82-B8. Stanford, Calif.: Institute for Research on Educational Finance and Governance, Stanford University, 1982.

Lightfoot, S. L. Portraits of exemplary secondary schools, *Daedalus*, 1981, *110*, 17-38.

Lindsay, A. W. Institutional performance in higher education: The efficiency dimension. *Review of Educational Research*, 1982, *52*, 175-199.

Lynton, E. A. The economic impact of higher education. *Journal of Higher Education*, 1983, *54*, 693-708.

McCartan, A. The community college mission: Present challenges and future visions. *Journal of Higher Education*, 1984, *54*, 676-692.

Mackenzie, D. Research for school improvement: An appraisal of some recent trends. *Educational Researcher*, 1983, *12*, 5-17.

McLaughlin, M., and Berman, P. *Federal Programs Supporting Educational Change*. Santa Monica, Calif.: Rand Corporation, 1978.

McPherson, M. S., and Schapiro, M. O. Economic public policy implications of an "outmoded" work force. *Educational Record*, 1983, *64*, 50-55.

Maeroff, G. I. *Don't Blame the Kids: The Trouble with America's Public Schools*. New York: McGraw-Hill, 1982.

Maeroff, G. I. *School and College: Partnerships in Education*. Princeton, N.J.: Carnegie Foundation, 1983.

Morgan, A. W. College and university planning in an era of contraction. *Higher Education*, 1982, *11*, 553-566.

Morgan, A. W., and Newell, L. J. Strategic planning at a small college: To be comprehensive or to be distinctive? *Planning for Higher Education*, 1981, *9*, 29-33.

National Association of Secondary School Principals. *College Admissions: New Requirements by the State Universities*. Reston, Va., 1982.

National Commission on Excellence in Education. *A Nation at Risk*. Washington, D.C., April 1983.

National Commission on Higher Education Issues. *Action to Advance Quality in Higher Education, Draft Edition*. Washington, D.C.: American Council in Higher Education, September 1982.

National Commission on Higher Education Issues. *To Strengthen Quality in Higher Education: Summary Recommendations of the National Commission on Higher Education Issues*. Washington, D.C.: American Council on Education, November 1982.

National Science Board Commission on Precollege Education in Mathematics, Science and Technology. *Educating Americans for the 21st Century*. Washington, D.C., 1983.

Passow, A. H. *Secondary Education Reform: Retrospect and Prospect*. New York: Teachers College, 1976.

Perkinson, H. J. *The Imperfect Panacea: American Faith in Education, 1865-1965*. New York: Random House, 1968.

Peters, T. J., and Waterman, R. H. *In Search of Excellence: Lessons from America's Best-Run Companies*. New York: Harper & Row, 1982.

Porter, M. The contributions of industrial organization to strategic management. *Academy of Mangement Review*, 1981, *6*, 609-620.

Ravitch, D. Forgetting the questions: The problem of educational reform. *American Scholar*, 1981, *50*, 329-40.

Ravitch, D. The Paideia Proposal in perspective. *Harvard Educational Review*, 1983(a), *53*, 380-383.

Ravitch, D. *The Troubled Crusade: American's Education 1945-1980*. New York: Basic Books, 1983(b).

Resnick, L. B., and Resnick, D. P. Standards, curriculum, and performance: An historical and comparative perspective. A report to the National Commission on Excellence in Education, August 31, 1982.

Rohlen, T. P. *Japan's High Schools*. Berkeley: University of California Press, 1983.

Royster, V. Watching the pendulum in education. *American Scholar*, 1983, *52*, 193-204.

Rutter, M., Maughan, B., Mortimer, P., Ouston, J., and Smith, A. *Fifteen Thousand Hours: Secondary Schools and Their Effects on Children*. Cambridge, Mass.: Harvard University Press, 1979.

Samuelson, R. J. From crisis to crisis. *National Journal*, 1983, *15*, 1424-1456.

Sarason, S. B. *The Culture of the School and the Problem of Change*. 2d ed. Boston: Allyn & Bacon, 1982.

Schultz, T. W. *Investment in Human Capital*. New York: Free Press, 1971.

Sizer, T. R. High school reform: The need for engineering. *Phi Delta Kappan*, 1983, *64*, 679-683.

Sizer, T. R. *Horace's Compromise: The Dilemma of the American High School*. Boston: Houghton Mifflin, 1984.

Southern Regional Education Board Task Force on Higher Education and the Schools. *Meeting the Needs for Quality in the South*, June 1981.

Task Force on Education for Economic Growth. *Action for Excellence*. Denver: Education Commission of the States, June 1983.

Task Force on Federal Elementary and Secondary Education Policy. *Making the Grade*. New York: Twentieth Century Fund, 1983.

Thomas, J. A. Governmental cooperation to improve efficiency in education. In S. M. McMurrin (ed.), *The Schools and the Challenge of Innovation*. New York: McGraw-Hill, 1969.

Tomlinson, T. M. The troubled years: An interpretive analysis of public schooling since 1950. *Phi Delta Kappan*, 1981, *62*, 373-376.

Trow, M. Reflections on the transition from mass to universal higher education. *Daedalus*, 1970, *99*, 1-42.

U.S. General Accounting Office. *The Federal Role in Fostering University-Industry Cooperation*. Washington, D.C.: U.S. Government Printing Office, 1983.

Watts, D. Four views of NCATE's role and function. *Phi Delta Kappan*, 1983, *64*, 646-649.

Wildavksy, A. *Budgeting: A Comparative Theory of the Budgetary Process*. Boston: Little, Brown, 1975.

Wildavksy, A. On the uses of adversity in higher education. *Review of Higher Education*, 1982, *6*, 19-28.

Willie, C. V. Educating students who are good enough: Is excellence an excuse to exclude? *Change*, 1982, *14*, 16-21.

Wise, A. Why educational policies often fail: The hyper-rationalization hypothesis. In J. V. Baldridge and T. Deal (eds.), *The Dynamics of Organizational Change in Education*. Berkeley, Calif.: McCutchan, 1983.

Zald, M. N., and Wamsley, G. L. *The Political Economy of Public Organizations*. Lexington, Mass.: Heath, 1973.

BEYOND BACKGROUND MUSIC:
Historical Research on Admissions and Access in Higher Education

John R. Thelin, *The College of William and Mary*

At several major university libraries Hugh Hawkins' 1960 work, *Pioneer*, is shelved among the Western Americana collection. This would be appropriate if the book dealt with the settlement of the Great Plains or how the West was won. However, on closer inspection one discovers it is a carefully researched study of the innovations Johns Hopkins University contributed to American higher education in the late 19th century. Little wonder, then, that historians of higher education harbor some fears that their works are misread, misplaced, and misunderstood — assuming they are read at all.

This chapter responds to those qualms by examining the place of historical writing, methods, and logic within the study of higher education. A primary question is whether historians are equal participants in the concert of scholars who systematically analyze colleges and universities. Or, rather, are historians now merely providing the background music which most higher education researchers hear but fail to absorb?

To explore these questions this essay first will review some major trends in concepts and analytical strategies which historical studies have made available to research on higher education over the past quarter-century. Second, these broad contours will be examined for signs of cross-fertilization with other disciplines, especially the social sciences. Third, the essay will include a search for ways in which historical research and thinking on higher education may have shaped contemporary practices and policies in American colleges and universi-

Research for this project was made possible in part by a grant from The College of William and Mary. I owe special thanks to two people who worked with me on the manuscript: A. S. T. Blackburn provided timely information and insights on admissions at selective colleges, and Marsha V. Krotseng assisted with research and editing.

349

ties. Finally, the concluding section will discuss the problems involved in formulating an agenda for higher education research which acknowledges both the
strengths and limits of historical studies since 1960.

These ground rules already suggest that a modest proposal runs the risk of
growing into an overly ambitious project. Hence, to build in both a focus and a
constraint, the essay will pay particular attention to one strand of historical research in higher education: namely, the study of admissions and access. In sum,
discussion of historiography since 1960 will be monitored carefully to see how
key works have altered the perspectives, data collection, and research questions
in one significant (albeit limited) area — admissions and access — within the
sprawl of higher education as a field of systematic inquiry.

An essay review at worst degenerates into an indulgent *Festschrift*, plagued
by inflated homage to writers and works. Here the assignment is at once more
troublesome and more interesting than providing congratulations because this
essay heeds well the thoughtful comments, criticisms, and disagreements which
historians of higher education have about their works. To whet the reader's ap-
petite for candor and controversy, one need look no further than one
historian's recent statement: "The past decade has been a strange and somewhat disappointing one for historians of American higher education" (Leslie,
1980, p. 3). But this intriguing point jumps ahead of the story. The first order
of business is to go back about twenty-five years to unravel and reconstruct the
ways in which historical research in higher education came to be characterized
by *extension*, *criticism*, *cross-fertilization*, and *revision*. It is no less than the
complex story of decades of interesting scholarship and the diffusion of
knowledge.

THE EXTENSION MANIFESTO: BUILDING THE BASE

The exciting development in the history of higher education during the early
1960s was what might be termed an "extension manifesto"; i.e., those who
studied the past of colleges and universities were encouraged to extend the
study of a particular campus to encompass the wider sphere of social context
and change. Extension of subject matter *per se* also brought about a shift in the
historian's scope and tone. In short, the challenge was to make organizational
chronicles part of social history. As Wilson Smith wrote in his landmark 1961
article, "The New Historian of American Education" (p. 136):

> A new kind of historian is coming to the old problem of telling how man has learned
> and taught. Although he may be new to the field of educational history, he is not a
> newcomer to the writing of history. Earlier he may have been devoted to general his-
> tory or to social or intellectual history. From whatever interest, however, he is one
> who has the opportunity to rejuvenate an old subject with novel inquiries.

The two-step process was that use of broad historical research sources would
reinforce a broad frame of reference. Put another way, an extended notion of
institutional history would lead to increasingly critical questions of significance

and interpretation in the history of higher education. An institution still could be the object of study, but according to Smith, "It is now the external story of education that the new historian wants most to tell so that he may more skillfully and critically display the inner structure of institutions" (p. 137).

Implicit in the manifesto was an assault on the so-called "house history" genre. The complaint was that all too often the history of higher education was limited to institutional chronicles which told the official, predictable, and sanitized story of a particular college or university. The formula was to chronicle the story of Alma Mater from its founding (usually with a chapter on "humble beginnings") through decades of struggle to eventual success and triumph. These works often were commissioned by institutional officials to coincide with a campus anniversary, whether it be a centennial or a sesquicentennial. Authors of house histories seldom asked searching questions about the topic and relied heavily on official documents and records. Nor was there any guarantee that authors were educated as serious, professional historians, since long-time familiarity with the campus often was the first priority. Such commissioned works usually were tedious, with little interest to audiences beyond the institution's alumni and immediate campus constituency. For Smith, the rejuvenation of the history of higher education meant in large measure the rescue of the topic from the hackneyed house-history approach. If the extension manifesto were successful, the result would be a new generation of scholars who would study colleges and universities without being hamstrung by the orthodoxy of the "old grad" or "true believer."

Smith's landmark article was both an invitation and an acknowledgment. He was careful to point readers to exemplary work in the history of education which already had been published or was in progress. This acknowledgment is important because, as shall be discussed later, in subsequent decades the advocates of new, critical dimensions in the history of higher education would take little favorable notice of predecessors. Thus the Smith article signaled some healthy achievements as well as provided a call to action with some blueprints for further research. Here was both a precedent and a rationale for extending the scope, tone, sources, and context of the history of higher education.

Wilson Smith practiced what he preached. Along with Richard Hofstadter he compiled and edited a two-volume anthology, *American Higher Education: A Documentary History* (1961). The aim was to fill a void — the absence of readily available primary sources and documents dealing with the major trends and essential controversies in the history of American higher education. To reaffirm the new spirit of scholarship, the editors noted: "We are living in an age of heightened educational criticism and increasing interest in the educational past. There is every reason to believe that among general students of American history a minor boom in studying the history of education is beginning that will eventually fill many of the gaps in our present knowledge" (Hofstadter and Smith, 1961, p. vii).

The concentration of disparate documents from many institutions served to provide an alternative to single-campus insularity. Documents ranged from royal charters to irate correspondence over contested faculty appointments, from familiar and successful campuses to some unfamiliar and unsuccessful pleas before state legislatures. Gone was the facile excuse among institutional historians that there were no convenient anthologies of documents by which to compare or contrast local trends. Editors Hofstadter and Smith made clear the focus of their anthology: historical trends in the structure of colleges and universities, with considerable attention to legal and political episodes. And they stated in a straightforward manner that their anthology had little on such topics as student life or academic and professional organizations. A decade later, some scholars would point out other limits in the editing — namely, relatively little attention to conflicts and divergences in higher education and heavy reliance on official documents. The documentary history was still in the domain of history written "from the top down." Nonetheless, the anthology represented a substantial breakthrough in providing incipient scholars with basic documents which attested to the complexity of higher education's structural past.

At the same time, other historians were scouring hundreds of campus archives and gleaning secondary sources to respond to Wilson Smith's invitation to write the history of higher education intertwined with social history. By the early 1960s one had at least three lively single-volume generic histories of American higher education: Ernest Earnest's *Academic Procession* (1953), John S. Brubacher and Willis Rudy's *Higher Education in Transition* (1958), and Frederick Rudolph's *The American College and University: A History* (1962).

These works were traditional in the sense that there was a chronological ordering to issues and fidelity to the historian's role as storyteller. Important to note was the tone: part of the complexity of higher education's past was its blend of gravity and folly, significa and trivia. The extracurriculum, ranging from literary societies to riots over rancid butter in dining commons, warranted attention along with solemnities of board meetings. In fact, Rudolph's chapter on the 19th-century extracurriculum led to the argument that many of the now-familiar aspects of the official and formal institution evolved from persistent-yet-prohibited student activities. A historian had used numerous case studies and specific examples to show how students "voted with their feet." This was an example of primary-source and secondary research across many institutions which stimulated a rethinking of organizational behavior. For the institutional historian who wishes to explain the development of such officially approved services and activities as libraries, varsity sports, seminars, science laboratories, and modern language study, Rudolph's work sends the message that one must delve outside the formal records into the elusive and informal world of student life.

As was the case with Wilson Smith and Richard Hofstadter, Frederick Rudolph emphasized his debt to earlier scholars. With characteristic good humor and modesty, Rudolph (1962, p. 497) wrote in his bibliographic essay:

There is a notion current among historians that educational history is a recent interest among them and that this interest promises to save the subject from professional educators and old grads, to whose care they have heretofore been content to leave it. This view of the matter is approaching the level of myth, even though the first significant volumes on the history of higher education in the United States were the work of professional historians under the guidance of that early master of the research seminar, Herbert Baxter Adams of Johns Hopkins.

Indeed, probably the most underappreciated contribution which Rudolph made was his resurrection of numerous forgotten works which represented sound scholarship in the history of higher education. So the weakness of historical writing on higher education, circa 1960, was not simply the absence of good research, but also the neglect and ignorance of good scholarship from earlier periods. Rejuvenation and rescue also included rediscovery.

The paradox of rejuvenation for the history of higher education in the early 1960s is that promising new scholars were attracted to the field — but only temporarily. A good example of this syndrome is George Peterson's *The New England College in the Age of the University* (1964). The book fulfilled the wishes of Smith, Hofstadter, Rudolph, Hawkins et al. by placing the story of the late 19th-century liberal arts college within the context of social history — with thoughtful attention to national and regional circumstances. Second, the work went beyond the *bête noire* of preoccupation with a single institution by drawing from case studies of Amherst College, Williams College, Wesleyan University, and Dartmouth College to construct a composite profile of the New England college. Third, Peterson dared to look elsewhere than the "obvious" story of *university* ascent during the late 19th and early 20th centuries and accepted the challenge of looking at an allegedly declining institution — hardly the recipe for a "success story." Fourth, this bold work acknowledged and built on a base of earlier scholarship — namely, Thomas LeDuc's study of piety and intellect at Amherst College (1947). Finally, Peterson paid attention to student activities and groups not listed in the course catalogue and tracked student influence beyond the campus into such areas as the YMCA, the settlement house movement, and urban social work. As a result, one now had to recalculate the vitality and influence of the "collegiate way" in American life during a period when the growth of the university often was depicted as the dominant story.

All this was well and good. Yet for the history of higher education as a sustained, professional activity, it was puzzling. Peterson was a mystery man. Where was the sequel to his excellent work? At which conferences would he join with colleagues on panels? The answer was, "None of the above." Peterson wrote his book as an undergraduate honors thesis at Amherst College — after which he turned to a career in foreign affairs and Latin American studies. On the one hand, this demonstrated that fresh, good work could be done in the history of higher education; novitiates could be brought into the field promptly. On the other hand, the residual problem was whether there was a system of rewards, fellowship, reinforcement, and affiliation which could retain talent.

One who did stay with the history of higher education was Laurence Veysey. As a doctoral student in American history at the University of California at Berkeley under his mentor Henry F. May, Veysey sought to answer the question "How did the American university acquire its familiar form?" It was an answer which took five volumes — more than 1,500 pages — a feat which assured the author a secure place in the lore of graduate students. A condensed version was published in 1965 as *The Emergence of the American University*. For Veysey, the research problem centered on a fundamental flaw in institutional histories: the tendency to see the past as the present writ small. As Veysey noted, the danger was that we attribute the logic and the results of the present to an earlier period — with the tacit assumption that "things had to turn out the way they did." Instead, his finding was that to those involved in American higher education from roughly 1870 to 1910 there was little consensus or certainty as to how institutions would develop (p. vii):

> The most striking thing about the American university in its formative period is the diversity of mind shown by the men who spurred its development. Here lies the excitement of their story. . . . Although by the end of the century one can properly speak of "the" university, characterized by a particular structure, not even a powerful trend toward uniformity of procedure could obliterate the profound differences of opinion which subdivided the academic population.

Now the history of American colleges and universities had not only diversity, but also conflict, avoidance, and uncertainty. In Veysey's terms, organizational development involved numerous skirmishes and campaigns among "rival conceptions of learning." *The Emergence of the American University* made a case of sorts for intellectual history as significant for institutional history — but with the caveat that implementation of ideas about higher education into actual structures seldom went as fast or smoothly as advocates expected. Institutional history was absorbing the sociologist's notion of "unexpected consequences." Not unlike Rudolph's wit, Veysey exhumed incredible anecdotes from campus archives to use as humorous episodes illustrating important points about university leadership and administration. "Leadership style" and "organizational development" go beyond dry annual reports when one follows Veysey's account of how President William Rainey Harper of the University of Chicago was so enamored of the ceremonies of academic life that he worked out the intricacies of his elaborate funeral procession (complete with faculty in full academic regalia) while on his deathbed (p. 380).

Veysey's emphasis on the interplay among rival conceptions of learning within and among institutions countered in part another fallacy often cited as a weakness in the history of higher education: the tendency to "follow the flag." By this is meant the tendency to write history as a succession of vignettes about whichever ideal or institution happened to be triumphant at the time. In fact, there was juxtaposition, coexistence, and competition; there was no assurance the "university" ideal would prevail — or, if it did, what that ideal entailed. In another interesting wrinkle, Veysey devotes the second half of his work to a thematic account within a historical period in which he argues that institutional structures crystallized into a more or less familiar "standard American university."

Veysey's *Emergence of the American University* exemplifies another paradox in the development of historical writing on higher education: the perils of success. The work was exhaustive and formidable — so much so that it may have scared off subsequent or alternative interpretations. The danger is that a single work dominates a field by default, rather than fostering healthy debate and exchanges. There are recent signs of a thaw in this big freeze. Paul Mattingly, for example, contends that despite Veysey's description of flux and uncertainty about "the university" in the late 19th century, he tends to treat the emergent institution as a static phenomenon. And Veysey's organizational analysis is top-heavy in its reliance on data from about a dozen enduring, successful major universities (Mattingly, 1983, pp. 43-45).

That American historians were paying attention to the history of higher education represented only one lane in the scholarly traffic. The other trend was that colleges and universities were cropping up as important institutions in social history. Two works which illustrate this latter trend were E. Digby Baltzell's controversial study of elites, *The Protestant Establishment* (1964), and Richard Hofstadter's *Anti-intellectualism in American Life* (1964). For Baltzell, the city was the crucial unit of analysis — whether Boston, Philadelphia, or New York — and the campus was to be studied along with law firms, corporations, churches, city clubs, country clubs, fraternal lodges, and professional societies as threads in the web of organizations and affiliations which constituted an urbane American society. Privilege, along with the double-edged sword of opportunity and exclusion, were the dominant themes in an America where tension, and often conflict, characterized the elaborate network of multiple elites and diverse institutions.

Hofstadter, in turn, brought attention to the role of the college and university in the gentrification and professionalization of American life. Higher education certainly was not the primary focus, but its institutions did play a strong part in placing Americans of the late 19th and early 20th centuries within society and in occupational worlds. His controversial notion of *status protest* — the alleged "shrinking ground" of college-educated established elites — made an intriguing case for connections between the collegiate ethos and progressivism. Furthermore, Hofstadter's analyses gave some early distant warnings of diversity and multiple constituencies within American colleges at the turn of the century. The notion that there were sharply contrasting reasons why various groups chose to go to college was a social fact upon which a later group of scholars would seize.

Today the works of the early 1960s discussed in this section are criticized by radical historians of the left for sins of omission; i.e., failure to pay sufficient attention to conflicts and class differences in America and neglect of women and minorities as participants in social and institutional history. And since about twenty years have elapsed since their publication, there is the inevitable complaint that they do not cover the events and issues of the recent past.

Given these criticisms, the remarkable fact is that the works from the early 1960s still endure as models of rigorous research, good writing, and interpretive analysis. If indeed the anthologies by Smith and Hofstadter or the general histories by Rudolph, Brubacher, and Rudy are obsolete, where are the sequels and counterparts written in and for the 1980s? The lags and voids today may be more a reflection on current scholarship and publication than on the works published twenty years ago. Even though readers and writers are now ready to move on, this ought not diminish the substantial contributions made in the 1960s.

Most of the authors cited in this section were American historians who had only incidental connections with higher education as a formal professional affiliation. This was not the complete story, however. The works by Rudolph, Hofstadter, Smith, Veysey et al. were being used as texts in graduate seminars in Higher Education doctoral programs. The extension manifesto had led to the construction and diffusion of a knowledge base. An important step, then, is to look for cross-fertilization — a central process in the hybrid field of higher education.

CROSS-FERTILIZATION: ADMISSIONS AND ACCESS AS A THEME
Were the historians of higher education prophets without passports? Who beyond their immediate circle read and responded to their findings? Relations with neighbors from other disciplines who shared an interest in higher education were limited. Consider, for example, the place of the "new historian of higher education" in the monumental anthology edited by Nevitt Sanford in 1962, *The American College: A Psychological and Social Interpretation of the Higher Learning.* Only one of twenty-nine selections had what could be called a historical focus — and this was an elementary and breezy tour of higher education from antiquity to the twentieth century (Stewart, 1962). In fact, inclusion of this selection was counterproductive because it did not present the kinds of issues and research which characterized the true state of the art.

This was not to say that the outlook for historical perspective in the social study of higher education was wholly bleak. Within the Sanford anthology one could find definite signs that social and behavioral scientists were starting to acknowledge and rely on the methods and insights of historians. Conspicuous examples were the two chapters co-authored by sociologists David Riesman and Christopher Jencks: "The Viability of the American College" (Riesman and Jencks, 1962) and "Patterns of Residential Education: A Case Study of Harvard" (Jencks and Riesman, 1962). The former work introduced the notion of "campus ethnography," in which the historical and cultural dimensions of a particular institution were plumbed in depth to make sense out of the respective curricula and administrative styles at San Francisco State College, the University of Massachusetts at Amherst, and Boston College. In the latter selection,

Jencks and Riesman drew from archival materials and other historical documents, oral history, and student lore and stereotypes to trace over time the evolution of Harvard's student housing and residential patterns. The message was that institutional analysis was greatly enhanced by attention to the details of historical context.

Elsewhere, Wilson Smith's extension manifesto prospered most when first-rate historians and sociologists compared notes. During the decade 1960-70 this alliance resulted in some of the richest and most imaginative research on higher education. Notable figures in this interdisciplinary phase included sociologists Burton Clark, Martin Trow, David Kamens, Howard Becker, Harold Hodgkinson, and the previously mentioned David Riesman and Christopher Jencks. Some historians who in turn were indebted to developments in sociology were Laurence Veysey, Oscar and Mary Handlin, Walter Laqueur, John Talbott, and Lawrence Stone.

How to explain this cross-fertilization? To use the apt analogy of the mating dance among academic disciplines, it did take two to tango — and for a while historians and sociologists mutually benefited from one another's company in the interdisciplinary study of higher education. On the one hand, sociologists were intrigued by the methods and sources favored by historians: historians' ease with memorabilia, artifacts, clutter, unwieldy documents, and voluminous organizational records allowed them to explore all the closets and corners of complex institutions. Second, historians were able to take advantage of unexpected discoveries in the documents and sources far more easily than behavioral scientists' experimental design research. Third, if a social scientist were concerned with organizational *change*, a historical approach was well suited to handling a temporal dimension.

The fair exchange was that sociologists provided historians of higher education with concepts and themes which constituted an escape route from the formula of linear chronicles associated with the "house histories." A historian no longer was confined to narrating the story of a single campus when one could draw from such sociological concepts as stratification, organizational structure, social class, and functional analysis. Put another way, the sociological concepts assisted in shifting historical writing on colleges and universities from vertical to horizontal analyses. One could now focus on a theme (e.g., governance) which cut across many institutions over time.

A good example of this reciprocity was in the study of college and university admissions. Usually the institutional histories had little to say about the topic beyond tribute to a longtime dean of admissions, or there might be a quotation from the obligatory president's address on Parents Day in which the entering freshmen were praised as the "best class yet." There was seldom attention to the structural and bureaucratic changes which altered the role of the admissions staff. Nor would one find much data on the composition of applicant pools — especially those who did not enroll at Alma Mater. The official histories were written for an audience of alumni and other "insiders," with limited concern or information on those outside the campus. All this would change dramatically, however, when one added the sociological issue of *access* to the topic of college and university admissions. The following list of related themes suggests — yet hardly exhausts — the research questions which were opened to the new historians of higher education who were interested in access and admissions:

1. Higher education and social mobility
2. Socialization as a function of higher education
3. Institutional selection and differentiation
4. Self-selection in students' applications and college choice
5. Institutional reputation and image
6. Exclusion, sorting, and tracking within social and educational systems
7. Articulation among segments within education
8. Attrition, retention, transfers, and degree completion

The critical research revolved around the questions "Who went to which college — and why?" "How did going to college change over time and from one campus to another?" "Were there good reasons for *not* going to college?" Admissions, then, was a social as well as an institutional phenomenon; both insiders and outsiders played active roles in the configurations. And the upshot was that historians and sociologists alike had to acknowledge how little was known about access and admissions.

Perhaps the best example of sociology's contribution to historical thinking about access and admissions was Ralph Turner's 1960 study of "sponsored mobility" versus "contest mobility." Using the educational systems and social rewards apparatus of Great Britain and the United States as polarities, Turner described contrasting ideal types (p. 855):

> Under the American norm of *contest mobility*, elite status is the prize in an open contest, with every effort made to keep lagging contestants in the race until the climax. *Sponsored mobility*, the English norm, involves controlled selection in which the elite or their agents choose recruits early and carefully induct them into elite status. Differences between the American secondary school and the British system, in the value placed upon education, the content of education, the system of examinations, the attitude toward students working, the kind of financial subsidy available to university students, and the relation of social class to clique formation may be explained on the basis of this distinction.

One disquieting part of Turner's "sponsored mobility" which he associated with the British system was that it also described the socialization, recruitment, selection, and upward mobility patterns associated with social groups and campuses in the United States. This resulted in historians analyzing the composition of student bodies at prestigious colleges and universities. Martin Trow (1970) assisted the social and historical analysis by suggesting that "going to college" in America had undergone since the late 19th century a series of transformations — from elite to mass and toward universal access to higher education. The complication was twofold: on the one hand, even within an era of mass access to higher education, one could find significant pockets of selective admissions; on the other hand, the increasing numbers of high school graduates who enrolled in postsecondary education put considerable strain on structures and practices.

To analyze institutional differentiation within an era of mass access to higher education was both important and difficult. Burton Clark's 1959 article, "College Image and Student Selection," illustrated the potential for collaboration among historians and sociologists (pp. 167-168):

> Research is needed to identify the public images of colleges, to show how these images were determined, and to trace their effects . . . . One necessary step is intensive analysis of a few colleges that have highly salient images of academic quality. The central matter is to identify the way in which such colleges have constructed and communicated desired images, how they happen to initiate and maintain a "snowballing" effect of reputation and student quality . . . . Historical analysis needs to show how the rise and persistence of distinct image can affect the recruitment patterns of a college over a period of time, as for example, in moving from a locally to a nationally based student body.

Historian Allan Nevins' 1962 book, *The State Universities and Democracy*, meshed closely with sociologist Burton Clark's research concerns. For Nevins, a key theme in the history of the land grant institutions was the new state universities' quest for acquisition of a distinct campus character and historical image (p. 82):

> One of the more difficult obligations of these new institutions has been the creation of an atmosphere, a tradition, a sense of the past, which might play as important a part in the education of sensitive students as any other influence. This requires time, sustained attention to cultural values, and the special beauties of landscape and architecture. It is the immemorial grace of towers and lawns, the recollections of great ideas and causes, the fame of eminent leaders, that makes the name of Oxford fall like a chime of music on the ears of men in Delhi and Melbourne. It is this which for generations has made men wake at night with memories of Old Nassau at Princeton or the Colonnade at Charlottesville, their warm brick and ivy, their atmosphere redolent with scholarship and principle . . . . This spiritual grace the state universities cannot quickly acquire, but they have been gaining it.

By 1970 Clark had contributed good insights and answers to the research questions posed a decade earlier. For Clark, the lesson for admissions, administration, or fund raising was that belief and loyalty were dimensions of "normative bonding" essential to a healthy college or university (Clark, 1970*a*). In a subsequent book, *The Distinctive College* (Clark, 1970*b*), he used case studies of three colleges — Reed, Swarthmore, and Antioch — to develop the notion of organizational *saga*. By this was meant that some colleges acquired over time a combination of actual and embellished history which they transmitted to new students, faculty, staff, board members, deans, presidents, and alumni. Its saga was the institution's historic identity, without which the place ceased to be special. In a closely related work, David Kamens (1974) analyzed the concept of *charter* — an institution's historic mandate as accepted both by those within the institution and such external groups as prospective students and employers. According to Kamens, "Colleges have different kinds of

charters, depending upon the cultural beliefs and values of their historical constituencies in the wider society" (p. 355).

Jencks and Riesman's 1968 work, *The Academic Revolution*, used historical
sociology to question the conventional wisdom about connections between
higher education and social mobility. To say that this monumental study dealt
exclusively with access and admissions would be presumptuous and incorrect.
It did, however, synthesize literally hundreds of research reports and studies to
analyze the folklore of "going to college" in American life. Jencks and Riesman argued, for example, that cleavages in taste and cultural style, not income,
were the major consequence of the college experience. Drawing from the "social science fiction" of *The Rise of the Meritocracy, 1870–2033* (Young, 1958),
they contended that for the American upper-middle class, sending children to a
prestigious college was less an avenue of upward mobility than a hedge against
downward mobility. This reinforced a major point advanced by social historians in the 1960s: "going to college" often served to *confirm* or *ratify* one's existing social status, as distinguished from the popular conception that a college
education raised one's social standing.

In a similar vein, historians Oscar and Mary Handlin thought "socialization
as a function of higher education" was a sufficiently important and underappreciated focus to serve as the organizing theme for a survey of American colleges and universities over 300 years. Their warning was that within each era
one had to discern the particular risks and gains which faced American youth
of college-going age. This caveat was especially useful in guarding against
anachronism in educational research; i.e., historians reminded social and behavioral scientists about the fallacy of applying the values and assumptions of
our own era to the past. Hence, according to the Handlins' argument, the 17th-
century colleges' commitment to educating a learned clergy ought not be
compared to today's seminaries; a profession which today we view as specialized or apart from practical affairs may well have been integral to practical affairs in preceding centuries. The Handlins also provided a healthy counter to
the assumption that going to college is desirable or necessary; their research
suggests that in 19th-century America a college degree had only a marginal connection with occupations and the economy — even for medicine, law, the ministry, journalism, or science. Such external factors forced higher education researchers to review carefully the proposition that large numbers of Americans
were necessarily deprived of or excluded from going to college (Handlin and
Handlin, 1970).

TAKING STOCK, CIRCA 1970
What was the condition of the "new" history of higher education a decade after Wilson Smith's manifesto? The works discussed in the preceding section
suggest the topic had spawned interesting scholarship and attracted an enthusi-
astic following — omens of a promising future. But despite its richness in vigor
and research contributions, the history of higher education remained marginal

as a proportion of the total educational research enterprise (Cronbach and Suppes, 1969). For over half a century educational psychology and concern for tests and measures had dominated research in education. There was scant indication that this was changing in the late 1960s and early 1970s when massive federal funding for educational research and development became available. Within graduate schools of education, historical studies seldom were acknowledged as pertinent to applied research efforts.

Fame without fortune, then, was the progress report. At least for a brief time in the early 1970s the social history of colleges and universities enjoyed applause among the American intelligentsia, thanks to coverage in such publications as *The New York Review of Books* (Stone, 1971) and *Daedalus* (Talbott, 1971). Lawrence Stone's article, "The Ninnyversity?" published in *The New York Review of Books*, was especially important for gauging the real and symbolic state of the art. The symbolic achievement was that the history of higher education, far from being obscure, was for the moment in the nation's scholarly and intellectual mainstream. The "real" dimension of Stone's article was its critical analysis of the logic and methods of scholars in the field. Using a review of *Scholars and Gentlemen: Universities and Society in Pre-Industrial Britain, 1500-1700* (Kearney, 1970) for his entry vehicle, Stone proceeds to prepare a report card on recent research trends. For example, he applauds Kearney for having examined the "social and political role of the universities, the intellectual content of the curriculum, and the relationship of the one to the other." Stone praised Kearney's book as a *tour de force* (p. 20):

He ties up all the social and intellectual threads and provides an explanation of how the university fitted into contemporary society and contemporary culture and how it acted and reacted upon them. This is therefore an important book which is likely to be widely read and to serve as a model for fresh work in the rapidly expanding field of educational history. Apart from Professor Bernard Bailyn's brilliant essay on American education, it is the only work I know which tries so comprehensively to link what went on in the university to the society in which it was embedded.

Stone's review offered high praise with a few disclaimers. The fusion of social history with the study of educational institutions had yet to reach full maturity. Subsequent research would do well to avoid the tendency to depict a university as a monolithic "social and intellectual control system to strengthen the monopoly of the existing elite over high status positions, to formalize and reinforce class distinctions and to propagate conservative ideology" (p. 22). Stone wanted to steer the history of higher education away from crude class analyses and conspiracy theories because colleges and universities were sufficiently complicated and internally diverse to resist gross simplifications. Another flaw of simplistic logic and weak data which Stone spotted was especially pertinent for the study of access and admissions (p. 24):

. . . the assumption that there is a one-to-one correlation between what goes on in the university and the needs of the outside society. This is to take the misguided functionalist notions of modern sociologists far too seriously. As every historian knows, all the institutions of society are partly functional and partly antiquated, vestigial, or even frankly "dysfunctional." This is because they all have a history and a life of their own, and their response to outside pressure is consequently imperfect, stumbling, tardy, and even reactive.

Stone's reminder was that a campus was never wholly "conservative" or "liberal" One could argue that colleges and universities had "organizational personalities" so long as one was careful to note that this could include personality change over time and a split personality at any given time. The fusion of social and institutional history would have to develop more sophistication than facile generalizations about how a university was "meeting societal needs."

Historian John Talbott, writing in *Daedalus*, reinforced Stone's warnings. The extensionist impulse in educational history had made the topic so broad and amorphous that it was becoming "hopelessly ill-defined" (Talbott, 1971, p. 134). Raising questions about connections between college and society was far easier than answering them (p. 135):

> Conventional histories of education are filled with generalizations about relationships between education and social structure. It has been a common practice, for example, to attach a class label to an educational institution, which is then held to respond to the "needs" or "demands" of a particular social class. Who determines these needs, or whether, if such needs exist, the institution in fact responds to them, is left unclear. Moreover such static descriptive statements, based on implicit assumptions about how the class system works, explains very little about the dynamics of interaction between education and the structure of society.

A good illustration, according to Talbott, was the fondness of some historians for describing the American university as "middle class" — a description which told little about either the American university or American society. As an antidote to such careless generalizations, he offered the following proposition (p. 136):

> To be sure, education and social class have been, and continue to be, intimately connected. But the complexity of the historical connections between them has only begun to receive the carefully nuanced analysis it requires. One would expect to find a large number of aristocrats' sons in an institution labeled "aristocratic." But one would also find some people who were not the sons of aristocrats. Who were they? Furthermore, one might also find aristocrats' sons in fairly large numbers in institutions not traditionally associated with the aristocracy. What were they doing there? Detailed research has only recently begun on who actually received the education a particular society has offered, how this has changed, and what the causes and consequences of changes have been.

Both Talbott and Stone gave wise counsel for the future direction of historical writing on higher education. Their concerns about sloppy and erroneous connections between institutions and society were especially timely. The one disappointing aspect of both articles was oversight which bordered on hubris. Talbott and Stone needlessly maligned the "house histories" as a prelude to their essays even though that genre had been amply criticized long ago. The following excerpt from Stone's article indicates that this might have been "news" in 1961 — but by 1971 he was wasting time and energy beating a very dead horse (p. 21):

Like education itself, the history of education is in a bad way today, having been left far too long in the hands of professional educators. Too many educational historians write either stupefyingly boring books about educational theory, or else pious hagiographies of individual schools or universities, without reference to the larger society or even the educational system of which they are a part, and with a careful glossing over of discreditable events.

Talbott's obligatory preface was that (p. 133):

A good share of the institutional history has been the work of antiquaries and devoted alumni, who uncovered much valuable information but rarely sought to interpret it. With the professionalization of schoolteaching and the establishment of teachers' colleges educational history became a separate discipline, isolated from the mainstream.

To dwell on such obvious, dated targets was unfortunate because it meant slighting the excellent works published since 1960. Had Stone and Talbott done their homework thoroughly they might have been pleasantly surprised to find that historians already had published articles and monographs which put into practice the research agenda which Stone and Talbott were advocating for the 1970s.

Nowhere was this better demonstrated than in the 1967 anthology edited by Walter Laqueur and George L. Mosse, *Education and Social Structure in the Twentieth Century*. The work brought together thirteen polished studies by *bona fide* historians whose special interests were united by a common theme. In contrast to most works discussed in this essay, *Education and Social Structure* was not confined to analysis of the American experience. The essay topics included the historical study of student cultures (MacRae, 1967); higher education in France, 1848–1940 (Zeldin, 1967); connections between 19th-century German universities and the civil service (Ringer, 1967; Rohl, 1967); an analysis of elite views on American education (Karier, 1967); and a cross-national historical study of the education of military elites (Barnett, 1967). The topics were broad and significant, the research tools sharp. True, this anthology was exceptional — but this meant it warranted attention as the advanced state of the art.

To fault Lawrence Stone for his oversight is a quibble. The greater error of oversight would be to ignore his own contributions to fulfilling the research agenda he had outlined. Stone the critic was also a working historian. As director of the Shelby Cullom Davis Center for Historical Studies at Princeton University, he focused attention from 1969 to 1974 on the history of education. One superb product of this thematic focus was publication of a two-volume anthology, *The University in Society* (1974). The first volume dealt with Oxford and Cambridge Universities from roughly the 16th through 19th centuries. Selections in the second volume encompassed Europe, Scotland, and the United States.

To correct a tendency toward broad generalizations about relationships between a university and society, the contributors favored a tactic of studying "specific problems" in which they replaced "ignorance or wild guesses by solid quantifiable evidence, wherever it is both available and appropriate" (Stone, 1974, pp. vi-vii). The shared conviction among the authors was that before historians could construct grandiose "macro" theory about the university and society, one first needed careful studies about the size and composition of student bodies and faculty, about patterns of alumni professions and social rank, and about analysis of student subcultures and clubs.

Interest in hard data, case studies, and "micro" analyses did not mean that the history of higher education was destined to become a dreary science. To the contrary, the selections in Stone's anthologies showed that such emphases could be exciting both in the process of conducting research and in the findings. Stone's own essay, "The Size and Composition of the Oxford Student Body, 1580 to 1909," and James McConica's study, "Scholars and Commoners in Renaissance Oxford," show the cat-and-mouse game between historians and institutional records in the attempt to work out a scheme for determining a student's socioeconomic standing. Matriculation records often were incomplete; gentlemen-scholars may have been charged different fees than students designated as "servitors" or "plebeians." Special scholarship funds intended for poor-but-bright young men were subject to corrupt administration — with monies being unscrupulously awarded to the undeserving sons of wealth. Or, as Richard Kagan wrote in his study "Universities in Castile, 1500–1810," the academic integrity of a university could be compromised by its connection with such procedures as examination fees or its access to job opportunities in the civil service. The historian's appreciation of the details of institutional life did not have to degenerate into an obsession with trivia.

The University in Society showed that the heroic years of the extension manifesto had been followed by self-criticism within the ranks of educational historians, followed by readjustment and refinement in the research act. On balance, the ledger sheet read that the history of higher education had gained legitimacy and was approaching maturity. Nor was Stone's leadership and scholarship the entire story. Elsewhere one finds a steady flow of good books and articles. *The History of Education Quarterly*, for example, featured numerous articles both by established and new historians of higher education; under the editorship of Paul Mattingly the journal served throughout the decade of the 1970s as a consistently good forum for articles and essay reviews which were provocative and well researched. The history of higher education had entered into a period which combined revision with refinement.

REFINEMENT AND REVISION: THE "ELITISM" QUESTION
For scholars, the ultimate damnation by faint praise is the eulogy that one "wrote without fear — and without research." So, although extension promoted revision in historical writing on higher education, daring new works which rejected earlier interpretations could be dismissed as merely polemical unless grounded in fresh information and sound analyses. Hence, the element which gave substance and credibility to the revisionist impulse was the refinement of analytic strategies and data collection. During the 1970s historians of higher education were at their best when they reexamined institutional stereotypes which often were careless or inaccurate, then followed by carefully recon-

structing episodes and events as the foundation of a new interpretation. An obvious contribution was that historians dismantled works which presented American schooling as an unblemished success story or a morality play. Equally important, and often overlooked, was that many of the bold, brave attempts at revision were themselves subjected to yet another round of scrutiny. The process of revising the revisionists fostered lively point-counterpoint exchanges.

A good example of multiple revisions and research complications is the question of "elitism" as a historic characteristic of college and university admissions and access. Revisionists threw down the gauntlet by depicting the historic colleges as largely inaccessible except to the sons (and sometimes, the daughters) of families graced by privilege and wealth. Consider the interpretation rendered by Kearney in his postscript to *Gentlemen and Scholars* (1970). After devoting most of his attention to the British universities between 1500 and 1700, he closed with some strong parting shots about the relative isolation and exclusion of the older colleges in the United States of the 19th century. To Kearney, "in a sea of rising democracy, the colleges were 'citadels of privilege,' " and "Harvard was the only Eastern college to go any way towards adapting itself to the new conditions of social revolution. The *elitist* traditions of Princeton and Yale remained unchanged well into the twentieth century" (p. 189).

Kearney's statements would have made for an exciting hypothesis, but as a postscript his broad depictions invited controversy. Possibly he was correct, but he certainly did not present detailed information which would enable a reader to follow his logic or unequivocally share his conclusion. Fortunately, although Kearney lacked data, other historians did not. The story of their work is the high pont of the research and writing for the decade.

The "elitism" charge against American colleges and universities in the 19th and early 20th centuries elicited no single finding or consensus. One complication was that many of the New England colleges now regarded as "selective" or "elitist" were not always so. David Allmendinger (1971, 1975) spent years carefully reviewing institutional records and the biographies of students and alumni at Amherst College and constructed an institutional profile which challenged the charge of 19th-century elitism. In the early and mid-19th century the New England colleges charged relatively low tuition, had substantial scholarship funds (often via missionary societies), and were sending alumni into such fields as teaching, the ministry, and service abroad as missionaries. Indeed, one could identify a "social revolution" in the colleges, as these institutions were attracting students who often were older than "traditional" college age of 18 to 22. Students at Amherst College included military veterans and the displaced sons of modest New England farmers. There may well have been incidents of wealth and snobbery at Amherst College in the 1910s and 1920s — but to call the 19th-century campus a "citadel of privilege" was erroneous. More perplexing for our notion of improved access over time was the haunting question posed by Allmendinger's work: "Had access to higher education for modest income students *declined* since the 19th century?"

Elsewhere, a thorough case study of the social composition of Harvard from 1800 to 1870 documented that those who entered Harvard College were becoming an increasingly homogeneous group, characterized by high income and local (Boston) patrician family background (Story, 1975). Yet this was not the pervasive trend at Harvard. Detailed analyses from the early 20th century indicated that there were "many Harvards" — an institution which was diverse in composition and accommodated glaring extremes of wealth, heritage, and academic ability in its student body.

One could not extrapolate from Harvard the totality of colleges and universities. The demand was for more case studies. A study of two Philadelphia institutions — the University of Pennsylvania and Temple College — for the years 1873 to 1906 impeded any quick resolution of debates over access and exclusion (Angelo, 1981). The predictable hypothesis was that the University of Pennsylvania would show a pattern of elitism: students from locally prominent families who opted for the prestigious liberal arts curriculum, followed by passage into the advanced schools for such learned professions as law and medicine. Temple, in turn, was founded to provide for the instruction of workers and probably would illustrate the "tracking" syndrome of the American class structure. Indeed, Angelo did find some confirmation of this pattern — but with numerous exceptions so as to warrant hesitation. One datum was that even the allegedly "working class" institution could not, did not, enroll workers; its student body was dominated by young men and some women in modest white-collar jobs who were ambitious and sought either advancement or options for lateral job change. Although the temptation was to depict historic Penn as the city's favored institution, Angelo noted that his data on composition of the student bodies at the two institutions did not strongly support such a conclusion. There were, for example, a substantial number of Penn students who had neither wealth nor Philadelphia family ties. Above all, Angelo argued against depicting Penn and Temple as the institutional symbols of class division and career tracking for two reasons: first, such polarization imposed backward from the 1980s to the 1880s was wrongheaded because it misread and oversimplified socioeconomic arrangements for Philadelphia in that era; second, the process and criteria for admission both at Penn and Temple were not at all comparable to those we associate with colleges and universities today. True, a century ago the liberal arts college and the schools of medicine and law dominated Penn's enrollments — but Angelo points out this did not necessarily imply high status or exclusion. One did not need a bachelor's degree or even a high school diploma to gain admission to Penn's medical or law school in the late 19th century. There was no tight connection between secondary schools and university admissions at either Penn or Temple. The research mistake would be to attribute our mid-twentieth-century conception of selective admissions to an earlier period. The first order of research business would be to understand education and social mobility in late 19th-century cities on their own terms.

Where and why a student chose to go to college — then as now — was thought to be closely associated with institutional image and reputation. Most of the historical research published in the 1950s emphasized the "rise of the modern university" as the success story of the late 19th century — accompanied by a correspondingly depressing demise of the "old-time college." In the 1970s several historians worked to produce an impressive body of literature which disputed the grandiose claims of university ascension. By looking beneath the self-serving claims and rhetoric of the "university builders," historians devised tests to see whether there really were substantial differences between what a "university" offered and what a "college" did not (Axtell, 1971; Hawkins, 1971). Often the allegedly small, stagnant colleges surpassed the state universities of the 1880s in such quantitative categories as student enrollment, number of electives and courses, laboratory and research facilities, library holdings, and evidence of faculty publication and scholarship. A recent intense study of Dartmouth College during the last two decades of the 19th century confirms the gist of the 1971 studies with evidence that the small college was robust and attractive to an increasingly ambitious and cosmopolitan group of prospective students, donors, and alumni (Tobias, 1982). Until a few years ago, most historians were content to accept at face value the conventional wisdom that the numerous private colleges founded between 1800 and 1900 faced a high mortality rate. Now, however, Colin Burke's prodigious work of "macro" historical statistics on college foundings, closing, and enrollments indicates that the tenacity and appeal of these 19th-century colleges have been seriously underestimated (Burke, 1982). The neat categories of "rising universities" and "declining colleges" explained less and less about institutional realities at the turn of the century.

Religious affiliation long had been acknowledged as an important source of a college's attraction. The contribution of social historians was to go beyond the obvious rationale that denominations built colleges to educate (and retain) the children of the faithful. In fact, church-related colleges in the 19th and 20th centuries behaved in a more interesting, complicated manner. Some were built as part of real estate ventures in the Midwest and West. Others were chameleon-like in character; i.e., the same college, although founded by a particular denomination, shifted its institutional image over time — it at first emphasized religious ties; then, in the wake of declining enrollments, projected itself as a "local" or "community" campus, open to all students regardless of church affiliation; later on, it might experiment with coeducation or professional education as a recruiting magnet; and, in the decades since World War II, shifted to "selective admissions" and a liberal arts orientation (Potts, 1971). One interesting modification was the argument that a college's religious affiliation was best understood as an indication of ethnic heritage: e.g., Lutheran colleges educated the children of immigrants from Germany and Scandinavia; Catholic colleges served a predominantly Irish and Italian constituency (Jencks and Riesman, 1968, pp. 316-320).

The 1970s case studies showed some interest in recognition of state and regional differences. All too often the colleges and universities on the East Coast and in New England had received inordinate attention. The worst abuse was that these institutions, although important, were mistaken as the *national* pattern or model. Studies of institutional reputation and administrative strategies in such states as Pennsylvania (Leslie, 1977; Potts, 1971) and California (Thelin, 1977) tempered the geographical imbalance. However, a handful of historic institutions — Harvard, Yale, Princeton, and Columbia — persisted as the favorite objects of curiosity and analysis among revisionist historians even though literally thousands of other institutions dotted higher education's historical landscape. From time to time a brilliant article would "rediscover" the prestige and fame once associated with Horace Holley's Transylvania University of the 1840s or Philip Lindsley's great hopes for a modern university in Nashville (Borrowman, 1961). Yet, for the most part, these "forgotten" stories of innovation and success remained lost to readers of the mid-20th century.

Some established institutional reputations were bruised in the wake of revisionism. Campuses which had received a great deal of praise and prestige for traditions of coeducation were subject to scrutiny, with the finding that although such colleges as Cornell or Oberlin did enroll women, there was curricular tracking and institutional regulations which made women students less than equal partners within the walls (Conable, 1977). Another surprise was the finding that even the prestigious colleges of the late 19th century admitted substantial numbers of "special students" who needed remedial work (Brier, 1984). The tarnish on the image of allegedly egalitarian state universities was the finding that by the early 1900s the Midwestern public universities were hardly "open" institutions serving all sectors of the state population, as student life came to be dominated by a "fast set" and a social elite (Veysey, 1965).

The sense of urgency in historical research on access and admissions increased as historians' case studies came closer and closer to the familiar forms and practices of meritocracy and selective admissions. Institutional history took on a new dimension when it was extended beyond the campus to other, integral organizations directly involved with college admissions. Historical studies of the Carnegie Foundation and the College Entrance Examination Board were essential for making sense out of the elaborate curricular requirements and sorting mechanisms developed in the twentieth century (Schudson, 1972). And for the large public universities of the Midwest and West, one had to understand the evolution of the "certificate system" and the relations among public high schools and state universities as an important mechanism in the attempt to maintain academic standards while moving into an era of mass higher education (Wechsler, 1977, pp. 16-61).

For historians of the late 1970s, however, the main event was the study of selection and exclusion at the prestigious colleges and universities from 1900 to the present. The recent past was an intriguing subject when the research question was "How has sponsored mobility fared in an era of contest mobility and almost universal access to some form of postsecondary education?" Two significant works which addressed the issue were Harold Wechsler's *The Qualified Student: A History of Selective College Admissions in America* (1977) and Marcia Graham Synnott's *The Half-Opened Door: Discrimination and Admissions at Harvard, Yale, and Princeton, 1900-1970* (1979).

Institutional differences and historical changes in admission policies prevented either Wechsler or Synnott from claiming to have covered the complete story of access in American higher education since 1900. Wechsler's chapter on the University of Michigan's certificate system at the turn of the century and his later chapter on open admissions at the City University of New York in the late 1960s made good contributions to understanding the issue of mass higher education. Yet ultimately Wechsler was most concerned with the policies and practices whereby a relatively few aspiring students ended up at prestigious colleges. As Synnott's title clearly indicates, her study dealt almost totally with the "Big Three" of Harvard, Yale, and Princeton.

Taken together, the books by Wechsler and Synnott were powerful in their documentation and dissection of overt discrimination at the private Eastern colleges, circa 1900 to 1970. Wechsler's case study of Columbia and Synnott's profiles of Harvard, Yale, and Princeton presented overwhelming evidence that presidents, deans, and trustees at these institutions consciously adopted and enforced systems of quotas whereby academically qualified Jews were denied admission. Rich documentation and detailed quotations from internal memoranda and letters displayed expertise in historical research. The materials, often embarrassingly candid, moved charges of discrimination from the vague realm of innuendo into established fact. At worst, then, colleges' construction of selective admission policies in the 1920s and 1930s was a subterfuge for exclusion based on birth, heritage, and religion — although public pronouncements claimed that the policies were designed to achieve geographical balance and diversity in entering classes.

Still, Wechsler and Synnott leave a new generation of historians with more questions than answers in the sensitive areas of access and exclusion. Were deans of admission totally bigoted and sinister in matters of access? The paradox of the quotas is that in the cases of Harvard and Columbia, these were devised at two institutions which had high proportions of Jews enrolled as students in the 1920s and 1930s — markedly different from the situation at, e.g., Yale or Princeton. And there is good evidence to show that selective admissions also were used to raise academic standards and to recruit in regions and areas heretofore unrepresented in the student body. Finally — and most odious — was the fact that often the officials of the university were less bigoted than were the alumni or the undergraduate student culture within the institution.

Wechsler and Synnott presented interpretations which concurred with Jencks and Riesman's (1968) conclusion that selective admissions of the post-World War II era represented the "partial triumph of meritocracy" (pp. 8-12). Or, to borrow from Synnott's terminology, academically strong applicants would find that the elite college's door was at least partially opened — and would be opened wider by the 1970s. To hail institutional policy as a part of social progress was to hail the colleges' identification and sponsorship of a new elite — allegedly, an elite of talent.

However, the meritocrats' celebration was muted in the 1970s by a conflict between belief in rewarding talent and proposals to correct social and racial injustices by adopting — rather than ending — quotas. After having traced more than a half-century campaign to eliminate quotas which excluded minorities from colleges, historians were hard pressed to shift suddenly to justify quotas which favored underrepresented groups. Although Wechsler and Synnott cited parallels between the exclusion which Jews faced in the 1920s and 1930s and the small percentage of blacks and Hispanics enrolled in elite colleges in the 1960s, the comparisons were not convincing. Neither author ventured to discuss in depth the ramifications of the 1973 *DeFunis v. Odegaard* case for the thorny issue of reverse discrimination. So, although readers had incredibly thorough accounts of admissions episodes, historians had not spelled out clearly their own criteria by which to determine what appropriate admissions practices were or what they ought be in the future. Selective admissions was a difficult, ambiguous task in which deans and admissions officers were expected to fill a scarce number of places for entrance into prestigious colleges while abiding by the norms and codes of a democratic society. It was a situation which was destined to have "left-outs" and "left-overs." Meritocracy, then, received only muffled applause from the revisionist historians.

CONNECTIONS WITH POLICIES AND PRACTICES

Before faulting historians Wechsler and Synnott for not commenting at length on the 1973 *DeFunis v. Odegaard* case on reverse discrimination, one should bear in mind that both the university and the Supreme Court dodged this interesting, volatile case. Since the plaintiff, Mario DeFunis, was granted belated admission to the University of Washington law school (after having been initially rejected) before the case had reached the Supreme Court, the Justices declared the case moot.

Furthermore, the numerous articles, monographs, and books discussed in the previous section on the elitism question showed that historians of higher education have been very much involved in controversial and contemporary issues. Given the relatively slow pace of historical research and publication, the fact that many pertinent studies were published by the late 1960s and early 1970s indicates that historians had been working seriously with the complexities of access and selective admissions several years before courts, institutions, foundations, blue ribbon commissions, and legislatures took public stands or released reports on these issues. A work such as *The Rise of the Meritocracy, 1870–2033* (Young, 1958) anticipated by almost two decades the topics addressed in such reports as the Carnegie Council on Policy Studies in Higher Education's *Selective Admissions in Higher Education* (Manning, Willingham, and Breland, 1977). A generation of revisionist historians already had plunged into campus archives by the early 1970s to attempt to *answer* questions about access and admissions which many public officials and campus administrators were just starting to *ask*. Far from being harmless antiquarians, historians who used demographic data and institutional records to analyze patterns of selection and differentiation at colleges and universities were running ahead of public policy and institutional practice.

Sometimes this meant that historians caused problems for college presidents and deans. At Sarah Lawrence College in New York, for example, the commissioned author of the college's centennial history came across files dating back to the 1920s which documented in graphic detail the existence of formal procedures by which quotas on the admission of Jewish applicants were implemented. Since the college officials had often denied the existence of such a system, the historian's accidental and belated discovery was a source of institutional embarrassment. The subsequent discussions between the author and college officials raised fundamental questions about editorial jurisdiction for the commissioned "house history" genre (Rose, 1983; Steinberg, 1971).

For the most part, however, historians had great potential to provide research which was attractive to deans of admission. One strategy was for colleges and universities to open archives and files to historians and to acknowledge the strengths and weaknesses of past practices. *The Qualified Student* (Wechsler, 1977) and *The Half-Opened Door* (Synnott, 1979) were among the few works — historical or otherwise — which traced the evolution of admissions offices. "Micro" analysis which described how admissions offices of various eras and campuses actually operated was invaluable for understanding structural changes in American colleges and universities. It also pointed out how little the higher education research literature dealt with connections between middle-level administrators and campus policy. Above all, some recent historical research has brought attention and enhancement to the development of admissions as a profession and a career with its own expertise, responsibilities, powers, constraints, and codes (Lowery and Associates, 1982; Thelin, 1982). How has the role of the dean of admissions changed over time? How have institutions differed in defining the dean's role? Historians interested in closing the gap between scholarly research and professional administration would do well to consider doing case studies which examine admissions offices at colleges and universities which heretofore have received scant research attention.

To illustrate the dearth of information on admissions as an office and as a profession, consider the sources available before publication of Wechsler's and Synnott's books in the late 1970s. There were almost no detailed accounts of admissions procedures in the 19th century apart from the extraordinary memoir by a young Yale College alumnus (Bagg, 1871). His clinical reconstruction of the entrance examination offered in New Haven a few days before the start of classes contrasts dramatically with the deferred gratification, intricate record keeping, and elaborate review which applicants to Yale College faced a century later (Sacks and Anderson, 1978). Not until the early 1960s can one find a thorough description of the office procedures and annual cycle associated with an admissions staff at a selective college; *How an Ivy League College Decides on Admissions* (Kinkead, 1961) was written for parents of academically ambitious high school students who were about to begin the prolonged ritual of college applications. Beyond these scattered works we simply do not have many accounts or analyses. In the past year Keller (1983, p. 6) has given brief mention to the late 19th-century practice of combining external fund raising with student recruitment in the position of "college agent" — but this is not sufficient.

Part of the research problem is that institutions and offices do not always cooperate with posterity. Admissions offices, which handle an enormous bulk of paper, have storage problems. All too often the solution has been to discard records rather than send them to the archives. Another fact of institutional life is that most colleges and universities have led unexamined lives. Beyond the Ivy League and the major state universities, most institutions have been neglected by outside scholars and by internal researchers. Most campuses are "invisible colleges" (Astin and Lee, 1972) which have not acquired a strong sense of historic saga or identity. The popular "inside" guides to colleges usually are confined to about one hundred prominent campuses (Fiske, 1982).

If historical researchers have neglected most admissions offices, the converse also holds. Unfortunately, there is little evidence that deans of admission over the past twenty-five years have kept abreast of articles on access written by historians of higher education. From time to time a dean will leave "business as usual" to write an explanation of the innards and historic rationales for the procedures associated with selective admissions (Moll, 1980). The year-to-year press of recruitment and folder reading certainly works against admissions staff devoting much time to internal research and analysis beyond calculating the "yield" of admissions offers to actual enrollments. Ironically, when universities do set aside resources and personnel to study particular admissions problems, the results can be useful and important. At the University of California, Berkeley, for example, a research team solved a complex riddle about charges of gender discrimination in admissions as ostensibly reflected in enrollments in graduate and professional schools. The key strategy was to distinguish university-wide data on applications and admissions from program-by-program records. The surprising finding was that the underrepresentation of women in certain fields was not due to discrimination or exclusion at the admission juncture; rather, prior socialization to *not* apply to such programs as law, engineering, and chemistry explained the enrollment trend (Brickel, Hammel and O'Connell, 1974). What had started out as an "obvious" case of institutional discrimination turned into an elusive social problem.

In the late 1970s and 1980s a swell of interest in long-range planning and comprehensive marketing brought administrators and historians together. The

College Entrance Examination Board's national conference on marketing and admissions featured historian Laurence Veysey's address on the past and future of college admissions (Veysey, 1980). The University of Maryland's ambitious vision of becoming the archetypal "post-land grant university" fused a historical account of the state and institutional saga into a blueprint for the 21st century (Moos, 1981). In a similar vein, *Academic Strategy: The Management Revolution in American Higher Education* depended on a lively historical approach to the analysis of institutions to advance novel ideas about campus planning and administration (Keller, 1983). A rare yet promising sign that the historical study of higher education need not be divorced from admissions was the example of Virginia's John T. Casteen III: a leader and spokesman who combined experience as a dean of admissions, a faculty member, and as a state secretary of education — and who found time to write forcefully and with historical perspective on policy issues both for members of the admissions profession and the general public (Casteen, 1982, 1984).

The residual message is that historical research has been from time to time compatible with policy analysis and formulation. Historians can be invaluable to agencies whose charge it is to review and discuss "macro" policy in education — whether with a state higher education council, a private foundation, a federal legislative staff, or possibly with an association or consortium of colleges and universities. Much of the policy research conducted in the 1970s dealt with access and choice in higher education, but with primary attention to matters of financial aid rather than to admissions *per se* (Spies, 1973). Historians are well suited to reconstructing the traditions and beliefs from decades ago which provided state legislators with the rationales for adopting policies of low tuition or no tuition at public universities. Have the policies worked over time? Were the assumptions about tuition charges erroneous — or archaic? Have lower-income families taken advantage of low tuition to send their children to the state colleges? Do other factors (e.g., tracking and admissions criteria) cancel out low tuition as incentives to enrollment? How have the states' independent colleges and universities compared over time with the public institutions in enrolling students from a range of income levels? All these are essentially historical questions whose answers are central to reviewing and formulating state policy.

At the federal level, Chester Finn drew historical materials from the recent past to compose an iconoclastic and influential work which caused an uproar in Washington. *Scholars, Dollars, and Bureaucrats* (Finn, 1978) tracked down the roots of legislation and political debates to show that many of the major federal policies associated with the support of higher education were fundamentally flawed. This and the other examples cited in this section were exceptional. Historical research and thinking hardly dominated the policy research effort. At very least, however, these scattered works provided good models to show that historians could have a rightful place in contemporary policy analysis.

ENDPOINT: THE RESEARCH DILEMMA AND AGENDA

The research dilemma for the 1980s and 1990s is thus: after more than two decades of quality scholarship, the history of higher education stands as a fragile enterprise which lacks security, support, or clear affiliation. The tragedy of this bleak situation is that on the whole this has been a strand of educational research which has matured over the past decades and, at times, has even sparkled. All this was done with modest funding from external sources or even from campus programs and departments. The concern of this essay is that this distinctive research effort faces lean times and, at worst, may be on borrowed time.

The peak of fame for the history of higher education was in the early 1970s for two reasons: first, many of the scholars associated with the topic were eminent and established, either at the height or in the golden years of their respective careers; second, the widespread attention afforded Lawrence Stone's essay review (Stone, 1971) and the projects he directed at Princeton (Stone, 1974) made the history of higher education "news" beyond its own practitioners. More important for the future was that in the period 1970 to the present several younger scholars (Axtell, Allmendinger, Synnott, Wechsler, Angelo, Mattingly, Tobias, and Burke, to name a few) published refined, lively works which led to the reasonable expectation that exciting research in the history of higher education would be forthcoming for a long time. Why then, given such promise, does this essay conclude with fears and lament — or, at best, cautious optimism?

For some (Leslie, 1980), the disappointment is that the new generation of researchers failed to replace the "standard" major works by Rudolph (1962), Hofstadter and Smith (1961), and Veysey (1965) with fresh syntheses. Possibly the fault is with the younger scholars, but there may be another consideration: large-scale research and the revision of major works require sustained support and funding. Where is there evidence that such support and resources have materialized? The promising scholarship of the past five to ten years may fade not because of lack of skill and interest by the new scholars but, rather, for lack of ample resources, rewards, career routes, and opportunities to do research and write.

Part of the problem is that the logic and methods of historical analysis remain accidental or marginal in higher education as a field of study. Certainly this neglect persists in Higher Education doctoral programs and in graduate schools of education. The corollary is that historical analysis has yet to be incorporated into the "applied research" endeavors associated with large-scale educational research and development. In the late 1970s the good news was that the National Institute of Education announced competition for projects dealing with the historical development of organizations in higher education; the bad news was that the agency's research funds were small (and getting smaller) compared to the research support of the preceding five years. It is unfortunate that recognition of the contributions which historians might make to educational research is belated.

How might the history of higher education salvage a place in the higher education research enterprise? The earlier section "Connections with Policies and Practices" alludes to some readily available opportunities where historical analysis of access might be in demand: institutional reports on admissions and fund raising as part of a serious marketing strategy; long-range and strategic planning; state and federal policy analysis. The problem is that the successful examples cited earlier are the exceptional high points. The prospects for historians of higher education working with and as planners and analysts remain more in the realm of potential than accomplishment. One clear point is that if historical studies are to be integral to large-scale "applied" research, historians of higher education must learn to work as part of a team. Historians writing for fellow historians may be essential to the craft, but it is insufficient as a strategy for support and survival. Nor should cooperation with other research orientations and administrators be undertaken reluctantly. At the very least, coordination and interaction with other researchers can be an opportunity to demonstrate the worth of historical methods and logic in approaching significant issues in higher education.

Where, then, are some likely areas for this incorporation of history into the higher education research effort to take place in the immediate future? First, most institutions are unexamined and have a superficial or weak sense of organizational saga. Historical research can assist in reconstructing and analyzing the institutional history as part of long-range planning or marketing strategies. This skill also could be integral to the ubiquitous ten-year regional accreditation self-studies which most campuses undertake. Presidents, deans, and trustees need help in these assignments — but it probably will require historians to look elsewhere than the handful of highly prestigious, overstudied colleges and universities.

Second, if most colleges and universities are in an era of unselective admissions, both institutions and state councils will be attempting to cope with problems of retention and remediation. Although this may seem to be a "new" problem for administrators, the leverage which historians of higher education have is familiarity with comparable situations from the 19th century.

A third topic is the problem of reluctant students. The conventional wisdom since World War II has been that the United States can provide access to higher education for more and more students if only classrooms, dormitories, and scholarship programs can be put into place on time to meet the demand. Now there is evidence from California that, in addition to a decline in the college-age population, there is a decline in interest about going to college among high school students. Again, this "new" problem which baffles administrators and planners is not especially surprising to historians who encountered such episodes in the study of Wayland at Brown and other 19-century colleges which had to scrounge for students.

Fourth, and most important, is the possibility that dissatisfaction with the limits of survey research may turn higher education research toward the particular skills, sources, and methods one associates with historians. In the late

1960s there was a spurt of interest in "unobtrusive measures" as supplements and alternatives to attitudinal surveys (Webb et al., 1966). This research redirection, however, remains incidental to most institutional research offices. During the past two years the Association for the Study of Higher Education's national conferences have included sessions and panels dealing with the importance of institutional context for the study of organizational theory. Ironically, most of the related studies and presentations were based on data drawn from attitudinal surveys administered to college and university administrators. How can one truly study institutional context without paying attention to organizational saga, to monuments, to spatial arrangements, to historical development? The obvious void in this area of organizational theory is that historians, who would work well with the documents, records, and memorabilia which shape the context of an organization, are not participating in the research effort.

A partial solution is that historians of higher education must actively seek out such new research assignments. It will call for a shift in tone, attitude, and activity. Furthermore, if historians wish to be taken seriously in the applied research of higher education and public policy, they must first unlearn some indulgent habits. Specifically, historians of higher education can no longer afford to spend time and energy congratulating themselves that their scholarship has corrected the weaknesses of uncritical campus "house histories." Lawrence Stone (1971) lapsed into this syndrome of self-congratulations more than a decade ago. And again in 1983 the pattern is repeated. Consider the following summary of the state of historical research on education.

> In the field of education, for example, many of us are just beginning to get used to the idea that everything we learned in graduate school a decade or so ago — about how the Great American Public School had opened the door of opportunity to us all — was at the very least a romantic myth if not a deliberate lie. But now that all seems to be overturning. [Best, 1983, p. 2]

Doesn't this slight the solid scholarship and teaching which took place in graduate schools of education in the late 1960s and early 1970s? Advanced research and graduate seminars in higher education programs and in social foundations of education programs had moved beyond celebration of educational institutions much earlier than a decade ago.

The 1980s self-congratulations are misplaced for another reason: although researchers and scholars of education may have abandoned the simplistic and flawed celebrations of the rise of schools and colleges, this does not mean that we now have institutional histories of colleges and universities which are researched and written according to the ground rules and guidelines espoused by the extensionist and revisionist historians of higher education.

It may well be that the new historians of higher education have yet to show the vitality and worth of their insights, findings, and methods to such constituencies as presidents, trustees, alumni, and administrators. The unfortunate result is that advanced scholarship in the study of higher education moves in one direction while colleges and universities continue to commission the familiar centennial "house histories" which scholars maligned in 1960. This mutual avoidance need not continue indefinitely. Perhaps one element in the research agenda for the next decade is that historians of higher education will look beyond writing for members of their own circle. Advocates and practitioners of the historical study of higher education would do well to devote some thought to the *logistics* of the research effort, as well as the necessary concern for the content of scholarship. One task, then, is to work actively and effectively to show the uninitiated audiences that the history of higher education can and does offer much more than background music.

REFERENCES

Allmendinger, D. F., Jr. New England students and the revolution in higher education, 1800–1900. *History of Education Quarterly*, 1971, *11*, 381-389.

Allmendinger, D. F., Jr. *Paupers and Scholars: The Transformation of Student Life in Nineteenth Century New England*. New York: St. Martin's Press, 1975.

Angelo, R. The students at the University of Pennsylvania and the Temple College of Philadelphia, 1873-1906: Some notes on schooling, class and social mobility in the late nineteenth century. *History of Education Quarterly*, 1981, *19*, 179-204.

Astin, A., and Lee, C. B. T. *The Invisible Colleges*. New York: McGraw-Hill, 1972.

Axtell, J. The death of the liberal arts college. *History of Education Quarterly*, 1971, *11*, 339-352.

Bagg, L. H. *Four Years at Yale: By a Graduate of '69*. New Haven: Chatfield, 1871.

Baltzell, E. D. *The Protestant Establishment: Aristocracy and Caste in America*. New York: Vintage Books, 1964.

Barnett, C. The education of military elites. In W. Laqueur and G. L. Mosse (eds.), *Education and Social Structure in the Twentieth Century*. New York: Harper & Row, 1967.

Best, J. H. (ed.), *Historical Inquiry in Education: A Research Agenda*. Washington, D.C.: American Educational Research Association, 1983.

Borrowman, M. The false dawn of the state university. *History of Education Quarterly*, 1961, *1*, 6-20.

Brickel, P. J., Hammel, E. A., and O'Connell, J. W. Sex bias in graduate admissions: Data from Berkeley. *Science*, 1974, *187*, 398-404.

Brier, E. M. The controversy of the underprepared student at Vassar College and Cornell University, 1865-1890. Association for the Study of Higher Education, 1984.

Brubacher, J. S., and Rudy, W. *Higher Education in Transition: An American History, 1636-1956*. New York: Harper, 1958.

Burke, C. B. *American Collegiate Populations: A Test of the Traditional View*. New York: New York University Press, 1982.

Casteen, J. T., III. Functions of postsecondary education for individuals and society. In W. R. Lowery and Associates (eds.), *College Admissions Counseling: A Handbook for the Profession*. San Francisco: Jossey-Bass, 1982.

Casteen, J. T., III. Higher education and public policy. Paper presented at The College of William and Mary, April 12, 1984.

Clark, B. R. College image and student selection. *Selection and Educational Differentiation*. Berkeley: University of California Center for Research and Development in Higher Education, 1959.

Clark, B. R. Belief and loyalty in college organization. *Journal of Higher Education*, 1970(a), *42*, 499-515.

Clark, B. R. *The Distinctive College: Antioch, Reed, and Swarthmore*. Chicago: Aldine, 1970(b).

College Entrance Examination Board. *Marketing College Admissions: A Broadening of Perspectives*. New York: College Entrance Examination Board, 1980.

Conable, C. W. *Women at Cornell: The Myth of Equal Education*. Ithaca, N.Y.: Cornell University Press, 1977.

Cronbach, L. J., and Suppes, P. (eds.), *Research for Tomorrow's Schools: Disciplined Inquiry for Education*. New York: Macmillan, 1969.

Earnest, E. *Academic Procession: An Informal History of the American College, 1636-1953*. New York: Bobbs, 1953.

Finn, C. E., Jr. *Scholars, Dollars, and Bureaucrats*. Washington, D.C.: Brookings Institution, 1978.

Fiske, E. B. *The New York Times' Selective Guide to Colleges, 1982-83*. New York: New York Times, 1982.

Foster, M. S. *"Out of Smalle Beginnings . . . "*: *An Economic History of Harvard College in the Puritan Period, 1636 to 1712*. Cambridge, Mass.: Belknap Press of Harvard, 1962.

Handlin, O., and Handlin, M. F. *The American College and American Culture: Socialization as a Function of Higher Education*. New York: McGraw-Hill, 1970.

Hawkins, H. *Pioneer: A History of the Johns Hopkins University, 1874-1889*. Ithaca, N.Y.: Cornell University Press, 1960.

Hawkins, H. The university-builders observe the colleges. *History of Education Quarterly*, 1971, *11*, 353-362.

Hodgkinson, H. L. Social mobility and success: Who stole the Protestant ethic? In *Education, Interaction, and Social Change*. Englewood Cliffs, N.J.: Prentice-Hall, 1967.

Hofstadter, R. *Anti-intellectualism in American Life*. New York: Vintage Books, 1964.

Hofstadter, R., and Smith, W. (eds.), *American Higher Education: A Documentary History*. Chicago: University of Chicago, 1961.

Jarausch, K. H. (ed.), *The Transformation of Higher Learning, 1860-1930*. Chicago: University of Chicago, 1961.

Jencks, C., and Riesman, D. Patterns of residential education: A case study of Harvard. In N. Sanford (ed.), *The American College: A Psychological and Social Interpretation of the Higher Learning*. New York: Wiley, 1962.

Jencks, C., and Riesman, D. *The Academic Revolution*. Garden City, N.Y.: Doubleday, 1968.

Kagan, R. L. Universities in Castile, 1500-1810. In L. Stone (ed.), *The University in Society*. Princeton: Princeton University Press, 1974.

Kamens, D. Colleges and elite formation: The case of the prestigious American colleges. *Sociology of Education*, 1974, *47*, 354-378.

Karier, C. J. Elite views on American education. In W. Laqueur and G. L. Mosse (eds.), *Education and Social Structure in the Twentieth Century*. New York: Harper & Row, 1967.

Kearney, H. *Scholars and Gentlemen: Universities and Society in Pre-Industrial Britain, 1500-1700*. Ithaca, N.Y.: Cornell University Press, 1970.

Keller, G. *Academic Strategy: The Management Revolution in American Higher Education*. Baltimore: Johns Hopkins University Press, 1983.

Kinkead, K. *How an Ivy League College Decides on Admissions*. New York: Norton, 1961.

Laqueur, W., and Mosse, G. L. (eds.), *Education and Social Structure in the Twentieth Century*. New York: Harper & Row, 1967.

LeDuc, T. *Piety and Intellect at Amherst College, 1865-1912.* New York: Columbia University Press, 1946.

Leslie, W. B. Localism, denominationalism, and institutional strategies in urbanizing America: Three Pennsylvania colleges, 1870-1915. *History of Education Quarterly,* 1977, *17,* 235-256.

Leslie, W. B. From tumult to benign neglect: The strange career of the history of American higher education in the 1970's. *Review of Higher Education,* 1980, *3,* 3-7.

Lowery, W. R., and Associates. *College Admissions Counseling: A Handbook for the Profession.* San Francisco: Jossey-Bass, 1982.

McConica, J. Scholars and commoners in Renaissance Oxford. In L. Stone (ed.), *The University in Society.* Princeton, N.J.: Princeton University Press, 1974.

MacRae, D. G. The culture of a generation: Students and others. In W. Laqueur and G. L. Mosse (eds.), *Education and Social Structure in the Twentieth Century.* New York: Harper & Row, 1967.

Manning, W. H., Willingham, W. W., and Breland, H. M. *Selective Admissions in Higher Education.* San Francisco: Jossey-Bass, 1977.

Mattingly, P. H. Structures over time: Institutional history. In J. H. Best (ed.), *Historical Inquiry in Education: A Research Agenda.* Washington, D.C.: American Educational Research Association, 1983.

Moll, R. *Playing the Private College Admissions Game.* New York: New York Times, 1980.

Moos, M. *The Post-Land Grant University: The University of Maryland Report.* College Park: University of Maryland, 1981.

Nevins, A. *The State Universities and Democracy.* Urbana: University of Illinois Press, 1962.

Park, J. *The Rise of American Education: An Annotated Bibliography.* Evanston, Ill.: Northwestern University Press, 1965.

Peterson, G. E. *The New England College in the Age of the University.* Amherst, Mass.: Amherst College Press, 1964.

Potts, D. B. American colleges in the nineteenth century: From localism to denominationalism. *History of Education Quarterly,* 1971, *11,* 363-380.

Rainsford, G. N. Change, growth, and entrepreneurial opportunity in higher education administration. *Educational Record,* 1983, *64,* 20-22.

Riesman, D., and Jencks, C. The viability of the American college. In N. Sanford (ed.), *The American College: A Psychological and Social Interpretation of the Higher Learning.* New York: Wiley, 1962.

Ringer, F. K. Higher education in Germany in the nineteenth century. In W. L. Laqueur and G. L. Mosse (eds.), *Education and Social Structure in the Twentieth Century.* New York: Harper & Row, 1967.

Rohl, J. C. G. Higher civil servants in Germany, 1890-1900. In W. Laqueur and G. L. Mosse (eds.), *Education and Social Structure in the Twentieth Century.* New York: Harper & Row, 1967.

Rose, L. B. The secret life of Sarah Lawrence. *Commentary,* 1983, *64,* 52-56.

Rudolph, F. *The American College and University: A History.* New York: Random House, 1962.

Sacks, H. S., and Associates. *Hurdles: The Admissions Dilemma in American Higher Education.* New York: Atheneum, 1978.

Sanford, N. (ed). *The American College: A Psychological and Sociological Interpretation of the Higher Learning.* New York: Wiley, 1962.

Schudson, M. Organizing the "meritocracy": A History of the College Entrance Examination Board. *Harvard Educational Review,* 1972, *42,* 34-69.

Smith, W. The new historian of American education: Some notes for a portrait. *Harvard Education Review,* 1961, *31,* 136-143.

Spies, R. R. *The Future of Private Colleges: The Effects of Rising Costs on College Choice.* Princeton, N.J.: Princeton University Industrial Relations Section, 1973.

Steinberg, S. How Jewish quotas began. *Commentary*, 1971, *52*, 67-76.

Stewart, C. The place of higher education in a changing society. In N. Sanford (ed.), *The American College: A Psychological and Sociological Interpretation of the Higher Learning.* New York: Wiley, 1962.

Stone, L. The Ninnyversity? *New York Review of Books.* January 28, 1971, pp. 20-29.

Stone, L. The size and composition of the Oxford student body, 1580-1909. In L. Stone (ed.), *The University in Society.* Princeton, N.J.: Princeton University Press, 1974.

Story, R. Harvard students, the Boston elite, and the New England preparatory system, 1800-1870. *History of Education Quarterly*, 1975, *15*, 281-298.

Synnott, M. G. *The Half-Opened Door: Discrimination and Admissions at Harvard, Yale, and Princeton, 1900-1970.* Westport, Conn.: Greenwood Press, 1979.

Talbott, J. E. The history of education. *Daedalus*, 1971, *100*, 133-150.

Thelin, J. R. California and the colleges. *California Historical Quarterly*, 1977, *56*, 140-163 and 230-249.

Thelin, J. R. Auditing the admissions office: Applied research and evaluation at the small, selective college. *College and University*, 1979, *54*, 96-108.

Thelin, J. R. Gatekeepers and headhunters: Admissions, exclusion, and sorting. In *Higher Education and Its Useful Past.* Cambridge, Mass.: Schenkman, 1982.

Tobias, M. *Old Dartmouth on Trial: The Transformation of the Academic Community in Nineteenth-Century America.* New York: New York University Press, 1982.

Trow, M. Reflections on the transition from mass to universal higher education. *Daedalus*, 1970, *99*, 1-42.

Turner, R. Sponsored and contest mobility and the school system. *American Sociological Review*, 1960, *25*, 855-867.

Veysey, L. R. *The Emergence of the American University.* Chicago: University of Chicago Press, 1965.

Veysey, L. R. Undergraduate admissions: Past and future. In *Marketing in College Admissions: A Broadening of Perspectives.* New York: The College Entrance Examination Board, 1980.

Webb, E., Campbell, D. T., Schwartz, R. D., and Sechrest, L. *Unobtrusive Measures: Nonreactive Research in the Social Sciences.* New York: Rand McNally, 1966.

Wechsler, H. S. *The Qualified Student: A History of Selective College Admissions in America.* New York: Wiley, 1977.

White, H. The burden of history. *History and Theory*, 1966, *5*, 111-134.

Young, M. *The Rise of the Meritocracy, 1870-2033.* Middlesex, England: Penguin Books, 1958.

Zeldin, T. Higher education in France, 1848-1940. In W. Laqueur and G. L. Mosse (eds.), *Education and Social Structure in the Twentieth Century.* New York: Harper & Row, 1967.

APPLICATIONS OF CAUSAL MODELS IN HIGHER EDUCATION

Lee M. Wolfle, *Virginia Polytechnic Institute and State University*

A theory is a systematic statement about relationships among variables for the purpose of understanding and explaining the phenomenon at hand. Causal models specify these relationships in ways that permit the application of rigorous and generalized methods for testing hypothesized relationships specified by theory. Thus causal models hold great promise for unraveling many of the phenomena studied in higher education by providing a statistically rigorous quantitative assessment of theoretical relationships. It is my contention that causal modeling should play a central role in higher education research, and this chapter endeavors to show how such models have been usefully applied in the past and how they might be applied in the future.

Causal modeling techniques originated with the work of the geneticist Sewall Wright (1921, 1934). Wright's path analysis starts by displaying a diagram with one-way arrows pointing from causal variables to their directly affected variables. Most of Wright's work expressed these variables in standard form, and the terms "path analysis" and "path coefficients" came to be associated with standardized variables and their coefficients. In contrast, the term "structural equation model" has been applied to causal models incorporating unstandardized coefficients. However, most analysts now use the terms "structural equation model," "causal model," and "path model" interchangeably (Bielby and Hauser, 1977). Despite the early preference for standardized coefficients, the use of causal models does not require standardized variables, and there are several good reasons to prefer unstandardized coefficients, the primary one being that they come closer to conveying the meaning of the scientific relationships contained in the theory being tested (Blalock, 1964; Duncan, 1975; Kim and Mueller, 1976).

Although the method of path analysis was devised over 60 years ago, it was introduced to the social sciences only recently. While several people (e.g., Blalock, 1961, 1964; Boudon, 1965; Land, 1969; Simon, 1957) helped to introduce causal modeling techniques to the social sciences, the expository paper by Duncan (1966) was of primary importance. He illustrated the method with several empirical models, and showed how the analysis of these models led to insights not obtained through ordinary regression analysis. He followed this with a comprehensive study of American occupational mobility (Blau and Duncan, 1967), which included a three-equation model of the process of occupational achievement. This seminal work built a framework for studying occupational mobility that has been widely adopted by researchers in the field.

Applications of path analysis to other substantive problems in sociology quickly began to appear in the journals, and soon began to permeate the other social sciences. Werts and Linn (1970) introduced path analysis to educational psychologists, and Hauser (1971) applied the method in his study of the influence of socioeconomic background on school performance. Gintis (1971) used path analysis to study the effects of education on worker productivity. Several studies of the causes and consequences of educational achievement employed path analysis (Duncan, Featherman, and Duncan, 1972; Griliches and Mason, 1972; Sewell and Hauser, 1975). The introduction of expository articles in educational research journals soon followed (Anderson, 1978; Anderson and Evans, 1974; Wolfle, 1977; 1980a), and now causal models are often to be found in the pages of educational journals.

The use of path analysis usually requires that all of the variables are manifest (i.e., actually measured).[1] Yet it is often useful to include latent variables that are not directly observable (e.g., intelligence, attitudes, motivation). Indeed, Wright's (1925) analysis of fluctuations in corn and hog prices included unmeasured hog breeding variables (see Goldberger, 1972). Recent methodological advances now make the analysis of such models commonplace. Building on the work of Lawley (1943), Joreskog (1966, 1967, 1969, 1973) discovered an efficient computational procedure that combined confirmatory factor analysis with linear structural models among the latent factors. Joreskog and van Thillo (1972) have since provided a computer program called LISREL, now in its sixth edition (Joreskog and Sorbom, 1983), that is revolutionizing the way social scientists test hypothesized relationship among theoretical variables (Kerlinger, 1977).

Before going any further, several preliminary topics need to be discussed. The first topic distinguishes structural equation modeling as a heuristic device from the statistical procedures used to estimate coefficients in the models. The second topic sets forth the notation that will be used in drawing path diagrams and specifying the causal equations. The third topic touches briefly on the subject of causality.

THE HEURISTIC VALUE OF CAUSAL MODELS

Unlike correlation, stepwise regression, or factor analyses, structural equation modeling requires the researcher to think about cause, particularly systems of intercausal connections, and provides an explicit link between *a priori* theoretical notions of causal connections and quantitative estimates of causal impact. It is important to recognize that the methods used to estimate coefficients in structural equation models add little mathematically or statistically to methods already available in regression and factor analysis.

If structural equation models add so little mathematically and statistically, why are they so useful? The first reason is that the formulation of a problem in a causal framework forces a degree of explicitness that is often absent in research reports that rely solely on regression or factor analysis. The drawing of the path diagram, the arrangement of variables with causal arrows, all force the researcher to confront his model of reality.[2] Once a causal arrow has been drawn, the researcher knows, and others will know, that the model explicitly specifies one variable to be a cause of another.

One draws these causal arrows on the basis of what one knows *a priori*, or theoretically, about the subject matter under investigation. Once the arrows have been drawn, there can be no misinterpretation about hypothesized causes and effects. The researcher may, of course, be wrong; but he won't be misunderstood. It is this degree of explicitness in the presentation of causal models that led Wolfle (1980*a*) to conclude a recent article on causal models with the comment that explicit communication was the most important strategy of path analysis.

There is a second reason why causal models are useful: they provide a powerful aid to the substantive interpretation of results. Causal models not only allow the assessment of hypothesized direct causal links, but the researcher can also obtain estimates of the extent to which intervening variables account for relationships between predetermined and subsequent variables. These are interpreted as indirect causal effects (Finney, 1972). In addition, the researcher may obtain estimates of the extent to which antecedent variables account for relationships between subsequent variables. These may be interpreted as spurious or noncausal effects. More will be said about decomposing effects in causal models below.

THE PATH DIAGRAM

While not necessary for estimating the coefficients in causal models, most researchers present their structural equation models in diagrammatic form. One such model is shown in Figure 1. It is a basic model of the process of socioeconomic achievement, originally analyzed by Duncan, Featherman, and Duncan (1972) and subsequently by several others (Alwin and Hauser, 1975; Sobel, 1982; Wolfle and Ethington, 1984). The three variables on the left-hand side of the diagram are called exogenous variables, because they are determined by variables outside of the present model. They may, of course, covary with each other, though for reasons unanalyzed in this particular model. These covariances are depicted by the curved, double-headed arrows.

The other variables in the model are called endogenous variables, because they do have explicit causes in the model. The straight, unidirectional arrows in the model represent hypothesized causal effects. The arrows point from the variables taken as causes to the variables taken as effects. These arrows may be interpreted to mean, for example, that father's education (X_1) is a cause of education (X_4) or alternatively that a change in father's education produces a change in education. An endogenous variable that is specified to be caused by some variables may itself be a cause of subsequent variables. Thus education is seen to be dependent on father's education, father's occupation, and number of siblings, but is seen to be a cause of occupational prestige and income.

The endogenous and exogenous variables shown in Figure 1 are explicitly measured. Other variables in the model are not explicitly measured; these are called "disturbances," or "errors," or "residuals." They represent all other sources of variation in the endogenous variables not jointly explained by the independent variables. These other sources may include variables not included in the model, deviations from linearity, random errors, and the like. These effects are depicted in Figure 1 as the short arrows that point to the endogenous variables from outside the model.

Figure 1 is merely a diagrammatic representation of a set of structural equations. The equations implied by Figure 1 are:

$$X_4 = b_{41}X_1 + b_{42}X_2 + b_{43}X_3 + e_4$$

$$X_5 = b_{51}X_1 + b_{52}X_2 + b_{53}X_3 + b_{54}X_4 + e_5$$

$$X_6 = b_{61}X_1 + b_{62}X_2 + b_{63}X_3 + b_{64}X_4 + b_{65}X_5 + e_6$$

In these equations, the six X_i variables are measured as deviations from their respective means.[3] Consequently, the intercept terms are all zero. The parameter estimates b_{ij} in recursive causal models can be estimated with ordinary least-squares regression.[4] They are interpreted as the average amount that X_i changes when X_j changes by one unit when the other independent variables in the equation are held constant. The e_i variables are residual terms representing deviations of predicted scores from actual scores. In those instances when the variables have been standardized, the standardized regression coefficients (sometimes called "beta weights") are interpreted as the average number of standard deviations that X_i changes when X_j changes by one standard deviation when the other independent variables in the equation are held constant.

The set of three equations shown above may look like regression equations, but they are more. They are structural equations. They not only express a mathematical relationship between the endogenous variables and their predictors, but they also express a theoretical relationship between hypothesized causal variables and their effects. Structural equation models therefore require a blend of mathematics and theory, and it is the translation of theory into mathematical relationships that is by far the more difficult undertaking. As Duncan (1975, p. 149) noted, "The study of structural equation models can be divided into two parts: the easy part and the hard part." The easy part is mathe-matical. The hard part is constructing causal models that are consistent with sound theory. In short, causal models are no better than the ideas that go into them.

THE CONCEPT OF CAUSATION
The role of causal modeling is not to accomplish the impossible task of deter-mining causal relationships from the values of correlations or covariances (Wright, 1934).[5] Its purpose, rather, is to provide quantitative estimates of the impacts of causes on their effects, and to interpret these coefficients in the con-text of the theory being expressed in the model. Thus causal relationships exist in models because theories posit them. The data may demonstrate the absence of a causal relationship, but not its presence. While models can be discon-firmed, in contrast causal relationship at best fail to be disconfirmed; they can never be confirmed (Cliff, 1983; Kenny, 1979; pp. 1-2).

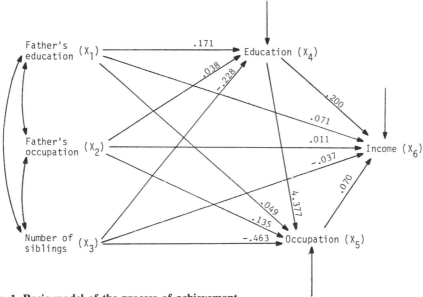

Fig. 1. Basic model of the process of achievement.
Source. Duncan, Featherman, and Duncan, 1972, p. 39.

The correlations among variables in causal models may be suggestive of causal effects, but additional conditions must hold. As Kenny (1979), among others, has pointed out, in order to infer the existence of a causal relationship between *X* and *Y*, three conditions must hold. The first of these is that *X* must precede *Y* in time. For example, models of social mobility posit that the socio-economic achievements of parents are causes of the socioeconomic achieve-ments of offspring, but never the opposite. When the temporal order of variables is not clear, researchers often include them in causal blocks with no causal nexus posited among them. Thus when Hauser (1973) and his associates (Hauser, Tsai, and Sewell, 1983; Sewell and Hauser, 1975) measured the influence of significant others on educational plans and subsequent socioeconomic achievements, they included the influence of parents, teachers, and best friends as one block of variables.

The second condition for causation is that a functional relationship exists between X and Y. Neither X nor Y may be a constant, and the association between them should not be independent. If X and Y are independent, then knowing the value of one variable yields no advantage in predicting the value of the other variable.

The third condition for causation is that the association between X and Y is not spurious. That is, for X to be a cause of Y, there must not exist a causally antecedent Z (or set of Z's) such that when Z is controlled the association between X and Y disappears. This is the view of causality adopted by Good (1961, 1962) and Suppes (1970). In essence, the probabilistic view of causality states that X is a cause of Y if a change in X produces a change in Y after controlling for everything else in the universe. Of course, one can never control everything. Rather, the researcher must include in his model the *relevant* controls as dictated by the substance of the model at hand. Including the relevant controls is a matter of insight, and led Cooley (1978, p. 13), a self-declared number cruncher, to remark that Paul Lazersfeld, using contingency tables, was the better causal analyst because "he was aware of the major alternative explanations that had to be guarded against and took that into account when he decided upon the four or five variables that were crucial to include."

If relevant antecedent causes have been omitted from a causal model, then the coefficients commonly used to measure causal impacts are biased. Yet it is not enough to criticize a causal model by *saying* that confounding variables have been omitted from the model. One must identify these variables, measure them, include them in the model, and demonstrate that causally subsequent relationships are spurious. This is, to cite a personally familiar example, exactly what Wolfle (1980*b*) did in reanalyzing the work of Hyman, Wright, and Reed (1975).

DECOMPOSITION OF EFFECTS ON CAUSAL MODELS

An attractive feature of causal models is the ability to decompose zero-order measures of association into a sum of simple and compound paths, some of which are interpretable as direct causal effects and some as indirect causal effects. Direct causal effects are estimated by the magnitude of partial regression coefficients. Indirect causal effects are estimated by the magnitude of the sum of products of causal effects through intervening variables. These decompositions provide a basis for substantively interpreting the causal effects that variables have on each other in a causal model. For example, occupational mobility data are frequently analyzed with contingency tables (e.g., Rogoff, 1953), and analyses of intergenerational occupational mobility typically show that the occupations of fathers and sons are positively related. In one of the first applications of path analysis, Duncan and Hodge (1963) demonstrated how this association is mediated by educational attainment. They found that "education was an appreciably more important determinant [of occupational prestige] than was father's occupation; and the latter factor, moreover, was influential in large part because of its association with education" (p. 644). Thus father's occupation and son's occupation are associated predominantly because fathers with high prestige have sons who acquire the education necessary to obtain occupations of high prestige.

The decomposition of effects in causal models can be done in a number of ways. For example, one way of measuring zero-order associations in causal models is with correlation coefficients. These may be decomposed into three substantive components using the fundamental theorem of path analysis. The three substantive components consist of direct causal effects, indirect causal effects, and noncausal, or spurious, components. The sum of the direct and indirect effects is commonly called the "total effect." The fundamental theorem of path analysis may be written:

$$\varrho_{ij} = \Sigma p_{iq} \varrho_{jq}$$

where p denotes a standardized regression coefficient, ϱ denotes a population correlation coefficient, i and j denote two variables in the model, and the index q runs over all variables from which direct paths lead to X_i. Wolfle (1980a) has given a number of examples of this approach toward decomposing effects in causal models. The resulting equations, however, can be tedious, and there are several less cumbersome ways of calculating these decompositions. One way is to read the simple and compound paths directly from the path diagram according to rules established by Wright (1934) and reiterated by Duncan (1966, p. 6):

Read *back* from variable i, *then forward to* variable j, forming the product of all paths along the traverse; then sum these products for all possible traverses. The same variable cannot be intersected more than once in a single traverse. In no case can one trace back having once started forward. The bidirectional correlation is used in tracing either forward or back, but if more than one bidirectional correlation appears in the diagram, only one can be used in a single traverse. The resulting expression . . . may consist of a single direct path plus the sum of several compound paths representing all the indirect connections allowed by the diagram.

When the variables in the model have been standardized, the sums of such products yield the correlation coefficient, ϱ_{ij}. When the variables have been measured in their original metrics or as deviation scores, the coefficients are partial regression coefficients, and the sum of their products along the appropriate traverses yields the zero-order population slope, β_{ij}. With standardized variables a bidirectional association is measured by the correlation between the two variables since $\varrho_{gh} = \varrho_{hg}$. With metric coefficients, however, one may no longer use the correlation coefficient for bidirectional associations, but must use the regression slope β_{gh} or β_{hg}, as appropriate, since in general $\beta_{gh} \neq \beta_{hg}$.

Consider the sample decomposition of the association between father's occupation (X_2) and respondent's occupation (X_5) in Figure 1. The direct effect of X_2 on X_5 is estimated by b_{52}. The indirect effect of X_2 on X_5 through education (X_4) is estimated by the product, $b_{54}b_{42}$. All of the other possible traverses between X_2 and X_5 involve bidirectional associations, to which no causal interpretations were attached. Hence, no causal interpretation is warranted in the traverses that use these associations. The decomposition into direct and indirect effects for all of the causal links implied by Figure 1 are shown in Table 1.

TABLE 1. Decomposition of Causal Effects in a Basic Model of the Process of Achievement

Variables	Direct Effect	Indirect Effect	Total Effect	Direct Effect	Indirect Effect
x_1 to x_4	b_{41}	—	.171	.171	—
x_2 to x_4	b_{42}	—	.038	.038	—
x_3 to x_4	b_{43}	—	-.228	-.228	—
x_1 to x_5	b_{51}	$b_{41}b_{54}$	.796	.049	.747
x_2 to x_5	b_{52}	$b_{42}b_{54}$	.303	.135	.168
x_3 to x_5	b_{53}	$b_{43}b_{54}$	-1.461	-.463	-.998
x_4 to x_5	b_{54}	—	4.377	4.377	—
x_1 to x_6	b_{61}	$b_{41}b_{64} + b_{51}b_{65} + b_{41}b_{54}b_{65}$	.161	.071	.090
x_2 to x_6	b_{62}	$b_{42}b_{64} + b_{52}b_{65} + b_{42}b_{54}b_{65}$	.040	.011	.029
x_3 to x_6	b_{63}	$b_{43}b_{64} + b_{53}b_{65} + b_{43}b_{54}b_{65}$	-.186	-.037	-.149
x_4 to x_6	b_{64}	$b_{54}b_{65}$	.508	.200	.308
x_5 to x_6	b_{65}	—	.070	.070	—

In complex causal models, decomposing associations with either the fundamental theorem or the tracing method can be tedious and subject to computational errors. Fortunately, there are several methods for decomposing causal components that alleviate this tedium. Alwin and Hauser (1975) showed for just-identified[6] recursive models that reduced-form equations[7] could be used to estimate total effects. Indirect effects could then be obtained by subtracting the appropriate final-equation coefficients from their respective coefficients in the reduced-form equation. Applying Alwin and Hauser's method to the model in

Figure 1 to obtain the indirect effect of father's occupation (X_2) on occupation (X_5), one would first regress occupation on the three exogenous variables. One would next add education to the regression. The difference between $b_{52.13}$ and $b_{52.134}$ is equal to the indirect effect of X_2 on X_5. Alwin and Hauser's technique thus allows the computation of indirect effects on mainframe computers with only minor arithmetic computations, and Wolfle (1982a) has provided a microcomputer program that calculates all direct and indirect effects in just-identified recursive models utilizing this method.

Fox (1980) has introduced a more efficient and general technique for calculating indirect effects. His strategy for calculating total indirect effects involves raising a matrix of direct effects to successive powers, until a zero matrix is obtained, and summing the results. Joreskog and Sorbom (1983, III.39) have since provided a more general procedure that holds for models with or without latent variables, for recursive or nonrecursive models, and for just-identified or overidentified models.[8] Graff and Schmidt (1982) have shown how the LISREL decompositions can be usefully applied to evaluation studies of unintended consequences of social programs.

Despite the enormous interest in estimating indirect causal effects, their probability distribution was for a long time unknown. Thus most users of causal modeling techniques treated estimates of indirect effects as if they were population parameters and did not test whether they were statistically significant. Bobko and Rieck (1980) and Sobel (1982) have independently corrected this uncertainty by deriving the asymptotic distribution of indirect effects for large sample sizes. Following the work of Sobel, Wolfle and Ethington (1984) discovered an algorithm for calculating partial derivatives of indirect-effect coefficients with respect to their direct-effect components, and incorporated this algorithm into a FORTRAN computer program called SEINE that makes the calculation of standard errors in recursive causal models a relatively easy task.

Cliff (1983) has said that the development of rigorous methods for statistically testing hypotheses in covariance structures is one of the most important statistical revolutions in the social sciences. The easy calculation of indirect effects and their standard errors adds an important component to that revolution. It has always been good practice to publish standard errors of direct-effect coefficients, so readers may draw their own conclusions about the precision of estimates (Duncan, 1975, p. 49). The easy calculation of standard errors of indirect effects now makes it advisable to include these coefficients as part of the presentation of structural equation results along with the standard errors of direct effects.

APPLICATIONS OF CAUSAL MODELS IN HIGHER EDUCATION

In recent years, researchers in higher education have been showing a steadily growing interest in utilizing structural equation models to study relationships among variables. Several examples will be presented. The first of these will involve recursive causal models. These are models in which there are no causal feedback loops; that is, the causal flow in the model is unidirectional. The second category involves nonrecursive models, which include reciprocal causal effects.

Recursive Causal Models in Higher Education

Vincent Tinto (1975) reviewed an extensive literature on withdrawal from college and came to two main conclusions. First, he found that withdrawal has typically been poorly defined, and studies often fail to distinguish among voluntary dropouts, academic failures, temporary withdrawers, and intercollegiate transfers. Second, he found that prior studies had failed to develop theoretical models that explained the process of college withdrawal. Following the lead of Spady (1970), Tinto built a theoretical model of dropout from college based on the degree of integration of individual students into the social and academic systems of the college and their identification with the institution. In the words of Pascarella, Duby, and Iverson (1983, p. 88):

> The model suggests that students come to a particular college or university with a range of background traits (e.g., race, secondary school achievement, academic aptitude, family educational, and financial context). These background characteristics lead to initial commitments, both to the goal of graduation from college and to the specific institution attended. Together with background traits, these initial commitments are hypothesized as influencing, not only how well the student will perform academically, but also how he or she will interact with, and subsequently become integrated into, the institution's social and academic systems. Other things being equal, the greater the individual's level of social and academic integration, the greater his or her subsequent commitment to the institution and commitment to the goal of college graduation, respectively. These subsequent commitments, in turn, are seen, along with levels of integration, as having a positive influence on persistence.

Since the publication of Tinto's (1975) paper, a number of investigators have incorporated his conceptual scheme in their own causal models of persistence in higher education. Munro (1981) used data from the National Longitudinal Study of the High School Class of 1972 to test Tinto's model. She found that a commitment to the goal of completing an educational program was the strongest predictor of persistence in higher education. Contrary to Tinto's hypotheses about the predictors of goal commitment, however, Munro found that educational aspirations were more important than academic integration.

In the meantime, Bean (1980), using data from the freshman class of a major Midwestern university, discovered that the process of persistence differed for men and women. For both men and women, the most important predictor of persistence was institutional commitment, but for women the second most important predictor was academic performance in high school, while for men the second most important predictor was academic performance during their freshman year. In another test of Tinto's model, Bean (1982) continued to find interactions in the process of withdrawal/persistence. In this new set of analyses, Bean found for three of the four groups he analyzed that intent to leave and university grades were the two most important predictors of withdrawal.

Pascarella and his associates (Pascarella and Chapman, 1983; Pascarella, Duby, and Iverson, 1983; Pascarella and Terenzini, 1980, 1983; Terenzini and Pascarella, 1977) have tested the validity of Tinto's model in a number of settings, and in general have obtained results consistent with the model's expectations. As Pascarella and Terenzini (1983) point out, however, most tests of Tinto's model are deficient in the sense that not all of the salient constructs specified by Tinto are represented in the models that purport to test the theory. Pascarella and Terenzini (1983) provide one of the first comprehensive tests of Tinto's model of withdrawal.

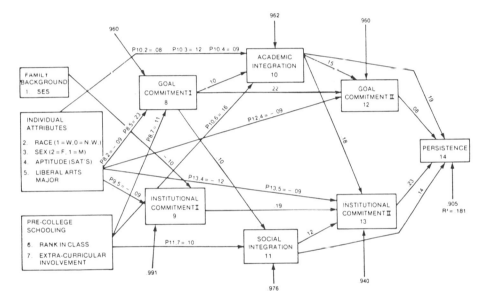

Fig. 2. Causal model of freshman-year persistence/withdrawal.
Source. "Predicting Voluntary Freshmen Year Persistence/Withdrawal Behavior in a Residential University: A Path Analytic Validation of Tinto's Model" by Ernest T. Pascarella and Patrick T. Terenzini, *Journal of Educational Psychology,* 1983, *75,* 221. Copyright 1983 by the American Psychological Association, Washington, D.C. Reprinted by permission.

The model tested by Pascarella and Terenzini (1983) is shown in Figure 2. Only the statistically significant effects are indicated, and the coefficients shown are standardized regression coefficients (or beta weights). Pascarella and Terenzini discuss these results in detail (pp. 221-222). With respect to the direct causes of persistence, as hypothesized by Tinto (1975), the influences of academic integration and social integration were about equal in value. The influences of goal commitment and institutional commitment, however, were not equal, a result that Pascarella and Terenzini attributed to the academic selectivity of the institution being studied.

With respect to the several indirect effects in Pascarella and Terenzini's (1983) model, they note that both academic and social integration possess both direct and indirect causal effects on persistence, but that none of the background characteristics had significant direct effects. The authors wrote, "Rather, their effects were indirect, being transmitted through social and academic integration or subsequent institutional and goal commitment" (p. 222). Like nearly all users of causal models, Pascarella and Terenzini made these statements about indirect effects without testing whether or not the indirect-effect coefficients were statistically significant.

Using a new FORTRAN program described by Wolfle and Ethington (1984), the Pascarella and Terenzini (1983) model was reanalyzed by the author and the standard errors of indirect effects estimated. These results are partially reproduced in Table 2 for the direct and indirect effects of the causes of persistence.[9] These results show, as indicated by Pascarella and Terenzini, that both the direct and indirect effects of academic and social integration on persistence are statistically significant at the .05 level of probability. With respect to the effects of background variables, it is true that none of their direct effects were statistically significant. The authors were overoptimistic, however, to conclude therefrom that their indirect effects were all significant. As Table 2 clearly shows, only high school extracurricular activities, high school rank, and sex had significant indirect effects on persistence. The indirect effects of socioeconomic status, race, SAT performance, and liberal arts major were statistically insignificant. These last four background variables apparently have no effect on persistence, either directly or indirectly.

The studies that were inspired by Tinto's (1975) conceptual model were interested in explaining persistence or withdrawal from institutions of higher education. In a related area of inquiry, Robertshaw and Wolfle (1983) were interested in the effects on educational attainment of delayed entry into college and interruptions in college educations. That is, they investigated the causes and consequences of educational discontinuities rather than educational terminations. Using a structural equation model suggested by Featherman and Carter (1976), Robertshaw and Wolfle found that their model did not explain very well why people delay entry into postsecondary institutions or interrupt their educations once enrolled. However, it was clear from their analysis that if students do either, it costs them about one-half year of education, net of the effects of their social background, ability, and especially the length of time they were in school. Those people who attain more education are not only those who attend institutions of higher education, but also those who enter them immediately after high school, and once enrolled in college, remain there without interruption.

Two final illustrations of the applications of recursive structural equation models to higher education will suffice to indicate the interpretive advantages to be gained from such analyses. Bruton and Crull (1982) examined the intervening effects of instructional quality in an introductory sociology course on two outcome variables: whether students would recommend the course to

TABLE 2. Summary of Causal Effects on College Persistence/Withdrawal from Pascarella and Terenzini (1983)[a]

Predetermined Variables	Direct Effect	Indirect Effect
Institutional commitment 2	.040 (.006)	—
Goal commitment 2	.027 (.013)	—
Social integration	.015 (.004)	.003 (.001)
Academic integration	.016 (.003)	.005 (.001)
Institutional commitment	.017 (.011)	-.010 (.005)
Goal commitment	.013 (.011)	.024 (.005)
High school extracurricular activities	-.018 (.019)	.021 (.008)
High school rank	-.001 (.001)	.001 (.000)
Liberal arts major	-.003 (.023)	-.013 (.011)
SAT performance	.000 (.000)	-.000 (.000)
Sex	.024 (.022)	.025 (.010)
Race	-.025 (.038)	.006 (.017)
Socioeconomic status	.004 (.008)	.001 (.003)

[a] Standard errors shown in parentheses.

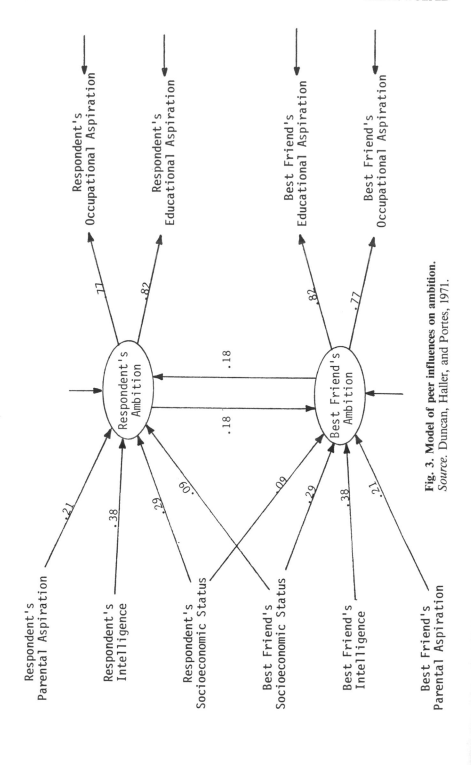

Fig. 3. Model of peer influences on ambition.
Source. Duncan, Haller, and Portes, 1971.

others, and whether they planned to take more courses in the discipline. Positive evaluations of the lecturer and the textbook led to higher course evaluations, which in turn had strong effects on both outcome variables. The authors concluded that departments concerned about enrollments should staff introductory courses with highly able instructors, for perceived quality of instruction has an important effect on future enrollment plans.

Roberson, Keith, and Page (1983) were interested in determining the motivating factors in the decision to enter the teaching profession. Using a causal model of the decisional process to enter teaching, they studied the relative importance of various background variables, attitudes, and motivations for a sample of 1980 high school seniors. The two most important effects on teaching aspirations were gender and the importance of a "good income." It is primarily females who aspire to teach, while those who feel that a good income is important opt not to teach.

Nonrecursive Causal Models in Higher Education
The models examined above were all recursive; that is, the assumed direction of causal flow was unidirectional. Another class of models specifies the existence of two-way causal relationships. These are called nonrecursive models. In nonrecursive models it is implausible to assume that residual disturbances are uncorrelated with causal variables in an equation, which is a necessary assumption for estimating structural coefficients with ordinary least-squares multiple regression. Consequently, two-stage least-squares solutions are required. Identification of such models, however, requires that the model contain so-called instrumental variables, which are exogenous variables assumed *a priori* to have zero effects on one or more endogenous variables. Nevertheless, it is difficult to conceive that such variables exist in most substantive situations, which makes most nonrecursive models implausible for social science applications.

A notable exception is the model used by Duncan, Haller, and Portes (1971) to analyze the hypothesis that adolescent boys influence each other in forming their socioeconomic aspirations. It is clear that children of similar socioeconomic backgrounds form friendships. It is also clear that a positive relationship exists between the parental aspirations for children's achievements among parents of similar background. The Duncan et al. study controlled for these associations while estimating the extent to which one's best friend's ambitions influenced one's own. Yet it is immediately evident that the relationship must be reciprocal; if the best friend influences the respondent, the respondent must influence the best friend. The reciprocal relationship between respondent's and best friend's ambitions led Duncan et al. to specify a nonrecursive model, which is depicted in Figure 3.

The model shown in Figure 3 is not only more complicated by virtue of being nonrecursive than the recursive models discussed above, but it also contains two latent, unmeasured constructs. These latent constructs are thought to be respondent's ambition and best friend's ambition. They are thought to be indexed by manifest measures of occupational and educational aspirations. The exogenous variables in the model measure parental aspirations, intellectual ability, and parental socioeconomic status (SES), for both the respondent and his best friend. The model specifies that all three of his background variables influence the respondent's ambition, while the same is true for the best friend and his background characteristics. Furthermore, the model specifies a direct influence of friend's SES on the respondent's ambition, and of the respondent's SES on the best friend's ambition. However, it is assumed that there is no direct effect of respondent's IQ or respondent's parental aspiration on the best friend's ambition, and vice versa. (In their respective equations these are the instrumental variables that identify the model.) Rather, the influence of these variables occurs only indirectly through the ambition variables.

In estimating this model, Duncan et al. (1971) determined that intellectual ability and SES had the greatest influence on the formulation of socioeconomic ambitions for both respondent and friend. But the effects of friend's ambition, and vice versa, were also important. Peer groups do indeed play a role in the formation of socioeconomic ambitions.

In their original paper, Duncan et al. (p. 243) noted that it was only a coincidence that the effects of respondent and friend on each other were equal when rounded to two decimal places. Yet it may not be a coincidence at all. The effects may be equal in the population, and within normal sampling error limits in any particular sample. This hypothesis was tested explicitly by Joreskog and Sorbom (1983, III.81–93) in their reanalysis of the Duncan et al. model. Using LISREL, and specifying that the reciprocal effects had to be equal, they found that $\chi^2 = 0.01$ with 1 degree of freedom. Clearly, the hypothesis that friend's effect on respondent and respondent's effect on best friend were equal cannot be rejected. Joreskog and Sorbom went on to suggest that the whole model could be symmetric, in which, say, the effect of IQ on ambition for the friend was equal to the corresponding effect for the respondent. When they reestimated such a model, they found it to be more parsimonious and to have a better fit than Duncan et al.'s original model. Their results are shown in Figure 3; all the coefficients are significant at the .05 level of probability.

In the models specified by both Duncan et al. (1971) and Joreskog and Sorbom (1983), the effects from respondent's IQ to best friend's ambition, and vice versa, were specified to be zero. In addition, the effects from respondent's parental aspirations to best friend's ambition, and vice versa, were also specified to be zero. How realistic were these assumptions? No definite test is possible, since to include these variables in their respective equations with non-zero coefficients would yield a model with no unique solution. However, a partial test is possible, first by allowing the two coefficients from IQ to ambition to be non-zero, then specifying that the two effects from parental aspiration to ambition are zero. Maintaining the specification about symmetric effects for respondent and best friend, the test of non-zero effects from IQ was conducted by the author. This test yielded a $\chi^2 = 0.73$ with 1 degree of freedom. Hence, the null hypothesis of zero effects from IQ may not be rejected. A second partial test allowed the two coefficients from parental aspiration to be non-zero. This test yielded a $\chi^2 = 0.47$ with 1 degree of freedom. Clearly this null hypothesis cannot be rejected either. Thus the zero effects posited by Duncan et al. apparently are indeed zero in the population.

CAUSAL MODELS WITH LATENT CONSTRUCTS
With the exception of the Duncan et al. (1971) analysis, all of the structural equation models considered above were based on explicitly measured variables. Yet there is a long history of latent, unmeasured constructs in social science research. Examples include the latent construct intelligence, as indexed by tests of quantitative and verbal ability; locus of control, as indexed by the items on Rotter's (1966) scale; and socioeconomic status, as indexed by education, occupation, and earnings. While latent constructs may not be observable, their effects on manifest variables are observable and hence measurable. Factor analysis, for example, is concerned with finding unmeasured factors that can explain why manifest variables are intercorrelated. Until recently, however, the factors were rarely conceived of as being causally related, only intercorrelated, when they were allowed to covary at all.

Among others, it was Joreskog (1967, 1969, 1970, 1973) who wedded the techniques of causal modeling to factor analysis, and has thus provided a powerful new data analysis tool. Joreskog's procedure, commonly called Lisrel (for linear structural relationships), is available in a computer program, LISREL (Joreskog and Sorbom, 1983), that allows structural equation models among latent constructs, which are often the variables of real theoretical interest. Lisrel has thus made possible the rigorous testing of theories that have until now been very difficult to test adequately (Kerlinger, 1977).

Lisrel also incorporates measurement models rooted in the psychometric literature (Alwin and Jackson, 1980; Joreskog, 1971) — both classical true-score models (Lord and Novick, 1968) and the common-factor model (Lawley and Maxwell, 1971). From a formal point of view, assuming measurement error in structural equation models is much the same as assuming variables to be latent, theoretical constructs. In the former case, one assumes that the true variable is observable, but only with error; in the latter, one assumes that the true variable is unobservable even in the population (Bentler, 1982), but that its effects on manifest variables are observable.

Structural equation models containing unobserved variables have been a part of the literature for years (Bielby, Hauser, and Featherman, 1977; Duncan, 1969; Hauser, 1969; Hauser and Goldberger, 1971; Hodge and Treiman, 1968; Siegel and Hodge, 1968; Wiley and Wiley, 1970) and have been nicely summarized by Bentler (1980). Applications in higher education have been slower to develop, but are beginning to show promise of yielding substantive insights not available through more traditional methods of analysis. Several examples will help to demonstrate the promise of using latent variable methods in higher education research.

Multicolinearity is a situation that exists when independent variables in an equation are so closely related that structural parameter estimates become unstable and their standard errors inflated (see Gordon, 1968). Several solutions to the problem have been proposed, including ridge regression (Hoerl and Kennard, 1970; Rozeboom, 1979) and principal components regression (Gunst and Mason, 1977). Multicollinearity was a problem among the data analyzed by Muffo and Coccari (1982). They were interested in the causes of the number and amount of external funds for research among members of the American Association of State Colleges and Universities. They concluded that the institutions most successful in securing external research support placed greater emphasis on both graduate teaching and funded research.

At one point in Muffo and Coccari's presentation of results, they reported that the standardized regression coefficient for the presence of an educational doctoral program was 871.86 (which implies that a one-standard-deviation change in the education doctorate variable produced a change of 872 standard deviations in external funding!), but that the presence of an arts and sciences doctorate produced a *negative* change of -423.74, although the zero-order correlation was a positive .37. These results are exceedingly unlikely in their substantive interpretations.

Wolfle (1982*b*) suggested a more useful analytic approach by which multicolinear data could be analyzed. Identifying several theoretical constructs that apparently underlay the variables involved in Muffo and Coccari's (1982) analysis, Wolfle used LISREL to reanalyze the data, using the highly correlated manifest variables as indicators of underlying latent constructs. The effects of these latent constructs on external research support indicated that the only important determinant of funding was past success in securing such funds.

Lisrel is also a very useful methodology for analyzing longitudinal data. A typical design for longitudinal studies is the measurement of a construct of interest followed by a subsequent remeasure of the same construct. After controlling for initial scores of the construct, one asks whether intervening events, either natural or experimental, have an influence on subsequent scores of the construct. Yet it is unreasonable to assume that response errors incurred in measuring the construct at one point in time are necessarily uncorrelated with response errors in subsequent measurements. Ignoring these measurement errors will tend to inflate stability estimates of the construct over time. Lisrel avoids these problems by permitting one to specify that the response errors of the manifest variables used to index the construct are correlated.

Wolfle and Robertshaw (1982) used this approach to analyze the effects of college attendance on locus of control. Using a sample of 1972 high school seniors, who were resurveyed four years later, and using LISREL to analyze the data, they were able to determine that a model which assumed random response errors among the manifest measures of locus of control yielded a stability estimate that exceeded the stability estimate in a model with correlated response errors by nearly a third.

Wolfle and Robertshaw's substantive question addressed the question of whether the acquisition of postsecondary education had an effect on locus of control, after controlling for initial expressions of locus of control. They found that postsecondary educational attendance and locus of control had a correlation of .25, but over 80% of this association was spurious due to the mutual dependence of postsecondary education and locus of control on their antecedent causes — primarily the earlier measures of locus of control and ability. When the proper control variables are included, and with an appropriate analytic approach, it is apparent that the acquisition of education beyond high school does not substantially increase one's internal control expectancies.

In yet another application of Lisrel, Wolfle (1983) examined interracial differences between blacks and whites in the postsecondary educational attainment process. Previous research in the area of educational attainment had indicated that social background variables are more important determinants of educational attainment among whites than among blacks. Thus whites with higher socioeconomic origins possess greater opportunity for the successful completion of additional years of schooling than those of lower origins, but among blacks the process of educational attainment relegates them to the same, equal, and comparatively low opportunity for success regardless of their status origins.

Wolfle (1983) argued, however, that the process needed to be reexamined because previous studies had been based on manifest variables measured with error. Ignoring measurement error can result in biased structural parameter estimates (e.g., Blalock, 1964), and when levels of measurement error differ between groups, interracial comparisons of parameter estimates can exaggerate interracial differences.

The model of postsecondary educational attainment used in the analysis considered education to be a function of father's occupational status, father's education, mother's education, respondent's ability, high school curriculum, and high school grades. The model is shown diagrammatically in Figure 4; the theoretical, latent variables of interest are shown within ellipses. With the exception of educational attainment, each of the latent constructs has two manifest indicators. In the case of the exogenous variables, the respondents were asked to report these variables in both the base year and the first follow-up of the survey. Ability was indexed with tests of math and reading, while curriculum and grades were reported by both the respondents and the schools they had attended.

In analyzing the model, Wolfle first tested whether the factor patterns were the same for whites and blacks. These are the regression coefficients that connect manifest variables with their true constructs. He found these to be the same for whites and blacks. The analysis then turned to interracial comparisons

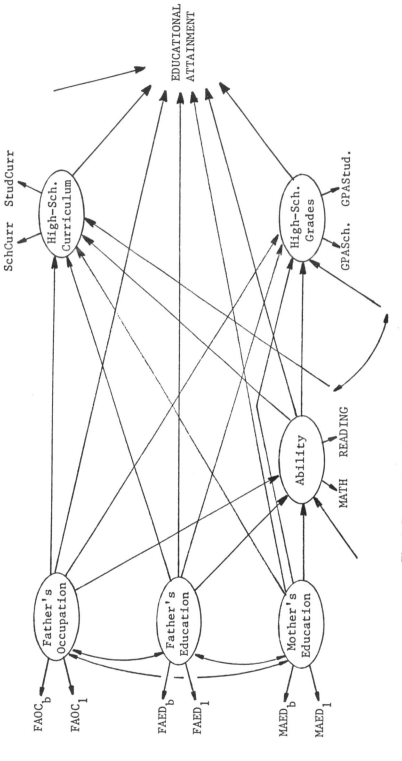

Fig. 4. Structural equation and measurement models of educational attainment among white and black 1972 high school graduates. *Source.* Wolfle, 1983.

of structural parameter estimates. Using the multigroup model in LISREL, equality constraints between whites and blacks were imposed on all structural estimates in the model. These constraints yielded a $\chi^2 = 17.25$ with 18 degrees of freedom. Thus the hypothesis that the process of educational attainment is the same for whites and blacks cannot be rejected.

Previous studies of interracial differences in educational attainment have suggested multiple social theories to explain the differences they found between whites and blacks (e.g., Porter, 1974; Portes and Wilson, 1976). Wolfle's (1983) study suggested a more simplified theory of educational attainment in which the process works the same for both whites and blacks.

PRECAUTIONS IN APPLYING CAUSAL MODELS

There are many ways that complexities can enter into the analysis of causal models, which if unrecognized can lead to implausible models, faulty analyses, or biased causal parameter estimates. The book by Namboodiri, Carter, and Blalock (1975) suggests several ways to avoid these problems, while Cliff (1983) and Miller (1977) summarize several principles to keep in mind when applying causal models.

Implausible Models
Duncan (1975) noted that the hard part of "doing" path analysis is constructing causal models that are consistent with sound theory. Thus all causal models are no better than the ideas invested in them, and a number of causal analyses fail on that basis alone, regardless of the statistical complexity used to estimate them. In my role as journal referee I have seen a number of causal models that were so implausibly constructed that the conclusions drawn from them were worthless. Two come readily to mind. One potential author constructed a model in which father's education was specified to be a cause of respondent's gender. Supposedly these were temporally ordered such that the parents completed their educational careers before bearing children, but temporal order is not sufficient to establish a causal relationship; there must also exist a functional relationship, and I can think of no plausible argument to suggest that "a change in parental education causes a change in the sex of offspring." Another model crossed my desk that included 30 variables with a sample size of only 26! Such a model is obviously not identified (see below). In order to estimate the model the author specified *a priori* a number of paths to be zero, but whether or not a causal effect is zero is more properly an empirical question and not a constraint to be specified *a priori*. Fortunately, most implausible models never make it into print, because one of the advantages of structural equation models is that the presentation of the model often reveals the lack of fit between the model and reality.

As in the example just cited, it has been my experience that neophytes in causal modeling tend to include in their models only those causal paths thought *a priori* to be non-zero. That is, without good reason to include a path, it is specified to be zero, which is a fairly strong assumption. The danger in this practice is that such assumptions go untested. A much better practice is to include such paths in one's analysis and use normal statistical procedures to decide whether or not the parameter was zero. Kenny (1979) has suggested that recursive causal models should always be just-identified, even if theory specifies that some parameters should be zero. It is good advice.

Standardized Coefficients

In reporting parameter estimates, many authors publish only the standardized path coefficients. It is a practice that should be discouraged. As demonstrated by Namboodiri, Carter, and Blalock (1975), among others, standardized coefficients are population-specific, and cannot be compared across populations or even within populations over time. No particular difficulty arises in using standardized coefficients for population-specific generalizations, but it is often the case that researchers want to compare results from one population to another. The author who reports only standardized coefficients precludes anyone from making such comparisons. A related and equally unfortunate practice is to fail to report the standard deviations of variables when reporting their zero-order correlations. One might be excused for reporting standardized coefficients if one also included the standard deviations; then the interested reader could calculate metric coefficients for himself. But without standard deviations, the situation is hopeless. Generally, reports of analyses of causal models should include a zero-order correlation or covariance matrix for the variables in the model along with their means and standard deviations.

Identification

Identification is yet another complexity with which the causal analyst must deal. Identification becomes a problem when there are more unknown parameters in an equation than there are knowns. Thus the equation has multiple solutions, which may be considered to be no solution at all. Failure to recognize the identification problem has trapped the unwary (e.g., Inverarity, 1976; and see comment by Bohrnstedt, 1977). Fortunately, in recursive causal models identification typically is not a problem. In nonrecursive models, as mentioned above, the identification problem is solved only by specifying the existence of instrumental variables, which may serve to identify the set of equations but often leads to substantively implausible models. In Lisrel models identification can also be a problem that can trap the unwary. While LISREL will print estimates for underidentified parameters, it is almost impossible for the program to estimate their standard errors. Thus users of LISREL should always specify that the standard errors be calculated. Not only is it good practice, it is also a good check on whether all of the equations in the model are identified.

Another form of underidentification exists in the presence of multicollinearity. That is, an equation may be algebraically identified but one or more variables could be so highly intercorrelated that the parameter estimates become unstable. Consequently, parameter estimates, and presumably the substantive interpretations drawn from them, may vary widely from sample to sample. Gordon (1968) gives a good review of multicollinearity, and Kenny (1979) discusses the issue in the context of causal modes.

Precautions in Using Lisrel

In addition to the general precautions already mentioned, there are some additional precautions unique to Lisrel. The first of these is the strong assumption required to estimate parameters by the method of maximum likelihood. In order to implement the maximum likelihood method, Joreskog (1967) chose to estimate the parameters with reference to a multivariate normal distribution. Yet in many situations the distributions of variables are unknown, or if known, known to be far from normal. While the maxiumum likelihood fitting function may be used if the observed variables do not deviate too much from normality, the standard errors must be interpreted with a great deal of caution. Furthermore, deviations from normality have a substantial influence on the magnitude of the likelihood ratio chi-square statistic often used to assess the fit of the model. Questions about the appropriateness of Lisrel estimation procedures have led to the inclusion in the LISREL program of several alternative estimation procedures, including the method of instrumental variables, two-stage least squares, unweighted least squares, and generalized least squares.

Because of questions with regard to the appropriateness of maximum likelihood estimation procedures used in Lisrel, at least two other methodological approaches to the estimation of coefficients in latent variable models have been proposed. One of these is called the partial least squares (PLS) method, which is essentially an extension of principal component and canonical variables analyses. The method was proposed by Wold (1966), and is available in a computer program by Lohmoller (1981). Both Bentler (1982) and Dijkstra (1983) have done excellent jobs comparing the estimation procedures in LISREL and PLS.

Another approach to the analysis of latent variable models has been proposed by Bentler and Weeks (1980) and reviewed by Bentler (1983). The parameters in the Bentler and Weeks EQS-system model can be estimated by a Gauss-Newton algorithm, and the model has a simpler parametric structure than Lisrel. It was designed to accommodate a wide range of models, most of which can also be accommodated in Lisrel with some contorted setups, yet requires the specification of only three matrices (compared to the eight used in Lisrel). More important, the EQS-system contains a statistically superior method for calculating the difference between the observed and the expected covariance matrices.

Cliff (1983) has pointed out another difficulty with the Lisrel approach, namely, the tendency to treat *ex post facto* analyses as if they were confirmatory. Users of Lisrel not uncommonly estimate a model, find its parameter estimates do not adequately reproduce the observed covariance matrix, make reference to LISREL's modification indices, and reestimate the model with additional free parameters added to the model. Eventually a model is found that results in a good statistical fit. Unfortunately, such models do not have the same probability of occurrence as truly confirmed models.

In an analogous situation, analysis of variance designs permits one to make overall tests of *a priori* hypotheses, followed by a number of *post hoc* comparisons among individual cell means. But the appropriate statistical corrections for *post hoc* comparisons mean that the confidence intervals are several times larger than those used in *a priori* comparisons. In Lisrel, however, no one knows how to treat *post hoc* comparisons. Indeed, the problem may be insoluble (Cliff, 1983).

This difficulty has been compounded in the latest version of LISREL by the unfortunate inclusion of an automatic model modification option. Invoking this option in LISREL automatically frees fixed parameters in sequential fashion until no further changes would be statistically significant. This procedure invites abuse. In the first place, the unwary analyst may allow the program to free a parameter that cannot be interpreted from a substantive point of view. In the second place, using automatic model modification makes LISREL a semi-exploratory analytic tool, rather than the useful confirmatory tool it was designed to be. Using automatic model modification is akin to using stepwise regression to estimate a recursive causal model, and stepwise regression has no place in structural equation modeling (Kenny, 1979, p. 53; Wolfle, 1980*a*, p. 206).

One final precaution needs to be mentioned, which Cliff (1983) has called the nominalistic fallacy. That is, just because someone gives a name to a latent variable does not mean he understands it, or that the manifest measures used to estimate it actually do. The nominalistic fallacy can show up in one's data in a variety of ways. Kenny (1979, p. 113), for example, has pointed out in a one-factor, three-indicator model that it must hold that $\varrho_{12}\varrho_{13}\varrho_{23} > 0$; otherwise, one of the construct loadings must be imaginary. It must also hold empirically that the loadings be of moderate size. Finally, it is mathematically possible to estimate construct loadings that imply correlations greater than unity, which usually indicates in some way that the model has been misspecified.

Even when manifest variables are all positively correlated and their correlations at least modest in size, there remains the problem of validity. The variables may be highly correlated but not measuring what one thinks they are measuring. Thus the usefulness of analyses of relationship among latent variables is no better than the validity and reliability of the manifest measures thought to index those latent constructs.

RECENT DEVELOPMENTS IN CAUSAL MODELING
Until very recently, people who analyzed causal models compared direct causal effects in structural equation models to their standard errors, and thus determined whether inferences to non-zero population parameters were warranted, yet treated estimates of indirect causal effects as if they *were* population param-

eters. Sobel (1982) has recently derived the asymptotic distribution of indirect effects, and thus made possible a determination of their statistical significance. Wolfle and Ethington (1984) have since produced a FORTRAN program that provides the causal modeler with standard errors of indirect effects for recursive causal models. Developments in this area are likely to continue. More general programs will be written to estimate standard errors for nonrecursive and latent variable models. We can expect that routines will be made available that permit the estimation of structural equation models, including the standard errors of indirect causal effects, in one step. One possible approach would be to use the USERPROC facility in SPSS[x].

Another development likely in the near future is the availability of sophisticated microcomputer programs for analyzing structural equation models. Wolfle (1982a) has already provided a microcomputer program for analyzing recursive causal models, and it is not unreasonable to expect that future microcomputer programs will include algorithms for estimating standard errors of indirect effects in addition to the traditional estimates of standard errors of direct effects. LISREL, as it currently exists, is a mainframe FORTRAN computer program; despite its sophistication, however, it requires only about 7,000 lines of source code and occupies only about 140K of computer memory. Rewriting LISREL for microcomputers would therefore not be a difficult undertaking, and it is likely to be available in microcomputer form in the not too distant future.

Despite the sophistication of latent variable models such as Lisrel, the statistical theory involved has been developed only in rudimentary form (Bentler, 1980). Recent developments promise that advances will be made in understanding the statistical theory behind latent variable models. For example, standard errors of latent variable parameter estimates have been developed only for large samples. Recently, however, Boomsma (1982a, 1982b) has investigated the robustness of LISREL estimates for various sample sizes and deviations from normality. He concluded in general that sample sizes should exceed 200 in order to obtain reliable standard errors of the maximum likelihood estimates. New programs such as Bentler's EQS-system and improvements in the Lisrel model will allow the estimation of models that are not based on the assumption that a random sample has been drawn from a multivariate normal population. A lot of these statistical developments will be technically difficult, but as they develop should show up in the common computer programs available to the user. As these statistical developments show up in the programs, many of the changes will be transparent to users, but their transparency should not detract from an appreciation of their importance.

Developments in Categorical Data Analysis
Both Wold's (1966) PLS model and Bentler and Weeks's (1980) EQS-system were developed in part out of an appreciation for the fact that continuous multivariate normality is the exception rather than the rule in social data. Many of the variables used in the social sciences merely classify individuals into a small

number of categories, and there are well-developed statistical procedures for analyzing such data (e.g., Bishop, Fienberg, and Holland, 1975). Recently, B. Muthen (1978, 1981, 1983a, 1984) has developed a drastic modification to the analysis of categorical data, which brings the analysis of such data within the framework of latent variable models. Muthen assumes that there exist latent response variables that intervene between latent constructs and the observed categorical data. The observed data are related to the latent response variables by a step function. This specification is an important generalization of Pearson's (1913; Pearson and Pearson, 1922) system of tetrachoric, polychoric, biserial, and polyserial correlation coefficients. Muthen has illustrated the usefulness of his statistical techniques in analyses of American attitudes toward abortion (B. Muthen, 1981), and in a longitudinal model of neurotic illness (B. Muthen, 1983a).

Implicit in Muthen's (1978) development of methods for analyzing latent variable models with categorical data is the well-known fact (e.g., Carroll, 1961) that product-moment correlation coefficients are downwardly biased estimates of associations among categorical variables. Recent studies (B. Muthen, 1983b; L. Muthen, 1983) clearly demonstrate the advantages to be gained from using polychoric and polyserial correlations in latent variable models, and applications (e.g., Ethington and Wolfle, 1984) are beginning to appear.

SUMMARY

Good (1961, 1962) and Suppes (1970) have argued that a causal relationship exists when a change in one variable produces a change in another when everything else has been controlled. Where applicable, experiments do a nice job demonstrating such relationships by randomly assigning subjects to treatments and controls. In naturalistic settings, however, such assignment simply is not possible. In these situations applications of causal modeling techniques have proven to be a very useful analytic strategy. Causal models allow the measurement and decomposition of causal effects in models that explicitly include important control variables.

It is easy enough to say that the important control variables must be explicitly included. It is quite another thing actually to do it. The parameters of human behavior are numerous and complex, much more numerous and complex than the analytic tools we have available. Duncan (1975) made the distinction between the easy part of structural equation models, by which he meant the essential tools of matrix algebra and mathematical statistics, and the hard part of causal modeling, by which he meant the formulation of creative ideas that are necessary to construct good causal models. Consequently, the application of causal models alone to research in higher education will not automatically yield good research. To believe otherwise confuses the tool with the aim. Causal modeling is a useful analytic tool, but the aim is a thriving line of research with theories that have scope and coherence and that yield predictions of unexpected new facts. Thus the techniques of causal modeling are indeed useful, but they are merely tools to be used by those who first know their subject matter.

Latent variable causal models represent a major breakthrough in combining the techniques of factor analysis and simultaneous equation theory into a single comprehensive model. The major advantages of such models is their capability of specifying causal models with well-defined measurement properties. While the weakest part of Lisrel-type models is their statistical component, recent developments promise to alleviate this shortcoming. Furthermore, B. Muthen's (1978, 1981, 1983a, 1984) work promises to make such models even more practical for the kind of data typically analyzed in higher education research. Yet the sophistication of such techniques should not detract from the general rule: causal models are no better than the substantive ideas that go into them.

Acknowledgements. I would like to express my deep appreciation to Corinna Ethington, whose advice and criticisms have contributed greatly to this work, and to Ernest Pascarella and Dael Wolfle for their very helpful comments on an earlier draft.

NOTES

1. This is an oversimplification. Some path models can be estimated with piecemeal data or from diverse sets of data, no one of which contains all of the intercorrelations among the variables included in the model. While such exercises cannot be expected to yield definitive results, they can be extremely useful. Examples can be found in Duncan (1968), Jencks et al. (1972), and Wolfle (1980b).
2. In the absence of an epicene personal pronoun or possessive adjective, I have used "he" and "his" fairly consistently, since I believe "he or she" and "his or hers" are awkward. Except when referring to a specific individual, everything I say applies to women as it applies to men.
3. Expressing these variables as deviations from their respective means serves merely to drop from the equation the irrelevant intercept term. The b_{ij} regression coefficients are algebraically equivalent to the regression coefficients one would obtain from analyzing raw data.
4. A recursive causal model has no causal feedback loops, either directly or indirectly. That is, the causal flow of influences among variables in the model is unidirectional. In contrast, a nonrecursive model is one in which a variable thought to be a cause of another is also thought to be caused by it, either directly or indirectly. In other words, an independent variable in one equation is, in another equation, regressed on the dependent variable in the first equation. In nonrecursive models, unbiased estimates are no longer obtainable through ordinary least-squares procedures.
5. Campbell (1963) suggested that cross-lagged correlations in two-wave, two-variable models could be used to infer causal relationships from data. Nevertheless, as Duncan (1969) noted, some *a priori* causal assumptions are required in order to make these causal inferences. These rather restrictive assumptions are often ignored by researchers (e.g., Yap, 1979), and the use (or misuse) of such models continues to draw criticism (e.g., Rogosa, 1980; Wolfle and McGee, 1979).

6. A just-identified model is one in which there are just as many unknown parameters as there are independent pieces of information in an equation system. For example, in Figure 1 there are 15 correlations among the 6 variables in the model, and 15 parameters to be estimated — 12 regression coefficients and 3 correlations among the exogenous variables. If the model were to be respecified such that the effect from father's education to occupation, b_{51}, was zero, the model would then be overidentified, with 15 correlations but only 14 unknowns.

7. A reduced-form equation is one in which the dependent variable is expressed in terms only of exogenous variables. For example, in Figure 1, X_5 could be expressed as a function of X_1, X_2, and X_3 by substituting $(b_{41}X_1 + b_{42}X_2 + b_{43}X_3 + e_4)$ for X_4.

8. The table of decompositions shown in Joreskog and Sorbom (1983, III.39) contains two errors. The direct effect on Y by ϵ is given as $\Delta_y \Gamma$ but should be 0 (zero), and in the expression for the indirect effect the term $- \Delta_y \Gamma$ should be deleted. These two errors exist only in the table, and do not affect the LISREL program estimates.

9. The coefficients shown in Table 1 differ from those shown in Figure 2, since Pascarella and Terenzini (1983) reported their results in standardized form, whereas the reanalysis shown in Table 1 was conducted with the variables measured in their original metrics.

REFERENCES

Alwin, D. F., and Hauser, R. M. The decomposition of effects in path analysis. *American Sociological Review*, 1975, *40*, 37-47.

Alwin, D. F., and Jackson, D. J. Measurement models for response errors in surveys: Issues and applications. In K. F. Schuessler (ed.), *Sociology Methodology 1980*. San Francisco: Jossey-Bass, 1980.

Anderson, J. G. Causal models in educational research: Nonrecursive models. *American Educational Research Journal*, 1978, *15*, 81-97.

Anderson, J. G., and Evans, F. B. Causal models in educational research: Recursive Models. *American Educational Research Journal*, 1974, *11*, 29-39.

Bean, J. P. Dropouts and turnover: The synthesis and test of a causal model of student attrition. *Research in Higher Education*, 1980, *12*, 155-187.

Bean, J. P. Student attrition, interactions, and confidence: Interaction effects in a path model. *Research in Higher Education*, 1982, *17*, 291-320.

Bentler, P. M. Multivariate analysis with latent variables: Causal modeling. *Annual Review of Psychology*, 1980, *31*, 419-456.

Bentler, P. M. Linear systems with multiple levels and types of latent variables. In K. G. Joreskog and H. Wold (eds.), *Systems Under Indirect Observation: Causality, Structure, Prediction*. Amsterdam: North-Holland Publishing Co., 1982.

Bentler, P. M. Simultaneous equation systems as moment structure models. *Journal of Econometrics*, 1983, *22*, 13-42.

Bentler, P. M., and Weeks, D. G. Linear structural equations with latent variables. *Psychometrika*, 1980, *45*, 289-308.

Bielby, W. T., and Hauser, R. M. Structural equation models. In A. Inkeles (ed.), *Annual Review of Sociology*. Palo Alto, Calif.: Annual Reviews, 1977.

Bielby, W. T., Hauser, R. M., and Featherman, D. L. Response errors of black and nonblack males in models of the intergenerational transmission of socioeconomic status. *American Journal of Sociology*, 1977, *82*, 1242-1288.

Bishop, Y. M. M., Fienberg, S. E., and Holland, P. W. *Discrete Multivariate Analysis: Theory and Practice*. Cambridge, Mass.: MIT Press, 1975.

Blalock, H. J., Jr. Correlation and causality: The multivariate case. *Social Forces*, 1961, *39*, 246-251.

Blalock, H. M., Jr. *Causal Inferences in Nonexperimental Research*. Chapel Hill: University of North Carolina Press, 1964.

Blau, P. M., and Duncan, O. D. *The American Occupational Structure*. New York: Wiley, 1967.

Bobko, P., and Rieck, A. Large sample estimators for standard errors of functions of correlation coefficients. *Applied Psychological Measurement*, 1980, *4*, 385-398.

Bohrnstedt, G. W. Use of the multiple indicators–multiple causes (MIMIC) model. *American Sociological Review*, 1977, *42*, 656-663.

Boomsma, A. On the robustness of LISREL (maximum likelihood estimation) against small sample size and nonnormality. Unpublished doctoral dissertation, University of Groningen, The Netherlands, 1982(a).

Boomsma, A. The robustness of LISREL against small sample sizes in factor analysis models. In K. G. Joreskog and H. Wold (eds.), *Systems Under Indirect Observation: Causality, Structure, Prediction*. Amsterdam: North-Holland Publishing Co., 1982(b).

Boudon, R. A method of linear causal analysis: Dependence analysis. *American Sociological Review*, 1965, *30*, 365-373.

Bruton, B. T., and Crull, S. R. Causes and consequences of student evaluation of instruction. *Research in Higher Education*, 1982, *17*, 195-206.

Campbell, D. T. From description to experimentation: Interpreting trends as quasi-experiments. In C. W. Harris (ed.), *Problems in Measuring Change*. Madison: University of Wisconson Press, 1963.

Carroll, J. B. The nature of the data, or how to choose a correlation coefficient. *Psymetrika*, 1961, *26*, 347-372.

Cliff, N. Some cautions concerning the application of causal modeling methods. *Multivariate Behavioral Research*, 1983, *18*, 115-126.

Cooley, W. W. Explanatory observational studies. *Educational Researcher*, 1978, *7*, 9-15.

Dijkstra, T. Some comments on maximum likelihood and partial least squares methods. *Journal of Econometrics*, 1983, *22*, 67-90.

Duncan, O. D. Path analysis: Sociological examples. *American Journal of Sociology*, 1966, *72*, 1-16.

Duncan, O. D. Ability and achievement. *Eugenics Quarterly*, 1968, *15*, 1-11.

Duncan, O. D. Some linear models for two-wave, two-variable panel analysis. *Psychological Bulletin*, 1969, *72*, 177-182.

Duncan, O. D. *Introduction to Structural Equation Models*. New York: Academic Press, 1975.

Duncan, O. D., Featherman, D. L., and Duncan, B. *Socioeconomic Background and Achievement*. New York: Seminar Press, 1972.

Duncan, O. D., Haller, A. O., and Portes, A. Peer influences on aspirations: A reinterpretation. In H. M. Blalock (ed.), *Causal Models in the Social Sciences*. Chicago: Aldine-Atherton, 1971.

Duncan, O. D., and Hodge, R. W. Education and occupational mobility: A regression analysis. *American Journal of Sociology*, 1963, *68*, 629-644.

Ethington, C. A., and Wolfle, L. M. A structural model of sex differences in mathematics achievement using tetrachoric and polyserial measures of association. Paper presented at the meeting of the American Educational Research Association, New Orleans, April 1984.

Featherman, D. L., and Carter, T. M. Discontinuities in schooling and the socioeconomic life cycle. In W. H. Sewell, R. M. Hauser, and D. L. Featherman (eds.), *Schooling and Achievement in American Society*. New York: Academic Press, 1976.

Finney, J. M. Indirect effects in path analysis. *Sociological Methods & Research*, 1972, *1*, 175-186.

Fox, J. Effect analysis in structural equation models: Extensions and simplified methods of computation. *Sociological Methods & Research*, 1980, *9*, 3-28.

Gintis, H. Education, technology, and the characteristics of worker productivity. *American Economic Review*, 1971, *61*, 266-279.

Goldberger, A. S. Structural equation methods in the social sciences. *Econometrica*, 1972, *40*, 979-1001.

Good, I. J. A causal calculus (I). *British Journal for the Philosophy of Science*, 1961, *11*, 305-318.

Good, I. J. A causal calculus (II). *British Journal for the Philosophy of Science*, 1962, *12*, 43-51.

Gordon, R. A. Issues in multiple regression. *American Journal of Sociology*, 1968, *73*, 592-616.

Graff, J., and Schmidt, P. A general model for decomposition of effects. In K. G. Joreskog and H. Wold (eds.), *Systems Under Indirect Observation: Causality, Structure, Prediction*. Amsterdam: North-Holland Publishing Co., 1982.

Griliches, Z., and Mason, W. M. Education, income, and ability. *Journal of Political Economy*, 1972, *80*, S74-S103.

Gunst, R. F., and Mason, R. L. Biased estimation in regression: An evaluation using mean squared error. *Journal of the American Statistical Association*, 1977, *72*, 616-628.

Hauser, R. M. Schools and the stratification process. *American Journal of Sociology*, 1969, *74*, 587-611.

Hauser, R. M. *Socioeconomic Background and Educational Performance*. Rose Monograph Series. Washington, D.C.: American Sociological Association, 1971.

Hauser, R. M. Disaggregating a social-psychological model of education attainment. In A. S. Goldberger and O. D. Duncan (eds.), *Structural Equation Models in the Social Sciences*. New York: Seminar Press, 1973.

Hauser, R. M., and Goldberger, A. S. The treatment of unobservable variables in path analysis. In H. L. Costner (ed.), *Sociological Methodology 1971*. San Francisco: Jossey-Bass, 1971.

Hauser, R. M., Tsai, S. L., and Sewell, W. H. A model of stratification with response error in social and psychological variables. *Sociology of Education*, 1983, *56*, 20-46.

Hodge, R. W., and Treiman, D. J. Social participation and social status. *American Sociological Review*, 1968, *33*, 723-740.

Hoerl, A. E., and Kennard, R. W. Ridge regression: Biased estimation for nonorthogonal problems. *Technometrics*, 1970, *12*, 55-67.

Hyman, H. H., Wright, C. R., and Reed, J. S. *The Enduring Effects of Education*. Chicago: The University of Chicago Press, 1975.

Inverarity, J. M. Populism and lynching in Louisiana, 1889-1896: A test of Erikson's theory of the relationship between boundary crises and repressive justice. *American Sociological Review*, 1976, *41*, 262-280.

Jencks, C., Smith, M., Acland, H., Bane, M. J., Cohen, D., Gintis, H., Heyns, B., and Michelson, S. *Inequality: A Reassessment of the Effect of Family and Schooling in America*. New York: Basic Books, 1972.

Joreskog, K. G. *UMLFA: A Computer Program for Unrestricted Maximum Likelihood Factor Analysis*. Research Memorandum 66-20. Princeton: Educational Testing Service, 1966.

Joreskog, K. G. Some contributions to maximum likelihood factor analysis. *Psychometrika*, 1967, *32*, 443-482.

Joreskog, K. G. A general approach to confirmatory maximum likelihood factor analysis. *Psychometrika*, 1969, *34*, 183-202.

Joreskog, K. G. A general method for analysis of covariance structures. *Biometrika*, 57, 1970, *57*, 239-251.

Joreskog, K. G. Statistical analysis of sets of congeneric tests. *Psychometrika*, 1971, *36*, 109-133.

Joreskog, K. G. A general method for estimating a linear structural equation system. In A. S. Goldberger and O. D. Duncan (eds.), *Structural Equation Models in the Social Sciences*. New York: Seminar Press, 1973.

Joreskog, K. G., and Sorbom, D. *LISREL VI: Analysis of Linear Structural Relationships by Maximum Likelihood and Least Squares Methods*. Chicago: National Educational Resources, 1983.

Joreskog, K. G., and van Thillo, M. *LISREL: A General Computer Program for Estimating a Linear Structural Equation System Involving Multiple Indicators of Unmeasured Variables*. Research Bulletin 72-56. Princeton: Educational Testing Service, 1972.

Kenny, D. A. *Correlation and Causality*. New York: Wiley, 1979.

Kerlinger, F. N. The influence of research on education practice. *Educational Researcher*, 1977, *6*, 5-12.

Kim, J., and Mueller, C. W. Standardized and unstandardized coefficients in causal analysis: An expository note. *Sociological Methods & Research*, 1976, *4*, 423-438.

Land, K. C. Principles of path analysis. In E. F. Borgatta (ed.), *Sociological Methodology 1969*. San Francisco: Jossey-Bass, 1969.

Lawley, D. N. The application of the maximum likelihood method to factor analysis. *British Journal of Psychology*, 1943, *33*, 172-175.

Lawley, D. N., and Maxwell, A. E. *Factor Analysis as a Statistical Method*. New York: American Elsevier, 1971.

Lohmoller, J. B. LVPLS 1.6 program manual: Latent variables path analysis with partial least-squares estimation. Forschungsbericht 81.04. Hochschule der Bundeswehr München, Fachbereich Padagogik, Munich.

Lord, F. M., and Novick, M. R. *Statistical Theories of Mental Test Scores*. Reading, Mass.: Addison-Wesley, 1968.

Miller, M. K. Potentials and pitfalls of path analysis: A tutorial summary. *Quality and Quantity*, 1977, *11*, 329-346.

Muffo, J. A., and Coccari, R. L. Predictors of outside funding for research among AASCU institutions. *Research in Higher Education*, 1982, *16*, 71-80.

Munro, B. H. Dropouts from higher education: Path analysis of a national sample. *American Educational Research Journal*, 1981, *18*, 133-141.

Muthen, B. Contributions to factor analysis of dichotomous variables. *Psychometrika*, 1978, *43*, 551-560.

Muthen, B. Factor analysis of dichotomous variables: American attitudes toward abortion. In D. J. Jackson and E. F. Borgatta (eds.), *Factor Analysis and Measurement in Sociological Research: A Multidimensional Perspective*. London: Sage, 1981.

Muthen, B. Latent variable structural equation modeling with categorical data. *Journal of Econometrics*, 1983(a), *22*, 43-65.

Muthen, B. Categorical vs. continuous variables in factor analysis and structural equation modeling. Paper presented at meeting of the American Educational Research Association, Montreal, April 1983(b).

Muthen, B. A general structural equation model with dichotomous, ordered categorical, and continuous latent variable indicators. *Psychometrika*, 1984, *49*, 115-132.

Muthen, L. Estimation of variance components for dichotomous dependent variables. Paper presented at the meeting of the American Educational Research Association, Montreal, April 1983.

Namboordiri, N. K., Carter, L. E., and Blalock, H. M. *Applied Multivariate Analysis and Experimental Design*. New York: McGraw-Hill, 1975.

Pascarella, E. T., and Chapman, D. W. A multiinstitutional, path analytic validation of Tinto's model of college withdrawal. *American Educational Research Journal*, 1983, *20*, 87-102.

Pascarella, E. T., Duby, P. B., and Iverson, B. K. A test and reconceptualization of a theoretical model of college withdrawal in a commuter institution setting. *Sociology of Education*, 1983, *56*, 88-100.

Pascarella, E. T., and Terenzini, P. T. Predicting persistence and voluntary dropout decisions from a theoretical model. *Journal of Higher Education*, 1980, *61*, 60-75.

Pascarella, E. T., and Terenzini, P. T. Predicting voluntary freshman year persistence/withdrawal behavior in a residential university: A path analytic validation of Tinto's model. *Journal of Educational Psychology*, 1983, *75*, 215-226.

Pearson, K. On the measurement of the influence of "broad categories" on correlation. *Biometrika*, 1913, *9*, 116-139.

Pearson, K., and Pearson, E. S. On polychoric coefficients of correlation. *Biometrika*, 1922, *14*, 127-156.

Porter, J. N. Race, socialization and mobility in educational and early occupational attainment. *American Sociological Review*, 1974, *39*, 303-316.

Portes, A., and Wilson, K. L. Black-white differences in educational attainment. *American Sociological Review*, 1976, *41*, 414-431.

Roberson, S. D., Keith, T. Z., and Page, E. B. Now who aspires to teach? *Educational Researcher*, 1983, *12*, 13-21.

Robertshaw, D., and Wolfle, L. M. Discontinuities in schooling and educational attainment. *Higher Education*, 1983, *12*, 1-18.

Rogoff, N. *Recent Trends in Occupational Mobility*. Glencoe, Ill.: Free Press, 1953.

Rogosa, D. A critique of cross-lagged correlation. *Psychological Bulletin*, 1980, *88*, 245-258.

Rotter, J. B. Generalized expectancies for internal versus external control of reinforcement. *Psychological Monographs*, 1966, *80* (Whole No. 609).

Rozeboom, W. W. Ridge regression: Bonanza or beguilement? *Psychological Bulletin*, 1979, *86*, 242-249.

Sewell, W. H., and Hauser, R. M. *Education, Occupation, and Earnings: Achievement in the Early Career*. New York: Academic Press, 1975.

Siegel, P. M., and Hodge, R. W. A causal approach to the study of measurement error. In H. M. Blalock and A. B. Blalock (eds.), *Methodology in Social Research*. New York: McGraw-Hill, 1968.

Simon, H. A. *Models of Man*. New York: Wiley, 1957.

Sobel, M. E. Asymptotic confidence intervals for indirect effects in structural equation models. In S. Leinhardt (ed.), *Sociological Methodology 1982*. San Francisco: Jossey-Bass, 1982.

Spady, W. Dropouts from higher education: An interdisciplinary review and synthesis. *Interchange*, 1970, *1*, 64-85.

Suppes, P. *A Probabilistic Theory of Causality*. Amsterdam: North-Holland Publishing Co., 1970.

Terenzini, P. T., and Pascarella, E. T. Voluntary freshman attrition and patterns of social and academic integration in a university: A test of a conceptual model. *Research in Higher Education*, 1977, *6*, 25-43.

Tinto, V. Dropout from higher education: A theoretical synthesis of recent research. *Review of Educational Research*, 1975, *45*, 89-125.

Werts, C. E., and Linn, R. L. Path analysis: Psychological examples. *Psychological Bulletin*, 1970, *74*, 193-212.

Wiley, D. E., and Wiley, J. A. The estimation of measurement error in panel data. *American Sociological Review*, 1970, *35*, 112-117.

Wold, H. O. A. Nonlinear estimation by iterative least squares procedures. In F. N. David (ed.), *Research Papers in Statistics: Festschrift for J. Neyman*. New York: Wiley, 1966.

Wolfle, L. M. An introduction to path analysis. *Multiple Linear Regression Viewpoints*, 1977, *8*, 36-61.

Wolfle, L. M. Strategies of path analysis. *American Educational Research Journal*, 1980(a), *17*, 183-209.

Wolfle, L. M. The enduring effects of education on verbal skills. *Sociology of Education*, 1980(b), *53*, 104-114.

Wolfle, L. M. PASE: Program for analysis of structural equations. *Behavior Research Methods & Instrumentation*, 1982(a), *14*, 548-550.

Wolfle, L. M. Predictors of outside funding for research among AASCU institutions: A reanalysis. *Research in Higher Education*, 1982(b), *17*, 99-104.

Wolfle, L. M. Postsecondary educational attainment among whites and blacks. Paper presented at the meeting of the American Educational Research Association, Montreal, April 1983.

Wolfle, L. M., and Ethington, C. A. A program for standard errors of indirect effects in recursive causal models. Paper presented at the meeting of the American Educational Association, New Orleans, April 1984.

Wolfle, L. M., and McGee, L. M. On the determination of causal ordering between vocabulary and comprehension. *Journal of Reading Behavior*, 1979, *11*, 273-277.

Wolfle, L. M., and Robertshaw, D. Effects of college attendance on locus of control. *Journal of Personality and Social Psychology*, 1982, *43*, 802-810.

Wright, S. Correlation and causation. *Journal of Agricultural Reseach*, 1921, *20*, 557-585.

Wright, S. *Corn and Hog Correlations*. Washington, D.C.: U.S. Department of Agriculture Bulletin #1300, 1925.

Wright, S. The method of path coefficients. *Annals of Mathematical Statistics*, 1934, *5*, 161-215.

Yap, K. O. Vocabulary: Building blocks of comprehension? *Journal of Reading Behavior*, 1979, *11*, 49-59.

TOWARD A NEW PARTNERSHIP FOR FINANCING A COLLEGE EDUCATION: The Changing Roles of the Public, Students, and Colleges

Michael L. Tierney, *University of Pennsylvania*

Prior to the passage of the Education Amendments of 1972, there was widespread discussion of the financing of postsecondary education (Bowen and Servelle, 1968; Carnegie Commission, 1973; Orwig, 1971). The fundamental issue concerned how the burden of the full costs of a college education should be distributed among various parties. Of particular concern in these pre-1972 discussions was the attention given to the substantial burden represented by the income forgone by students and their families while enrolled. Partly in recognition of this problem, the Education Amendments of 1972 marked a shift in federal policy in which financial assistance would be provided directly to students. By 1981–82, the Pell grant program (formerly known as Basic Education Opportunity Grants, or BEOG's) was estimated to be providing approximately 2.6 million college students with $2.4 billion in assistance (Office of Student Financial Assistance, 1982).

Subsequent to the Education Amendments of 1972, a series of modifications have led to a significant redistribution in the burden of financing a college education away from parents and onto the taxpayers and the future earnings of the students. The amount parents were expected to contribute to their son's or daughter's college education declined in real terms, the level of student indebtedness increased, and federal and state grant programs ballooned. Such trends are not likely to continue into the next century for several reasons. First, the federal government shows little inclination to increase either appropriations for Pell awards or the ceiling on borrowing under the Guaranteed Student Loan program. Second, student resistance to increasing levels of indebtedness appears to be on the rise. When this indebtedness is coupled with new financing instruments (e.g., adjustable rate mortgages) for young families, the specter of perpetual debt is raised. Third, there is a growing concern over the erosion in the historical pattern of family financing of a college education. Such erosion is not surprising given that parents continue to have little incentive to save for their children's education.

The purpose of this chapter is to revitalize the discussion of who should pay for a college education. To initiate the debate, four basic propositions will be developed which essentially stand the Education Amendments of 1972 on their heads:

1. Parental contributions toward a child's education should return to the levels attained prior to the mid-1970s.
2. Federal and state governments should coordinate efforts to improve access to a wider array of postsecondary education programs by allocating Pell grants according to an absolute measure of financial need.
3. Federal loan subsidies, particularly the Guaranteed Student Loan program, should be eliminated gradually if and only if the repayment period is lengthened and maximum loan ceilings are increased.
4. Colleges and universities must become more active in assisting students and their parents in acquiring capital to attend the institution.

In the interest of professional self-preservation, the author is not necessarily advocating any one or all of these propositions. They are intended to serve as a rhetorical device to make explicit certain unstated assumptions concerning financial aid policies and practices.

THE COSTS OF POSTSECONDARY EDUCATION

Prior to developing each of these propositions, it is necessary to review briefly the full costs associated with college attendance. Table 1 provides a very preliminary estimate of how the current full costs are distributed among various groups. These data are considered preliminary for two reasons: the role of direct student financial assistance is ignored, and the magnitude of various types of indirect costs are either not readily available or impossible to partition among various groups. Thus question marks in the table indicate a need for additional research before basic financial questions can be answered fully.

Table 1 shows that the education and general expenditures of public institutions was more than $30.6 billion in 1980. This category of direct expense includes expenditures for instruction, research, and scholarships and fellowships. For several reasons it is not possible to determine how much of the $3.4 billion in research expenditures was paid for by the federal government or other parties, and thus research expenditures must remain in the larger education and general category. However, since instruction and research are jointly produced, education and general costs are less than would be the case if these two services were produced separately. Similarly, scholarships and fellowships include both unrestricted institutional funds ($324 million in the case of public institutions) and restricted funds ($646 million). Included in this latter category are federal appropriations for the three campus-based programs: Supplemental Education Opportunity Grants (SEOG), National Direct Student Loans (NDSL), and

TABLE 1. Who Pays How Much: A Very Preliminary Estimate

Cost Category	Total 1980 Expenditures (in millions of dollars)	Percentage Paid by			
		Students and Families	Federal Govt.	State/Local Govt.	Other
Public institutions					
Direct costs					
Education and general	30,627	16	16	63	5
Auxiliary enterprises	4,132	100	0	0	0
Indirect costs					
Forgone income	38,650 (?)	100	0	0	0
Forgone tax revenue	775 (?)	0	34 (?)	66 (?)	0
Private institutions					
Direct costs					
Education and general	13,915	51	29	4	25
Auxiliary enterprises	2,354	100	0	0	0
Indirect costs					
Forgone income	12,055 (?)	100	0	0	0
Forgone tax revenue	731 (?)	0	67 (?)	33 (?)	0

Source. National Center for Education Statistics, *Financial Statistics of Institutions of Higher Education*, 1981.

College Work-Study (CWS). In 1980, total federal appropriations for these programs came to more than $1.2 billion. Because this money goes to paying part of the student's and his or her family's cost of attending college, one begins to appreciate the financing implications of these federal programs, i.e., shifting the burden away from the family and onto the taxpayer.

Table 1 provides similar information for private institutions. A comparison with the figures for public institutions leads to the obvious conclusion that students attending private institutions, through their tuition and fee payments, pay a substantially larger proportion of the education and general expenditures relative to their peers at public institutions. Lacking substantial appropriations from state and local governments, private institutions are forced to charge higher prices in order to provide educational services of at least comparable quality. The issue of price differences between public and private institutions will be discussed later.

Estimating the indirect costs of college attendance is a very uncertain business. A crude estimate of the income forgone by students while in college is provided by the Bureau of the Census Current Population Survey (Tierney, 1984). In 1980, high school graduates who entered the labor force immediately after graduation and were between 18 and 22 years of age earned $7,363 annually. This earnings estimate is based on the median weekly earnings before taxes and the median weeks worked. Taking three-fourths of this estimate as the amount of forgone earnings (adjusting for summer and part-time earnings), the total earnings forgone by full-time students in 1980 was $37.5 billion. An estimate for part-time students during the regular, nine-month academic year is $13.2 billion. Thus the total earnings forgone is approximately the same as the total direct costs of public and private institutions. As indicated in Table 1, the entire burden of the earnings forgone is borne by students and their families.

More problematic is the magnitude of the tax revenues forgone due to either the tax deductions taken by individuals and corporations who make gifts to colleges and universities and the property tax exemption enjoyed by charitable institutions. If the average marginal tax rate is assumed to be 26.8%, then each dollar contributed to a college or university costs the donor 73.2 cents. Applying this estimate of donor marginal tax rates to the total gifts to public institutions yields an estimate of $262 million in forgone tax revenues by the federal government. For private institutions, forgone tax revenues attributable to charitable tax deduction amounted to $490 million.

Forgone tax revenues attributable to the property tax exemption of colleges and universities are more difficult to determine. Borrowing from Nelson (1978) and assuming a constant ratio between tax subsidy and the book value of college properties, an estimate of the forgone tax revenues from this exemption is $241 million for private institutions and $513 million for public institutions. It should be noted that the burden of these forgone tax revenue falls predominantly on local taxpayers in whose communities the colleges and universities are to be found. It is no wonder that Bok urges increased sensitivity to the complaints of local government representatives; their constituents are bearing a substantial part of the cost (via higher local tax rates) associated with the operation of the college (Bok, 1982).

Aggregating these various categories of direct and indirect costs leads to the following conclusion: the total cost of providing the instructional activities of colleges and universities was approximately $103.2 billion in 1979–80. If one were to examine this total cost without reference to various types of student financial assistance, it will be found that students and their families pay approximately 67%. This percentage compares quite closely to the Carnegie Commission's 1971 estimate of 64% (Carnegie Commission, 1973). The qualification is important, however. The provision of unrestricted grants and scholarships and highly subsidized loans shifts some of this financial burden from the family to other parties.

TABLE 2. Average Student Expense Budgets for 1979–80 by Institutional Category

Institutional Category	Tuition	Room and Board	Books and Supplies	Other	Total
Public					
Four-year [a]	680	1,550	229	799	3,258
Two-year [b]	389	942	208	967	2,506
Private					
Four-year [a]	2,923	1,629	231	743	5,526
Two-year [b]	2,043	1,018	228	905	4,194

[a] For residential students.
[b] For nonresidential students.
Source. College Entrance Examination Board, *College Costs*, 1981.

As one would expect, tuition charges at private institutions are substantially higher than those at public institutions. In 1979–80 the difference was $2,243 for four-year institutions and $1,654 for two-year institutions. This difference, usually referred to as the "tuition gap," constitutes the price disadvantage at which private institutions find themselves relative to their public competitors. Their higher tuition and fees are necessary due to the absence of state appropriations on a level comparable to those provided to public colleges.

In order to begin to understand the role of direct student assistance in the financing of a college education, it is necessary to examine college tuition and fees in more detail (see Table 2). As one would expect, tuition charges at private institutions are substantially higher than those at public institutions. In 1979–80 the difference was $2,243 for four-year institutions and $1,654 for two-year institutions. This difference, usually referred to as the "tuition gap," constitutes the price disadvantage at which private institutions find themselves relative to their public competitors. Their higher tuition and fees are necessary due to the absence of state appropriations on a level comparable to those provided to public colleges.

Student expense budgets are more than tuition and fees. Table 2 also provides estimates of the average amounts full-time students will spend on room and board, books, supplies and other items (i.e., transportation and miscella-

neous expenses) during the academic year. One should note in particular the
room and board charges, which are quite similar for public and private institutions. This class of student expenditure constitutes the bulk of the auxiliary enterprise expenditures for most colleges and universities.

The total student expense budgets for colleges and universities thus would
seem to reflect how much of the education and general plus auxiliary enterprise
expenditures are paid by students and their families. But this is not the case for
many college students today because part of these costs are borne by the federal
and state grants and loans that are provided directly to students. For instance, a
student attending a four-year public institution full time may have estimated
expenses of $3,258, but he may receive a Pell award of $800, a state grant of
$350, and a Guaranteed Student Loan of $2,100. In this example, the student
and his family would not be required to make any payments out of current income. As a result, the burden of financing their part of a college education
would not be borne by the family unit, but by the student after graduation and
by the taxpayer. If the costs of direct student financial assistance are aggregated
across all families, the percentage paid by students and their families would be
reduced from its current level of 67% (Table 1) and the federal and state share
of the burden would increase by a corresponding amount. The policies and
practices through which this redistribution occurs are described in the next
section.

NEED-BASED FINANCIAL AID

The central feature of need-based financial aid policies is that it is essentially a
relative measure of need. Specifically, student financial need is defined as the
total cost of attendance less expected family contribution, or:

$$\text{Need} = \text{Student budget} - \text{Expected family contribution} \qquad (1)$$

Consequently, a student's financial need is a function of both the cost of attending a particular college and what her family is expected to contribute to a
college education. Because the total direct costs of attendance have already
been examined (Table 2), attention will be focused on the calculation of the expected family contribution, a calculation which involves summing estimated
parental and student contributions.

Table 3 presents the estimated parental contribution for families of varying
size and income. For purposes of simplification, the treatment of parental assets is not incorporated in this example. The first issue to note is the incorporation of a standard maintenance allowance (SMA). This allowance is based on
the Bureau of Labor Statistics lower standard of living expenditures for families of varying sizes (Bureau of Labor Statistics, 1967a). While one may argue
whether a lower or middle standard of living ought to be employed, the major
question surrounding the SMA involves its original derivation. One problem
with its derivation involves the use of the consumption behavior of families

headed by adults in their late thirties in the mid-1960s. The adequacy of these budgets in measuring consumption behavior has been subject to severe criticism (Watts, 1980). Second, the adjustments for families of differing sizes with older or younger heads of household is determined through the construction of a series of equivalency scales (Bureau of Labor Statistics, 1967b), all of which require some form of validation. In other words, it is very difficult to determine whether the SMA adjustment used in current financial aid systems is even close to being accurate.

TABLE 3. Expected Parental Contribution for a Dependent, Undergraduate Student (1979–80)

	Income after Taxes and Allowances		
	$10,000	$15,000	$20,000
Standard maintenance allowance			
Family size of 3	$6,670	$6,670	$ 6,670
Family size of 4	8,240	8,240	8,240
Family size of 5	9,720	9,720	9,720
Available income			
Family size of 3	3,330	8,330	13,330
Family size of 4	1,760	6,760	11,760
Family size of 5	280	5,280	10,280
Expected parental contribution			
Family size of 3	733	2,090	4,348
Family size of 4	387	1,577	3,610
Family size of 5	62	1,176	2,914

Source. American College Testing Program, *Handbook for Financial Aid Administrators*, 1981.

Nonetheless, the SMA is subtracted from parents' after-tax income in order to yield the adjusted available income (AAI). The AAI is subjected to a progressive tax schedule based on the rationale that as family income increases, a larger proportion is available for discretionary spending. Thus families with larger incomes are able to pay more for a college education than families with less income. Ultimately, this "ability to pay" judgment rests on a series of value judgments made by the various financial aid policies (Goggin, 1968).

Based on the taxation schedule in effect in 1979–80, parental contributions are as estimated in Table 3. These expected parental contributions have the advantage of expecting greater contributions from more affluent families of a given size, and smaller contributions from larger families with a given income level. Thus some sense of equity is attained in determining expected parental contributions.

However, one must remember that the current financial aid system is based on a relative definition of financial need. Ignoring for the moment expected student contributions, consider how equation (1) yields different estimates of student financial need by subtracting Table 3 estimates from Table 2 student budgets. For instance, a student from a family of three with after-tax income of $15,000 would have an estimated financial need of $1,168 if he attended a four-year public college or a need of $416 if attending a two-year public college. Clearly, the more expensive the postsecondary education option, the more needy any particular student is. One scholar has applied a food stamp analogy to this method of determining financial need, in which the amount of food stamps one receives is partially determined by whether one purchases steak or chicken (Finn, 1978).

As difficult as this relative measure of need may be to swallow, it leads to more serious problems, particularly when used in conjunction with the half-cost rule for the distribution of Pell awards. This rule, which was considered a gesture of congressional support for private postsecondary education, stated that an individual's Pell award would be the lesser of $1,800 (the 1979–80 maximum Pell award authorization) or half the cost of attending a college. For instance, a student from a family size of three and parental after-tax income of $10,000 who chose to attend a community college would receive $1,253 (i.e., the lesser of $1,800 or one-half of $2,506). His Pell award would be only slightly greater than that of a student from a family of the same size but with a $20,000 after-tax income who opted to attend a four-year private college (i.e., $1,178). If individual institutions were used instead of average student budgets, it would be easy to demonstrate that students from more affluent families were receiving larger Pell awards to attend an Ivy League college than students from less affluent families who attended a low-cost public institution. Given that students from low-income families disproportionately enroll at public two-year colleges, it would appear that the original legislative intent to provide equal access to postsecondary education is not being achieved (Davis and Van Dusen, 1978).

The previous estimates of financial need would have to be adjusted for the expected student contribution. This contribution is determined by multiplying student savings and other assets by a fixed percentage (35% in 1979–80) and adding to this product estimated summer earnings, veterans benefits, and Social Security benefits where applicable. When this result is added to the expected parental contribution, the total contribution of the family toward a child's college education is determined.

Once the total family contribution is determined and subtracted from the anticipated student budget, his or her financial need is derived. It should be noted that approximately 70% of all institutions recently surveyed reviewed the expected family contribution, and made changes in over one-fifth of those cases that were reviewed (College Scholarship Service, 1984). This estimate of financial need is to be met through a combination of grants, loans, and college work-study programs. At this stage, institutions have tremendous latitude in determining how much of the financial need they will meet and what combination of scholarships, loans, and work will be offered a particular student.

There are a wide variety of programs providing direct, non-repayable assistance to students. By far the largest of these programs is the Pell grant program of the federal government. In 1979–80 this program awarded $2.5 billion to approximately 2.5 million students. One reason for focusing upon 1979–80 is that it was the most generous year in terms of financial aid opportunities. The effective Pell award ceiling was $1,800, and there were no income ceilings on Guaranteed Student Loans. For 1983–84 Pell awards are estimated to total $2.4 billion, or a decline of $100 million. Such shrinkage constitutes evidence of the increasing reluctance of the federal government to appropriate funds for this program. Federal cutbacks have placed substantial pressure on state grants and institutional scholarship budgets, and have been a major stimulant for reviewing the present pattern of financing higher education.

While there has always been some ambiguity regarding the intent behind the original BEOG legislation (Carnegie Council, 1979; Hartman, 1978), at least part of the impetus for this program was an attempt to offset some of the burden of the earnings forgone by students from low-income families. The burden imposed on low-income families of doing without the earnings that a young adult could supply is substantially greater than is the case for more affluent families. In order to determine the extent to which this objective was being realized, the distribution of Pell grant awards among 28,253 Pennsylvania residents who applied for Pell awards for the first time in 1981–82 was examined. Table 4 describes the number of applicants, average Pell award, and the distribution of dollars awarded according to family income level and institutional type. For comparison purposes, one should bear in mind that the effective Pell ceiling in this year was approximately $1,670 and the average Pell award nationwide was $928 (Office of Student Financial Assistance, 1982).

Even a cursory examination of Table 4 indicates the impact of basing the distribution of Pell grants on a relative measure of need. A student from a low-income family matriculating at a public four-year college would receive an almost 50% greater Pell award than if the same student matriculated at a public two-year institution. Because students from low-income families tend to be much less geographically mobile in terms of the types of colleges they can attend, the imposition of the half-cost rule constitutes a substantial reduction in the availability of Pell grant assistance precisely for those students who have the least choice in the type of college they attend (Zemsky and Oedel, 1983).

Removing the half-cost rule affects only these individuals from low-income families attending public two-year institutions. Retaining the original average family contribution, an estimate of the average Pell award for these students would be $1,605. Substituting this value in Table 4 and multiplying by the number of applicants yields a very modest increase of $175,000 for these students, or slightly more than 1%. Students attending public two-year colleges would be the beneficiaries of a 75% increase in their average Pell grants, or an additional $689. Nonwhite students from low-income families in particular would benefit from the removal of the half-cost rule, since they are disproportionately enrolled in public two-year colleges (9% versus 5% for white students).

In addition to the Pell grant program, the federal government provides grants through several other programs, most notably the Supplementary Educational Opportunity Grant (SEOG) and the State Student Incentive Grant (SSIG). This latter program was originally intended as a federal incentive (in the form of matching grants) to states for the development of state grant programs. In 1983–84 state grants totaling some $1 billion were awarded to almost 1.3 million students (National Association of State Scholarship and Grant Programs, 1983). Since the Reagan administration took office, this program has been targeted for elimination and appropriations have been reduced. If the program is reduced, states will either have to appropriate additional funds to maintain their current grant programs or reduce their own programs by a corresponding amount (NASSGP, 1983). In some states (e.g., Maine and Alabama), the elimination of the SSIG program could result in the total elimination of the state grant program.

TABLE 4. Distribution of a Selected Sample Pell Grant Award by Income Level and Institutional Type, 1981–82

Income Level	Public		Private	
	2-year	4-year	2-year	4-year
Less than $12,000				
Number of applicants	280	2,496	61	1,635
Average Pell award	$916	$1,364	$1,225	$1,257
Distribution of dollars awarded (in thousands)	$256	$3,405	$ 75	$2,005
$12,000–$24,000				
Number of applicants	445	5,537	100	3,773
Average Pell award	$462	$ 647	$ 545	$ 553
Distribution of dollars awarded (in thousands)	$206	$3,582	$ 54	$2,086
Greater than $24,000				
Number of applications	332	7,488	82	6,024
Average Pell award	$166	$ 137	$ 102	$ 108
Distribution of dollars awarded (in thousands)	$ 55	$1,026	$ 8	$ 651

Source. M. L. Tierney, *Price, Prestige, and College Choice*, unpublished manuscript, 1984.

The remaining source of non-repayable grants and scholarships is the colleges and universities themselves. In 1979–80 institutions are estimated to have awarded $1.9 billion in aid to their students (Gillespie and Carlson, 1983). This assistance constitutes a type of price discrimination practiced by most colleges and universities. Such practices may be viewed as part of institutional efforts to enhance equal educational opportunity. Specifically, colleges and universities will charge students from high-income families a nondiscounted price (Table 2) in order to finance aid to students from low-income families. When coupled with third-party payers (i.e., federal and state government grant programs), colleges become little more than collection agencies for redistributing educational opportunity.

However, college and university officials are becoming increasingly concerned over the rate of growth in their unrestricted financial aid expenditures. If these rates of growth were to continue, particularly in a period of declining enrollments of affluent college students, colleges will be forced to divert scarce resources from investments in new programmatic opportunities or current academic programs to their unrestricted financial aid budgets. Under the worst possible scenario, a bitter price war could break out among colleges under the guise of the widespread use of merit scholarships. In such a scenario, all colleges — even those that survive — would suffer.

If the various grant programs discussed above were aggregated for 1979–80, expenditures would total $5.7 billion. By this amount would the burden of financing a college education be shifted from students and their families to other parties, principally taxpayers. In this case, the student/family share of the total instructional costs of postsecondary education would be reduced to 61%. If one were to examine federal grant programs only, expenditures would total slightly over $3 billion in 1979–80. But as noted above, this year was a high-water mark in financial assistance. For 1983–84 federal grant programs are estimated to total slightly under $2.9 billion. Federal grant programs thus have declined by over $1 billion, or 26.8% (Gillespie and Carlson, 1983).

During the same period, federal expenditures for student loan programs grew by almost $1.6 billion, or by about 27.8% (Gillespie and Carlson, 1983). By far the largest of these loan programs is the Guaranteed Student Loan (GSL) program, which made 2,314,200 loans averaging $2,091 each in 1979–80 (Office of Student Financial Assistance, 1982). While the average loan has increased slightly since then (to an estimated $2,238 for fiscal 1983), the number of students borrowing under this program had increased to nearly 3.3 million by 1982–83 (Office of Student Financial Assistance, 1982). Thus it would appear that more students and their families have been required to offset the reductions in direct federal grant assistance by borrowing. Such a pattern would seem to involve another fundamental shift in the burden of financing a college education, this time to the future earnings of college students.

But appearances can be deceiving, given the fact that the federal GSL and National Direct Student Loan (NDSL) programs are heavily subsidized. At the time of this writing, the NDSL program offers student loans at 5% interest and the GSL program at 9%. Depending upon the size of the loan, these programs provide up to ten-year repayment plans commencing six months after graduation. Thus individuals participating in these programs are receiving subsidies in two ways: the interest rates charged are below current market rates, and the interest on the loans is paid by the government while the student is in college. The difficulty is to estimate the size of these subsidies.

Table 5 provides an example of one approach to such estimates. Essentially, it is necessary to calculate the present value of the repayments made by a student under these two programs. For instance, a student entering college in the fall of 1979 who borrowed $2,091 under the GSL program would make monthly payments of $26.49 at a 9% interest rate. Over a ten-year repayment period, the student would repay $3,178.55. However, the final payment of $26.49 in 1995 is worth considerably less than the first payment 1985. Consequently, the total repayments are discounted by the interest rate on six-month U.S. Treasury Bills, which averaged 9.61% in 1979–80. While there are several rates that could be applied, employing T-Bill rates captures the cost to the government of financing these programs (Hartman, 1971). With this discount rate, the present value of the student's total repayments in $221.

TABLE 5. Estimates of the Public Subsidies in the GSL and NDSL Programs

	NDSL	GSL
Amount borrowed [a]	$679	$2,091
Interest	5%	9%
Monthly payments [b]	$7.20	$26.49
Total repayment	$864.22	$3,178.55
Discount rate	9.61%	9.61%
Present value of total repayment	$221	$813
Public subsidy	$458	$1,278

[a]Average loan in 1979–80. Office of Student Financial Assistance, 1982.
[b]Assumes that the student takes the maximum of 10 years to repay the loan after four years of college.

It is quite easy to determine the level of public subsidy involved in these programs: it is the difference between the amount borrowed and the present value of student repayments. For a student borrowing $2,091 under the GSL program, the value of the subsidy is $1,278; for the NDSL program, it is $458. Note that this estimated cost to the government does not include the special allowance built into the GSL program or the cost of administering either program. Approximately three-fourths of the dollars borrowed under federal loan programs (approximately $5.5 billion in 1979–80) constitute a redistribution of the financial burden away from families' current earnings, or approximately $4.1 billion. This $4.1 billion is picked up by the taxpayer, with the remaining $1.4 billion being shifted to the future earnings of the sons and daughters of these families.

The computation of the present value of various loan programs allows one to derive the net price of attending a particular college or university. This net price is defined as

$$\text{Net price} = \text{Student budget} - \text{Grants} - \text{Loan subsidies} \qquad (2)$$

For instance, a student attending a private college would have an expected cost of $5,526 (Table 2). This student might also be receiving a Pell award for $553 (Table 4), a state grant of $1,100, and an institutional scholarship of $300. In addition, she might borrow $2,000 under the GSL program, three-fourths of which is an outright grant to the student and her family. With this financial aid package, the actual current cost to the student and her family is $2,073 ($5,526 − $553 − $1,100 − $300 − $1,500). This discounted price of $2,073 is paid by either the parents (whose expected contribution might be $1,500; see Table 3) or the student from her summer and part-time earnings.

In 1979–80 over 900,000 college students held some type of employment, earning a total of $600 million in the process. For many financial aid analysts and practitioners, college work-study programs — together with borrowing under one or more of the available programs — constitute the student's self-help portion of the financial aid package. The Carnegie Council (1979) made the adoption of a required self-help component its first recommendation for modifying the Pell grant program for a variety of reasons, not the least of which was to help redress an imbalance created by the extension of student grants to young people from middle-income families. An additional rationale underlying the recommendation was to encourage a return to the work ethic, in which students are expected to work for their college education. The work ethic rationale is not only intended to build character, but also is thought to be easier to sell to a more conservative Congress and administration.

Before preceding to the four propositions presented at the beginning of this chapter, it is useful to summarize how current financial aid policies and practices affect the distribution of the burden of paying for a college education. Initially, it was estimated that students and their families bore approximately two-thirds of the burden of postsecondary education's direct and indirect costs. This estimate must be revised in the face of almost $10 billion in direct grants and loan subsidies provided by other parties (principally the taxpayer). Taking this assistance into account yields a rough estimate that students and their families are paying approximately 58% of total postsecondary costs. Moreover, the increasing use of various loan programs signals a further shift in the pattern of postsecondary education finance involving less dependence on parents' current earnings and increased emphasis on students' future earnings.

EXPECTED PARENTAL CONTRIBUTIONS

The first proposition addresses directly the decreasing contribution of parents to their children's college education. Historically, financing a college education has involved a substantial intergenerational transfer of wealth. Parents were expected to sacrifice current consumption (e.g., an improved family food budget, a vacation, or a second car) in order to support the educational aspirations of their sons and daughters. Such sacrifices constituted the major means of assisting one's children to do better than oneself, to start them on the ladder of upward social mobility.

This historical pattern has been changing since the mid-1970s. This change has involved more than increased use of loan programs that shift the burden of financing a college education from parents' current income to students' future earnings. The primary engine of this change has been a relative reduction in what parents are expected to contribute to their children's education.

Returning to Table 3, one can begin to understand how this reduction occurred. The table contains a contribution schedule which was judged to approximate what parents should be able to pay for a college education. While parental gross incomes and the standard maintenance allowance should be increased from year to year in order to reflect increases in the cost of living, changes in parental contribution should occur only when fundamental changes in parental ability to pay have occurred.

However, adjustments in the contribution schedule are made *annually* in accordance with Department of Education regulations. Such adjustments are intended to reflect increases in the cost of living, even though such increases already have been reflected in the standard maintenance allowance. The impact of this adjustment in the parental contribution schedule varies with family income level. For families with incomes below $24,000, expected parental contributions increased between 1976–77 and 1979–80. For instance, a family with an income of $16,000 experienced a 9.3% increase (College Scholarship Service, 1982). For families with incomes above $24,000, expected parental contributions decreased, with the rate of decline increasing with family income. For instance, a family with an income of $32,000 would have experienced a 2.5% decline in these three years (College Scholarship Service, 1982).

It would seem unlikely that fundamental changes in parents' ability to pay for a college education would occur on an annual basis. In fact, parental contribution schedules should be returned to the levels that obtained prior to the imposition of these annual adjustments. While periodic reviews are needed to ensure basic fairness, such reviews should be based on a thorough understanding of family consumption budgets. As mentioned in the earlier discussion of the standard maintenance allowance, acceptable data on family consumption budgets are not available.

More needs to be done to prevent further erosion in the historical pattern of intergenerational financing of a postsecondary education. Specifically, income tax incentives need to be provided in order to induce parents to start saving for their children's education as early as possible. A college education "IRA" is an appealing device, particularly if it is coupled with a favorable asset treatment in financial aid policies and practices. Under current practices, family assets (savings, home equity, etc.) are estimated and an asset protection allowance is applied. The difference between the family's total assets and the asset protection allowance (if greater than zero) is assessed at a flat rate of 12% in 1979–80. Under a college IRA, these savings should be exempted from this assessment due to the fact that they are intended entirely for a son's or daughter's college education.

It is impossible to estimate the impact of a nonexistent program. However, holding parental contribution schedules at mid-1970's levels would return the share of the total cost borne by parents to their historical levels. Coupling this policy with a college IRA could induce families to plan for a college education rather than being faced by the trauma of trying to get together sufficient funds to pay for the college costs of their 18-year-old. It is even possible that a policy could be established in which the amount saved by the federal government (due to the reduction in grants and loans required by the now less needy students) could just match the forgone tax revenues due to the implementation of a college IRA.

PELL AWARDS BASED ON AN ABSOLUTE MEASURE OF NEED

As discussed earlier, basic grants were originally intended to provide targeted assistance for those families for whom the burden of forgone earnings was especially onerous. By the time the Education Amendments of 1972 emerged from Congress, basic grants were to be distributed on the basis of a relative measure of need with the half-cost rule stipulation. The result of this legislation and the ensuing regulations was discussed above.

TABLE 6. Distribution of Pell Awards Based on an Absolute Measure of Need: Maximum Pell of $1,670

Income Level	Public		Private	
	2-year	4-year	2-year	4-year
Less than $12,000				
Average Pell award	1,605	$1,505	$1,568	$1,468
Distribution of dollars awarded (in thousands)	449	3,756	96	2,400
$12,000–$24,000				
Average Pell award	159	65	150	102
Distribution of dollars awarded (in thousands)	71	360	15	385
Greater than $24,000				
Average Pell award	0	0	0	0
Distribution of dollars awarded (in thousands)	0	0	0	0

Source. M. L. Tierney, *Price, Prestige and College Choice*, unpublished manuscript, 1984.

An alternative set of policies might more closely approximate the original spirit of the Education Amendments of 1972. This alternative set might involve the adoption of an absolute measure of need as the basis for distribution of Pell awards. Such an alternative would has two components. First, every high school graduate would be entitled to a grant to attend some form of postsecondary institution (not necessarily limited to traditional institutions of higher education). The amount of this entitlement could be indexed to estimates of the earnings forgone while enrolled. Lacking a method of generating such estimates, the maximum Pell award would be tagged to non-tuition and fee direct costs of college attendance (Carnegie Council, 1979; Hartman, 1978). Second, the maximum grant that a student could receive would be reduced by the amount of the expected family contribution. In other words, family ability to pay for a college education would constitute a direct offset against this entitlement.

Assuming that $1,670 continued to represent the maximum Pell grant award, Table 6 displays the impact of this alternative for the sample studied earlier (Table 4). Comparing the average awards in this table with Table 4 indicates that students from low-income families would receive larger grants on average, students from middle-income families would receive substantially smaller grants on average, and students from families earning more than $24,000 would not receive any Pell grant assistance.

It is clear from Table 6 that the Pell grant program could be reduced by 44% by such an alternative (to the extent that the distribution of student enrollment in Pennsylvania is generalizable to the United States as a whole). Students from low-income families attending public two-year colleges again would be the primary beneficiaries of the increased benefits that would follow the implementation of this alternative policy. The $5.3 million "saved" under this alternative could be used to increase the average Pell grant received by students. Under the constraint that total Pell grant expenditures would remain at around $13.5 million for these students, it would be possible to increase the maximum Pell award to $2,100. With this maximum, average Pell awards would be distributed as in Table 7.

With this revision, the grants available to students from low-income families increase on average by 28%. Making this alternative more attractive politically is the increase in the average Pell award to students from middle-income families. In fact, the average award in Table 7 is approximately the same as the values in Table 4 for these individuals. As should be obvious, the elimination of Pell awards to students from upper-income families is the primary means by which the redistribution is achieved. The aggregate effect of this alternative Pell grant program also is displayed in Table 7. While the total amount expended on these students was constrained to remain constant, students from low-income families now receive 63% of all Pell awards, with students from middle-income families receiving the remaining 37%.

Consideration might be given to widening the definition of postsecondary education activities for which young adults could use their basic grant entitlement. In particular, basic grants might be made available for young adults entering job-training or apprenticeship programs. Such assistance would provide an efficient means of producing the basic skills required by young labor force entrants, thereby making them less subject to frequent and/or prolonged bouts of unemployment. It would also reduce a source of inequality in current financial aid programs involving public support only for those indivduals enrolled in more traditional forms of postsecondary education.

TABLE 7. Distribution of Pell Awards Based on an Absolute Measure of Need: Maximum Pell of $2,100

Income Level	Public		Private	
	2-year	4-year	2-year	4-year
Less than $12,000				
Average Pell award	$2,035	$1,935	$1,998	$1,898
Distribution of dollars awarded (in thousands)	$ 570	$4,830	$ 122	$3,103
$12,000–$24,000				
Average Pell award	$ 589	$ 495	$ 580	$ 532
Distribution of dollars awarded (in thousands)	$ 262	$2,741	$ 58	$2,007
Greater than $24,000				
Average Pell award	$ 0	$ 0	$ 0	$ 0
Distribution of dollars awarded (in thousands)	$ 0	$ 0	$ 0	$ 0

Source. M. L. Tierney, *Price, Prestige, and College Choice*, unpublished manuscript, 1984.

CHANGES IN THE GSL PROGRAM

In the preceding discussion, Pell grant awards were tied to the cost of forgone income or its surrogate, non-tuition and fee costs of college attendance. Such a policy would mean that tuition and fee costs would have to be financed out of current family income or by borrowing on the part of college students. Private institutions in particular might oppose Pell grants based on an absolute measure of need, given their relatively higher tuition and fees. Attending a private institution could become out of the reach of all but the most affluent if most if not all of escalating tuition costs were to be borne by increasing levels of student indebtedness.

Concern over levels of student indebtedness highlight the fundamental problem of all college loan programs: forcing young college graduates to pay for their education in the early, family-raising years even though the benefits of this education accrue throughout one's life. Clearly, the most direct solution to this problem is to lengthen the repayment period in order that the cost of financing a college education more clearly approximates the period during which the benefits of that education are received.

Currently, if a student were to borrow the GSL maximum of $10,000 (i.e., $2,500 for each undergraduate year), his or her monthly payment would be

$127 (at a 9% interest rate). If the repayment period were extended to 15 years, monthly payments would drop to $101; for a 20-year repayment period, monthly payments would be $90. The maximum loan could be raised to $12,500 while the monthly repayment would remain at $127 if the repayment period could be increased to 15 years. Or, if students were allowed to borrow $15,000 and a monthly repayment of $127 were to be maintained, the repayment period would have to be extended to 24 years, or just about the time their own children would be going off to college. While a variety of loan ceilings and repayment periods may be considered, the fundamental question is, When does the scheduled monthly payment become "too big" or burdensome?

Two different approaches have been suggested to answer this question: (1) a modified need analysis procedure in which a varying contribution schedule is applied to a college graduate's discretionary income, and (2) a "value-added" approach in which college graduates are assumed to be willing to repay the entire incremental earnings attributable to a college education (Hartman, 1971). The most difficult aspect of the first approach is to determine the amount of income that is "discretionary," i.e., income that is available after allowance has been made for individual (or family) consumption and taxes. Estimates of these two categories of expense are similar to the determination of parental contributions (Table 3). In fact, if those contribution schedules were used for young college graduates, annual loan payments would be limited to between 8.6% and 18.1% for single adults with adjusted gross incomes between $15,000 and $35,000 in 1980; between 6.2% and 17.5% for married couples with the same incomes; and between 2.2% and 14.0% for married couples with one child. Note that these estimates constitute lower repayments than in the parental contribution schedules, since they are based on what a young college graduate might be able to repay for his or her college education.

An upper bound estimate of oppressive loan payments is arrived at by calculating the increment in a college graduate's income attributable to his or her college education. Two steps are required in this calculation. First, the ratio of the earnings of college graduates 23-30 years of age to those of high school graduates the same age must be estimated. In 1980–81 this rate was 1.28 (Tierney, 1984). Second, since it is widely recognized that part of this earnings differential is attributable to factors other than one's college education, most notably a college graduate's initial academic achievement level and socioeconomic background, the earnings differential should be reduced by approximately 25% (Solmon and Taubman, 1973). If three-fourths of the differential is attributable to a college education, then a college graduate would be expected to earn about 21% more annually than a high school graduate solely due to his or her collegiate experience. Thus, if college graduates are assumed to be able to repay at a rate equal to the increment in their age 23-30 incomes attributable to a college education, then their annual repayment would be approximately 17% of their adjusted gross income.

What do these two approaches indicate for the college graduate who has bor-

rowed the maximum amount under the GSL program? The college graduate
would be expected to repay $127 per month, or $1,524 annually. For a single
adult earning $15,000 immediately after graduation, this annual repayment
would constitute 10.2% of his or her gross income, a percentage that exceeds
the amount calculated under the need analysis approach but is clearly less than
the 17% calculated in the preceding paragraph. In fact, annual earnings would
have to be less than $8,964 before the upper bound estimate of burdensome re-
payments was reached. However, this level of repayment is 4 percentage points
higher than the estimated need analysis repayment ceiling for married couples
(with no children) and 8 percentage points higher for married couples with one
child. It is no wonder that many college graduates, particularly those that have
married and started a family, find GSL payments burdensome. Note that this
example assumes only one college graduate in the family unit. What if both
adults had attended college and borrowed the maximum possible?

Even if agreement could be reached on what constitutes a burdensome level
of repayment, what should be done if this level is exceeded? One possible answer is to stretch out the length of the repayment period. As should be clear
from the earlier example, the repayment period would have to be at least dou-
bled if maximum loans were increased to $15,000. A second possible answer is
to employ some type of graduated repayment plan that tracks the growth in the
college graduate's income. Historically, the rate of growth in the earnings of
college graduates has been approximately equal to inflation plus 2.5 percentage
points (Becker, 1975). Ultimately, the growth in a college graduate's earnings
would catch up with the maximum monthly repayments at a level that is not
burdensome. If combined with the lengthened repayment period, the debt
could be manageable.

One final aspect of the current GSL program needs to be considered: the in-
school interest subsidy. As noted earlier (Table 5), the federal government
makes the interest payments for the student while enrolled and for six months
after graduation. This direct subsidy amounts to approximately $2,500 in four
years if the student were to borrow the maximum each year. If this in-school interest subsidy were capitalized, the repayment period would have to be extended to 15 years in order to maintain the current monthly payment of $127.
Otherwise, a student's monthly payment would increase to $158. It should be
noted that the National Commission on Student Financial Assistance recently
concluded that the in-school interest subsidy is an essential component of the
GSL program (American Council on Education, 1984).

Colleges and Capital

The current limits on borrowing under the GSL program have forced many
higher-priced private colleges and universities to consider a variety of alternatives for assisting students in financing their education. These programs are intended to assist all students — with or without financial need as defined by current financial aid policies — in meeting the costs of a college education. Such

programs should not be considered a prerogative of the major private research universities but should be seen as a harbinger of things to come for all colleges and universities as college costs continue to increase while federal financial assistance remains constant or declines.

The University of Pennsylvania has developed a comprehensive plan which incorporates most of these alternatives while adopting a few innovations of its own. The primary objectives of the PENN Plan are to (1) maintain a need-blind admissions process that will permit the university to attract and admit qualified students, and (2) provide a mechanism for leveraging the university's unrestricted financial aid budget. Thus the PENN Plan seeks to maintain if not enhance the diversity of the undergraduate student body while limiting the rate of growth in unrestricted aid to the rate of growth in the university's total unrestricted income. It should be noted that this rate of growth in unrestricted aid is less than under prior institutional policy, which based increases in unrestricted aid on the rate of growth in tuition revenues.

In order to accomplish these objectives, Penn has developed four basic options to financing an education. Plan A — the Guaranteed Tuition/Extended Payment Plan — fixes the cost of the university education at four times the first year's tuition. Under this plan, non-aided students are expected to make an initial payment equal to one-fourth of the first year's tuition and the family borrows the difference between the total cost and this down payment. The plan offers students and their families a stable financing program in which monthly payments are fixed over a repayment period of approximately ten years. For its part, the university provides a mechanism for financial planning for the families in terms of how the family might split the monthly payments between parents and students, and acquires the capital against its own line of credit. In a very real sense, the university is an active partner in assisting students and their families in financing a college education.

Plan B — the Annual Tuition/Extended Payment Plan (non-aided students) — allows non-aided students and their parents the flexibility of deciding when and how much to borrow from the university. Students are expected to make an initial payment equal to one-fourth of the first year's tuition, and monthly payments are fixed. However, families are charged the actual annual tuition rate for each year, and interest rates may vary in accordance with market rates. Consequently, the length of the repayment period may vary, generally estimated to be between seven and eleven years.

Plan B for aided students involves the same option as set forth in the preceding paragraph with the notable difference that the university's Office of Student Financial Aid designs an aid package based on the family's financial situation. For instance, the university may make part or all of the student's initial payment and/or make up the difference between the estimated monthly payment and the amount parents are expected to contribute. (Note that a relative measure of financial need is being employed by the university.)

By far the most innovative aspect of the PENN Plan for aided students is the fact that the university will continue to contribute to the student's account even after graduation if the student's payment schedule is determined to be burdensome. Thus, if a student from a low-income family were to enter a field that is not characterized by substantial earnings (e.g., teaching or social work), the university will continue to make up the difference between the monthly payment and the sum of the expected parental and student contributions. Thus the university has provided yet another answer to the question of what to do if an alumni's monthly payments are considered burdensome — continue providing financial assistance. Note that this policy applies only those students judged to have financial need initially.

Plan C — the Guaranteed Tuition/Single Payment Plan — sets the total cost of the university education at four times the first year's tuition and allows the student to pay the entire amount in one payment at the beginning of the freshman year. Thus, if a student has a rich relative who has been saving for his or her college education, the university provides an incentive (i.e., no tuition increases) for a lump-sum payment. The limited experience of other institutions suggests that only 1% to 2% of entering freshmen will take advantage of this option.

Plan D — the Annual Tuition/Semester or Monthly Payment Plan — allows families to spread annual tuition payments over the year rather than paying a semester's tuition at the beginning of each semester. A number of colleges employ this option and sometimes contract with an external agency (e.g., a bank) to collect these funds.

These four options suggest a new role for colleges and universities. No longer will they simply struggle to meet estimated student need through their unrestricted financial aid budgets, but will play an increasingly important role in assisting families with the planning necessary to finance a college education. This shift from financial aid to financial planning constitutes one of the important new roles of colleges and universities in the financing of postsecondary education.

Increasingly, colleges and universities will be called upon to use their own lines of credit in order to provide student access to the capital necessary to finance a college education. There is clearly some financial risk in such ventures, and colleges differ in their credit worthiness. It may be good government policy to encourage institutions to develop such plans by either underwriting part of the risk being assumed by colleges and/or providing a partial interest subsidy. In Pennsylvania, for instance, the Pennsylvania Higher Education Assistance Agency is currently authorized to sell financial aid bonds, the proceeds to be used to assist students generally in meeting increasing postsecondary education costs.

For its part, the University of Pennsylvania will continue to face trade-offs between its unrestricted aid budget and other university priorities. With the PENN Plan, the university is able to leverage its unrestricted aid budget, thus ensuring the continuation of need-blind admissions policies into the 21st century. Such a policy is not without its problems. In addition to the risk to which the university is exposed, it also must develop an ever more stringent fiscal discipline. By fixing tuition rates for four years for a potentially large proportion of its student body, the university must keep its annual expenditures from exceeding this predetermined level of income. As in the case of the other parties involved in the financing of a postsecondary education, colleges and universities also will be expected to contribute to a changing pattern of postsecondary education finance.

CONCLUSIONS

The fundamental intention of this chapter is to reinvigorate the discussion surrounding the financing of postsecondary education. It began with a rough approximation of who currently bears the burden of financing a college education. This approximation suggests that students and their parents pay an average 58% of the direct and indirect costs associated with a college education. This percentage is between 6 and 9 percentage points lower than was estimated to be the case at the beginning of the 1970s. Clearly, federal and state governments have taken on a larger share of the burden formerly assumed by parents. If one were to include the level of indebtedness assumed by increasing numbers of students, the historical pattern of intergenerational transfer has been altered even further.

The obvious question raised by this 58% estimate is whether it is too high or too low. With such a question, the discussion shifts from a descriptive to a normative mode, a shift that must be held constantly in mind. While it is beyond the scope of this chapter to address the variety of normative issues that could be raised, at least three principles will be suggested to help guide the discussion of these issues.

First, the burden of financing a college education needs to be socially efficient. Since at least the middle of the nineteenth century, the need for governmental intervention to produce the optimal level of social benefits has been recognized. If students and their families had to pay the full cost of a college education, fewer would go on to college, with resultant social benefits that are less than optimal. Few people would argue that the social benefits associated with a college education are zero (Bowen, 1978). However, it is equally difficult to accept the proposition that the social benefits of a college education have increased substantially relative to those benefits accruing to individuals, particularly when the social costs associated with the college-educated displacing less educated workers are taken into consideration (Levin, 1977). Ultimately, this problem will be either increased or decreased through a variety of federal and state actions. What is needed is a well-documented rationale to support these changes.

Second, the burden of financing a college education needs to be distributed fairly. The operative word in this principle is "fairly." Currently, the concept of fairness is raised in a variety of financial aid contexts. For instance, parental contribution schedules incorporate a somewhat radical conception of fairness, i.e., from each according to ability to pay, to each according to need. On the other hand, the adoption of a relative measure of financial need for basic grant programs, particularly when used in conjunction with the half-cost rule, would seem to run counter to this conception of fairness. What is required is the adoption of a uniform standard of fairness so that the burden of financing a college education can be applied consistently to meet the unique circumstances of each individual. In other words, the average burden of financing a college education can be adjusted upward or downward depending on a student's family income and other contingencies.

Third, the burden of financing a college education needs to be reconsidered without reference to differences between public and private institutions. Students who attend private colleges or universities bear a larger share of the financial burden than their counterparts in public institutions. It would be extremely difficult to argue that the undergraduate education programs of private colleges produce lower levels of social benefits on average than is the case for public colleges. Similarly, it is also difficult to argue that the individual benefits associated with attending private college are larger relative to the social benefits produced than is the case for public colleges, particularly when one controls for institutional academic reputation (and its correlates of average faculty salaries, teaching load, class size, etc.). Without empirical substantiation of either proposition, differences in the burden of financing a private versus a public education would appear to be both inefficient and unfair by almost any standard.

REFERENCES

American Council on Education. *Policy Brief.* Washington, D.C., Division of Policy Analyses and Research, January 1984.

American College Testing Program. *Handbook for Financial Aid Administrators.* Iowa City, Iowa: American College Testing Program, 1978.

Becker, G. S. *Human Capital.* New York: National Bureau of Economic Research, 1975.

Bok, D. *Beyond the Ivory Tower.* Cambridge, Mass.: Harvard University Press, 1982.

Bowen, H. R., and Servelle, P. Who benefits from higher education and who should pay? Washington, D.C.: ERIC Clearinghouse on Higher Education, 1968.

Bowen, H. R. *Investment in Learning.* San Francisco: Jossey-Bass, 1978.

Bureau of Labor Statistics. *Three Standards of Living for an Urban Family of Four.* Washington, D.C.: U.S. Department of Labor Bulletin, No. 1570.5, 1967(a).

Bureau of Labor Statistics. *Revised Equivalence Scale for Estimating Equivalent Incomes or Budget Costs by Family Type.* Washington, D.C.: U.S. Department of Labor Bulletin, No. 1570-2, 1967(b).

Carnegie Commission. *Higher Education: Who Pays? Who Benefits? Who Should Pay?* New York: McGraw-Hill, 1973.

Carnegie Council on Policy Studies in Higher Education. *Next Steps for the 1980s in Student Financial Aid.* San Francisco: Jossey-Bass, 1979.

College Scholarship Service, *The Uniform Methodology: Past, Present, and Future.* New York: The College Board, 1982.

College Scholarship Service. *A Survey of Undergraduate Need Analysis Policies, Prac-*

tices, and Procedures. New York: The College Board and the National Association of Student Financial Aid Administor, 1984.

Davis, J. S. D., and Van Dusen, W. *Guide to the Literature of Student Financial Aid.* New York: The College Board, 1978.

Finn, C. *Scholars, Dollars, and Bureaucrats.* Washington, D.C.: Brookings Institution, 1978.

Gillespie, D. A., and Carlson, N. *Trends in Student Aid: 1963 to 1983.* Washington, D.C.: The College Board, 1983.

Goggin, W. J. *The Measurement of Economic Well-Being in Need Analysis Models.* Iowa City, Iowa: American College Testing Program, 1968.

Hartman, R. W. *Credit for College.* New York: McGraw-Hill, 1971.

Hartman, R. W. Federal option for student aid. In D. W. Breneman and C. E. Finn (eds.), *Public Policy and Private Higher Education.* Washington, D.C.: Brookings Institution, 1978.

Levin, H. Is a college education worth it? Paper presented at the annual meeting of the American Council of Education, Washington, D.C., October 1977.

National Association of State Scholarship and Grant Programs. *15th Annual Survey.* Harrisburg, Pa.: Pennsylvania Higher Education Assistance Agency, 1984.

Nelson, S. Financial trends and issues. In D. W. Brennan and C. E. Finn (eds.), *Public Policy and Private Higher Education.* Washington, D.C.: Brookings Institution, 1978.

Office of Student Financial Assistance. *Program Book.* Washington, D.C.: U.S. Department of Education, 1982.

Orwig, M. *Financing Higher Education: Alternatives for the Federal Government.* Iowa City, Iowa: American College Testing Program, 1971.

Solmon, L. C., and Taubman, P. J. *Does College Matter?* New York: Academic Press, 1973.

Tierney, M. L. Price, prestige, and college choice. Unpublished manuscript. Higher Education Finance Research Institute, University of Pennsylvania, 1984.

Watts, H. W. Special panel suggests changes in BLS family budget program. *Monthly Labor Review,* December 1980, pp. 3-10.

Zemsky, R., and Oedel, P. *The Structure of College Choice.* New York: College Entrance Examination Board, 1983.

INTERNATIONAL STUDENTS IN COMPARATIVE PERSPECTIVE:
Toward a Political Economy of International Study

Y. G.-M. Lulat and Philip G. Altbach, *State University of New York at Buffalo*

Foreign students are a "growth industry" in higher education. It has been estimated that in the United States more than $2.5 billion is devoted to the education of students from other countries each year. More than 336,000 international students are studying in American colleges and universities, constituting about 3% of the total enrollment in postsecondary education. International students are even more important in graduate education, constituting about 15% of the total, and in some fields, such as engineering and computer science, comprising about half of the total enrollment. Other countries (such as Canada, France, the United Kingdom, and the Soviet Union) also have large numbers of international students (see Table 1).

While the "sending" nations are often ignored in discussions on international students, the issues are important in these nations as well. In fact, in a number of Third World countries their total internal university student population is less than their total external student population (examples include Malaysia, Hong Kong, Saudi Arabia, and most of the Arabian Gulf nations). A few of the smaller nations, such as Cyprus, have virtually no postsecondary educational institutions and rely on foreign institutions for their training needs. While there are no firm statistics, it can be estimated that there are more than one million students worldwide studying outside their native countries.

This essay has two primary purposes: to provide a balanced discussion of major themes, and to present an overview of the literature as a whole — with a view toward suggesting gaps in the literature that need to be filled, as well as avenues of further research in a relatively new area that we have termed "the political economy of international study."

FOREIGN STUDY IN HISTORICAL PERSPECTIVE

While current interest in issues relating to international study may give the impression that the phenomenon is of recent origin, this is not so. International study has a long tradition going back to the very beginning of universities as institutions of higher learning. (An important study, and probably the only one of its kind that extensively documents the historical origins of international study, is Brickman's *Two Millennia of International Relations in Higher Education*, published in 1975. Other studies of relevance here include Dedijer, 1968, and Hess, 1982.) Indeed, universities throughout much of their history have been truly international institutions, enrolling students from many nations as an integral part of their policies and practices. It was only with the rise of the modern nation-state in Europe that universities began to teach in the national language rather than the "international" language, Latin.

TABLE 1. International Student Flows: Major Indicators

The Top 20 of the World's Leading Hosts of International Students (1980/81)		*The Top 20 of the World's Leading Senders of International Students (1980/81)*	
Country	Total Number of Students	Country of Origin	Total Number of Students
United States	325,628	Iran	65,521
France	114,181	Malaysia	35,693
USSR[a]	62,942	Greece	31,509
Germany, Federal Republic of	61,481	China	30,127
United Kingdom	56,003	Nigeria	26,863
Canada	32,303	Morocco	20,876
Italy	27,784	Hong Kong	20,625
Lebanon	26,343	United States	19,843
Egypt	21,751	Japan	18,066
Australia	17,694	Venezuela	17,755
Switzerland	15,515	Canada	17,714
Saudi Arabia	14,298	Jordan	17,030
Austria	12,885	Germany, Federal Republic of	16,983
Belgium	12,875	United Kingdom	15,776
India[a]	11,761	Palestine (Refugees)	15,414
Spain	10,997	Lebanon	15,117
Vatican	9,104	India	15,238
Argentina[b]	8,649	Turkey	14,606
Greece[c]	8,304	Italy	13,848
Philippines	7,901	Syria	13,701

Source. Based on data from *UNESCO Statistical Yearbook*, 1983.
[a] 1978.
[b] 1976.
[c] 1979.

Although the Western higher education model is now dominant throughout the world, this was not always the case, and non-Western academic systems were also international in scope. The Islamic university, still exemplified by the Al-Azhar in Cairo, sees itself as an international institution, serving Islamic civilization rather than any one country (Dodge, 1961). The Al-Azhar uses Arabic as the medium of instruction — the international language of Islamic culture. The traditional Hindu and Buddhist universities, such as the Universities of Taxila and Nalanda in India (which are among the earliest known universities, going back as far as 600 B.C.), also were international in scope and welcomed both teachers and students from other countries (see Altekar, 1948; Nurullah and Naik, 1956). These institutions used international languages — Sanskrit or Pali — as the medium for teaching, and thus students from other countries that used these languages could attend the universities. These institutions were largely religious in orientation, but secular subjects were often taught as well. It should be remembered that the great Islamic libraries of Egypt and Spain kept much of Western culture alive during the European "Dark Ages" (see, for example, Parsons, 1952). It was when Western scholars again came into contact with this knowledge through the Islamic universities that the Renaissance, in part, got its start. Thus continuing international contacts in higher education have proved important to the preservation and transmission of knowledge — and at some periods of history, Western scholars were dependent on academic institutions and traditions in other parts of the world.

The medieval universities in Europe (such as Bologna, Cordova, Florence, Louvain, Paris, and Salerno) were, of course, the forerunners of contemporary institutions, and these institutions were basically international in nature (Cobban, 1975; Haskins, 1966; Rashdall, 1936). The language of instruction was Latin. The faculty, too, was generally international in nature. (In Italy, the medieval university itself often moved from town to town in search of more congenial surroundings.) Thus the core of the medieval university was international. Foreign students were the norm, not the exception. This tradition of openness to foreign currents has been a powerful force in higher education ever since the medieval period. Later, as European nationalism grew and universities came under the domination of local princes and later of the nation-states, gradually shifting the medium of instruction from Latin to the various national languages, some of the previous internationalism was lost; but access to universities remained open to students from various countries. The concept of the "wandering student" was a strong one, and sometimes these sojourns included studying in another country. The metropolitan nations of Europe — France, and later Germany and to some extent Austria — provided a powerful magnet for students from other countries. For certain periods, universities in Poland, the Netherlands, and Sweden also attracted many foreign students.

In the 19th century, when the United States was building its academic system and graduate education was being established, young scholars typically studied in Europe, especially in Germany during the latter part of the century, in order to ensure an academic career in the United States. In this period, American higher education was, in a sense, an intellectual colony of Europe (Veysey, 1965). The flow of foreign students was almost completely from America to Europe. The United States did not emerge as a major center of foreign study for international students until after World War II, when American higher education expanded rapidly and dramatically improved its quality.

Turning to the modern period, once again one perceives a long historical tradition in the migration of students — especially Third World students going to the West. During the colonial era, students from the colonies often studied in the colonizing country to prepare themselves for the colonial civil service or for positions in emerging trade and industrial enterprises. While their numbers were small, these individuals were often very influential in the intellectual development, in nationalist and revolutionary movements, and eventually in the politics of the emerging nations after World War II. The French, who were slow to establish academic institutions in their colonies, brought many students from Indochina (including Ho Chi Minh) and from their dependencies in Africa to France to study. The British, especially in India, who were quicker to found colleges and universities and encouraged local educational initiatives, brought fewer students to England, but many did study there (including Jawaharlal Nehru). Sukarno, the founder of the Indonesian nation, studied in the Netherlands when his country was under colonial rule, and many of the concepts of Indonesian nationalism were forged in the universities of Holland by colonial students.

It is possible to see discernible patterns in the transnational migration of students over a long period of time. Indeed, historical trends buttress the general concept that students migrate from the peripheries to the centers and that foreign study is very much part of an international knowledge system. None of the problems that are evident at present — the brain drain, adjustment issues, the relevance of the curricula, language issues — are entirely new.

In the medieval period, students were sometimes so unpopular that the entire university was forced to move from place to place. Issues relating to the cosmopolitanism of the international academic community versus local populations created disputes. For example, King Henry III of England in an address to the townspeople of the city of Cambridge warned them: "Unless you conduct yourselves with more restraint and moderation towards them [international students] . . . they will be driven by your exactions to leave your town and, abandoning their studies, leave the country, which we by no means desire" (Williams, 1982, pp. 10-11). The medieval universities, in comparison to their modern counterparts, were considerably more international in terms of not only the curricula, but student and staff composition as well.

While the flow of students across borders has deep historical precedents, the characteristics of the present flow of international students differs from that of previous times in several respects: the numbers involved are much greater today than was the case in the past; the students of the past were scholars in their own right; and the staff of the institutions were very heterogeneous in terms of national origins. But perhaps the most important distinction between the present and the past is that today the general pattern of international student flow is close to unilinear, that is, it is skewed in the direction of a largely south-to-north movement (from less industrialized to more industrialized nations).

INTERNATIONAL STUDENT FLOW PATTERNS

The numbers of students traversing the globe are considerable. Table 2 indicates some of the contemporary flows of students and Table 3 provides a basic overview of the flows. The magnitude and direction of the flows have over the years remained fairly stable, though slight variations do occur. This section discusses the nature of some of these flows and some of the reasons for them.

TABLE 2. Regional Destinations of International Students from the Top 10 of the Industrialized Market Economies with the Largest Numbers of International Students Abroad (1980/81)

Home Country	Total Number of Students Abroad	Regions of Destination		
		Industrialized Market Economies	Planned Economies	Third World Countries
Greece	31,509	30,282	748	479
United States	19,843	19,071	339	433
Japan	18,066	17,498	381	187
Canada	17,714	17,594	82	38
Germany, Federal Republic of	16,983	16,765	120	98
United Kingdom	15,776	14,669	73	1,034
Italy	13,848	13,014	90	744
France	11,159	10,312	82	765
Spain	7,035	6,080	10	945
The Netherlands	5,178	5,145	14	19

Source. Based on data from *UNESCO Statistical Yearbook*, 1983.

While the major international flow of students is from the Third World to the industrialized market-economy nations, an important flow of students is among the industrialized nations themselves (see Table 2). Here, motivations for study abroad differ from those of Third World students and the length of study is generally shorter. Relatively few stay to complete their entire degree program abroad. More typical is the American pattern of "study abroad" programs which typically provide undergraduate students with a year's experience overseas, usually in Western Europe (Brown, 1983). It is significant that of the 30,000 American college students who participate in study-abroad programs each year, only about 5% study in Third World nations. This period of overseas

TABLE 3. Flow Patterns of International Students

Third World students	to	Industrialized market-economy nations
Third World students	to	Socialist nations
Third World students	to	Other Third World nations
Industrialized market-economy students	to	Other industrialized market-economy nations
Industrialized market-economy students	to	Third World nations
Socialist nation students	to	Other Socialist nations
Socialist nation students	to	Industrialized market-economy nations
Industrialized market-economy students	to	Socialist nations

study is generally counted as part of the American undergraduate degree. An exception to this generalization is in the field of medical education, where many Americans, generally those unable to gain admission to U.S. medical schools, study abroad for their entire medical degrees.

In Western Europe, the Council of Europe, the European Economic Community (Common Market), the CRE (the organization of European higher education administrators), and other groups have supported a variety of student exchanges. The Common Market, for example, guarantees that students from member states pay fees equivalent to those of domestic students and provides relatively open access to the universities. Under these circumstances of relative freedom it is surprising that only a very small percentage of European students choose to study abroad. Thus, while there is movement across European borders for academic exchange and study, the total numbers involved are modest. Very often, European students perceive that a foreign degree will put them at a disadvantage in terms of professional advancement in their own countries, and with the exception of students of language and perhaps international affairs, higher education tends to be fairly insular (Roeloffs, 1982).

There is also considerable mobility among students from the Socialist nations. Arrangements exist among the COMECON nations of Eastern Europe to exchange students, but it seems that the largest flow is from nations such as East Germany, Cuba, Czechoslovakia, and Bulgaria to the Soviet Union, with relatively few Soviet students studying abroad.

There is a good deal of mobility from one Third World nation to another, although this is a phenomenon not widely researched (see Table 4). India and the

Philippines host large numbers of foreign students. The Indian government provides scholarships for study in India for students from the South Asia region and also from Africa. Many students from Southeast Asia gravitate to India, in part because costs are very much lower than in most other parts of the world and in part because admission in many fields is easier. To some degree the curricula are more attuned to conditions in the Third World. The Philippines, with its large educational system functioning in English and with many private universities, also attracts a great number of international students, mostly from Southeast Asia. Mexico and Argentina serve as foci for Latin American students because of their well-developed academic systems, and Egypt has been a traditional center for students from the Middle East. Lebanon, with its English- and French-language universities, until recently also served as a destination for many Middle Eastern students (see Smith, Woesler de Panafieu, and Jarousse, 1981).

TABLE 4. The Top 10 of the Third World Nations Hosting the Largest Numbers of International Students, and a Breakdown of the Students by World Regions of Origin (1980/81) [a]

Host Country	Total Number of International Students	Africa, Asia, South America	Europe	USSR	North America	Oceania	Other (Not specified)
Lebanon	26,343	14,308	255	—	216	—	11,564
Egypt	21,751	21,618	110	1	22	—	—
Saudi Arabia	14,298	12,987	28	58	38	—	—
India [b]	11,671	11,145	211	8	97	210	—
Argentina [c]	8,649	6,327	2,005	15	301	1	—
Philippines	7,901	6,105	830	—	966	—	—
Turkey	6,378	5,571	449	—	9	1	348
Kuwait	3,153	2,701	6	—	4	—	442
Senegal	3,065	2,732	318	—	15	—	—
Ivory Coast	2,314	1,988	293	—	19	2	12

Source. Based on data from *UNESCO Statistical Yearbook*, 1983.
[a] Note that disaggregation of data is not possible along the same regional lines as those determined for Table 2.
[b] 1978.
[c] 1976.

The host country's internal flow pattern (or "intranational pattern") is also very important in understanding overall flows. International students are not distributed randomly in an academic system. They tend to concentrate in particular institutions and fields of study. For example, engineering is the choice of 25% and business and management studies of another 16% of the foreign students studying in the United States. More than one-third of all foreign students (35.9%) are graduate students (Boyan, 1981). In engineering and management studies, foreign students constitute about half of the total enrollment at the graduate level in many universities. The five leading states in foreign student enrollments (California, New York, Texas, Florida, and Massachusetts) had 41% of all such students in the United States. Foreign students tend to congregate in the larger colleges and universities. Particular nationality groups often choose particular institutions, due to informal contacts and for other reasons. This non-random internal flow pattern of international students is replicated in other nations as well.

We have in general terms described some of the key elements of the international flow of students. There are many reasons that account for these flows or may induce changes (see Table 5). Despite minor variations, the stability in the general flow since World War II is clear and is related to the overall trend of students to go from the peripheries (by and large the Third World) to the centers (mainly the industrialized market-economy nations that use the major international languages — English and French). In our following section concerning dependency and international students, many of the factors related to this major theme are discussed, with attention to the basic elements that produce flows of students and that effect changes, usually within the broader framework of the movement from the periphery to the center of the world economic system.

Flows of students are affected by policy changes in the host countries. In general, economic problems in the industrialized market-economy nations in the 1970s stimulated a reevaluation of policies regarding the education of international students, and some countries — several of the American states, Australia, Britain, and West Germany — made moves to reduce the flow or significantly raise fees. (For a synoptic account of these changes in selected countries see Appendix F in Williams, 1982.) Political factors in the host countries can also have an impact on student flows. In the postwar years, foreign policy considerations induced many industrialized nations to welcome larger numbers of international students and even to provide scholarship assistance. Host-country policies concerning particular countries may affect flows; for example, the American government has been less sympathetic toward granting visas to students from Iran since the revolution in that country. And educational and cultural factors play their part. In the United States, for example, a commitment to "internationalizing" the curriculum in higher education has made many universities more conscious of their role as international institutions. In Western Europe, efforts have been made to make intra-European mobility easier.

Policy changes in the home nations also determine student flows. Economic factors are a key element. The changes in oil prices have affected flows of students from such nations as Venezuela and Nigeria, which have had to dramatically curtail their scholarship programs and limit the availability of foreign exchange for their students studying abroad. Political upheaval can bring an abrupt change in student flows. A well-known example is Iran, where the over-

TABLE 5. Variables Affecting the Magnitude and Direction of Major Flow Patterns

Host Country Variables	Home Country Variables
1. Economic difficulties leading to restrictions on international students via measures such as higher tuition fees, e.g., United Kingdom, Australia.	1. Economic difficulties leading to reduction in available state funds as well as available foreign exchange, e.g., Nigeria, Venezuela.
2. Population changes leading to increase in available student places, e.g., some states in the United States.	2. Economic boom leading to expansion of demand for trained personnel and hence an increase in numbers of students going abroad, e.g., oil-producing nations before the oil glut on the world market.
3. Changes in foreign policy leading to completion of bilateral agreements, e.g., between China and the United States or Ethiopia and the USSR.	3. Economic policy changes leading to emphasis in areas with a dearth in requisite training facilities, and hence necessitating students going abroad, e.g., China.
4. Reemphasis of political commitments leading to increase in inflow of international students from a politically volatile region, e.g., Afghanistan.	4. Political changes (such as revolution) leading to changes in foreign policy and hence change in flow direction, e.g., Nicaragua.
5. Education policy changes leading to emphasis on international area and language studies and hence a greater commitment to study-abroad programs, e.g., the United States.	5. Educational changes such as completion of appropriate training facilities, hence leading to reduction in numbers of students abroad, e.g., India.

TABLE 6. Key Variables Affecting the Personal Decision to Study Abroad by Third World Students

Key Variables Pertaining to Home Country (Push Factors)	Key Variables Pertaining to Host Country (Pull Factors)
1. Availability of scholarships for study abroad.	1. Availability of scholarships to international students.
2. Poor-quality educational facilities.	2. Good-quality education.
3. Lack of research facilities.	3. Availability of advanced research facilities.
4. Lack of appropriate educational facilities.	4. Availability of appropriate educational facilities with likely offer of admission.
5. Failure to gain admission to local institution(s).	5. Presence of relatives willing to provide financial assistance.
6. Enhance value (in the market place) of a foreign degree.	6. Congenial political situation.
7. Discrimination against minorities.	7. Congenial socioeconomic and political environment to migrate to.
8. Politically incongenial situation.	8. Opportunity for general international life experience.

throw of the Shah caused major alterations in student numbers and induced many Iranian students abroad not to return. Political changes in countries such as South Vietnam, Angola, Ethiopia, Nicaragua, Somalia, and others also have affected the direction of student flows as well as the numbers of students going abroad. International educational changes also impact on student flows overseas. At one time India was a major "exporter" of students, but with the growth of Indian higher education, fewer Indian students now study abroad.

MOTIVATIONS FOR STUDY ABROAD

Research indicates that there are a myriad of "push" and "pull" factors involved in foreign study (Glaser and Habers, 1978; Rao, 1979; also Table 6). Students and their families have their own interests and concerns, as do governments of Third World nations, and at the same time funding agencies and governments in the industrialized nations also have priorities. Therefore, in many instances there is more than one motivation involved; for example, American authorities are interested in "internationalizing" American higher education, providing assistance to students from the Third World, and expanding American influence abroad (Jenkins, 1983b). It is useful to consider some of these motivations as a means of understanding some of the important implications of foreign study.

It seems likely that a majority of the world's international students provide their own financial support and are not sponsored by any agency or government. Some eventually are able to obtain support from a university or other agency, while many rely on personal or family resources for their entire sojourn. Thus the decision to undertake foreign study is largely an individual one. Individual decisions are made for many reasons. Some international students see their studies as a preliminary to emigration, and statistics on the "brain drain" from countries such as Taiwan, South Korea, and several others support this idea (Glaser and Habers, 1978; Myers, 1972; Rao, 1979). Obtaining visas for study overseas is relatively easy, and such students hope that the sojourn can be turned into permanent residency. Such hopes are often realized, though this is now becoming increasingly difficult.

Probably the largest number of international students — particularly those from Third World nations — wish to improve their professional opportunities at home by studying abroad. In many cases, they obtain training in technological or other fields which are not available at home. In others, the prestige value of a foreign degree is a major motivation. Both the skills obtained abroad and the benefits of having studied abroad are highly valued. In most Third World countries, such foreign qualifications are quite useful on the job market and usually yield higher salaries and better prospects for promotions.

Students who are unable to obtain admission to academic institutions at home often choose to go abroad for their education. In some countries, the higher education system is very small and highly selective and large numbers of well-qualified individuals cannot obtain entry to local institutions. In other cases, policies regarding entrance favor specific groups in the population and some racial or ethnic groups find themselves excluded. The vicissitudes of privately funded international students are often considerable. Changes in home-country policies, economic crises, or personal circumstances may make support from home difficult or impossible and students are left without funds. When students go abroad for study for political reasons, they sometimes find it difficult to return home, leading to considerable problems for themselves and the host country. Despite tightened immigration policies and other restrictions, privately funded students remain a large and important portion of the total population. The motivations of privately funded students differ, and they tend to study where they can obtain admission and where the cost of education suits their ability to pay. In recent years, India and the Philippines have become more popular among foreign students because of the relatively inexpensive education offered.

Generally, the motivations of Third World governments in providing oppor-

tunities for study abroad are clear: in most instances, they cannot provide sufficient educational opportunities at home. As secondary education expanded, increasing numbers of middle-class young people demanded access to higher education and local academic systems were unable to absorb these increased numbers. Governments began to provide scholarships for study abroad to meet this
demand. In other cases, needed academic specializations — from nuclear physics to management studies — were not available at home and thus funding was
provided for overseas study. Countries such as Saudi Arabia, Kuwait, Venezuela, and Malaysia have spent very large sums of money on overseas study
programs, although there have been massive cutbacks recently because of difficult economic circumstances in these countries. There has also been a rethinking of priorities as a result of problems with some of the returning students.
Questions concerning the relevance of foreign training to local needs have been
raised, and there have been some difficulties in readjustment. From the point
of view of Third World governments, foreign study programs are a way of reducing pressure on indigenous academic resources — although the costs are
quite high — as well as a means of quickly providing needed expertise without
making a permanent investment in local academic institutions.

The motivations of the host countries are even more complex and combine
altruistic, pragmatic, and foreign policy factors. The American debate has
stressed the value of foreign students on campus in "internationalizing" the
American higher education system. Western governments wish to maintain
their influence overseas and see foreign study opportunities as a means of doing
this (Coombs, 1964). The United States, which has no colonial heritage (except
in the Philippines) to draw on, has tried for thirty years to build links with
Third World nations. The Fulbright program has a new "International Linkages" component which attempts to foster such connections. French policy
seeks to continue relationships with France's former colonies and to foster the
French language overseas. In the Third World, policies have also contributed to
the maintenance of ties. Malaysia has traditionally sent its government-funded
students to England and altered this policy only when the British government
dramatically raised fees for foreign students. Thus official policies and informal relationships tend to maintain contacts. In the case of the United States,
scholarship programs, institutional development efforts, and other policies
over a thirty-year period have built up some linkages as well. (For analyses of
several American efforts see Coleman, 1984; Hanson, 1968; and Mazrui,
1975.)

The motivations for study abroad among students from the industrialized
nations differ significantly from those of Third World students. These students
typically do not obtain a foreign academic degree but rather go abroad for linguistic training, cultural enrichment, or the experience of living in another environment. Many academic institutions in North America and Western Europe
provide academic credit for foreign study, and in some fields, such as foreign
languages, overseas study is an important part of the curriculum. In most in-

dustrialized countries a foreign academic degree is less valued than a domestic degree, so the impetus for obtaining such degrees is limited. The most extreme case is probably Japan, where foreign degrees in some fields are not recognized. In Western Europe, the European Community has made it easier and less costly to study in its member states. There has been no comprehensive study of the motivations of students from the industrialized nations who study abroad, but it seems clear that the impetus is more personal and cultural than it is professional or economic.

Motivations are difficult to discern, and "push" and "pull" factors vary considerably. The equation for students from the Third World is quite different than for those from industrialized nations. Politics, economics, and prestige as well as desire for knowledge enter into the motivating forces for international study. Recently, in a number of host nations (such as Australia, Canada, and Britain) foreign policy aims and altruistic goals regarding international study have come into conflict with economic and political pressures to restrict educational opportunities for Third World students (see, for example, Williams, 1982). The result has usually been an ambivalent response by the government concerned: a reemphasis of commitment to provide educational opportunities for international students at the rhetorical level and at the practical level the establishment of legal and economic restrictions.

THE ECONOMICS OF FOREIGN STUDY

This section considers some of the major policy issues relating to the economics of international study. Later, we discuss in detail some of the important components of research on this topic. There is probably no more complex topic, nor one more hotly debated at present, than the relative costs and benefits of foreign study. Much of the literature recently has focused on the costs to the host countries of educating international students (Blaug, 1981; Jenkins, 1983a; Sims and Stelcner, 1981; Winkler, 1981). This literature has been stimulated by debates in the host nations, with policymakers often arguing that large numbers of international students are costly and that they add a new and sometimes difficult element to the educational equation. It is argued that the education of international students is subsidized by general tax revenues, since in almost all countries higher education is subsidized by the state or in some cases provided virtually without cost to the individual. Britain, Canada, and Australia have raised questions about whether they can afford these subsidies. Several states in the United States have also questioned the wisdom of large enrollments of foreign students.

In federal systems like the United States, Canada, and Australia the situation is particularly complex, since the national government may have policies which reflect broader national concerns while the bulk of funding comes from the governments of the states or provinces, whose policymakers may have little interest in national affairs and are mainly concerned with serving the needs of local residents and protecting their immediate fiscal interests. In the United

States, private universities generally charge tuition fees that reflect the cost of education and public institutions have generally charged more to students from other states (and countries) while providing subsidies to all students by charging fees that are less than the cost of the education. There has been increasing pressure in some states to raise "out of state" tuition rates even higher as a revenue-creating measure. A few states have discussed quotas on foreign students. There has been particular concern over the large proportion of foreign students in graduate fields such as engineering, computer science, and management, which are relatively "high cost" fields. The Western European nations have also been concerned about the costs of educating foreign students. A few, such as West Germany, have placed restrictions on the enrollment of foreign students in certain fields of study. Others have been debating how to deal with the rising costs of postsecondary education. The European nations are somewhat limited in their options by the agreements they have in the context of the European Community.

The economic costs for the home countries are, if anything, even less well understood than those of the host nations. For a number of Third World nations, the cost of sending students abroad for education is very high. The costs can be calculated in many ways. The expenditure in foreign exchange, a rare commodity in many Third World nations, includes funds spent by individuals as well as by government agencies and the private sector. Some nations, such as India, restrict the amount of foreign exchange that can be taken out of the country for foreign study (as well as for other purposes), and for many fields in which India has self-sufficiency in higher education, students are not permitted to matriculate abroad unless they have scholarships from external sources. Other countries permit virtually anyone to study abroad as long as the student is able to obtain admisssion to a foreign school. It is therefore very difficult to calculate the costs for study abroad — but without question the amount is very substantial.

The direct economic costs to public agencies in the Third World are quite large in a number of countries. Malaysia, Saudi Arabia, Kuwait, Venezuela, and Colombia, among others, have central agencies responsible for providing funding and guidance for their students studying abroad. Sometimes the infra-structures of these agencies are impressive and include not only placement and counseling assistance but also guidance on curricular questions and the choice of institutions, job assistance on return, and of course disbursement of funds while studying. There is also some monitoring of academic progress while abroad. These agencies have very large budgets and sometimes sponsor thousands of students abroad. They have full-time staff abroad to assist their students. Even such small countries as Singapore and Kuwait maintain full-time overseas offices for their students. The costs for scholarships and stipends are substantial, as are the overhead costs. The cost of educating a student overseas is generally higher than that of a domestic education, but the equation becomes complex if the very high infrastructural costs of universities, particularly in the sciences and medicine, are added.

Most countries build universities as a matter of national independence and do not wish to rely on foreign training for their students. Nevertheless, in many fields and specializations, foreign training remains a necessity where domestic facilities do not exist or cannot provide the needed numbers of graduates. There are also severe pressures from the educated middle class for access to higher education and this is also a motivation for public expenditures for foreign study.

Funding for international students comes from many sources in the industrialized nations. Direct financial assistance in the form of scholarships is provided by many agencies — foreign student assistance bodies, philanthropic foundations, academic institutions, professional societies, and even industrial firms. According to the Institute of International Education (1983), fewer than 15% of the foreign students studying in the United States in 1983 were directly financed by American sources, with the largest part (8.9%) of funding coming directly from colleges and universities as scholarships and assistantships.

It is possible to argue — from the perspective of "home" or "host" countries, of budget managers or foreign policy analysts, of world-conscious humanitarians or narrow-minded legislators — about the relative economic costs and benefits of international study. Further, it is often possible to determine the outcome of economic analysis on this topic by manipulating the variables. In a later section, we suggest some of the key factors that must be considered in any analysis of the economics of foreign study. But it is clear that while economic analysis can add to a debate, it cannot be the determining factor. The issues are too complicated and necessarily extend beyond what is measurable by economic analysis. It has been argued that the presence of international students and faculty enriches the academic life and the ambience of a university. It is impossible to measure this enrichment. International graduate students in some fields provide needed research and teaching assistance at low cost (Bailey, Pialorsi, and Zukowski-Faust, 1984). The foreign policy interests of some countries are enhanced by providing education to international students. It is hoped that long-term trade and other relationships will be cemented by the experience of international study. And altruistic and noneconomic goals of mutual understanding and cooperation may be realized as well. Thus, while it is theoretically possible to measure some of the direct and indirect costs of international students, economically measurable costs and benefits are only part of the equation.

INTERNATIONAL STUDY AS EDUCATIONAL DEPENDENCE

An important element in any consideration of international study is that it takes place in a context of global economic, technological, and political inequality. The inequality is particularly dramatic precisely where the largest flows of students take place — between the Third World nations and the industrialized market-economy countries. Discussion of the inequalities between nations has been rare in debates concerning international study, and it is our conviction that in order to understand the political economy of international study it is necessary to comprehend this factor. It was stated earlier that it is possible to see the historical and contemporary international flows of students to centers of knowledge and power from peripheries. Third World nations look to the industrialized nations as models of how to "modernize." The norms and values learned during overseas study are brought home along with technological knowledge. International study, as a phenomenon, is therefore a relationship of considerable inequality (Weiler, 1984). While there is increasing concern that foreign study implies the transformation of the Third World according to the models and policies of the industrialized nations (Fuenzalida, 1981), most discussions of foreign study are couched in terms of exchanges, mutual understanding, cooperation, and related issues. Few observers have discussed foreign study from the perspective of global inequalities and the continuing domination of the industrialized nations over the Third World. Yet it is important to consider foreign study in the broader international context of global inequality — which foreign study both helps to alleviate, by bringing skills to the Third World, and helps to perpetuate, by continuing the dependent relationships of the Third World on the industrialized nations.

It is not the purpose of this discussion to claim that all foreign study is necessarily detrimental to the Third World but rather to point out the paradoxical character of foreign study from the perspective of the Third World — the principal generator of international student flows. International study for Third World nations must represent a mixed blessing (Altbach, 1981, 1983; see also Glimm and Kuper, 1980, and Stauffer, 1979). Thus, as international students from the Third World participate in a flow from the periphery to the center, they imbibe the values of their new environment as well as the skills learned in the university. They must not only be proficient in the language of the host country, but if they are to succeed in meeting their academic goals they have to internalize the methodological and often the substantive concerns of the academic systems in which they study. When they return home, they naturally seek to replicate the institutions and practices they experienced in the industrialized nations (Bochner, 1979). This informal and often invisible bond to the industrialized nations is one of the positive outcomes of a liberal international student policy, and ought to be pursued by the industrialized nations (Wallace, 1981).

Thus there are many kinds of expertise that are learned as a result of foreign study. In addition to scientific and technological knowledge, international students also obtain what might be called the "cultural capital" that permits them to function in technological societies (Bourdieu and Passeron, 1977). The term "cultural capital" has been applied in an American context to indicate that middle-class children learn from family and school a particular set of behavioral skills and attitudes that permit them to flourish in the mainstream of American society. The same concept can be applied internationally to that minority (the elite) in the Third World that becomes proficient in the language, technologies, and orientations of the industrialized nations. These skills not only permit this group to hold the reins of power, but the elite also develop a particular lifestyle which is more attuned to the West than to realities in many Third World nations. (For further discussion of these and related issues, see Dagnino, 1980, and Sauvant and Mennis, 1980.) International students thus learn not only Western technical skills but also the cultural styles, languages, and orientations of the West. They learn to use Western consumer products and tend to import these when they return home. The problems of readjustment to the local environment are related to these factors: it has been a common complaint of foreign graduates that they are unable to work effectively in their native countries, that scientific facilities are not up to an international standard, and that working conditions are inadequate (Gama and Pedersen, 1977).

Foreign students become acclimated to working in an international language — usually English or French — and often find it difficult to use an indigenous language for scientific work at home. Language issues are a very important part of the international student experience, but in this context it is not so much the problem of adequate knowledge of the foreign language at the beginning of the sojourn (a much researched topic; see Kaplan, 1984) but rather the ties to the language and its culture that are forged during the sojourn. On the one hand, graduates are acclimated to using an international language in research, teaching, and intellectual discourse generally. They make use of the major international journals — largely published in English or French — and they tend to focus their scholarship on the concerns of these journals and of the international scientific community. They are in effect socialized through language into the scientific ethos of the West. The use of a foreign language provides a link with current developments in a field of knowledge. In many disciplines, scientific terms do not exist in the indigenous languages and appropriate textbooks have not been published and thus access to an international language is necessary.

There are also potentially negative consequences of working in an international language. The scholar is sometimes cut off from discourse in the local language and very frequently does not help to develop a scientific life in that language. There is a complete reliance on the international language. Those with foreign qualifications are sometimes unwilling to shift their work into an indigenous language or to assist in preparing textbooks or learning materials. The continued use of an international language, then, has far-reaching implications for the Third World.

The question of indigenization is a complex one which is only partly related to foreign study. Third World nations have tried with varying degrees of success to utilize indigenous languages for instruction and research (Gopinathan, 1984). Many have found that it was necessary to retain an international language, ususally the language of colonialism, for a variety of political, academic, and other reasons. A few countries — Malaysia and Indonesia among them — have made the shift from a colonial to an indigenous language for education. Others, such as China, Thailand, and the Latin American nations, did not face this problem. There are also other aspects of indigenization that relate to foreign study. The research foci of the industrialized nations are often brought back by those who have studied overseas along with textbooks, laboratory equipment, and ideas about the curriculum. There are many reasons for the expansion of American ideas about university organization and the curriculum in the Third World. One of them is the fact that many returning scholars have brought back their experiences and tried to implement Western ideas at home (Hawkins, 1984). While foreign study may be valuable in many respects, it does not assist in the building of indigenous models of higher education or the growth of original curricula aimed at local problems.

There is a natural tendency to look toward the international centers of knowledge for research guidelines and methodologies and for innovations in most scientific fields (Kumar, 1980). The major internationally circulated journals are published in the Western nations, and these tend to dominate their fields. Most scientific discoveries take place in the West. Even without foreign-returned graduates, these trends would be a powerful force, but individuals who have studied in the West have been particularly good conduits for the continuing involvement with Western models and ideas. After all, these individuals were trained to respect and use these ideas. In short, the links forged during the foreign sojourn tend to last into the professional careers of those who have undergone this often powerful experience.

In many Third World countries, foreign study adds a measure of prestige and perhaps power to an individual. In Africa, the term "been to" signifies that an individual has studied overseas and it is a measure of considerable achievement. Foreign training permits an individual in many situations to have more ready access to positions of authority, leadership, and power than one who has not had foreign training. It is assumed that "the best and the brightest" are sent overseas and that the quality of training has been high — a powerful combination. While there has been no careful research that has correlated foreign study with rapid advancement, whether in the educational system, government, or in industry and commerce, there are indications that foreign training does provide certain advantages.

The location of foreign study may also make a difference, not only in one's outlook and attitudes but also in professional opportunities. The methodological and sometimes the ideological approach to fields of study differ from one country to another and this will make a difference in outlook and orientation. A student who has obtained an academic degree in the Soviet Union in economics will probably have a quite different approach to the field than one who has studied in the United States. Even academic systems which are closer, such as the British and the American, exhibit considerable variations. An academic degree from a particular country may create intellectual loyalties to that country. Certainly, there will be a tendency to look back on the overseas experience when thinking of textbooks, the purchase of imported equipment, or perhaps the hiring of expatriate advisers. As more students are sent to study in the United States, there is a trend toward looking to American models of higher education for reform efforts in the Third World.

The locale of foreign study also creates important linguistic affinities. Students who have studied in Francophone nations naturally have an orientation toward French-language journals, universities, and expertise. Those who have studied in Anglophone institutions have similar loyalties. Indeed, there are generally closer links between, for example, universities in Anglophone Africa and those in Britain, Canada, or the United States than between Anglophone and Francophone universities within Africa. Politics can also play a role. To give an extreme example, when revolution came to Ethiopia, many American-trained academics and policymakers were killed by the new pro-Soviet revolutionary government. Politics also plays a part in determining the preferred locale of foreign study or the influence of graduates of particular countries. At present, the graduates of Soviet-bloc universities are regarded with some suspicion in many Third World nations; this has created problems since large numbers of graduates are being produced in Eastern Europe.

Links between industrialized and Third World nations are key determinants of the nature of international student flows and of continuing intellectual and academic relationships between those countries. Most important, of course, are the continuing links between France and Britain and their former colonial posessions. Traditionally, students from the colonies tended to go to the universities of the colonial powers. Linguistic factors, perceptions of educational quality and prestige, links between examination systems, an "old boy" network, and official policies of governments all contribute to this situation. In many instances, there has been an official recognition of these traditional links through acceptance of secondary school examinations, etc. Current British debates concerning numbers of foreign students and fees to be charged have included discussions of the traditional role of Britain as educator of large numbers of students from such countries as Cyprus (which has no university of its own), Hong Kong, and Malaysia.

The experiences of students from the Third World and their roles on returning to their home countries reinforce links to the host country, its culture, language, academic styles, and values. (There are, of course, many international students who return home only to reject Western values. The government of Malaysia, for example, is concerned about the fundamentalist Islamic values which many of its students adopt while overseas, perhaps as a reaction to the secularism of the West.) Further, the technical skills learned abroad are of great importance for development. Thus it is not inevitable that foreign study will build dependence on the industrialized nations. But there is evidence that in many ways foreign study does make for close ties and reinforces traditional patterns of inequality.

THE INTERNATIONAL EDUCATION INFRASTRUCTURE: AN EMERGING PROFESSION

There is a growing community of professional educators and support personnel who deal with issues concerning international students and broader questions of international education policy and practice. This emerging profession is best developed in the United States, where it is represented by organizations such as the National Association for Foreign Student Affairs (NAFSA) and the American Association of Collegiate Registrars and Admissions Officers (ACCRAO). Backman (1984) describes the scope of international education activities of many American colleges and universities. Year-abroad programs for undergraduates, services for visiting scholars and faculty, foreign student admissions personnel, advisers for international students, and campus-wide administrators for international programs are some of the services now common in many institutions. These activities are fairly new in American higher education, and the emergence of professional staff to deal with the many aspects of international education is also recent. In general, there are no specific training programs for international education staff, although some hold advanced degrees in such fields as higher education administration, comparative and international education, student personnel, and related areas.

International education responsibilities in the larger institutions are becoming increasingly differentiated. Foreign student admissions is a good example. In many universities, specialized staff now deal with this task and increasingly specialized knowledge is required. The nuances of overseas credentials, visa problems, and other matters require specialized knowledge. Communications networks, through NAFSA and AACRAO as well as other agencies, are developing. Specialized publications, such as AACRAO's "World Education Series," have been developed to provide guidance to those responsible for foreign student admissions. The Institute of International Education also provides statistical information and other publications that are helpful to this emerging community. Organizations like the American Council on Education have taken an interest in international education as well.

Universities and colleges are still struggling with appropriate definitions, functions, and responsibilities for the newly emerging profession in the field of international education. And in a period of fiscal constraint, it is always a problem to ensure that sufficient personnel are assigned to those functions. There is nevertheless a growing recognition that the developing international role of academic institutions demands competent professional staff to ensure the effective administration of these programs. The United States, with its large administrative cadres in higher education, has been quick to recognize the need for professionals in the field of international education. Other countries have also developed professional expertise. In Canada, the Canadian Bureau for International Education is quite active in developing data, issuing reports, and representing the international education community. Similar groups exist in Britain, West Germany, and Japan. Australia has been very much concerned with international education issues.

Professionalism in dealing with international education is essential in higher education. The various functions involved require both expertise and long-term professional commitment. Few have thus far thought about the implications of a growing group of professionals in the field. It is imperative that these functions be met, but it is not as yet clear how the emerging profession will fit into academic systems or what its role or status will be.

A REVIEW OF PAST RESEARCH ON INTERNATIONAL STUDENTS

We have considered some of the important issues relating to international students. Now we turn to a more detailed discussion of the research on international students undertaken over the past two and a half decades. Naturally, our consideration can only touch the surface of a varied literature. We have attempted to organize this analysis according to some of the major themes of the literature. Some of these themes overlap with topics discussed earlier; others do not. Our aim is to provide an overview of the literature and then to present some suggestions for future research.

The literature concerning international students is by now extensive, but for the most part it is of relatively recent origin. American researchers are responsible for the bulk of the literature to date — our guess is that perhaps 70% of the research uses American data. This fact will naturally affect the topics of the research, since the concerns and methodological orientations of American researchers will be largely reflected in the literature. Further, issues of student adjustment, cross-cultural relations, and similar topics seem to dominate the literature. There is relatively little that directly addresses policy, economics, or the politics of foreign study. The topic of international study has not attracted much attention from social scientists, although as issues have become more complex and as funding from external agencies has become available, there has been a growth of interest from a wider community of scholars. One of the problems is that there is at present no research community — organizations such as the National Association for Foreign Student Affairs have been largely concerned with concrete issues rather than with research. Related fields like comparative education have not been directly concerned with issues of international study.

In reviewiing the extensive research on international students to date, one is immediately struck by three distinct characteristics of this research. (1) A great proportion of it, as mentioned above, is based on American data. (2) Much of this U.S. research is lopsided in the direction of exploring either the cross-cultural consequences of studying abroad or the conditions and means necessary to help international students adapt and succeed in an alien institutional and cultural environment. (3) The research is characterized by a great deal of haphazard diversity in terms of topics covered, findings, and conclusions; it is not uncommon for two or more studies on the same topic to emerge with radically different conclusions and recommendations (throwing the prospective policy-maker into a quandary). Given this character of the research, what follows is not a synopsis of all the findings in the research but a summary of *recurrent* themes supported by usually more than one study.

What, then, are the major findings of the bulk of the research undertaken in the United States?

The "U-Curve" Hypothesis

To take the cross-cultural studies first: there does not seem to be much empirical support for the celebrated "U-curve" hypothesis first advanced by Sverre Lysgaard following his study of Norwegian Fulbright grantees in 1953, and which states: "Adjustment as a process over time seems to follow a U-shaped curve: adjustment is felt to be easy and successful to begin with; then follows a 'crisis' in which one feels less well adjusted, somewhat lonely and unhappy; finally one begins to feel better adjusted again, becoming more integrated into the foreign community" (Lysgaard, 1955; see also Gullahorn and Gullahorn, 1963). Yet in one of the few truly international studies designed to identify the cross-cultural problems that international students face while abroad, and the strategies used to cope with these problems, Klineberg and Hull (1979) concluded that their data presented almost no support for the U-curve hypothesis.[3] They found that the frequency of occurrence of the key variables (depression, loneliness, homesickness, and so on) pertaining to the hypothesis had no relationship to the duration of the foreign sojourn.

Cross-Cultural Contact

If Lysgaard's hypothesis has turned out to be questionable, his formulation of it at least has not been without benefit: he alerted researchers to the fact that international study was potentially fraught with stress for those who undertook it. That is, stress arising from residence in an alien cultural setting and taking such forms as loneliness, depression, or various psychosomatic illnesses (Boer, 1981; Horner et al., 1981). Research shows that the principal cause of this stress is what may be referred to as the cross-cultural isolation factor. International students almost everywhere complain about isolation. Unless the student is able to establish frequent (or as desired), easy, and harmonious interrelationships with the natives of the host country, it is almost absolutely predictable that his or her sojourn will be one of considerable dissatisfaction. For next to academic success, positive contact with natives of the host country ranks at the very top of international student needs. Thus, as Hull (1978) found in his study of this issue, those international students who reported frequent positive cross-cultural contact with Americans (via such interpersonal experiences as joint academic work, visits, outings, discussions, participating in artistic/social/communal activities, and so on) were the ones most likely to report "less loneliness and homesickness, more favorable attitudes about their experience in general, less desire to return home, less discrimination, and basically fewer negative reactions to experiences during their sojourn in the United States.'' This finding is corroborated by similar findings for international students studying in other countries such as Brazil, Canada, France, India, Iran, Japan, and Kenya (Klineberg and Hull, 1979).

Among the variables that stand out in determining positive cross-cultural contact, research indicates the following four to be very important: language proficiency, previous travel experience, absence of discrimination, and cultural background. Adequate facility with the language of the host country is, to state the obvious, not only an important determinant of academic success but also success in breaking down cross-cultural isolation.

Klineberg and Hull (1979) found that those international students who had had travel experience away from their home countries for a minimum period of at least one month tended to be better adapted at establishing positive contact. But language proficiency and previous travel experience by themselves are of little use if the response from the host natives is one of hositility. Insofar as discrimination against peoples of other races, religion, etc., exists in a given country, positive cross-cultural contact for international students is to that extent curtailed. It is interesting to note on this point that the Klineberg/Hull study found that those international students most likely to report the existence of racial discrimination were to be found in France, followed by the United States, then the United Kingdom, and finally Canada. However, when it came to experiencing *personal* discrimination, international students studying in Japan were the largest number of respondents to report such discrimination (44.4%, followed by those in Hong Kong (36.6%), France (35.8%), Kenya (34.5%), Canada (34.2%), the United States (30.6%), India (30.4%), Iran (22.2%), United Kingdom (22.0%), West Germany (17.9%), and Brazil (11.6%). A recent study involving international students from a number of East African countries found that the United States scored the lowest, followed by Western Europe, in terms of satisfaction rating for cultural and racial relations. The score for Eastern Europe was the highest (Maliyamkono et al., 1982). For an illuminating article on discrimination against international students in Japan see Michii (1981).

The fourth important factor in inhibiting or facilitating cross-cultural contact is the international student's own cultural background. In their comparative study of Indian and Chinese students, White and White (1981) report that the factor of cultural background appeared to be so significant that it even overrode the language proficiency factor when they tried to correlate it to social adjustment. They state: "English language proficiency may be related to acculturation but this relationship appears to be neither strong nor consistent across groups of foreign students whose national origins differ" (p. 65) (see also Dunnett, 1981).

An important dimension of research in the area of cross-cultural contact issues is that which aims toward developing formal programs to enhance cross-cultural contact via educational activities. For example, programs would be developed to use international students and faculty as educational resources in the classroom on campus, as well as in schools off campus. (Relevant studies in this particular area include Christensen and Thielen, 1983; Mestenhauser, 1981; Neff, 1981; Paige, 1978; Robinson and Hendel, 1981.)

Attitudes

While studies pertaining to stress dominate within the area of cross-cultural consequences of studying abroad, there are a significant number of studies that look at the attitudinal dimension (see, for example, Bowman, 1978; Hasan, 1976; Hegazy, 1968; Hensley and Sell, 1979; Kelman, 1975; Kumagai, 1977). That is, studies that examine attitudes of international students toward the host country, as well as attitudinal change regarding self. With regard to the former, available evidence does not suggest any clear-cut pattern in the attitudes of international students, except that positive or negative attitudes toward the host country were principally a matter of social and academic adjustment and to a much lesser extent national origin. Hull (1978) found that in general European and African students had negative attitudes toward the United States, whereas Asian students had much more positive attitudes. There does not seem to be much support for the "national status" hypothesis, which states that a student's attitude toward the host country will be influenced by his perception of the status (superior or inferior) of his own country in relation to the host country. Certainly the Klineberg/Hull study found only limited evidence in support of the hypothesis, to the extent that the data were able to address the matter. As for change in attitudes toward the host country, there does not seem to be any evidence to demonstrate a consistent change during the sojourn, though this certainly is not the case with attitudes pertaining to self. Here there is strong evidence that those international students who are abroad for at least two years demonstrate a consistent change in their attitudes during their stay, though not necessarily of an overwhelming magnitude. Generally, it seems, change is in the direction of liberal (understood here to mean less rigid or more open-minded) attitudes with regard to such matters as religion or sexual behavior for those international students in the West coming from Third World countries, but without altering fundamental beliefs, which tend to remain stable. It is in the matter of personal and intellectual growth that change is most noticeable. As evidence from research in the United States indicates: "The sojourn and educational experience tends to engender a more sophisticated, differentiated, personalized and concretized knowledge and perception of the host society, its achievements and problems, its peoples and policies, and of its way of life as compared to 'knowledge' and images held before. The result is a soberer appraisal of some of its features, values, and practices and of their relevance to one's own role, one's field of activity, and one's own country" (Flack, 1976). This conclusion is borne out by the Klineberg and Hull (1979) study.

A number of studies have looked at attitudes of international students toward those with whom, among the host natives, they share a common racial heritage. Two groups of international students studying in the United States quickly come to mind: European students and African students. Strangely, it appears that both groups of students display negative attitudes toward those Americans who on the surface bear the closest resemblance to them. Thus Europeans tend to have a negative attitude about the United States in general, and Africans are similarly negative toward black Americans — explained in part by basic sociocultural differences, in part by their perception of a supposed superiority complex shared by black Americans vis-à-vis Africans, and in part by a tangible lessening of discrimination toward the Africans, once they are identified, by white Americans (Becker, 1973; Heath, 1970; Markham, 1967; Miller, 1967; Odenyo, 1970; Pierce, 1969; Wakita, 1971).

Does the presence of international students have any impact on the attitudes of the host population? This question has unfortunately not received adequate attention in international student research. What little research there is indicates a nonconclusive finding. If, however, one is to go by indirect evidence on the matter, then the conclusion to be reached is that the mere act of studying in a foreign country does not of itself assist in breaking down cultural barriers — in fact it may even reinforce these barriers. Thus, in a comparative study (Miller et al., 1971) on the ability of students from East Asia studying in the United States, and U.S. students studying in East Asia, to achieve "warm friendship and understanding" with host nationals, it was found that for both groups of students the only source of such friendship and understanding was themselves. Similarly, Klineberg and Hull (1979) report that overall, with respect to international students in all eleven countries of their study, they found "a tremendous amount of disappointment and even discouragement when respondents were seeking, were open to, or were expecting more social contact with local students and individuals than they found" (p. 178). (For other relevant studies on the impact of international students on the host population, see Brickman, 1967; Cowser, 1978; Deutsch, 1970; Ebbers, 1981; Marion and Thomas, 1980; Matross et al., 1982; and Neville, 1981.)

Sadly, the general conclusion to be drawn from the overall research on the cross-cultural dimension of international study is that the potential for an enriching cross-cultural experience for both hosts and guests has yet to be realized. However, this is not to say that there are no nonacademic benefits of international study — at least from the perspective of the individual student. On the contrary, evidence indicates a consistent finding that among the almost assured nonacademic benefits an international student can expect from his foreign sojourn are intellectual development, personal development, independence, and self-confidence (Brislin, 1980; see also Goodwin and Nacht, 1984).

At first glance it may appear, when reviewing the research on international students, that studies on the cross-cultural consequences of studying abroad dominate the research. This, however, is not so. It is in the area of assisting international students in adjusting to and succeeding in an alien academic environment that the majority of the studies are to be found. And the topics covered in this area range widely: admissions; advising and counseling; language proficiency; academic achievement; curricular relevance. And here again, the bulk of the research is dominated by U.S. data.

Recruitment and Admission
Within the area of admissions there are two major concerns reflected in the literature: the absence of specific institutional policy regarding admission of international students, and the problem of effective evaluation of international credentials. A number of studies strongly lament the fact that almost no university in the United States has specific policies regarding such issues as optimum number of international students, balance in fields of study they pursue, balance in their geographical origins, balance in gender division, and so on. This situation is perhaps not surprising, since in many instances the top-level administrators responsible for institutional policy are far removed from those who deal directly with international students.

Admissions officers seem to be perpetually grappling with the problem of developing an effective system for evaluating credentials of international applicants — which of course is to be expected given the complex diversity of educational systems throughout the world. To assist admissions officers with their onerous task, one of the major organizations in the field of international study in the United States, the National Association for Foreign Student Affairs, has published a number of guides. Supplementing these guides are the World Education Series materials produced by the American Association of Collegiate Registrars and Admissions Officers. (For this particular area, the following studies are relevant: Dixon et al., 1976; Fisher and Dey, 1979; Patrick, 1983; and Turner, 1979).

One issue pertinent to the area of admissions that has recently come to the fore is the matter of recruitment of international students by U.S. institutions. Faced with declining enrollments, some institutions are aggressively venturing into the international student market, with the result that in some instances unsavory practices have come to light — such as making ability to pay the *only* criterion for granting admission to the prospective applicant. To eliminate such practices, efforts, are under way to come up with an ethical code of conduct that institutions must subscribe to — if they are not to lose to the government their highly prized prerogative of who, how, and when to admit international student applicants (Berendzen, 1983; Fiske, 1981; Jenkins, 1980, 1983*b*; Williams, 1984).

Advising and Counseling
A fairly large number of studies concern the role and effectiveness of international student advisers (Benson, 1968; Higbee, 1961; Miller, 1968; Pedersen, 1981; Woolston, 1983). While many U.S. institutions with significant interna-

tional student populations cannot do without international student advisers, they are not usually accorded the necessary top-level academic and administrative authority. In fact with regard to academic authority, their offices seem to have almost none whatsoever, with the result that not only is there lack of coordination between academic advisement and general advisement of the international student, but often there is no provision at all of academic advisement services specifically geared to the needs of the international student.

On the whole, the conclusion regarding the effectiveness of international student advisers is that, when viewed from within the context of administrative and budgetary constraints, they seem to be performing their functions fairly well (Lockett, 1970). This general finding, however, applies mainly to four-year institutions. As for two-year institutions, evidence suggests a bleak picture: often those appointed to the role of international student advisers are poorly qualified, and even those who may be qualified are severely hampered in effectively performing their functions by administrative constraints.

Before turning to the area of counseling, one further observation that needs to be made is the important finding by Hull (1978) of the need for advisers to "reemphasize their functions as educators within the educational community as well as within the surrounding communities" (p. 188). That is, they must develop resources and skills aimed at the creation and implementation of programs that can facilitate more meaningful cross-cultural contact with Americans (both on and off campus). Such programs would move beyond formal receptions and mass gatherings and emphasize one-to-one interpersonal interaction. The equivalent of the traditional host-family program off-campus needs to be developed on-campus via local student peers.

International students present special problems when it comes to provision of psychological counseling services, for three major reasons: first, a very significant proportion of them report suffering from acute depression (one-quarter of the sample in the Klineberg and Hull study, 1979); second, for cultural reasons they are not generally prone to seeking counseling help, and hence by the time they do so they are usually in very serious need of it; and third, the varied cultural backgrounds of the international students render counseling that much more difficult for the counselor. To elaborate on the last point: The values and assumptions that American counselors bring to the counseling situation will be very different from those of the international student. For instance, many Third World students come from cultures that tend to see one's life circumstances as essentially determined by external factors (political, economic, etc.) beyond one's control. Americans, on the other hand, generally believe that one's life circumstances are very much within the control of the individual. To take another example, many Third World students come from cultural backgrounds that do not allow outsiders access to their personal problems. In contrast, Americans believe that an individual's personal problems can be made the legitimate business of a stranger (a "professional") with a view toward arriving at a solution. (For further discussion of these and other differences see Stewart,

1975, and Sue, 1978.) Given these circumstances of international students, it is surprising that many institutions do not consider provision of counseling services a special need separate from the general advisement service provided by the international student office. (Among the studies relevant to this area are: Akoff, Thayer, and Elkind, 1966; Alexander et al., 1981; Higginbotham, 1979; Horner et al., 1981; Story, 1982; Yeh, 1972; and Zunin and Rubin, 1967.)

Language Proficiency

A number of studies have documented the pivotal character of proficiency in the language of instruction for adjustment and success in meeting academic goals. They have found a high correlation between success on English-as-a-foreign-language tests (such as the test administered worldwide by the Educational Testing Service in Princeton, New Jersey) and academic success (Heil and Aleamoni, 1974; Martin, 1971; Melendez-Craig, 1970; Uehara, 1969). There are, however, almost no studies that go beyond this finding, such as attempting to evaluate the success rates of language remedial programs at various U.S. institutions, or to determine the major factors encouraging or inhibiting rapid acquisition of proficiency among different international groups.

The importance of ascertaining proficiency in the language of instruction is beginning to receive greater attention in countries that traditionally assumed such proficiency to be present among international applicants. A case in point is New Zealand, where the issue of a mandatory language proficiency test for all international applicants has been raised — though not without some controversy. The reason for this, of course, is the increasing diversity in the backgrounds of international students coming to these countries in comparison to those students who came in the past (who were usually from countries that used English as their official language).

Academic Achievement

Besides language proficiency, research indicates a number of other variables of significance that come into play in predicting academic achievement among international students. These variables include the student's academic background prior to enrollment in the foreign institution; source of financial support (scholarship/assistantship students, for self-evident reasons, have been found to perform better than self-supported students); and national origin (again for self-evident reasons, students from countries with educational systems similar to the American model seem to perform better academically than those from countries with dissimilar education systems).

A number of studies that attempt to correlate variables such as age, sex, and marital status with academic achievement have found that these variables are of comparatively little significance, and attempts to correlate personal and social adjustment with academic achievement have run into the "chicken and egg" problem — which comes first? The use of aptitude tests in American institutions has been the subject of some studies, and the general finding surprisingly (considering the pervasive use of these tests) is that they seem to have little prognosticatory value, perhaps because of cultural bias creeping into the tests (Sharon, 1971; Sugimoto, 1966). Evidence suggests that institutions would do better by relying on two principal indicators of academic ability: the applicant's prior academic record and his or her performance on a language proficiency test.

An interesting question that has been raised but not yet properly addressed in the literature concerns success rates of international students meeting academic goals. How many international students manage to get the degrees, certificates, etc., that they set out to obtain? Hull (1978) surmises (on the basis of a random investigation of U.S. universities) that nearly all international students do eventually obtain the credentials they set out to get. And as for comparative studies on success rates among both international students and local students, there seem to be almost none of significance. And what little evidence there is turns out to be conflicting, either suggesting that international students do better than local students, or suggesting they perform less well than local students (Rao, 1979, p. 75). Blaug (1981) notes that he found general agreement among British university teaching staff that international students seemed to perform academically less well than native students. However, he goes on to say: "But all these statements were no more than several impressions: despite persistent probing by the research team, nobody produced hard facts about the differential performance rates of home and overseas students" (p. 64; see also Bie, 1976).

Curricula

Are the academic programs offered by U.S. institutions relevant to the needs of international students? A few studies have looked at this issue — which is an important question considering that the majority of international students (roughly 85%) do not remain in the United States upon completion of their studies. In general, the conclusion was that U.S. curricula are not particularly suited to the needs of international students coming from Third World countries — especially with respect to the technical disciplines (engineering, agriculture, etc.) at the advanced levels. These studies also indicate that international student returnees find technical knowledge (gained from practical training experience where this has been possible to obtain following completion of studies) more useful than the theoretical knowledge obtained from their training. There is also evidence to suggest that those students with set or predetermined career goals (usually sponsored students) tend to express dissatisfaction with their academic programs more often than those with less specific career goals.

Research in this area of curricular relevance is still in its infancy, and hence much still needs to be done. (Relevant studies include Baron, 1979; Harari, 1970; Moock, 1984; Myer, 1979; Ronkin, 1969; Stone, 1969; Susskind and Schell, 1968.)

Needs

Numerous studies have looked at the nebulous issues of "international student needs" relating to such nonacademic matters as finance, housing, health, information, leisure, etc. Of particular relevance here is an extensive study by Lee, Abd-Ella and Burks (1981), under the auspices of the National Association for Foreign Student Affairs on needs of international students from developing nations at U.S. colleges and universities. Among their principal findings were the following: Ranking at the top of the list of needs of respondents were, first, adequate finance; second, acquisition of credentials; third, acquisition of specialized skills and knowledge; fourth, obtaining a job at home commensurate with one's training; and fifth, obtaining relevant practical training experience in the United States before returning home. Ranking near the bottom of the list of needs were, first, need for information on obtaining one's customary food; second, need for information on English courses; third, need for sharing housing with U.S. nationals; and fourth, need for observing religious practices. There were other needs that ranked even lower than these, such as the need to get used to American food or for information on dating customs.

The other findings of this thorough study include the following: Scholarship/assistantship students were more satisfied with their overall sojourn than self-supported students (this finding conflicts with that of Hull, 1978); many respondents, particularly agricultural students, emphasized the need for relevant curricula; national origin was a determining factor in the identification and weighting of needs (Lee et al., [p. 32] note: "One of the groups which perceived the least satisfaction in receiving equal acceptance by faculty and human respect by U.S. students was the group most likely to return home, i.e. African students"); those students who already had jobs waiting for them at home tended to be more satisfied with their overall experience than those who did not; and those whose roommates were local students tended to be more satisfied than those who did not have local roommates. This latter finding is supported by both Hull (1978) and Klineberg and Hull (1979). However, the Klineberg and Hull study cautions that "the person with whom one shares a residence may not be *the* most important factor at the sojourn location in terms of the overall coping and adaptation processes . . . data would rather suggest, as already indicated, that *access* to local people (amount of contact and kinds of contact) is more important than sharing residence with a local student" (p. 187).

Besides these two major areas of international student research (the cross-cultural consequences of studying abroad, and the academic adjustment and success factors) there are two other areas of research that must be examined: one well represented in the literature and the other underrepresented. Beginning with the latter, there exists some research on international students who have returned home. The general thrust of this research has been essentially to poll returnees on their experiences and attitudes during their sojourn. The information obtained via these studies generally corroborates the findings of studies on similar issues conducted among students still present in the host country (see, for example, Galtung, 1965). There are almost no studies on such an important matter as the overall impact of returnees on the development of their societies. This and related issues will be raised again below.

Brain Drain

The better represented research topic referred to above is on what is generally called "brain drain," that is, the voluntary nonreturn of Third World students following completion of their studies abroad, and hence constituting a "brain drain" on their home countries (which are less developed than the host countries). (The term "brain drain" is also used in the case of voluntary migration of skilled persons who are not necessarily students from their home countries to other nations. It should be pointed out that the migration or nonreturn is *voluntary* and not as a result of political persecution or other threat where remaining or returning to the country may imply placing life or livelihood in jeopardy.) Since the percentage of officially sponsored students coming under various bilateral agreements who do not return home is extremely small — around 2% according to one study (Rao, 1979, p. xii) — brain drain should generally be understood to refer to privately sponsored students.

Factors that have been identified as prominent in the voluntary nonreturn of international students are as follows: Given that a preponderant number of self-sponsored Third World students are minorities of one kind or another (racial, religious, etc.) seeking to achieve upward social mobility via higher education abroad, there is already an in-built self-selection bias among them toward considering not returning home as a serious option (barring host-country legal restrictions). This is especially so in circumstances where the student's minority status may subject him or her to discrimination because of nepotism or corruption in employment and promotion practices at home. (This is not to say that self-sponsored students are usually from low socioeconomic classes. The very fact that they are self-sponored points to the opposite.)

Besides the economic advantages to be gained from remaining in the host country, there may also be a career advantage. A very able Third World student with a deep commitment to pursue research in his or her field may be tempted to remain in the host country because returning home may mean curtailing the research due to lack of support (funds, equipment, peers, etc.). In fact, one international study concludes that a very large proportion of international students who have returned home end up being underemployed — that is, they are employed in jobs for which their training is not fully used (Glaser and Habers, 1978). This of course also applies to highly talented artists, especially if their art is of a type that is almost unmarketable at home through lack of demand — for example, a symphony director.

The brain drain as it pertains to international students is considered a highly undesirable phenomenon from the perspective of both the home country and the host country — and more so by the latter than the former. Hence, among the measures that have been implemented or advocated to discourage international students from remaining after completion of their studies are: (a) tightening the legal restrictions in the host country that allow international students to remain (such as the proposed American Simpson/Mazzoli bill); (b) encouraging home countries to accord the same employment opportunities as those enjoyed by the sponsored students; and (c) developing joint training agreements between host-country institutions and home-country institutions that would specify the training of international students (private and sponsored) according to the skill and knowledge requirements of the home country without necessarily involving major redefinitions of graduate curricula of host institutions. The benefit deriving from the latter arrangement would be bilateral: the opportunity for the international students to remain would be lessened because their training would be of greater relevance to the home country than to the host country, and the host institutions would be assured of a more steady, homogeneous flow of students — one amenable to planning.

While statistics on the number of international students who do remain in the host countries following completion of studies are hard to come by, if one is to judge by the figure for the United States (roughly 15%), then it is likely that international students constitute a smaller fraction than the total brain-drain migrants. Nevertheless, it is a problem that must be addressed — especially from the perspective of developing and implementing solutions, something that is distinctly lacking in this area of international student research.

Evaluation of Exchange Programs
A significant amount of research on international study has been devoted, not surprisingly, to the area of program evaluation. Sponsoring agencies, such as the U.S. Agency for International Development (AID), have funded research projects to evaluate the effectiveness of some of their exchange programs. An obvious example is the massive study conducted by American University's Development Education and Training Research Institute on behalf of AID's Office of International Training of some 10,000 AID scholarship holders from approximately 75 countries over the period 1966 to 1972 (Kimmel, Ockey, and Sander, 1972). The aim of the study was to determine the satisfaction ratings of the students with respect to their overall training and life experiences in the United States and their general evaluation of the exchange programs via "exit interviews" as they left for home after completion of studies. The conclusions of the study were, in general, in conformity with findings of other research on international student issues, though there were some in conflict. For example, the study found little correlation between sojourn satisfaction and language proficiency problems, problems of access to orientation programs, and financial problems. Overall, the study concluded that roughly 50% to 70% of the students found their training and life experiences in the United States highly or near highly satisfactory. (Other relevant studies pertaining to this area include evaluation studies based on a survey of returned students in their home coun-

tries published by AID in 1966, but separately under four regional headings: Far East, Latin America, North Africa and Near East, and South Asia; Collin, 1979; Crespi, 1978; International Research and Exchanges Board, 1980; and Uhlig, Crofton, and Thompson, 1978.)

GAPS IN PAST RESEARCH

These, then, are some of the major issues that have dominated research on international students over the last two decades. Other issues have been examined too, but on a less emphatic scale, such as alumni issues (Dolibois, 1976; Goodwin and Nacht, 1984; Rogers, 1983), physical and mental health (Coelho, 1973; Cole, Allen, and Green, 1980, Klineberg, 1980), legal issues (Anthony, 1980; Bedrosian, 1983; Gray, 1982; Smith, 1981), academic disciplines, specific issues (Babiker, Cox, and Miller, 1980; Fouad and Jones, 1979; Rogers, 1971; Shaw, 1982). But with all these issues, as with all the issues mentioned above, the underlying theme has been to find ways and means of aiding international students in achieving their goals; that is, to make their sojourn both productive and pleasant. It is research that has been conducted almost entirely from the perspective of the international student to the exclusion of other perspectives; such as that of the department, or the institution, or the host country, or even the home country.

It is necessary now to direct research attention toward these other perspectives — especially in the direction of what might be called the "political economy of international study." This, of course, is not to say that the research conducted hitherto has been misguided or irrelevant; in fact, this traditional, micro-level, student-oriented research was very necessary during the growth of international student population flows, but the stage has now been reached where the present sizable population of international student flows demands the examination of other dimensions of it — that is, dimensions of the macro level. Before turning to what the research agenda aimed toward a political economy of international study may look like, mention should be made of some of the major research gaps in the traditional literature that still remain to be filled.

International Student Impact

An area of considerable importance that to date has not received sufficient attention is that of the impact of international students on the academic life of their host institutions, as well as on the attitudes of the host population — both students and non-students. Taking the latter point first, of particular interest is the issue of change in attitudes (in a positive direction) and gain in knowledge about other cultures, peoples, etc., through interaction with international students. It may well be that the "internationalizing" influence that high-level administrators so often speak of when called upon to justify the presence of international students on their campuses is merely well-meaning rhetoric. That is, it is likely that only those campus and off-campus communities already inclined toward internationalizing their knowledge and life experiences (usually a small minority) make the effort to know and interact with international students. The vast majority prefer to remain aloof and uninvolved. Or it could be that the appropriate communication structures (constructed through creative programing) are simply lacking, and hence the potential for an internationalizing influence from the presence of international students goes unrealized. In any case, this is an area that must be looked at closely for both educational reasons (the host students' educational experience on campus needs to be broadened and enriched) and for reasons of general goodwill (that is, creating understanding between peoples — perhaps, to cite an example, the presence of Russian students on American campuses and vice versa, along the lines of the U.S./ China exchange programs, would lead to reduced tension between these two powerful adversaries).

Do international students have any impact on the academic life of the host institutions? This is an important question that must be asked in light of the fact that in a significant number of institutions in the United States (as well as France, Britain, and Canada) the physical sciences and engineering departments are dominated by international students at the graduate level. The statistics for the United States in this regard are sobering: whereas in 1960 international students claimed 33.5% of all Ph.D.'s awarded in the engineering sciences (Business Higher Education Forum, 1982), by 1982 this figure had climbed to 51%. The magnitude of international graduate student participation in the engineering sciences becomes even more dramatic when viewed from the perspective of individual departments. At the State University of New York at Buffalo, for example, international students make up 61% of the total graduate enrollment in the department of mechanical engineering.

Given this pronounced shift toward a greater presence of international graduate students in selected fields in many institutions, questions such as the following must be raised and answered: What effects, if any, do international students have on the number of courses offered, the content of these courses, and the general curricula of the departments? What impact, if any, do international students have on the kinds of research undertaken and the quantity of research accomplished, by both faculty and students? To what extent do the departments rely on international students for teaching assistants, and how does this affect the quality of undergraduate teaching? Does the presence of international students encourage departments in developing international programs, consultancy agreements, training projects, etc.? Does such encouragement come from alumni contacts?

An important dimension for future research would be an inquiry into attitudes of faculty toward international students regarding the students' competence, diligence, achievement, and the general presence of international students in the department. Preliminary investigations suggest that the dramatic increases in graduate-level enrollment of international students have been accompanied by a general lowering of morale among faculty as they face nontraditional students with unfamiliar cultural and educational backgrounds. Goodwin and Nacht (1983) state that they found considerable animosity among faculty toward international students, with frequent use of derogatory analogies such as "wet noodles soaking up anything you pour over them," and "bazaar merchants haggling over grades." If their preliminary findings represent a general situation prevalent in institutions throughout the United States, then research needs to be done on the causes of such negative attitudes, their effect on international students, and ways and means of ameliorating the situation.

Institutional Policy

It could well be that there is a certain numerical threshold beyond which any increase in international student presence leads to disruption in the academic life of the department and a general breakdown in morale among faculty. If this is so, then it is necessary to determine what that numerical threshold is. This point brings one to the whole question of institutional policy. Surprisingly, many institutions lack a coherent institutional policy. A call has been made for research to rectify this situation by determining a general institutional policy on international students (American Council on Education, 1982; Carrigan, 1977; Goodwin and Nacht, 1983; Williams, 1982; see also National Association for Foreign Student Affairs, 1972, as an example of the kind of study that is needed in this area). Such an institutional policy would comprise policy statements on the following elements:

Admissions procedures and criteria. For example, must international students meet the same admissions requirements as domestic students?

Student profile. How many international students should be admitted in a given department? How should the balance be struck in terms of their geographical origin, gender, fields of study, and so on?

Financial aid. Should international students be allowed access to university scholarships; and if so, what should be the qualification criteria?

Student services. What services specifically geared to international students must be provided by the university, and who should bear the cost of providing these services? For example, should international students be charged a fee to pay for these services?

Housing. Does the university have an obligation to ensure that the housing needs of international students are met via specific campus and off-campus arrangements?

Curricular and program relevance. Does the university have an obligation to make every arrangement possible (without disrupting its basic academic programs geared to the domestic clientele) to provide international students access to courses or programs designed for their needs? For example, there is a critical omission among graduate programs of public administration and management courses for international students. The need for such courses is absolute, considering that an overwhelming majority of international students who return home end up in administrative and managerial positions that demand powerful skills and initiative as they confront problems unique to the political and economic circumstances of Third World nations (Dunnett, 1982).

Practical training and inducement to return. Does the university have an obligation to develop programs and services (even if only at the basic level of information exchange akin to that provided by campus career placement offices) that can assist international students to gain practical training? (Research indicates that such training comprises the most valuable dimension of an international student's overall education.) Does the university have an obligation to develop programs that would encourage and assist self-sponsored students to return home rather than remain in the host country?

Alumni contact. Should the university develop an aggressive alumni program for its international students? For example, helping to form international chapters and a viable liaison system between the alumni office and the chapters.

Health

A subject that is woefully underrepresented in the literature is research pertaining to the health of international students — both physical and mental health. Very little is known about the disease pattern among international students and whether the pattern is general (akin to that found among the host population) or more specific to international students. For example, one can surmise that international students are prone to suffer more from stress-related disorders such as stomach ulcers or high blood pressure than do the rest of the student population. Very little is known about patterns of alcohol and drug abuse among international students. Again, one may surmise that, given the high incidence of depression among international students, their use of alcohol and drugs may be at levels higher than that for the native students. Or the reverse may also be true, given that many international students come from cultures where use of alcohol and drugs is (in comparison to Western nations) at very low levels.

As for research comparing disease patterns among the different nationalities represented within the international student group, there is almost none. It is possible, to suggest one hypothesis, that even if a high incidence of stress-related diseases is common among international students, it is not likely that such incidence is uniform throughout the international student population. Depending upon the cultural background of the particular nationality, the incidence may be greater or less.

While some research on the mental health of international students exists, there is need to broaden it. Mental health (to be understood here in its broad sense) is in many respects culture bound — especially when it comes to treatment. This, therefore, necessitates an understanding of the varied counseling needs of the different nationalities represented among international students.

Post-sojourn Issues

How does the international student fare after returning home? What problems does he or she encounter in terms of "counter-culture shock" — locating a job, making use of his or her training, and so on? These and other issues pertain to what may be termed post-sojourn issues, and here again research is still in its infancy, and requiring redress. One organization that has begun to concern itself with these matters, the National Association for Foreign Student Affairs, has published a very helpful monograph on the subject (Hood and Schieffer, 1983), which covers a number of very pertinent topics such as the professional integration of women, developing a professional library, and continuing research and publication. (Other studies relevant to this area of research include Adler, 1981; Bochner, Lin, and McLeod, 1980; Gama and Pedersen, 1977; and National Association for Foreign Student Affairs, 1972.)

POLITICAL ECONOMY OF INTERNATIONAL STUDY

The issues of further research raised so far are issues that are still within the realm of traditional international student research. The dramatic increase in the population of international students throughout the world over the last decade, however, requires a new area of research that earlier would not have been necessary or viable to conduct because the numerical magnitude of the population of international students was not large enough. This new area of research may be termed "the political economy of international study." The principal objective of this research area would be twofold: to begin the examination in depth of a host of questions that pertain to the macro-level dimension of international study (in contrast to the micro-level dimension represented by such concerns as factors inhibiting satisfactory social adjustment, or evaluating the effectiveness of an orientation program for international students, etc.), and to enlist the theoretical and conceptual tools of a variety of relevant disciplines in the social sciences (economics, politics, sociology, etc.) for the task of examining phenomena pertinent to international study. In other words, a political economy of international study is a research study via an interdisciplinary approach characterized by sound methodologies. What, then, are the principal elements for further research (since some sporadic research has already commenced in this area — see, for example, Barber, Altbach, and Myers, 1984, and Williams, 1981) that would constitute the research agenda for this new area that we have termed the political economy of international study? They include the following.

ECONOMIC COST-BENEFIT ANALYSIS — HOST COUNTRY

As a consequence of two unrelated factors — the rapid increase in international student flows, and the world economic recession experienced by many countries throughout the world, including the host nations of the West — governments and institutions among the host nations have begun to raise the issue of the cost of educating thousands of international students at the expense of tax-payers. (Several important studies relating to this theme include the Canadian Bureau for International Education, 1977; Grubel and Scott, 1977, in the United States; Mark Blaug, 1981, in England.)

Costs

Unlike most other situations where costs are relatively easy to determine, in the case of international students the costs are just as difficult to calculate as the benefits. Blaug (1981) enumerates the key points of economic analysis that must be considered when undertaking research in this area:

1. The difference between *marginal* costs and *average* costs, and their relative importance, must be determined. If the problem is to assess capacity in educational institutions and ways and means of using excess capacity, or conversely, reducing excess pressure on limited capacity (depending upon what the situation is), then analysis must center on the calculation of marginal costs — that is, the additional cost incurred as a consequence of either adding or subtracting a student from the total student population. If, on the other hand, the issue is to determine how much subsidy that the institutions must receive (from whatever source, public or private) — since almost all institutions of higher education rely on some sort of subsidy — then it is the average cost that is of importance. That is, the cost calculated in terms of per capita total capital plus recurrent expenditure. The two costs are of course related in the sense that a reduction in average cost becomes possible in that situation where the marginal cost is lower than the average cost, by enrolling more students; and vice versa.

2. The relationship between marginal costs and marginal *savings* is not necessarily a one-to-one relationship — that is, the relationship is not always an inverse one. The reason is that cutbacks in student enrollment cannot always be matched by corresponding cutbacks in staff — especially tenured staff. (In the long run, however, savings may be realized via natural attrition, sale of excess equipment, sale of physical plant stock, etc.)

3. The calculation of costs and savings has to take into consideration the fact that the distribution of international students by fields of study (as well as institutions) is not an even one. For example, in the United Kingdom international students at the graduate level comprise nearly 57.6% of total enrollment in engineering and technology fields, while only 16.1% in education (Williams, 1981). Obviously, the cost of providing training in engineering is significantly higher than that of training in education.

4. The calculation of costs and savings is further bedeviled by the problem of determining *teaching* costs and *research* costs. In all research universities it is an accepted understanding that teaching staff will devote some of their time to research, and it follows therefore that an increase or decrease in student enrollment will have an impact on research costs. These costs will also vary by field of study.

Benefits

In the calculation of benefits, the research situation becomes even more complex. Thus any calculation of benefits accruing to the host country from the presence of international students must devise appropriate methodology to measure the following key dimensions of benefits.

1. International students at the graduate level provide benefit via the research they carry out in the process of producing their doctoral dissertations (and in some cases master's theses) — especially considering that they tend to be concentrated in fields such as engineering sciences, computer sciences, medicine, and so on. The problem here is to determine the value to the host country of this research.

2. A sizable number of international students provide research and teaching assistance through their roles as stipended research/teaching assistants in their institutions. Thus they provide labor to the institution at a lower cost than full-time professional staff.

3. If the international research assistant or teaching assistant received his or her pre-graduate-level education outside the host country, then the host country is deriving further benefit in that it did not have to pay for this part of the student's education.

4. The host country derives benefit from the presence of international students at the graduate level if their presence implies that local students can be "freed" from graduate studies in order to take up jobs that need to be filled in an unsaturated labor market — this is most likely the situation in the engineering sciences in the United States. (Very crudely, the benefit is the difference between the salary received by a graduate engineer and the per annum cost of educating him or her at the graduate level.)

5. The host country derives benefit from those international students who are legitimately granted residence/work permits because of their much-needed services in the economy — that is, as long as their pre-graduate-level education was undertaken outside the host country.

6. If the host country is in a situation of a chronic balance-of-payments deficit (as the United States is today), then the host country benefits from the foreign exchange the international students bring in. The benefit can become more dramatic when viewed from the perspective of a state-level economy (as in the situation of the United States, where the economy is geographically fragmented). For example, the state of New York (a state with many international students) received during the academic year 1982–83 foreign exchange equivalent to $145 million in the form of living expenses (Institute of International Education, 1983).

7. If the large presence of international students leads to an increase in export orders for goods produced in the host country in the long run, via alumni preference for host-country goods, then the host country will benefit. The problem here of course is the construction of an appropriate methodology to measure

this benefit — an immensely difficult task.

8. A benefit almost impossible to calculate (at least in monetary terms) is that of cross-cultural understanding and enlightenment that the host population would derive from the presence of international students — provided, of course, that an effort is made to produce positive contact. More feasible as a means of placing a numerical figure on this type of benefit is to calculate the benefits derived from a program such as that operated by the Oregon State System of Higher Education, under which needy international students earn tuition assistance credit by providing 80 hours of educational service per academic year. "Educational service" is broadly defined to include providing assistance to local school with their cross-cultural programs, advising the Oregon import/export business community, and so on (Van de Water, 1983).

To conclude this section, it is important to stress that in undertaking a cost-benefit analysis of the presence of international students, the implication is not that there is an automatic case for doing away with international students if the finding is that the cost far outweighs the benefit (from the perspective of economics). What it does imply is that whatever reasons may be adduced in favor of the presence of international students (foreign aid, foreign policy, etc.), they will have to be made more explicit and convincing to the taxpayer. Or, in the case of foreign aid, it may well be more sensible for the host country to provide funds for the development of educational facilities within the home country.

COST-BENEFIT ANALYSIS — HOME COUNTRY

Just as the economic recession has impelled host nations to subject previously unquestioned expenditures to cost-benefit calculations, the home countries (many of which are in the Third World and hence in even more serious economic straits than the host countries) need to undertake cost-benefit analyses of their international student programs. To our knowledge no one has yet done a thorough study of this area, though the work of Maliyamkono et al. (1982) does touch on the subject.

Costs

In determining the costs from the perspective of a Third World country, the problems the researcher would encounter would not only be those of methodology (akin to those pertaining to host-country cost-benefit calculations) but also of access to statistical data. The dearth of relevant statistical data in the Third World on many issues is legendary. But assuming that some data were available, the key elements of the calculations relating to the cost side of the equation would be the following.

1. Marginal costs (assuming that the home country has some comparable educational facilities available) must be calculated and compared with the cost of sending the student abroad. If the country does not have comparable educational facilities (for example, the home-country university may not have a medical department to train doctors), then the average cost must be calculated

and compared with the cost of sending the student abroad. Since it is unlikely that the cost of sending the student abroad will be greater than the average cost of training him or her at home (because if this were so, one can assume that the home country would quickly establish the relevant facility), the average cost must be calculated in terms of projections over a number of years. This will involve further calculations of two types: projections of economic growth, and projections of demand on human resources. The question then arises as to whether the number of years are too many (before the average cost begins to equal the cost of sending the student abroad) to warrant an immediate establishment of the facility in question, or whether the number of years are few enough to justify development of the facility.

2. Considering the heavy reliance of Third World countries on imports for almost all their needs (including the raw materials that go into manufacturing — as a result of the import-dependent strategies pursued by many Third World countries in the late fifties and sixties), a very important cost that these countries have to take into consideration is foreign exchange outlays. If the shortage of foreign exchange is critical (which is the case for most non-oil-producing Third World nations today), then there arises the need for comparing costs between international study in the industrialized countries and in the more advanced of the Third World countries (such as India), in order to conserve the scarce foreign exchange. This would of course mean curtailing the freedom of choice of the student (including the privately funded student) regarding which host country to go to.

3. The cost of non-returning students must be taken into consideration. This involves calculating the cost of educating the student plus lifetime contributions forgone, then comparing this total against the benefit of money sent back to relatives by the student (something that is common among Third World student non-returnees whose relatives are still at home).

4. Many international students come back home with knowledge and skills that are not relevant to the needs of the home country (usually because the curricula of the host institutions were inappropriate); to the extent that the student remains underemployed, this represents a cost to the home country.

5. The cost of sending a student to a host country using a different language of instruction from that used by the student must also be taken into account.

In addition to these costs, there are others that are almost impossible to measure but are nevertheless observable. These costs include: returnees helping to forge new personal consumption patterns learned from the affluent host countries of the West but wholly inappropriate to the home country's level of economic development; returnees helping to implement development strategies appropriate to the circumstances of the host country but not the home country (for example, advocacy of capital-intensive production techniques in situations of scarce capital and abundant labor supply); returnees becoming a political liability as a result of a mismatch between their rising expectations generated in the host country and the reality of the situation facing them upon returning

home — consequently leading them to embark on a course of political desta-
bilization. Many of these issues are discussed in Kumar (1980), though not with
specific reference to the international student.

Benefits

We now turn to a discussion of benefits, and once again the methodological implications involved are daunting. Among the benefits that require analysis are
the following.

1. The benefit of new knowledge and skills gained, and their application in
employment, must be calculated. This would require comparison with similar
workers who received their training locally (that is, where such workers exist).
It should be noted that a subjective assessment by employers of the relative productive worth of the two sets of workers is a method not to be favored, if one is
to go by the experience of Maliyamkono et al. (1982). (In taking this methodological route, they found an overwhelming tendency for locally trained employers to favor locally trained workers, and vice versa.) A method that measures
productivity more objectively would have to be devised — perhaps along the
lines of comparing production output between those units under locally trained
management and those units under overseas-trained management. (One fairly
easy study that can be conducted according to this principle is to compare the
research output of locally trained university staff with that of the overseas-
trained university staff.) Another alternative would be to devise some form of
time-and-motion study. Of course the problem would be greatly simplified if
the conventional micro-economic approach of correlating incomes with place
of training could be used as a basis for calculating benefit. But the difficulty
with this approach is twofold: it would be impossible to factor out the "prestige" factor (since in most Third World countries some prestige is associated
with training obtained overseas, and in a significantly large number of countries (such as those in Africa) the approach is rendered redundant by virtue of
the fact that the labor market is not a market in the conventional sense of the
term (because of the state ownership of the major means of production and the
consequent determination of wage and salary levels on political rather than
economic grounds).

2. In those situations where a country has no choice but to send its students
abroad for higher education because of lack of appropriate facilities at home,
benefit can be measured in terms of those workers (who invariably are foreign)
that they replace after returning home.

3. Benefits accrue to the home country in those situations where international study is funded not by the home country, but by the host country via some
form of bilateral aid. Here the only costs to be taken into consideration would
be those relating to appropriateness of training received.

As with costs, there are also benefits that are almost impossible to measure.
An example is the general personal and intellectual development the individual

undergoes as a result of foreign travel — an individual benefit that also has an indirect benefit for the home country.

It is obvious that the calculation of costs and benefits for the home country is infinitely more difficult than for the host country. Yet cost-benefit analyses for the home countries of the Third World are sorely needed as their economies slowly grind to a halt as a result of a combination of past errors and malpractices and global economic problems.

INTERNATIONAL STUDENTS AND FOREIGN AID

An important if implicit corollary to allowing Third World students to study in the institutions of the advanced host country (irrespective of whether the students are self-supported or officially sponsored) is the issue of providing development assistance to the Third World. Further research is necessary to determine how best this assistance can be provided — assuming that the host country does feel obligated to provide some form of aid. (Studies pertinent to this subject include Danckwortt, 1980; Fry, 1984; Hunter, 1963; Jenkins, 1983c; Oxenham, 1981; United Kingdom, 1980; and Williams, 1981b.) Related issues on this matter include the following.

1. The relevance of the training the international student obtains needs to be evaluated, and if necessary, weaknesses redressed.

2. There is need to provide opportunities for international students to gain practical experience following completion of formal classroom studies, via both legal measures (relaxing anti-work laws) and liaison programs between institutions and industry.

3. Consideration must be given to developing measures to dissuade international students from remaining in the country following completion of their studies. This is especially important in the case of those students who are considered to be bright (that is, the ones who are most likely to be granted residence permits by the host country).

4. In keeping with the democratic traditions of the host nations, channels must be developed to extend aid to those Third World students who would ordinarily be bypassed by bilateral scholarship programs as well as home-country scholarship programs because of racial discrimination, their political or religious beliefs, etc. Such students would necessarily be financially needy, but they would also be exceptionally promising.

5. Similarly, there is need to focus attention on those nations that are finding it increasingly difficult to finance international study for their students in the face of rising tuition costs — that is, the non-oil-producing nations such as Tanzania, Guatemala, or Sri Lanka.

6. Research attention should be directed to identifying the benefits accruing to the host country from providing foreign aid of this type (that is, providing access to study facilities). Does aid here constitute merely a humanitarian gesture, or can other grounds be adduced in its support? For example, can such aid help to create allies, develop (indirectly) democratic forms of government

and thereby promote world peace and stability, and perhaps most important of all, assist in the economic development of these nations? The importance of the last point cannot be overemphasized. The development of Third World nations to levels where they can play the same role in capital investment and commodity markets as do the industrialized host nations with respect to each other can only be in the long-term benefit of the host nations.

Turning now to the perspective of the home country on the issue of foreign aid, there is need for research to address the following matters.

1. The sending countries must consider the alternative places (that is, other Third World nations) to educate their students, and thereby lessen the problems of excessive foreign exchange costs, incompatible curricula, and cultural dependency. Hence a bilateral aid program might provide for students to be sent to a third country.

2. Measures must be developed to decrease the tendency for overseas-trained nationals to exacerbate inequality — international students upon returning home tend to become members of a "super-elite" within the Third World.

3. In the case of countries such as India with fairly well developed higher education systems, it is necessary to devise measures that prevent foreign exchange leakage by allowing access to it only in circumstances where there is a bona fide need for the type of training the student wishes to undertake abroad.

4. Third World nations must develop programs that would encourage privately sponsored students to return home rather than becoming part of the "brain drain" phenomenon.

International Students and Foreign Policy

For the host country, international students constitute an additional element in the realm of diplomacy and foreign policy. A concrete example can be seen in the relations between the United States and Guinea-Bissau. As soon as it became clear (following the coup in Guinea-Bissau) that the new administrators wished to realign themselves away from their long-time benefactor, the Soviet Union, the United States quickly began an aid program for Guinea-Bissau — an important element of which included scholarships to students in Guinea-Bissau to study in the United States. The United States thereby established a tangible relationship as well as an intangible one — of the sort that comes with having top-level foreign administrators as alumni of one's own institutions.

Of course, the matter of furthering the foreign policy interests of the host country (in terms of cultivating allies, trading partners, etc.) via the education of international students is in a sense an act of faith. It is almost impossible to accurately evaluate the extent to which international students develop long-term positive attitudes toward the host country and thereafter translate these attitudes into positive behavior after returning home. Of interest in this area is the extent to which the presence of large numbers of international students from a given country may serve to stabilize relations between that country and the host country. For example, could it be that the presence in the United States of a larger number of international students from Iran during the Iranian hostage crisis helped prevent the crisis from deteriorating any further than it did?

An area that requires research attention, and that holds out the promise of a more tangible payoff, is that of developing an international alumni program. It is an area whose potential has yet to be realized.

CONCLUSIONS

In addition to the need for further research discussed in the preceding sections, there are a number of areas in which research of almost any kind (including the traditional socio-psychological and adaptation variety) is severely lacking. For example:

1. *International students studying in other Third World countries.* There is a sizable flow of international students between Third World countries themselves. Do these students exhibit the same kinds of problems as do Third World students who come to study in the industrialized nations? Do they receive a more relevant education than do those who study in the industrialized nations? These and many other questions need to be answered. (One study that has been done in this area is that by Ganguli, 1975, which looks at international students in India, and a study by Hafeez-Zaidi, 1975, examines the cross-cultural problems of social adjustment of international students in Pakistan.)

2. *International students involved in military training.* A significant amount of aid via bilateral agreements takes the form of military training assistance. Very little is known about the non-military aspects of this training — such as the attitudes and adjustment problems of the Third World trainees.

3. *International students studying in China and Eastern-bloc countries — specifically international students from non-Communist countries.* The flow of international students to the Communist countries is fairly large (see Table 7), yet the amount of research on such students is very meager indeed. What little is known has tended to portray the experience of studying in these countries as usually less than satisfactory (Robinson, 1982).

4. *Female international students.* The general increase in the participation in higher education by women throughout the world in recent years has also been reflected in an increase in the number of female international students to the point where, in the United States, roughly one out of every three of the students is female. Yet despite this trend very little attempt has been made by researchers to disaggregate variables and data by gender. Female international students, by virtue of their gender, encounter special problems both in the host countries and upon return in the home countries. Research on female international students should also include data on women who go overseas not as students but as spouses. A pertinent study to this end is that by Ntiri (1979), who discusses the efforts of wives of African international students in the United States to upgrade their education. (For a general study in this particular area, see Rowe and Sjoberg, 1981.)

**TABLE 7. The Flow of International Students from Third World Countries
(Non-Communist) to China and Eastern Bloc Countries (1965 and 1969)**

Home Regions	Countries and Regions of Destination							
	USSR		Eastern Europe		China		Total	
	1965	1979	1965	1979	1965	1979	1965	1979
Africa	5,065	14,690	2,800	12,400	275	240	8,140	27,330
Asia	2,310	6,660	965	3,060	175	95	3,450	9,815
Latin America	935	2,860	305	2,150	—	—	1,240	5,010
Middle East	2,125	6,745	955	6,405	5	10	3,085	13,160
Total	10,435	30,955	5,025	24,015	455	345	15,915	55,315

Source. Based on data from the National Foreign Assessment Center, Central Intelligence Agency, 1980.

5. *Informal international students.* This is a category of people who are not students in the strictest sense of the word, yet they form part of what Vente (1980) calls "non-organized" exchange. These are people who go abroad on assignment for their employers (either the government, an international organization, or a multinational corporation). Research needs to be undertaken to document the direction and magnitude of this kind of international flow, and the similarities and dissimilarities between the cross-cultural problems they encounter and those that ordinary international students encounter.

The rapid increases in the number of international students witnessed during the past decade will inevitably slow, and indeed there is evidence from the United States and Britain that rates of increase have slowed. As opportunities for domestic study in some of the large sending nations such as Nigeria, Malaysia, and Venezuela grow, more of their students will remain at home for their higher education. It is also likely that economic necessity and national priorities will cause additional countries to restrict the exit of their nationals for overseas study — as India has done in recent years. It is also possible that some of the host nations may raise their fees so high as to deter international students from studying in these countries. Recent trends in Britain, traditionally the country of choice for many Commonwealth students, indicate that the fee increases did in fact direct students to other countries.

Similarly, as circumstances and policies change, the mix of international students is also likely to change. For example, with fewer Iranians and Nigerians coming to study in the United States, their numbers have been partly made up by Malaysians and an ever-growing number of students from Hong Kong, Taiwan, and other Southeast Asia nations. The People's Republic of China has dramatically increased the number of students studying abroad.

In determining the magnitude and direction of future international student flow, the orientations of the major "donor" agencies in the industrialized nations will also play an important role. During the 1960s, organizations like the U.S. Agency for International Development, the Ford Foundation, and Britain's Overseas Development Administration placed greater emphasis on the training of high-level personnel and provided more scholarships and other assistance to higher education; and while this is no longer the case, there are signs that this may be changing.

While it is difficult to predict the economic circumstances or political imperatives that might account for further shifts, given current trends it seems unlikely that the rates of increase of recent years can be sustained, but it is also unlikely that the absolute numbers of international students will dramatically decline. It is likely that numbers will grow modestly, although the configuration of sending and receiving countries may significantly alter and the fields of specialization may change as well.

This essay has presented a multifaceted overview of issues related to international students and foreign study. We have pointed to some of the priorities for future research. Without question, the topic is of considerable importance as a policy issue and as a matter for applied concern by professionals working with international students. It is our conviction that research on international students has achieved some level of coherence and sophistication with a potential for yielding fruitful generalizations. Further, there is an emerging research community, and consequently this is a field that has the potential to "come of age." Of course, much still remains to be done. There is a need to temper the heavy policy-oriented research that has been the hallmark of research on international students over the last two or three decades with academically oriented theory if generalizations are to be generated — something that has not been easy to do with past research — and by way of providing methodological guidance.

The issue of methodology is a crucial one, for it has been among the major weaknesses of past research. The problem has not simply been of proper or "scientific" research designs for many of the studies undertaken but also of formulation of research questions themselves — arising primarily out of the failure to perceive the fundamentally "behavioral" character of much of the data gathered in the areas of cross-cultural contact and social adjustment. It is the kind of data that can be immensely difficult to characterize because of the complexity of the variables involved, ranging as they do from the personality of the person to the characteristics of the cultural environment.

REFERENCES

Adler, N. Re-entry: Managing cross-cultural transitions. *Group and Organisation Studies*, 1981, *6*, 341-356.

Akoff, A., Thayer, F, and Elkind, L. Mental health and counseling ideas of Asian and American students. *Journal of Counseling Psychology*, 1966, *13*, 219-223.

Alexander, A. A., et al. Psychotherapy and the foreign student. In P. P. Pedersen et al. (eds.), *Counseling Across Cultures*. Honolulu: University Press of Hawaii, 1981.

Altbach, P. G. The university as center and periphery. *Teachers College Record*, 1981, *82*, 601-621.

Altbach, P. G. The dilemma of success: Higher education in advanced developing countries. *Prospects*, 1983, *12*, 293-312.

Altekar, A. S. *Education in Ancient India*. Benares, India: Nand Kishore, 1948.

American Council on Education. *Foreign Students and Institutional Policy: Toward an Agenda for Action*. Washington, D.C.: American Council on Education, 1982.

Anthony, M. W. Suspension of deportation: A revitalized relief for the alien (*Kamheangpatiyooth* vs. *Immigration and Naturalization Service*). *San Diego Law Review*, 1980, *18*, 65-88.

Babiker, I. E., Cox, J. L., and Miller, P. M. The measurement of cultural distance and its relationship to medical consultations, symptomatology and examination performance of overseas students at Edinburgh University. *Social Psychiatry*, 1980, *15*, 109-116.

Backman, E. *Approaches to International Education*. New York: Macmillan, 1984.

Bailey, K. M., Pialorsi, F., and Zukowski-Faust, J. *Foreign Teaching Assistants in U.S. Universities*. Washington, D.C.: National Association for Foreign Student Affairs, 1984.

Barber, E., Altbach, P. G. and Myers, R. (eds.). *Bridges to Knowledge: Foreign students in Comparative Perspective*. Chicago: University of Chicago Press, 1984.

Baron, M. *The Relevance of U.S. Graduate Programs to Foreign Students from Developing Countries*. Washington, D.C.: National Association for Foreign Student Affairs, 1979.

Becker, T. Black Africans and black Americans on an American campus: The African view. *Sociology and Social Research*, 1973, *57*, 168-181.

Bedrosian, A. Alien status: Legal issues and institutional responsibilities. In H. M. Jenkins et al. (eds.), *Educating Students from Other Nations: American Colleges and Universities in International Educational Exchange*. San Francisco: Jossey-Bass, 1983.

Benson, A. G. On-the-job behavior of college and university foreign student advisers as perceived by knowledgeable faculty members. Unpublished doctoral dissertation, Michigan State University, 1968.

Berendzen, R. Ethics in international higher education. In M. C. Baca and R. H. Stein (eds.), *Ethical Principles, Practices and Problems in Higher Education*. Springfield, Ill.: Thomas, 1983.

Bie, K. N. Norwegian students at British universities: A case study of the academic performances of foreign students. *Scandanavian Journal of Education Research*, 1976, *20*, 1-24.

Blaug, M. The economic cost and benefits of overseas students. In P. Williams (ed.), *The Overseas Student Question: Studies for a Policy*. London: Heinemann, 1981.

Bochner, S. Cultural diversity: Implications for modernization in international education. In K. Kumar (ed.), *Bonds Without Bondage*. Honolulu: University Press of Hawaii, 1979.

Bochner, S., Lin, A., and McLeod, B. M. Anticipated role conflict of returning overseas students. *Journal of Social Psychology*, 1980, *110*, 265-272.

Boer, E. E. Some psychosocial factors affecting adaptation and orientation of foreign students. In S. C. Dunnett (ed.), *Factors Affecting the Adaptation of Foreign Students in Cross Cultural Settings*. Buffalo, N.Y.: Council on International Studies, State University of New York at Buffalo, 1981.

Bourdieu, P., and Passeron, J. C. *Reproduction in Education: Society and Culture*. London: Sage, 1977.

Bowman, J. S. Learning about American government: Attitudes of foreign students. *Teaching Political Science*, 1978, *5*, 181-191.

Boyan, D. (ed.). *Profiles: The Foreign Student in the United States*. New York: Institute of International Education, 1981.

Brickman, W. W. *Foreign Students in American Elementary and Secondary Schools*. Philadelphia: International House, Ogontz Plan Committee, 1967.

Brickman, W. W. *Two Millennia of International Relations in Higher Education*. Norwood, Pa.: Norwood Editions, 1975.

Brislin, R. Outcomes, human relations, and contributions to task effectiveness as key variables in educational exchanges. In German Academic Exchange Service, *Research on Exchanges: Proceedings of the German-American Conference at Wissenschafts-Zentrum, Bonn, November 24-28, 1980*. Bonn, 1980.

Brown, M. A. U.S. students abroad. In H. M. Jenkins et al., *Educating Students from Other Nations: American Colleges and Universities in International Education Interchange*. San Francisco: Jossey-Bass, 1983.

Business-Higher Education Forum. *America's Competitive Challenge: The Need for a National Response*. Washington, D.C., 1983.

Canadian Bureau for International Education. *A Question of Self-interest: A Statement on Foreign Students in Canada*, Ottawa, Canadian Bureau for International Education, 1977.

Carrigan, O. *The Right Mix: The Report of the Commission on Foreign Student Policy in Canada*. Ottawa, Canadian Bureau for International Education, 1977.

Christensen, G. C., and Thielen, T. B. Cross-cultural activities: Maximizing the benefits of educational interchange. In H. M. Jenkins et al., *Educating Students from Other Nations: American Colleges and Universities in International Educational Interchange*. San Francisco: Jossey-Bass, 1983.

Cobban, A. B. *The Medieval Universities: Their Development and Organization*. London: Methuen, 1975.

Coelho, G. V. *An Investigation of the Consequences of International Educational Exchanges*. Washington, D.C.: National Institute of Mental Health, 1973.

Cole, J. B., Allen, F. C. L., and Green, J. S. Survey of health problems of overseas students. Part A, "Medical Sociology," *Social Science and Medicine*, 1980, *14*, 627-631.

Coleman, J. S. Professional training and institution building in the Third World. *Comparative Education Review*, 1984, *28*, 180-202.

Collin, A. E. *Education for National Development: Effects of U.S. Technical Training Programs*. New York: Praeger, 1979.

Coombs, P. *The Fourth Dimension of Foreign Policy: Education and Cultural Affairs*. New York: Harper & Row, 1964.

Cooper, K. Increasing the international relevance of U.S. education. In H. M. Jenkins et al., *Educating Students from Other Nations*. San Francisco: Jossey-Bass, 1983.

Cowser, R. L., Jr. Foreign student: New nigger on campus. *Community College Review*, 1978, *6*, 4-7.

Crespi, Leo P. *The Effectiveness of the Exchange Program*. Washington, D.C.: U.S. Office of Research, 1978.

Dagnino, E. Cultural and ideological dependence: Building a theoretical framework. In K. Kumar (ed.), *Transnational Enterprises: Their Impact on Third World Societies and Cultures*. Boulder, Colo.: Westview Press, 1980.

Danckwortt, D. Where does educational aid for the Third World stand at the end of the second development decade? In Institute for Foreign Cultural Relations, *International Cultural Relations — Bridge Across Frontiers. Symposium '80: A Documentation*. Stuttgart, 1980.

Dedijer, S. "Early" migration. In W. Adams (ed.), *The Brain Drain*. New York: Macmillan, 1968.

Deutsch, S. E. *International Education and Exchange: A Sociological Analysis*. Cleveland, Ohio: Case Western Reserve University, 1970.

Dixon, R., et al. Controversial issues in interpreting foreign academic records. *College and University*, 1976, *51*, 462-468.

Dodge, B. *Al-Azhar: A Millennium of Muslim Education*. Washington, D.C.: Middle East Institute, 1961.

Dolibois, J. E. Alive and well: International alumni program. *International Educational and Cultural Exchange*, 1976, *11*, 32-34.

Dunnett, S. C. A study of the effects of an English language training and orientation program on foreign student adaptation. In S. C. Dunnett (ed.), *Factors Affecting the Adaptation of Foreign Students in Cross Cultural Settings*. Buffalo, N.Y.: Council on International Studies, State University of New York at Buffalo, 1981.

Dunnett, S. C. *Management Skills Training for Foreign Engineering Students: An Assessment of Need and Availability*. Washington, D.C.: National Association for Foreign Student Affairs, 1982.

Ebbers, K. D. The seductivity of stereotypes: Examining American attitudes toward foreign students. In S. C. Dunnett (ed.), *Factors Affecting the Adaptation of Foreign Students in Cross Cultural Settings*. Amherst, N.Y.: Council on International Studies, State University of New York at Buffalo, 1981.

Fisher, S. H., and Dey, W. J. *Forged Educational Credentials: A Sorry Tale*. New York: World Education Services, 1979.

Fiske, E. B. Ethical issues in recruiting students. *New Directions for Higher Education*, 1981, *9*, 41-48.

Flack, J. Results and effects of study abroad. *Annals of the American Academy of Political and Social Science*, 1976, *424*, 107-115.

Fouad, A. A., and Jones, E. C. Electrical-engineering curriculum and the education of international students. *IEEE Transactions on Education*, 1979, *22*, 95-98.

Fry, G. W. The economic and political impact of study abroad. *Comparative Education Review*, 1984, *28*, 203-220.

Fuenzalida, E. U.S. education for the Third World: How relevant? *World Higher Education Communique*, 1981, *4*, 15-19.

Galtung, I. E. The impact of study abroad: A three-by-three nation study of cross-cultural contact. *Journal of Peace Research*, 1965, *3*, 258-275.

Gama, E. M. P., and Pedersen, P. Readjustment problems of Brazilian returnees from graduate studies in the U.S. *International Journal of Intercultural Relations*, 1977, *1*, 46-59.

Ganguli, H. C. *Foreign Students: The Indian Experience*. New Delhi: Sterling, 1975.

Glaser, W., and Habers, G. C. *The Brain Drain: Emigration and Return*. New York: Pergamon, 1978.

Glimm, H., and Kuper, W. (eds.). *University, Science and Development in Africa*. Bonn: Deutscher Akademischer Austauschdienst, 1980.

Goodwin, C. D., and Nacht, M. *Absence of Decision: Foreign Students in American Colleges and Universities*. New York: Institute of International Education, 1983.

Goodwin, C. D., and Nacht, M. *Fondness and Frustration: The Impact of American Higher Education on Foreign Students with Special Reference to the Case of Brazil*. New York: Institute of International Education, 1984.

Gopinathan, S. Intellectual dependency and the indigenization response: Case studies of three disciplines in two Third World universities. Unpublished doctoral dissertation, State University of New York at Buffalo, 1984.

Gray, J. H. The status of foreign students under the Immigration Act, 1976 (Canada). *McGill Law Journal*, 1982, *27*, 556-562.

Grubel, H. G., and Scott, A. *The Brain Drain: Determinants, Measurements and Welfare Effects*. Waterloo, Ontario: Wilfrid Laurier University Press, 1977.

Gullahorn, J. T., and Gullahorn, J. E. An extension of the U-curve hypothesis. *Journal of Social Issues*, 1963, *19*, 33-47.

Hafeez-Zaidi, S. M. Adjustment problems of foreign Muslim students in Pakistan. In R. W. Brislin, S. Bochner, and W. J. Lonner (eds.), *Cross-cultural Perspectives on Learning*. New York: Wiley, 1975.

Hanson, J. W. *Education Nsukka: A Study of Institution Building Among the Modern Ibo*. East Lansing, Mich.: Michigan State University, 1968.

Harari, M. Priorities for research and action in the graduate foreign student field. *Exchange*, 1970, *6*, 60-67.

Hasan, R. Socialization and cross-cultural education (Indo-Pakistani students studying in Britain). *Linguistics*, 1976, no. 175, 7-25.

Haskins, C. H. *The Rise of Universities*. Ithaca, N.Y.: Cornell University Press, 1966.

Hawkins, J. N. Educational exchanges and the transformation of higher education in the People's Republic of China. In E. G. Barber, P. G. Altbach, and R. G. Myers (eds.), *Bridges to Knowledge: Foreign Students in Comparative Perspective*. Chicago: University of Chicago Press, 1984.

Heath, G. L. Foreign student attitudes at International House, Berkeley. *Exchange*, 1970, *5*, 66-70.

Hegazy, M. E. Cross-cultural experience and social change: The case of foreign study. Unpublished doctoral dissertation, University of Minnesota, 1968.

Heil, D., and Aleamoni, L. *Assessment of the Proficiency in the Use and Understanding of English by Foreign Students as Measured by the Test of English as a Foreign Language*. Urbana: University of Illinois, Office of Instructional Resources, 1974.

Hensley, T. R., and Sell, D. K. Study abroad program: An examination of impacts on student attitudes. *Teaching Political Science*, 1979, *6*, 387-411.

Hess, Gerhard. *Freshmen and Sophomore Abroad*. New York: Teachers College Press, 1982.

Higbee, H. D. *The Status of Foreign Student Advising in United States Universities and Colleges*. East Lansing: Michigan State University, 1961.

Higginbotham, H. N. Cultural Issues in providing psychological services for foreign students in the United States. *International Journal of Intercultural Relations*, 1979, *3*, 49-85.

Hodgkin, M. C. The Asian student in an Australian university. *The Educand*, 1958, *3*.

Hood, M. A. G., and Schieffer, K. J. *Professional Integration: A Guide for Students from the Developing World*. Washington, D.C.: National Association for Foreign Student Affairs, 1983.

Horner, D., et al. Cross-cultural counseling. In G. Althen (ed.), *Learning Across Cultures: Intercultural Communication and International Educational Exchange*. Washington, D.C.: National Association for Foreign Student Affairs, 1981.

Hull, W. F., IV. *Foreign Students in the United States of America*. New York: Praeger, 1978.

Hunter, G. *Education for a Developing Nation: A Study in East Africa*. London: Allen & Unwin, 1963.

Institute of International Education. *Open Doors 1981/82*. New York: Institute of International Education, 1983.

International Research and Exchanges Board. *A Balance Sheet for East-West Exchanges: Working Papers*. New York, 1980.

Jarousse, J.-P., Smith, A., and Woesler de Panafieu, C. *Etrangers: Comparaison internationale des flux et des politiques, 1960-1980*. Paris: Institut Européen d'Education et de Politique Sociale, 1982.

Jenkins, H. M. (ed.). *Foreign Student Recruitment: Realities and Recommendations*. New York: College Entrance Examination Board, 1980.

Jenkins, H. M. Economics: Analyzing costs and benefits. In H. M. Jenkins et al., *Edu-*

cating Students from Other Nations: American Colleges and Universities in International Educational Interchange. San Francisco: Jossey-BAss, 1983(a).

Jenkins, H. M. Recruitment: Ensuring educational and ethical standards. In H. M. Jenkins et al., *Educating Students from Other Nations: American Colleges and Universities in International Educational Interchange.* San Francisco: Jossey-Bass, 1983 (b).

Jenkins, H. M. (ed.). *The Role of the Foreign Student in the Process of Development.* Washington, D.C.: National Association for Foreign Student Affairs, 1983(c).

Jenkins, H. M., et al. *Educating Students from Other Nations: American Colleges and Universities in International Educational Interchange.* San Francisco: Jossey-Bass, 1983.

Kaplan, R. English as a second language: An overview of the literature. In E. G. Barber, P. G. Altbach, and R. G. Myers (eds.), *Bridges to Knowledge: Foreign Students in Comparative Perspective.* Chicago: University of Chicago Press, 1984.

Kelman, H. C. International interchanges: Some contributions from theories of attitude change. *Studies in Comparative International Development,* 1975, *10*, 83-99.

Kimmel, P., Ockey, W. C., and Sander, H. J. *Final Report: International Training Assessment Program.* Washington, D.C.: Development Education and Training Research Institute, 1972.

Klineberg, O. Mental health aspects of international student exchange. In German Academic Exchange Service, *Research on Exchanges: Proceedings of the German-American Conference at Wissenschafts-Zentrum, Bonn, November 24-28, 1980.* Bonn, 1980.

Klineberg, O., and Hull, W. F., IV. *At a Foreign University: An International Study of Adaptation and Coping.* New York: Praeger, 1979.

Kumagai, F. The effects of cross-cultural education on attitudes and personality of Japanese students. *Sociology of Education,* 1977, *50*, 40-47.

Kumar, K. (ed.). *Transnational Enterprises: Their Impact on Third World Societies and Cultures.* Boulder, Colo.: Westview Press, 1980.

Lee, M., Abd-Ella, M., and Burks, L. A. *Needs of Foreign Students from Developing Nations at U.S. Colleges and Universities.* Washington, D.C.: National Association for Foreign Student Affairs, 1981.

Lockett, B. A. A study of the effectiveness of foreign student advisers at American colleges and universities as reported by foreign students sponsored by the United States Agency for International Development. Unpublished doctoral dissertation, American University, 1970.

Lysgaard, Sverre. Adjustment in a foreign society: Norwegian Fulbright grantees visiting the United States. *International Social Science Bulletin,* 1955, *7*, 45-51.

Maliyamkono, T. L., et al. *Training and Productivity in East Africa: A Report of the Eastern African Universities Research Project on the Impact of Overseas Training and Development.* London: Heinemann, 1982.

Marion, P. B., Jr., and Thomas, H., Jr. Residence hall proximity to foreign students as an influence on selected attitudes and behaviors of American college students. *Journal of College and University Student Housing,* 1980, *10*, 16-19.

Markham, J. W. *International Images and Mass Communication Behavior.* Iowa City: University of Iowa School of Journalism, 1967.

Martin, G. M. A model for the cultural and statistical analysis of academic achievement of foreign graduate students at the University of North Carolina at Chapel Hill. Unpublished doctoral dissertation, University of North Carolina, 1971.

Martin, J. N. The intercultural re-entry conceptualization and directions for future research. *International Journal of Intercultural Relations,* 1984, *8*, 115-134.

Matross, R., et al. American student attitudes toward foreign students before and during an international crisis. *Journal of College Student Personnel,* 1982;, *23*, 58-65.

Mazrui, A. A. The African university as a multi-national corporation: Problems of penetration and dependency. *Harvard Educational Review*, 1975, *45*, 191-210.

Melendez-Craig, M. A study of the academic achievement and related problems among Latin American students enrolled in the major Utah universities. Unpublished doctoral dissertation, Brigham Young University, 1970.

Mestenhauser, J. A. Foreign students as teachers: Lessons from the program in learning with foreign students. In G. Althen (ed.), *Learning Across Cultures: Intercultural Communication and International Educational Exchange*. Washington, D.C.: National Association for Foreign Student Affairs, 1981.

Michii, T. N. Problems of cross-cultural education: The Japanese case. In S. C. Dunnett (ed.), *Factors Affecting the Adaptation of Foreign Students in Cross Cultural Settings*. Amherst, N.Y.: Council on International Studies, State University of New York at Buffalo, 1981.

Miller, J. C. African students and the racial attitudes and practices of Americans. Unpublished doctoral dissertation, University of North Carolina, 1967.

Miller, M. H., et al. The cross-cultural student: Lessons in human nature. *Bulletin of the Menninger Clinic*, 1971, *35*, 128-131.

Miller, R. E. A study of significant elements in the on-the-job behavior of college and university foreign student advisers. Unpublished doctoral dissertation, Michigan State University, 1968.

Moock, J. L. Overseas training and national development objectives in Sub-Saharan Africa. *Comparative Education Review*, 1984, *28*, 221-240.

Myer, R. B. *Curriculum: U.S. Capacities, Developing Countries' Needs*. New York: Institute of International Education, 1979.

Myers, R. G. *Education and Emigration*. New York: McKay, 1972.

National Association for Foreign Student Affairs. *An Inquiry into Departmental Policies and Practices in Relation to the Graduate Education of Foreign Students*. Washington, D.C., 1972.

National Foreign Assessment Center, Central Intelligence Agency. *Communist Aid Activities in Non-Communist Less Developed Countries 1979 and 1954–79: A Research Paper*. Washington, D.C.: Photoduplication Service, Library of Congress, 1980. (Superintendent of Documents No. ER80-10318U)

Neff, C. B. (ed.). *New Directions for Experiential Learning: Cross-cultural Learning, No. 11*. San Francisco: Jossey-Bass, 1981.

Neville, A. Alienation from the second homeland: German difficulties in dealing with foreigners. *Western European Education*, 1981, *13*, 65-69.

Ntiri, D. W. Continuing education efforts of African students' wives in the United States. *Journal of the National Association for Women Deans, Administrators, and Counselors*, 1979, *42*, 16-21.

Nurullah, S., and Naik, J. P. *A Student's History of Education in India*. Bombay: Macmillan, 1956.

Odenyo, A. O. Africans and Afro-Americans on campus: A study of some of the relationships between two minority sub-communities. Unpublished doctoral dissertation, University of Minnesota, 1970.

Oxenham, J. Study abroad and development policy: An enquiry. In P. Williams (ed.), *The Overseas Student Question: Studies for a Policy*. London: Heinemann, 1981.

Paige, R. M. Foreign students as learning resources. In *Proceedings of the Central Region Conference on International Agricultural Training*. Urbana-Champaign: University of Illinois Press, 1978.

Parsons, E. A. *The Alexandrian Library: Glory of the Hellenic World*. Amsterdam: Elsevier, 1952.

Patrick, W. S. Admissions: Developing effective selection practices. In H. M. Jenkins et al., *Educating Students from Other Nations: American Colleges and Universities in International Educational Interchange*. San Francisco: Jossey-Bass, 1983.

Pedersen, P. Personal problem solving resources used by University of Minnesota foreign students. In S. C. Dunnett (ed.), *Factors Affecting the Adaptation of Foreign Students in Cross Cultural Settings*. Buffalo, N.Y.: Council on International Studies, State University of New York at Buffalo, 1981.

Pierce, F. N. Foreign student views and attitudes toward advertising in the United States. Unpublished doctoral dissertation, University of Illinois, 1969.

Prince, R. Mental health workers should be trained at home: Some implications of transcultural psychiatric research. Paper presented at the American Psychological Association Conference, Montreal, August 1973.

Rao, G. L. *Brain Drain and Foreign Students: A Study of the Attitudes and Intentions of Foreign Students in Australia, the U.S.A., Canada and France*. New York: St. Martin's Press, 1979.

Rashdall, H. *The University of Europe in the Middle Ages*. London: Oxford University Press, 1936.

Robinson, B. E., and Hendel, D. D. Foreign Students as teachers: An untapped educational resource. *Alternative Higher Education*, 1981, *5*, 256-269.

Robinson, L. *An American in Leningrad*. New York: W. W. Norton, 1982.

Roeloffs, K. International mobility in higher education: The experiences of an academic exchange agency in the Federal Republic of Germany. *European Journal of Education*, 1982, *17*, 27-36.

Rogers, K. A. *Improving the Latin American Engineering Student's Experience in the U.S. University*. Washington, D.C.: National Association for Foreign Student Affairs, 1971.

Rogers, K. A. Alumni networking. In M. A. G. Hood and K. J. Schieffer (eds.), *Professional Integration: A Guide for Students from the Developing World*. Washington, D.C.: National Association for Foreign Student Affairs, 1983.

Ronkin, R. R. Modifying the Ph.D. program for foreign students. *Science*, 1969, *163*, 20.

Rowe, L., and Sjoberg, S. (eds.). *International Women Students: Perspectives for the 80s. Report of the International Women Student Conference (Boston, Mass., August, 1981*. Washington, D.C.: National Association for Foreign Student Affairs, 1981.

Sauvant, K. P., and Mennis, B. Sociocultural investments and the international political economy of north-south relations: The role of transnational enterprises. In K. Kumar (ed.), *Transnational Enterprises: Their Impact on Third World Societies and Cultures*. Boulder, Colo.: Westview Press, 1980.

Sharon, S. T. *Test of English as a Foreign Language as a Moderator of Graduate Record Examination Scores in the Prediction of Foreign Students' Grades in Graduate School*. Princeton, N.J.: Educational Testing Service, 1971.

Shaw, R. A. The stranger in our midst: Liability or asset? *Engineering Education*, 1982, *72*, 310-313.

Sims, W. A., and Stelcner, M. *The Costs and Benefits of Foreign Students in Canada: A Methodology*. Ottowa: Canadian Bureau for International Education, 1981.

Smith, A., Woesler de Panafieu, C., and Jarousse, J.-P. Foreign student flows and policies in an international perspective. In P. Williams (ed.), *The Overseas Student Question: Studies for a Policy*. London: Heinemann, 1981.

Smith, S. K. Alien students in the United States: Statutory interpretation and problems of control. *Suffolk Transnational Law Journal*, 1981, *5*, 235-250.

Stauffer, R. B. Western values and the case for Third World cultural disengagement. In K. Kumar (ed.), *Bonds Without Bondage*. Honolulu: University Press of Hawaii, 1979.

Stewart, E. C. *American Culture Patterns: A Cross-cultural Perspective.* Washington, D.C.: Society for International Education, Training and Research, 1975.

Stone, B. Gaps in graduate training of students from abroad. *Science*, 1969, p. 1118.

Story, K. E. The student development professional and the foreign student: A conflict of values. *Journal of College Student Personnel*, 1982, *23*, 66-70.

Sue, D. W. Eliminating cultural oppression in counseling: Toward a general theory. *Journal of Counseling Psychology*, 1978, *25*, 419-428.

Sugimoto, R. A. The relationship of selected predictive variables to foreign student achievement at the University of California, Los Angeles. Unpublished doctoral dissertation, University of Southern California, 1966.

Susskind, C., and Schell, L. *Exporting Technical Education: A Survey and Case Study of Foreign Professionals with U.S. Graduate Degrees.* New York: Institute of International Education, 1968.

Turner, S. M. (ed.). *Evaluation of Foreign Educational Credentials and Recognition of Degree Equivalences.* Boston: Northeastern University, Center for International Higher Education Documentation, 1979.

Uehara, S. *A Study of Academic Achievement of F-1 Classed Aliens and Other Nonimmigrant Temporary Students at Kapiolani Community College.* Honolulu: Kapiolani Community College, 1969.

Uhlig, S. J., Crofton, H. E. M., and Thompson, J. H. *Industrial Training for Kenya: An Evaluation of ODM's Technical Co-operation Programme.* London: Ministry of Overseas Development, 1978.

United Kingdom. House of Commons. Foreign Affairs Committee, Overseas Development Sub-committee. *Minutes of Evidence Taken Before the Overseas Development Sub-committee and Appendices. Overseas Student Fees: Aid and Development Implications.* London: Her Majesty's Stationery Office, 1980.

Van de Water, J. Financial aid for foreign students: the Oregon Model. *National Association for Foreign Student Affairs Newsletter*, 1983, *34*, 97, 106.

Vente, R. The "technological mind" and other issues of current exchange research. In German Academic Exchange Service, *Research on Exchanges: Proceedings of the German-American Conference at Wissenschafts-Zentrum, Bonn, November 24-28, 1980.* Bonn, 1980.

Veysey, L. *The Emergence of the American University.* Chicago: University of Chicago Press, 1965.

Wakita, K. *Asian Studies Survey — Spring 1970.* Los Angeles: Los Angeles City College, 1971.

Wallace, W. Overseas students: The foreign policy implications. In P. Williams (ed.), *The Overseas Student Question: Studies for a Policy.* London: Heinemann, 1981.

Weiler, H. The political dilemmas of foreign study. *Comparative Education Review*, 1984, *28*, 168-179.

White, S., and White T. G. Acculturation of foreign graduate students in relation to their English language proficiency. In S. Dunnett (ed.), *Factors Affecting the Adaptation of Foreign Students in Cross-Cultural Settings.* Buffalo, N.Y.: Council on International Studies, State University of New York at Buffalo, 1981, pp. 59-77.

Williams, P. (ed.). *The Overseas Student Question: Studies for a Policy.* London: Heinemann, 1981.

Williams, P. *A Policy for Overseas Students: Analysis-Options-Proposals.* London: Overseas Students Trust, 1982.

Williams, P. Britain's full-cost policy for overseas students. *Comparative Education Review*, 1984, *28*, 258-278.

Winkler, D. R. *The Economic Impacts of Foreign Students in the United States.* Los
    Angeles: University of Southern California, School of Public Administration, 1981.
Woolston, V. Administration: Coordinating and integrating programs and services. In
    H. M. Jenkins et al., *Educating Students from Other Nations: American Colleges and
    Universities in International Educational Interchange.* San Francisco: Jossey-Bass,
    1983.
Yeh, D. K. Paranoid manifestations among Chinese students studying abroad: Some
    preliminary findings. In W. P. Lebra (ed.), *Transcultural Research in Mental Health.*
    Honolulu: University Press of Hawaii, 1972.
Zunin, L. M., and Rubin, R. T. Paranoid psychotic reactions in foreign students from
    non-Western countries. *Journal of American College Health Association,* 1967, *15,*
    220-226.

AUTHOR INDEX

*Names in parentheses identify senior author for "et al." references.

SUBJECT INDEX